D0687025

IP Telephony with H.323

Architectures for Unified Networks and Integrated Services

Vineet Kumar
Markku Korpi
Senthil Sengodan

Wiley Computer Publishing

John Wiley & Sons, Inc.

NEW YORK • CHICHESTER • WEINHEIM • BRISBANE • SINGAPORE • TORONTO

Publisher: Robert Ipsen
Editor: Margaret Eldridge
Managing Editor: Micheline Frederick
Text Design & Composition: D & G Ltd, LLC

This book is printed on acid-free paper. ∞

Published by John Wiley & Sons, Inc.
Published simultaneously in Canada.

Library of Congress Cataloging-in-Publication Data:

Kumar, Vineet, 1958-
IP telephoney with H.323: architectures for unified networks and integrated services/Vineet Kumar, Markku Korpi, Senthil Sengodan.
p. cm.
Includes bibliographical references and index.
ISBN 0-471-39343-6 (cloth: alk. paper)
1. Internet telephony. I. Korpi, Markku. II. Sengodan, Senthil, 1970- III. Title.

TK5105.8865 K86 2000
621.'12—dc21 2001017821

Printed in the United States of America.

10 9 8 7 6 5 4 3 2 1

DEDICATION

To my role models: My mother for shaping my life; my father for inspiring me.

Vineet

With gratitude to my father and mother and to my lovely wife, Tellervo, and our daughters, Anne-Maria and Johanna.

Markku

To Appa, Amma and Kothai: For your guidance, support, and undying love.

Senthil

CONTENTS

	Preface	**xv**
	Acknowledgments	**xvii**
Chapter 1	**Introduction**	**1**
	Functional Entities	3
	H.323 Protocols	5
	H.323 System Model	7
	Administrative Domain X	7
	Administrative Domain Y	9
	Administrative Domain Z	9
	Call Scenarios	9
	Book Outline	11
	Chapter 2: Multimedia Transport on IP Networks	11
	Chapter 3: Point-to-Point Call: Signaling	12
	Chapter 4: Multi-Point Conference	12
	Chapter 5: Inter-Domain Communication	13
	Chapter 6: Supplementary Services: Overview and Approach	14
	Chapter 7: Third-Party Supplementary Services in H.450	14
	Chapter 8: Call Diversion Services in H.450	15
	Chapter 9: Call Completion Services for Unsuccessful Calls in H.450	15
	Chapter 10: Stimulus Signaling	15
	Chapter 11: Service-Independent Transport by Using HTTP	15
	Chapter 12: Principles of Interworking	16
	Chapter 13: H.323 Security	16
	Chapter 14: H.323, Generic Security Protocols, and Firewalls	16
	Chapter 15: H.323 Mobility	16
	Chapter 16: QoS Principles and Application Level QoS	17
	Chapter 17: Network-Provided QoS for H.323	17
	Recommended Reading	17
	References	17

Chapter 2 Multimedia Transport on IP Networks **19**

Voice 19
- Transmission of Digitized Voice 20
- Voice Coders 20
- Basic Attributes of Voice Coders 22
- End-to-End Delay 24

Conversational Text 26
- Text Transmission Using T.140 as a Coder 26
- End-to-End Delay 27

Facsimile 27
- G3 Facsimile Architecture 27
- G3 Facsimile Communications Protocol 28

Video 30
- Transmission of Digitized Video 30
- Bit-Stream Syntax Overview 33
- Video Coder Summary 34

Transport of Conversational Media on the Internet by Using RTP 36
- RTP Header 39
- RTP Payload 41
- End-to-End Delay and Header Compression on the IP Network 51
- Synchronization of Streams 53
- Real-time Transport Control Protocol 53

Transport of Facsimile over the Internet 54

References 56

Problems 57

Chapter 3 Point-to-Point Call: Signaling **59**

Call-Signaling Protocol: H.225.0-Q.931 62
- H.225.0-Q.931 Signaling 64
- H.225.0-Q.931 Messages 66

Call-Control Protocol: H.245 69
- Description of Some H.245 Messages 70
- Scenarios 99

Call Control Embedded in Call Signaling 110
- H.245 Tunneling 110
- Fast Connect 111

The Registration, Admission, and Status Protocol: H.225.0-RAS 115
- H.225.0-RAS Message Flows 117
- H.225.0-RAS Transport Protocol 133

Call Models 134
- Gatekeeper-Routed Call Signaling 135

References 143

Problems 143

Chapter 4 Multi-Point Conference 145

Conference Basics 145
- Conference Types 146
- Network Configurations 148
- Network Configurations Used in H.323 151
- Conference Types Used in H.323 153

Small- and Medium-Scale Conferences Using H.323 153
- Additions to Call Control Protocol–H.245 155
- Additions to RTP 166
- Additions to Call Signaling Protocol 170
- Scenarios 171
- Scalability of Voice and Video on the Access Link 180

Large-Scale Conferences Using RTP/RTCP and SDP 181
- Session Description Protocol (SDP) 182
- RTP Control Protocol (RTCP) 187

Large-Scale Conference Using H.332 210
- Conference Configuration 210
- Extensions to SDP 211
- Invitation from the Panel 211
- Generation of SSRC Identifiers in H.323 and RTP 212

Recommended Reading 212

References 212

Problems 213

Chapter 5 Inter-Domain Communication 215

Organization of Administrative Domains 217

H.225.0 Annex G Messages and Message-Flows 220

Address Templates for Routing Calls 225

Pre-Call Population of Address Resolution Table 235
- Border Element Discovery 235
- Service Relationship Establishment 235
- Populating the Address Resolution Table 237

Address Resolution, Authorization, and Usage Reporting during the Call 238
- Address Resolution and Authorization 239
- Resource Usage Reporting 240

Recommended Reading 242

Reference 242

Problems 242

Chapter 6 Supplementary Services: Overview and Approach 245

Purpose of Supplementary Services 246

Categories of Call Control Applications 247
- First-Party Call Control Applications 248

Third-Party Call Control Applications 249
Call Management Applications 250
Signaling Architecture for Services in H.323 251
A Centralized Approach Using Stimulus Signaling 252
A Web-Based Approach Using HTTP 254
Distributed Peer-to-Peer Approach Using H.450 256
Introduction to H.450 Supplementary Services 258
Requirements for H.450 258
The Embedding of H.450 in H.323 System Architecture 260
The Status of H.450 Recommendations 261
H.450.1–Generic Functional Protocol 261
H.450.12–Common Information 267
H.450.8–Name Information 268
Recommended Reading 272
References 272
Problems 273

Chapter 7 Three-Party Supplementary Services in H.450 275

General 275
Call Hold 276
Near-End Hold Invocation and Operation 277
Remote-End Hold Invocation and Operation 279
Near-End Hold/Retrieve Performed by Gatekeeper 281
Remote-End Hold/Retrieve Performed by Gatekeeper 281
Consultation 283
Alternating 284
Call Transfer 285
Invocation and Operation 285
Signaling Protocol 286
Unsuccessful Transfers 287
Call Transfer Performed by Gatekeeper 288
Consultation Transfer 290
Invocation and Operation 290
Signaling Protocol 291
Consultation Transfer Performed by Gatekeeper 292
Conference Out of Consultation 295
Invocation and Operation 296
Signaling Protocol 297
Recommended Reading 298
References 299
Problems 299

Chapter 8 Call Diversion Services in H.450 301

General 301

Common Characteristics of Call Diversion Services 302

Remote Registration of Call Forwarding 303

Call Forwarding on All Calls and on Busy 304

Invocation and Operation 305

Signaling Protocol 306

Call Forwarding on No Reply and Call Deflection 307

Invocation and Operation 307

Signaling Protocol 308

Call Forwarding Performed in the Gatekeeper 309

Call Diversion when Terminal Is Out of Service 312

Interaction with Other Supplementary Services 313

References 314

Problems 315

Chapter 9 Call Completion Services for Unsuccessful Calls in H.450 317

General Information 317

The Treatment of Unsuccessful Calls 319

The Definition of Busy and the Handling of Multiple Calls 321

Call Waiting–H.450.6 323

Invocation and Operation 324

Signaling Protocol 324

Conclusion of the H.450.6 Call Waiting Services 325

Message Waiting Indication–H.450.7 326

Invocation and Operation 326

Signaling Protocol 327

Conclusion of the H.450.7 Message Waiting Indication Services 328

Message Waiting Callback–H.450.7 329

Invocation and Operation 329

Signaling Protocol 329

Conclusion of the H.450.7 Message Waiting Callback Services 331

Call Completion Services–H.450.9 331

Invocation and Operation 331

Signaling Protocol 333

Additional Implementation Aspects 335

Conclusion of the H.450.9 Call Completion Services 335

Call Offering–H.450.10 336

Invocation and Operation 336

Signaling Protocol 337

Conclusion of the H.450.10 Call Offering Services 340

Call Intrusion–H.450.11 340

Invocation and Operation 341

Signaling Protocol 342
Conclusion of the H.450.11 Call Intrusion Service 344
References 344
Problems 346

Chapter 10 Stimulus Signaling 347
General Information 347
Variants of Stimulus Signaling 348
Centralized versus Distributed Stimulus Call Control 349
H.323 Stimulus Signaling 350
The Goals 350
Programming Model 351
Functional Units 354
Protocol Framework 355
Stimulus Signaling Protocol in H.248 363
The H.248 Connection Model 363
Recommended Reading 368
References 369
Problems 369

Chapter 11 Service-Independent Transport by Using HTTP 371
Characteristics and Purpose 371
Comparison to Stimulus Signaling 372
Supported Features 373
Application Scenarios 373
Protocol Mechanisms 375
Non-Call-Related Service Control 376
Call-Related Service Control 378
Recommended Reading 382
References 382
Problems 383

Chapter 12 Principles of Interworking 385
QSIG Interworking with H.323 387
QSIG Gateway-Layer Architecture 388
Gateway Signaling 389
Interworking of Consultation Transfer 390
The Interworking of Single-Step Call Transfer 396
ISUP Interworking with H.323 398
ISUP Gateway-Layer Architecture 399
Gateway Signaling 399
Trunking Gateways 401
QSIG Trunking 401
ISUP Trunking 401

BICC Interworking 402
Residential H.323 Gateways 402
References 404
Problems 404

Chapter 13 H.323 Security 405

Security Services for H.323 Systems 405
Generation of a Secret Key 406
Key Generation from a Password 407
Key Generation by Using Diffie-Hellman 408
User Authentication 410
Authentication by Shared Secret-Based Encryption 411
Authentication by Shared Secret-Based Hash 413
Authentication by Using a Digital Signature 414
Message Authentication/Integrity 415
Mechanisms to Achieve Message Integrity 416
Securing H.225.0 and H.245 Channels 417
Securing the H.225.0 Channel 417
Securing the H.245 Channel 417
Secure H.235 Control Channel 419
Security Capability Exchange 419
Receiver Requesting a Security Mode 421
Media-Stream Encryption 421
Opening a Logical Channel for the Encrypted Media Stream 423
Encryption Key Generation, Distribution, and Refresh 424
Use of RTP-Based Techniques for Media-Stream Encryption 428
Use of IPSec for Media-Stream Encryption 432
Anonymity 432
Security Profiles 435
Baseline Security Profile 436
Signature Security Profile 437
Recommended Reading 439
References 439
Problems 440

Chapter 14 H.323, Generic Security Protocols, and Firewalls 443

Generic IP Security Protocols and Algorithms 443
Security Protocols 444
Security Algorithms 454
Firewall Traversal 458
Issues Surrounding Firewall Traversal of H.323 Streams 459
Types of Firewalls 461
Network Topology and Firewall Placement 469

Private Addressing 471
Network Address Translation 471
Realm Specific IP 473
Using RADIUS within H.323 Systems 475
RADIUS Overview 475
H.323 and RADIUS 476
Recommended Reading 479
References 480
Problems 481

Chapter 15 H.323 Mobility 483
Types of Mobility 483
User Mobility 484
Terminal Mobility 485
Service Mobility 485
H.323 Mobility Architecture 487
Initial Gatekeeper Discovery and Registration 487
Location Update 489
Call Signaling to an Endpoint 490
Authenticating Function (AuF) 491
Interworking Function (IWF) 491
User Mobility between PLMN and H.323 Systems 492
Subscriber Identifiers 492
Achieving User Mobility with IWF 493
Non-Application Layer Wireless Issues 499
Error Correction 499
Link and Network Layer Handoff 500
Recommended Reading 501
References 501
Problems 502

Chapter 16 QoS Principles and Application Level QoS 503
Motivation and Drivers 503
Factors Affecting H.323 System Quality 506
Quality in the RAS, H.225.0, and H.245 Channels 508
Quality in the Media Stream 509
Application Level QoS 513
Feedback Mechanisms 513
Source Acting on the Feedback 515
Overhead Reduction Techniques 519
IP/UDP/RTP Header Compression 519
Multi-frame packets 519
Recommended Reading 520

References 520
Problems 521

Chapter 17 Network Provided QoS for H.323 523

Motivation 523
Basic Network QoS Building Blocks 527
Traffic Characterization Using Token Bucket 527
Packet Classifiers 533
Rate Controllers 534
Packet Schedulers and Queue Management 536
RAS Operations for H.323 QoS 541
H.323 Entity Controlling QoS 541
Call Bandwidth 544
RSVP/Intserv Based QoS for H.323 Systems 544
Integrated Services (Intserv) 545
RSVP 549
H.323 and RSVP/Intserv 552
H.323 with RSVP/Intserv over 802 LANs 555
Diffserv-based QoS for H.323 systems 556
Default PHB 559
Class Selector PHB 559
Assured Forwarding (AF) PHB 559
Expedited Forwarding (EF) PHB 562
Policy, Resource Management, and Multi-Domain Issues 565
QoS Functional Entities and Reference Points 565
Role of Policy in H.323 QoS 566
Scenario 1 567
Scenario 2 568
Scenario 3 569
EP/GK Controlled QoS 569
Recommended Reading 570
References 571
Problems 572

Glossary 575

Acronym List 583

Index 591

PREFACE

Internet Protocol (IP) Telephony enables users to collaborate using multimedia telephones on IP networks, just as traditionally users have been collaborating using voice telephones on Public Switch Telephone Networks (PSTN). IP Telephony enables any combination of voice, video, image, and data to be used for collaboration. Traditionally, the Internet was developed for data, and PSTN was developed for voice. The services developed for these two networks were also different—for example, e-mail for the Internet and voice mail for the PSTN. Two trends in the middle 1990s gave rise to IP Telephony. The first trend was the acceptance of the Internet for commercial use. The second trend was the use of the Internet to bypass the PSTN for cheaper phone calls. Other trends followed, chief among them was the standardization of IP Telephony protocols by the ITU-T in a series of H.323 recommendations. This standardization enabled vendors to manufacture interoperable IP Telephony products with the rapidly declining cost curves associated with the development of IP products in general. The ability to develop rich multimedia services, and the promise of unification of the corporate LANs and the private telephone network into one network were other factors that drove the use of IP Telephony.

Objectives

The primary purpose of this book is to explain the various protocols and architectural components of IP Telephony through the use of the ITU-T's H.323 standard. Although the H.323 subject matter for IP Telephony is well understood by the standard's developers and by those who implemented the standard, the authors of this book attempt to expand the understanding of this subject matter beyond that select group.

This book is a result of the authors' direct involvement in the creation of the H.323 family of related standards and the IP Telephony industry. Not only does this book explain how H.323 works, but it also provides insights into the use and implementation of the standard. H.323 has evolved through four revisions. The first version was developed for video conferencing. The second and higher versions were optimized for IP Telephony. All standards are open to interpretation, and this book provides the authors' interpretation of H.323. Implementers and others involved in the development of H.323 products must use the H.323 specifications as the definitive text specifying this standard.

Intended Audience

This book is intended for both academics and professionals. As a textbook, it is meant to be a single-semester senior- or graduate-level course in IP Telephony. Various types of readers can benefit from this book. The students can gain a deep practical understanding of how IP Telephony works. The exercises at the end of each chapter provide a good way to use the concepts described in the chapter by solving the problems. The system engineer will find this book ideal because it lays out a complete system view of IP Telephony and explains how each component in that system interworks. Executives and marketing managers will find this book easy to read and will gain a complete picture of IP Telephony. The researcher can get a good understanding of the protocols and components involved and how they work together; this basic knowledge can be used to develop more powerful protocols and components to improve the overall architecture being standardized and deployed today. The implementers often do not get a complete picture; this book provides that image, which is needed to appreciate what might otherwise appear to be magic. This book also helps readers understand the H.323 specifications and the more complex technical features of this standard.

ACKNOWLEDGMENTS

The authors wish to thank David Graumann and Tom Gardos, both with Intel Corporation, for their help in reviewing the audio and the video sections, respectively, of this book.

The ITU-T H.323 family of specifications is the result of the dedicated effort and contribution of several folks over the span of a few years, and the authors would like to acknowledge each of them.

I, Markku, wish to thank my former colleagues from Siemens Information and Communication Networks for shaping the H.450 vision. I am especially grateful to Karl Klaghofer who worked with me in the ITU-T and helped to design and draft the ITU-T H.450 series of recommendations.

The authors would like to thank the entire Wiley team that assisted us from start to finish. You ensured that the book got published on schedule.

I, Senthil, would like to thank Vineet for initiating this project and inviting me to be a coauthor. Completing a project of this nature takes commitment from each author, and I'd like to thank both Markku and Vineet for sticking it out until the end.

I would like to thank Dr. Raj Bansal, Senior Manager, Nokia Research Center (NRC), Boston, for his continued support and encouragement throughout the course of writing this book. My colleagues—past and present—at NRC/ Boston helped create an environment fostering intellectual and professional development, an ingredient that was vital to my embarking on and successfully completing the writing of this book.

I would like to thank my teachers—all the way from kindergarten to graduate school—you paved the road that led to my writing this book. I would like to thank all my friends—you know who you are—for the many good times we've had together. My sister, Kothai, has been a pillar of strength and friendship during my entire stay in the United States, for which I am thankful. My gratitude to my parents knows no bounds. I am what I am because of you; you are the wind beneath my wings.

Senthil

CHAPTER 1

Introduction

This chapter describes the H.323 concepts and terminology that we will use in the rest of this book. H.323 consists of a series of *International Telecommunications Union—Telecommunications Sector* (ITU-T) recommendations that specify protocols on packet-based networks, such as the *Internet Protocol* (IP) or *Asynchronous Transfer Mode* (ATM), in order to enable multimedia collaboration among two or more entities. Because they are transport independent, H.323 protocols can operate on virtually any network but are optimized for the IP network. This book describes the operation of H.323 protocols on IP networks (including the Internet) and the interoperation of H.323 with the *Switched-Circuit Network* (SCN).

The H.323 network is divided into administrative domains. We define an administrative domain as a collection of H.323 functional entities that one administrative entity administers. We do not have to expose the internal structure of the domain to other domains. Figure 1.1 shows an H.323 network that has three administrative domains: X, Y, and Z. Domain X is a corporate network belonging to Corporation X. Domain Y belongs to a *third-generation* (3G) cellular service provider that connects its subscribers to the Internet. Domain Z belongs to a service provider that provides its subscribers with seamless connectivity between the *Public Switched Telephone Network* (PSTN) and the Internet.

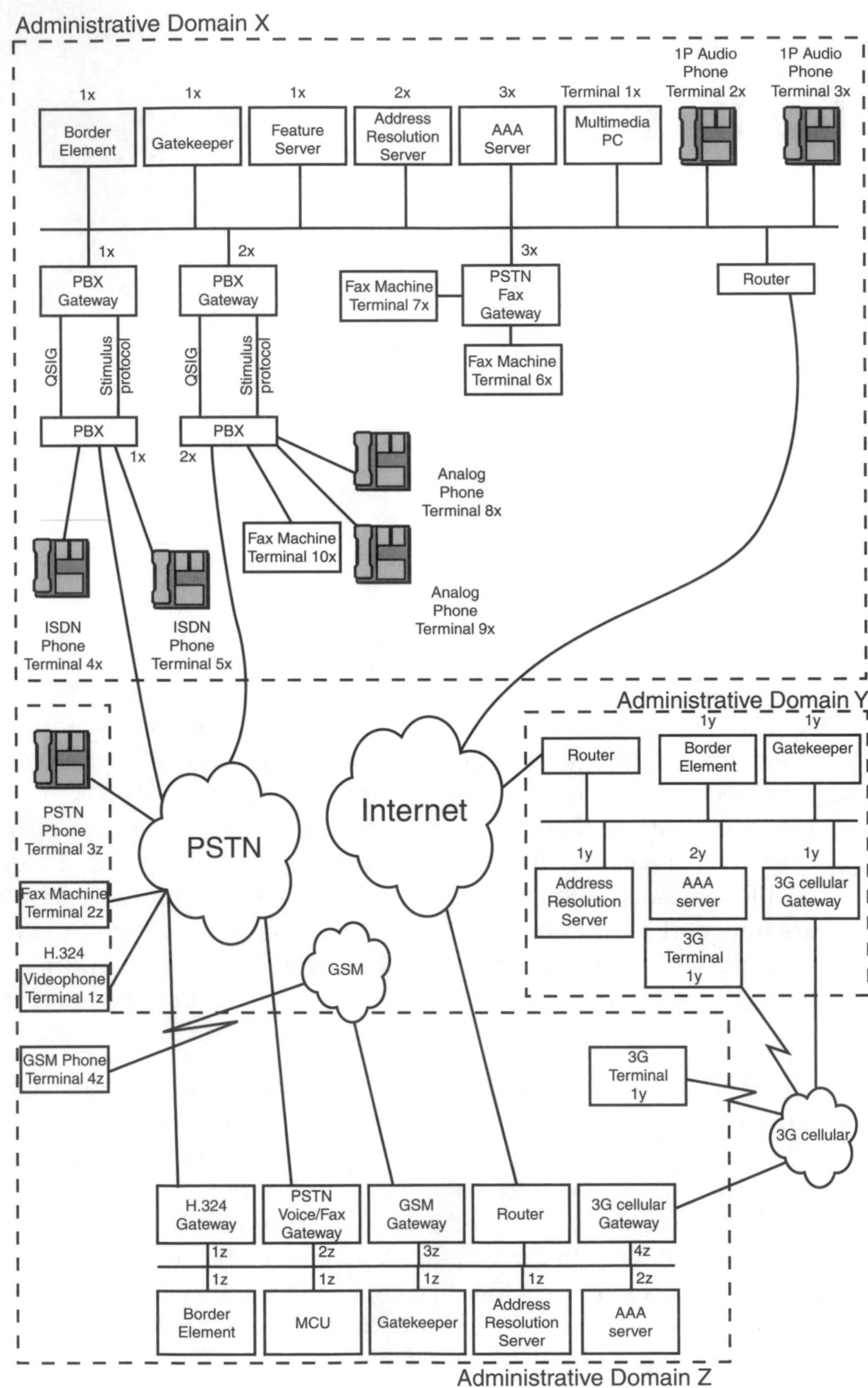

Figure 1.1 H.323 IP telephony networks.

Functional Entities

The H.323 series of recommendations consists of a number of functional entities specified as follows:

- *Terminal*. The terminal terminates signaling and media at the end-user's location. Some examples of terminals are multimedia PC (Terminal 1_X), IP audio phone (Terminal 2_X), H.324 PSTN videophone (Terminal 1_Z), PSTN audio phone (Terminal 3_Z), 3G multimedia phone (Terminal 1_Y), and GSM audio phone (Terminal 4_Z). We can also call the terminal a client.
- *Gateway*. The gateway interconnects the H.323 network and the SCN and converts signaling protocols as well as media transmission formats between the two networks. Some examples of gateways are as follows:
  - *PSTN/voice gateway*. This gateway interconnects voice calls between the H.323 and PSTN networks. As an example, Gateway 2_Z converts voice calls between the PSTN telephone (Terminal 3_Z) and the H.323 phone (Terminal 2_X).
  - *PSTN/fax gateway*. This gateway interconnects facsimile calls between the H.323 and PSTN networks. As an example, a call between the PSTN facsimile machines 6_X and 2_Z involves two PSTN facsimile gateways: 3_X and 2_Z. Both gateways convert facsimile calls between the H.323 and PSTN networks.
  - *PSTN/H.324 gateway*. This gateway interconnects the H.323 and H.324 networks. As an example, it converts voice and video calls between the PSTN H.324 videophone (Terminal 1_Z) and the H.323 multimedia PC (Terminal 1_X).
  - *GSM gateway*. This gateway interconnects the H.323 and GSM networks. As an example, it converts voice calls between the *Global Systems for Mobile* (GSM) phone (Terminal 4_Z) and H.323 multimedia PC (Terminal 1_X).
  - *PBX gateway*. This gateway interconnects the H.323 network with the *Private Branch Exchange* (PBX). As an example, it converts voice calls between *Integrated Services Digital Network* (ISDN) phone (Terminal 4_X) and H.323 multimedia PC (Terminal 1_X).
- *Multi-Point Control Units (MCUs)*. MCUs enable multimedia conferencing among three or more terminals. They mix the voices and usually pick the video of the participant whose voice has the highest energy (in other words, the person who is talking the loudest) and provides this video for all of the terminals. As an example, Terminals 1_X, 2_X, 1_Z, and 4_Z use MCU 1_Z to host a conference. We also call the MCU a conference server.

- *Endpoint*. The endpoint terminates the signaling and media. We collectively refer to terminals, gateways, and MCUs as endpoints.
- *Gatekeeper*. The gatekeeper provides services to endpoints and routes H.323 calls to their destinations. The services that it provides include *Authentication, Authorization, and Accounting* (AAA) and address resolution (for example, resolving an E.164 address of a terminal to a routable IP address). Normally, the gatekeeper interfaces with various servers and acts as a proxy for the endpoint when obtaining the services. As an example, Gatekeeper 1_Z interfaces with the address resolution server 1_Z and with the AAA Server 2_Z.
- *Border element*. The border element provides public access to an administrative domain for the purposes of address resolution, access authorization, and resource usage reporting. As an example, each of the domains X, Y, and Z has a border element.
- *Address resolution server*. This server resolves nonroutable addresses such as *Universal Resource Locators* (URLs), e-mail addresses, E.164 addresses, and so on of an H.323 entity to a routable IP address. The protocol that this server uses to communicate with the functional entities is not standardized in H.323. Normally, this server does not directly communicate with the endpoints. Instead, the gatekeeper acts as a proxy for the endpoints when communicating with this server. As an example, Terminals 1_X and 2_X might communicate with the address resolution server 2_X via Gatekeeper 1_X.
- *AAA server*. This server authenticates the user, authorizes the user for the services requested, and performs accounting for the call in order to bill the user. The protocol that this server uses to communicate with the functional entities is not standardized in H.323. Normally, the gatekeeper acts as a proxy for the endpoints when communicating with this server. As an example, Terminals 1_X and 2_X might communicate with AAA Server 3_Z via Gatekeeper 1_X.
- *Feature server*. This server provides supplementary services such as Call Park/Call Pickup. The protocol that this server uses to communicate with the functional entities is standardized in H.323. The endpoints can communicate directly with this server or use the gatekeeper as a proxy in order to communicate indirectly with this server. As an example (as we will see later), Terminals 1_X and 2_X communicate directly with Feature Server 1_X, and Terminal 3_X communicates with Feature Server 1_X via Gatekeeper 1_X.

Note that H.323 defines functional or logical entities and not physical entities. You can integrate these functional entities in any combination as a single product. As an example, you can integrate the gatekeeper and the border element as a single product or the gateway, gatekeeper, and the border element as a single product.

H.323 Protocols

These functional entities communicate through a series of protocols that we collectively know as the H.323 protocols. Some H.323 protocols have multivendor, interoperable implementations deployed on various networks while others have not yet been implemented in any measurable form. In this book, we describe some of the protocols that have multivendor implementations. Figure 1.2 shows the placement of these H.323 protocols on the *Transmission Control Protocol/Internet Protocol* (TCP/IP) stack. All H.323 protocols are higher than the transport layer; therefore, they can work on various networks such as ATM (although they are optimized for IP networks).

We define the H.323 protocols as follows:

- *H.225.0-Q.931.*This protocol defines the procedures and signaling between two endpoints for setting up and releasing a call. This signaling is derived from Q.931 ISDN signaling by using a subset of the Q.931 messages and adding functionality in the User Information fields of the H.225.0-Q.931 messages. Using Q.931 makes the interconnection with ISDN networks easier.
- *H.245.* This protocol defines procedures and signaling between two endpoints in order to exchange capabilities and control media streams. The endpoints have a variety of capabilities, but the call that you establish only uses the capabilities that are common to both endpoints.

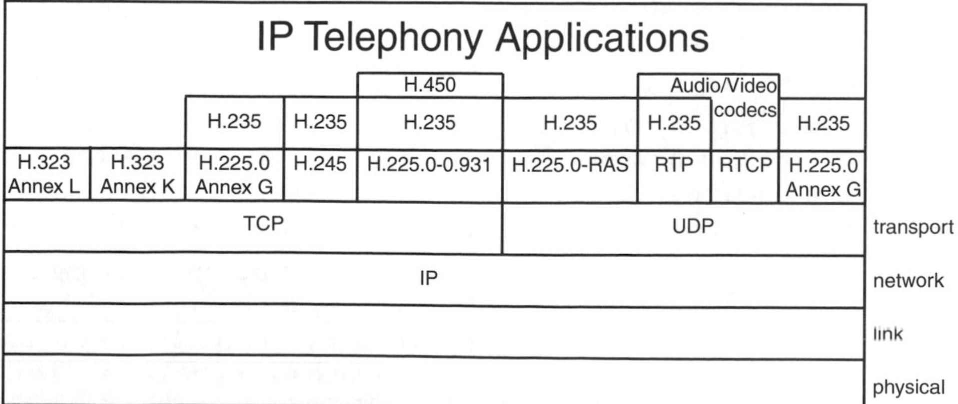

Figure 1.2 H.323 protocols on a TCP/IP stack.

- *H.225.0-RAS (Registration, Admission, and Status).* This protocol defines the procedures and signaling between the endpoint and the gatekeeper so that the endpoint can obtain services from the gatekeeper, and the gatekeeper can provide service notifications/commands to the endpoints. Some of the services include AAA and address resolution. The endpoints use this protocol to request these services. The gatekeeper acts on behalf of the endpoint in order to obtain these services from the AAA and from the address resolution server. The protocol between the gatekeeper and the AAA or the address resolution server is not standardized in H.323.
- *Real-time Transport Protocol (RTP).* This protocol defines the delivery of real-time data from one endpoint directly to another endpoint in the case of unicast or to multiple endpoints in the case of multicast.
- *Real-time Transport Control Protocol (RTCP).* This protocol is RTP's companion protocol and primarily gathers statistics about the quality of the network on which the RTP packets are transmitted.
- *H.450.* This protocol defines the procedures and signaling between two intelligent H.323 entities for the execution of supplementary services. This protocol also uses H.225.0-Q.931 messages with added functionality in the User Information fields of the H.225.0-Q.931 messages. You use this protocol when the supplementary service-execution software is distributed between the two entities involved and when the services are executed without the intervention of the network entities. The two entities are the endpoints or the endpoint and the feature server.
- *H.225.0 Annex G.* This protocol provides procedures and signaling between two border elements, in different administrative domains, for the exchange of addressing information, accessing authorization for a call, and resource usage reporting for a call. The address resolution server, the authorization server, and the accounting server all use the border elements in their domain in order to communicate addressing, authorization, and accounting information (respectively) to border elements in other domains.
- *H.323 Annex K.* This protocol specifies the use of the standard *Hypertext Transport Protocol* (HTTP) protocol between two H.323 entities for the execution of supplementary services. You can use the standard HTTP along with standard *Hypertext Markup Language* (HTML) to develop and execute certain supplementary services with or without the aid of H.450.
- *H.323 Annex L.* This protocol defines procedures and signaling between an unintelligent H.323 terminal (for instance, a telephone) and the feature server for the execution of supplementary services. We use this protocol when the supplementary service execution software is centralized in the feature server and the unintelligent H.323 terminal simply provides stimuli corresponding to the service to be executed. The feature server can

also be a back-end server of the gatekeeper. In this case, this protocol is between the endpoint and the gatekeeper, and the gatekeeper acts as a proxy for the endpoint in requesting the execution of the service at the feature server.

- *H.235.* This protocol provides the security framework to enable authentication, nonrepudiation, privacy/confidentiality, and integrity on the H.323 networks. The security information is carried in the H.225.0-Q.931, H.225.0-RAS, H.245, H.225.0 Annex G, and RTP protocols through the use of new fields in the messages of these protocols.

You should note that all H.323 protocols except for RTP and RTCP were developed by the ITU-T. The *Internet Engineering Task Force* (IETF) developed the RTP and RTCP protocols.

H.323 System Model

The H.323 environment consists of administrative domains that offer functional entities that communicate through H.323 protocols on packet-based networks in order to enable multimedia collaboration among two or more entities. Figure 1.1 shows three domains: X, Y, and Z.

Administrative Domain X

Domain X is a corporate network consisting of *Local Area Networks* (LANs) for the data network and the traditional private telephone network. The H.323 entities connect to the LAN in order to provide multimedia services to the users. H.323 Terminals 1_X, 2_X, and 3_X are connected to the LAN. Terminal 1_X is a multimedia terminal, and Terminals 2_X and 3_X are audio-only terminals. The traditional private telephone network consists of PBXs 1_X and 2_X. PBX 1_X connects to *Integrated Services Digital Network* (ISDN) telephones 4_X and 5_X. PBX 2_X connects to analog telephones 8_X, 9_X, and facsimile machine 10_X. PBX gateways 1_X and 2_X connect PBXs 1_X and 2_X (respectively) to the LAN. PSTN Facsimile Gateway 3_X connects two traditional PSTN facsimile machines 6_X and 7_X to the LAN. Gatekeeper 1_X, Border Element 1_X, Feature Server 1_X, Address Resolution Server 2_X, and AAA Server 3_X are all connected to the LAN.

Basic Service

Basic service includes multimedia calls between two or more terminals. The three terminals—1_X, 2_X, and 3_X—implement the basic H.323 protocols that include the call control protocols (H.225.0-Q.931, H.225.0-RAS, and H.245) and the media transfer protocols RTP and RTCP. Terminals 2_X and 3_X are audio-only terminals whereas Terminal 1_X is a multimedia terminal consisting of audio, video, and data. PSTN Facsimile Gateway 3_X provides interworking between the call control and facsimile formats on the H.323 IP network with those in the PSTN network. This gateway enables facsimile calls between the H.323 facsimile entity and the PSTN facsimile machine to complete. PBX Gateways 1_X and 2_X provide interworking between the call control and voice/facsimile formats on the H.323 IP network with those in the PBX. These gateways enable voice/facsimile calls between the H.323 endpoint and the PBX telephone/facsimile machine to complete.

Supplementary Services

In addition to basic service, you have optional supplementary services. Terminals 1_X and 2_X implement the H.450 protocols that include widely used supplementary services such as call forwarding, call transfer, call hold, call waiting, message waiting, and multiple call handling. Therefore, Terminals 1_X and 2_X are essentially software PBXs. Terminal 3_X does not implement H.450 but instead relies on Gatekeeper 1_X to act as its proxy for the execution of H.450 supplementary services. Gatekeeper 1_X uses Feature Server 1_X as its back-end server in order to provide H.450 supplementary services. Terminal 3_X and Gatekeeper 1_X communicate supplementary services signaling through the H.323 Annex L stimulus protocol. The protocol between the gatekeeper and any back-end server is not standardized in H.323. The feature server also implements H.450 supplementary services that cannot be distributed in the endpoints. In an automatic call distribution environment, services such as call park/pickup are not directed toward any specific terminal. Incoming calls are parked in the feature server and are picked up by the first available agent on the terminal.

The PBX provides more than 300 supplementary services that have not currently been replicated in the H.323 environment. H.450 currently provides only the most widely used supplementary services. When Terminal 1_X communicates with Gateway 1_X by using H.450, Gateway 1_X identifies itself to PBX 1_X as a PBX and communicates with it by using the QSIG protocol. Gateway 1_X provides interworking between the QSIG protocol of the PBX and the H.450 protocol of the H.323 terminal. Because H.450 is derived from QSIG, the interworking functionality in the gateway is rather easy to implement. When Terminal 3_X communicates with Gateway 1_X by using H.323 Annex L, Gateway 1_X identifies itself to PBX 1_X as a telephone and communicates with it by using the stimulus protocol of PBX 1_X. Gateway 1_X provides interworking functionality between the H.323 Annex L stimulus protocol and the stimulus protocol that the PBX uses. In the former case, the execution of supplementary services is distributed in Terminal 1_X and PBX 1_X.

In the latter case, Terminal 3_X has access to more than 300 supplementary services centralized in PBX 1_X.

Administrative Domain Y

Domain Y is a 3G wireless cellular service provider that connects its subscribers to the Internet. Gatekeeper 1_Y, Border Element 1_Y, 3G cellular GW 1_Y, Address Resolution Server 1_Y, and AAA Server 2_Y are all connected to the LAN. H.323 Terminal 1_Y accesses the Internet through GW 1_Y. Terminal 1_Y implements the basic H.323 protocols and the H.450 protocols for supplementary services.

Administrative Domain Z

Domain Z is a service provider that seamlessly connects its subscribers to the Internet, PSTN, GSM, and 3G cellular networks. H.324 videophone Terminal 1_Z, Facsimile Terminal 2_Z, and PSTN phone terminal 3_Z are on the PSTN. GSM phone terminal 4_Z is on the GSM. Terminal 1_Y is mobile and is in this domain on the 3G cellular networks. H.324 Gateway 1_Z, PSTN fax/voice Gateway 2_Z, GSM Gateway 3_Z, and 3G cellular Gateway 4_Z connect the *Switched-Circuit Networks* (SCNs) to the service provider's LAN. The gateways provide interworking between the call control and media formats on the H.323 IP network with those in the SCNs. Gatekeeper 1_Z, MCU 1_Z, Border Element 1_Z, Address Resolution Server 1_Z, and AAA Server 2_Z are all connected to the LAN.

Call Scenarios

We describe the following call scenarios as follows:

Multimedia calls between administrative domains. Assume that a user at H.324 videophone terminal 1_Z connects to H.324 Gateway 1_Z and dials the E.164 address of the user at multimedia PC terminal 1_X. Gateway 1_Z uses Address Resolution Server 1_Z to resolve the E.164 address to the IP address of Terminal 1_X. Address Resolution Server 1_Z might instruct its border element 1_Z to resolve the address by using the H.225.0 Annex G protocol. After the address is resolved, Address Resolution Server 1_Z provides the IP address of Terminal 1_X to Gateway 1_Z. Gateway 1_Z makes an H.323 call over the Internet to the IP address of Terminal 1_X by using H.225.0-Q.931 and H.245 signaling. If the call is successful, Accounting Servers 2_Z and 3_X start accounting for the resource usage of this call. Terminals 1_Z and 1_X can start audio/video collaboration. RTP audio and video streams are transmitted between Terminals 1_Z and 1_X. Gateway 1_Z provides interworking between the H.324 protocols/media and the H.323

protocols/media. After the call ends, Accounting Servers 2_Z and 3_X use Border Elements 1_Z and 1_X (respectively) to exchange accounting information for the purpose of settlement between the two domains.

Multimedia calls within an administrative domain. Assume that a user at Terminal 3_X calls Gatekeeper 1_X with the E.164 address of the user at Terminal 1_X. Gatekeeper 1_X uses Address Resolution Server 2_X to resolve the E.164 address to the IP address of Terminal 1_X. Gatekeeper 1_X calls Terminal 1_X. The user at Terminal 1_X is forwarding calls to Terminal 2_X. So, Terminal 1_X starts the H.450 signaling for call forwarding with the back-end Feature Server 1_X forwarding the call to Terminal 2_X. The call between Terminal 3_X and Terminal 2_X is then established with Gatekeeper 1_X as the proxy for Terminal 3_X. Terminals 3_X and 1_X can start audio collaboration. RTP audio streams are transmitted between Terminals 3_X and 1_X. You can use the same Accounting Server 3_X to provide accounting for this call.

Trunking over IP networks. Assume that a user at Terminal 4_X calls PBX 1_X with the E.164 address of the user at Terminal 8_X. PBX 1_X calls PBX 2_X, which then completes the call to Terminal 8_X. Traditionally, a *Primary Rate Interface* (PRI) would connect the two PBXs (1_X and 2_X). Gateways 1_X and 2_X, however, connect the PBXs to the LAN instead. The reason to use the LAN over PRI is the enormous cost savings. The calls between the PBXs are tunneled in H.225.0-Q.931 between the gateways.

Facsimile over IP networks for toll bypass. Assume that a user at Facsimile Terminal 7_X connects to Facsimile Gateway 3_X and dials the E.164 address of the user at Facsimile Terminal 2_Z. Gateway 3_X uses Address Resolution Server 2_X to resolve the E.164 address to the IP address of Facsimile Gateway 2_Z that is close in proximity to Terminal 2_Z. Facsimile Gateway 3_X establishes an H.323 call over the Internet with Facsimile Gateway 2_Z, which in turn establishes a PSTN call with Terminal 2_Z. The two PSTN terminals 7_X and 2_Z communicate over the Internet, thereby bypassing most of the PSTN for toll bypass.

Mobility and execution of supplementary services without need for network entity. Assume that a user at Terminal 1_X calls the E.164 address of a user at Terminal 1_Y. Terminal 1_X uses Address Resolution Server 2_X to resolve the E.164 address to the IP address of 3G cellular gateway 4_Z. Note that Terminal 1_Y is roaming in domain Z. Terminal 1_X makes an H.323 call to Gateway 4_Z, which then completes the call to Terminal 1_Y. If Terminal 1_Y is already in a call, the H.450 signaling for call waiting executes between Terminals 1_X and 1_Y.

- Note that the mechanism through which the address resolution server locates a mobile user is not standardized as part of H.323 protocols as of this writing. This work is underway in the ITU-T and is expected to finish in the year 2001.

Book Outline

This book can be broken down into five sections:

- Chapters 2 through 5 describe protocols among two or more entities that enable users to collaborate in a multimedia call/conference. The service providers who are involved in the call/conference can record the network resources that are used for the purpose of billing the end-user.
- Chapters 6 through 11 describe protocols between two H.323 entities that enable supplementary services to execute. The supplementary services that are standardized for the H.323 IP telephony networks are those that are already available in traditional telephony networks.
- Chapter 12, "Principles of Interworking," describes the architecture and deployment scenarios of various types of gateways (including network access gateways, trunking gateways, and residential gateways).
- Chapters 13 through 15 cover security and mobility on H.323-based networks. On the subject of security, these chapters describe how you can implement security in H.323-based signaling protocols and media streams. On the subject of mobility, these chapters describe how user, terminal, and service mobility is accomplished on H.323 networks.
- Chapters 16 and 17 introduce *Quality of Service* (QoS) and describes application- and network-level techniques in order to provide QoS to the H.323 network.

In the next section, we provide a summary of the chapters in this book. Figure 1.1 serves as an aid in summarizing the contents of each chapter.

Chapter 2: Multimedia Transport on IP Networks

This chapter describes the media that we commonly use in IP telephony and the transport of this media between two endpoints (for instance, between Terminals 1_X and 1_Y, Terminal 3_Z, and PSTN Gateway 2_Z) on IP networks. This media consists of audio, video, data, and images. In IP telephony, the types of media that we normally use are conversational voice for audio, conversational video for video, conversational text for data, and facsimile for images. For each media type, we describe the components that generate, compress, and transmit the media on the network and that receive, uncompress, and render the media. For real-time media, we normally use RTP to transfer media on the IP networks. On the Internet, routers drop packets when they become congested, so some packets that are transmitted will not be received. Therefore, we will describe mechanisms such as

Redundancy and *Forward Error Correction* (FEC) that we can use to recover the lost information at the receiver. Also, this chapter examines the rather important topic of end-to-end delay in conversational voice. In order for humans to converse at a natural pace, there is a limit on the round-trip delay of voice. The Internet was developed for nonreal-time data; therefore, unlike the PSTN that was especially developed for conversational voice, it does not guarantee a maximum boundary on network delay and jitter. Implementing conversational voice on the Internet poses an engineering challenge.

Chapter 3: Point-to-Point Call: Signaling

This chapter describes the signaling for each of the H.225.0-Q.931, H.245, and H.225.0-RAS protocols for the purpose of establishing, collaborating, and finally releasing a call between two endpoints (for example, Terminals 1_Y and 1_Z). Also, we show example scenarios in order to illustrate the use of these protocols. This chapter describes the signaling portion of the call (we cover the media portion of the call in Chapter 2, "Multimedia Transport on IP Networks"). The call is normally between two humans on terminals, but it can also include nonhumans (such as answering machines or servers that provide various types of services). Deploying IP telephony commercially requires the use of AAA servers in order to authenticate users, providing services for which they are authorized, and performing accounting on resources that are used for billing the user. In this chapter, we also describe the interaction of these servers with the endpoints through the use of the gatekeeper as a proxy.

The Internet and the PSTN have different models based on where the intelligence lies. On the Internet, the intelligence lies in the endpoints; the network is dumb and essentially performs the routing. On the PSTN, the intelligence lies in the network; the endpoints are dumb and essentially provide a stimulus to the network switch. The H.323 recommendation enables both types of models, which we will examine in this chapter. In fact, in H.323, the PSTN model is much like the ISDN model where the endpoints have some intelligence, but the network is still where most of the intelligence lies.

Chapter 4: Multi-Point Conference

This chapter describes how multiple (three or more) users on different terminals collaborate in a multimedia conference. This chapter essentially extends the point-to-point signaling of Chapter 3 to multipoint involving three or more endpoints (for example, MCU 1_Z is connected to Terminals 1_X,

2_X, 1_Y, and 1_Z). This chapter also describes extensions to the H.225.0-RAS, H.225.0-Q.931, and H.245 protocols for their operation in the H.323 multipoint conference. Also, we show example scenarios in order to illustrate the use of these protocols. These protocols are for small and medium-scale conferences involving fewer than five and 100 terminals, respectively. For large-scale scalability involving hundreds and thousands of terminals, we make adjustments to these protocols. Here, we also describe RTP's companion protocol, RTCP. RTCP gathers statistics about the quality of the network on which the RTP packets are transmitted. RTCP, in general, was developed for large-scale conferences; hence, we describe it here.

Chapter 5: Inter-Domain Communication

This chapter describes the communication between administrative domains (for example, domains X and Y, domains X and Z, and so on) for the purpose of address resolution, access authorization, and resource usage reporting in order to complete a call from the originating to the terminating administrative domain. You accomplish this communication between administrative domains with the use of the H.225.0 Annex G protocol between border elements. The H.225.0 Annex G protocol is specified between domains when calls originate (for instance, Terminal 1_X) and terminate (for example, Terminal 1_Y) in different domains. This specification ensures that a standard protocol exists between domains that are maintained by different service providers so that the equipment between different service providers interworks. Within a domain that is maintained by the same service provider, there is no need to standardize a protocol (although you can use the H.225.0 Annex G protocol for calls that originate and terminate in the same domain). The H.225.0 Annex G protocol puts no restrictions on how the administrative domains are organized for the purpose of resolving alias addresses. You can organize the administrative domains in a hierarchical, distributed, or clearinghouse format (or in a hybrid of distributed and clearinghouse formats or in any other fashion).

A URL, e-mail address, or an E.164 address represents the address of the endpoints. The H.225.0 Annex G protocol resolves these addresses to routable transport addresses consisting of the IP address and port. Access authorization is performed at the terminating administrative domain in order to enable a specific call from the originating administrative domain to finish. Also, both the originating and the terminating administrative domains report resource usage for the purpose of settlement of the call.

Chapter 6: Supplementary Services: Overview and Approach

This chapter describes the basic architectures for implementing supplementary services in the H.323-based IP telephony environment. These architectures vary based on whether the service execution software is distributed among functional entities or is centralized in some network functional entity, such as the feature server. In a distributed architecture, the endpoints communicate with their peer entities (feature servers, terminals, or gateways) directly without any network intervention by using the ITU-T's H.450 series of recommendations. In the administrative domain X of Figure 1.1, Terminals 1_X and 2_X have the software to execute certain supplementary services. In a call between Terminals 1_X and 2_X, these services are executed without the need for any other entity. We describe this distributed architecture for various services in Chapters 7 through 9.

In the centralized architecture, all service execution software is executed in the feature server. The feature server might interact directly with the endpoints or indirectly through the gatekeeper as a back-end server. The endpoints provide the stimulus to the feature server. The stimulus can consist of the coordinates of the key that the user presses. The feature server executes the service software that is associated with the stimulus. In the administrative domain X of Figure 1.1, software for certain supplementary services might only be executed in the feature server or PBX. In that case, the user at Terminal 1_X might provide a stimulus to the feature server/PBX in order to invoke those centralized services. We describe this architecture in Chapter 10, "Stimulus Signaling."

You can use the standard HTTP protocol along with standard HTML in order to implement services. This situation requires support of an HTTP browser in the endpoint. The advantage of using HTTP is that you can deploy new services without upgrading the endpoints. Also, you can download software upgrades and commercials to the terminals through the HTTP channel. In Chapter 11, "Service-Independent Transport by Using HTTP," we describe this use of Web protocols to implement supplementary services.

Chapter 7: Third-Party Supplementary Services in H.450

This chapter describes the protocols and usage scenarios for third-party supplementary services. These services enable a user to manage two related point-to-point calls simultaneously. These services include call hold/retrieve, call transfer, and conference. These services are reusable as building blocks for the development of more complex services, such as consultation. Services such as consultation are known as compound services; we also describe these concepts in this chapter.

Chapter 8: Call Diversion Services in H.450

This chapter describes the protocols and usage scenarios for call diversion services. These services enable the called user (in other words, the user who is being called) to send all or specific incoming calls to another destination. These services include various flavors of call forwarding.

Chapter 9: Call Completion Services for Unsuccessful Calls in H.450

This chapter describes the protocols and usage scenarios for call completion services. This chapter also describes services that can be invoked for calls that cannot be completed because the called user is either busy or is not answering the call. These services enable an unsuccessful call to be turned into a call that can continue to progress and finally be answered. These services include multiple call handling, call waiting, message waiting, call offering, call intrusion, and call completion on busy subscriber and on no reply.

Chapter 10: Stimulus Signaling

This chapter describes the protocols and usage scenarios for stimulus signaling. The service execution software is centralized in the feature server and can be accessed by any endpoint by providing a stimulus that is associated with the service to be executed. The ITU-T's H.323 Annex L recommendation provides a framework through which the centralized entity can control the stimulus endpoints.

Chapter 11: Service-Independent Transport by Using HTTP

This chapter describes how you can use Web protocols to execute supplementary services in the H.323 environment. The architecture divides the call control plane from the service plane. The call control plane involves H.323 entities executing H.323 call control protocols whereas the service control plane involves a Web browser and a Web server executing supplementary services with the use of Web protocols such as HTTP and HTML. We present scenarios relating to the usage of HTTP and HTML with and without the use of H.450.

Chapter 12: Principles of Interworking

This chapter describes the system architecture of gateways and the scenarios in which you can deploy them. We cover three types of gateways in this chapter: network access gateways, trunking gateways, and residential gateways. We also describe the deployment of trunking gateways and network-access gateways on public and private networks. Also, we explore the deployment of residential gateways in order to interface with existing user-premises telephone networks.

Chapter 13: H.323 Security

In general, there are five fundamental security services: authentication, integrity, confidentiality, nonrepudiation, and authorization. The H.235 recommendation provides a framework for implementing these security services in H.323 systems. This chapter describes this framework and shows how it is applied to H.323-based signaling protocols and media streams.

Chapter 14: H.323, Generic Security Protocols, and Firewalls

H.323 networks make use of the widely available, IP-based, generic security protocols and algorithms. These protocols and algorithms include IPSec, *Transport-Layer Security* (TLS), *Internet Key Exchange* (IKE), *Data Encryption Standard* (DES), *Secure Hash Algorithm* (SHA), *Message Digest 5* (MD5), and so on. This chapter provides a detailed description of these security protocols and algorithms and their usage in the H.323 environment. This chapter also discusses issues with H.323 protocol traversal through firewalls and *Network Address Translators* (NATs). This chapter also describes how you can use RADIUS, the AAA server, in an H.323 environment.

Chapter 15: H.323 Mobility

The H.323 Annex H recommendation will specify how mobility is accomplished within the H.323 networks. As of this writing, the work in H.323 Annex H is not yet complete. Therefore, this chapter provides a general discussion of three types of mobility: user, terminal, and service—followed by a discussion of the architecture that we have specified so far in H.323 Annex H for the H.323 networks.

Chapter 16: QoS Principles and Application Level QoS

The Internet was developed for nonreal-time data. Transporting real-time media on the Internet requires providing QoS to that media. This chapter describes the principles governing QoS, some models that you can use for gauging QoS, and factors affecting QoS on H.323 IP networks. We also describe application-level techniques for providing QoS on H.323 IP networks.

Chapter 17: Network-Provided QoS for H.323

This chapter describes network-level techniques for providing QoS on H.323 IP networks. These techniques include the use of the *Resource Reservation* (RSVP) and differentiated services protocols for QoS signaling. We also explore the use of these techniques on H.323 IP networks.

Recommended Reading

The messages for H.225.0-Q.931 and H.225.0-RAS are described in the ITU-T recommendation H.225.0 [00H2250], and the procedures on the usage of these messages are described in the ITU-T recommendation H.323 [00H323]. The messages and the procedures for the H.245 protocol are described in the ITU-T recommendation H.245 [00H245]. The RTP and RTCP protocols are specified in the IETF standard [CAS96]. The H.450 protocol consists of a series of ITU-T recommendations starting with H.450.1 [98H4501]. The H.450.1 recommendation provides a framework for all H.450-based supplementary services. As a new supplementary service is standardized, it is provided the next higher number in the H.450.x series. The ITU-T recommendation H.225.0 Annex G is specified in [H225G99]. The ITU-T recommendation for security on H.323 networks is specified in H.235 [H.235v3]. The ITU-T recommendation for videoconferencing on PSTNs is specified in H.324 [96H324].

References

00H2250 ITU-T Recommendation H.225.0: *Call signalling protocols and media stream packetization for packet-based multimedia communication systems.* November 2000.

H225G99 ITU-T Recommendation H.225.0: Annex G. *Communication Between Administrative Domains*. May 1999.

00H235V3 ITU-T Recommendation H.235, Version 3: *Security and Encryption for H-series (H.323 and other H.245-based) multimedia terminals*. November 2000.

00H245 ITU-T Recommendation H. 245: *Control Protocol for Multimedia Communication*. February 2000.

00H323 ITU-T Recommendation H. 323: *Packet-based multimedia communications systems*. November 2000.

00H323K ITU-T Recommendation H.323: Annex K. *Service Independent Transport Using HTTP*. November 2000.

00H323L ITU-T Recommendation H.323: Annex L. *Stimulus signaling procedures for H.323*. November 2000.

96H324 ITU-T Recommendation H.324: *Terminal for low bit rate multimedia communication*. November 1996.

98H4501 ITU-T Recommendation H.450.1: *Generic functional protocol for the support of supplementary services in H.323*. November 1998.

CAS96 Casner, S. et al., RTP: *A transport protocol for real-time applications*. RFC 1889, January 1996.

CHAPTER 2

Multimedia Transport on IP Networks

The authors wish to thank David Graumann and Tom Gardos, both of whom work for the Intel Corporation, for their help in reviewing the audio and video sections of this chapter (respectively).

This chapter covers the commonly used media in *Internet Protocol* (IP) telephony and the transport of these media on IP networks. Traditional telephony consists of voice-only calls whereas IP telephony brings the richness of multimedia. Multimedia consists of audio, data, images, and video. Audio consists of music, speech, and animal or other types of sounds. Audio-based systems include the telephone, *Interactive Voice Response* (IVR), and audio conference. Data consists of symbols representing various human languages. Images consist of photographs, drawings, or writing. Image-based systems include facsimiles, medical imaging, and digital cameras. Video consists of a sequence of pictures that occur at a certain rate. Video-based systems include television, videoconferencing, and movies. In this section, we will describe the various media comprising IP telephony—speech and background noise for audio, text conversation for data, facsimile for images, and videoconferencing for video—and the transport of these media over IP networks.

Voice

Voice is fundamental to IP telephony. This section describes voice coders and the transmission of voice over digital networks. Later in this chapter, we will describe how to transmit voice over IP networks.

Transmission of Digitized Voice

If you transmit human voice or speech digitally, you must first digitize it by using an *Analog-to-Digital* (A/D) converter (as shown in Figure 2.1). Voice is limited to frequencies below 4kHz on analog telephone networks. Therefore, sampling at the Nyquist rate of 8kHz can completely characterize the analog telephony voice, producing 8,000 digital samples *per second* (/s). The telephone network uses *Pulse Code Modulation* (PCM) to convert the analog signal to digital samples by quantizing the amplitude of the analog signal to a digital level. You must quantize the digital sample in such a way that it can be accurately converted back to an analog signal. If samples are represented in one of 16-bit levels and are sent on the digital network, they can be reproduced faithfully by the *Digital-to-Analog* (D/A) converter back to the original analog signal and played back as speech in the speaker. The quantization error by the D/A in reproducing an analog signal from the 16-bit digital sample is negligible to the human ear.

Voice Coders

The bit rate on the digital network from each stream of voice is 128 kbps (8,000 samples/s × 16 bits/sample). If voice is transferred hundreds and thousands of miles from one end to another, it becomes economical to reduce the bit rate and still be able to provide the quality that is acceptable to humans. You perform this task by using coders, as shown in Figure 2.2. A coder, also known as a codec, consists of an encoder and a decoder. The encoder compresses the digital samples from the A/D by removing

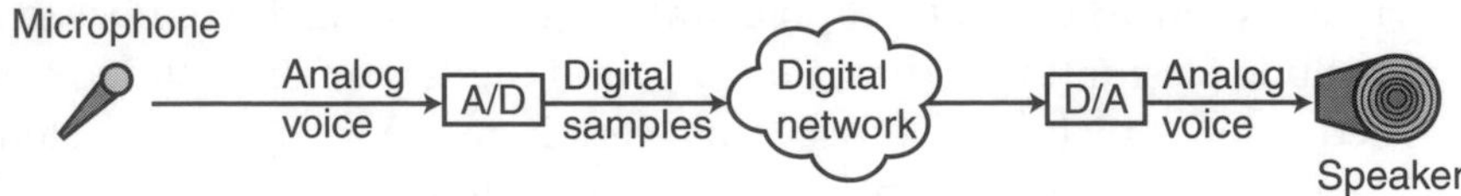

Figure 2.1 Voice transmissions on a digital network.

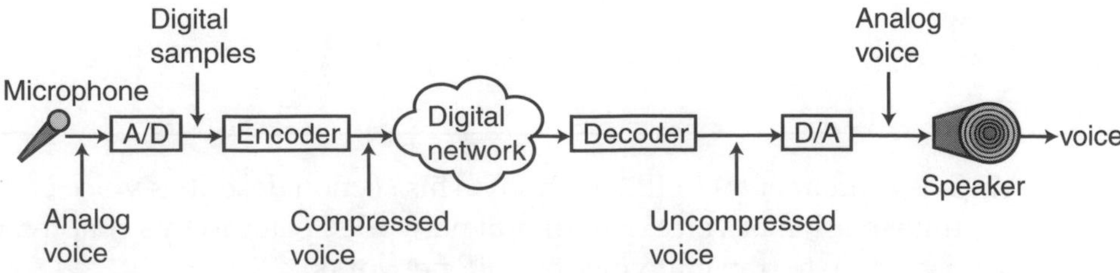

Figure 2.2 Using a voice coder to reduce the bit rate.

predictable and redundant information. The decoder takes the output from the encoder and recreates the original digital samples. There are two types of coders: audio and voice. Audio coders cover a range of sounds and noises so they have a lower compression ratio than voice coders. Voice coders exploit the characteristics of human voice in order to achieve much higher compression ratios. In the quest to reduce the bit rate, you will find it tempting to not send silence on the network. Studies have shown, however, that listeners prefer the background noise of the speaker to dead silence. Most encoders that are developed for multimedia applications distinguish between silence (when the person is not speaking) and speech and compress speech at one rate and silence at a much lower rate. Silence compression consists of the *Voice Activity Detector* (VAD) and the *Comfort Noise Generator* (CNG) algorithms. You implement the VAD in the encoder, and it determines whether the digital samples are from speech or from silence. You implement the CNG in the decoder, and it reconstructs background noise for the listener.

The ITU-T has standardized a number of coders, including the following:

G.711. The G.711 coder is specified in [72G711] and is widely used on digital telecommunications networks. In North America and Japan, G.711 is known as μ-law, and in Europe it is known as A-law. G.711 μ-law and A-law compress 14-bit linear *Pulse-Code Modulation* (PCM) samples and 13-bit linear PCM samples, respectively, into 8-bit logarithmic samples—producing a bit rate of 64 kbps.

G.723.1. The G.723.1 coder is specified in [96G723] and uses the *Multi-Pulse Maximum Likelihood Quantization* (MP-MLQ) algorithm to compress 30 ms blocks of 240 16-bit samples into 24-byte frames, producing a bit rate of 6.3 kbps. Another algorithm, *Algebraic Code-Excited Linear Prediction* (ACELP), compresses 30 ms blocks to 20-byte frames—producing a bit rate of 5.3 kbps. G.723.1 produces one of three frame sizes: 24 bytes, 20 bytes, or four bytes. The 4-byte frame specifies comfort noise parameters. There is no restriction on how 4-, 20-, and 24-byte frames are intermixed. The least significant 2 bits of the first byte in the frame determine the frame size and codec type as follows: bits 00 imply a 24-byte frame; bits 01 imply a 20-byte frame; bits 10 imply a 4-byte frame; and bits 11 are reserved for future use. We can switch between the two rates at any 30 ms frame boundary. G.723.1 also specifies the VAD and CNG algorithms in [G723A96].

G.726. The G.726 coder is specified in [90G726]. This coder uses the *Adaptive Differential Pulse Code Modulation* (ADPCM) algorithm to compress 8-bit samples of 64 kbps G.711 to 2-bit, 3-bit, 4-bit, or 5-bit samples at the bit rate of 16, 24, 32, or 40 kbps, respectively. You can convert samples from G.726 back to G.711 samples.

G.728. The G.728 coder is specified in [92G728]. This coder uses the *Low Delay —Code-Excited Linear Prediction* (LD-CELP) algorithm to compress 0.625 ms blocks of five 16-bit samples into 10-bit samples at the bit rate of 16 kbps.

G.729. The G.729 coder is specified in [96G729] and [G729A96]. This coder uses the *Conjugate Structure—Algebraic Code-Excited Linear Prediction* (CS-ACELP) algorithm to compress 10 ms blocks of 80 16-bit samples into one of two frame sizes: 10-byte (8 kbps) or two-byte. The two-byte frame specifies comfort noise parameters. G.729 also specifies the VAD and CNG algorithms in [G729B97].

Basic Attributes of Voice Coders

Reduction in bit rate by the encoders comes at the expense of delay and reduction in the quality of voice. There are four basic attributes that determine the characteristics of the coders: bit rate, complexity, delay, and quality. Table 2.1 shows how each of these coders compare based on these attributes:

Bit rate. A lower bit rate is important from at least two standpoints. First, it is economical to squeeze more voice streams into the same bandwidth network. Second, in multimedia applications, the savings in bit rate from voice can be allocated to other streams such as video or data. It is no coincidence that the bit rate of G.723.1 is the lowest among the codecs mentioned here. G.723.1 was primarily developed for videophones where the channel bandwidth is shared between voice and video.

Complexity. The number of *Millions of Instructions per Second* (MIPS) that is needed to execute the encoder and the decoder algorithms measures the complexity of the codec. For portable applications, the usage of *Read Only Memory* (ROM) and *Random Access Memory* (RAM) is also important, but

Table 2.1 Comparison of Voice Coders Based on Basic Attributes

Codec	Bit rate in kbps	Complexity compared with 6.726	Algorithmic Delay	Quality MOS
G.711	64	very low	0.125	4.0
G.723.1	5.3	8	37.5	3.9
G.723.1	6.3	8	37.5	3.6
G.726	32	1	0.125	3.85
G.728	16	15	0.625	3.61
G.729	8	10	15	3.9
G.729A	8	6	15	3.7

for PC applications, memory is of little concern. More complexity translates to higher *Central Processing Unit* (CPU) and memory usage, resulting in more cost and power usage. Measuring the complexity of a coder depends on a number of factors, and chief among them are the processor being used, the memory requirements, and the implementation of the algorithm. The G.728 codec is the most complex—about 15 times more complex than G.726 and about twice as complex as G.723.1. On the other hand, G.711 is the simplest and takes a negligible amount of processing power.

Delay. The delay that is introduced by the coder depends on three factors: frame size, look-ahead, and processing delay. The coders work on sets of samples called frames. G.723.1 has a frame size of 30 ms, which is equal to 240 samples, and G.729 has a frame size of 10 ms, which is equal to 80 samples. In addition to waiting for a complete frame, some encoders also wait to collect some samples ahead of the frame for analysis in compressing the frame. This additional waiting time is the look-ahead time. The look-ahead time for G.723.1 is 7.5 ms, and for G.729 it is 5 ms. Delay due to frame size and the look-ahead is called the algorithmic delay. Algorithmic delay for G.723.1 is 37.5 ms, and for G.729 it is 15 ms. Other encoders in Table 2.1 do not have look-ahead. G.711 and G.726 are sample-based coders with a frame size of one sample.

The algorithmic delay is constant for the given codec, but the processing delay depends on the processing power of the hardware that you use. The processing delay also depends on the complexity of the codec. The delay is equal to the time that it takes to encode and decode one frame. Thus, codec delay equals the algorithmic delay plus the processing delay.

Quality. The quality of the codec is commonly measured through the *Mean Opinion Score* (MOS). This rating is subjective, where 1 is bad and 5 is excellent. Experts assign an MOS score by comparing the quality of voice from a specific codec with other known codecs. The MOS score of G.711 is 4, which is the quality of voice on standard telephone lines (also known as toll quality). Both G.729 and the high bit rate version of G.723.1 have a near-toll quality.

Besides the basic attributes that we described, there are a number of other attributes that might be equally important depending on the environment and the application. Consider Figure 2.3, where a connection has been established between a telephone and the *Interactive Voice Response* (IVR) system. In this scenario, it might be desirable to pass *Dual-Tone Multi-Frequency* (DTMF) tones through the codec along with voice data. DTMF is an international standard for encoding telephone digits (0123456789*#). When you press a digit on the telephone, the DTMF generator encodes the digit as a sum of sinusoids corresponding to a row and column frequency of that digit.

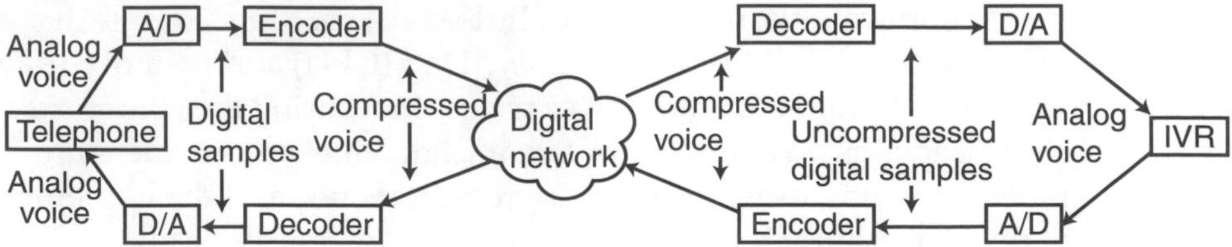

Figure 2.3 DTMF passing to the coder.

The A/D then converts this DTMF tone to digital samples and travels to the encoder. The encoder should encode the DTMF so that the decoder can accurately reproduce it. Among the coders described, only G.723.1 cannot accurately reproduce DTMF.

End-to-End Delay

The end-to-end delay for the setup in Figure 2.2 is the time that it takes voice to travel from the microphone to the speaker. In order to model this delay, let's follow the path that the first voice sample takes. When a person speaks into the microphone, the A/D digitizes the voice and stores it in memory. The samples are held until there are enough to fill a frame size and look-ahead to process into a frame. The frame is then encoded and transmitted through the network to the decoder. The decoder converts the frame back to samples and feeds this first sample to the D/A. The D/A converts this digital sample back to analog and plays the sound on the speaker. All of the following frames and samples are pipelined one behind the other and appear at a constant frequency of 8,000 samples/s at the D/A. The delays that this first sample experiences exist in the following components: microphone, A/D, encoder, transmission, decoder, D/A, and speaker. The delays in the endpoint depend on the hardware and on the *Operating System* (OS) used. Generally, the delays in the microphone, A/D, D/A, and the speaker are negligible, so we will ignore them here. The delays in the encoder are due to the algorithmic delay plus the processing delay. The delay in the decoder is entirely due to the processing delay. The combined delay in the encoder and the decoder is known as the coder delay. The transmission delay is the time that it takes the frame to travel from the output of the encoder to the input of the decoder. This delay depends on the network used. So, we can essentially characterize the end-to-end delay ($d_{end\text{-}end}$) as the coder delay (d_{coder}) plus the transmission delay (d_t), as shown in Figure 2.4. You should hold this end-to-end delay for a full-duplex voice conversation to a minimum. An end-to-end delay that is greater than about 300 ms can make the conversation awkward; therefore, $d_{end\text{-}end} < 300$ ms is desirable.

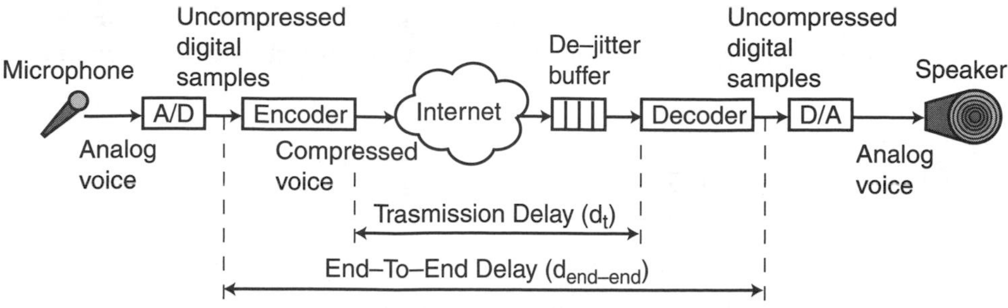

Figure 2.4 End-to-end delays.

The coder delay depends on the coder that you use. For G.723.1, the typical processing delay in the encoder and the decoder is about 4 ms and 1 ms, respectively. With the algorithmic delay of 37.5 ms, the G.723.1 coder delay is about 42.5 ms.

The transmission delay depends on the network you use. Later in this chapter, we will describe specific details about transmission delays on the IP network. The two essential components of transmission delay are the network delay (d_{net}) and the variability in the delay, which we call jitter (j_{net}). Therefore, $d_t = d_{net} + j_{net}$. We can model this equation as shown in Figure 2.4, where the dejitter buffer absorbs the jitter on the network so that when the first frame has been played to the speaker, there is a guarantee that another frame is ready to be played. The size of the dejitter buffer (j_{buf}) in milliseconds depends on the maximum network jitter and the frame size (fs):

i. $\max(j_{net}) =< fs$, then $j_{buf} = 0$

ii. $\max(j_{net}) > fs$, then $j_{buf} = \max(j_{net}) - fs$

You only need the dejitter buffer when the jitter on the network is greater than the frame size. The PSTN has a typical network delay of about 75 ms for 6,000 miles; the network jitter is almost zero because the resources on the network are allocated end-to-end for the transmission of voice. The end-to-end delay in the telephone system should be less than 100 ms.

On the Internet, the end-to-end delay and jitter depends on whether the network is lightly loaded, highly loaded, or just outright congested. Because the Internet was developed for nonreal-time data, the network does not provide *Quality of Service* (QoS) in order to guarantee a maximum boundary on network delay and jitter. A typical network delay is about 80 ms for 6,000 miles; the network jitter fluctuates considerably. On networks where the network delay and jitter numbers are not available, the receiver can use $d_{end\text{-}end} < 300$ ms to calculate the size of the dejitter buffer in milliseconds to be j_{buf}

$< 300\ j_{net} - d_{coder} - fs$. You can approximately determine the value of d_{net} through message exchanges during the call setup time before transmitting voice.

Conversational Text

In the online world of the Internet, we often refer to conversational text as chat. Text is generated from the keyboard or from any other input device, such as voice-to-text or handwriting-to-text. This input method is also an alternative to the telephone and provides remote communication capabilities to people who are hearing impaired

Text Transmission Using T.140 as a Coder

You use the T.140 recommendation [99T140] much like a codec in order to encode the characters before transmission and to decode them after reception, as shown in Figure 2.5. There is one fundamental difference between T.140 and a codec, however: The text is not compressed. Characters from the keyboard in ASCII or any other format are encoded in the T.140 format before transmission on the network. Upon reception, characters are decoded back to a format that the output device requires (such as a display).

T.140 specifies the following requirements for encoding:

- The character set is encoded according to 16-bit *International Standards Organization* (ISO)/International Electotechnical Commission (IEC) 10646-1 level 3, as described in [ISO93]. Characters in the IRV and Latin-1 supplement of ISO/IEC 10646-1 will be supported.
- Editing and control functions such as new line, backspace, alerting user, and selecting graphic rendition are coded according to ISO/IEC 6429 and ISO/IEC 10646-1 as described in [ISO92] and [ISO93], respectively.

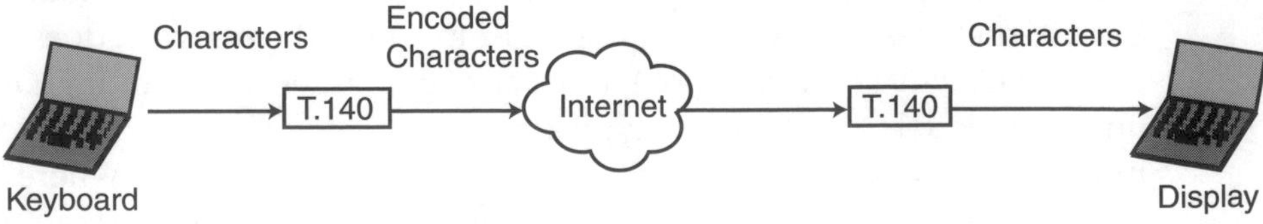

Figure 2.5 Text conversation using T.140.

The only requirement imposed by T.140 on the transport protocol is that the data that is delivered to the T.140 receiver must be in the same order sent by the T.140 transmitter. There are two requirements for received characters:

1. Unrecognized characters must be treated as text and displayed.
2. Unsupported characters must be displayed as some representation of a character.

End-to-End Delay

The majority of the delay occurs because of the speed at which characters are typed. Normally, characters are typed at a rate of about two per second. For conversational text, an end-to-end delay of less than two seconds is acceptable. Although characters can be buffered, they are normally sent to the display as soon as they are available in order to give a real-time feel to the receiving user.

Facsimile

Facsimile (commonly known as fax) machines digitize printed images and transmit the image over the telephone network. The receiving fax machine reconstructs the image on paper. Groups 1 and 2 were standards for analog fax machines; *Group 3* (G3) was for digital fax machines; and Group 4 was designed for ISDN. More than 90 percent of all fax machines worldwide are G3. G3 consists of two standards: T.4 [96T4] and T.30 [96T30]. T.4 specifies all aspects of the image, including the dimensions of the documents, the resolution of the scanner and printer, the coder for image compression, in-band line synchronization and the escape sequence, and the addition of fill bits in order to accommodate slow output devices. T.30 specifies the protocol to enable two fax machines to communicate.

G3 Facsimile Architecture

The architecture of a G3 fax machine appears in Figure 2.6. This design consists of an optical scanner, which scans the document and generates the image in terms of an array of analog amplitudes. The A/D converts the analog amplitudes to digital. The resolution of the fax image is expressed as *dots per inch* (DPI), or dots per inch in the horizontal direction × dots per inch in the vertical direction. The standard resolution is 204-by-98 dpi, and the

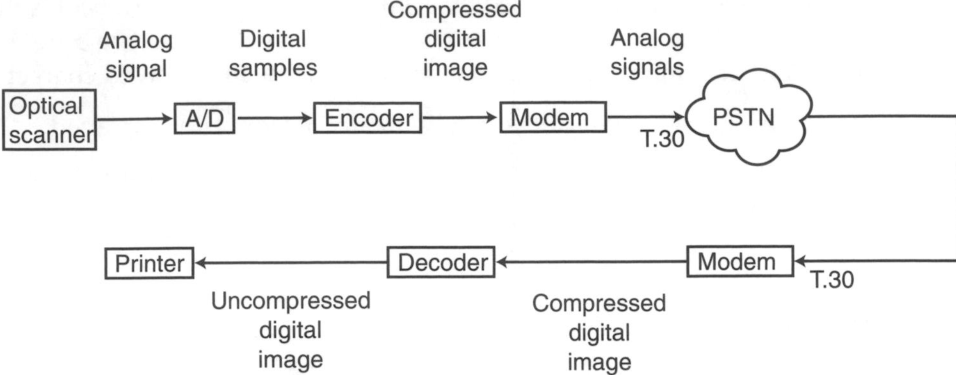

Figure 2.6 Architecture of the facsimile machine.

fine resolution is 204-by-192 dpi. The size of the black-and-white image on a standard 8.5-by-11 square-inch paper is 234 KB. The encoder compresses this image by using *Modified Huffman* (MH), *Modified Read* (MR), or *Modified Modified Read* (MMR) and then giving the image to the modem. The modem converts the digital image into analog signals for transmission over the telephone line. The received image is converted from analog signals back to the digital image by the modem, decompressed by the decoder, and printed.

G3 Facsimile Communications Protocol

The protocol between the transmitter and the receiver is specified in [96T30] and consists of five phases. We show an example in Figure 2.7:

1. *Phase A—Call establishment*. The calling machine dials the telephone number and emits the *calling* (CNG) tone every three seconds. The tone identifies the call as a facsimile and not a voice call. The called machine answers the call by emitting the *answering* (CED) tone. If the CED is not emitted within 30 to 40 seconds, the calling machine disconnects.
2. *Phase B—Pre-message procedure*. The called machine sends its capabilities in the *Digital Identification Signal* (DIS). The calling machine compares its capabilities with those of the called machine, and they send their joint capabilities in the *Digital Command Signal* (DCS). The calling machine then sends a series of training signals followed by a *Training Check Frame* (TCF). If the TCF is received successfully, the called machine sends a *Confirmation to Receive* (CFR); otherwise, it sends a *Failure to Train* (FTT) to the calling machine. Then, the calling machine can send a new DCS that has a lower transmission rate.

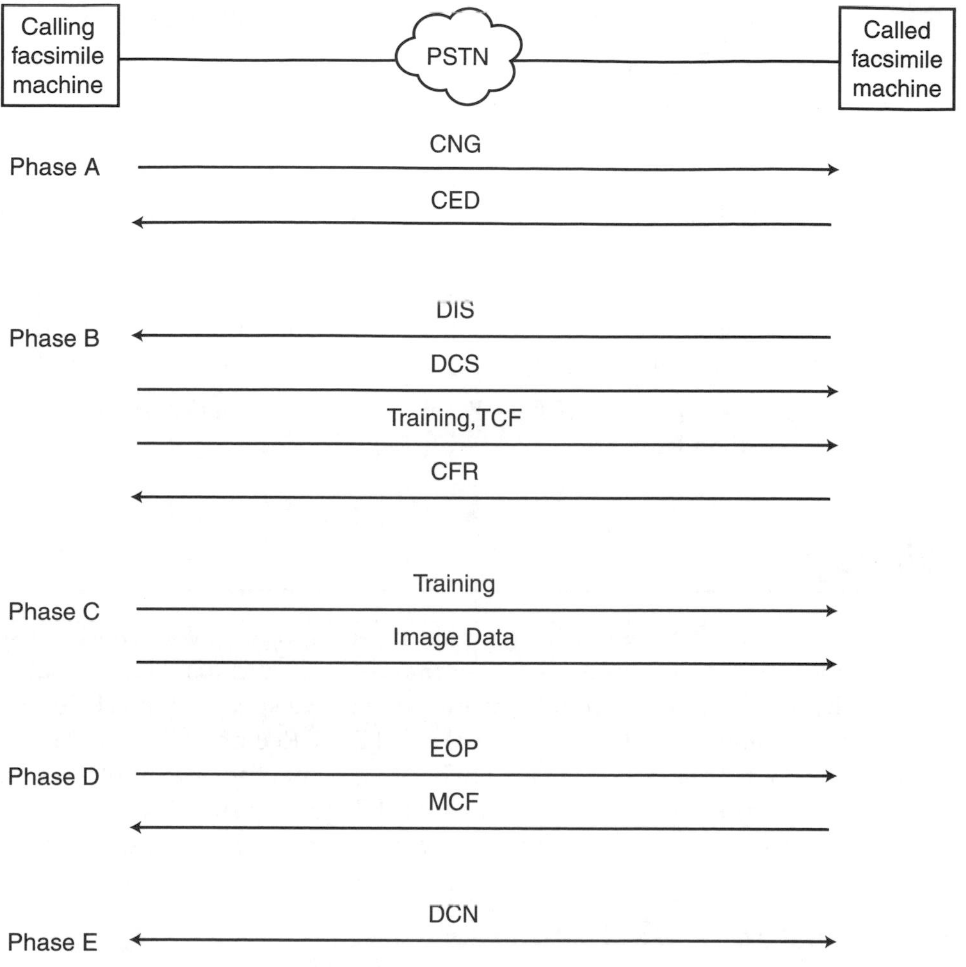

Figure 2.7 G3 facsimile communication protocol.

3. *Phase C—Message transmission.* T.4 covers the procedure for message transmission. The calling machine sends a single page of T.4 images.
4. *Phase D—Post-message transmission.* The calling machine sends one of the following:
   - An *End of Procedure* (EOP) in order to indicate the end of a page and to move to Phase E after the called machine sends an acknowledgement
   - A *Multi-Page Signal* (MPS) in order to indicate the end of a page and to return to Phase C for another page to send after the called machine sends an acknowledgement
   - An *End of Message* (EOM) in order to indicate the end of a page and to return to Phase B

The called machine responds with one of the following items:

- A *Message Confirmation* (MCF) in order to indicate that the page quality was acceptable. This message is a positive acknowledgement to MPS, EOM, or EOP.
- A *Retrain Positive* (RTP) in order to indicate that the page quality was barely acceptable; therefore, additional pages should follow after the training and CFR.
- A *Retrain Negative* (RTN) in order to indicate that the page quality was not acceptable; therefore, this page should be retransmitted after training and CFR.

5. *Phase E—Call release*. The calling machine sends a *Disconnect* (DCN), and the call ends.

Video

Video telephony requires the capability to capture, encode, and transport video over networks to a receiver that decodes and displays the data. The video decoder and bit stream syntaxes are specified in ITU-T Recommendation H.261 [93H261] and ITU-T Recommendation H.263 [96H263]. This section covers the basic concepts that are involved with transporting video over digital networks in H.261 or H.263 format. Later in this chapter, we will describe how video is transmitted on IP networks.

Transmission of Digitized Video

Figure 2.8 shows the basic functional elements that are necessary in order to capture, encode, transport, decode, and display video in a video telephony system. Video consists of a sequential series of pictures or frames that are displayed at a rate that we call the frame rate. Video from the camera can be either an analog signal such as *Networking and Telecommunication Standing Committee* (NTSC) or a *Phase Alternating Line* (PAL) format, or it can be a digital signal such as *Digital Video* (DV) format. The video signal is fed into the capture subsystem. The capture subsystem consists of the A/D conversion, color transformation, and resampling subsystems. The A/D conversion subsystem only converts the analog video signal to a digital representation. The digital representations of NTSC and PAL video are defined in [95BT601] as having a frame resolution and a frame rate of 720 pixels by 480 lines at 29.97Hz and 720 pixels by 576 lines at 25Hz, respectively.

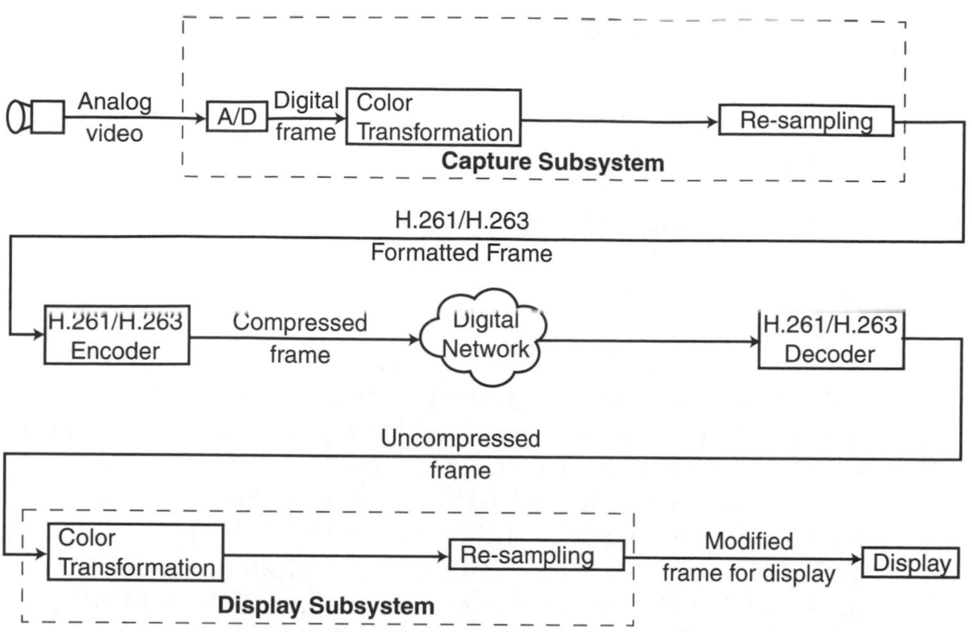

Figure 2.8 Video transmissions on a digital network.

The digital video from the A/D conversion subsystem or directly from the digital video camera is then fed into the color transformation subsystem in order to convert the data into a format that is acceptable to H.261 and H.263. The color representation of NTSC and PAL is defined in [95BT601], and we refer to it as YC_rC_b with a 4:2:0 pixel subsampling ratio. A simple way to describe this representation is to first assume that the digital video is initially represented in a *Red, Green, and Blue* (RGB) format where each picture or frame consists of red, green, and blue color planes. Similarly, each pixel is represented by a red, green, and blue pixel. In the case of digitized NTSC, each video picture has three color planes, each of which have a resolution of 720-by-480. The Y (or luminance) plane of the YC_rC_b format represents the intensity value of each color pixel in the picture. The C_b plane, referred to as a color difference or chrominance plane, represents the values of the blue plane subtracted from Y, and the C_r plane similarly represents the values of the red plane subtracted from Y. The color transformation is implemented as a 3-by-3 matrix transform of RGB pixel values to YC_rC_b pixel values. Recommendations H.261 and H.263 also require the color difference planes to be subsampled by two, relative to the luminance plane, both in vertical and horizontal directions. This process constitutes a first step toward data compression by exploiting the fact that the human visual system has lower spatial resolution sensitivity to color than to luminance. Assuming that the luminance plane is still 720-by-480, the chrominance planes are now each 360-by-240.

The output from the color transformation subsystem is fed into the resampling subsystem that resizes the frames to one of the formats that are acceptable to H.261 or H.263. These formats are nominally specified as some multiple or fraction of *Common Intermediate Format* (CIF). CIF specifies the frame resolution ([width-by-height], [horizontal-by-vertical], or [pixels/line-by-the number of lines]) to be 352-by-288 for luminance and 176-by-144 for chrominance. Moreover, it specifies that these pixels occupy a display window where the ratio of horizontal to vertical dimensions is 4:3. Because 352 horizontal pixels are not related to 288 vertical pixels by a 4:3 ratio, a display system must use nonsquare pixel representations. Recommendation H.261 accepts frame resolutions of CIF and *Quarter Common Intermediate Format* (QCIF), which is 176-by-144. Recommendation H.263 Version 1 accepts frame resolutions of SQCIF (128-by-96), QCIF (176-by-144), CIF (352-by-288), 4CIF (704-by-576), and 16CIF (1408-by-1152). The frame resolution expressed in pixels for the C_B and C_R components consists of Sub-QCIF (64-by-48), QCIF (88-by-72), CIF (176-by-144), 4CIF (352-by-288), and 16CIF (704-by-576), respectively. Recommendation H.263 Version 2 relaxes the constraints on input dimensions to any multiple of four in both horizontal and vertical dimensions from a minimum of 4-by-4 to a maximum of 2048-by-1152.

The output from the capture subsystems is so-called uncompressed video, which still requires a high bandwidth network for transmission. As an example, video with a frame rate of 10 frames/s, QCIF resolution, and 12 bits/pixel requires a bandwidth of about 4.5 Mbps. Today's access networks do not provide such a high bandwidth as required by uncompressed video. The *Public-Switched Telephone Network* (PSTN) modem provides an access bandwidth of only 28.8 kbps to 56 kbps. Even the 128 kbps to 384 kbps access bandwidth of the *Integrated Services Digital Network* (ISDN) is not sufficient. This situation is one reason why the encoder (H.261 or H.263) compresses video before transmission on the network.

The decoder (H.261 or H.263) receives the compressed video that the encoder transmits. The decoder then creates frames consisting of Y, C_B, and C_R components for the display subsystem. The display subsystem consists of the color transformation and resampling subsystems. The color transformation subsystem up-samples the C_b and C_r planes to the resolution of the Y plane and converts the Y, C_B, and C_R components to the RGB components that most digital displays require. The resampling subsystem can then convert the frame resolution to a format that the digital display requires (for example, interpolating to twice the resolution both horizontally and vertically if required). The resampling subsystem could alter a CIF frame provided by the color transformation subsystem to a much larger frame (for instance, 800-by-600) that completely covers the display screen.

Bit-Stream Syntax Overview

Gaining an understanding of the various elements of the compressed video bit stream of H.261 and H.263 is beneficial for anyone who is developing video telephony systems. The bit stream is defined by H.261 and H.263, and we refer to it as the bit-steam syntax. An encoder must comply with the recommended bit-stream syntax if it wishes for a compliant decoder to operate on the bit stream without error. This section gives a high-level overview of the bit-stream syntax. Both H.261 and H.263 operate on some basic principles involving a hybrid of intra-frame, inter-frame, and bidirectional frame coding. Intra-frame coding reduces spatial redundancy within each frame, whereas inter-frame and bidirectional frame coding reduces temporal redundancy between frames of the video along with spatial redundancy. The video frames are further broken down into smaller syntactical elements (as we describe next).

Intra-frame (also known as I-frame) coding takes place on a frame without referring to any other frames in the video sequence. An I-frame is required at the beginning of a video sequence because there are no prior frames to which you can refer. You can insert I-frames periodically in a coded video sequence for use as random access key frames and to eliminate errors that might have accumulated in the previous sequence of frames. I-frame coding is similar to the JPEG still-picture compression standard in that an 8-by-8 pixel *Discrete Cosine Transform* (DCT) is employed (as well as quantization and variable-length coding).

Inter-frame (also known as Predictive-frame or P-frame) coding occurs on the current frame that is being encoded based on a prediction by using the prior frame. P-frame coding relies on the fact that the content changes little from frame to frame. The encoder codes differences between frames and transmits them over the network to the decoder. These inter-frame differences can be significantly reduced (and in turn, coded much more efficiently) by taking advantage of the fact that you can approximate most changes by displacing 16-by-16 or 8-by-8 pixel blocks in the previous frame by a few pixels and subtracting them from the corresponding blocks in the target frame. The use of spatial displacement is known as motion compensation, and a motion vector specifies the spatial displacement for each block. Coding of this difference due to displacement is known as *Displaced Frame-Difference* (DFD) coding. The frame differences are then coded in a manner similar to the I-frames; that is, employing DCT, quantization, and variable-length encoding.

Bidirectional frame (also known as B-frame) coding is very similar to P-frame encoding with the addition of a prediction from the frame located immediately before the current frame to be encoded. You use the previous frame, the future frame, or a weighted average of both in order to predict each block to be encoded in the target frame. In some cases, the predictions fail to improve the coding efficiency for a given block—at which time the block is coded as if it were in an I-frame. Each block is thus coded along with a representation of zero, one, or two motion vectors. As with the P-frame encoding, the displaced frame difference is then encoded by using DCT, quantization, and variable-length encoding.

The bit-stream syntax for each picture is divided into smaller syntactical elements. The picture is divided into *Groups of Blocks* (GOBs), GOBs into *Macro Blocks* (MBs), MBs into blocks, and blocks into pixels. Normally, the encoder is restricted to producing its output within a certain bit rate based on the bandwidth of the network. On a 28.8 kbps modem, the encoder might be limited to a bit rate of, say, 15 kbps. Such a low bit rate is possible on a low frame resolution and on a frame rate of, for example, QCIF at 5Hz.

Video Coder Summary

Although at a high level the H.261 and H.263 coders share many common elements, there are some important differences between them. Some of the characteristics of H.261 and H.263 coders are as follows:

H.261. The H.261 coder is specified in [93H261] and is designed for low coding delay and low bit rates at multiples of 64 kbps, from 64 kbps to 1.92 Mbps. This coder operates on video with a frame rate of 29.97Hz (30,000/1001) and a frame resolution of QCIF and CIF. A frame is divided into GOBs, MBs, and blocks. As an example, the luminous component of the QCIF frame consists of 1-by-3 GOBs, each of which consists of 11-by-3 MBs. In turn, each MB consists of 2-by-2 blocks, and each block consists of 8-by-8 pixels of Y. H.261 uses motion compensation on 16-by-16 pixel blocks in order to remove temporal redundancy and uses DCT coding to remove spatial redundancy.

H.263 (original version). Recommendation H.263 [96H263] was first published in 1996. Since then, this recommendation has been superseded by version 2 (published in 1998), although it maintained complete backward compatibility in that a 1998 H.263-compliant decoder can decode a 1996 H.263-compliant encoder's bit stream. The converse of this statement is not necessarily true, however, because the 1998 version of H.263 contains new features. A 1996 H.263 decoder should be capable of detecting and rejecting newer bit streams by checking the version field in the H.263 bit-stream picture header. Although it is designed for very low bit rates starting at 10 kbps, H.263 works well at rates of up to 2 Mbps. H.263 has many of the same elements as H.261, but through improvements in motion compensation, quantization, and variable-length encoding, it performs more efficiently at all bit rates. In addition to the QCIF and CIF frame resolutions of H.261, H.263 also includes Sub-QCIF, 4CIF, and 16CIF. A frame is divided into GOBs, MBs, and blocks. As an example, the luminous component of the QCIF frame consists of 1-by-9 GOBs, each GOB consisting of 11-by-1 MBs and each MB consisting of 2-by-2 blocks. Also, each block consists of 8-by-8 pixels of Y. Among other options, H.263 also adds 8-by-8 pixel block motion compensation and improved Intra-frame coding.

H.263 Version 2. H.263 Version 2 coder, also known as H.263+, is specified in [98H263]. This coder contains improvements leading to increased compression efficiency as well as better error resilience and bit-stream scalability that is necessary for wireless and packet-based networks. This coder adds new, optional features to H.263 and is backward compatible with H.263. This version essentially covers any bit rate, frame rate, and frame resolution. In addition to the frame resolutions of H.263, it also includes custom frame sizes.

The following options of H.263+ address the needs of wireless and packet-based networks:

Slice Structured Mode. This mode provides flexibility in partitioning the frame and transmitting the partitions in any order. The partitions must be on MB boundaries. You can compare this mode with fixed partitions and the fixed order of transmission of the GOBs in earlier coders. This mode can enhance error resilience and reduce video delay.

Independent Segment Decoding Mode. In this mode, the segments of the frame are encoded in such a way that you can independently decode them. This feature prevents errors in a segment from propagating to other segments of the frame.

Reference Picture Selection Mode. Normally, the most recently encoded frame is used as the reference frame for inter-frame prediction. But this mode avoids the use of an erroneous frame for reference by enabling an older error-free frame to be used instead. In this mode, there is a back channel through which the decoder provides the encoder information about which reference frame to use.

Bit-Stream Scalability Mode. In this mode, the bit stream consists of layers that represent different levels of video quality. The base layer guarantees a minimum level of video quality, and the enhancement layers progressively add higher levels of quality to the base layer. This mode enables receivers that have varying processing and bandwidth capabilities to receive different qualities of video. For example, if the bit rates of the base layer, enhancement layer 1, and enhancement layer 2 are 10 kbps, 20 kbps, and 60 kbps (respectively), then a receiver that is connected to a 28.8 kbps link will only pick the base layer with minimum video quality. The receiver on a 56 kbps link will additionally pick the enhancement layer 1 with higher video quality, and the receiver on a 128 kbps link will pick all three video layers that have the highest video quality.

We define three types of scalability modes as follows. You can use these three modes separately or together in order to create a layered, scalable bit stream:

Temporal Scalability. In this mode, the base layer consists of I- and P-frames and the enhancement layer consists of B-frames. This mode provides a considerably higher frame rate with little increase in bit rate. As an example, the base layer consists of QCIF, 10 frames/s, and 60 kbps while the enhancement layer consists of QCIF, 20 frames/s, and 80 kbps.

Spatial scalability. In this mode, the base layer consists of I- and P-frames that are down-sampled horizontally and vertically by two before being coded. The enhancement layer frames are horizontally and vertically two times the base layer. This mode provides a higher frame resolution. As an example, the base layer consists of QCIF, 10 frames/s, and 60 kbps while the enhancement layer consists of CIF, 10 frames/s, and 300 kbps.

SNR scalability. In this mode, the base layer consists of I- and P-frames and the enhancement layer consists of the difference between the original frames and the base-layer frames. This mode provides higher-fidelity frames with the same frame resolution. As an example, the base layer consists of QCIF, 10 frames/s, and 60 kbps, and the enhancement layer consists of QCIF, 10 frames/s, and 100 kbps. The decoded enhancement plus the base-layer video would be noticeably better than the decoded base-layer video only.

Transport of Conversational Media on the Internet by Using RTP

The Internet was developed for nonreal-time data and does not provide *Quality of Service* (QoS). There is no boundary on delay or jitter; packets do not arrive at the destination when congested routers drop them; and packets from the same source might take different routes and arrive in a different order at the destination.

The *Transmission Control Protocol* (TCP) or User Datagram Protocol (UDP) transports data on IP networks. TCP provides a connection-oriented stream of bytes without any message boundaries. TCP also provides a guarantee, through the use of receiver acknowledgements and sender timeouts, to the application that the packet sent will arrive at its destination. TCP provides flow control by having receiving endpoints specify the amount of data that they can receive. TCP receivers reorder out-of-order data and discard duplicate data. All TCP packets have a checksum that the receiver can use in order to detect errors. Finally, TCP provides a mechanism to adjust the rate of traffic based on network conditions. The rate increases when the network has the capacity and decreases when it detects congestion.

UDP, on the other hand, is a simple datagram-oriented protocol that does not provide any of the functionality that TCP provides. UDP does not provide a guarantee to the application that the sent packet will arrive at its destination. If a guarantee is required, then you can implement a procedure similar to TCP in the application itself. Although the maximum UDP packet is 64K, the endpoint does not have to accept a datagram that is larger than 576 bytes. Many UDP applications restrict application data to 512 bytes in order to stay within the 576-byte limit. If the datagram is not within this limit, it can exceed the network *Maximum Transmission Unit* (MTU) and become fragmented on the network. Then, it would have to be reassembled at the IP layer of the receiving endpoint. Fragmentation has two disadvantages: first, it leads to performance degradation, and second, a loss of a fragment makes the entire datagram useless.

In H.323, conversational text is transported by using TCP (as specified in [H323G00]) or UDP (as specified in [HEL00]). The maximum allowable end-to-end delay for conversational text is large enough to enable the retransmission of lost packets. For conversational voice and video, however, the maximum allowable end-to-end delay is too short to enable retransmissions to occur. For this reason, TCP is not used to transport conversational voice and video (we only use UDP). UDP, however, does not provide mechanisms to identify lost and out-of-order packets to the receiver so that the receiver can compensate. Packets that become out-of-order through the network have to be identified to the receiver so that the receiver can reorder them. The RTP protocol [CAS96] provides this level of functionality. If voice and video are lip-synchronized at the sender's location, then there should be additional information in the packets in order to enable the receiver to synchronize the separate streams. RTP also provides this information.

RTP is independent of the underlying transport and network layers and runs on both Unicast and multicast networks. The RTP header is not treated as a separate layer of protocol. Instead, it is integrated with the application according to the principles of application-layer framing [CLAR90]. RTP provides the functionality to packetize the real-time data for transmission on

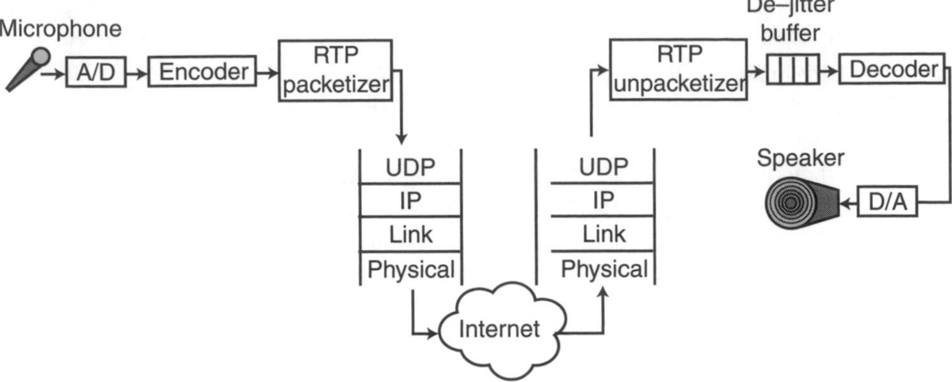

Figure 2.9 Role of RTP in an end-to-end voice transmission.

the network so that the data can be reconstructed into the original sequence upon reception. Figure 2.9 illustrates the role of RTP in an end-to-end voice transmission by using the G.723.1 codec. Every 30 ms, the encoder provides a G.723.1 frame to the RTP packetizer. The RTP packetizer constructs the packet and gives it to the IP network stack. The packet goes through the UDP/IP/link layers with each layer putting its header on its way onto the network. Upon reception, the packet goes through the link/IP/UDP layers before being delivered to the RTP unpacketizer. The RTP unpacketizer removes the frames from the packet and puts them in the dejitter queue.

The RTP packet that the packetizer creates consists of the header and the payload, as shown in Figure 2.10. You should not confuse the RTP packet

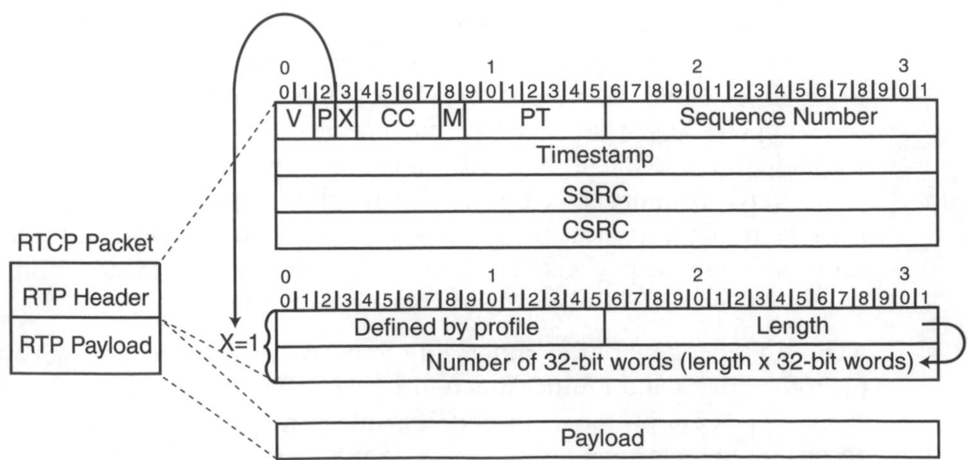

Figure 2.10 RTP header and payload.

with the packet that is sent on the network, however. The packetizer can pack one or more RTP packets into one network packet before delivering to the UDP layer.

RTP Header

The first 12 bytes are always present in the RTP header (the remaining bytes are optional). In this chapter, we describe the fields in the header that are applicable to point-to-point calls. In Chapter 4, "Multi-Point Conference," we discuss the remaining fields that are applicable to multi-point conferences. Although these fields are divided between the two chapters, the H.323 recommendation requires all fields to be implemented even if the applications cover only point-to-point calls. The fields in the header that are applicable to two-party calls include *Version* (V), *Padding* (P), *Extension* (X), *Marker* (M), *Payload Type* (PT), sequence number, and timestamp. The remaining fields for multi-point calls: Contributing Source Count (CC), Synchronization Source Identifier (SSRC), and the Contributing Source Identifiers (CSRC).

Two fields are not defined in the RTP header: Marker and Payload Type. Specific RTP profiles define these fields. By not defining the Marker and Payload Type fields, you can tailor the 12-byte header to a specific profile without extending the header. Specific RTP profiles can also use the Extension field in order to extend the header to fit the environment where the header will be used. As of this writing, there is only one RTP profile for voice and video applications in [SCHU96]. This profile describes the fields of the header for the point-to-point call as follows:

- *Version (two bits)*. This field provides the version of RTP that the application is using. RFC 1889 is version 1 [CAS96].
- *Padding (two bit)*. This field aligns the network packet to a boundary that the link layer or the application requires. If the padding bit is set, the last byte in the RTP packet contains the count of the number of redundant bytes at the end of the RTP packet to be ignored.
- *Extension (one bit)*. This field extends the RTP header. Some implementations use this for experimentation purposes. Other implementations that are not aware of the specifics of the extension can ignore it. If this field is set, the header is extended by two more fields: Defined By Profile and Length. The interpretation of Defined By Profile is specific to the implementation. The Length field provides the number of 32-bit words that follow. The Extension field is normally set to zero (its use is rare).

- *Marker (one bit)*. The RTP profile in RFC 1890 specifies the use of this bit for voice and video applications. For voice applications, this bit is set only in the first packet following silence suppression. Note that during silence suppression, packets are not generated. The receiver can use this indication to dynamically adjust the delay in the play-out buffer. For video applications, this bit is set to one in the last packet of a video frame; otherwise, it is set to zero.
- *Payload Type (seven bits)*. The RTP profile in RFC 1890 specifies the use of this field to identify the format of the RTP payload. The 128 payload type numbers are divided into static and dynamic payload types as follows: 0–34 is assigned statically; 35–71 is currently unassigned; 72–76 is reserved; 77–95 is unassigned; and 96–127 is assigned dynamically. A static payload type is permanently assigned to the payload format. Examples are a payload type of 4 for G.723.1 and 34 for the 1996 version of H.263. The conference control protocol assigns the dynamic payload type. The trend is to do away with static payload types and have payload types assigned only dynamically. Static payload types are no longer assigned to new payload formats that are developed. The 1998 version of H.263, also known as H.263+, does not have a static payload type.
- *Sequence Number (16 bits)*. This field increases by one for each RTP packet that is sent on the network. The receiver uses this field to detect packet loss and to correctly order any out-of-order packets.
- *Timestamp (32 bits)*. Three clocks are used in the end-to-end transmission of media: a sampling clock to sample the analog media, an RTP clock to generate the timestamp, and a reference clock to correlate the timestamps from separate media for the purpose of synchronizing the media streams. The timestamp reflects the instant at which the first sample in the payload was sampled. The timestamp is derived from a clock that increments monotonically and linearly with sufficient resolution to enable various calculations (such as synchronization and packet arrival jitter). The frequency of the RTP clock depends on the payload format. The RTP clock for voice payload formats normally equals the sampling clock. The voice payload formats use the RTP clock from the set 8000Hz, 11025Hz, 16000Hz, 22050Hz, 24000Hz, 32000Hz, 44100Hz, and 48000Hz. Video payload formats use an RTP clock of 90000Hz, which yields exact integer timestamp increments for most widely used frame rates—24Hz for *High-Definition Television* (HDTV), 25Hz (PAL), 29.97Hz (NTSC), and 30Hz (HDTV). All packets belonging to the same video frame have the same timestamp. Video frames are distinguished by a change in timestamp. In the layered scenario, all frames corresponding to the same temporal reference use the same timestamp.

RTP Payload

The RTP payload consists of media to be transported. The format of the payload depends on the media, the codec, and the resiliency for recreating lost packets. The payload formats of some voice and video codecs are provided in [SCHU96]. There are a number of voice codecs that do not have built-in *Voice Activity Detector* (VAD) and Comfort Noise Generator (CNG) algorithms. So, [SCHU96] also specifies a payload format for comfort noise. In specifying a payload format for voice codecs, it is normally sufficient to just provide the frequency of the RTP clock for the media and codec to be used. The H.245 control protocol in H.323 negotiates the length in bytes of the payload, usually based on the environment of the operation. Later in this section, we will describe payload formats for G.723.1, Comfort Noise, T.140, and H.263+.

On the Internet, packets are lost due to congestion. The majority of losses occur with single packets. Short-burst losses are less frequent, and long-burst losses are rare. Losses degrade the quality of media. For conversational voice, the degradation is more noticeable than in other media. The end-to-end delay for voice and video is so high and unpredictable on the Internet that it is not possible to retransmit the lost packets. Therefore, the sender applies resiliency techniques to the packets so that the receiver can recreate the lost packets. These techniques are either applied at the codec level (such as H.263+) or at the packet level. Techniques applied in the H.263+ codec, described previously in this chapter, include Slice Structure, Independent Segment Decoding, and Reference Picture Selection. Two techniques applied at the packet level are Redundancy and Forward Error Correction. Later in this section, we will describe the payload formats for both of these techniques. Any media and codec can use these techniques at the packet level.

Payload Format for G.723.1

The G.723.1 payload format includes the following components:

- The frequency of the RTP clock is the same as the sampling clock of 8000Hz.
- The payload consists of one or more G.723.1 frames. The number of frames in the payload is signaled through the H.323 Control Protocol (H.245), which we will describe later in Chapter 3, "Point-to-Point Call: Signaling."
- A static payload type of 4 is assigned.

Payload Format for Comfort Noise

The payload format for comfort noise is specified in [SCHU96] and includes the following components:

- The frequency of the RTP clock is 8000Hz.
- The payload consists of a single byte whose most significant bit is set to zero, and the least-significant seven bits contain the absolute noise level expressed in -dBov. This payload provides an absolute noise level between 0 and -127 dBov.
- A static payload type of 13 is assigned.

Voice coders such as G.711 that do not have a built-in CNG use this payload format. Such coders have a separate payload format for speech and comfort noise. Coders such as G.723.1, on the other hand, have a built-in CNG. Therefore, speech and comfort noise packets use the same payload format. Normally, a comfort noise packet is not sent along with speech packets. The first comfort noise packet is sent as soon as silence is detected. After that, the next comfort noise packet is sent when there is a change in the background noise.

Another payload format to generate comfort noise is specified in [00G711A2]. This payload format replaces [SCHU96].

Payload Format for T.140

The payload format for the conversational text is specified in [HEL00] and includes the following components:

- The frequency of the RTP clock is 1000Hz. This timestamp is useful only for synchronizing with other media streams.
- The payload consists of one or more characters. We recommend that you send one character at a time as soon as the character is typed. Characters are normally typed at the rate of about two per second. Each character that is encoded by using T.140 is two bytes. Although sending one character at a time in the payload provides a good real-time experience at the receiver display, it also introduces a huge header overhead. More characters can be packed into the payload, but that would degrade the experience of the receiver at the expense of utilizing the network bandwidth more efficiently.
- A static payload type is not assigned.

We should note that you can also transport conversational text by using TCP, as specified in [H323G00]. In this case, RTP is not required.

Payload Format for H.263

The H.263+ (H.263 version 2) payload format is specified in [WEN98] and includes the following components:

- The frequency of the RTP clock is 90kHz.
- The payload consists of the payload header followed by the H.263-bit stream.
- A static payload type is not assigned.

Figure 2.11 shows the payload header. The header contains a mandatory 16-bit basic header followed by an optional 8-bit *Video Redundancy Coding* (VRC) header, which is then followed by an optional variable-length extra picture header. The VRC mechanism provides error resilience at the packet level. This feature is in addition to the error resilience that is provided at the coder level in the H.263+ coder. VRC enables the transmission of multiple threads of independently coded P-frames so that errors in a frame cause distortions only within the thread that contains that frame. The effect of a packet loss, for example, would result in video being displayed at half the

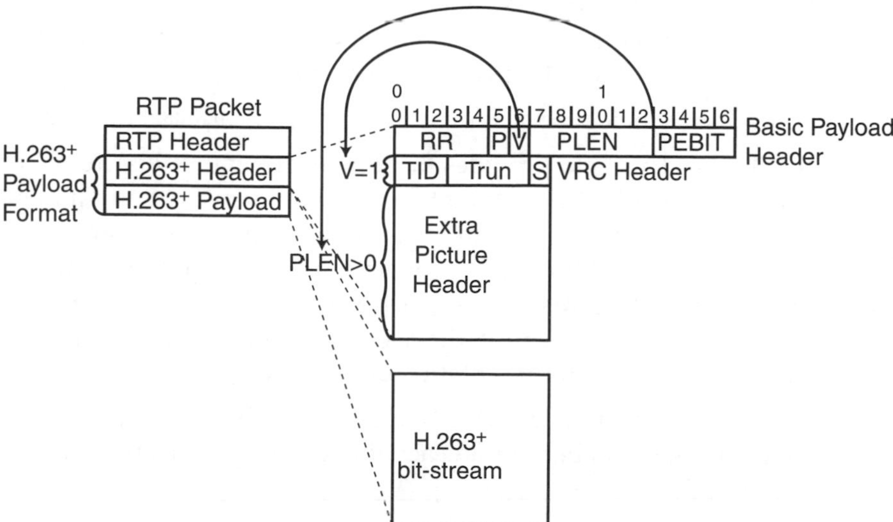

Figure 2.11 RTP packet containing the H.263+ payload format.

original frame rate (as opposed to no video displayed at all without VRC). The drawback of VRC is that coding efficiency is reduced, however, so you should only use it when you anticipate errors and when you find the other error-resiliency schemes of H.263 to be insufficient.

We specify the fields in the 16-bit basic header as follows:

RR (5 bits). This field is reserved for future use; we will assign it a value of zero.

P (1 bit). The start code in the H.263-bit stream begins with two bytes of zeros. The start code is unique and cannot occur anywhere else in the bit stream. This field specifies the beginning of a frame, GOB, slice, or the end of a video sequence. The P field, when set to 1, enables you to remove these two bytes of zeros—thus resulting in the reduction of the bit stream for transmission. The receiver recreates the bit stream by substituting two bytes of zeros in the start code when this field is set.

V (1 bit). If this field is set to 1, then it specifies the presence of the optional VRC header.

PLEN (6 bits). If this field is not zero, then it specifies the presence and size (in bytes) of the optional extra picture header. You can insert the extra picture header into packets that do not contain the start of a coded picture and that would otherwise not include the bit-stream picture header. Inserting extra picture header information in these cases improves the resiliency of the representation.

PEBIT (3 bits). This field is valid only if the extra picture header is present. This field specifies the number of least-significant bits of the last byte in the extra picture header that you should ignore.

We specify the fields in the 8-bit optional VRC header as follows:

TID (3 bits). This field provides the identification number from 1 to 7 of up to seven threads. A thread that has a lower identification number should provide a better representation of the synchronization frame than the higher-numbered thread. We conventionally assign the identification number 0 to the thread from which the synchronization frame should be used. If thread 0 is corrupt, the decoder should use the next-higher error-free thread for the representation of the synchronization frame.

Trun (4 bits). This field provides a monotonically increasing modulo 16 count of the packet number within each thread. We use this field to detect packet loss within a thread.

S (1 bit). If this field is set to 1, then it specifies that the H.263+ bit stream contains a representation of the synchronization frame.

Payload Format for Redundancy

The main idea behind redundancy is to send information about the previous packet in the following packet. If the previous packet is lost, the following packet will provide the lost information. The disadvantage is in the increase in bandwidth and the extra delay. The payload format for redundancy is specified in [PERK97] and consists of multiple secondary or redundant payloads along with the primary nonredundant payload. An RTP packet containing a redundancy payload format appears in Figure 2.12. The RTP header provides information about the primary payload. The Payload Type field in the RTP header is of type Redundancy in order to indicate the format of the payload. The payload format consists of one or more headers for each secondary payload and the last header for the primary payload. The length of each secondary header is four bytes, and the primary header is one byte. Each header contains information about its media payload.

The fields in the header are as follows:

First (1 bit). If this field is set to 1, then another header follows. If this bit is 0, then this header is the last. The last header contains information about the primary payload.

Block Payload Type (7 bits). This field specifies the type of the payload format used.

Timestamp Offset (14 bits). This field contains the offset from the timestamp in the RTP header. This value is an unsigned number, and you should

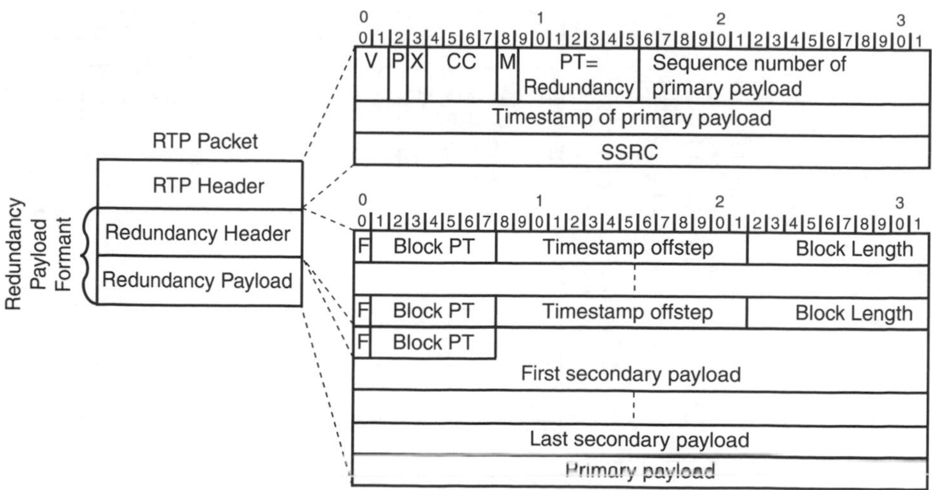

Figure 2.12 RTP packet containing the redundancy payload format.

subtract it from the RTP timestamp in order to determine the timestamp of the secondary media. The timestamp for the primary media is in the RTP timestamp.

Block Length (10 bits). This field contains the length (in bytes) of the payload that this header describes.

In Figure 2.13, we show an example RTP packet using voice redundancy. The RTP header specifies that the RTP payload will use the Redundant Payload Format described in Figure 2.12, and the primary payload has a timestamp of 150. The RTP payload consists of one primary and two secondary headers followed by their payloads. The first secondary header specifies that the payload has a format of G.723.1 and a timestamp offset of 60, which translates to a timestamp of 90, and a size of 20 bytes. The second secondary header specifies that the payload will have a format of G.723.1 with a timestamp offset of 30, which translates to a timestamp of 120, and a size of 20 bytes. The last header is the primary header, which specifies that the payload will have a format of G.711. Note that the primary header does not specify the length of the payload because you can determine this information from the RTP packet length. Also note that the RTP packet is not aligned on a word (four-byte) boundary. If there is a requirement to align on a word

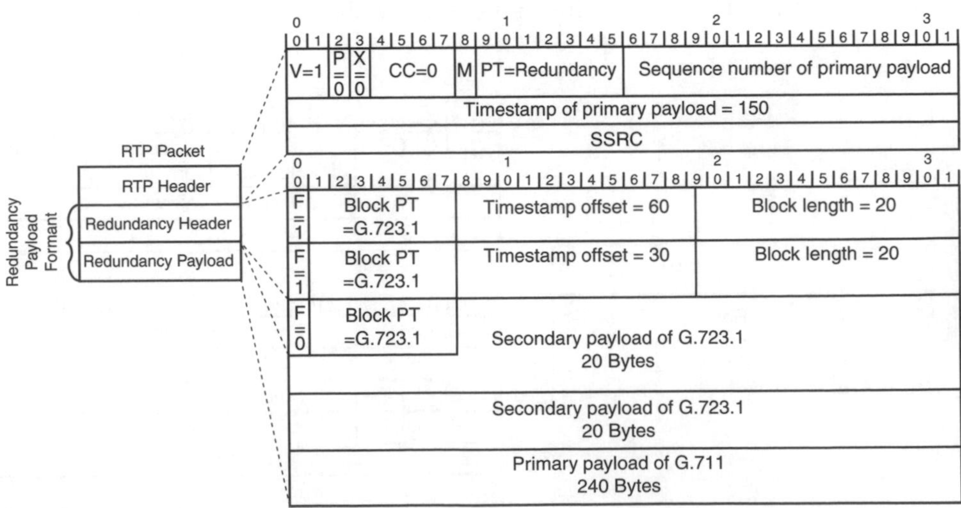

Figure 2.13 An example RTP packet with a voice-redundancy payload.

boundary, you can use the Padding bit in the RTP header to specify redundant bytes at the end of the RTP packet.

The example packet is sent every 30 ms. If a burst of two packets is lost, the receiver can still recreate the media sequence from the secondary payloads in the third packet. This benefit comes at the cost of 16.3 percent (a 252-byte RTP packet without redundancy versus a 301-byte RTP packet with redundancy) overhead per RTP packet due to redundancy and 60 ms of extra delay in the play-out buffer in order to allow for time to play the two redundant payloads if up to two packets are lost.

The overhead in the previous example is low because the secondary payload has much lower bandwidth than the primary payload. For redundancy to be economical, it must add as low an overhead as possible with reduced but acceptable quality. This situation is not always the case, however—especially if the primary payload has low bandwidth. On a low-bandwidth link using a modem at 28.8 kbps or 56 kbps, you cannot use G.711, so you must use a low bit rate codec such as G.723.1 as the primary payload. If you use redundancy, then the secondary payload can also be G.723.1. If single packet losses are covered and the primary payload has one G.723.1 frame, then the overhead per RTP packet due to redundancy is 43.8 percent with an additional delay of 30 ms at the receiver. This overhead is quite high, and you should use it if the voice quality is unacceptable due to a high number of single packet losses on the network.

Payload Format for FEC

The main idea is to first generate a *Forward Error Correction* (FEC) packet by applying an Exclusive-OR type of operation on a set of non-FEC packets and then send the FEC packet on a separate RTP session than the one on which you are sending non-FEC packets. Instead of sending the non-FEC and FEC packets on separate RTP sessions, you can send them on the same RTP session. Then, however, you will have to demultiplex the two packet types on the basis of the Payload Type field in the RTP header that distinguishes them. The advantage of using FEC is that the receiver can reconstruct the lost non-FEC packets from the information in the FEC packets. The disadvantage of using FEC is the increase in bandwidth and the extra delay due to the extra FEC packets.

The payload format for FEC is specified in [ROSE00]. This format is generic enough to include a wide variety of FEC algorithms (such as Parity, Hamming Codes, and Reed-Solomon). Figure 2.14 shows an RTP packet generated for FEC. This packet consists of a 12-byte RTP header, an FEC

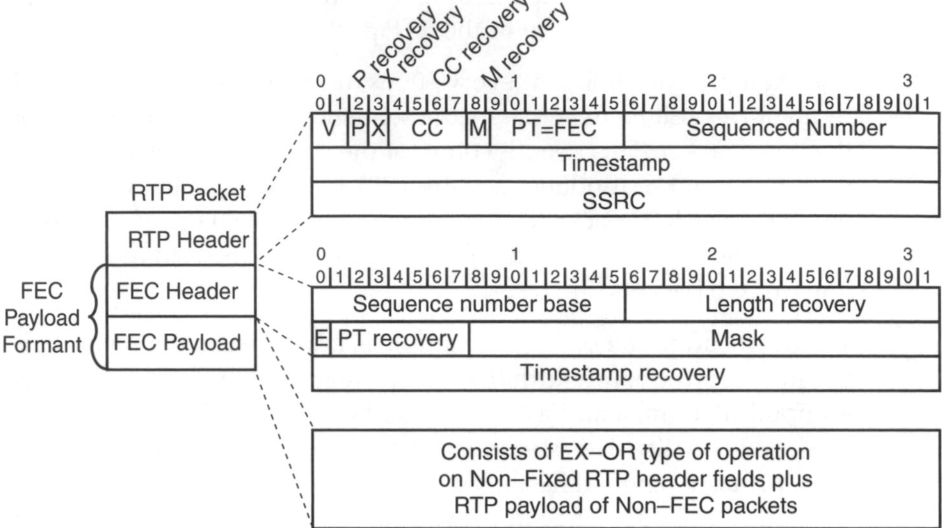

Figure 2.14 RTP packet containing the FEC payload format.

header, and an FEC payload. Because the RTP header of the FEC packet is never more than 12 bytes, we always assume the Padding, Extension, and Contributing Source Count fields to be zero, and we reuse them instead for recovering the respective fields in the lost packets. The value of the Marker field is also reused in order to recover the Marker field in the lost packets. All of the fields in the 12-byte RTP header are generated in accordance with the rules of RTP (except for the following fields):

Padding recovery (1 bit). An Exclusive-OR type of operation is applied to the padding bits in the non-FEC packets that are associated with this FEC packet.

Extension recovery (1 bit). An Exclusive-OR type of operation is applied to the extension bits in the non-FEC packets that are associated with this FEC packet.

Contributing Source Count recovery (4 bits). An Exclusive-OR type of operation is applied to the contributing source-count bits in the non-FEC packets.

Marker recovery (1 bit). An Exclusive-OR type of operation is applied to the marker bits in the non-FEC packets that are associated with this FEC packet.

Timestamp (32 bits). Using the timestamp value in the non-FEC packets might result in nonmonotonically increasing the timestamp for some FEC algorithms. Therefore, this field is generated from the value of the RTP clock at the instant the FEC packet is sent. Note that this field is not used to recover the timestamps for lost packets.

The FEC payload format consists of a 12-byte header that contains information about the FEC payload that follows this header. The fields in the FEC header areas follows:

Sequence Number Base (16 bits): This field is equal to the minimum sequence number of the non-FEC packets that are used to generate this FEC packet.

Length recovery (16 bits): This field is generated by an Exclusive-OR type of operation on the lengths of non-FEC packets that are used to generate this FEC packet. The length is an unsigned number (in bytes) determined by subtracting the first 12 bytes of the RTP header from the length of the RTP packet. If the RTP header of a non-FEC packet is extended beyond the first 12-bytes, then the extended bytes are treated as part of the payload for the purpose of generating the length.

Extension (1 bit). This field might be used in the future by the next version of this specification in order to extend the FEC header. The extension header is not currently defined, so you should set this field to zero.

Payload Type recovery (7 bits). An Exclusive-OR type of operation is applied to the payload type bits in the non-FEC packets that are associated with this FEC packet.

Mask (24 bits). This field contains the list of sequence numbers of those non-FEC packets that generated this FEC packet. Instead of listing all of the 32-bit sequence numbers, this field contains a 24-bit mask that calculates the sequence numbers. The least-significant bit in the mask is i = 0, and the most significant bit is i = 23. If bit i is set, then the non-FEC packet with the sequence number that is equal to the sequence number base + i is present. You can use up to 24 non-FEC packets in order to generate this FEC packet.

Timestamp recovery (32 bits). An Exclusive-OR type of operation is applied to the padding bits in the non-FEC packets that are associated with this FEC packet.

You generate the FEC payload by applying an Exclusive-OR type of operation across the bit strings of non-FEC packets that are associated with this FEC packet. The bit string of a non-FEC packet consists of the extended RTP header fields (if present) and the RTP payload. You should make all bit strings of a non-FEC packet equal in length to the longest bit string by padding the shorter bit strings with either a 1 or a 0.

Figure 2.15 shows how you can use FEC to recover from single packet losses. Non-FEC packet A is sent first, followed by non-FEC packet B. The FEC packet

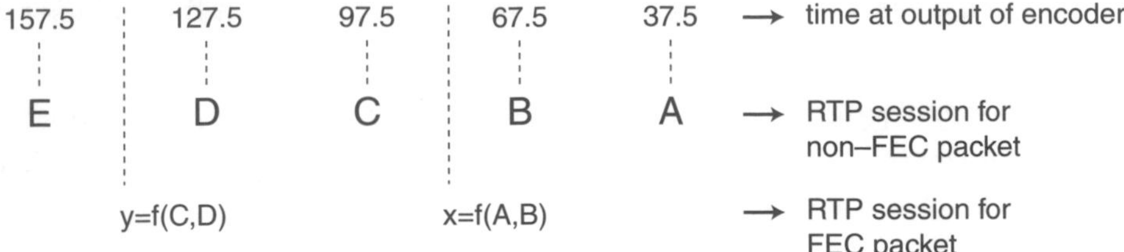

Figure 2.15 Scenario for recovering single packet losses by using FEC.

X originates from non-FEC packets A and B and is sent immediately after non-FEC packet B. The non-FEC and the FEC packets are sent on separate RTP sessions so that the receiver can demultiplex them based on different UDP ports. If packet A is lost, it can be recovered from packet B and X.

Table 2.3 shows the generation of packet X from packets A and B. Packets A and B contain a 6.3 kbps and 5.3 kbps frame of G.723.1, respectively. The payload type of packets A and B is a static payload type of 4 for G.723.1 and a dynamic payload type for FEC. The payload of packets A and B is 24 and 20

Table 2.3 Generation of an FEC Packet from Two Non-FEC Packets

		Packet A	Packet B	Packet X = f(A,B)
RTP Header	Version (V)	1	1	1
	Padding (P)	0	0	0 ($P_A \oplus P_B$)
	Extension (X)	0	0	0 ($E_A \oplus E_B$)
	Contribution Source Count (CC)	0	0	0 ($CC_A \oplus CC_B$)
	Marker (M)	0	1	1 ($M_A \oplus M_B$)
	Payload Type (PT)	4	4	FEC
	Sequence Number (SN)	5	6	20
	Timestamp (T)	0	30	38
	Synchronization Source (SSRC)	6	6	6
FEC Header	Sequence Number Base	–	–	5
	Length Recovery (L)	24	20	12 ($L_A \oplus L_B$)
	Extension	–	–	0
	Payload Type Recovery	–	–	0 ($PT_A \oplus PT_B$)
	Mask	–	–	3
	Timestamp Recovery	–	–	30 ($T_A \oplus T_B$)
FEC Payload	FEC Payload in Hexadecimal	A′	B′	X = A′ $\oplus$ B′

bytes, respectively. Therefore, packet B is padded by four bytes of zeros in order to calculate packet X's payload.

This FEC approach introduces an overhead of about 41 percent (116 bytes in packets A, B, and X and 48 bytes of redundancy overhead in packet X) and an additional delay of 30 ms + GFEC + RFEC, where GFEC is the computational time that is necessary to generate packet X at the sender and RFEC is the computational time needed to recover the lost packet B at the receiver.

End-to-End Delay and Header Compression on the IP Network

We will illustrate end-to-end delays by using conversational voice as the multimedia of choice, because voice has the most stringent delay requirements and it is most important for a good multimedia experience. As we described in Section 1.1, the end-to-end delay must be less than 300ms, and the maximum allowable jitter on the Internet expressed in ms is $j_{buf} < 300 - d_{net} - d_{coder} - fs$. If we use G.723.1, then $j_{buf} < 227.5 - d_{net}$. To calculate the network delay (d_{net}), let's use the setup in Figure 2.16. This figure shows two terminals/endpoints accessing the Internet through low-bandwidth 56 kbps modem links. The components that are involved in the one-way network delay include the following: packetization, modems, the Internet, modems, and the unpacketizer. The one-way delay in the modems is about 90 ms. The delay on the Internet when it is not congested is about 80 ms for 6,000 miles. Assume that the endpoints measure a one-way delay of 40 ms, then $d_{net} = 130 + d_{pkt}$ (where d_{pkt} is the packetization delay and the unpacketization delay is low enough that we can assume it is zero). The maximum allowable jitter will then be $j_{buf} < 97.5 - d_{pkt}$.

The packetization delay is quite low, and we can assume that its value is zero for one frame of voice per packet. This value puts the size of the jitter buffer

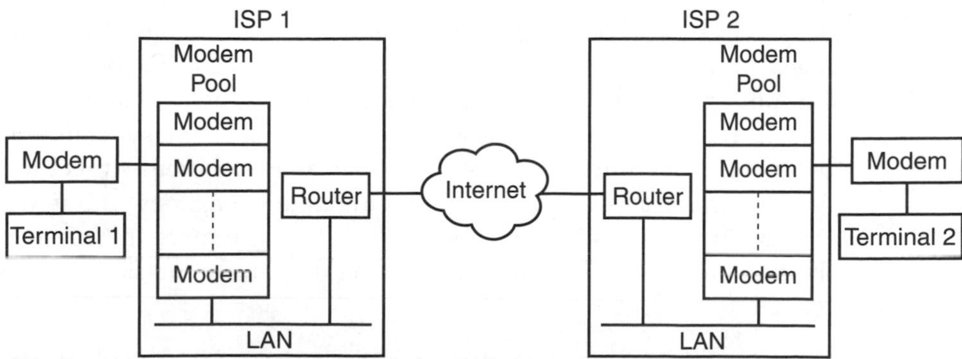

Figure 2.16 Components of the transmission delay of the IP network.

at 97.5 ms. In this scenario, jitter on the Internet that is greater than 97.5 ms will essentially make the conversation half-duplex.

Although one frame per packet produces the minimum delay possible, it also produces the maximum overhead in bandwidth due to the headers of the packet. On the *Point-to-Point Protocol* (PPP) link, the headers (RTP + UDP + IP + PPP and 12 + 8 + 20 + 4) occupy at least 44 bytes. A 5.3 kbps G.723.1 frame has a duration of 30 ms and occupies 20 bytes. If one frame/packet is sent on the network, it produces an overhead of 68.75 percent and utilizes a bandwidth of 17.1 kbps. This situation leaves about 38.9 kbps of bandwidth for two voice or other multimedia streams. Packing four frames per packet reduces the overhead and bandwidth utilization to 35.5 percent and 8.3 kbps (respectively) but increases the packetization delay of three extra frames to $d_{pkt} = 90$ ms. The size of the jitter buffer should then be $j_{buf} < 7.5$ ms in order for full-duplex conversation to occur. Assuming a maximum jitter of 7.5 ms on the Internet is not practical.

Another method of reducing the header overhead is to compress the headers. This method of compressing the 40-byte RTP/UDP/IP headers is described in [CAS99]. The main idea is to first send an uncompressed header followed by compressed headers. The compressed header is created through three types of compression:

1. The constant fields are removed from the compressed header. The Version field in the RTP header is an example of a field that remains the same.
2. Fields that change by a constant number from packet to packet are removed from the compressed header. You can construct these fields by adding the constant change to the compressed header that you receive. The sequence number field in the RTP header is an example of a field that changes by one per RTP packet.
3. Fields that change by a nonconstant number from packet to packet can be encoded by their difference. The difference can be represented in fewer bits compared to the full number of bits in the field itself. The timestamp field for H.263 video is an example of a field that changes by a non-constant number. In this case, the frequency of the RTP clock is 90kHz. Assuming that the H.263 frame rate is 29.97Hz, the RTP timestamp would increment by about 3,003 between frames. An RTP packet containing data from the same frame as the previous packet will increment its timestamp by 0, whereas an RTP packet containing data from a new frame will increment its timestamp by about 3,003. The difference in timestamp can be encoded in 12 bits, thus compressing the timestamp field from 32 bits to 12 bits.

The resulting compressed header is two bytes for most packets. If you use the UDP checksum, then the compressed header is four bytes. You can apply the compression end-to-end or link-to-link. If it is end-to-end, then all intermediate routers on the Internet must have knowledge about the structure of compressed packets in order to properly route these packets. If it is link-to-link, then only the links that implement header compression will participate. The real savings from header compression is when it is applied to packets on low-bandwidth links (such as between the endpoint modem and the ISP modem pool in Figure 2.16). You can uncompress these packets for the Internet backbone, where bandwidth is less of a constraint and where there is no guarantee that the backbone routers will implement header compression.

Synchronization of Streams

RTP recommends the use of separate RTP sessions in order to transmit different streams, such as voice and video. This feature enables the UDP ports of the destination endpoint to demultiplex the streams before handing it to the voice and video RTP applications. This feature also enables the source endpoint to request different QoS (for example, high QoS for voice and lower QoS for video) for the two streams and have the network provide it. If the voice and video streams were to be lip-synchronized at the destination endpoint, however, there is no coupling between the two sessions at the RTP level. Each stream has its own timing space, and the only way to synchronize is to correlate the timing spaces in the two sessions with a reference clock. If two different applications are generating the streams from the same endpoint, then you can use a system clock or a clock that is common to the two applications as the reference clock. If separate endpoints generate the streams, then you will have to use NTP [MILL92]. The source endpoint periodically provides this reference clock to the destination endpoint through the *Real-time Transport Control Protocol* (RTCP).

Real-time Transport Control Protocol

RTCP is RTP's companion protocol that gathers statistics about the quality of the network on which the RTP packets are transmitted. RTCP performs this procedure by gathering statistics on the RTP packets that it receives and then periodically sending these statistics to the sender of the RTP packets. RTCP is a control protocol whose functionality overlaps with H.245's features. The design philosophy of RTCP and H.245 are quite different, however. RTCP is designed for large-scale conferences that scale to thousands of participants, whereas H.245 is designed for small-scale conferences that scale to fewer than 100 participants. The design choices in these two protocols are based on satisfying this level of scalability. We cover H.245 in Chapters 3 and 4 ("Point-to-Point Call: Signaling" and "Multi-Point Conference," respectively). We cover RTCP in Chapter 4, where we can better understand its concepts.

Transport of Facsimile over the Internet

Group 3 facsimile machines were developed in order to communicate on the PSTN. Due to cost savings in using the Internet instead, however, we are using IP gateways to bypass the PSTN (as shown in Figure 2.17). These IP gateways can be single-port or multi-port. A single port gateway has a single G3 fax interface on one side and an IP interface on the other. A multi-port gateway has multiple G3 fax interfaces so that multiple G3 fax machines can operate simultaneously. The calling G3 fax machine communicates with the calling gateway as if it were a peer G3 fax machine. Similarly, the called fax machine communicates with the called gateway as if it were a peer G3 fax machine. The calling gateway encapsulates the T.4 data or the T.30 control information from the calling fax machine in the T.38 [98T38 and 99T38] packet and sends it to the called gateway by using either the TCP or the UDP transport protocol. The called gateway extracts the T.4 or the T.30 information from the T.38 packet and sends it to the called fax machine. The T.30 information sent by the called fax machine is similarly encapsulated by the called gateway and is sent to the calling gateway. The calling gateway removes the T.30 information from the T.38 packet and sends it to the calling fax machine. The T.38 packet consists of T.30 indications and T.30/T.4 data. The T.30 indications include CNG and CED signals, High-level Data Link Control (HDLC) preamble flags, and modem modulation training. The T.30/T.4 data includes T.30 HDLC Control and T.4 images.

If you use TCP as a transport protocol, the T.38 packet is sent unchanged. If you use UDP, then a 16-bit sequence number (and optionally, redundancy or FEC) is added to T.38. The sequence number provides information about lost and out-of-order packets to the called gateway. The optional redundancy or FEC enables the called gateway to reconstruct lost packets. Note that the RTP header is not used here because the only information that is needed from the 12-byte RTP header is the two-byte sequence number field (and the rest of the 10 bytes are overhead).

Figure 2.7 showed an example of the communication between two fax machines. Figure 2.18 shows the use of a gateway to route that

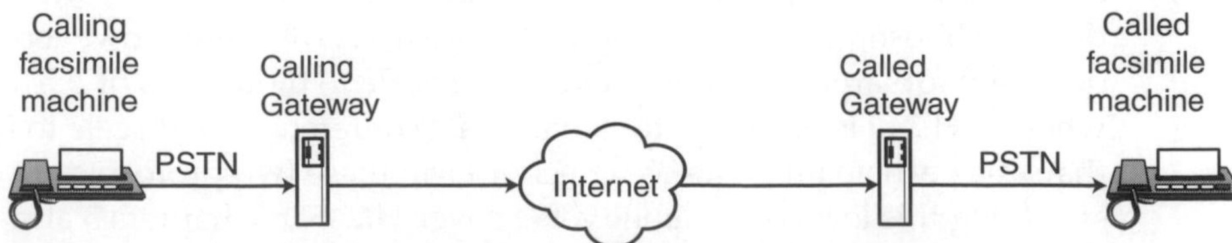

Figure 2.17 Using gateways to route G3 facsimile communication over the Internet.

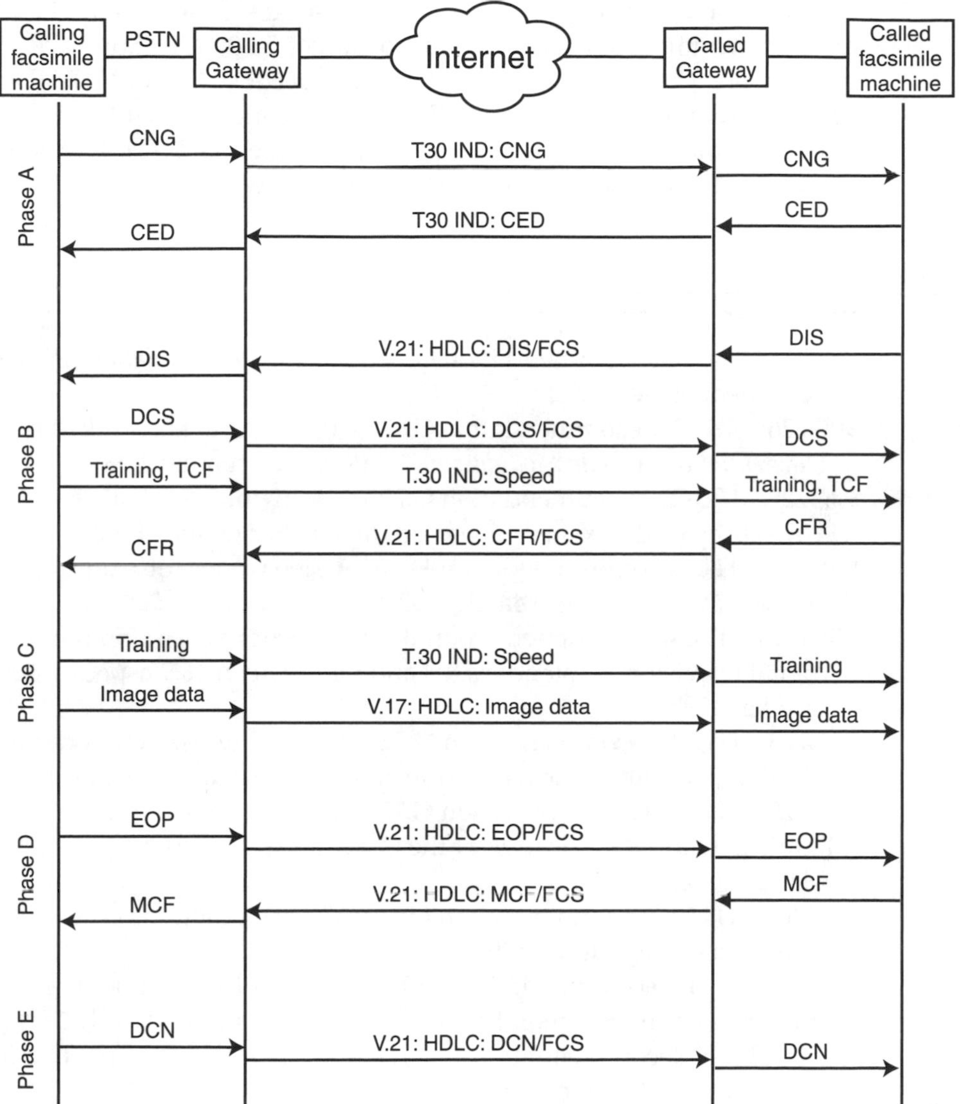

Figure 2.18 G3 facsimile communication over the Internet through gateways.

communication over the Internet in T.38 packets. The CNG and the CED tones are transferred as T.30 indications. Upon reception of these indications, the gateway can locally generate the tone for its fax machine. The Digital Identification Signal (DIS) is sent by the gateway as a T.30 control consisting of a V.21 HDLC packet with a DIS field and an FCS field. The DCS is also sent as a T.30 control packet. The modem training is sent as a T.30 indication with the proper speed. The TCF signal is transferred between gateways if UDP is used as the transport protocol. If TCP is used as a transport protocol, TCF is not transferred; instead, the called gateway locally generates it. The CFR and modem training is sent as a T.30 control and as T.30 indication packets, respectively. The image data is sent as T.4 data consisting of V.17 HDLC packets with image data, and the final packet is marked with FCS-Sig-End. The rest of the signals are appropriately packetized as T.30 indications, T.30 control, or T.4 data and are sent to the other gateway.

References

72G711 ITU-T Recommendation G.711: *Pulse Code Modulation* (PCM) of voice frequencies. 1972.

90G726 ITU-T Recommendation G.726: 40, 32, 24, 16 kbps *Adaptive Differential Pulse Code Modulation* (ADPCM). December 1990.

92G728 ITU-T Recommendation G.728: Coding of Speech at 16 kbps using Low-Delay Code Excited Linear Prediction. September 1992.

93H261 ITU-T Recommendation H.261: Video Codec for Audiovisual Services at p x 64 kbits. March 1993.

95BT601 ITU-R Recommendation BT.601-5: Studio encoding parameters of digital television for standard 4:3 and wide screen 16:9 aspect ratios. October 1995.

96G723 ITU-T Recommendation G.723.1: Dual Rate Speech Coder for Multimedia Communications Transmitting at 5.3 and 6.3 kbps. March 1996.

96G729 ITU-T Recommendation G.729: C source code and test vectors for implementation verification of the G.729 8 kbps CS-ACELP speech coder. March 1996.

96H263 ITU-T Recommendation H.263: Video Coding for Low Bit Rate Communication. March 1996.

96T30 ITU-T Recommendation T.30: Procedures for document facsimile transmission in the general switched telephone network. July 1996.

96T4 ITU-T Recommendation T.4. Standardization of Group 3 Facsimile apparatus for document transmission. July 1996.

98H263 ITU-T Recommendation H.263: Video Coding for Low Bit Rate Communication. January 1998.

98T38 ITU-T Recommendation T.38: Procedures for real-time Group 3 facsimile communication over IP networks. June 1998.

99T38 ITU-T Recommendation T.38 (Amendment 1): Procedures for real-time Group 3 facsimile communication over IP networks. April 1999.

99T140 ITU-T Recommendation T.140: Protocol for multimedia application text conversation. February 1998 with addendum 1 to T.140 in February 2000.

00G711A2 ITU-T Recommendation G.711, Appendix II: A comfort noise payload definition for ITU-T G.711 use in packet-based multimedia communication systems. February 2000.

CAS96 Casner, S., et al. *RTP: A transport protocol for real-time applications*. RFC 1889, January 1996.

CAS99 Casner, S., and Jacobson, V. *Compressing IP/UDP/RTP Headers for Low-Speed Serial Links*. RFC 2508, February 1999.

CLAR90 Clark, D., and Tennenhouse, D. Architectural considerations for a new generation of protocols. SIGCOMM Symposium on Communications Architectures and Protocols, September 1990. Computer Communications Review, September 1990.

G723A96 ITU-T Recommendation G.723.1, Annex A: C reference code, test signals and test sequences for the fixed point 5.3 and 6.3 kbps dual rate speech coder and for the silence compression scheme, version 5.1. November 1996.

G729A96 ITU-T Recommendation G.729, Annex A: C source code and test vectors for implementation verification of the G.729 reduced complexity 8 kbps CS-ACELP speech coder. November 1996.

G729B97 ITU-T Recommendation G.729, Annex B: C source code and test vectors for implementation verification of the algorithm of the G.729 silence compression scheme. August 1997.

H323G00 ITU-T Recommendation H.323, Annex G: Text Conversation and Text SET. February 2000.

HEL00 Hellstrom, G. RTP Payload for Text Conversation. RFC 2793, May 2000.

ISO92 ISO/IEC 6429. Information technology—Control functions for coded character sets. 1992.

ISO93 ISO/IEC 10646-1. Information technology—Universal Multiple-Octet Coded Character Set (UCS)—Part 1: Architecture and Basic Multilingual Plane. 1993.

MILL92 Mills, D. Network time protocol (version 3) specification, implementation. RFC 1305. March 1992.

PERK97 Perkins, C., et al. RTP Payload for Redundant Voice Data. RFC 2198, September 1997.

ROSE00 Rosenberg, J., and Schulzrinne, H. An RTP Payload Format for Generic Forward Error Correction. RFC 2733, December 1999.

SCHU96 Schulzrinne, H., and Casner, S. RTP profile for voice and video conferences with minimal control. RFC 1890, January 1996.

WEN98 Wenger, S., et al. RTP Payload Format for the 1998 Version of ITU-T Recommendation H.263 Video (H.263+). RFC 2429, October 1998.

Problems

1. The RTP Profile RFC 1890 suggests for the transmitter to set the marker bit in the first packet after silence suppression. The receiver can then use this

indication to dynamically adjust the delay in the playout buffer. How should you adjust the delay in the playout buffer if this packet is lost?

2. In this chapter, we describe a method to generate an FEC packet. Develop a method to recover the lost non-FEC packet.

CHAPTER 3

Point-to-Point Call: Signaling

The protocols that we use in point-to-point calls include H.225.0-RAS, H.225.0-Q.931, and H.245. The *International Telecommunications Union-Telecommunication* (ITU-T) recommendation H.225.0 [00H2250] describes messages for H.225.0-Q.931 and H.225.0-RAS, and the procedures on the usage of these messages appear in ITU-T recommendation H.323 [00H323]. ITU-T recommendation H.245 [00H245] describes the messages and the procedures for the H.245 protocol. We collectively know these protocols as H.323 protocols, and we use them between functional entities (such as terminals, gateways, Multi-Point Control Units or MCUs, and gatekeepers). The terminals terminate the signaling and media at the end user's location. The gateways interconnect the H.323 with the circuit-switched networks. The MCUs provide centralized multi-point conferences. Functional entities such as terminals, gateways, and MCUs that terminate H.323 signaling and media are collectively known as endpoints. The gatekeepers provide services to endpoints and can also route H.323 packets.

The H.225.0-RAS protocol is between the endpoint and the gatekeeper, and the endpoints use it in order to obtain services from the gatekeeper. The H.225.0-Q.931 protocol is between the endpoints, and you use this protocol for call setup and call termination. The H.245 protocol is also between endpoints and controls the multimedia. The H.225.0-RAS and H.245 messages are encoded in ASN.1. The H.225.0-Q.931 protocol consists of a

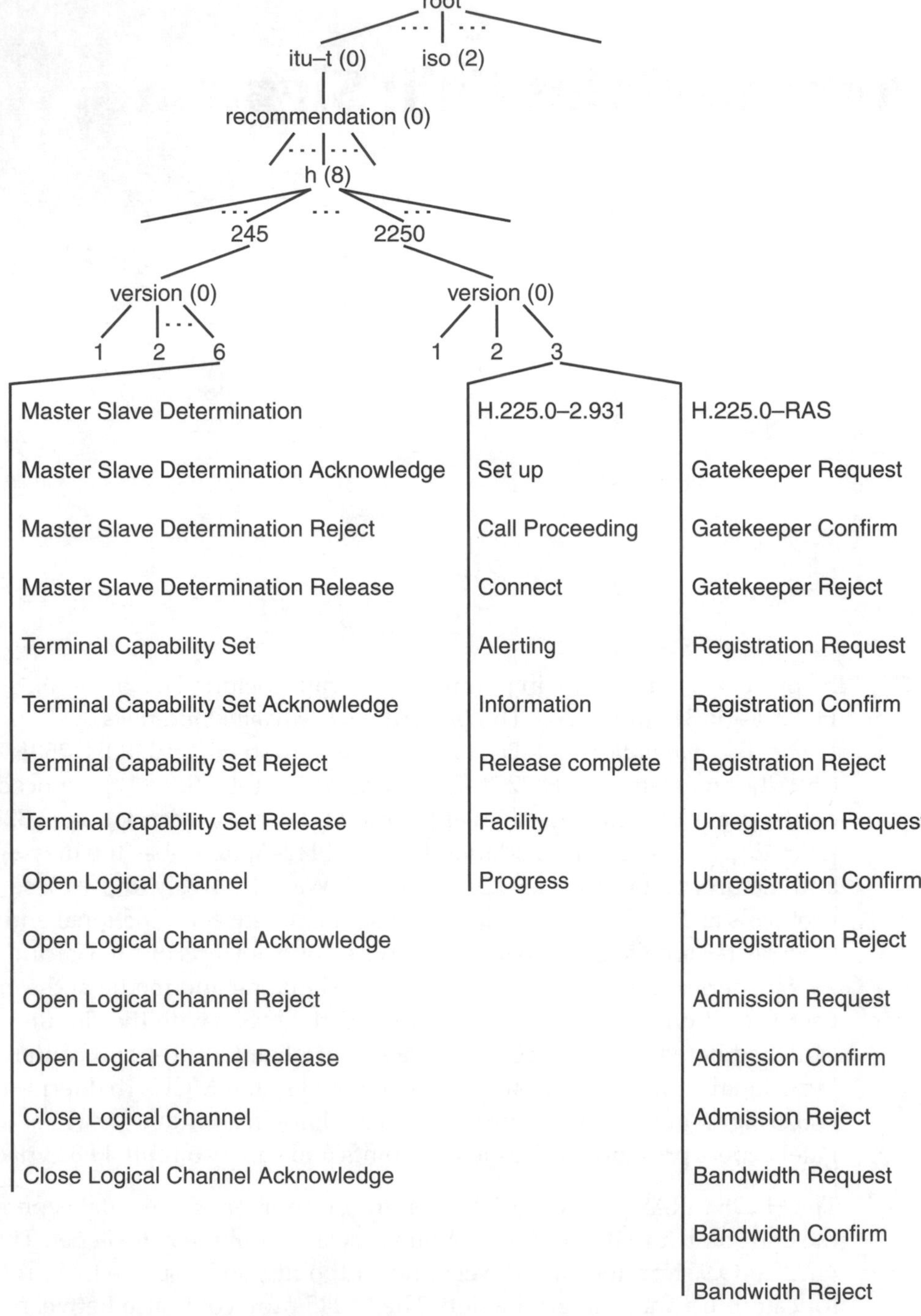

Figure 3.1 H.323 (H.225.0-RAS, H.225.0-Q.931, and H.245) messages and object identifiers.

Request Channel Close
Request Channel Close Acknowledge
Request Channel Close Reject
Request Channel Close Release
Request Mode
Request Mode Acknowledge
Request Mode Reject
Request Mode Release
Round Trip Delay Request
Round Trip Delay Response
Conference Request
Conference Response
Communication Mode Command
Send Terminal Capability Set
Flow Control Command
End Session Command
Miscellaneous Command
Function Not Understood
Function Not Supported
Conference Command
Miscellaneous Indication
Conference Indication

Disengage Request
Disengage Confirm
Disengage Reject
Location Request
Location Confirm
Location Reject
Info Request
Info Request Response
Non Standard Message
Unknown Message Response
Request In Progress
Resource Available Indicate
Resource Available Confirm
Info Request Ack
Info Request Nak

Figure 3.1 H.323 (H.225.0-RAS, H.225.0-Q.931, and H.245) messages and object identifiers. (Continued)

subset of messages from ITU-T recommendation Q.931 [98Q93]. The Q.931 messages are binary-encoded and consist of fields known as Information Elements. The User-to-User Information Element consists of one or more fields that are encoded in ASN.1. These fields in the User-to-User Information Element are not part of Q.931; rather, they were developed for the H.225.0-Q.931 protocol for operation on IP networks. H.323 protocols are assigned object identifiers under the ITU-T object identifier tree (shown in Figure 3.1, along with all messages that are used in H.323).

The root of the tree where the object identifiers start is unnamed. The nodes that are one level below the root are assigned to various organizations. The ITU-T is assigned an object identifier of 0; the *International Standards Organization* (ISO) is assigned 1, and so on. Each organization has the responsibility of maintaining the branch under its node as the tree traverses from the organization downwards. An object identifier is a sequence of integers that are separated by decimal points. The H.245 version 6 has the object identifier of 0.0.8.245.0.6, and H.225.0 Version 4 has the object identifier of 0.0.8.2250.0.4. Note that both H.225.0-RAS and H.225.0-Q.931 protocols have the same object identifier.

This chapter describes the H.225.0-RAS, H.225.0-Q.931, and H.245 protocols and their operation in the H.323 point-to-point call.

Call-Signaling Protocol: H.225.0-Q.931

Call signaling helps connect one terminal with another so that the users who are using those terminals can collaborate. Once collaboration completes, call signaling terminates the connection. Figure 3.2 shows terminals, gateways, and the networks: *Integrated Services Digital Network* (ISDN), *Public Switched Telephone Network* (PSTN), and the *Internet Protocol* (IP). The gateways interconnect two disparate networks and provide interworking between the signaling and media on one network and that of the other network. H.323-PSTN Gateways 1 and 4 provide interworking between the H.225.0 and H.245 signaling on the IP network with the ISDN User Part (ISUP) signaling on the PSTN network and the packetized media streams on the IP network with the *Pulse-Code Modulation* (PCM) voice streams on the PSTN network. H.323-ISDN Gateway 2 similarly provides interworking of signaling and media between the H.323 and ISDN networks. You can address the PSTN and the H.320 gateways with an IP address and *Transmission Control Protocol* (TCP) port by entities on the IP network and by using an E.164 address by entities on the PSTN and ISDN networks (respectively). The residential gateway 3 provides interworking between the H.323 network and the wireless and analog interfaces and protocols in homes and offices. You can

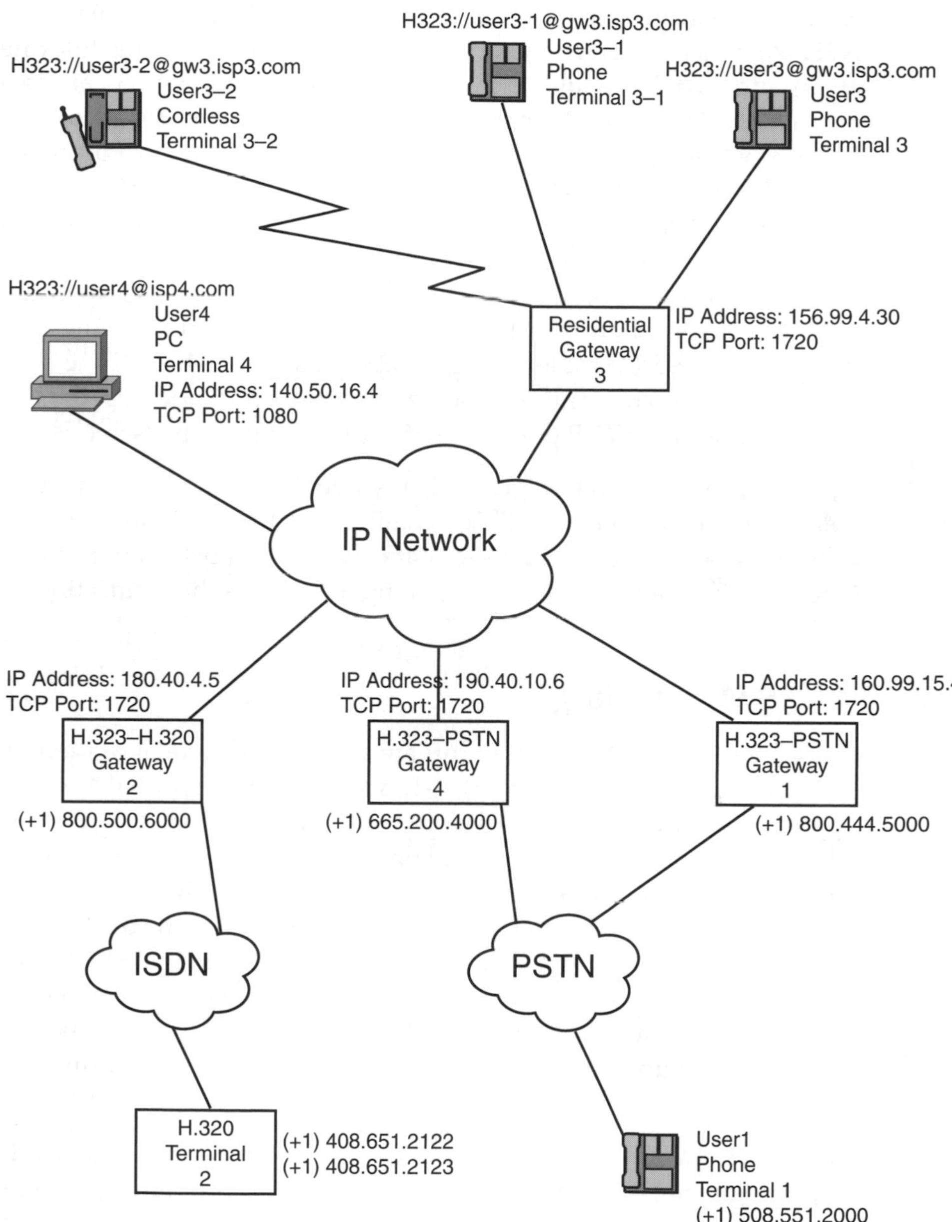

Figure 3.2 Call signaling on the networks.

address the residential gateway with an IP address and TCP port by entities on the IP network. The terminals terminate the signaling and media at the end user's location. Users and terminals have addresses through which they can be contacted. Terminal 1 is connected to the PSTN network and is addressable through an E.164 address of (+1) 503.551.2000. User 1 can be contacted by using Terminal 1's address. Terminal 2 is a 128 kbps H.320 [97H320] videoconferencing terminal that is connected to the ISDN network and is addressable through two E.164 addresses of (+1) 408.651.2122 and (+1) 408.651.2123. User 2 can be contacted by using Terminal 2's addresses. Users 3, 3-1, and 3-2 are addressable though the H.323 URL of the form h323://user@domain as h323://user3@gw3.isp3.com, h323://user3-1@ gw3.isp3.com, and h323://user3-2@ gw3.isp3.com, respectively. The domain part of the *Uniform Resource Locator* (URL), gw3.isp3.com, should resolve to the transport address (the IP address of 156.99.4.30 and the TCP port of 1720) of Gateway 3. The user part of the URL contacts the appropriate user. User 4 is addressable through h323://user4@isp4.com. The domain part of the URL, isp4.com, should resolve to the transport address (the IP address 140.50.16.4 and the TCP port 1080) of Terminal 4 (which User 4 uses).

With the setup shown in Figure 3.2, any two users who have terminals can collaborate on the network. Call signaling uses the destination user's address in order to set up a connection so that collaboration between users can begin. Once collaboration is over, call signaling terminates the connection.

H.225.0-Q.931 Signaling

If User 4 at Terminal 4 wants to initiate a multimedia collaboration with User 3 (h323://user3@gw3.isp3.com) at Terminal 3, then Terminal 4 must first obtain the transport address of User 3's Gateway 3. In Chapter 5, "Inter-Domain Communication," we explain the mechanism that obtains the transport address from the URL. In this chapter, we will assume that Terminal 4 obtains Terminal 3's transport address, which consists of an IP address of 156.99.4.30 and a TCP port number of 1720. Note that port 1720 is the well-known call-signaling port for H.323. The following steps, as we illustrate in Figure 3.3, show the exchange of H.225.0-Q.931 messages that are required to set up and tear down the connection between Terminal 4 and Gateway 3:

Call initiation. Terminal 4 opens a TCP connection with Terminal 3 for the Call Signaling channel. The terminal then sends the setup message to Gateway 3. This message consists of Terminal 4's transport addresses (IP address 140.50.16.4, TCP port 1080, IP address 140.50.16.4, and TCP port 1090) at which Gateway 3 should send call signaling (H.225.0-Q.931) and call control (H.245) messages, respectively. Terminal 4 will wait at least four seconds for an H.225.0-Q.931 message response from Gateway 3 before disconnecting.

Call proceeding. Upon receiving the setup message, Gateway 3 can respond with the optional call proceeding message in order to inform Terminal 4

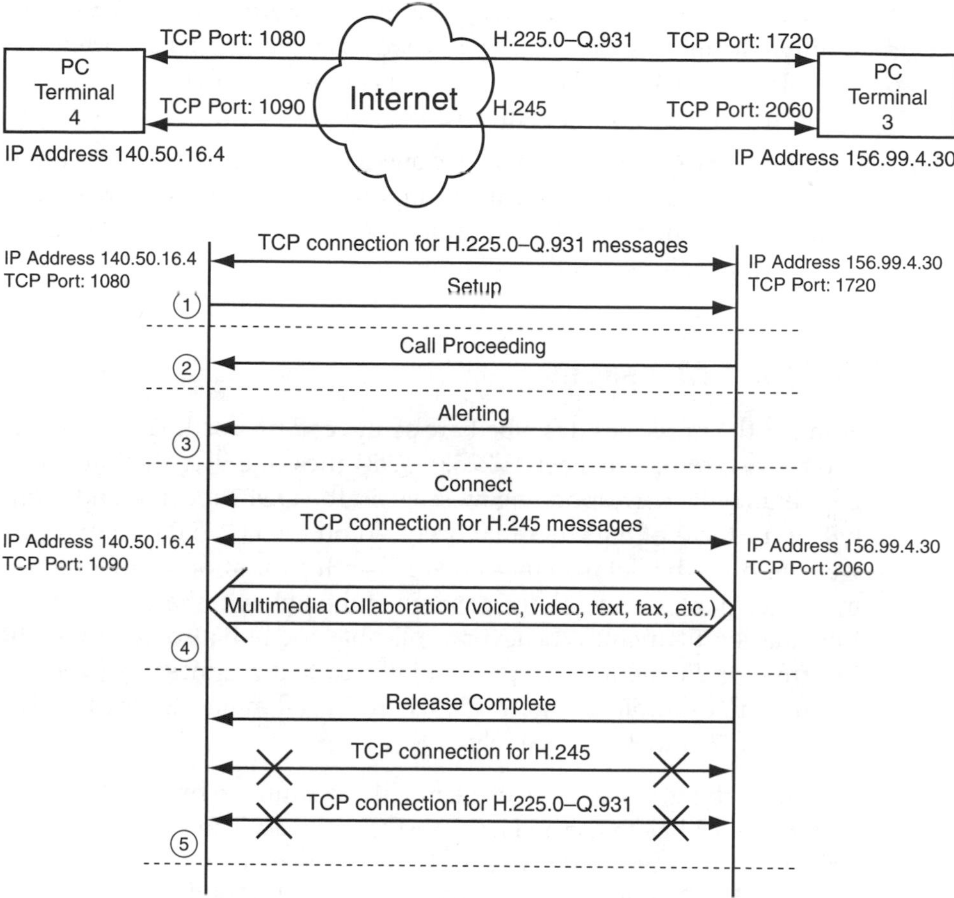

Figure 3.3 Call establishment and termination.

that it has received the setup message. Gateway 3 responds with call proceeding only if it cannot send an appropriate H.225.0-Q.931 message to Terminal 4 within the timeout value of four seconds.

Call alerting. Upon receiving the setup message, Gateway 3 alerts User 3. This alert takes place in the form of a ringing tone, popping a dialog box on the user-interface display, or by any other means. The gateway then sends an alerting message to Terminal 4, indicating this occurrence. Terminal 4 in turn alerts its User 4, and waits at least 180 seconds for another H.225.0-Q.931 message from Gateway 3 before disconnecting.

Call connection. If User 3 takes the call, Gateway 3 stops alerting and sends a connect message indicating this occurrence to Terminal 4. Terminal 4 notifies User 4 by stopping the alert. The connect message consists of Terminal 3's transport addresses (IP address 156.99.4.30 and TCP port

2060) at which Terminal 4 will send the call control (H.245) messages. Either Terminal 4 or Gateway 3 will open the second TCP connection for the H.245 call control channel. At this point, the call has been established—and multimedia collaboration can begin.

Call termination. When users are done collaborating or User 3 does not answer the call in step 4, either endpoint sends the release complete message to the other. The endpoints close the H.225.0-Q.931 and H.245 TCP connections and the call terminates.

H.225.0-Q.931 Messages

Some of the messages described are setup, call proceeding, alerting, connect, and release complete. Each H.225.0-Q.931 message uses the Information Elements of its corresponding message in the Q.931 recommendation [98Q931]. Most of the work that occurred on the H.225.0 recommendation was defining the fields in the User-to-User Information Element for each message. Here, we will describe some of the fields in the User-to-User Information Element. Whenever applicable, we will also describe other Information Elements. Later, we will illustrate these messages and their fields through an example in Figure 3.5, where User 4 makes three calls (1, 2, and 3) to Users 1, 2, and 3, respectively.

For call 1, the E.164 address of Terminal 1 is routable by the PSTN network, so Terminal 4 has to use an H.323-PSTN gateway. The terminal has a choice between Gateway 1 and Gateway 4. Call 1 (using Gateway 1) will mostly traverse the IP network and then hop onto the PSTN that is closest to Terminal 1, whereas Call 1 (using Gateway 4) will quickly hop on and traverse the PSTN, mostly. Usually, the desired routing depends on the cost and the *Quality of Service* (QoS) that you want. PSTN calls are usually more expensive and provide much better QoS. Let's assume that Call 1 uses Gateway 1. Terminal 1 must be capable of obtaining the transport address of Gateway 1 and then sending the setup message to it.

For Call 2, Terminal 1 needs to know in advance that the two E.164 addresses belong to the H.320 terminal. The terminal can then obtain the transport address of H.320 Gateway 2 and send the setup message to it. For Call 3, the domain part of User 3's address of h323://user3@ gw3.isp3.com must resolve to the transport address of Gateway 3, and Terminal 4 should then send the setup message to Gateway 3.

We can describe some of the fields in the setup message as follows:

sourceAddress. This field consists of a list of addresses, known as alias addresses, that belongs to User 4. You can display the information in this field at the destination terminal. These addresses can include the URL, E.164 address, a character string (for example, containing the name of the person who is making the call), and so on. User 4 can provide the URL of h323://user4@isp4.com in this field.

sourceCallSignalAddress. This field consists of the transport address of Terminal 4 at which the destination endpoint will send H.225.0-Q.931 messages for this call. You should not use this field if Terminal 4 is behind an H.323-unaware firewall. Some firewalls such as *Network Address Translation* (NAT) change the TCP port and IP address in the TCP and IP headers, respectively, of the setup message to their own transport address. The H.225.0-Q.931 messages from the destination endpoint should be sent to the transport address of the firewall, which will then send the messages to Terminal 4. If the destination endpoint always extracts the transport address from the TCP and IP headers of the setup message, then it will respond with H.225.0-Q.931 messages to either the transport address of the firewall or to the transport address of the terminal from where the setup message originated (if there is no firewall).

destinationAddress. This field consists of the E.164 address of the destination endpoint. The same information should also be present in the Called Party Number Information Element. In Call 1, PSTN Gateway 1 will use the E.164 address of (+1) 508.551.2000 in this field in order to connect to Terminal 1. In Call 2, H.320 Gateway 2 will use the E.164 address of (+1) 408.651.2122 in this field in order to connect to the first 64 kbps ISDN channel of the videoconferencing Terminal 2. In Call 3, we do not use this field because the E.164 address is not involved.

destExtraCallInfo. This field consists of a list of additional E.164 addresses. The PSTN and the IP gateways, respectively, do not use this field in Calls 1 and 3. In Call 2, H.320 Gateway 2 will use the E.164 address of (+1) 408.651.2123 in this field in order to connect to the second 64-kbps ISDN channel of the videoconferencing Terminal 2. For a 128 kbps H.320 call, the E.164 address of the first channel is provided in the destinationAddress field; the second E.164 address is provided in this field.

remoteExtensionAddress. This field contains the destination user's alias address in case the H.323 gateways need it when routing the call to the destination terminal. You should always fill in the destination user's non-routable alias address in case you need it when the call is being routed. In Calls 1 and 2, we do not need the routable E.164 addresses in this field. In Call 3, the non-routable address of h323://user3@gw3.isp3.com in this field is absolutely critical for the residential Gateway 3 to determine the user (3, 3-1, 3-2, and so on) to which it should route the call. user3 in the URL implies that the call is for User 3.

endpointIdentifier. This field is used in the gatekeeper-routed call model, which we will describe later in this chapter.

The setup, call proceeding, alerting, and connect messages have some common fields in the User-to-User Information Element of the message. The release complete message has two of these common fields: callIdentifier and cryptoTokens:

callIdentifier. This field consists of a 128-bit globally unique identification number for the call that is unique in space and time. This number is generated through a procedure that is described in [00H2250]. No two H.323 calls have the same callIdentifier. This field is present in the User-to-User Information Element of all of the H.225.0-Q.931 messages and is generated by Terminal 1, which initiates the call with the setup message. This field enables multiple calls to be multiplexed and demultiplexed on the same TCP connection between two entities (such as gateways).

fastStart. This field consists of all information regarding the media streams that are involved with this call. We will describe this field later in this chapter in the section dealing with Fast Connect.

h245Address. This field consists of the transport address (IP address and TCP port) of the endpoint at which call control (H.245) messages are received. Terminal 4 will provide its H.245 transport address (IP address 140.50.16.4 and TCP port 1090) in this field of the setup message, and the destination endpoint (such as the residential Gateway 3) will provide its H.245 transport address (IP address 156.99.4.30 and TCP port 2060) in the call proceeding, alerting, or connect message.

cryptoTokens. This field provides user authentication and message integrity. You can also use it to encrypt media streams. We will provide a detailed description of security in H.323 in the chapters dealing with security.

multipleCalls. If *true*, the sender of the message is capable of multiple calls on the same call-signaling TCP connection. This function is useful between gateways that are handling multiple calls from various terminals. The *operating system* (OS) allocates a certain amount of memory resources for each TCP connection, and there is an upper limit on the number of TCP ports. By multiplexing multiple calls on the same TCP connection, the application can optimally manage memory resources without reaching the upper limit on the TCP ports that are opened.

maintainConnection. If *true*, the sender of the message is capable of maintaining the TCP connection even when there are no calls between the two entities. Usually, gateways maintain a TCP connection between them in order to eliminate the time that is required to establish the TCP connection for the call-signaling connection.

Call-Control Protocol: H.245

Once the call is established between two endpoints, the next step is to start multimedia collaboration. If one endpoint starts transmitting H.263-encoded video, it might not be decoded if the receiving endpoint only has the capability to decode H.261-encoded video. Therefore, the transmitter needs to know the receiver's capabilities before it can transmit media. The receiver provides this functionality to the transmitter through the TerminalCapabilitySet message of H.245 [00H245]. If the receiver has limited hardware capability, it might need to know the characteristics of the media that it will receive so that it can load the appropriate decoder, allocate memory, and perform other housekeeping functions in order to get ready to receive the media. The transmitter provides this functionality to the receiver through the OpenLogicalChannel message of H.245. Thus, the H.245 protocol provides the functionality to enable multimedia endpoints with varying hardware and software capabilities to collaborate. This reason is why we use H.245 in H.323.

The H.245 recommendation specifies the Call Control Protocol for H.323. This protocol consists of a set of messages and procedures. The messages are encoded in ASN.1. Some H.245 messages appear in Table 3.1. The messages are grouped into four categories: Request, Response, Command, and Indication l Control Protocol for H.323. This protocol consists of a set of messages and procedures. The messages are encoded in ASN.1. Some H.245

Table 3.1 H.245 Messages

	Request	Response	Command	Indication
Capability	MasterSlaveDetermination	MasterSlaveDeterminationAck		MasterSlave DeterminationRelease
		MasterSlaveDeterminationReject		
	TerminalCapabilitySet	TerminalCapabilitySetAck		TerminalCapability SetRelease
		TerminalCapabilitySetReject		
Channel Management	OpenLogicalChannel	OpenLogicalChannelAck		OpenLogicalChannel Confirm
		OpenLogicalChannelReject		
	CloseLogicalChannel	CloseLogicalChannelAck		
		CloseLogicalChannelReject	EndSession	
Channel Operations			FlowControlCommand	
			VideoFastUpdatePicture	
			VideoFastUpdateGOB	
			VideoTemporalSpatialTradeOff	
			VideoSendSyncEveryGOB	
			VideoSendSyncEveryGOBCancel	
			VideoFastUpdateMB	

messages appear in Table 3.1. The messages are grouped into four categories: Request, Response, Command, and Indication—(along the columns of the table), and they are also grouped into three categories: Capability, Channel Management, and Channel Operations—(along rows of the table). A request message results in an action along with a response message from the remote endpoint. A command message results in an action but no response from the remote endpoint. An indication message results in neither an action nor a response from the remote endpoint. A request message has a corresponding response and an indication message. When the endpoint sends a request message, it starts a timer. If the remote endpoint performs the action, the response is an acknowledgment message. If the remote endpoint does not perform the action, the response is a reject message. If the remote endpoint does not respond within the timeout period, the peer endpoint sends an indication that consists of a release message. The release message indicates to the remote endpoint that the corresponding request message that was sent earlier should be discarded.

The capability messages describe the multimedia capability of the endpoint to its peer. The set of messages consisting of MasterSlaveDetermination determines which endpoint is the master and which endpoint is the slave. The master resolves any conflicts for shared resources. The set of messages consisting of TerminalCapabilitySet specifies the capability of the endpoint to its peer.

The Channel Management messages manage logical channels between the endpoints. The set of messages consisting of RequestMode requests a specific media and its parameters. The set of messages consisting of OpenLogicalChannel opens a logical channel for the transmission of certain media and its parameters. Each logical channel has a logical channel number that is unique from the endpoint that opened the channel. The set of messages consisting of CloseLogicalChannel closes the logical channel when the associated media is no longer transmitted. The EndSession message terminates the H.245 channel.

The Channel Operation messages use the logical channel number to specify the channel on which the specific operation will take place. The FlowControlCommand temporarily changes the maximum bit rate of the channel that is specified through its logical channel number. The various video commands perform specific video operations on the video channel that is specified through its logical channel number.

Description of Some H.245 Messages

The following subsections describe some H.245 messages. Please note that we show only *some* fields in these messages. Refer to [00H245] for details. In the figures, fields that are not underlined are optional. In all of the messages, the assumption is that endpoint 1 and endpoint 2 are in a call, and they have a channel established on which they can send and receive H.245 messages.

MasterSlaveDetermination

When two endpoints are in a call, there is a possibility that both endpoints might simultaneously request the other for the same resource. In order to resolve this problem, one endpoint should be the master. The master can then resolve any conflicts for the same resource. The MasterSlaveDetermination, MasterSlaveDeterminationAck, and MasterSlaveDeterminationReject messages enable endpoints in a call to determine which endpoint is the master and which endpoint is the slave.

Messages

Figure 3.4 shows some fields of MasterSlaveDetermination. This message consists of the statusDeterminationNumber field. This field contains a random number in the range of 0 to $(2^{24} - 1)$. Assume that Endpoint 1 receives a statusDeterminationNumber of $t2_{num}$ from Endpoint 2 and sends a statusDeterminationNumber of $t1_{num}$ to Endpoint 2. If $t1_{num} > t2_{num}$, then Endpoint 1 is the master if $t1_{num} - t2_{num} > 2^{24}/2$. Otherwise, it is the slave. Endpoint 1 announces its determination by sending MasterSlaveDeterminationAck to Endpoint 2. The contents of this message appear in Figure 3.4. This message consists of a decision field whose value is either *master* or *slave*. If Endpoint 2 is the master, then the decision field is set to *master*; otherwise, it is set to *slave*. If $t1_{num} = t2_{num}$, then the result is

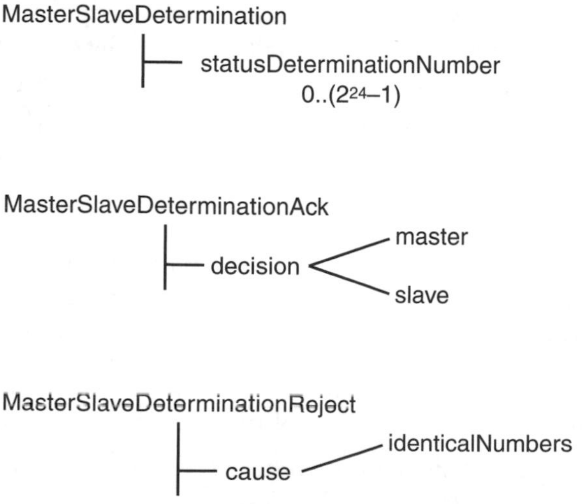

Figure 3.4 H.245 MasterSlaveDetermination messages.

inconclusive and must be repeated with new, random numbers. Endpoint 1 announces its determination by sending MasterSlaveDeterminationReject to Endpoint 2. We show the contents of this message in Figure 3.4. This message consists of a cause field whose value is identicalNumbers.

Usage

The MasterSlaveDetermination message from Endpoint 1 to Endpoint 2 consists of a statusDeterminationNumber of 2^{10}, as follows:

```
MasterSlaveDetermination.statusDeterminationNumber 2^10
```

Endpoint 2 sends MasterSlaveDetermination to Endpoint 1 with a statusDeterminationNumber of 2^{23}, as follows:

```
MasterSlaveDetermination.statusDeterminationNumber 2^23
```

Both endpoints independently determine that Endpoint 1 is the master. The MasterSlaveDeterminationAck message from Endpoint 1 to Endpoint 2 makes a decision of *slave* for Endpoint 2 as follows:

```
MasterSlaveDeterminationAck.decision.slave
```

Endpoint 2 also sends MasterSlaveDeterminationAck to Endpoint 1 with the decision field set to *master* as follows:

```
MasterSlaveDeterminationAck.decision.master
```

TerminalCapabilitySet

In order for endpoints to collaborate, they first have to know the multimedia capabilities of their peer endpoint. These capabilities are exchanged between endpoints in TerminalCapabilitySet. The endpoints acknowledge the reception of TerminalCapabilitySet with TerminalCapabilitySetAck. The TerminalCapabilitySetAck message does not have any field that needs to be described, so we will only describe the fields of TerminalCapabilitySet in this section.

Messages

Some fields of TerminalCapabilitySet and TerminalCapabilitySetAck appear in Figure 3.5. The TerminalCapabilitySet message consists of MultiplexCapability and CapabilityTable. We describe these fields as follows:

- *capabilityTable*. This field lists up to 256 capabilities of the endpoint. Each capability consists of CapabilityTableEntryNumber and Capability.
- *CapabilityTableEntryNumber*. This field references the specific capability of the endpoint.

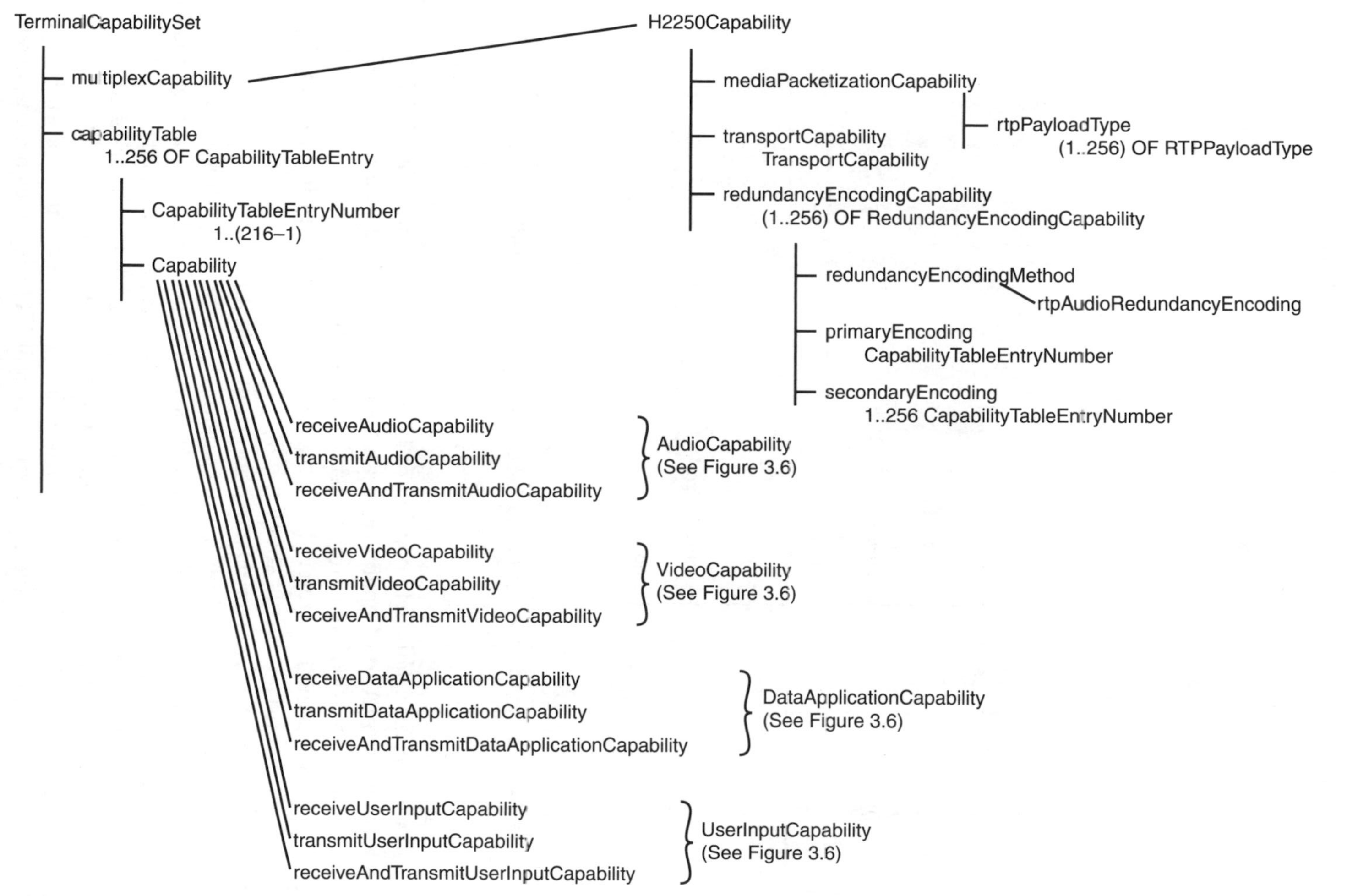

Figure 3.5 H.245 TerminalCapabilitySet message.

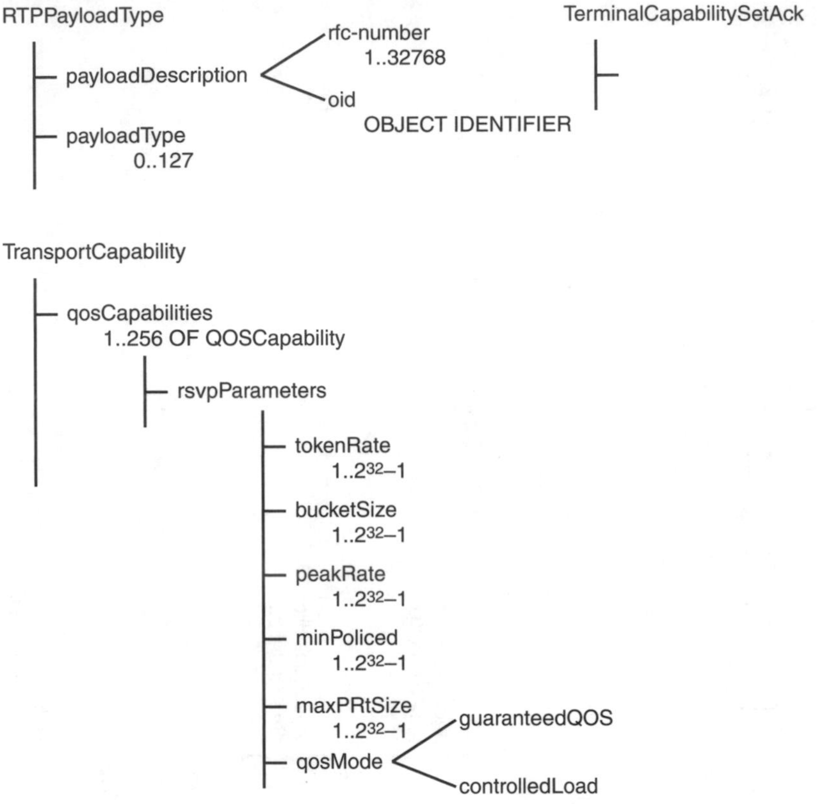

Figure 3.5 H.245 TerminalCapabilitySet message. (Continued)

- *Capability*. This field consists of 12 fields: receiveAudioCapability, transmitAudioCapability, receiveAndTransmitAudioCapability, receiveVideoCapability, transmitVideoCapability, receiveAndTransmitVideoCapability, receiveDataApplicationCapability, transmitDataApplicationCapability, receiveAndTransmitDataApplicationCapability, receiveUserInputIndication, transmitUserInputIndication, and receiveAndTransmitUserInputIndication. These fields are a combination of media (audio, video, and data) and receive, transmit, and receive-and-transmit capabilities. Receive capability describes the characteristics of the media that the endpoint can receive. Transmit capability describes the characteristics of the media that the endpoint can transmit. Receive-and-transmit capability describes the characteristics of the media that the endpoint can both receive and transmit. In practice, the endpoints specify their receive capabilities and enable the peer endpoint to transmit within those capabilities. TheAudioCapability, VideoCapability, and DataApplicationCapability specify the characteristics of the media, andUserInputCapability specifies the characteristics of the user interface. We show these fields in Figure 3.6 and describe them as follows:

- *AudioCapability*. This field consists of a list of audio codecs and their specific capabilities. The codecs that are listed are G.711, G.723.1, G.728, G.729, and G.729A. The capabilities of the listed codecs include the range of the size of the payload. The payload size is in frames. For sample-based codecs, a frame is equal to eight samples. So, the size of the G.711 payload is between eight and 2,048 samples, and the payload of G.723.1 is between one and 256 frames. Other capabilities include silence suppression for G.723.1. The G.711 codec is mandatory in H.323 systems in order to ensure that endpoints will always have one common codec. All other codecs in the list under AudioCapability are optional.

  Initially, each audio codec that the ITU-T standardized was listed under AudioCapability. Later, other recognized standards organizations also wanted their codecs listed. Soon, it became clear that there were too many new codecs being developed in the industry and that adding all of the codecs would tremendously increase the size of the H.245 document. A mechanism called the Generic Capabilities was developed in order to list newly developed codecs in H.245. Any new codec to be listed in H.245 gets a unique string of characters called the object identifier. The codec is identified through the value of its unique object identifier. The H.245 endpoints list the capabilities of new audio codecs through GenericAudioCapability. The capabilityIdentifier field has the standard field where the object identifier is listed. The main H.245 document does not describe the capabilities of the codec; rather, they are listed separately in a new annex to H.245.

- *VideoCapability*. This field consists of a list of video codecs and their specific capabilities. The first two fields list the two coders, H.261 and H.263. H.263+ justadds more capabilities to H.263 and is not listed as a separate coder. The third field, GenericVideoCapability, provides the same functionality for video coders as GenericAudioCapability provides for audio coders. The H.261 coder and the Quarter Common Intermediate Format (QCIF) frame resolution are mandatory in H.323 systems in order to ensure that endpoints will always interoperate. Normally, coders are subjected to the maximum bit rate that is allowed on the network in order to ensure that the network and decoder resources are properly allocated. We describe the capabilities of H.261 and H.263 coders as follows:

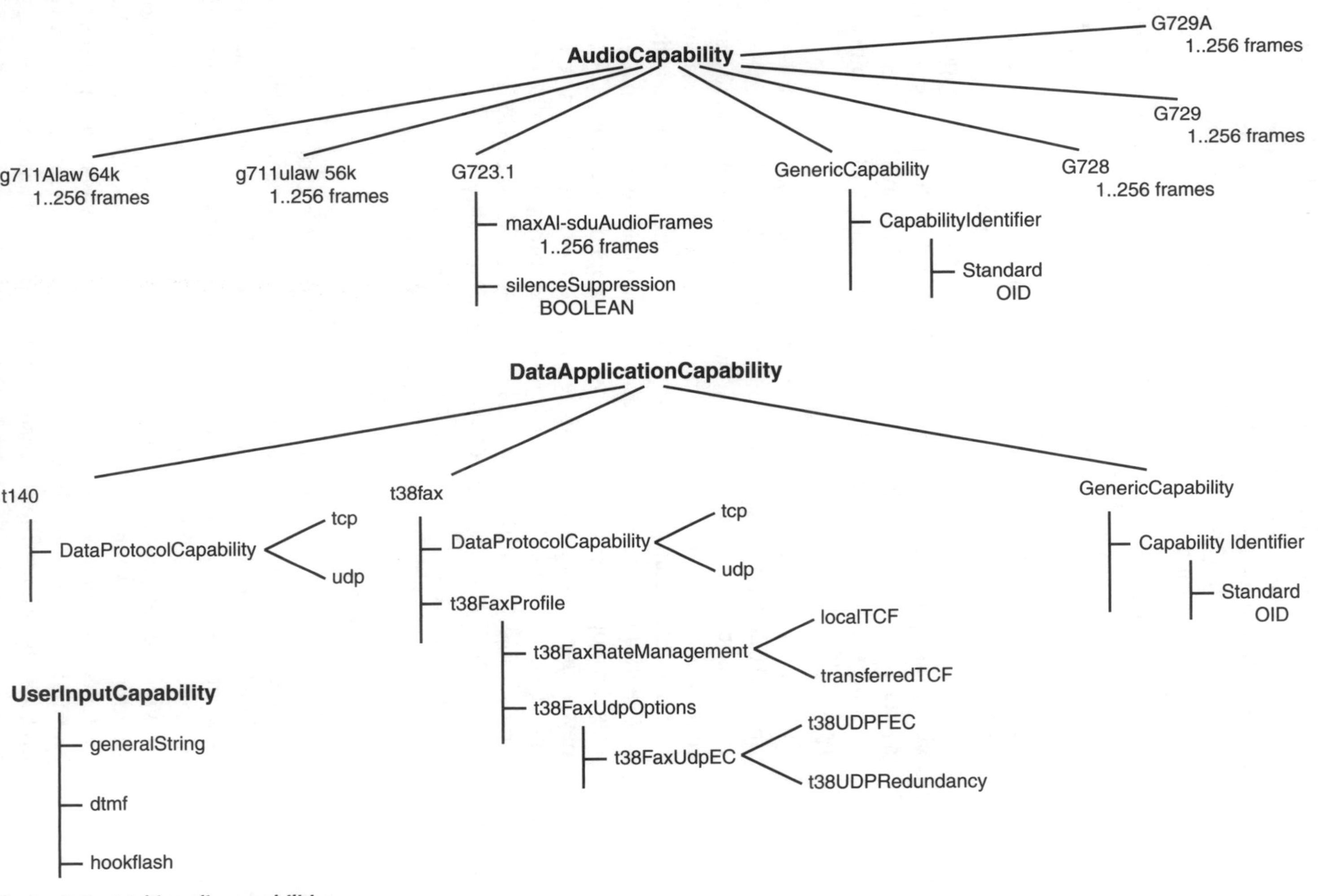

Figure 3.6 Multimedia capabilities.

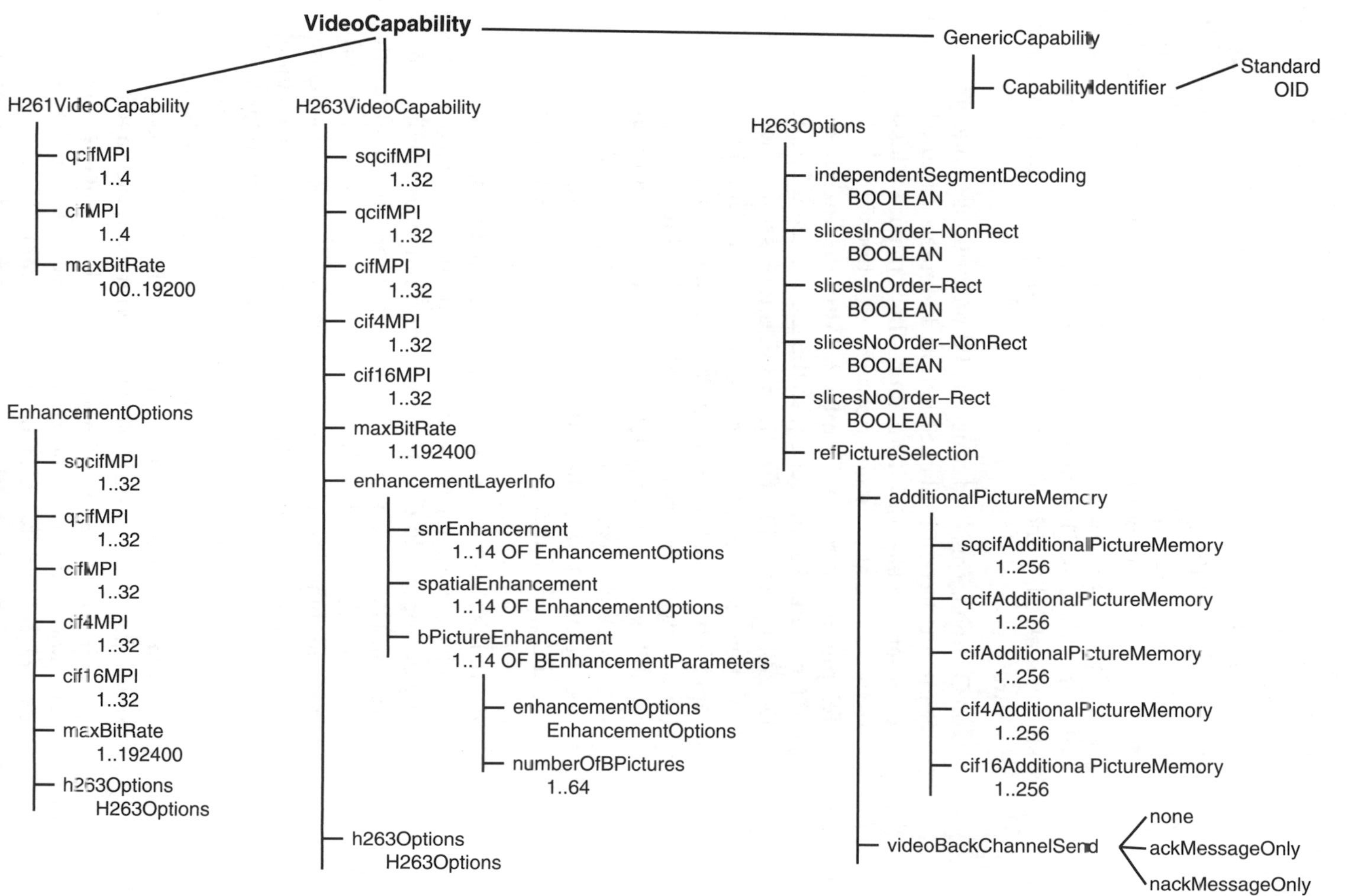

Figure 3.6 Multimedia capabilities. (Continued)

H261VideoCapability. This field consists of the frame resolution of QCIF and Common Intermediate Format (CIF), the minimum time interval between frames of 1/29.97 to 4/29.97 s, and the maximum bit rate in the range of 1×100 to 19200×100 bps.

H263VideoCapability. This field consists of the frame resolution of Sub Quarter Common Intermediate Format (SQCIF), QCIF, CIF, 4CIF, 16CIF, the minimum time interval between frames of 1/29.97 s to 32/29.97 s, and the maximum bit rate in the range of 1×100 to 192400×100 bps. This field also consists of H.263+ options on bit-stream scalability and error resiliency. We describe these options as follows:

h263 Options. This field consists of three options—Independent Segment Decoding, Slice Structure, Reference Picture Selection—in order to make the bit stream resilient to packet losses on the network. We already described these options in "Coders for Telephony" section of Chapter 2, "Multimedia Transport on IP Networks." If the coder has the Independent Segment Decoding capability, then it specifies it by setting the independentSegmentDecoding field to *true*. The Slice Structure capability consists of rectangular and nonrectangular slices and transmitting the slices in any order and in order. We express these capabilities by appropriately setting the slicesInOrder-NonRect, slicesInOrder-Rect, slicesNoOrder-NonRect, and slicesNoOrder-Rect fields to *true*. If the coder has the refPictureSelection capability, then it also specifies its capacity of storing frames and uses a back channel. The encoder specifies the number from 1 to 256 of the most recent reference frames that it can store. The decoder can use the back channel to request the encoder to pick any one of the stored reference frames when generating the bit stream. The decoder specifies whether it has the capability to use the back channel. If the back channel is used, then the decoder specifies whether it has the capability to use acknowledgement and negative-acknowledgement messages. The back channel consists of acknowledgement or negative-acknowledgement messages that are sent on the same channel as the reverse video bit stream; that is, sent by the encoder belonging to the same system as the decoder. If the acknowledgement message is used, then the decoder sends an acknowledgement message to the encoder for each frame that it receives. If the encoder does not get an acknowledgement message for a specific frame that it sent, it cannot use that frame as the reference frame. If the negative-acknowledgement message is used, then the decoder sends a negative-acknowledgement message to the encoder only for the frame that it received with errors. The encoder will not use this erroneous frame as the reference frame.

enhancementLayerInfo. This field consists of three options—Temporal, Spatial, and SNR—for scalability of the video bit stream. We already described these options in the "Coders for Video Telephony" section of Chapter 2. For each of the scalability options, the coder specifies the number of layers from 1 to 14 that it supports. For each of the layers, the coder specifies the H.263 video capability that we just described. This capability includes the frame resolution, maximum time interval between frames, maximum bit rate, and the H.263+ options for error resiliency. In the case of temporal scalability, the coder specifies the numberOfBPictures field. This field specifies the maximum number of B-frames that you can insert between other frames.

- *DataApplicationCapability*. This field consists of a list of data applications and their specific capabilities. Two data applications listed are *Text Conversation Using T.140* (t140) and *Facsimile Using T.38* (t38fax). The third field, GenericDataCapability, provides the same functionality for data applications as GenericAudioCapability provides for audio codecs. We describe the t140 and t38fax fields as follows:

  t140. This field consists of DataProtocolCapability, which lists the *Transmission Control Protocol* (TCP) and the User Datagram Protocol (UDP) as the transport protocol capabilities. Implementation of UDP is mandatory whereas TCP is optional if the H.323 system implements text conversation.

  t38fax. This field consists of DataProtocolCapability and t38FaxProfile fields. The DataProtocolCapability lists TCP and UDP as the transport protocol capabilities. Implementation of both UDP and TCP is mandatory if the H.323 system implements facsimile capabilities. The t38FaxProfile field lists the capabilities of T.38 as follows:

  t38FaxRateManagement. This field specifies the capability of transferring the Training Check Frame (TCF) training signal and having the far-end endpoint generate it locally. If you use TCP, then TCF is generated locally. If UDP is used, then TCF is transferred.

  t38FaxUdpOptions. You select this field only if you are using UDP as the transport protocol. The t38FaxUdpEC field provides error-correction mechanisms as either t38UDPFEC for FEC or t38UDPRedundancy for Redundancy.

- *UserInputCapability*. This field consists of the capabilities of the user interface. The generalString capability consists of alphanumeric characters; the dtmf capability consists of an emulation of *Dual-Tone Multi-Frequency* (DTMF); and the hookflash capability consists of the emulation of hookflash. Both DTMF and hookflash are found in analog telephones.

- *multiplexCapability*. This field consists of H2250Capability, which in turn consists of mediaPacketizationCapability, redundancyEncodingCapability, and transportCapability. We describe these three fields as follows:

  - *mediaPacketizationCapability*. This field consists of up to 256 RTPPayloadType fields. Each RTPPayloadType consists of payloadDescription and payloadType. The payloadDescription provides a reference to an RFC number or to an H.245 object identifier to the document that describes the payload format. A payload format that the IETF standardizes has a unique *Request for Comment* (RFC) number. A payload format that the ITU standardizes, however, has a unique object identifier. If the payload format has been assigned a static payload type, it should be specified in payloadType.

  - *redundancyEncodingCapability*. This field specifies up to 256 redundancy encoding capabilities. For each capability, the following fields exist:

    redundancyEncodingMethod. This field consists of a capability for one redundancy encoding method: rtpAudioRedundancyEncoding. In this method, the payload format is signaled through the redundancy header in the payload. We explained the format and description of the redundancy header in the "Payload Format for Redundancy" section of Chapter 2.

    primaryEncoding. This field provides the format of the primary encoding through a reference to CapabilityTableEntryNumber in capabilityTable.

    secondaryEncoding. This field provides the format of up to 256 secondary encodings through a reference to CapabilityTableEntryNumber in capabilityTable.

  - *transportCapability*. This field specifies up to 256 QoS capabilities, each consisting of rsvpParameters. The rsvpParameters field consists of the traffic characteristics of the single media stream that the endpoint sends. The following fields express the traffic characteristics: guaranteedQOS or controlledLoad, tokenRate, bucketSize, peakRate, minPoliced, and maxPktSize. The guaranteedQOS field specifies QoS from the network that guarantees delay and bandwidth. The controlledLoad field specifies QoS from the network that is equivalent to what the unloaded network provides even during times when the network becomes loaded. The endpoint should specify either guaranteedQOS or controlledLoad but not both. To date, all real-life deployments consist of controlledLoad, and guaranteedQOS has not been deployed. The tokenRate field specifies the average data rate (in bytes per second) from the endpoint. The bucketSize field specifies the largest burst of data (in bytes) from the endpoint. The peakRate field specifies the maximum short-term data rate in bytes per second from the endpoint. The minPoliced field specifies the smallest packet (in bytes) from the endpoint. The maxPktSize field specifies the largest packet (in bytes) from the endpoint. The size of the packet consists of the application data and all headers except the link-layer header. On the IP network, the headers in the media packet consist of the RTP, UDP, and IP headers adding to at least 40 bytes. The link-layer header is not considered in the calculation because it can change as the packet traverses the Internet.

Usage

Figure 3.7 shows the TerminalCapabilitySet of Endpoint 1. We describe it as follows:

1. Endpoint 1 supports the following seven RTP payload formats:
   a. RFC 1890 [SCHU96] with a static payload type of 0 (for G.711 μlaw)
   b. RFC 1890 [SCHU96] with a static payload type of 4 (for G.723.1)
   c. RFC 2198 [PERK97] (for the redundancy payload for voice; does not have a static payload type)
   d. RFC 2032 [TURL96] with a static payload type of 31 (for H.261)
   e. RFC 2190 [ZHU97] with a static payload type of 34 (the 1997 version of the payload format for H.263)
   f. RFC 2429 [WEN98] (for the 1998 version of the payload format H.263; does not have a static payload type)
   g. RFC 2793 [HEL00] (has the payload format for T.140 text conversation by using the UDP transport protocol; does not have a static payload type)
2. Endpoint 1 has the capability to perform packet resiliency by using the RTP Redundancy Encoding method. The primary encoding is G.723.1, which is referenced through the CapabilityTableEntry with the CapabilityTableEntryNumber of 1.
3. The endpoint has the capability to transmit two types of media streams with the following traffic characteristics:
   a. This traffic specification is for the constant bit-rate stream from the G.723.1 coder, which emits a voice frame of 20 bytes or a comfort noise

```
Point 1
TerminalCapabilitySet.multiplexCapability.h2250Capability.
mediaPacketizationCapability.rtpPayloadType 7 of RtpPayloadType
     RtpPayloadType.payloadDescriptor.rfc-number 1890
     RtpPayloadType.payloadDescriptor.payloadType 0
     RtpPayloadType.payloadDescriptor.rfc-number 1890
     RtpPayloadType.payloadDescriptor.payloadType 4
     RtpPayloadType.payloadDescriptor.rfc-number 2198
     RtpPayloadType.payloadDescriptor.rfc-number 2032
     RtpPayloadType.payloadDescriptor.payloadType 31
     RtpPayloadType.payloadDescriptor.rfc-number 2190
     RtpPayloadType.payloadDescriptor.payloadType 34
     RtpPayloadType.payloadDescriptor.rfc-number 2429
     RtpPayloadType.payloadDescriptor.rfc-number 2793
Point 2
TerminalCapabilitySet.multiplexCapability.h2250Capability.
redundancyEncodingCapability 1 OF RedundancyEncodingCapability
     Point 2 (a)
     RedundancyEncodingCapability.redundancyEncodingMethod.
     rtpAudioRedundancyEncoding
     RedundancyEncodingCapability.primaryEncoding 2
Point 3
TerminalCapabilitySet.multiplexCapability.h2250Capability.
transportCapability.qOSCapabilities 2 OF QOSCapability
     Point 3 (a)
     qOSCapabilities.rsvpParameters.qosMode.guaranteedLoad
     qOSCapabilities.rsvpParameters.tokenRate 2000
     qOSCapabilities.rsvpParameters.bucketSize 80
     qOSCapabilities.rsvpParameters.peakRate 2000
     qOSCapabilities.rsvpParameters.minPoliced 44
     qOSCapabilities.rsvpParameters.maxPktSize 80
     Point 3 (b)
     qOSCapabilities.rsvpParameters.qosMode.controlledLoad
     qOSCapabilities.rsvpParameters.tokenRate 4000
     qOSCapabilities.rsvpParameters.bucketSize 12000
     qOSCapabilities.rsvpParameters.peakRate  6000
     qOSCapabilities.rsvpParameters.minPoliced 100
     qOSCapabilities.rsvpParameters.maxPktSize 1000
Point 4
TerminalCapabilitySet.capabilityTable 9 OF CapabilityTableEntry
     Point 4 (a)
     CapabilityTableEntry.CapabilityTableEntryNumber 1
     CapabilityTableEntry.Capability.receiveAudioCapability.
     g711Ulaw64k 120
     Point 4 (b)
     CapabilityTableEntry.CapabilityTableEntryNumber 2
     CapabilityTableEntry.Capability.receiveAudioCapability.
```

Figure 3.7 Usage of TerminalCapabilitySet message.

```
g7231.maxAl-sduAudioFrames 4
CapabilityTableEntry.Capability.receiveAudioCapability.
g7231.maxAl-sduAudioFrames 4
CapabilityTableEntry.Capability.
receiveAudioCapability.g7231.silenceSuppression YES
Point 4 (c)
CapabilityTableEntry.CapabilityTableEntryNumber 3
CapabilityTableEntry.Capability.receiveVideoCapability.
h261VideoCapability.qcifMPI 4
CapabilityTableEntry.Capability.receiveVideoCapability.
h261VideoCapability.maxBitRate 320
Point 4 (d)
CapabilityTableEntry.CapabilityTableEntryNumber 4
CapabilityTableEntry.Capability.receiveVideoCapability.
h263VideoCapability.sqcifMPI 8
CapabilityTableEntry.Capability.
receiveVideoCapability.h263VideoCapability.qcifMPI 8
CapabilityTableEntry.Capability.receiveVideoCapability.
h263VideoCapability.maxBitRate 320
Point 4 (e)
CapabilityTableEntry.CapabilityTableEntryNumber 5
CapabilityTableEntry.Capability.
receiveDataApplicationCapability.t140.tcp
Point 4 (f)
CapabilityTableEntry.CapabilityTableEntryNumber 6
CapabilityTableEntry.Capability.
receiveDataApplicationCapability.t140.udp
Point 4 (g)
CapabilityTableEntry.CapabilityTableEntryNumber 7
CapabilityTableEntry.Capability.
receiveDataApplicationCapability.
t38fax.DataProtocolCapability.tcp
CapabilityTableEntry.Capability.
receiveDataApplicationCapability.t38fax.
t38FaxProfile.t38FaxRateManagement.localTCF
Point 4 (h)
CapabilityTableEntry.CapabilityTableEntryNumber 8
CapabilityTableEntry.Capability.
receiveDataApplicationCapability.t38fax.
DataProtocolCapability.udp
CapabilityTableEntry.Capability.
receiveDataApplicationCapability.t38fax.t38FaxProfile.
t38FaxRateManagement.transferredTCF
CapabilityTableEntry.Capability.
receiveDataApplicationCapability.t38fax.t38FaxProfile.
t38FaxUdpOptions.t38FaxUdpEC.t38UDPRedundancy
```

(Continues)

Figure 3.7 Usage of TerminalCapabilitySet message. (Continued)

```
Point 4 (i)
CapabilityTableEntry.CapabilityTableEntryNumber 9
CapabilityTableEntry.Capability.receiveUserInput
Capability.UserInputCapability.generalString
CapabilityTableEntry.Capability.receiveUserInput
Capability.UserInputCapability.dtmf
CapabilityTableEntry.Capability.receiveUserInput
Capability.UserInputCapability.hookflash
```

Figure 3.7 Usage of TerminalCapabilitySet message. (Continued)

frame of four bytes every 30 ms. The media stream requires guaranteed bandwidth and a delay specified by guaranteedLoad QoS. When transmitting media, the endpoint will either transmit two frames per packet or one frame per packet depending on the receive capability of the other endpoint. Because up to two frames can be packetized, the maximum packet size (maxPktSize) is 80 bytes, which includes 40 bytes of RTP/UDP/IP uncompressed headers and 40 bytes of payload. The minimum packet size (minPoliced) is 44 bytes, which includes four bytes of payload and 40 bytes of headers. The bucketSize is the maximum packet size of 80 bytes. If one frame is packetized every 30 ms, then the data rate is 2 kbps. For two frames per packet every 60 ms, the data rate is 1.33 kbps. For a constant bit rate, the tokenRate and peakRate are the same and are set to 2 kbps. Note that if G.711 is selected, then the traffic specification provided here will not work.

b. The media stream requires a controlled-load QoS. The average (tokenRate) and peak (peakRate) data rates are 4 kbps and 6 kbps, respectively. The maximum (maxPktSize) and minimum (minPoliced) packet sizes are 1,000 and 100 bytes, respectively. The bucketSize is 12,000 bytes. This traffic specification is for the variable bit-rate stream from the H.263 or H.261 coder.

4. Endpoint 1 has eight media capabilities that are described in eight entries of the CapabilityTableEntry:

   a. The first CapabilityTableEntry has a CapabilityTableEntryNumber of 1. This entry shows that the endpoint can receive G.711 μlaw at 64 kbps and a maximum of 120 frames per RTP packet (960 samples/RTP packet).

   b. The second CapabilityTableEntry has a CapabilityTableEntryNumber of 2. This entry shows that the endpoint can receive G.723.1 (a maximum of four frames per RTP packet) and can also perform silence suppression.

c. The third CapabilityTableEntry has a CapabilityTableEntryNumber of 3. This entry shows that the endpoint can receive H.261 video with QCIF resolution, a minimum time interval between frames of 4/29.97 s, and a maximum bit rate of 32,000 bps.

d. The fourth CapabilityTableEntry has a CapabilityTableEntryNumber of 4. This entry shows that the endpoint can receive H.263 video with Sub-QCIF and QCIF resolution, a minimum time interval between frames of 8/29.97 s, and a maximum bit rate of 32,000 bps.

e. The fifth CapabilityTableEntry has a CapabilityTableEntryNumber of 5. This entry shows that the endpoint can receive T.140 by using TCP as the transport protocol.

f. The sixth CapabilityTableEntry has a CapabilityTableEntryNumber of 6. This field shows that the endpoint can receive T.140 by using UDP as the transport protocol.

g. The seventh CapabilityTableEntry has a CapabilityTableEntryNumber of 7. This field shows that the endpoint can receive T.38 fax by using TCP as the transport protocol. This entry is also capable of locally generating Training Check Frame (TCF).

h. The eighth CapabilityTableEntry has a CapabilityTableEntryNumber of 8. This entry shows that the endpoint can receive T.38 fax by using UDP as the transport protocol. This entry is capable of transferring the TCF signal and uses redundancy for packet resiliency.

i. The ninth CapabilityTableEntry has a CapabilityTableEntryNumber of 8. This entry shows that the endpoint can receive user inputs from the remote terminal in the form of general string, DTMF, and hookflash.

Instead of the syntax in Figure 3.7, we can use a compact and easily readable syntax as follows:

```
Media packetization capability
     RFC 1890, Static payload type 0
     RFC 1890, Static payload type 4
     RFC 2198
     RFC 2032, Static payload type 31
     RFC 2190, Static payload type 34
     RFC 2429
     RFC 2793
Redundancy encoding capability
     Redundancy header in payload, Primary encoding G.723.1
QoS capability
   Guaranteed load, averate rate 2000 B/s, peak rate 2000 B/s, minimum
packet size 44 bytes, maximum packet size 80 bytes, bucket size 80 bytes
   Controlled load, averate rate 4000 B/s, peak rate 6000 B/s, minimum
packet size 100 bytes, maximum packet size 1000 bytes, bucket size
12000 bytes
```

```
Receive voice capability
     G.711 μlaw, 64 kb/s, Maximum 120 frames/RTP packet
     G.723.1, Maximum 4 frames/RTP packet, Silence Suppression
Receive video capability
     H.261, QCIF resolution, Minimum 4/29.97 s between frames, Maximum
     bit rate 32000 bits/s
     H.263, SQCIF and QCIF resolution, Minimum 8/29.97 s between frames,
     Maximum bit rate 32000 bits/s
Receive text capability
     T.140, TCP
     T.140, UDP
Receive fax capability
     TCP, locally generated TCF
     UDP, TCF transferred, redundancy encoding
Receive user-input capability
     general string, dtmf, hookflash
```

OpenLogicalChannel

The transmitter of media uses the OpenLogicalChannel message to specify the characteristics of the media to the receiver. The media characteristics will be within the capabilities of the endpoint that is receiving the media.

Message

Some of the fields in the OpenLogicalChannel message appear in Figure 3.8. The OpenLogicalChannel message consists of forwardLogicalChannelNumber, forwardLogicalChannelParameters, and reverseLogicalChannelParameters. We can describe these fields as follows:

- *forwardLogicalChannelNumber.* This field specifies the identification number that we use to refer to the logical channel. This field is unique among all logical channels that this endpoint opens.
- *forwardLogicalChannelParameters.* This field consists of fields that are associated with the logical channel that we will open in the forward direction from the sender to the receiver of this message. This field consists of the dataType and multiplexParameters fields (described as follows):
  - *dataType.* This field consists of audioData, videoData, and data (which in turn consist of AudioCapability, VideoCapability, and DataApplicationCapability, respectively). The fields that are associated with these capabilities appear in Figure 3.6, and we described them previously in this chapter.
  - *multiplexParameters.* This field consists of h2250LogicalChannelParameters, which in turn consist of a number of fields that we will now describe as follows:

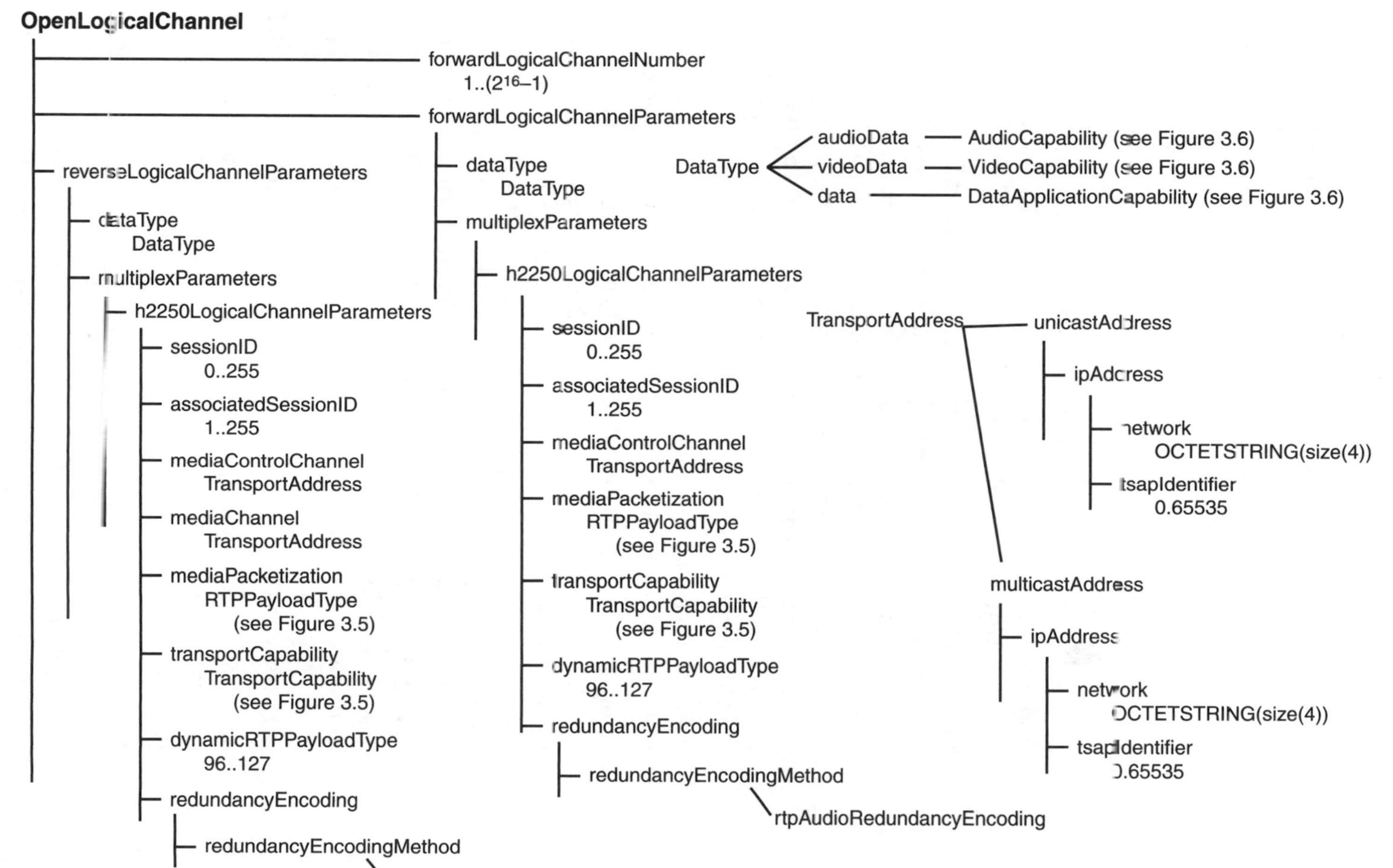

Figure 3.8 H.245 OpenLogicalChannel message.

sessionID. This field specifies an identifier that references the RTP session for this logical channel. Because the two endpoints can simultaneously open logical channels with the same identifier, the master generates this shared resource. The slave can propose a value for this field in OpenLogicalChannel, and the master ultimately decides the final value in OpenLogicalChannelAck.

associatedSessionID. This field specifies the RTP session with which this session is associated.

mediaControlChannel. This field specifies the RTCP IP address and port on which the transmitter of media will receive the RTCP reports from the receiver of the media. Note that the RTCP address can either be Unicast or multicast.

mediaPacketization. This field consists of rtpPayloadType, which in turn consists of payloadDescription and payloadType. The payloadDescription provides a reference through an RFC number or an H.245 object identifier to the document that describes the payload format. An IETF-standardized payload format has a unique RFC number. An ITU-standardized payload format has a unique object identifier. If the payload format is assigned a static payload type, it should be specified in payloadType.

transportCapability. This field was described in the transportCapability field of the TerminalCapabilitySet message.

dynamicRTPPayloadType. All new payload formats that are developed are preassigned a unique *object identifier* (OID). Static payload types are no longer used. During the call, the master assigns a dynamic payload type to the OID that is then used in the Payload Type field of each RTP packet. If the slave opens a logical channel, it does not use this field. The master provides the dynamic payload type in OpenLogicalChannelAck.

The Payload Type field is useful to the receiver of the media only if multiple logical channels are opened with different payload types. Then, the only way that the receiver can distinguish between packets with different payloads is through the Payload Type field.

redundancyEncoding. This field is used if the peer endpoint has the capability to receive redundant media. The following fields are defined:

redundancyEncodingMethod: This field consists of one redundancy encoding method: rtpAudioRedundancyEncoding. If the peer endpoint has the capability to receive media by using this method, then the transmitter can select it. Then, the payload format will be signaled through the redundancy header in the payload.

- *reverseLogicalChannelParameters.* This field consists of fields that are associated with the logical channel that will be opened in the reverse direction from the receiver to the sender of this message. This field is normally used to open a back channel and consists of the same fields as forwardLogicalChannelParameters plus the mediaControl field described as follows:
  - *mediaControl.* This field specifies the RTP IP address and port on which the media will be received. Note that the RTP address can either be Unicast or multicast.

Usage

Figure 3.9 shows the OpenLogicalChannel message for transmission of voice from Endpoint 1 to Endpoint 2. We describe this transmission as follows:

1. This logical channel has an identification number of 80.
2. We will transmit voice by using G.723.1 with a maximum of one frame per payload. Packets will not be sent during periods of silence. Normally, endpoints send a four-byte G.723.1 frame consisting of comfort noise at the beginning of silence.
3. This logical channel is part of an RTP session whose identification number is 1.
4. The sender of media (Endpoint 1) provides the RTCP transport address consisting of an IP address of 140.50.16.4 and port number (also known as the tsapIdentifier) of 1081. This address is the transport address to which the receiver of media (Endpoint 2) will send its RTCP packets. We assume the port to be UDP for voice (unless specified otherwise).
5. The format of the payload is specified in RFC 1890 [SCHU96], and it has a static payload type of 4. Each RTP packet will have a value of 4 in the Payload Type field of the header.
6. The traffic specification is for the constant bit-rate stream from the G.723.1 coder where one voice frame of 20 bytes or a comfort noise frame of four bytes is packetized every 30 ms, giving the data rate of 2 kbps:

Instead of the syntax in Figure 3.9, we can use a compact and easily readable syntax:

```
Forward logical channel number 80
G.723.1, 1 frames/RTP packet, Silence suppression
Session ID 1
RTCP IP address 140.50.16.4, Port 1081
RFC 1890, Payload type 4
```

```
Point 1
OpenLogicalChannel.forwardLogicalChannelNumber 80
Point 2
OpenLogicalChannel.forwardLogicalChannelParameters.dataType.audioData.
g7231.maxAl-sduAudioFrames 1
OpenLogicalChannel.forwardLogicalChannelParameters.dataType.audioData.
g7231.silenceSuppression YES
Point 3
OpenLogicalChannel.forwardLogicalChannelParameters.
multiplexParameters.h2250LogicalChannelParameters.sessionID 1
Point 4
OpenLogicalChannel.forwardLogicalChannelParameters.multiplexParameters
.h2250LogicalChannelParameters.mediaControlChannel.unicastAddress.
ipAddress.network 140 50 16 4
OpenLogicalChannel.forwardLogicalChannelParameters.
multiplexParameters.h2250LogicalChannelParameters.mediaControlChannel.
unicastAddress.ipAddress.tsapIdentifier 1081
Point 5
OpenLogicalChannel.forwardLogicalChannelParameters.
multiplexParameters.h2250LogicalChannelParameters.mediaPacketization.
rtpPayloadType.payloadDescriptor.rfc-number 1890
OpenLogicalChannel.forwardLogicalChannelParameters.
multiplexParameters.h2250LogicalChannelParameters.mediaPacketization.
rtpPayloadType.payloadType 4
Point 6
OpenLogicalChannel.forwardLogicalChannelParameters.
multiplexParameters.h2250LogicalChannelParameters.transportCapability.
qOSCapabilities.rsvpParameters.qosMode.guaranteedLoad
OpenLogicalChannel.forwardLogicalChannelParameters.
multiplexParameters.h2250LogicalChannelParameters.transportCapability.
qOSCapabilities.rsvpParameters.tokenRate 2000
OpenLogicalChannel.forwardLogicalChannelParameters.
multiplexParameters.h2250LogicalChannelParameters.transportCapability.
qOSCapabilities.rsvpParameters.bucketSize 60
OpenLogicalChannel.forwardLogicalChannelParameters.
multiplexParameters.h2250LogicalChannelParameters.transportCapability.
qOSCapabilities.rsvpParameters.peakRate 2000
OpenLogicalChannel.forwardLogicalChannelParameters.
multiplexParameters.h2250LogicalChannelParameters.transportCapability.
qOSCapabilities.rsvpParameters.minPoliced 44
OpenLogicalChannel.forwardLogicalChannelParameters.
multiplexParameters.h2250LogicalChannelParameters.transportCapability.
qOSCapabilities.rsvpParameters.maxPktSize 60
```

Figure 3.9 Usage of the OpenLogicalChannel message.

```
Guaranteed load, averate rate 2000 B/s, peak rate 2000 B/s, minimum
packet size 44 bytes, maximum packet size 60 bytes, bucket size 60 bytes
```

OpenLogicalChannelAck

The OpenLogicalChannelAck message informs the transmitter that the receiver is ready to receive media.

Message

Some of the fields in OpenLogicalChannelAck appear in Figure 3.10. The OpenLogicalChannelAck message consists of

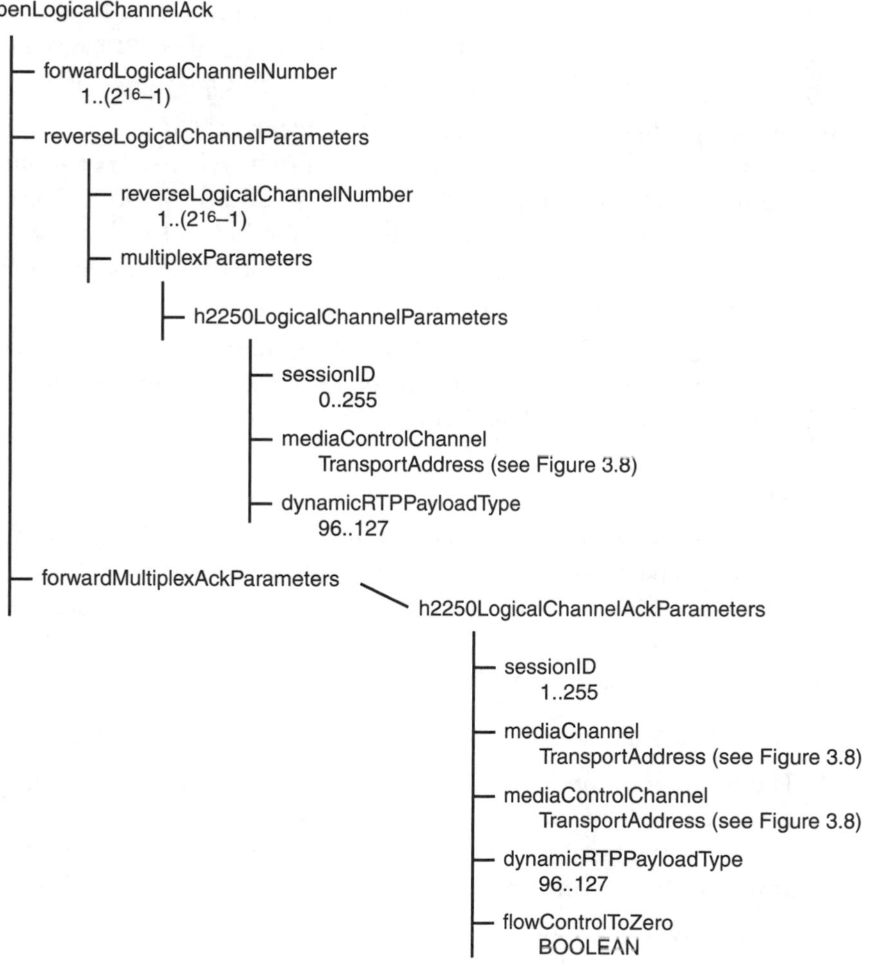

Figure 3.10 H.245 OpenLogicalChannelAck message.

forwardLogicalChannelNumber, reverseLogicalChannelParameters, and forwardMultiplexAckParameters. We describe these fields as follows:

- *forwardLogicalChannelNumber.* This field specifies the identification number of the logical channel that is being acknowledged.
- *reverseLogicalChannelParameters.* We use this field if OpenLogicalChannel specified the reverseLogicalChannelParameters field. This field contains the following fields:
  - *reverseLogicalChannelNumber.* This field specifies the identification number of the reverse logical channel, which will be unique among all logical channels that this endpoint opens.
  - *multiplexParameters.* This field consists of h2250LogicalChannelParameters, which in turn consists of sessionID, mediaControlChannel, and dynamicRTPPayloadType. We described these fields in the section on OpenLogicalChannel.
- *forwardMultiplexAckParameters.* This field consists of h2250LogicalChannelParameters, which in turn consists of sessionID, mediaChannel, dynamicRTPPayloadType, and flowControlToZero. We described the sessionID, mediaChannel, mediaControlChannel, and dynamicRTPPayloadType fields in the section on OpenLogicalChannel. The remaining field is as follows:
  - *flowControlToZero.* If this field is set to *true*, it specifies that media will not be transmitted until the receiver of media requests it in an H.245 message (such as flowControlCommand).

Usage

Upon receiving OpenLogicalChannel from Endpoint 1, Endpoint 2 allocates the resources (such as loading the G.723.1 decoder and allocating enough memory to receive two frames per RTP packet). When it is ready to receive the voice stream, it sends openLogicalChannelAck to Endpoint 1 (as shown in Figure 3.11). We describe the fields as follows:

1. This acknowledgement is to the logical channel with an identification of 80.
2. The receiver of media (Endpoint 2) provides the RTP transport address, which consists of an IP address of 179.6.8.20 and a port number (also known as the tsapIdentifier) of 2060. This address is the transport address at which the sender (Endpoint 1) of media will send its RTP packets.
3. The receiver of media also provides the RTCP transport address, which consists of an IP address of 179.6.8.20 and a port number of 2061. This address is the transport address at which the sender (Endpoint 1) of

```
Point 1
OpenLogicalChannel.forwardLogicalChannelNumber 80
Point 2
OpenLogicalChannel.forwardMultiplexAckParameters.
h2250LogicalChannelAckParameters.mediaChannel.unicastAddress.
ipAddress.network 179 6 8 20
OpenLogicalChannel.forwardMultiplexAckParameters.
h2250LogicalChannelAckParameters.mediaChannel.unicastAddress.
ipAddress.tsapIdentifier 2060
Point 3
OpenLogicalChannel.forwardMultiplexAckParameters.
h2250LogicalChannelAckParameters.mediaControlChannel.unicastAddress.
ipAddress.network 179 6 8 20
OpenLogicalChannel.forwardMultiplexAckParameters.
h2250LogicalChannelAckParameters.mediaControlChannel.unicastAddress.
ipAddress.tsapIdentifier 2061
```

Figure 3.11 Usage of the OpenLogicalChannelAck message.

media will send its RTCP packets. Note that it is customary, although not mandatory, to provide an even-numbered port for RTP and the next odd-numbered port for RTCP.

Instead of the syntax in Figure 3.11, we can use a compact and easily readable syntax as follows:

```
Forward logical channel number 80
RTP IP address 179.6.8.20, Port 2060
RTCP IP address 179.6.8.20, Port 2061
```

CloseLogicalChannel

The transmitter of media uses the CloseLogicalChannel message to close a specific logical channel that it opened with the receiver of media. The transmitter usually stops the transmission of media on the specified logical channel before sending this message to the receiver.

Message

The CloseLogicalChannel message consists of the forwardLogicalChannelNumber field. This message specifies the identification number of the logical channel and is described in the OpenLogicalChannel message.

Usage

The usage of CloseLogicalChannel is self-explanatory.

CloseLogicalChannelAck

The receiver of media uses the CloseLogicalChannelAck message to indicate to the transmitter that the logical channel can be closed. The receiver usually releases all resources that are tied to this specific logical channel before sending this message. Conversely, the transmitter usually releases all resources that are tied to this specific logical channel after this message is received.

Message

The CloseLogicalChannel message consists of the forwardLogicalChannelNumber field. This message specifies the identification number of the logical channel and is described in the OpenLogicalChannelAck message.

Usage

The usage of CloseLogicalChannel is self-explanatory.

FlowControlCommand

The receiver uses the FlowControlCommand message to throttle the flow of media.

Message

Figure 3.12 shows some of the fields in FlowControlCommand. The FlowControlCommand message consists of the following fields:

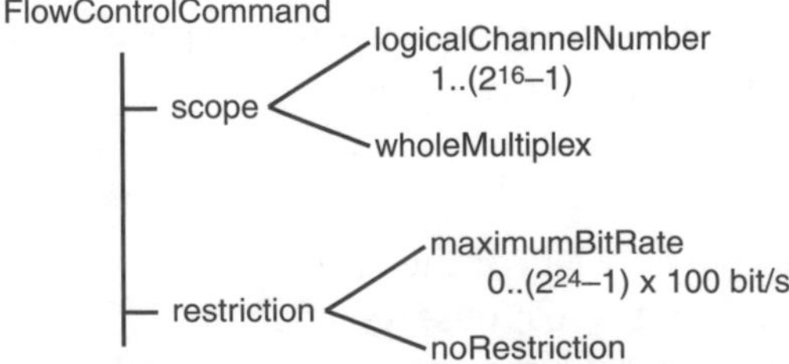

Figure 3.12 H.245 FlowControlCommand message.

- *scope.* This field specifies whether this message is applied to a specific logical channel or to all of the logical channels combined.
  - *logicalChannelNumber.* If selected, this field specifies the identification number of the logical channel.
  - *wholeMultiplex.* If selected, this field specifies that all of the logical channels should be combined.
- *restriction.* This field specifies the restriction on the bit rate of media from the transmitter.
  - *maximumBitRate.* If selected, this field specifies the maximum bit rate between 0 and (2^{24}x1) 100 bps.
  - *noRestriction.* If selected, this field removes any temporary restriction that is imposed on the maximum bit rate. The transmitter will still be within the restriction that is imposed in the receiver's TerminalCapabilitySet and that is reflected in the transmitter's OpenLogicalChannel.

Usage

The usage of FlowControlCommand is self explanatory.

UserInputIndication

The UserInputIndication message transmits inputs from the user interface to the receiver. The inputs can be from the user in the form of button presses.

Message

Some of the fields in UserInputIndication appear in Figure 3.13 and are described as follows:

- *alphanumeric.* This field is used to transmit characters from input devices (such as a keypad).
- *signal.* This field transmits characters from input devices (such as a keypad) as DTMF signals. You use this field in conjunction with the signalUpdate field in order to emulate the DTMF. This field provides information about the button press or the hookflash, the duration of the press, and timing information in order to synchronize the button press or hookflash with a media stream.
  - *signalType.* This field consists of the character "!" (exclamation point) for hookflash and one of the characters 0123456789*#ABCD to denote the corresponding button press.

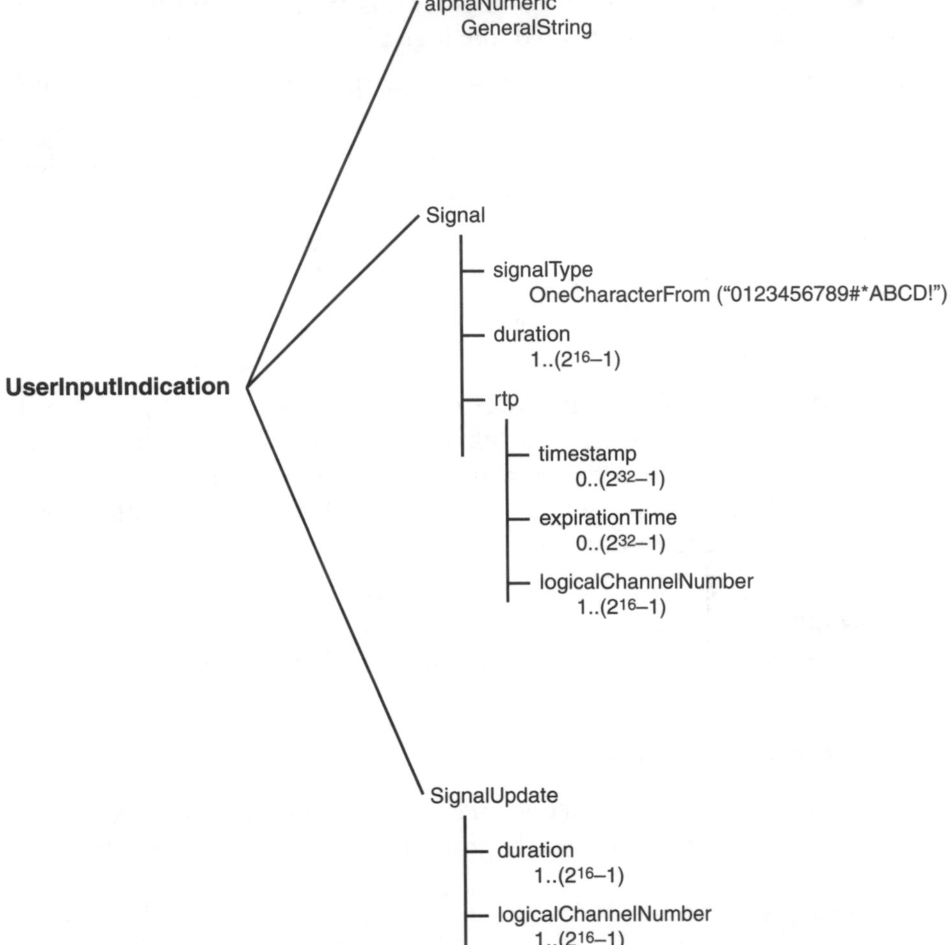

Figure 3.13 H.245 UserInputIndication message.

- *duration.* This field consists of the total duration of the button press in milliseconds or an estimate of the duration if the button is still pressed.
- *rtp.* This field consists of fields that associate the timing of the button press or hookflash with the media stream. These fields include the timestamp field in order to provide the RTP timestamp that corresponds to the start of the button press or hookflash and the expirationTime field in order to provide the RTP timestamp before the start of button press or hookflash should be played. Otherwise, they should be discarded. These fields also include the logicalChannelNumber field that specifies the identification number of the logical channel to which the RTP timestamps refer.

- *signalUpdate.* This field is used in conjunction with the signal field in order to revise the previous estimate of the duration of the button press or the hookflash. This field consists of the duration field that provides the revised total duration and the logicalChannelNumber field that specifies the identification number of the logical channel that is associated with this button press or hookflash.

Usage

Assume that User 1 on Endpoint 1 is interacting with an IVR via Endpoint 2. Assume that Endpoint 2 is a *Public Switched Telephone Network* (PSTN) gateway. The user presses a button for the character # (pound sign) for a duration of 130 ms in response to a command from the Interactive Voice Response (IVR) system. The button press from the user results in three messages from Endpoint 1 to Endpoint 2, as shown in Figure 3.14.

1. Endpoint 1 sends the first message to Endpoint 2, specifying that the user pressed a button with the letter # (pound sign) for an estimated duration of 100 ms. The start of the button press should be synchronized with audio from User 1 (having an RTP timestamp of 675440). The start of the DTMF tone from the button press should be played within the expiration time of 675480 in timestamp units. The timestamp and the expiration time belong to the logical channel with an identification number of 723.
2. Endpoint 1 sends the second message to Endpoint 2, specifying that the updated estimate for the duration of the button press is 200 ms and that the button press is associated with the logical channel that has an identification number of 723. Endpoint 2 should receive this message before the first estimated duration of 20 ms elapses.

```
Point 1
UserInputIndication.signal.signalType #
UserInputIndication.signal.duration 100
UserInputIndication.signal.rtp.timestamp 675440
UserInputIndication.signal.rtp.expirationTime 675480
UserInputIndication.signal.rtp.logicalChannelNumber 273
Point 2
UserInputIndication.signalUpdate.duration 200
UserInputIndication.signal.rtp.logicalChannelNumber 273
Point 3
UserInputIndication.signalUpdate.duration 130
UserInputIndication.signal.rtp.logicalChannelNumber 273
```

Figure 3.14 Usage of UserInputIndication message.

3. Endpoint 1 finally detects an end to the button press from User 1. The endpoint then sends the third message to Endpoint 2, specifying that the total duration of the button press should be updated to 130 ms and that the button press is associated with the logical channel that has an identification number of 723:

MiscellaneousCommand

The MiscellaneousCommand message consists of a variety of commands. In this section, we will only cover the commands pertaining to video. The receiver of video sends these commands to the transmitter.

Message

Figure 3.15 shows some of the fields pertaining to video commands, and we describe them as follows:

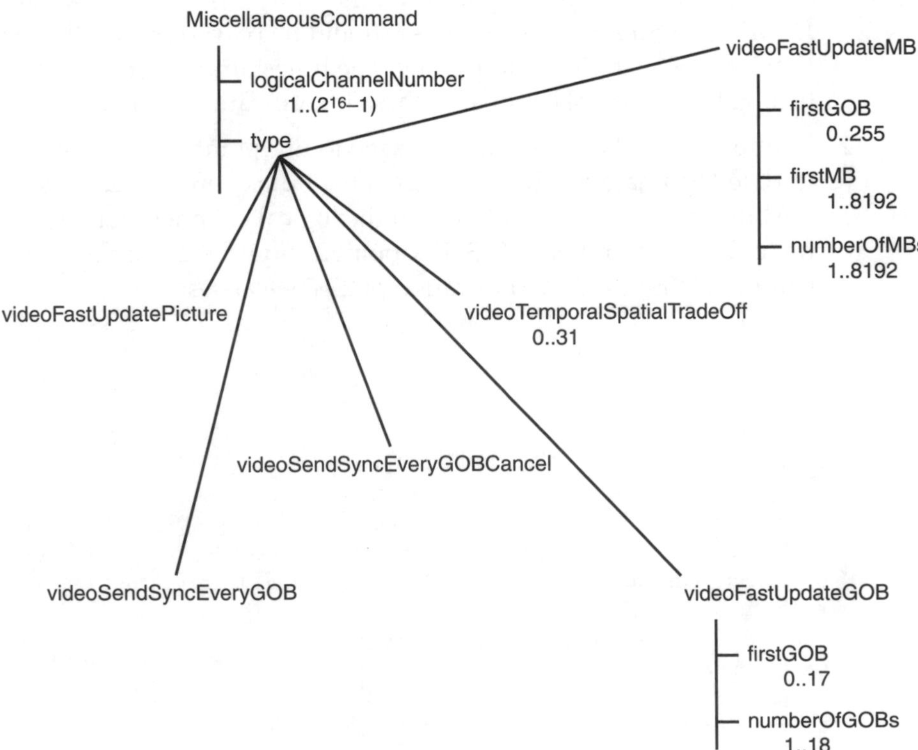

Figure 3.15 H.245 video commands.

- *logicalChannelNumber.* This field specifies the identification number of the logical channel.
- *type.* This field consists of a choice of commands that the receiver of video sends to the transmitter. These commands might be specific to a set of encoders and might not have any meaning to other encoders. For example, the H.263 encoder understands videoSendSyncEveryGOB, but it has no meaning to the H.261 encoder. These video commands are as follows:
  - *videoFastUpdatePicture.* If a partial or complete frame is lost, this command specifies for the encoder to update the entire frame.
  - *videoFastUpdateGOB.* If a few GOBs in the frame are lost, this command specifies for the encoder to update just those GOBs. The firstGOB field specifies the first GOB, and the numberOfGOBs field specifies the total number of GOBs (including the first GOB to be updated).
  - *videoFastUpdateMB.* If a few MBs in the frame are lost, this command specifies for the encoder to update just those MBs. The firstGOB field specifies the first GOB; the firstMB field specifies the first MB; and the numberOfMBs field specifies the number of MBs from the first MB to be updated.
  - *videoTemporalSpatialTradeOff.* This field specifies to the encoder a change in the tradeoff between temporal and spatial resolution. A range of 0 to 31 specifies the relative tradeoff (with 0 being the highest spatial resolution and 31 being the highest frame rate).
  - *videoSendSyncEveryGOB.* This field instructs the encoder to use sync for every GOB. This field is used in a high error-prone environment.
  - *videoSendSyncEveryGOBCancel.* This field instructs the encoder to cancel the videoSendSyncEveryGOB command. The encoder can now decide the frequency of GOB syncs.

Usage

The usage of MiscellaneousCommand is self-explanatory.

Scenarios

Let's consider some scenarios to show how we can use H.245 messages in H.323. Consider that Terminal 1 and Terminal 2 have just completed call signaling and have established a connection. The first scenario shows the message exchange that is needed in order to start the flow of multimedia. The second scenario shows the flow of facsimile activity from Terminal 1 to

Terminal 2. The last scenario shows how Terminal 1 handles network congestion in order to enable its User 1 to continue collaborating with User 2 on Terminal 2.

H.245 Messages to Start Multimedia Transmission

Once the call between two terminals is established by using call signaling, the two endpoints can start multimedia collaboration. Three sets of messages—TerminalCapabilitySet, MasterSlaveDetermination, and OpenLogicalChannel are used in order to start the flow of multimedia. The H.245 procedure that is required to start the flow of multimedia is shown in Figure 3.16.

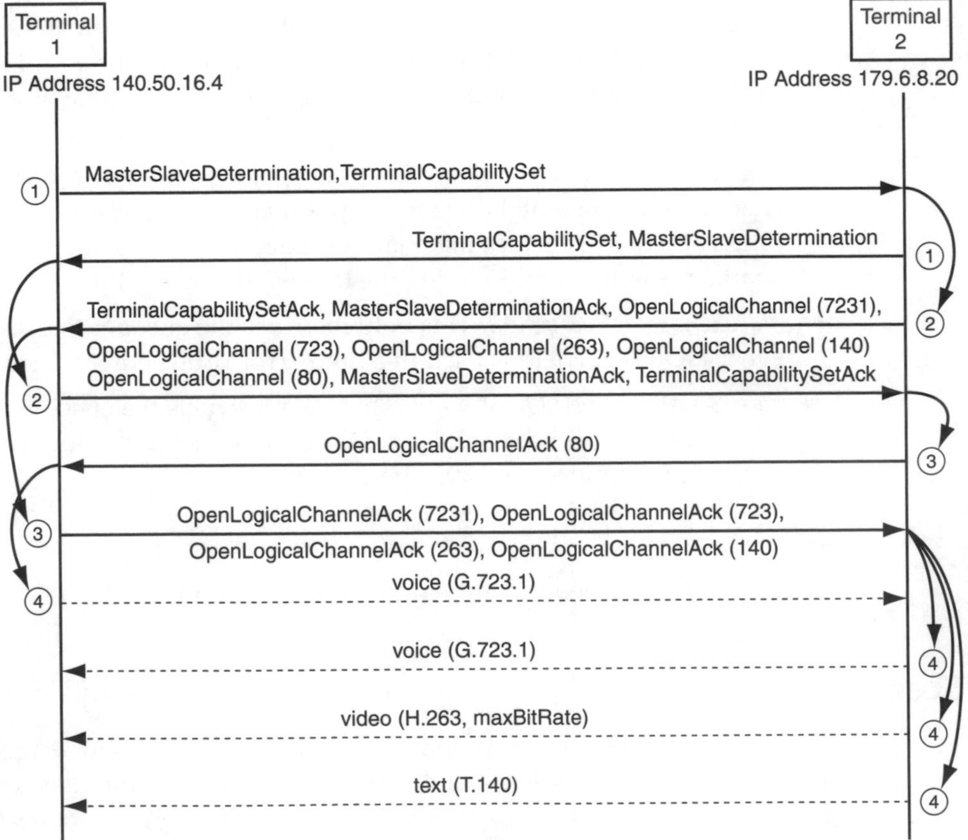

Figure 3.16 H.245 messages to start the flow of multimedia.

1. The terminals first need to provide their capabilities so that we can determine the extent of the collaboration. Terminal 1 sends TerminalCapabilitySet with the following parameters:

```
Media packetization capability
     RFC 1890, Static payload type 0
     RFC 1890, Static payload type 4
     RFC 2198
     RFC 2032, Static payload type 31
     RFC 2190, Static payload type 34
     RFC 2429
     RFC 2793
Redundancy encoding capability
     Redundancy header in payload, Primary encoding G.723.1
Receive voice capability
     G.711 µlaw, 64 kb/s, Maximum 960 samples/RTP packet
     G.723.1, Maximum 4 frames/RTP packet, Silence Suppression
Receive video capability
     H.261, QCIF resolution, Minimum 4/29.97 s between frames, Maximum
     bit rate 30000 bits/s
     H.263, SQCIF and QCIF resolution, Minimum 8/29.97 s between
     frames, Maximum bit rate 40000 bits/s
Receive text capability
     T.140, UDP
```

   a. Terminal 2 sends TerminalCapabilitySet with the following parameters:

```
Media packetization capability
     RFC 1890, Static payload type 0
     RFC 1890, Static payload type 4
     RFC 2198
     RFC 2032, Static payload type 31
     RFC 2190, Static payload type 34
     RFC 2429
     RFC 2793
Redundancy encoding capability
     Redundancy header in payload, Primary encoding G.723.1
Receive voice capability
     G.711 µlaw, 64 kb/s, Maximum 960 samples/RTP packet
     G.723.1, Maximum 4 frames/RTP packet, Silence Suppression
Receive video capability
     H.261, QCIF resolution, Minimum 4/29.97 s between frames,
     Maximum bit rate 40000 bits/s
     H.263, QCIF and CIF resolution, Minimum 8/29.97 s between
     frames, Maximum bit rate 90000 bits/s
Receive text capability
     T.140, UDP
     T.140, TCP
Receive fax capability
```

```
TCP, locally generated TCF
UDP, TCF transferred, redundancy
```

b. Next, the terminals need to determine who will be the master in resolving requests of conflicting resources. Terminal 1 sends MasterSlaveDetermination with the statusDeterminationNumber of 2^{10}, and Terminal 2 sends MasterSlaveDetermination with the statusDeterminationNumber of 2^{23}.

c. Note that MasterSlaveDetermination and TerminalCapabilitySet do not depend on each other, so they are sent in the same packet.

2. Upon reception of TerminalCapabilitySet and MasterSlaveDetermination, the terminals can independently determine the master and the capabilities of the call. From the MasterSlaveDetermination exchange, it is clear that Terminal 1 is the master. The capabilities of the call are an intersection of the capabilities of the two terminals. Note that the capabilities are only of the terminals, not of the access network to which the terminal is connected. If network access is through a 56 kbps modem, then you cannot use G.711 for voice because of bandwidth constraints. But before media transmission can start, the terminals need to specify the characteristics of each media in order to enable the receiving terminal to load the appropriate decoder, to allocate memory, and to perform any other housekeeping duties in order to get ready. This process occurs through the use of OpenLogicalChannel for each media.

   a. The terminals open a logical channel for each media that they will transmit. If the application on Terminal 1 automatically opens the voice channel, then Terminal 1 sends OpenLogicalChannel to Terminal 2 with the following parameters:

   ```
   Forward logical channel number 80
   G.723.1, 2 frames/RTP packet, Silence suppression
   Session ID 1
   RTCP IP address 140.50.16.4, Port 1081
   RFC 1890, Payload type 4
   ```

   b. If the application on Terminal 2 automatically opens the voice, voice redundancy, video, and text channels, then Terminal 2 sends four OpenLogicalChannel messages to Terminal 1 with the following parameters:

   ```
   Forward logical channel number 7231
   G.723.1, 2 frames/RTP packet, Silence suppression
   Session ID 1
   RTCP IP address 179.6.8.20, Port 2061
   RFC 1890, Payload type 4

   Forward logical channel number 723
   ```

```
Primary encoding G.723.1, 1 frames/RTP packet, Silence suppression
Session ID 1
RTCP IP address 179.6.8.20, Port 2061
Redundancy header in payload
Secondary encodings G.723.1, 1 frames/RTP packet, Silence
suppression
Timestamp offset 30 ms
RFC 2198

Forward logical channel number 263
H.263, QCIF resolution, Minimum 8/29.97 s between frames, Maximum
bit rate 40000 bits/s
Session ID 2
RTCP IP address 179.6.8.20, Port 4011
RFC 2429

Forward logical channel number 140
T.140, UDP
Session ID 3
RTCP IP address 179.6.8.20, Port 4021
RFC 2793
```

c. Although the terminals have independently determined the results of the master/slave determination, they also provide the result in MasterSlaveDeterminationAck. The terminals also send TerminalCapabilitySetAck in order to acknowledge the reception of TerminalCapabilitySet. The TerminalCapabilitySetAck, MasterSlaveDeterminationAck, and OpenLogicalChannel messages are sent in the same packet. Note that H.245 mandates for the terminal to wait until it receives MasterSlaveDeterminationAck before sending any other message, but the procedure shown here is different.

3. When the receiving terminal is ready to receive media, it sends an acknowledgement to OpenLogicalChannel messages in OpenLogicalChannelAck messages. Terminal 2 sends OpenLogicalChannelAck to Terminal 1 with the following parameters:

```
Forward logical channel number 80
RTP IP address 179.6.8.20, Port 2060
RTCP IP address 179.6.8.20, Port 2061
```

a. Terminal 1 sends four OpenLogicalChannelAck messages to Terminal 2 with the following parameters:

```
Forward logical channel number 7231
RTP IP address 140.50.16.4, Port 1080
RTCP IP address 140.50.16.4, Port 1081

Forward logical channel number 723
RTP IP address 140.50.16.4, Port 1080
RTCP IP address 140.50.16.4, Port 1081
```

```
Dynamic Payload Type 103
Flow control to 0

Forward logical channel number 263
RTP IP address 140.50.16.4, Port 1044
RTCP IP address 140.50.16.4, Port 1045
Dynamic Payload Type 104

Forward logical channel number 140
RTP IP address 140.50.16.4, Port 4010
RTCP IP address 140.50.16.4, Port 4011
Dynamic Payload Type 105
```

b. Note that logical channels 80, 723, and 7231 are in the same RTP session. The logical channel 723 for voice redundancy and 7231 for non-redundant voice are not used simultaneously, so they share the same transport addresses for RTP and RTCP on Terminal 1 and for RTCP on Terminal 2. Note that H.245 does not have an explicit way through which Terminal 1 can specify to Terminal 2 that the resources for logical channels 723 and 7231 will be shared and not used simultaneously. By specifying that logical channels 723 and 7231 use the same transport address for RTCP and temporarily halting the flow on 723, Terminal 1 provides an indication to Terminal 2 to allocate the same transport addresses for RTP and RTCP for these two logical channels.

4. Upon reception of OpenLogicalChannelAck, the transmitter can start sending media for that logical channel. Terminal 1 sends G.723.1-encoded voice to Terminal 2. Terminal 2 sends G.723.1-encoded voice, H.263-encoded video, and T.140 text. Note that if User 2 does not use the text application on Terminal 2, no data is sent on the text logical channel 140.

H.245 Messages for User-Initiated Facsimile Transmission

Terminal 2 has fax capabilities, but Terminal 1 does not. If a fax is to be transmitted, Terminal 1 must show fax capabilities. Terminal 1 has a G3 fax interface consisting of a device driver for the fax modem and a T.38 packetizer/depacketizer module. The device driver provides an interface between the external G3 fax machine and the T.38 module. The device driver receives T.30 control and T.4 data from the fax machine and sends it to the T.38 module. The T.38 module packetizes T.30/T.4 into T.38 packets and sends it on the IP network. The T.38 module converts T.38 packets from the IP network to T.30 and T.4 and gives them to the device driver for transmission to the fax machine.

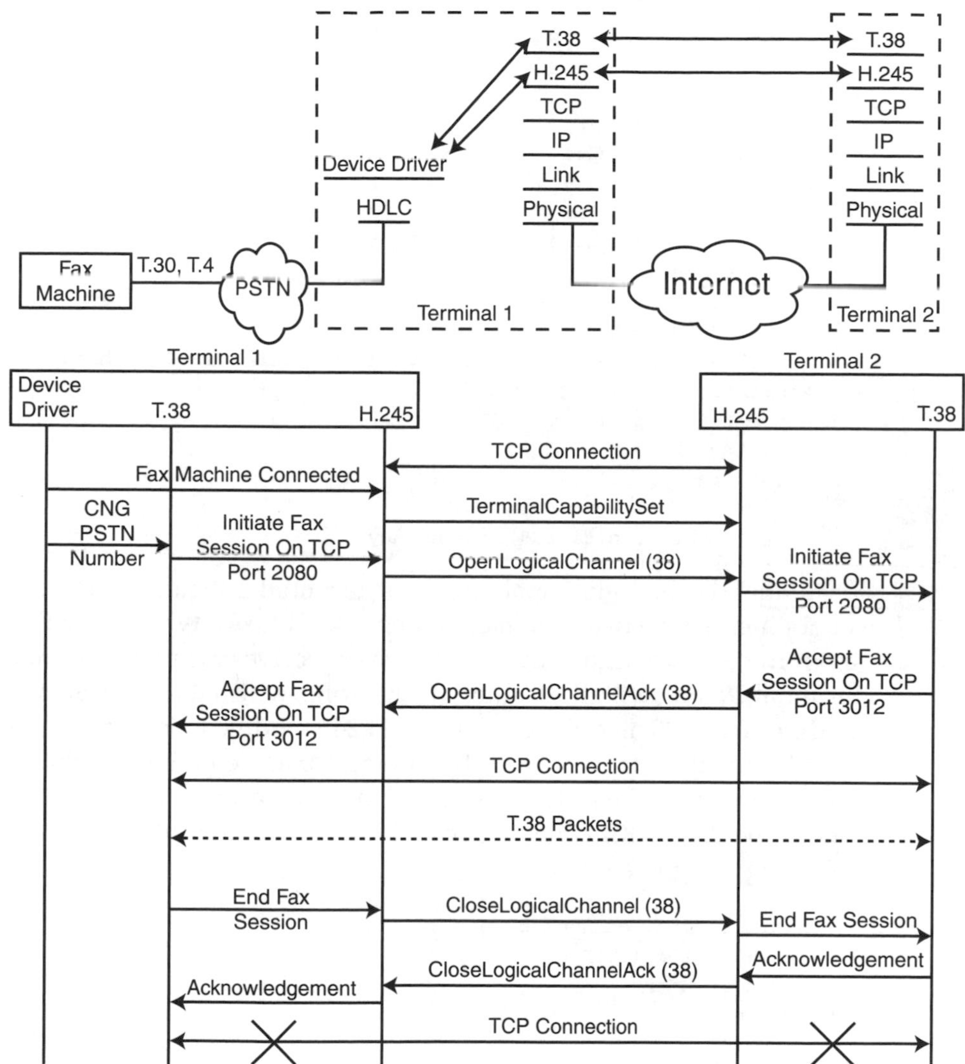

Figure 3.17 H.245 messages for user-initiated fax transmission.

When a fax machine is connected to Terminal 1 (as shown in Figure 3.17), the capabilities of Terminal 1 are updated. The T.38 module is loaded. The H.245 module sends the new TerminalCapabilitySet to Terminal 2 with the addition of fax capabilities as follows:

```
Media packetization capability
     RFC 1890, Static payload type 0
     RFC 1890, Static payload type 4
     RFC 2198
```

```
        RFC 2032, Static payload type 31
        RFC 2190, Static payload type 34
        RFC 2429
        RFC 2793
   Redundancy encoding capability
        Redundancy header in payload, Primary encoding G.723.1
   Receive voice capability
        G.711 µlaw, 64 kb/s, Maximum 960 samples/RTP packet
        G.723.1, Maximum 4 frames/RTP packet, Silence Suppression
   Receive video capability
        H.261, QCIF resolution, Minimum 4/29.97 s between frames, Maximum
   bit rate 30000 bits/s
        H.263, SQCIF and QCIF resolution, Minimum 8/29.97 s between frames,
   Maximum bit rate 40000 bits/s
   Receive text capability
        T.140, UDP
   Receive fax capability
        TCP, locally generated TCF
        UDP, TCF transferred, redundancy
```

Recall that the TerminalCapabilitySet of Terminal 2 already includes fax capabilities, so the two terminals can now send faxes. When User 1 sends a fax from the fax machine, the device driver receives the phone number of Terminal 2 along with the Calling (CNG) tone, which it forwards to the T.38 module. The T.38 module requests the H.245 module to initiate a fax session with Terminal 2 and to provide TCP port 2080 for receiving T.38 information from Terminal 2. The H.245 module follows the procedures in [H323D98] and sends OpenLogicalChannel to open a bidirectional logical channel with the following parameters:

```
Forward logical channel number 38
T.38, TCP, Local TCF
Session ID 4
T.38, TCP
Session ID 4
IP address 140.50.16.4, Port 2080
```

Upon receiving OpenLogicalChannel from Terminal 1, the H.245 module in Terminal 2 requests the T.38 module to initiate a fax session. The T.38 module responds with an acceptance on TCP port 3012 of T.38 information from Terminal 1. The H.245 module then sends OpenLogicalChannelAck to Terminal 1 with the following parameters:

```
Forward logical channel number 38
Reverse logical channel number 380
Session ID 4
Session ID 4
IP address 179.6.8.20, Port 3012
```

Upon receiving OpenLogicalChannelAck from Terminal 2, the H.245 module in Terminal 1 responds to the T.38 module with an acceptance of fax session on TCP port 3012. The T.38 module establishes a TCP connection with IP address 140.50.16.4, port 2080 of Terminal 1, IP address 179.6.8.20, and port 3012 of Terminal 2. We described the T.38 information that is exchanged between the two terminals in Chapter 2's section, "Transport of Facsimile on the Internet." When the fax session ends, the T.38 module in Terminal 1 indicates this information to the H.245 module, which then sends CloseLogicalChannel to the H.245 module in Terminal 2. The H.245 module in Terminal 2 sends an indication to its T.38 module to end the fax session. When the T.38 module responds with an acknowledgement, the H.245 module sends CloseLogicalChannelAck to the H.245 module in Terminal 1. The H.245 module then sends an acknowledgement to its T.38 module. The T.38 module in Terminal 1 then terminates the TCP connection with Terminal 2. Note that only the fax logical channel and its physical connection have been terminated. Any other opened logical channel is still operational.

H.245 Messages to Handle Network Congestion

QoS is normally not provided on the Internet. So, as network conditions change, the real-time streams must adapt to the changing conditions. For each stream, the receivers measure packet loss, inter-arrival packet jitter, and one-way delay of media. Based on these measurements, the receivers take appropriate actions on the streams. We can make measurements for these three parameters as follows:

- *Packet loss*. We can measure packet loss through gaps in the Sequence Number field in the RTP header of the packets that are received. As an example, if RTP packets with sequence numbers 1, 2, 4, 5, and 8 are received, then packets 3, 6, and 7 were lost in the network.
- *Inter-arrival packet jitter*. We can measure this value as an absolute value of the difference in delay from packet to packet as packets are received. If an RTP packet P_i has a capture timestamp of C_i units and is received at time R_i units, where C_i and R_i are the RTP timestamp units, then the jitter of P_i is $J_i = | (R_i - C_i) - (R_{i-1} - C_{i-1}) |$. For example, if packet 2 has a timestamp of 1280 units and is received at time 1060 units and packet 1 has a timestamp of 1240 units and is received at time 1000 units, then packet 2 has a jitter of 20 ms.
- *One-way delay.* We can measure this value by subtracting the NTP time that the received packet is played to the speaker from the NTP time that it

was captured, as calculated from the RTP timestamp of that packet. The transmitter uses RTCP to provide the receiver with the NTP timestamp (if available) and the corresponding RTP timestamp. The receiver uses this correlation between the NTP and RTP timestamps of the transmitter to determine the NTP timestamp of any packet that is received. If the NTP is not available from the transmitter or the receiver does not have access to it, then the receiver cannot calculate one-way delay.

Increases in jitter due to increases in delay over a certain period of time normally provide an indication of impending congestion on the network. If the jitter keeps increasing, an increase in packet loss usually follows. The H.323 terminals use RTCP to report these measurements to the transmitter of the media. Based on this feedback, the transmitter can make adjustments to the media. Because the receiver and the transmitter have already established an H.245 control channel, it is more effective for the receiver to provide explicit messages in order to direct the transmitter to make adjustments. Also, because the user at the receiving end is experiencing changes in quality of the media, it becomes effective when the receiver can directly change the characteristics of the media. Continuing from Figure 3.17, Figure 3.18 shows how Terminal 1 controls the flow of media from Terminal 2 due to changes in network conditions during the call. We describe this situation as follows:

1. When Terminal 1 perceives a packet loss on the voice channel that is sufficient enough to degrade the quality for the user, it requests for Terminal 2 to switch from non-redundant voice to redundant voice. Terminal 1 sends two FlowControlCommand messages to Terminal 2. The first FlowControlCommand requests Terminal 2 to start the transmission of voice redundancy on logical channel 723. The second FlowControlCommand requests Terminal 2 to stop the transmission of voice on logical channel 7231. Both messages can be sent in the same packet.
2. Terminal 2 switches to transmitting redundant voice. Because the primary encoding of G.723.1 is maintained between the two logical channels 723 and 7231, Terminal 2 maintains the fields of the RTP header (except for the Payload Type, which changes from 4 for G.723.1 to the dynamic payload type of 103 for Redundancy). By maintaining the RTP fields, the timing space and the sequence numbers are not disrupted.
3. When Terminal 1 perceives congestion due to an unusually large number of packet losses, you must enable the network to recover by reducing the bit rate on the network. Terminal 1 uses FlowControlCommand to request Terminal 2 to temporarily reduce the maximum video bit rate on logical channel 263 to a much lower value (say, 16 kbps).

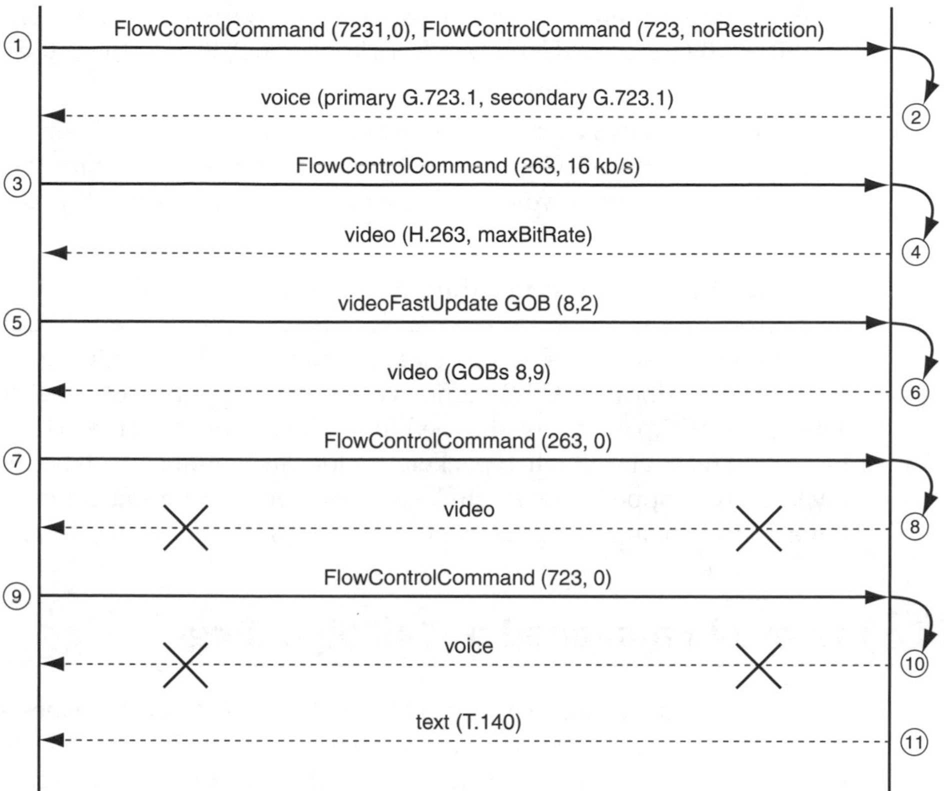

Figure 3.18 Scenario for handling network congestion.

4. Terminal 2 reduces the maximum bit rate of H.263 video to 16 kbps.
5. When Terminal 1 discovers that it did not receive an H.263 packet containing GOBs 8 and 9, it requests for Terminal 2 to resend a total of 2 GOBs starting from GOB 8 through the use of videoFastUpdateGOB.
6. Terminal 2 resends GOBs 8 and 9.
7. If congestion persists, Terminal 1 further reduces the overall bit rate on logical channel 263 of Terminal 2 by temporarily halting the transmission of video by reducing the bit rate to zero through the use of FlowControlCommand.
8. Terminal 2 stops the transmission of H.263 video.
9. Terminals normally monitor the one-way delay of voice to determine whether it is within the threshold for acceptable voice conversation. When the threshold is exceeded, Terminal 1 can request for Terminal 2 to temporarily halt the reception of voice on logical channel 723 by reducing

the bit rate to zero through the use of FlowControlCommand. This action will further reduce the bit rate from Terminal 2, thus helping the network recover from congestion.

10. User 2 now only has the use of text to communicate with User 1. Terminal 2 starts the transmission of text. At this point, User 1 is communicating with User 2 through voice, and User 2 is communicating with User 1 through text.

We make the assumption that during congestion, the H.245 messages can reach from Terminal 1 to Terminal 2. Because H.245 uses the TCP transport, the delivery of messages is eventually guaranteed. On the Internet today, routers give priority to UDP traffic over TCP during times of congestion. Therefore, TCP packets are dropped first. The reasoning is that TCP is well behaved and backs off when packets are lost and retransmits later. If UDP packets are dropped, they might be lost forever if peer applications do not have a protocol in order to detect lost packets and retransmit them.

Call Control Embedded in Call Signaling

In the previous sections, we showed how H.225.0-Q.931 establishes a connection between terminals, and we use H.245 next in order to allow terminals that have disparate hardware and software to perform multimedia collaboration. Version 1 of H.323 uses this architecture of cleanly separating the messages and procedures of H.225.0-Q.931 from H.245. Version 2 of H.323 improves the architecture by making the H.323 systems more scalable and by cutting down the delay in voice after the connection is established. We describe these improvements in the following sections.

H.245 Tunneling

Version 1 of H.323 uses different TCP ports at the receiver in order to de-multiplex between H.225.0-Q.931 and H.245. If the receiver (such as a gateway) is capable of handling hundreds of calls simultaneously, its scalability is reduced if each call takes two ports (because most operating systems have an upper limit on the total number of ports that can be opened). To solve this problem, version 2 of H.323 introduced H.245 tunneling so that H.245 messages could be encapsulated in any H.225.0-Q.931 message. This feature freed the H.245 port, reduced the port usage per call to one, and doubled the scalability of such receivers. But it also added an additional burden of having the receivers de-multiplex between the H.245 and the H.225.0-Q.931 messages on the same port. H.245 tunneling is optional and is used only if both of the endpoints have this capability.

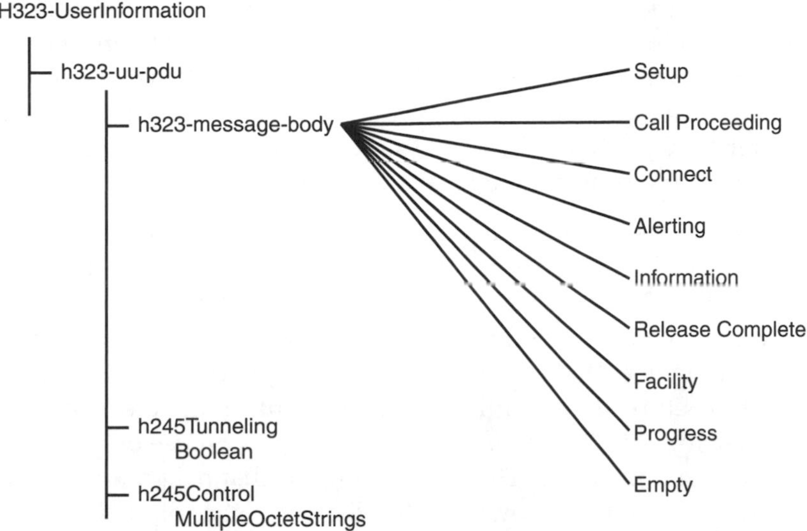

Figure 3.19 Message fields for H.245 tunneling.

Figure 3.19 shows the H323-UserInformation structure that contains the User-to-User Information Element of an H.225.0-Q.931 message along with two other fields: h245Tunneling and h245Control. The h245Tunneling field should be set to *true* in the Setup message and in all subsequent H.225.0-Q.931 messages by both endpoints in order to enable H.245 tunneling. You can encapsulate one or more H.245 messages in the h245Control field of any H.225.0-Q.931 message. If there is no H.225.0-Q.931 message to be sent at a time when H.245 messages are sent, then you use the Facility message (with an empty h323-message-body). In other words, no User-to-User Information Element is used.

Fast Connect

In version 1 of H.323, the H.245 messages are sent after the call has been established. This procedure introduces a delay before voice can flow, which can sometimes result in an unacceptable length of silence. This situation can also result in the initial voice being clipped. Both of these results are unacceptable in telephony. To solve this problem, version 2 of H.323 introduced Fast-Connect so that the logical channels could be opened before the connection is established. Then, when the connection is established, voice and other media can flow without any delay from the H.245 protocol overhead. Fast Connect is optional, and you should use it only if both of the endpoints have this capability.

In the Fast Connect procedure, one or more OpenLogicalChannel structures are embedded in the fastStart field of Setup. The forward logical channel parameters in OpenLogicalChannel suggest the characteristics of media that the calling endpoint wishes to transmit. The reverse logical channel parameters in OpenLogicalChannel suggest the characteristics of media that the calling endpoint wishes to receive from the called endpoint.

Upon receiving Setup, the called endpoint responds with one or more OpenLogicalChannel structures that are embedded in the fastStart field of any H.225.0-Q.931 message up to and including Connect. The OpenLogicalChannel structures consist of forward and reverse logical channel parameters that are picked from those provided by the calling endpoint in Setup. Note that the called endpoint cannot create new forward and reverse logical channel parameters; rather, it will use only those that the calling endpoint provides. The forward logical channel parameters of OpenLogicalChannel acknowledge the characteristics of media that the calling endpoint must transmit. The reverse logical channel parameters of OpenLogicalChannel acknowledge the characteristics of media that the called endpoint will transmit.

Figure 3.20 shows how Endpoint 1 establishes a voice channel with Endpoint 2 by using Fast Connect. The sequence of messages used are described as follows:

1. Endpoint 1 sends Setup with the fastStart field containing two OpenLogicalChannel structures with the following forward and reverse logical channel parameters:

```
Forward logical channel number 80
G.723.1, 1 frame/RTP packet, Silence suppression
Session ID 1
RTCP IP address 140.50.16.4, Port 1081
```

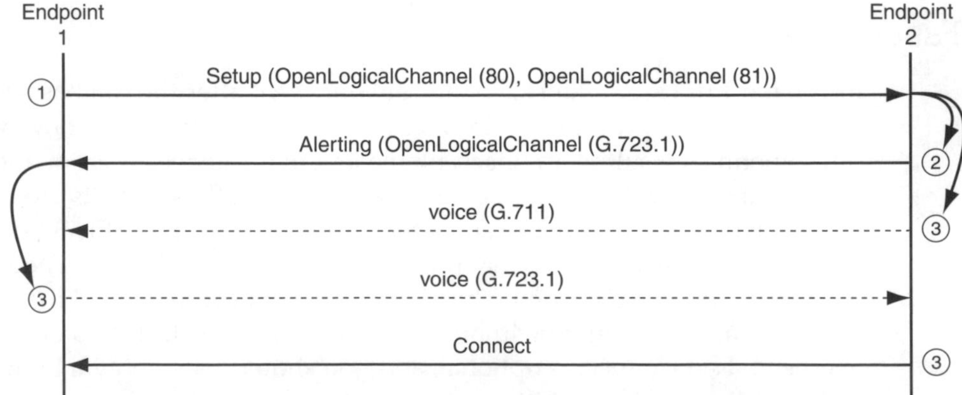

Figure 3.20 Using Fast-Connect to open voice channels.

```
RFC 1890, Payload type 4
Guaranteed load, averate rate 2000 B/s, peak rate 2000 B/s, minimum
packet size 44 bytes, maximum packet size 60 bytes, bucket size 60 bytes
G.723.1, 1 frame/RTP packet, Silence suppression
Session ID 1
RTP IP address 140.50.16.4, Port 1080
RTCP IP address 140.50.16.4, Port 1081
RFC 1890, Payload type 4
Guaranteed load, average rate 2000 B/s, peak rate 2000 B/s, minimum
packet size 44 bytes, maximum packet size 60 bytes, bucket size 60 bytes

Forward logical channel number 81
G.711 µlaw, 64 kb/s, 240 samples/RTP packet
Session ID 1
RTCP IP address 140.50.16.4, Port 1081
RFC 1890, Payload type 0
Guaranteed load, average rate 9333 B/s, peak rate 9333 B/s, minimum
packet size 41 bytes, maximum packet size 280 bytes, bucket size 280
bytes
G.711 µlaw, 64 kb/s, 240 samples/RTP packet
Session ID 1
RTP IP address 140.50.16.4, Port 1080
RTCP IP address 140.50.16.4, Port 1081
RFC 1890, Payload type 0
Guaranteed load, average rate 9333 B/s, peak rate 9333 B/s, minimum
packet size 41 bytes, maximum packet size 280 bytes, bucket size 280
bytes
```

a. The OpenLogicalChannel structures are listed in order of priority with the most preferred mode listed first. The OpenLogicalChannel structures for voice are listed first, followed by any other media. The mandatory codec for voice is also listed in order to ensure that both endpoints will have at least one common codec. All logical channels having the same Session ID provide alternatives out of which Endpoint 2 will only choose one. The forward logical channel parameters of the first OpenLogicalChannel structure lists G.723.1 as the most preferred codec that Endpoint 1 would use to transmit voice to Endpoint 2. The reverse logical channel parameters of the first OpenLogicalChannel structure also list G.723.1 as the most preferred codec for Endpoint 1 to receive voice from Endpoint 2.

b. The forward logical channel parameters of the second OpenLogicalChannel structure list G.711 as the next preferred codec that Endpoint 1 would use to transmit voice to Endpoint 2. The reverse logical channel parameters of the second OpenLogicalChannel structure also list G.711 as the next preferred codec for Endpoint 1 to receive voice from Endpoint 2. Both logical channels have the same session ID of 1, so Endpoint 2 will only select one logical channel.

2. Upon receiving Setup from Endpoint 1 with the fastStart field consisting of two OpenLogicalChannel structures, Endpoint 2 picks from among the alternatives offered by Endpoint 1 the forward logical channel parameters that Endpoint 1 will transmit, along with the reverse logical channel parameters that Endpoint 2 will transmit. This information is sent in a fastStart field of the OpenLogicalChannel structure in Alerting or in Call Proceeding, Facility, or Connect messages. After the connection is established, you cannot use the fastStart field in H.225.0-Q.931 anymore. The OpenLogicalChannel structure of Endpoint 1 consists of the following forward and reverse logical channel parameters:

```
Forward logical channel number 6973
G.723.1, 2 frames/RTP packet, Silence suppression
Session ID 1
RTP IP address 179.6.8.20, Port 2060
RTCP IP address 179.6.8.20, Port 2061
RFC 1890, Payload type 4
Guaranteed load, average rate 2000 B/s, peak rate 2000 B/s, minimum
packet size 44 bytes, maximum packet size 60 bytes, bucket size 60 bytes
G.711 μlaw, 64 kb/s, 480 samples/RTP packet
Session ID 1
RTCP IP address 179.6.8.20, Port 2061
RFC 1890, Payload type 0
Guaranteed load, average rate 2000 B/s, peak rate 2000 B/s, minimum
packet size 44 bytes, maximum packet size 60 bytes, bucket size 60 bytes
```

   a. The OpenLogicalChannel structure from Endpoint 2 to Endpoint 1 consists of an identification number of 6973. The forward logical channel parameters are for media to be transmitted from Endpoint 1 to Endpoint 2. The reverse logical channel parameters are for media to be transmitted from Endpoint 2 to Endpoint 1. Endpoint 2 can only pick the forward and reverse logical channel parameters from those that Endpoint 1 provides in the Setup message. Endpoint 2 picks the forward logical channel parameters of logical channel 80 and the reverse logical channel parameters of logical channel 81 from Endpoint 1.

3. Upon sending OpenLogicalChannel to Endpoint 1, Endpoint 2 can start sending G.711 voice. Upon receiving OpenLogicalChannel from Endpoint 2, Endpoint 1 can start sending G.723.1. If User 2 takes the call, Endpoint 2 sends Connect to Endpoint 1. If during the call new media is to be transmitted, then the H.245 procedure of master/slave determination, endpoint capability exchange, and opening logical channels will be performed before new media is transmitted.

The Registration, Admission, and Status Protocol: H.225.0-RAS

The H.225.0-RAS provides a single, unified protocol in order to enable the endpoint to obtain various services (such as address resolution and network QoS). The H.225.0-RAS protocol is between the endpoint and the gatekeeper, also known as the *Registration, Admission, and Status* (RAS) server. The front end of the gatekeeper consists of an interface with the endpoints; the back end of the gatekeeper consists of various servers that are required to provide the services that the endpoint requests. We illustrate this process in Figure 3.21.

In telephony, phone calls are routed to telephones based on phone numbers (E.164 address), and users are also identified by E.164 addresses. On the Internet, data is routed based on the IP addresses, and the users/hosts/servers/resources are identified by domain names, e-mail addresses, and URLs. The *Domain Name Server* (DNS) resolves domain names in e-mail addresses and URLs to IP addresses. The IP addresses are then used to route data to their destinations. In addition to using e-mail addresses and URLs, IP

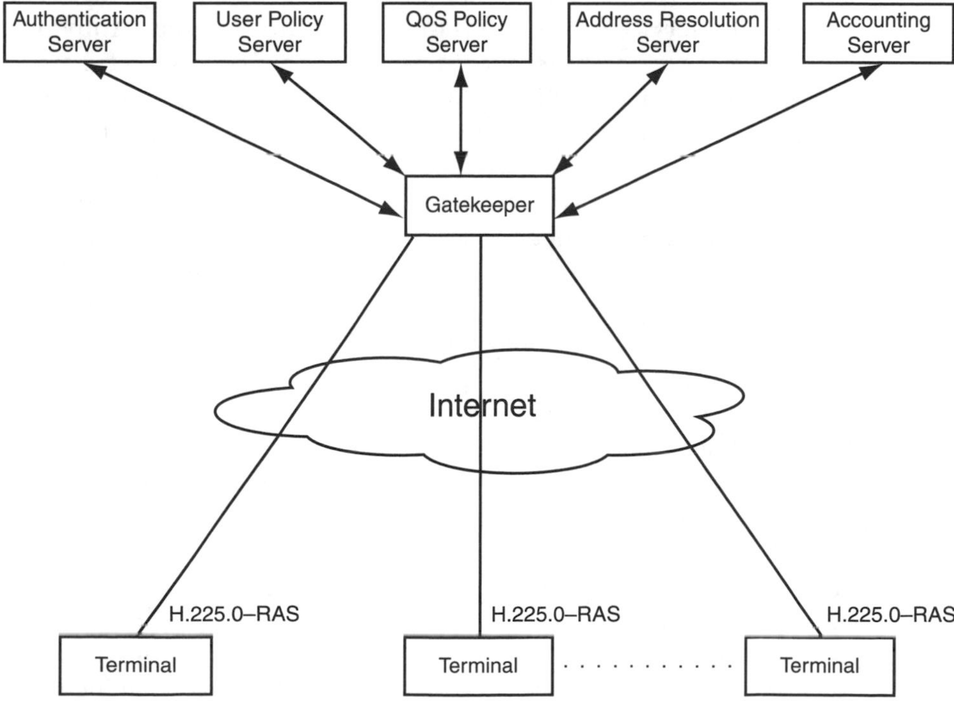

Figure 3.21 Endpoints, gatekeeper, and back-end servers.

telephony also uses E.164 addresses and unique names of users for identification. All of these address types are called alias addresses in H.323. These alias addresses in their various forms need to be resolved to IP addresses in order to route calls to their destinations. There are a number of address resolution servers, such as DNS and *Lightweight Directory Access Protocol* (LDAP), that you can use. The problem is that the endpoints need to have one or more client interfaces to the servers that will resolve the addresses. When the servers change, the client interfaces might also change. We solve this problem in H.323 by using the H.225.0-RAS protocol to carry the addressing information between the endpoint and the gatekeeper and by using the gatekeeper as a proxy for the endpoint to interface (with one or more address-resolution servers to resolve the alias addresses to an IP address and optionally to a port).

One problem with using the Internet is the unpredictable quality of the calls. The Internet was developed for nonreal-time data and provides best-effort service. The Internet does not provide QoS to real-time calls, however. In order to guarantee a certain level of QoS, the calls can be routed through the managed IP networks or through the PSTN when the Internet is congested. The service provider that invests in additional network infrastructure to provide QoS will charge the user who is requesting the service a higher fee than the best-effort service. In order to make sure that only the paying users get QoS, the service provider has to authenticate the users. Authentication involves some form of user identification and a shared secret. This information includes but is not limited to the following: 1) a username for identification and a password for authentication, 2) a prepaid card number for both identification and authentication of prepaid card users, 3) a calling-card number for both identification and authentication of calling-card users, and 4) a credit card number for authentication and an expiration date for authentication of credit card users. When the user is ready to call, he or she might have to be authorized based on some policy that is preconfigured for the user, along with the policy for providing the requested QoS. The policy for the user might include but is not limited to the following: 1) providing QoS only during certain times of the day, 2) providing no more than a certain amount of network bandwidth per call, 3) restricting calls only to certain geographic locations, and 4) restricting the duration of the call to the amount of prepaid credit. The policy for providing QoS can include but is not limited to the following: 1) checking the network for sufficient bandwidth in order to handle additional calls, and 2) setting up the edge routers to provide preferential treatment for certain calls. Once authorized (and once the user makes the call), the service provider can perform accounting in order to bill the user for the resources that he or she used. Resources can include but are not limited to the following: 1) the length of the call, 2) the amount of network bandwidth that is used, and so on.

In order to provide services such as address resolution and network QoS to users who are paying for these services, the service provider might authenticate, perform address resolution, authorize based on the policy for the user and the policy for providing QoS on the network, and perform accounting in order to bill the user for the services. This process might involve the use of various servers, such as the authentication server, the address resolution server, the user policy server, the QoS policy server, and the accounting server. Several authentication servers might be used, each having their own protocol based on whether the user has a prepaid card, calling card, or credit card. Different service providers might use, say, accounting servers from different manufacturers with their own unique protocols. Because millions of users use the terminals, it is quite expensive to load the client software that is needed by the special blend of servers that the service provider uses and to upgrade the client software in the terminals every time the servers change. So, we solve this problem in H.323 through the use of the H.225.0-RAS protocol and the gatekeeper. The H.225.0-RAS protocol enables the endpoints to request services and enables the gatekeepers to provide them. The gatekeeper is a proxy server acting on behalf of the endpoint with the various servers in order to obtain the services that the endpoint requests.

H.225.0-RAS Message Flows

Figure 3.22 shows how User 1 on Endpoint 1 makes a call to User 2 on Endpoint 2 by using the services of Gatekeeper 1. Endpoint 2 also uses the services of Gatekeeper 2. Most H225.0-RAS messages are of the request-response type. The endpoint first discovers its gatekeeper by sending a *Gatekeeper Request* (GRQ) message. The gatekeeper responds with a *Gatekeeper Confirm* (GCF) message if it can provide the services; otherwise, it responds with a *Gatekeeper Reject* (GRJ) message. Assuming successful discovery, the endpoint next registers with the gatekeeper by sending the *Registration Request* (RRQ) message. The gatekeeper responds with a *Registration Confirm* (RCF) message if it successfully registers the user; otherwise, it responds with a *Registration Reject* (RRJ) message. Once the endpoint is registered, it can use the gatekeeper services for which it is authorized. When User 1 makes a call to User 2, Endpoint 1 sends an *Admission Request* (ARQ) message to Gatekeeper 1 for an admission request to call. The gatekeeper responds with an *Admission Confirm* (ACF) message if admission is granted; otherwise, it responds with *Admission Reject* (ARJ). If admission is granted, the endpoint initiates the call to Endpoint 2 with the Setup message. When Endpoint 2 receives Setup, it requests admission to answer the call from Gatekeeper 2 with the ARQ message. Endpoint 2 also sends the call proceeding message to Endpoint 1. The gatekeeper grants admission in the ACF message; otherwise, it will refuse admission with an ARJ message. If admission is granted,

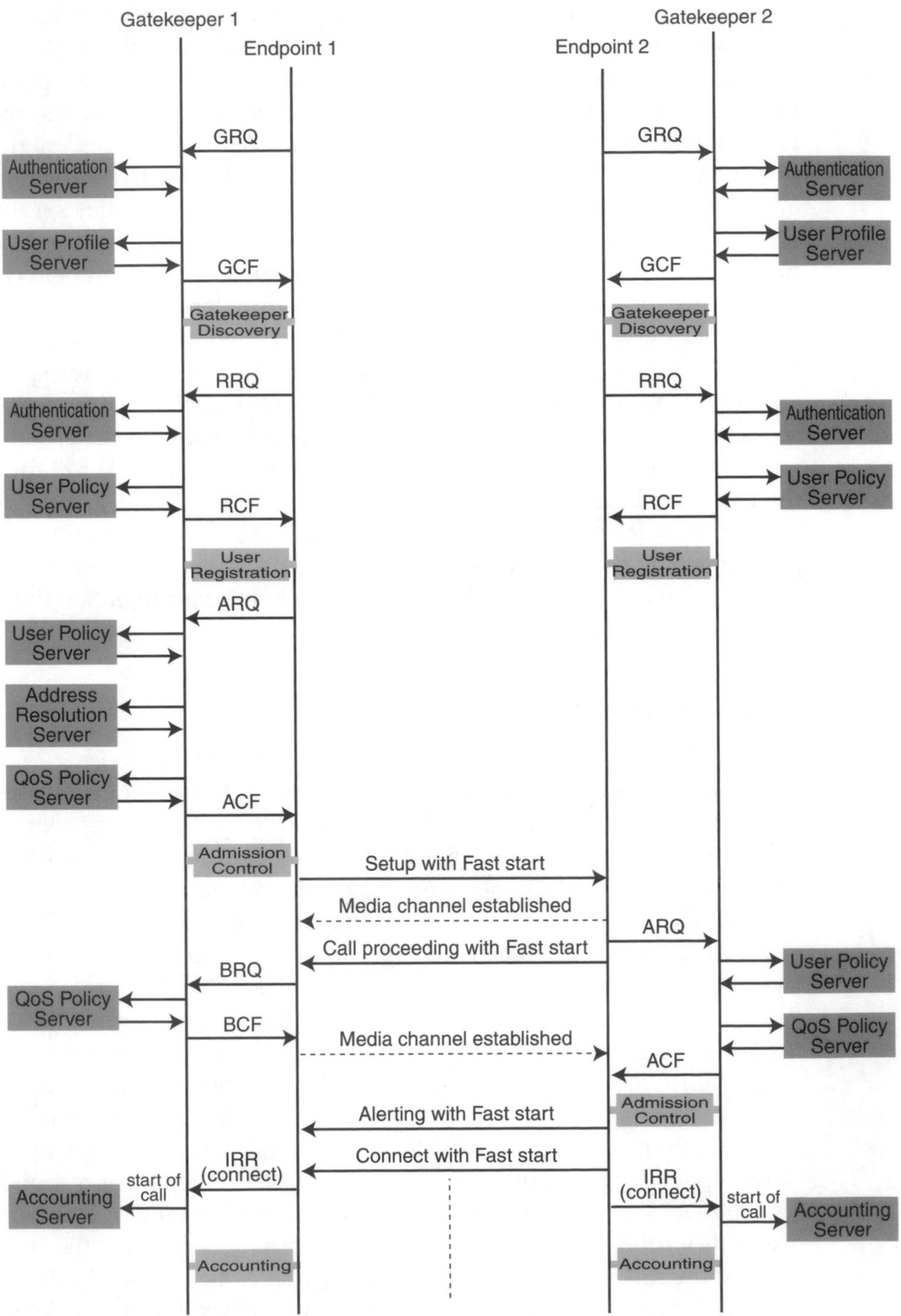

Figure 3.22 H.225.0-RAS message flows.

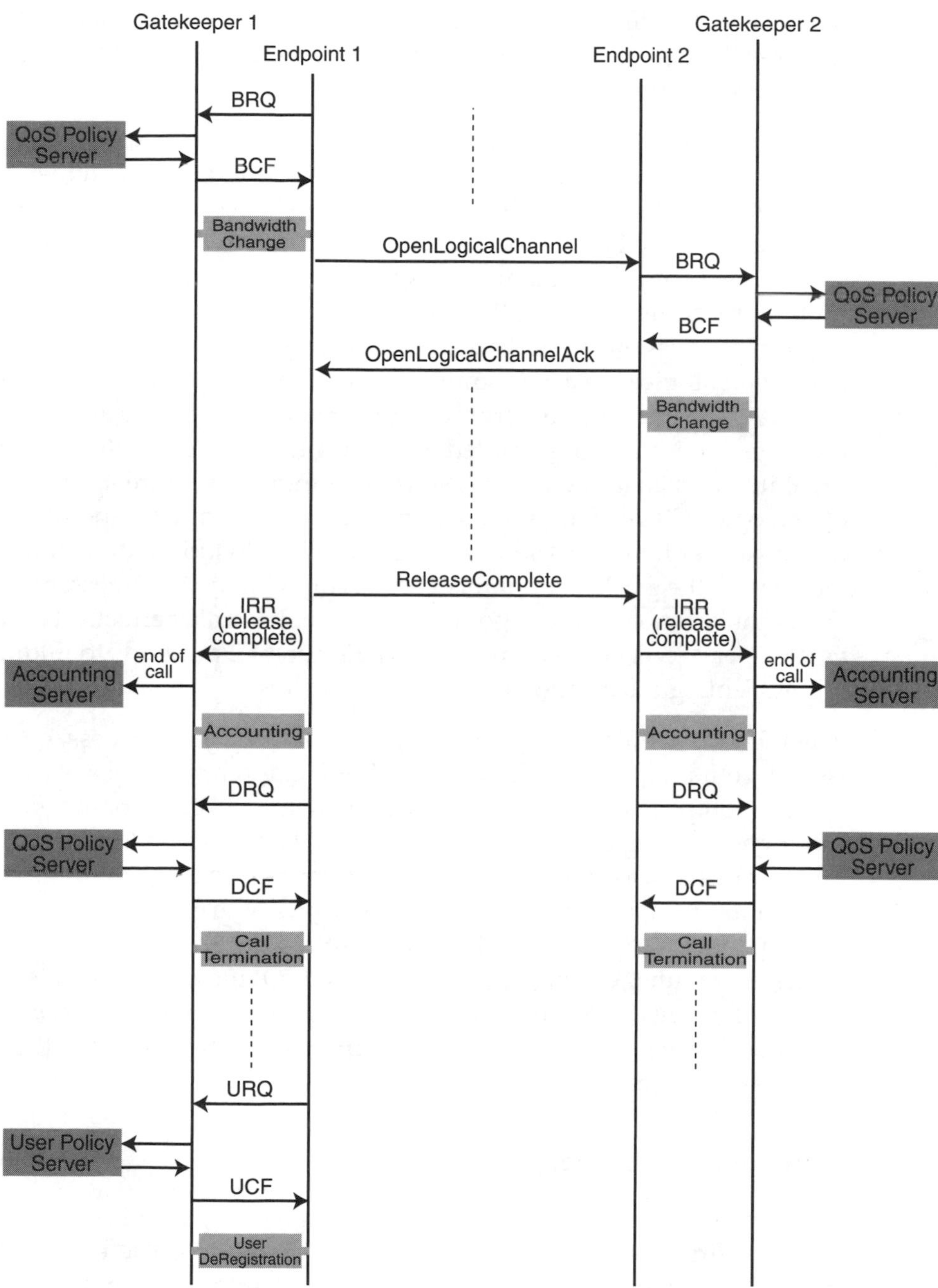

Figure 3.22 H.225.0-RAS message flows. (Continued)

Endpoint 2 alerts User 2 by ringing or by any other means and sends the alerting message to Endpoint 1. When User 2 answers the call, Endpoint 2 sends the Connect message to Endpoint 1. Media between endpoints are established. Both endpoints tunnel a copy of Connect in *Information Request Response* (IRR) in order to notify their gatekeepers of the start of the call for accounting purposes.

If H.245 messages are not exchanged after Fast Connect ends with the Connect message, then the call can proceed to termination with the ReleaseComplete message. If any H.245 message needs to be exchanged, however, then the H.245 procedure involving endpoint capability exchange and master/slave determination has to be performed first. During the call, if Endpoint 1 needs to change the traffic characteristics of the call, it first requests permission in the *Bandwidth Request* (BRQ) message to the gatekeeper. If the gatekeeper grants permission, it responds with a *Bandwidth Confirm* (BCF) message; otherwise, it responds with a *Bandwidth Reject* (BRJ) message. If permission is granted, Endpoint 1 will first have to perform capability exchange and master/slave determination before it sends the OpenLogicalChannel message with the new bandwidth. Endpoint 2 requests its gatekeeper for permission to use the new bandwidth with the BRQ message. If the gatekeeper grants permission with the BCF message, Endpoint 2 responds to Endpoint 1 with OpenLogicalChannelAck. If the gatekeeper rejects permission with BRJ, Endpoint 2 responds to Endpoint 1 with OpenLogicalChannelReject.

When User 1 is finished with the call, the ReleaseComplete message is issued from Endpoint 1 to Endpoint 2. Both endpoints tunnel a copy of ReleaseComplete in IRR in order to notify their gatekeeper of the end of the call for accounting purposes. The endpoints then send the *Disengage Request* (DRQ) messages to their gatekeepers in order to disengage the call. Endpoints can make or answer calls by starting with an ARQ message and ending with a DRQ message. The endpoint can deregister from the gatekeeper with the *Unregistration Request* (URQ) message. The gatekeeper cancels the registration and responds with an *Unregistration Confirm* (UCF) message. We explain the message flows in Figure 3.22 in detail in the following sections.

Gatekeeper Discovery

In order for the endpoint to use the services that the gatekeeper provides, the endpoint first has to discover its authorized gatekeeper. There are two methods for gatekeeper discovery: manual and automatic. In the manual method, the endpoint is preconfigured with the transport address of the gatekeeper. If the preconfigured transport address does not specify the port number, then the well-known port number of 1719 is used. The endpoint unicasts the GRQ message at the preconfigured transport address. The automatic method consists of multicast and the DNS. If multicast is used, the endpoint multicasts the GRQ message to the well-known transport address with an IP address of 224.0.1.41 and a port number of 1718. If DNS is used, the endpoint first has to obtain the transport address of its authorized gatekeeper before it can send the GRQ message. The endpoint performs this task by initiating a DNS resource record query for the transport address by using the gatekeeper's domain and the RAS service (if applicable).

The gatekeepers can be identified by e-mail addresses, such as gk-ID@gk-domain, or by URLs, such as ras://gk-ID@gk-domain or ras://gk-domain/gk-ID (where ras is the protocol used by the gatekeeper, gk-domain is the DNS domain name of the gatekeepers, and gk-ID is the identification of the gatekeeper in this gk-domain). The users who are subscribed for H.323 telephony to this gk-domain can be identified by e-mail addresses such as user-ID@gk-domain or by URLs such as h323://user-ID@gk-domain or h323://gk-domain/user-ID (where h323 is a service consisting of H.225.0-RAS and H.225.0-Q.931 protocols, gk-domain is the DNS domain name of the gatekeepers, and user-ID is the identification of the user in this gk-domain).

In order to discover the gatekeeper, the endpoint can perform an SRV [GUL00] or TXT [ROSE93] resource record query by using the domain name in the gk-domain of the user's e-mail address or in the URL. The SRV record query is made for the transport address of the ras service in the gk-domain. Because the SRV resource record is not widely supported, you should use the TXT resource record query next if the SRV record query fails. The TXT record response will consist of the transport address or an A-record containing the fully qualified domain name. The A-record query will then yield the transport address in the response. If the resource record response consists only of the IP address and not the port, then the well-known port of 1719 is used. The endpoint unicasts the GRQ message at the transport address of the discovered gatekeeper.

We describe some of the fields in GRQ as follows:

rasAddress. This field consists of the transport address of the endpoint at which the gatekeeper sends H225.0-RAS messages.

gatekeeperIdentifier. This field consists of a character string that identifies the gatekeeper that normally provides service to the endpoint. A null string implies that you can use any gatekeeper. As an example, if the Internet Service Provider (ISP; in this case, isp1) identified gatekeepers through e-mail addresses, then gk1@isp1.com refers to a gatekeeper with an identification of gk1 in the isp1.com domain. The string *@isp1.com, where * is the wild card, refers to any gatekeeper in the isp1.com domain.

endpointAlias. This field consists of a series of alias addresses that the service provider normally assigns that identifies the user or the endpoint. If the addresses belong to the user and not to the endpoint, the user can use any authorized endpoint. Otherwise, the user is tied to the endpoint. These addresses could be of various types, such as e-mail, E.164, a URL, or any unique character string. For example, the ISP (isp1) might provide User 1 with an E.164 address of (+1) 503-400-5000, an e-mail address of user1@isp1.com, and a URL of h323://isp1.com/user1 or h323://user1@isp1.com. A caller on an analog phone will use the E.164 address to reach User 1 because the analog phone only has digits available as a user interface. A caller on a PC that has a browser might use the URL to reach User 1 because that method is most convenient.

The gatekeepers listen for GRQ messages on the preconfigured and well-known transport addresses. When a gatekeeper receives a GRQ message, it performs a series of checks to determine whether to allow the terminal to use the services that it provides. The checks depend on the policy of the service provider. The policy might include checking the gatekeeperIdentifier and endpointAlias fields to verify that they include the domain that is serviced by this gatekeeper, authenticating the user, determining whether network resources are available, and so on. The gatekeeper might use the authentication server and the user policy server to perform the checks. If the checks pass, the gatekeeper responds to the endpoint with a GCF message; otherwise, it responds with GRJ at the transport address that is specified in the rasAddress field of the GRQ message. Some of the fields in GCF are described as follows:

gatekeeperIdentifier. This field consists of a character string that identifies the gatekeeper. The endpoint should use this string in all subsequent H225.0-RAS messages that it sends to the gatekeeper.

rasAddress. This field consists of the transport address of the gatekeeper at which the endpoint sends H225.0-RAS messages.

User Registration

After the endpoint has discovered a gatekeeper, its next step is to register the user and the associated endpoint with that gatekeeper. If the endpoint multicasts GRQ, multiple gatekeepers might respond with GCF. In this case, the endpoint should pick one gatekeeper with which to register. The endpoint initiates registration by sending RRQ to the gatekeeper at the transport address specified by the rasAddress field in the GCF message. Some of the fields in RRQ are described as follows:

callSignalAddress. This field consists of the transport address of the endpoint at which the gatekeeper sends H225.0-Q.931 messages. Note that H225.0-Q.931 signaling might not be directly between the endpoints;

instead, it can also be routed via the gatekeeper. We will cover H225.0-Q.931 signal routing later in the section titled, "Call Models."

terminalAlias. This field consists of one or more alias addresses that are assigned to the user. Refer to the description of the endpointAlias field in the GRQ message.

gatekeeperIdentifier. This field consists of the character string that is provided in the gatekeeperIdentifier field of the GCF message.

endpointIdentifier. This field consists of a character string that identifies the endpoint. If the gatekeeper provided this string in a prior registration, then the endpoint should use it in this field; otherwise, the string is null.

Upon receiving RRQ, the gatekeeper performs a series of checks to determine whether to allow the endpoint to register. The checks depend on the policy of the service provider. The gatekeeper might use the authentication server and the user policy server in order to perform the checks. If the checks pass, the gatekeeper responds to the endpoint with RCF; otherwise, it responds with RRJ. We describe some of the fields in RCF as follows:

callSignalAddress. This field consists of the transport address of the gatekeeper at which the endpoint sends H225.0-Q.931 messages. Note that H225.0-Q.931 signaling might not directly occur between the endpoints. Instead, it can also be routed via the gatekeeper. We will cover H225.0-Q.931 signal routing later in the section titled, "Call Models."

terminalAlias. This field consists of the user addresses that the gatekeeper registers. If the addresses registered are different from those that the endpoint in RRQ provides, then the endpoint should update its list of addresses to match the gatekeeper's. Refer to the description of the endpointAlias field in the GRQ message.

endpointIdentifier. This field consists of a character string that identifies the endpoint to the gatekeeper. The endpoint should use this string in subsequent messages as its identification.

preGrantedARQ. This field specifies whether the endpoint has to request authorization before making or answering calls with the use of the ARQ message or whether the endpoint has pregranted authorization for all incoming and outgoing calls.

At the end of a successful registration, the endpoint and the gatekeeper have exchanged the transport addresses at which they will receive H.225.0-Q.931 and H.225.0 RAS messages. You should note that the entity that was registered with the gatekeeper was the user and the associated endpoint. The user can use any authorized endpoint in order to register with the gatekeeper. The H.323 recommendation enables the user to register from multiple endpoints simultaneously and enables multiple users to register from the same endpoint simultaneously.

User/Gatekeeper Authentication and Message Integrity

All H.225.0-Q.931 and H.225.0-RAS messages have the cryptoTokens field. The sender of the message creates an authenticator in the cryptoTokens field. The receiver of the message uses the authenticator in the cryptoTokens field in order to authenticate the sender and to check the integrity of the message. Later in the chapters dealing with security, we will cover the details concerning how the authenticator is created along with all aspects of security in H.323.

The first message between the endpoint and the gatekeeper is a *Gateway Request* (GRQ) message (sent by the endpoint and received by the Gateway Confirm, or GCF). If security is used, the cryptoTokens field in GRQ will contain the authenticator that is generated from the shared secret, the fields of the message, a random number, and a timestamp, along with the use of the mandatory HMAC-SHA1 authentication algorithm. The gatekeeper extracts the user identification and the authenticator from the terminalAlias/ endpointAlias and cryptoTokens fields, respectively. With the identification and authenticator provided by the endpoint, the gatekeeper acts as a proxy in order for the endpoint to authenticate the user with some back-end authentication server. Credit card, calling card, or prepaid card users might all require different authentication servers. The choice of authentication servers can also vary from one service provider to another, and the protocols that you need in order to interact with the different authentication servers can also vary. These changes in the authentication protocols (depending on which authentication server you are using) are hidden from the endpoint. The endpoint has a consistent, unified H225.0-RAS protocol that it uses to provide the authentication information, and the gatekeeper provides the necessary interface in order to interact with the authentication server. The gatekeeper can also perform authentication, and in this case, the gatekeeper is also the authentication server.

If the authentication passes and other checks performed by the gatekeeper are also successful, then the gatekeeper creates an authenticator in the cryptoTokens field of the GCF message and sends the message to the endpoint. The endpoint uses the authenticator to check the message integrity and authenticates the gatekeeper.

The gatekeeper does not have to authenticate the user at the time of discovery, especially when GRQ is multicast and multiple gatekeepers might potentially have to authenticate the same user with the authentication server. The user can be authenticated later at the time the endpoint registers with the gatekeeper with the RRQ message. The endpoint will also authenticate the gatekeeper with the RCF message instead of the GCF message.

Authentication is computationally intensive, which might reduce the number of endpoints that the gatekeeper can simultaneously service. If the endpoints and the gatekeepers are operating in a relatively secure environment (such as an intranet), then it is possible to perform authentication and message integrity only at the time of discovery or registration. If the endpoints and gatekeepers are operating in an insecure environment (such as the Internet), then we recommend that message integrity and authentication be performed for all messages unless economic or other such important reasons outweigh the benefits from security.

Admission Control

The gatekeeper uses admission control to authorize each outgoing or incoming call to and from the endpoint. The endpoint requests alias address resolution and call authorization in the ARQ message, and the gatekeeper provides the resolved address and call authorization by responding with the ACF message or denies authorization by responding with the ARJ message. If admission control is on a per-registration basis and not on a per-call basis, then the gatekeeper informs the endpoint of this policy in the preGrantedARQ field of the RCF message. The endpoint can still use ARQ for alias address resolution but does not request call authorization. Some of the fields in the ARQ message are as follows:

endpointIdentifier. This field consists of the endpoint identification for the gatekeeper. The gatekeeper previously provided this identifier in the RCF message.

destinationInfo. This field consists of the destination user's (called party's) alias address.

bandwidth. This field consists of the total bandwidth that audio and video need (excluding the headers RTP/UDP/IP). Normally, calls are bidirectional, so this bandwidth includes audio and video in both directions. Bandwidth that data consumes, if any, is not included.

callIdentifier. This field is a 128-bit globally unique identifier [00H2250] that is unique in space and time. This identifier associates all H.225.0 messages, both H.225.0-RAS and H.225.0-Q.931, between all entities within the same point-to-point call. For example, if there are multiple simultaneous calls between the endpoint and the gatekeeper, then this field distinguishes between H.225.0-RAS messages belonging to different calls on the same UDP transport. Also, a call that receives admission through ARQ and ACF can subsequently be associated with the setup message through this field.

answerCall. This field specifies whether the endpoint is receiving or making a call.

willSupplyUUIEs. If this field is set to *true*, then the endpoint has the capability to provide H.225.0-Q.931 message information in IRR messages if the gatekeeper requests.

When the gatekeeper receives the ARQ message, it can use the user policy server and the QoS policy server to decide whether it should provide authorization for the call and can use the address resolution server to resolve the alias address. The user policy server contains the user's profile with information such as the geographic locations where calls can be made, restrictions on the duration of the call, restrictions on network QoS during certain times of the day, and so on. The QoS policy server configures the network with the QoS that is requested for the call. Some of the fields in the ACF message are as follows:

bandwidth. This field consists of the maximum network bandwidth that the audio and video streams can use.

destCallSignalAddress. This field provides the routable transport address (IP address and port) of the destination entity to which H.225.0-Q.931 messages should be sent.

destinationInfo. This field consists of the E.164 address that the gateway uses in order to complete the call to the destination terminal. We previously described the use of this field in this chapter in the destinationAddress field of the Setup message. The calling endpoint copies this field in the destinationAddress field of the Setup message that is destined for the gateway.

destExtraCallInfo. This field consists of additional E.164 addresses that the H.320 gateway uses. We previously described the use of this field in this chapter in the destExtraCallInfo field of the Setup message. The calling endpoint copies this field in the destExtraCallInfo field of the Setup message that is destined for the gateway.

remoteExtensionAddress. This field consists of the destination user's alias address in case the H.323 gateways need it in order to route the call to the destination terminal. We previously described the use of this field in this chapter in the remoteExtensionAddress field of the Setup message. The calling endpoint copies this field in the remoteExtensionAddress field of the Setup message that is destined for the endpoint.

uuiesRequested. This field consists of a list of H.225.0-Q.931 messages that the endpoint will provide to the gatekeeper in IRR messages during a call. This list includes all H.225.0-Q.931 messages in both directions between the two endpoints in a call. The gatekeeper can make this request only if the endpoint specified this capability in the ARQ message.

willRespondToIRR. If this field is set to *true* and the endpoint sets the needsResponse field in the IRR message to *true*, then the gatekeeper will respond to the unsolicited IRR message with an *Information Acknowledgement* (IACK) or *Information Request Negative Acknowledgement* (INAK) message.

Address Resolution

Normally, we do not use transport addresses to address users, because they are hard to remember. The ideal solution is to address users by their full names, but this action might not guarantee that two people who are using this service will not have the same full name. That is, full names might not generate unique addresses, and you might have to add some extra information in order to make them unique. H.323 enables various methods of addressing users, including the use of a unique string consisting of any information. These addresses are called alias addresses, and they are generally in the form of an E.164 address, e-mail address, URL, or a unique string. All of these alias addresses are not routable on the IP network, so they need to be resolved to the transport address (consisting of an IP address and port). If the alias address consists of the transport address, then we do not need to perform address resolution.

The user who is making a call uses his or her endpoint to provide one or more alias addresses of the destination user in the destinationInfo field of the ARQ message. In Chapter 5, "Inter-Domain Communication," we describe the method that the gatekeeper uses to resolve the alias address to the transport address (IP address and port). In this chapter, we will assume that the gatekeeper resolves the alias address through the use of some address resolution server and provides the transport address to the endpoint in the destCallSignalAddress field of the ACF message. If the alias address cannot be resolved, the gatekeeper responds with an ARJ message.

If the destination entity is another IP endpoint, then the transport address of the IP address and the port number is sufficient in order to route the call to its destination. If the destination entity is on a non-IP network, however, such as a telephone on the PSTN, then the transport address is for the gateway that connects to the non-IP network on which the destination resides. The routing instructions for the gateway are contained in the destinationInfo, destExtraCallInfo, and remoteExtensionAddress fields of the ACF message, and you should copy them to the destinationAddress, destExtraCallInfo, and remoteExtensionAddress fields of the H.225.0-Q.931 Setup message (respectively) by the calling endpoint in order to initiate the call.

QoS

In the chapters of this book that deal with QoS, we cover the topic of how the endpoint requests and receives QoS from the network. The simplistic view consists of Endpoint 1 and Gatekeeper 1 in Domain 1, Endpoint 2 and Gatekeeper 2 in Domain 2, and the backbone network separating the two domains. The QoS policy server manages QoS in its own domain, and based on the *Service Level Agreement* (SLA) between Domain 1 and the backbone network, the QoS policy server manages traffic to and from the backbone network. The following list shows how QoS is provided to a call from Endpoint 1 to Endpoint 2:

1. Endpoint 1 requests the maximum bandwidth needed by the audio/video call in the bandwidth field of the ARQ message. The callIdentifier field in the ARQ message identifies the call. The bandwidth request is essentially an estimate, because we do not know the capabilities of Endpoint 2. An audio call using G.711 will use a much higher bandwidth than a G.723.1 call. Also, if Endpoint 2 does not have video capabilities, then the bandwidth that is used in the call will be substantially less than the original estimate.
2. Gatekeeper 1 acts as a proxy for Endpoint 1 and requests its QoS policy server to configure the network in order to reserve the requested bandwidth for this specific call.
3. If the QoS policy server provides the bandwidth requested, it configures its Domain 1 and the backbone network. Then, its response is carried by the gatekeeper in the bandwidth field of the ACF message to Endpoint 1. If the QoS policy server cannot provide the bandwidth requested, Gatekeeper 1 responds with an ARJ message. Endpoint 1 can then decide whether to make a new request that has less bandwidth.
4. If admission is granted, Endpoint 1 sends a setup message to Endpoint 2 with the total bandwidth reflected in both the forward and reverse channels of the openLogicalChannel structures in the fastStart field. Endpoint 2 picks the coders among the choices that exist in the setup message and requests the exact maximum bandwidth in the ARQ message from its Gatekeeper 2. The QoS policy server for Gatekeeper 2 will reserve the bandwidth in its own Domain 2 and on the backbone network. Endpoint 2 responds to Endpoint 1 with the forward and reverse channels in a call proceeding, alerting, or connect message that it will use for the call.

5. Endpoint 1 adjusts downwards the new maximum bandwidth requested by sending the BRQ message to Gatekeeper 1. The callIdentifier field in the BRQ message identifies this call. Gatekeeper 1 requests for the QoS policy server to reduce the maximum bandwidth for the call, and it responds to Endpoint 1 with a BCF message.
6. During the call, if Endpoint 1 has to increase or decrease the bandwidth of the call, it sends the new total bandwidth in the bandwidth field of the BRQ message. The callIdentifier field in the BRQ message identifies this call.
7. Gatekeeper 1 requests the QoS policy server to configure the network with the new bandwidth requested for this call.
8. If the QoS policy server reserves the new bandwidth requested, Gatekeeper 1 then carries the response in the bandwidth field of the BCF message to Endpoint 1. If the QoS policy server cannot reserve the new bandwidth requested, Gatekeeper 1 responds with the BRJ message to Endpoint 1.
9. If Endpoint 1 receives a BCF message from Gatekeeper 1, it sends to Endpoint 2 the openLogicalChannel message containing the additional bandwidth in the traffic specification. Endpoint 2 requests the new total bandwidth in BRQ from its Gatekeeper 2. If Gatekeeper 2 responds with BCF, Endpoint 2 sends the openLogicalChannelAck message to Endpoint 1. If Gatekeeper 2 responds with a BRJ message, Endpoint 2 sends the openLogicalChannelReject message to Endpoint 1. Endpoint 1 can then request for Gatekeeper 1 to reduce the total bandwidth.

Note that the bandwidth requests in ARQ and BRQ include the total bandwidth of the call. This total bandwidth includes audio and video streams in both directions (streams from Endpoint 1 to Endpoint 2 and streams from Endpoint 2 to Endpoint 1), but we do not include the RTP/UDP/IP and link-layer headers in the calculation. In contrast, each openLogicalChannel message contains bandwidth that is needed by one stream that is being transmitted, and it also includes the RTP/UDP/IP headers in the calculation. The total bandwidth (adjusted for headers) that is granted for the call should be greater than or equal to all of the individual bandwidth requests in the openLogicalChannel messages from both endpoints.

Accounting

H.323 provides a mechanism through which we can measure the duration of a call. The start of the call normally occurs when the called party sends the H.225.0-Q.931 connect message to the calling party. The end of the call occurs when either the calling or the called party sends the H.225.0-Q.931

ReleaseComplete message to the other party. The accounting information regarding the call, known as the *Call-Detail Record* (CDR), can consist of information such as the identification of the two parties, the time the call started, the duration of the call, and so on. We describe the CDR in Chapter 5. The gatekeeper or the accounting server can generate the CDR. In fact, any network entity—such as a gateway—can generate the CDR. Terminals belonging to users are not normally trusted, so they are seldom used to generate the CDR. If the accounting server generates the accounting information, then the gatekeeper acts as a proxy for the endpoint in providing the information that is needed for the call. The accounting information for the call that is needed from the endpoint includes the beginning and the end of the call. This process occurs as follows:

1. The endpoint must be capable of providing information to the gatekeeper regarding the reception or transmission of certain H.225.0-Q.931 messages. These H.225.0-Q.931 messages are encapsulated in the IRR message to the gatekeeper. The endpoint sets the willSupplyUUIEs field to *true* in the ARQ message if it has this capability.
2. The gatekeeper sets up the endpoint as follows:
   - The gatekeeper specifies in the uuiesRequested field of the ACF message that it should be provided with the connect and ReleaseComplete messages when they occur in the call.
   - If the gatekeeper responds to the IRR message with a positive acknowledgement IACK message, then it sets the willRespondToIRR field of the ACF message to *true*. We recommend for the gatekeeper to provide an acknowledgement, because IRR messages containing critical accounting information might get lost on the network.
3. When the endpoint initiates a call, it performs the following tasks:
   - When it receives the connect message in a call, the endpoint encapsulates the message in IRR and sends it to the gatekeeper. This action marks the start of the call. The gatekeeper forwards the information to the accounting server.
   - When the endpoint receives the ReleaseComplete message in a call, it encapsulates the message in IRR and sends it to the gatekeeper. This action marks the end of the call. The gatekeeper forwards the information to the accounting server.

Call Termination

You can allocate the network resources (such as bandwidth) for the call during the ARQ/ACF exchange. The endpoint initiates the call with the setup message; the call is established after the connect message; and the call ends after the ReleaseComplete message. Note that closeLogicalChannel/ closeLogicalChannelAck and endSession messages are necessary in order to close the H.245 session and do not appear in Figure 3.22. At the end of the call, the network resources that are allocated for the call have to be reallocated. Because H 225.0-Q.931 signaling is between the endpoints, the gatekeeper needs to be informed of the end of the call. This action takes place by the endpoint with the DRQ message and the callIdentifier field that identifies the call that ended. The gatekeeper responds with the DCF message.

The gatekeeper can also send the DRQ message with the callIdentifier field in order to force the endpoint to terminate the call that is identified by the callIdentifier field. This action is performed if, say, the prepaid card user has run out of credit. The endpoint sends ReleaseComplete to the other endpoint in order to terminate the call and then responds with a DCF message to the gatekeeper.

User Deregistration

The endpoint or the gatekeeper can initiate deregistration by sending the URQ message with the endpointAlias and endpointIdentifier fields. If the endpoint receives the URQ message with the user who is specified by the endpointAlias field, it responds with a UCF message and the gatekeeper cancels the registration of the user who is specified in endpointAlias with the endpoint specified in endpointIdentifier. If the gatekeeper receives the URQ message from the endpoint, it responds with a URJ message if the registration does not exist or initiates a UCF message in order to cancel the existing registration of the user who is specified in endpointAlias (with the endpoint specified in endpointIdentifier).

The user might be registered on multiple endpoints—and an endpoint might have registered multiple users—but the URQ message uniquely specifies the user in endpointAlias who is associated with the endpoint in endpointIdentifier whose registration should be cancelled. If message security is used, each message can be authenticated and the integrity of the message can be checked.

Lightweight Registration

Deregistration does not always happen in an orderly manner with a URQ/UCF message exchange. Sometimes the endpoint fails unexpectedly and its registration lingers until detected by the gatekeeper. Stray registrations can cause new registrations to be rejected if the gatekeeper is at full capacity. To avoid this condition, either the gatekeeper can periodically ping each registered endpoint and delete the registration if the endpoint does not reply or the endpoints can periodically provide a heartbeat. We use the latter method, which is called lightweight registration. Lightweight registration is used to report to the gatekeeper when the registered endpoint fails and is implemented as follows:

1. The endpoint suggests an expiration time in the timeToLive field of the RRQ message, during which its registration with the gatekeeper must be refreshed.
2. The gatekeeper enables lightweight registration by providing the expiration time in the timeToLive field of the RCF message. The expiration time provided by the gatekeeper might be different from the expiration time that the endpoint provides.
3. The endpoint then periodically sends the RRQ message with the keepAlive field set to specify a lightweight RRQ for refreshing the registration. The lightweight RRQ message consists of the minimum number of fields (which is why we call it lightweight).
4. If the lightweight RRQ message is not received within the expiration time, the gatekeeper deregisters the endpoint.

Lightweight registration wastes network bandwidth because multiple endpoints periodically send heartbeat messages to the gatekeeper. You should limit its use on the Internet.

Gatekeeper Failure and Load Balancing

We have not yet discussed what happens when the endpoint's primary gatekeeper is not available. This situation can happen when the gatekeeper is non-operational, near full capacity, more loaded than other gatekeepers, close to down time due to scheduled maintenance, or for any other reasons. During normal conditions when the endpoint discovers and registers with the gatekeeper by using GRQ and RRQ (respectively), the gatekeeper provides a list of alternate secondary gatekeepers in the alternateGatekeeper field of the GCF and the RCF messages, respectively. For each alternate gatekeeper, the alternateGatekeeper field provides the transport address where the endpoint will send the H.225.0-RAS messages and provides the priority of the gatekeeper. The endpoint stores the alternate gatekeepers list. If the gatekeeper is non-operational at the time of discovery or unexpectedly goes down after discovery, the endpoint can discover and register with a secondary gatekeeper for the alternate gatekeeper list. The endpoint sends the GRQ message to the transport address of the gatekeeper that has the highest priority. If the highest priority gatekeeper is also unavailable, the endpoint will continue down the alternative gatekeeper list until some gatekeeper accepts registration or until the list is exhausted.

If the gatekeeper is near full capacity or is close to down time due to scheduled maintenance—or it has knowledge of other gatekeepers that are less lightly loaded—then at the time of discovery or registration, it responds to GRQ and RRQ with a list of alternate gatekeepers in the altGKInfo field of the GRJ and RRJ messages, respectively. In addition to the subfields in the alternateGatekeeper field, the altGKInfo field also specifies whether the alternate gatekeeper list consists of primary or secondary gatekeepers. A list of primary gatekeepers means that the first available alternate gatekeeper (according to priority) will become the endpoint's permanent gatekeeper. This situation changes the primary gatekeeper with which the endpoint must register every time at the time of discovery. A list of secondary gatekeepers means that the alternate gatekeeper list consists of temporary gatekeepers that will serve the endpoint only during the duration of one registration.

If the gatekeeper is close to scheduled maintenance, it can deregister all registered endpoints by sending URQ messages to them. This action will force the endpoints to deregister by responding with a UCF message to the gatekeeper and enables the gatekeeper to go down in an orderly manner.

H.225.0-RAS Transport Protocol

The transport protocol for H.225.0-RAS is UDP. H.225.0-RAS is designed to run on networks such as the Internet, where packets are lost due to congestion on the network. Because UDP does not provide protection against packet loss, you must implement resilience against packet loss into the H.225.0-RAS protocol. The following tools are provided in the protocol to enable the development of an algorithm in order to provide resiliency against packet loss between two entities (E_1 and E_2) on the Internet:

- A request message from E_1 has a corresponding response message from E_2, which enables E_1 to detect whether E_2 received the request message.
- All messages have a sequence number field (requestSeqNum). This field is monotonically increased for a request message from E_1. Request messages that are retransmitted should have the same requestSeqNum field.
- A request message from E_1 might have an associated retry counter and timeout timer. A response message that does not arrive within the timeout period is considered lost, and the request message is retransmitted. If

retransmission equals the maximum number of retries that are permitted, then the communication between E_1 and E_2 ends.

- The requestSeqNum field in the response message from E_2 has the same value as the requestSeqNum field in the request message from E_1.
- If E_2 is not ready to respond to the request message from E_1, it sends the RIP message within the timeout period. E_1 will then reset its timer. The recommended timeout period is three or five seconds for all H.225.0-RAS messages.
- If E_1 receives the RIP message before the timeout period, it resets its timeout timer.

Call Models

In Figure 3.22, the H.225.0-Q.931 signaling is between the two endpoints (1 and 2) that are involved in the call. This type of signaling is known as direct call signaling. There are some disadvantages of direct call signaling: 1) if the called endpoint (Endpoint 2) is powered down due to failure or for any other reason, then the incoming call will not complete; 2) if User 2 on Endpoint 2 is unavailable, then the call will not be answered unless there is a mechanism through which Endpoint 2 can complete the call through the answering machine; and 3) terminals that are in the hands of users are usually not trusted to provide accurate accounting information, such as the start and the end of the call. To overcome these disadvantages, H.323 provides a second type of signaling known as gatekeeper routed call signaling. In this signaling, the H.225.0-Q.931 signaling is routed via the gatekeepers that are involved in the call. The gatekeeper configures the endpoint for this routing at the registration time by providing its own transport address in the callSignalAddress field of the RCF message. The endpoint sends all H.225.0-Q.931 messages to the gatekeeper, and the gatekeeper routes the messages to their proper destinations. In this case, the gatekeepers act as an H.323application-level router and also as a firewall. They can inspect and change the messages to and from the endpoint in a call. Then, if the called endpoint is down, the gatekeeper can route the incoming call to voice mail (or to an answering machine). The gatekeeper that is routing the H.225.0-Q.931 messages can also start and stop the call for accounting purposes without relying on the terminal. Despite some advantages, gatekeeper-routed call signaling has an important disadvantage: it reduces the gatekeeper's scalability as far as the number of endpoints that can be serviced simultaneously (due to the extra computational burden of the H.225.0-Q.931 messages).

Gatekeeper-Routed Call Signaling

In gatekeeper-routed call signaling, the call-control signaling (H.245) can either be routed directly between the two endpoints or via the gatekeeper. Routing call control via the gatekeeper further decreases the scalability of the gatekeeper. Routing call control directly does not give the gatekeeper access to H.245 messages that are needed for services such as gatekeeper-controlled, ad-hoc multi-point conferences (described in Chapter 4, "Multi-Point Conference"). The direct routed call control signaling is for further study in the H.323 recommendations; therefore, both call signaling and call control are routed via the gatekeeper in the implementations that exist to date. Because call signaling and call control use two TCP connections, the scalability of the gatekeeper is reduced because most operating systems have an upper limit on the total number of ports that can be opened (which translates to a limit on the number of endpoints that can connect simultaneously to the gatekeeper). For this reason, H.245 is usually tunneled in H.225.0-Q.931, thereby reducing the TCP connections to one per endpoint-gatekeeper pair. Multiple calls between the same endpoint and the gatekeeper still use the same TCP connection because the callIdentifier field in H.225.0-Q.931 messages identifies the different calls.

Figure 3.23 illustrates a call flow for the gatekeeper-routed call signaling with H.245 tunneling and pregranted ARQ. We can compare this call flow with the call flow of the direct call-signaling model shown in Figure 3.22.

Gatekeeper Discovery and User Registration

Gatekeeper discovery and user registration involves the same steps as those that we show in Figure 3.22. As part of registration, the gatekeeper provides pregranted ARQ in the RCF message so that the endpoint does not have to request admission on a per-call basis. The gatekeeper also provides its own transport address in the callSignalAddress field of the RCF message in order to configure the endpoint for gatekeeper-routed signaling.

Call Initiation

When User 1 (who has an address of h323://user1@isp1.com) calls User 2 (who has an address of h323://user1@isp1.com), Endpoint 1 sends the setup message to Gatekeeper 1. Some of the fields in the setup message are as follows:

sourceAddress. This field identifies the user or subscriber to the gatekeeper and consists of alias addresses of User 1 that were returned by Gatekeeper

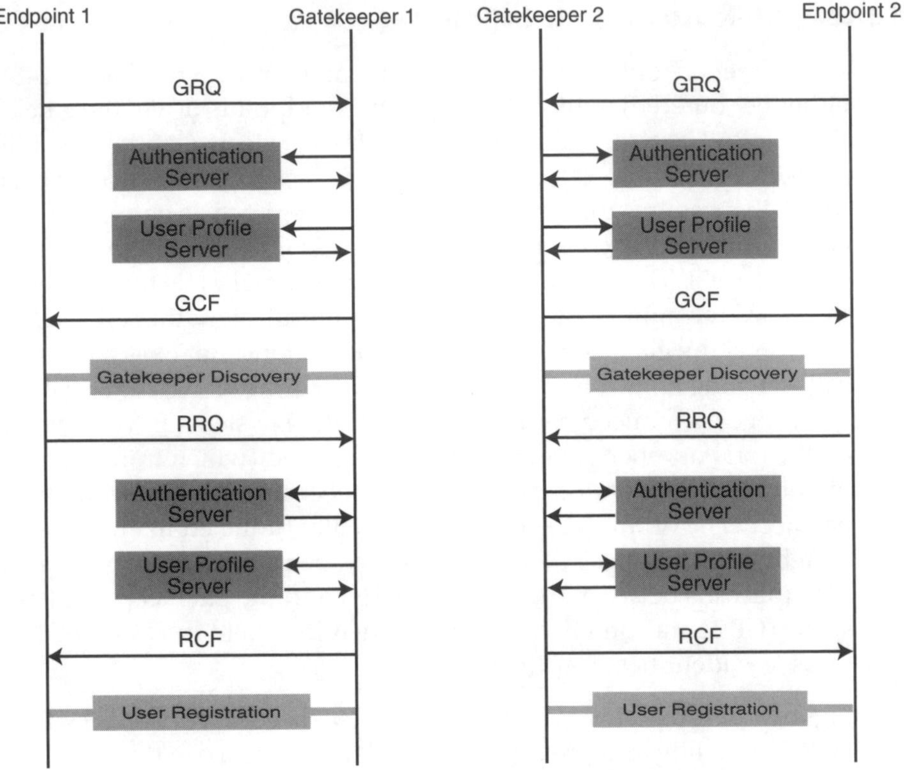

Figure 3.23 Gatekeeper-routed call signaling, H.245 tunneling, and a pregranted ARQ.

1 in the terminalAlias field of the RCF message. This field consists of the alias address h323://user1@isp1.com.

endpointIdentifier. This field identifies the endpoint to the gatekeeper and consists of the character string that was returned by Gatekeeper 1 in the endpointIdentifier field of the RCF message.

remoteExtensionAddress. This field consists of the alias address of User 2 that might have to be resolved to a routable address by various network entities. This field consists of the alias address h323://user2@isp2.com.

callIdentifier. This field consists of a globally unique identification number for this call (generated by Endpoint 1).

fastStart. This field consists of one or more openLogicalChannel structures. Each openLogicalChannel structure specifies the forward logical channel parameters and the reverse logical channel parameters. For example, Endpoint 1 might offer a choice of G.723.1 or G.711. The G.723.1 QoS parameters for both the forward and reverse logical channels of the first openLogicalChannel structure might include guaranteed load, average rate 2000 bps, peak rate 2000 bps, minimum packet size 44 bytes, maximum

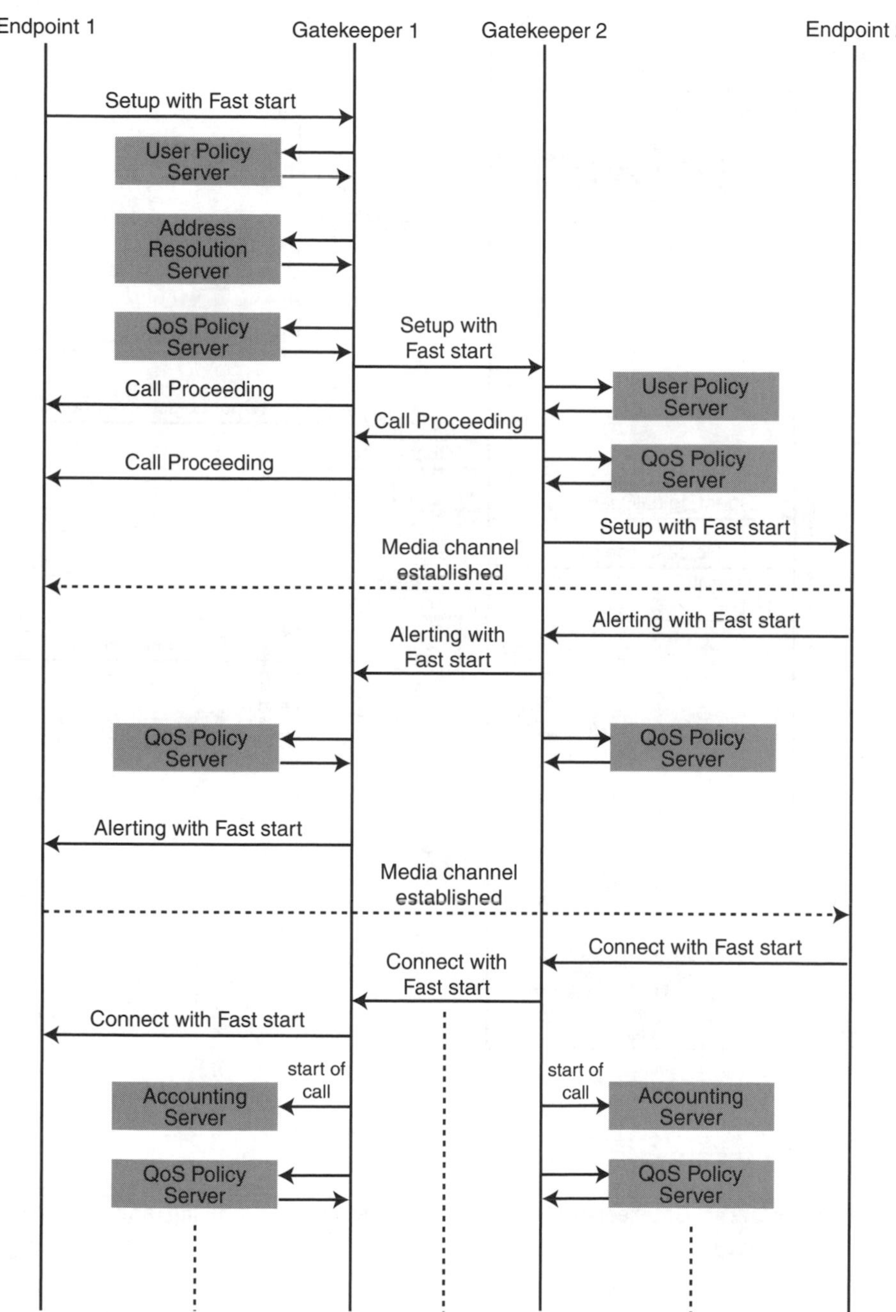

Figure 3.23 Gatekeeper-routed call signaling, H.245 tunneling, and a pregranted ARQ. (Continued)

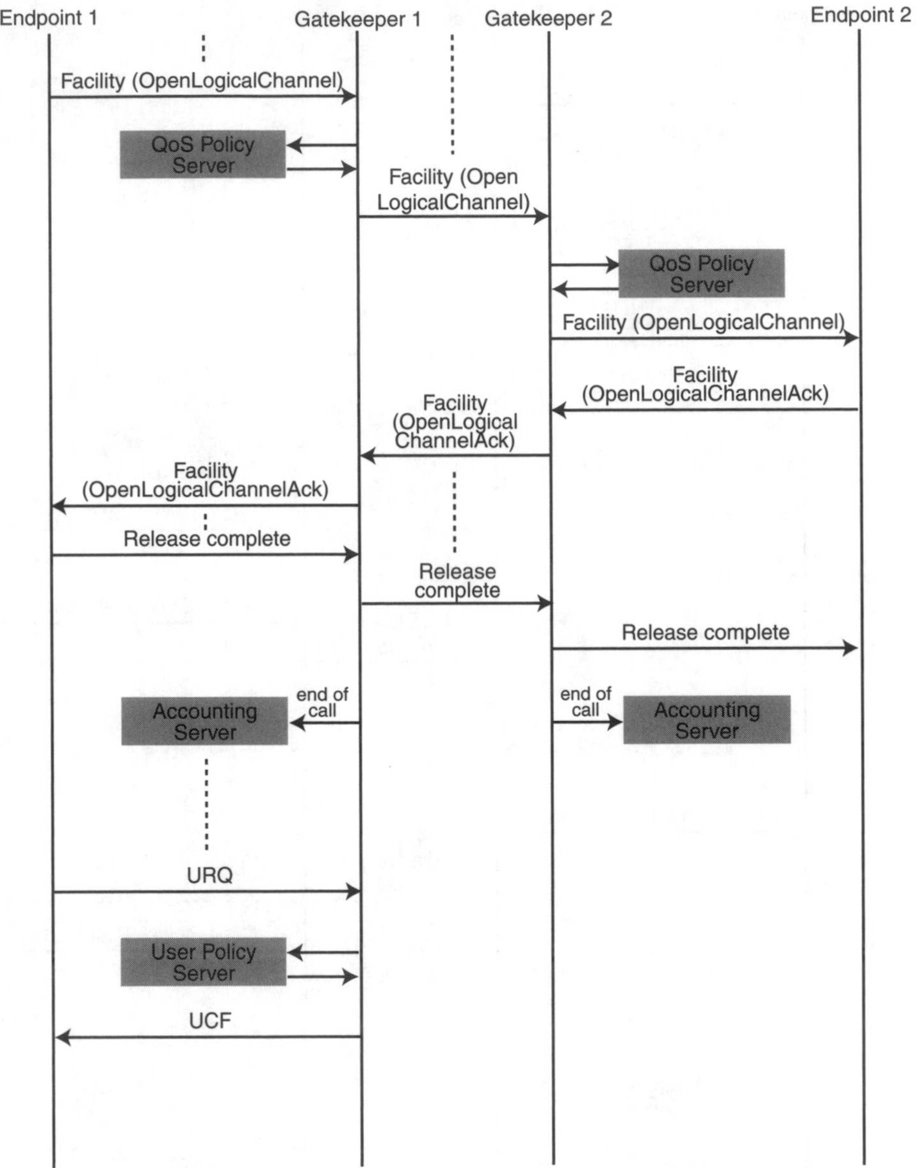

Figure 3.23 Gatekeeper-routed call signaling, H.245 tunneling, and a pregranted ARQ. (Continued)

packet size 60 bytes, and bucket size 60 bytes. The G.711 QoS parameters for both the forward and reverse logical channels of the second openLogicalChannel structure might include guaranteed load, average rate 9333 bps, peak rate 9333 bps, minimum packet size 41 bytes, maximum packet size 280 bytes, and bucket size 280 bytes. Because the openLogicalChannel structures also include the transport addresses of the media channels, the gatekeeper (acting as a firewall) might change these transport addresses.

Upon receiving the setup message, Gatekeeper 1 performs the following functions:

- Uses the address resolution server to resolve the alias address of h323://user2@isp2.com in the remoteExtensionAddress field to the transport address of Gatekeeper 2 (in Chapter 5, we explain the mechanism through which the address is resolved)
- Checks the policy that is preconfigured for h323://user1@isp1 in the sourceAddress field by the user policy server to determine whether to grant admission to User 1 to make the call
- Uses the traffic specification in the openLogicalChannel structures in order to estimate the QoS requirements for the call. (Because we do not know whether Endpoint 2 will pick G723.1 or G.711, Gatekeeper 1 might request the QoS policy server to make QoS reservations based on the higher bandwidth of 18666 bps for G.711, compared with 4000 bps for G.723.1.) Then, if Endpoint 2 picks G.723.1, Gatekeeper 1 can request the QoS policy server to adjust the QoS reservations downwards. If Gatekeeper 1 makes QoS reservations based on G.723.1 and Endpoint 2 picks G.711, however, then Gatekeeper 1 might not be capable of adjusting the QoS reservations upward if the network does not have the capacity. One solution is to wait for the call proceeding or alerting message that will contain the exact traffic specifications from openLogicalChannel structures picked by Endpoint 2.

  Another problem to consider is whether Gatekeeper 1 should make QoS reservations before or after the call is established via the connect message. Any QoS reservations that are made before the connect message might have to be cancelled if User 2 is not available to take the call. Making reservations after the connect message might run the risk of not getting a reservation if the network does not have the capacity for another call, however. Also, if the connect message arrives at Gatekeeper 1 after the first few voice packets from User 2 arrive at Endpoint 1, then the initial voice packets will not be provided the QoS that User 1 requested. Unfortunately, there is no clear solution to this problem. Each solution comes with its own advantages and disadvantages.

If User 1 is denied admission, Gatekeeper 1 responds to Endpoint 1 with the ReleaseComplete message that ends the call. If User 1 is granted admission to make the call, Gatekeeper 1 forwards the setup message to Gatekeeper 2. Gatekeeper 2 performs the following functions:

- Checks the policy that is preconfigured for h323://user2@isp2 in the remoteExtensionAddress field by the user policy server in order to determine whether to grant admission to User 2 so that he or she can receive the call

- Uses the traffic specification in the openLogicalChannel structures to estimate the QoS requirements of the call. Gatekeeper 2 might make estimated QoS reservations by using the QoS Policy Server, or it might wait on the alerting message from Endpoint 2 when the exact traffic specifications will be available based on the openLogicalChannel structures picked by Endpoint 2. Or, it might wait on the connect message from Endpoint 2 when the call is established and accounting for the call starts.
- Because User 2 registered with Gatekeeper 2, the gatekeeper has the routable address of Endpoint 2. If the routable address is an IP address and port, then the setup message can simply be forwarded to the transport address of Endpoint 2. If the routable address is an E.164 address of Endpoint 2, then the call will be routed through a gateway. In this case, the setup message needs to be modified in order to provide routing instructions to the gateway. Gatekeeper 2 performs this function by adding the resolved E.164 address in the destinationAddress field. Gatekeeper 2 then sends the setup message to the transport address of an appropriate gateway. The gateway uses the E.164 address in the destinationAddress field in order to complete the call to Endpoint 2. If the call gets routed through multiple gateways, then you can use the alias address in remoteExtensionAddress to find the next gateway.

  User 2 might have multiple, simultaneous registrations with Gatekeeper 2 when using multiple endpoints. In this case, the gatekeeper uses the user policy server to determine the policy for User 2 on multiple registrations. If the policy includes ringing all registered endpoints, then the gatekeeper sends the setup message to all of the endpoints. The call is then completed by the first endpoint that sends the connect message, and the ReleaseComplete message is sent to all other endpoints. If the policy includes ringing the endpoints one at a time in order of priority, then the gatekeeper sends the setup message to the highest-priority endpoint. If there is no answer, the gatekeeper sends ReleaseComplete to that endpoint and sends the setup message to the next-highest priority endpoint. The gatekeeper continues its search until the call is answered or until it runs out of endpoints. The policy could be made conditional based on caller identification, day, time, and other factors. Suffice it to say, there are many ways to treat an incoming call. The call can be routed to different endpoints based on various factors. The user can set policies by preconfiguring the user policy server on how his or her incoming calls can be treated, and the service provider can check for unauthorized configuration before executing the policies.

While going through the admission control checks, Gatekeeper 2 can send a call proceeding message to Gatekeeper 1 if it cannot respond with another H.225.0-Q.931 message within the timeout period. Gatekeeper 1 forwards the call proceeding message to Endpoint 1. If User 2 is denied admission, Gatekeeper 2 responds to Gatekeeper 1 with the ReleaseComplete message. Gatekeeper 1 forwards the ReleaseComplete message to Endpoint 1, which ends the call. If User 2 is granted admission to receive the call, Gatekeeper 2 forwards the setup message to Endpoint 2.

Call Alerting

Upon receiving the setup message, Endpoint 2 checks the openLogicalChannel messages in the fastStart field. Endpoint 2 has a choice of picking either G.711 or G.723.1. If it picks G.723.1, it constructs the appropriate openLogicalChannel structure in the fastStart field of the alerting message and sends the message to Gatekeeper 2. The endpoint also alerts User 2. At this point, the voice channel from Endpoint 2 to Endpoint 1 is established.

Based on the traffic specifications in alerting, Gatekeeper 2 performs one of following functions:

- Adjusting the QoS reservation (if it made the reservation at setup time)
- Making the QoS reservation (if it did not make the reservation at setup time)
- Postponing making QoS reservations until it receives the connect message when accounting of the call starts

Regardless of the policy regarding when to make a QoS reservation, Gatekeeper 2 forwards the alerting message to Gatekeeper 1. Gatekeeper 1 also has the same choices as Gatekeeper 2 as to when to make QoS reservations. Gatekeeper 1, in turn, forwards the alerting message to Endpoint 1. Endpoint 1 provides the alerting message feedback to its User 1 in the form of a ringing tone, text in a dialog box, or by any other user-interface means. At this point, the voice channel from Endpoint 1 to Endpoint 2 is established.

Call Connection

When User 2 takes the call, Endpoint 2 sends the connect message to Gatekeeper 2. If the QoS reservation has not been made, Gatekeeper 2 uses the fastStart field to calculate the traffic specifications and requests the QoS policy server to make the reservations. If QoS reservations cannot be made, Gatekeeper 2 can terminate the call by sending the ReleaseComplete message to both Gatekeeper 1 and Endpoint 2. If you make a QoS reservation for the call, Gatekeeper 2 signals the accounting server to start collecting accounting information for the call. Gatekeeper 2 forwards the connect message to Gatekeeper 1, which then starts its own accounting and QoS reservation (if not already done). Gatekeeper 1 forwards the connect message to its Endpoint 1, and the call is established. If Gatekeepers 1 and 2 make QoS reservations at the time of the connect message, then it is critical for the connect message to reach Endpoint 1 before the first media packet arrives from Endpoint 2. If QoS reservations are made before the connect message, then there is a possibility that a rogue Endpoint 2 implementation might delay the connect message but use the media channels before sending the connect message.

During the call, you can open more media channels with the openLogicalChannel message tunneled in the facility message. The gatekeepers will have to make QoS reservations if requested by the endpoint in the openLogicalChannel message.

Call Termination

If H.245 messages are not used after the connect message, then the call can be terminated with the ReleaseComplete message. If any H.245 message is used after the connect message, then you should follow the procedures of H.245. The procedures include starting with endpoint capability exchange and master/slave determination and ending with the endSession message. Also, if a channel is opened with openLogicalChannel, then you should properly close it by using closeLogicalChannel. Note that Figure 3.23 does not show these messages. Because H.245 tunneling is used, the H.245 messages are tunneled in the facility message.

When User 1 hangs up, Endpoint 1 sends a ReleaseComplete message to Gatekeeper 1. Gatekeeper 1 forwards the ReleaseComplete message to Gatekeeper 2 and signals to its accounting server that the call has ended. Gatekeeper 2 forwards the ReleaseComplete message to Endpoint 2 and signals its accounting server that the call has ended. Endpoint 2 notifies its User 2 that the call has ended.

Gatekeeper 1 can also terminate the call by sending a ReleaseComplete message to both Endpoint 1 and Gatekeeper 2. This action is performed if, say, the prepaid card user has run out of credit.

User Deregistration

User deregistration involves the same steps as those shown in Figure 3.22.

References

00H2250 ITU-T Recommendation H.225.0. Call signalling protocols and media stream packetization for packet-based multimedia communication systems. November 2000.

00H245 ITU-T Recommendation H. 245. Control Protocol for Multimedia Communication. February 2000.

00H323 ITU-T Recommendation H. 323. Packet-based multimedia communications systems. November 2000.

97H320 ITU-T Recommendation H.320. Narrow-band visual telephone systems and terminal equipment. 1997.

98Q931 ITU-T Recommendation Q.931. ISDN user-network interface layer 3 specifications for basic call control. 1998.

GUL00 Gulbrandsen, A., et al. A DNS RR for specifying the location of services (DNS SRV). RFC 2782, February 2000.

H323D98 ITU-T Recommendation H.323 Annex D. Real-time facsimile over H.323 systems. September 1998.

HEL00 Hellstrom, G. RTP Payload for Text Conversation. RFC 2793, May 2000.

PERK97 Perkins, C., et al. RTP Payload for Redundant Voice Data. RFC 2198, September 1997.

ROSE93 Rosenbaum, R. Using the Domain Name System To Store Arbitrary String Attributes. RFC 1464, May 1993.

SCHU96 Schulzrinne, H., and Casner, S. RTP profile for voice and video conferences with minimal control. RFC 1890, January 1996.

TURL96 Turletti, T., and Huitema, C. RTP payload format for H.261 video streams. RFC 2032. October 1996.

WEN98 Wenger, S., et al. RTP Payload Format for the 1998 Version of ITU-T Recommendation H.263 Video (H.263+). RFC 2429, October 1998.

ZHU97 Zhu, C. RTP payload format for H.263 video streams. RFC 2190, September 1997.

Problems

1. The RAS protocol does not specify the length of the timeout period from the time that the request message is transmitted to the time that a response message is received. Develop an algorithm through which the transmitter can calculate an appropriate value for the timeout counter.
2. The RAS protocol does not specify the number of times that the request message is retransmitted before the communication is disconnected due to network problems. How many times should the message be

retransmitted? Justify your choice. Also, show a relationship between the adjustment of the timeout value and the retransmission of the message.

3. The H.323 recommendation provides tools in the RAS protocol to enable RAS messages to be resilient to packet loss. Develop an algorithm to provide resiliency to RAS messages against packet loss.
4. The gatekeeper-routed call model can be improved to increase the scalability of gatekeepers by reducing the number of messages from the endpoints to the gatekeepers. In a call, which H.225.0-Q.931 and H.245 messages can be directed between the endpoints without compromising the gatekeepers' capability to provide address resolution, QoS reservation, admission control and accounting? Show with a diagram the message flow from the start to the end of a call.
5. Timer values that are used in call signaling are based on the Q.931 recommendation. The Q.931 timers are based on the switched-circuit network. Develop timer values for call signaling on the Internet.
6. Develop an intra-domain protocol that enables gatekeepers to balance the endpoint load among them. Note that in H.323, gatekeepers provide endpoints with a prioritized alternate gatekeepers list, and gatekeepers that are reaching full capacity can reject new endpoint registrations.
7. Show how H.245 can be used to signal the payload format for the RTP redundant header. This function removes the RTP redundant header overhead in each RTP packet.
8. Show how H.245 can be used to remove some of the fields in the 12-byte RTP header. Which fields in the RTP header cannot be removed, and why?
9. Switching between redundant and non-redundant voice modes can be performed through the use of two H.245 flowControlCommand messages. Show (with the use of a new H.245 message) how the transmitter can switch between the two modes without temporarily disrupting the flow of voice and without temporarily running two flows of voice.
10. Show how the calling endpoint can request the called endpoint to open two logical channels—one for non-redundant voice and another for redundant voice—in the same RTP session by using Fast connect.
11. When the delay and jitter is not known on the network, the size of the dejitter buffer is fixed so that the one-way delay does not exceed 300 ms. If one-way delay exceeds 300 ms, then voice conversation might be switched to text conversation. When one-way delay is less than 300 ms, however, the size of the dejitter buffer does not decrease in order to provide the user with a much better voice quality. Show how the size of the dejitter buffer can dynamically change based on calculations of one-way delay and inter-arrival jitter (made on a continuous basis).

CHAPTER 4

Multi-Point Conference

In this chapter we describe different types of multi-point conferences and network configurations. H.323 uses a subset of the conference types and network configurations described here. The H.225.0-RAS, H.225.0-Q.931, and H.245 protocols used in point-to-point calls are elaborated upon with descriptions of new messages and procedures for use in multipoint conferences involving three or more participants; these protocols do not scale to large-scale conferences involving thousands of participants. Therefore, adjustments are made to H.323 to cover small and large conferences.

Conference Basics

The basic concepts of multi-point conferences are described in this section. The different types of conferences are differentiated based essentially on the way in which they are set up. Different network configurations are used by the conferences; this use is determined essentially by the scalability of the endpoints. These concepts are described in the following subsections along with the conference types and network configurations used by H.323.

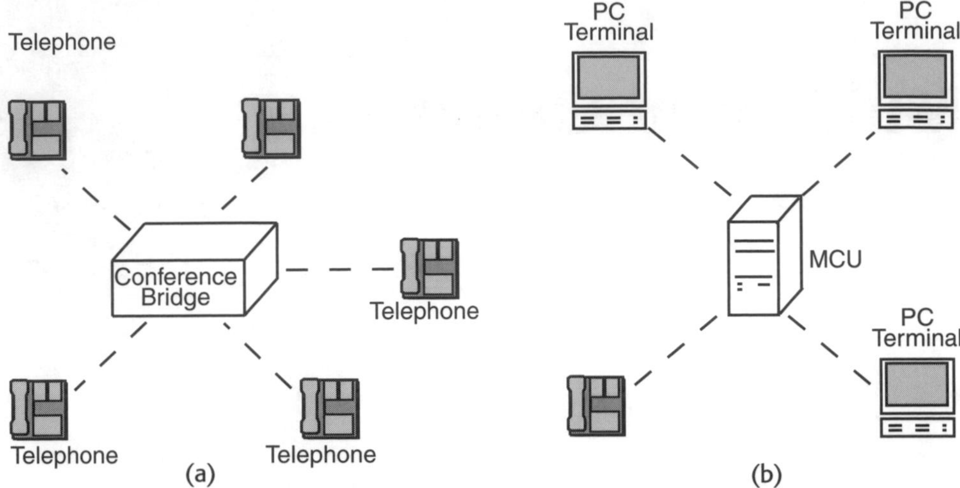

Figure 4.1 Meet-me conference.

Conference Types

The three types of conferences are meet-me, ad hoc, and interactive-broadcast. An example of the meet-me conference is shown in Figure 4.1. Figure 4.1(a) shows a conference bridge as a meeting place for the participants. The participants are provided the phone number of and call the bridge at some predetermined time to start the conference. The bridge mixes the voice from each participant and provides the mixed voice to the other participants connected to the bridge. Figure 4.1(b) shows an MCU as the meeting. The participants call the MCU at a predetermined time to start the videoconference. Each terminal provides the voice and the video of a participant. The MCU mixes the voice and usually picks the video of the participant whose voice has the highest energy (that is, the person talking the loudest) and provides it back to all the terminals. In meet-me conferences, participants usually join by calling the MCU/bridge. The MCU/bridge also can invite the participants by calling their terminals.

An ad hoc conference is shown in Figure 4.2. This conference starts as a point-to-point call and then grows to a multi-point conference when participants invite other people by calling their terminals. Unlike meet-me, an ad hoc conference may not be prearranged. An example of ad hoc in PSTN telephony is the three-way call in which after a point-to-point call is established, one participant puts the other on *hold* and then calls (invites) a third participant. The *held* call is then *retrieved*, and the two calls are joined in a three-way call. This method of establishing an ad hoc conference is covered

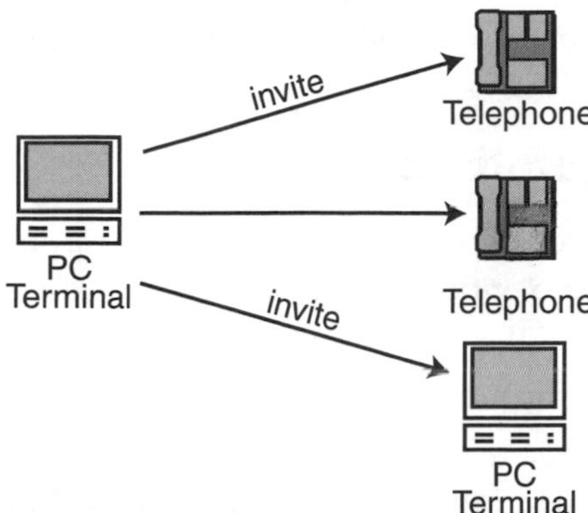

Figure 4.2 Ad hoc conference.

in Chapter 7, "Three-Party Supplementary Services in H.450." In this chapter, ad hoc conferencing without the use of hold/retrieve is discussed.

An interactive-broadcast conference is illustrated in Figure 4.3. In this type of conference, an entity usually broadcasts signaling and media to the terminals in the forward direction. The terminals have a reverse channel or back channel through which they provide feedback to the broadcast entity. Interactive broadcast normally requires conferences to scale to thousands of terminals. Meet-me and ad hoc conferences do not have such a requirement.

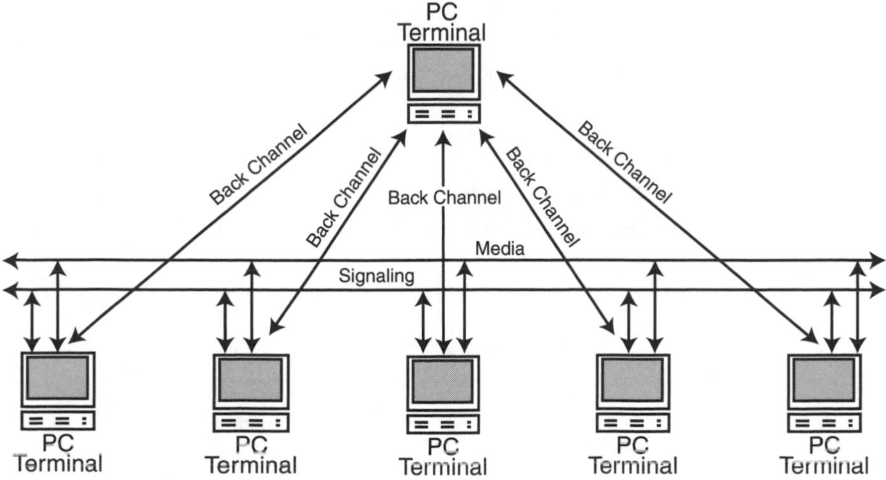

Figure 4.3 Interactivebroadcast.

Examples of interactive broadcasts include applications like *distance learning* in which the teacher and students are geographically dispersed.

Network Configurations

The network configuration for the point-to-point call is illustrated in Figure 4.4. Because two entities are involved, both the signaling and media packets are sent directly from one entity to another.

In the case of multi-point calls, more than two entities are involved, which leads to the three major network configurations shown in Figure 4.5. Figure 4.5(a) shows the multi-unicast configuration in which each terminal sends copies of signaling and media packets to every other terminal in the conference. Figure 4.5(b) shows the multicast or the bus configuration in which all terminals send and receive signaling and media packets on known multicast addresses. Figure 4.5(c) shows the master-slave or the star configuration in which one terminal is the master and the other terminals are slaves. Both signaling and media packets are unicast by the slave to the master who then multi-unicasts the information to the slave terminals. Each network configuration has its merits and demerits:

- *Simplicity in implementation of terminals.* The master-slave configuration is the easiest to implement for the slaves. The slave implementation is an extension of the point-to-point call because each slave is engaged in a point-to-point call with the master. The slaves send their signaling and media packets to the master. The master distributes the signaling packets to other slaves whenever appropriate. Voice from the slaves is mixed, and the mixed voice is provided to each slave. The master usually determines the person who is talking and provides that video to the slaves. The master has the complete state of the conference; the slaves are normally stateless.

  The multi-unicast and the multicast configurations are harder to implement because each terminal essentially has the functionality of the master. All terminals are peers and hold the same state of the conference.

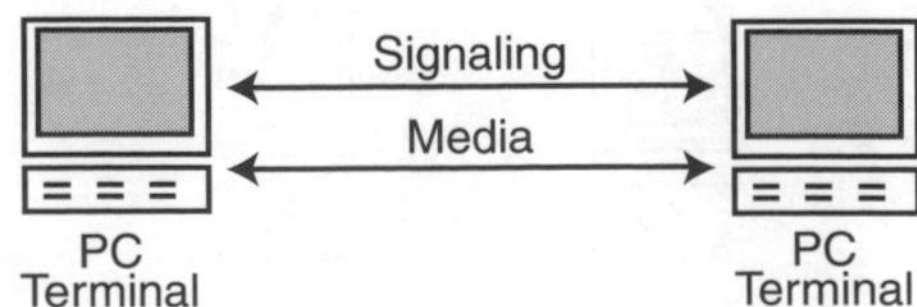

Figure 4.4 Network configuration for a point-to-point call.

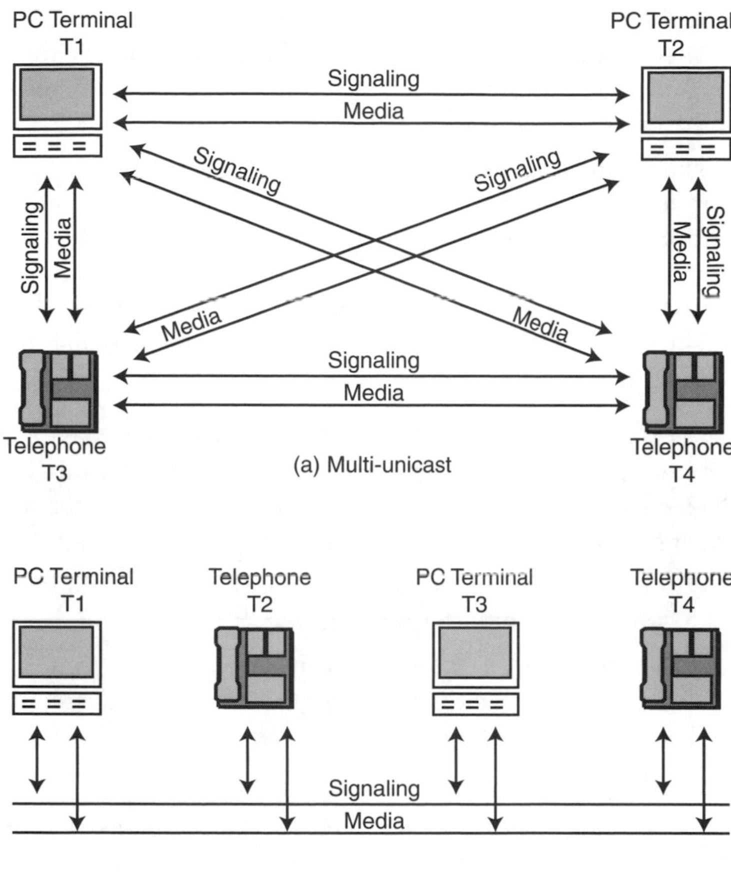

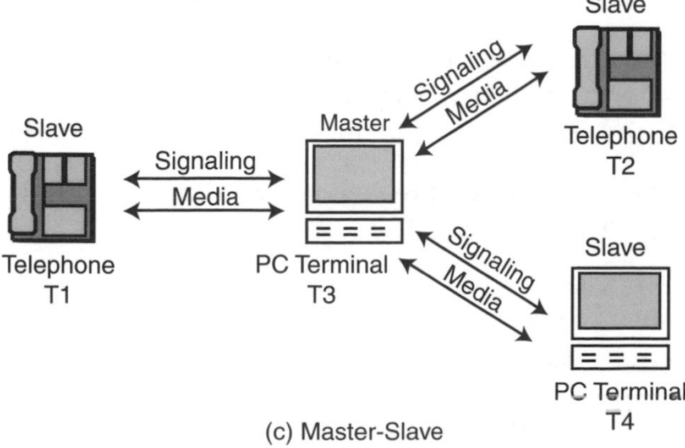

Figure 4.5 Network configurations for a multi-point conference.

- *Scalability of terminals.* The multicast configuration is the most scalable. Theoretically, it can scale to the full amount of traffic the network can handle. The master-slave configuration is as scalable as the scalability of the hardware with which the master is implemented.

  The multi-unicast configuration works best when the number of terminals involved is fewer than 10, such as a in a three-way conference. The multi-unicast consumes too much network bandwidth as the number of terminals grows. The master-slave configuration extends the scalability of terminals to double digits after which the cost of the master becomes impractical. The multicast configuration further extends the scalability to thousands of terminals.

- *Network usage.* Multicast is most efficient; master-slave is next; and multi-unicast uses the most network bandwidth. If n terminals are involved in a voice conference using no silence suppression, then the network bandwidth consumed by the three network configurations is as follows:
  - *Multicast.* n voice streams—network bandwidth increases by one voice stream with each terminal added.
  - *Multi-unicast.* $n(n-1)$ voice streams, $(n-1)$ from each terminal—network bandwidth increases by $(n-1)$ voice streams with each terminal added.
  - *Master-slave.*
    - *If the master is not the slave.* $2n$ voice streams, n to master, and n from master to each slave—network bandwidth increases by two voice streams with each terminal added.
    - *If the master is also the slave.* $2(n-1)$ voice streams, $(n-1)$ to master, and $(n-1)$ from master to each slave—network bandwidth increases by two voice streams with each terminal added.

On the other hand, if all terminals in the voice conference use silence suppression and one participant usually talks at a time, then the network bandwidth consumed by the three network configurations is as follows:

- *Multicast.* 1 voice stream—network bandwidth remains the same with each terminal added.
- *Multi-unicast.* $(n-1)$ voice streams—network bandwidth remains the same with each terminal added.
- *Master-slave.*
  - *If the master is not the slave.* $(1+n)$ voice streams, 1 to master, and n from master to each slave—network bandwidth increases by one voice stream with each terminal added.

- *If the master is also the slave.* 1 + (n − 1) voice streams if slave is participant; (n − 1) if master is the participant—network bandwidth increases by one voice stream with each terminal added.

- *Single point of failure.* The master-slave configuration has the master as the single point of failure. If the master becomes nonoperational during the conference, the conference comes to an end. In the multi-unicast or the multicast configurations, no single point of failure exists; the conference continues even if one or more terminals become nonoperational.
- *Point of contact.* For the master-slave configuration, the slaves call the master to enter the conference. For the multicast configuration, the multicast address is used for all communication. For the multi-unicast case, the conference is usually ad hoc, and participants are invited.
- *Delay.* Delay is critical for real-time media, especially conversational voice. The master-slave configuration will have the most delay because the slaves first send media to the master and the master then sends media back the resultant media. In the multi-unicast or the multicast configurations, media is sent directly from one terminal to all the other terminals.
- *Usability with conference types.* The master-slave configuration is usually used with meet-me and ad hoc conference types in which terminal scalability is limited (to double digit for meet-me and to single digit for ad hoc). The multi-unicast configuration is usually used with ad hoc conferences in which terminal scalability is low (single digit). The multicast configuration is usually used with interactive broadcasts in which terminal scalability is high (hundreds and thousands). The downside of multicast is that it is not widely deployed.

Network Configurations Used in H.323

The network configurations for signaling and media are different, as illustrated in Figure 4.6. Signaling is always centralized using the master-slave configuration. This centralized signaling entity is the master and is the MC. Each endpoint in the conference is the slave and has a TCP connection with the MC. The MC controls the endpoint in the conference through messages on this connection. The MC functionality resides in the terminal, MCU, gateway, or gatekeeper.

Media, on the other hand, is either centralized using the master-slave configuration shown in Figure 4.6(a) or is distributed using the multicast configuration shown in Figure 4.6(b). This centralized media entity is the MP.

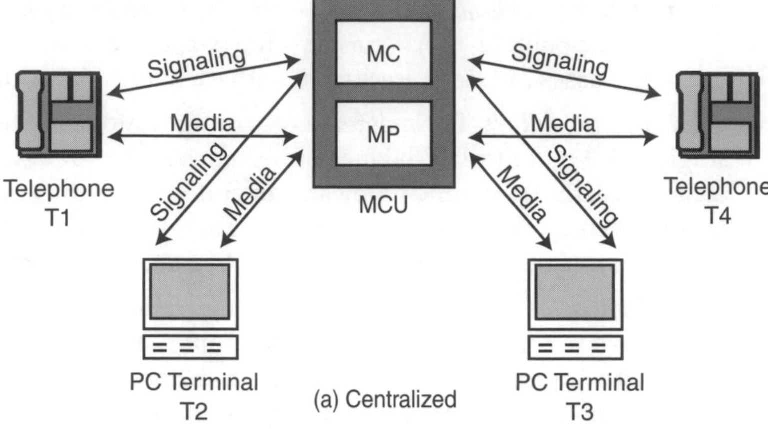

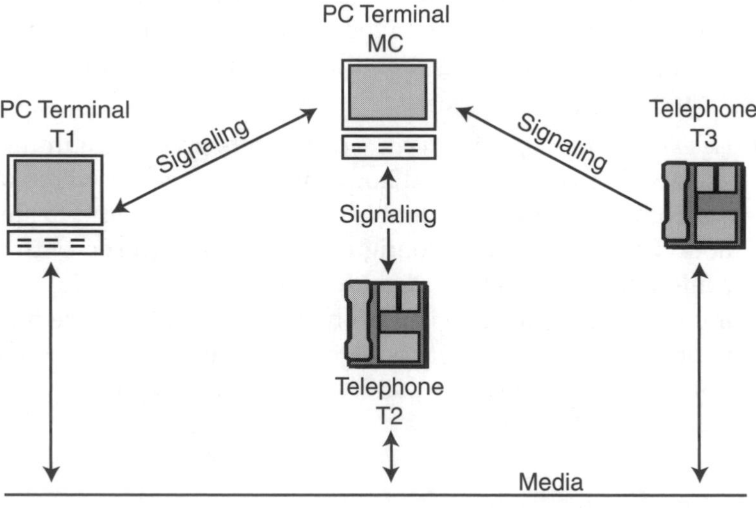

Figure 4.6 Network configurations used in H.323.

Each endpoint sends media packets to the MP. If the media is voice, the MP mixes the voice captured at the same time from the endpoints and sends the appropriate mix to the endpoints. If the media is video, the MP selects the video based on its defined policy and sends it to the endpoints. Voice and video packets are sent on the UDP channel. The MP functionality can reside in the MCU, gateway, or gatekeeper. Note that H.323 does not enable the MP to reside in the terminal, even though no reason exists for disallowing this combination.

If media are distributed, the MP does not exist. Endpoints send and receive all media on the specified multicast address. Each endpoint mixes voice and selects the video for its own use. This configuration, consisting of centralized signaling and distributed media, is known as *decentralized*. Besides the centralized and distributed configurations for media, a number of hybrid configurations involving both centralized and decentralized configurations exist. For example, endpoints can unicast media to the MP, and the MP can multicast the processed media back to the endpoints. Note that the multi-unicast network configuration is not used in H.323 because the state of the conference is not distributed. The state of the conference, including the addresses of the slave endpoints, resides in the MC. The endpoints send signaling packets to the MC; the MC multi-unicasts signaling packets to the endpoints.

Conference Types Used in H.323

H.323 is used for ad hoc and meet-me conferences. ad hoc conferences are usually small-scale conferences that scale to about five endpoints. Meet-me conferences are usually medium-scale conferences that scale to about 100 endpoints. Because H.323 uses the master-slave network configuration, the scalability of endpoints is limited to the number of signaling connections simultaneously sustained by the master. For this reason, interactive-broadcast uses another ITU-T recommendation, namely H.332 [00H332]. H.332 modifies the signaling part of the decentralized network configuration of H.323. The signaling connection between the master and the slave is made temporary; the slaves use it only when needed. All the slaves in the conference share the limited number of signaling connections with the master, which enables the number of endpoints in the conference to grow without increasing the hardware power of the master. Interactive-broadcast conferences are usually large-scale conferences that scale to thousands of endpoints.

Small- and Medium-Scale Conferences Using H.323

H.323 conferencing is illustrated by Figure 4.7. Users 1, 2, and 3 with Terminals 1, 2, and 3, respectively, access the Internet through their respective ISPs 1, 2, and 3. User 1 is addressed through the URL

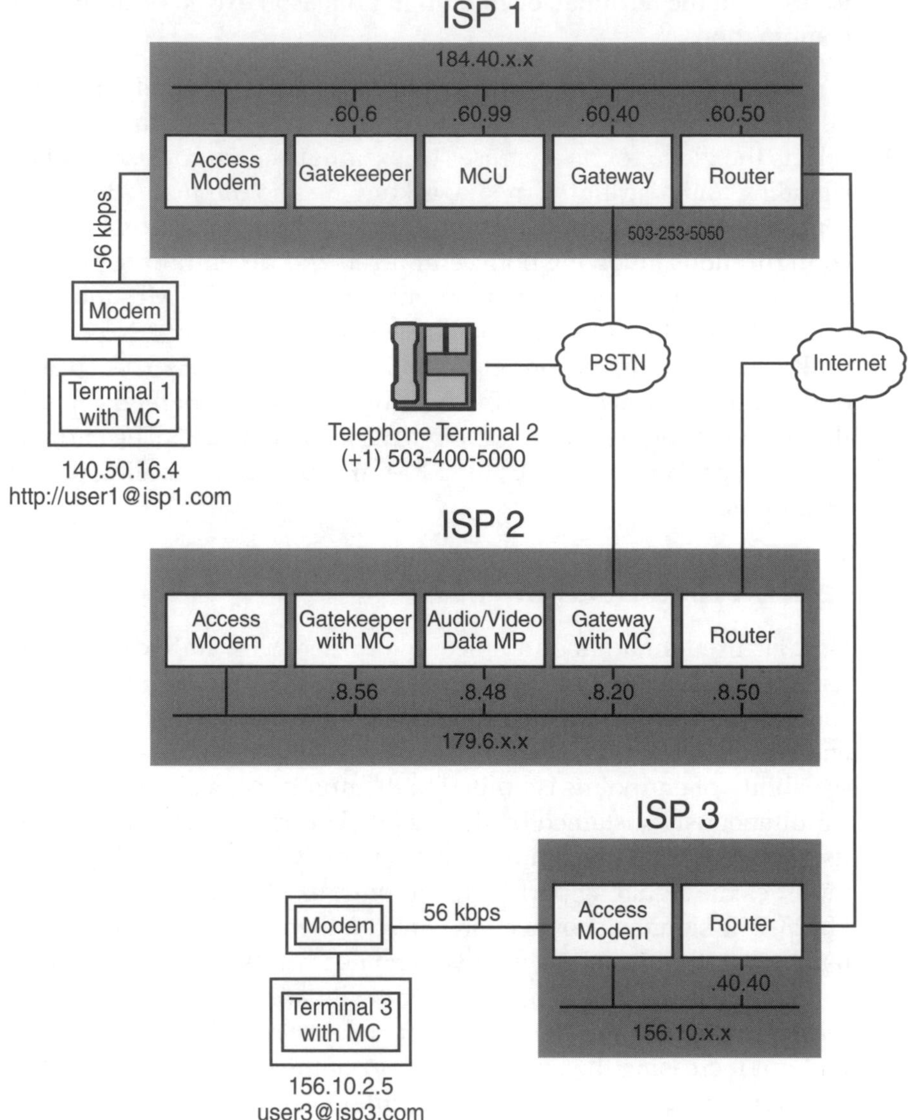

Figure 4.7 An H.323 conference.

h323://user1@isp1.com; User 2's Terminal 2 is addressed through the E.164 phone number (+1) 503-400-5000; and User 3 is addressed through the e-mail address user3@isp3.com. All three ISPs have multicast-capable routers.

Terminal 1 is multimedia- and multicast-capable; it has an MC; and it connects to ISP 1 using a 56 kbps modem. Being MC- and multicast-capable, Terminal 1 can host decentralized conferences. ISP 1 has a gatekeeper (ISP1-GK), gateway (ISP1-GW), and MCU (ISP1-MCU). The MC and the MP components of the MCU are collocated; both have the same IP address. ISP 1 uses ISP1-MCU for prearranged or scheduled (meet-me) conferences.

Terminal 2 is a PSTN phone that connects through the ISP 2 gateway (ISP2-GW) to the Internet. The ISP2-GW acts as an H.323 proxy for the phone. The ISP2-GW is voice-only-capable, because it connects on the PSTN to voice devices only. It also has an MC (ISP2-GW-MC), and it is multicast-capable. In addition to a PSTN gateway, ISP 2 has a gatekeeper (ISP2-GK) with an MC (ISP2-GK-MC). The ISP2-GK routes calls from and to IP terminals to do accounting for the calls. The ISP2-GK also provides other services to the IP terminal, such as address resolution in which an address in the form of a URL, e-mail address, or E.164 telephone number can be resolved into an IP address. Both ISP2-GK and ISP2-GW share the stand-alone audio/video/data MP (ISP2-MP). Note that ISP2-MP is not callable because it handles only media, not signaling. ISP 2 uses the MC and MP together for both meet-me and ad hoc conferences.

Terminal 3 is multimedia- and multicast-capable; it has an MC; and it connects to ISP 3 using a 56 kbps modem. Being MC- and multicast-capable, Terminal 3 can host decentralized conferences. For multicast to work in a conference, the terminals and the network must be multicast-enabled. ISP 3 is a traditional ISP providing only data services; it does not have any H.323 equipment to provide multimedia services.

To do multipoint conferencing, some of the messages for point-to-point calls in H.323 are extended, and new messages are developed. These extensions, along with new messages, are described in the following sections.

Additions to Call Control Protocol—H.245

To support multipoint conferences, H.245 is extended beyond the functionality it provides for point-to-point calls. Some of the additional messages needed for multipoint are shown in Table 4.1. The messages are

Table 4.1 H.245 Messages for Multipoint Conferences

	Request	Response	Command	Indication
Conference Management			CommunicationModeCommand	MiscellaneousIndication: MulitipointConference
Roster Management	Conference Request: enterH243TerminalID requestAllTerminalIDs requestTerminalID	ConferenceResponse: terminalIDResponse requestAllTerminalIDResponse mcTerminalIDResponse		Conference Indication: terminalNumberAssign terminalJoinedConferen terminalLeftConference

grouped into four categories— Request, Response, Command, and Indication —along the columns of the table and into two categories—Conference Management and Roster Management—along the rows of the table. The Conference Management messages are used to provide information about the conference. The Roster Management messages are used to develop a roster of participants in the conference. These messages are described in the following subsections. The following subsections also describe extensions to messages used for point-to-point calls.

NOTE

Only some fields in these messages are shown. Refer to the ITU-T H.245 Recommendation for details.

MasterSlaveDetermination

Because the MC functionality can reside in any endpoint or the gatekeeper, the potential exists for multiple MCs in the same conference. H.245 requires only one MC to be active in a conference, and the MasterSlaveDetermination set of messages is used to select the MC that will be used in a conference.

Message

The set of MasterSlaveDetermination messages was described in Chapter 3, "Point-to-Point Call: Signaling." An additional field, terminalType, is added to the MasterSlaveDetermination message as shown in Figure 4.8 to allow the selection of the MC in a conference. The value of terminalType is in the range of 0–255 and depends on two factors: the H.323 entity and MC and/or MP functionality in the entity as shown in Table 4.2. The MC of the H.323 entity with the highest value of terminalType is selected. Preference is given to network entities, such as a gatekeeper, over non-network entities, such as a terminal. A gatekeeper with an MC has a higher terminalType of 120 compared with the terminalType of 70 for the terminal with an MC. After the MC has been selected for a conference, its terminalType is elevated to 240 to end the MC selection process. If the entities have the same value for the

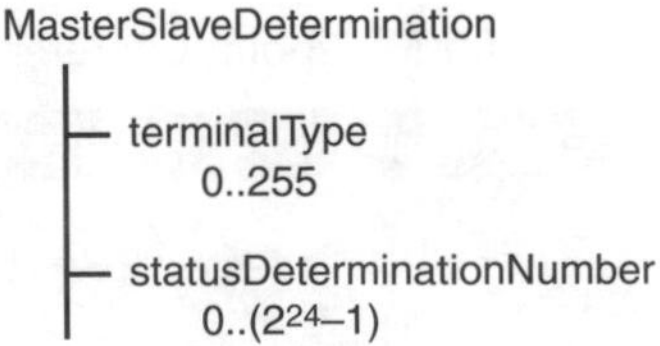

Figure 4.8 Additions to H.245 MasterSlaveDetermination message for multi-point.

Table 4.2 Value of terminalType in H.245 MasterSlaveDetermination Message

Functionality	H.323 Entity			
	Terminal	Gateway	Gatekeeper	MCU
No MC or MP	50	60	X	X
MC	70	80	120	160
MC with data and Voice MP	X	100	140	180
MC with Data, Voice and Video MP	X	110	150	190
Active MP	240	240	240	240

X = Not Applicable

terminalType, the statusDeterminationNumber is used to determine the master.

Usage

Assume the scenario used in Figure 4.7 with a call between Terminal 1 and Terminal 2 with a signaling path set up consisting of Terminal 1 with MC, ISP1-GK, ISP2-GK with MC, ISP2-GW with MC, and Terminal 2. Both Terminal 1 and ISP2-GW send the MasterSlaveDetermination message. The path of the message from Terminal 1 to ISP2-GW is as follows:

1. The content of the message from Terminal 1 to ISP1-GK is

   ```
   MasterSlaveDetermination.terminalType 70
   MasterSlaveDetermination.statusDeterminationNumber (2^24 - 40)
   ```

2. Because ISP1-MCU is not used for ad hoc conferences, ISP1-GK forwards the message unchanged to ISP2-GK.

3. ISP2-GK checks the message from ISP1-GK and determines that the terminalType is lower than its own terminalType. ISP2-GK can use its MC and MP, so it changes the content of the terminalType field in the MasterSlaveDetermination message and forwards the message to ISP2-GW as follows:

   ```
   MasterSlaveDetermination.terminalType 150
   MasterSlaveDetermination.statusDeterminationNumber (2^24 - 40)
   ```

ISP2-GW also sends its own MasterSlaveDetermination message to Terminal 1. The path of the message from ISP2-GW to Terminal 1 is as follows:

1. The content of the message from ISP2-GW to ISP2-GK is

   `MasterSlaveDetermination.terminalType 110`

   `MasterSlaveDetermination.statusDeterminationNumber` 2^3

2. Because ISP2-GK wants to use its MC, it changes the content of the terminalType field in the MasterSlaveDetermination message and forwards the message to ISP1-GK as follows:

   `MasterSlaveDetermination.terminalType 150`

   `MasterSlaveDetermination.statusDeterminationNumber` 2^3

3. ISP1-GK checks the message from ISP2-GK. Because ISP1-GK does not use its MCU, it forwards the message unchanged to Terminal 1.

Based on the exchange of MasterSlaveDetermination messages from Terminal 1 and ISP2-GW, each entity independently determines whether it is the master or the slave. The outcome has only one master. Terminal 1, ISP2-GW, and ISP1-GK are slaves; whereas ISP2-GK is the master. The entities also know that this point-to-point call has an audio/video/data MCU in a gatekeeper, so the call can be expanded to ad hoc multi-point and multimedia conference if desired. Terminal 1 and ISP2-GW send the MasterSlaveDeterminationAck message to acknowledge the outcome. The path of the message from Terminal 1 to ISP2-GW is as follows:

1. The content of the message from Terminal 1 to ISP1-GK is

   `MasterSlaveDeterminationAck.decision.master`

2. Because ISP1-GK is the slave, it forwards the message unchanged to ISP2-GK.

3. Because ISP2-GK is the master, it changes the message before forwarding it to ISP2-GW as follows:

   `MasterSlaveDeterminationAck.decision.slave`

ISP2-GW sends its own MasterSlaveDeterminationAck message. The path of the message from ISP2-GW to Terminal 1 is as follows:

1. The content of the message from ISP2-GW to ISP2-GK is

   `MasterSlaveDeterminationAck.decision.master`

2. Because ISP2-GK is the master, it changes the message before forwarding it to ISP1-GK as follows:

   `MasterSlaveDeterminationAck.decision.slave`

3. Because ISP1-GK is the slave, it forwards the message unchanged to Terminal 1.

This exchange of MasterSlaveDetermination and MasterSlaveDeterminationAck messages from Terminal 1 and ISP2-GW end the procedure required to determine the master for the point-to-point call, and the MC for the multi-point call if it is expanded. In the preceding example, if ISP2-GW receives MasterSlaveDetermination from Terminal 1 before it has sent its own MasterSlaveDetermination message, ISP2-GW instead will simply send MasterSlaveDeterminationAck, which will also end this procedure.

TerminalCapabilitySet

The TerminalCapabilitySet message is used by endpoints to provide their multi-point capabilities.

Message

The multi-point capabilities of the endpoint in the TerminalCapabilitySet are shown in Figure 4.9.

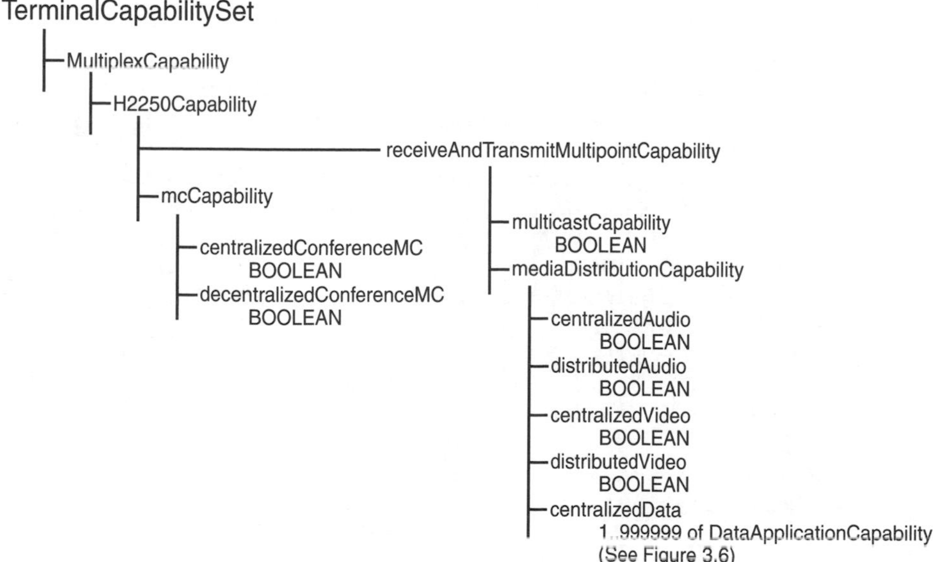

Figure 4.9 Additions to H.245 TerminalCapabilitySet message for multi-point.

multiplexCapability consists of H2250Capability, which in turn consists of receiveAndTransmitMultipointCapability and mcCapability. These two fields are described as follows:

- *receiveAndTransmitMultipointCapability*. It consists of the receive and transmit multi-point capabilities of the endpoint. These capabilities are as follows:
  - *multicastCapability*. It indicates whether the endpoint can multicast media.
  - *mediaDistributionCapability*. It indicates which media (voice, video, and data) is unicast (centralized) and which media is multicast (distributed).
- *mcCapability*. It indicates whether the endpoint has an MC and an MP. If the endpoint has a centralizedConferenceMC capability, it is an MCU. If it has a decentralizedConferenceMC capability, it has an MC and uses multicast to distribute media.

Usage

The usage of additional multi-point fields in TerminalCapabilitySet is shown in Figure 4.10:

```
Point 1
TerminalCapabilitySet.multiplexCapability.h2250Capability.
receiveAndTransmitMultipointCapability.multicastCapability YES
Point 2
TerminalCapabilitySet.multiplexCapability.h2250Capability.
receiveAndTransmitMultipointCapability.mediaDistributionCapability.
centralizedAudio YES
TerminalCapabilitySet.multiplexCapability.h2250Capability.
receiveAndTransmitMultipointCapability.mediaDistributionCapability.
distributedAudio YES
TerminalCapabilitySet.multiplexCapability.h2250Capability.
receiveAndTransmitMultipointCapability.mediaDistributionCapability.
centralizedVideo YES
TerminalCapabilitySet.multiplexCapability.h2250Capability.
receiveAndTransmitMultipointCapability.mediaDistributionCapability.
distributedVideo YES
Point 3
TerminalCapabilitySet.multiplexCapability.h2250Capability.
mcCapability.centralizedConferenceMC NO
TerminalCapabilitySet.multiplexCapability.h2250Capability.
mcCapability.decentralizedConferenceMC YES
```

Figure 4.10 Use of multi-point capabilities in TerminalCapabilitySet message.

1. Terminal 1 can multicast media.
2. Terminal 1 can unicast and multicast voice and video.
3. Terminal 1 has an MC and uses multicast for media.

Instead of the verbose syntax of Figure 4.10, the following compact syntax can be used:

```
Multipoint capability
     Can multicast
     Unicast and multicast voice
     Unicast and multicast video
MC and MP capability
     MC and multicast media
Chair control capability
     Chair control
```

CommunicationModeCommand

The CommunicationModeCommand is sent from the MC to the endpoints in the conference. It specifies precisely the media the endpoints are allowed to transmit to the MP and the transport addresses of the MP used to receive the media.

Message

Some of the fields in the CommunicationModeCommand message are shown in Figure 4.11. The CommunicationModeCommand message consists of a table of up to 256 entries. Each entry consists of the specifics of the media that the endpoint can transmit. For the description of the fields in each entry, refer to the OpenLogicalChannel message in Chapter 3.

Usage

Assume the same scenario as shown in Figure 4.7 exists. The CommunicationModeCommand from ISP2-GK-MC to all the endpoints in the conference is shown in Figure 4.12:

1. The first entry in the table consists of the following:
   a. This RTP session has an identification number of 1.
   b. Voice will be transmitted using G.723.1 with a maximum of two frames per payload. Packets will not be sent during periods of silence.
   c. The endpoints will transmit voice on the RTP transport address of 179.6.8.48 and a port number of 1140. This is the address of the MP. Note that the MP is not directly addressable by the endpoints; the address of the MP is given indirectly to the endpoints by the MC. Because all endpoints transmit to the same transport address, the

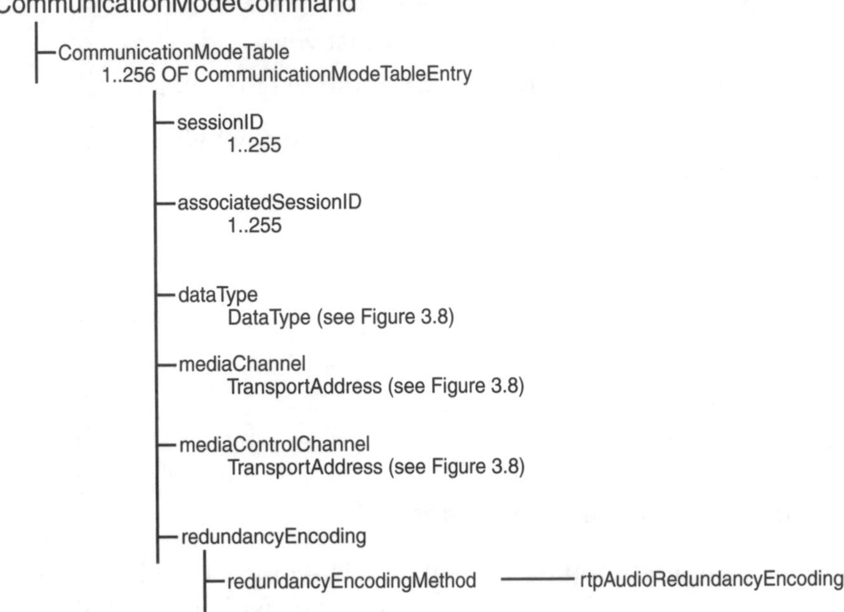

Figure 4.11 H.245 CommunicationModeCommand message.

mixer of voice uses the SSRC field in the RTP header to distinguish the payload from the different endpoints. The SSRC field is described later in section "Additions to RTP" of this chapter.

d. The endpoints will send RTCP reports on the RTCP transport address of 179.6.8.48 and a port number of 1141.

2. The second entry in the table consists of the following:
   a. This RTP session has an identification number of 2.
   b. This RTP session is associated with RTP session 1. This association specifies that voice in RTP session 1 can be lip synchronized with video in RTP session 2.
   c. Video will be transmitted using H.263 with QCIF resolution and with a minimum time interval between frames of 8/29.97 s and a maximum bit rate of 40,000 bits per s.
   d. The endpoints will transmit video on the RTP transport address of 179.6.8.48 and a port number of 1150. The mixer of video will use the SSRC field in the RTP header to distinguish the payload from the different endpoints. The SSRC field is described later in section "Additions to RTP" of this chapter.
   e. The endpoints will send RTCP reports on the RTCP transport address of 179.6.8.48 and a port number of 1151.

```
Point 1
CommunicationModeCommand.CommunicationModeTable 1 OF
CommunicationModeTableEntry
    Point 1 (a)
    CommunicationModeTableEntry.sessionID 1
    Point 1 (b)
    CommunicationModeTableEntry.dataType.audioData.g7231.
    maxAl-sduAudioFrames 2
    CommunicationModeTableEntry.dataType.audioData.g7231.
    silenceSuppression YES
    Point 1 (c)
    CommunicationModeTableEntry.mediaChannel.unicastAddress.
    ipAddress.network 179 6 8 48
    CommunicationModeTableEntry.mediaChannel.unicastAddress.
    ipAddress.tsapIdentifier 1140
    Point 1 (d)
    CommunicationModeTableEntry.mediaControlChannel.unicastAddress.
    ipAddress.network 179 6 8 48
    CommunicationModeTableEntry.mediaControlChannel.unicastAddress.
    ipAddress.tsapIdentifier 1141
Point 2
CommunicationModeCommand.CommunicationModeTable 2 OF
CommunicationModeTableEntry
    Point 2 (a)
    CommunicationModeTableEntry.sessionID 2
    Point 2 (b)
    CommunicationModeTableEntry.associatedSessionID 1
    Point 2 (c)
    CommunicationModeTableEntry.dataType.videoData.
    H263VideoCapability.qcifMPI 8
    CommunicationModeTableEntry.dataType.videoData.
    h263VideoCapability.maxBitRate 400
    Point 2 (d)
    CommunicationModeTableEntry.mediaChannel.unicastAddress.
    ipAddress.network 179 6 8 48
    CommunicationModeTableEntry.mediaChannel.unicastAddress.
    ipAddress.tsapIdentifier 1150
    Point 2 (e)
    CommunicationModeTableEntry.mediaControlChannel.unicastAddress.
    ipAddress.network 179 6 8 48
    CommunicationModeTableEntry.mediaControlChannel.unicastAddress.
    ipAddress.tsapIdentifier 1151
```

Figure 4.12 Use of CommunicationModeCommand message.

Instead of the verbose syntax shown in Figure 4.12, the following compact syntax can be used:

```
Session ID 1
    G.723.1, 2 frames/RTP packet, Silence suppression
```

```
        RTP IP address 179.6.8.48, Port 1140
        RTCP IP address 179.6.8.48, Port 1141
   Session ID 2, associated Session ID 1
        H.263, QCIF resolution, Minimum 8/29.97 s between frames, Maximum
        bit rate 40000 bits/s
        RTP IP address 179.6.8.48, Port 1150
        RTCP IP address 179.6.8.48, Port 1151
```

MiscellaneousIndication

The MiscellaneousIndication consists of a variety of indication messages. The multipointConference message is described here.

Message

The MiscellaneousIndication consists of two fields—logicalChannelNumber and type:

- *logicalChannelNumber*. It specifies the identification number of the logical channel. This field is used by a number of indication messages listed in the type field. Some messages apply to a specified logical channel; whereas others apply to all logical channels or to the conference. The multipointConference message applies to the conference and not to any specific logical channel. In this case, this field should be filled with a valid number of the logical channel even though it is ignored.
- *type*. It consists of a choice of indication messages. The message of interest is multipointConference, which is a message that notifies the slave endpoint that it must comply with the commands of the MC.

Usage

The usage of multipointConference is self-explanatory.

Roster Management

In a multi-point conference, an endpoint needs to provide a list of participants to the user. The messages used to manage the roster are included in ConferenceRequest, ConferenceResponse, and ConferenceIndication.

Messages

Some of the indication messages pertaining to roster management in ConferenceIndication are shown in Figure 4.13 and described as follows:

terminalNumberAssign. This indication message is sent by the MC to the slave endpoint to provide the endpoint with a two-byte identification, called the terminalLabel, that is unique within the conference. The least

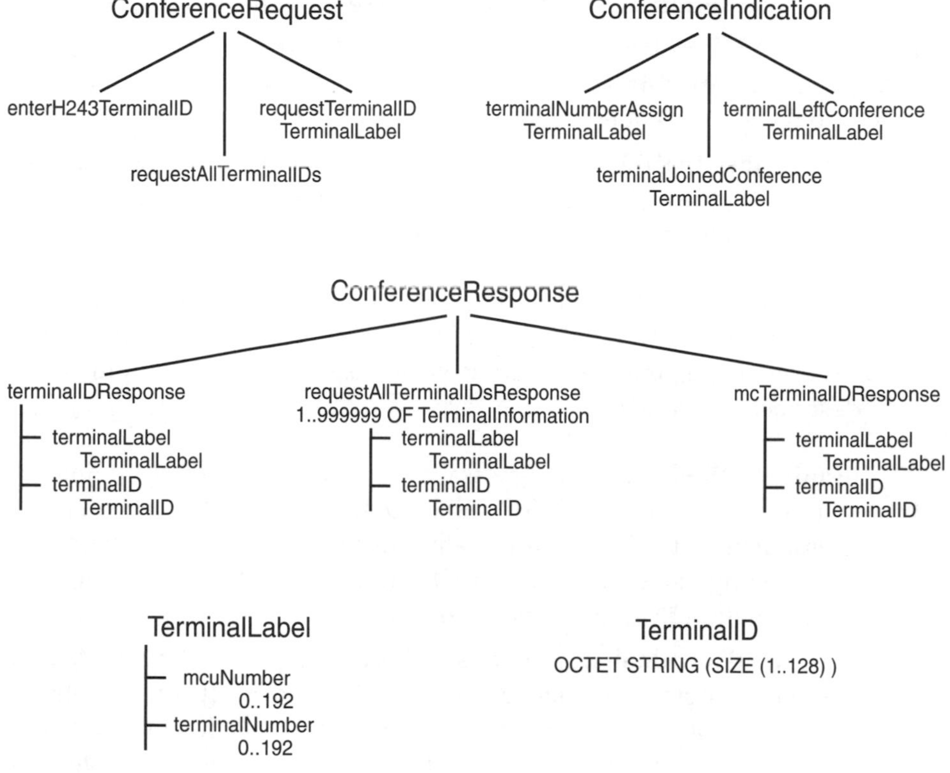

Figure 4.13 Roster management messages.

significant byte of terminalLabel consists of a value between 0 and 192 that is assigned uniquely to all endpoints in the conference. The most significant byte of terminalLabel is used when two or more conferences are merged. Because each of the merged conferences still has its own MC, this value between 0 and 192 is assigned uniquely to all MCs in the merged conference. Note that values above 192 for each of the two bytes in terminalLabel are reserved.

terminalJoinedConference. This indication message is sent by the MC to the slave endpoint to indicate that a new slave endpoint identified by a terminalLabel entered the conference.

terminalLeftConference. This indication message is sent by the MC to the slave endpoint to indicate that a slave endpoint identified by a terminalLabel left the conference.

Some of the request messages pertaining to roster management in ConferenceRequest are shown in Figure 4.13 and are described as follows:

enterH243TerminalID. This message is sent by the MC to the slave endpoint to request the participant's identification.

requestAllTerminalIDs. This message usually is sent by the slave endpoint to the MC to request identification of all participants in the conference.

requestTerminalID. This message usually is sent by the slave endpoint to the MC to request identification of the participant corresponding with the specified terminalLabel of the endpoint.

All request messages in ConferenceRequest have a corresponding response message in ConferenceResponse. These response messages pertaining to roster management in ConferenceResponse are shown in Figure 4.13 and described as follows:

terminalIDResponse. This message is sent by the slave endpoint to the MC in response to enterH243TerminalID. It consists of the terminalLabel assigned by the MC in terminalNumberAssign and the terminalID consisting of a string of up to 128 characters that usually includes information to identify the participant.

requestAllTerminalIDsResponse. This message is sent by the MC to the slave endpoint in response to requestTerminalID. It consists of a list of terminalLabel and the corresponding terminalID of all the participants in the conference. The MC assigned a terminalLabel to all the slave endpoints in the conference. The terminalID consists of a string of up to 128 characters that usually includes information to identify the participant.

mCTerminalIDResponse. This message is sent by the MC to the slave endpoint in response to requestTerminalID. It consists of the terminalLabel assigned by the MC in terminalNumberAssign and the terminalID consisting of a string of up to 128 characters that usually includes information to identify the participant.

Usage

The usage of roster messages is explained later in this chapter in "Scenarios."

Additions to RTP

The fields in the RTP header needed for the multi-point conference are: Contributing Source Count (CC), Synchronization Source (SSRC) Identifier, and the Contributing Source (CSRC) Identifiers. These fields are described as follows:

Contributing Source Count (CC) (4 bits). This field contains the count for the Contributing Source Identifiers. Up to 15 identifiers can be specified. For example, the MP uses this field to specify to the terminals the number of voice streams mixed in the payload.

Synchronization Source (SSRC) Identifier (32 bits). This field identifies the source of the RTP and the RTCP packets. In addition to being unique within an RTP session, the SSRC identifier shall also be unique across all related RTP sessions maintained by the MP. The SSRC space covers all related RTP sessions. In a centralized audio conference, the MP maintains an RTP session with each of the terminals. The SSRC identifiers across these related RTP sessions shall not conflict. For point-to-point calls, SSRC is not needed. For multi-point conference, the low-order byte of the terminalLabel provided by the MC is used in the low-order byte of the SSRC. This makes the SSRC unique because the terminalLabel is unique. The high 24 bits of SSRC are used by the endpoint to distinguish among the multiple streams it is sending in the same RTP session.

Contributing Source (CSRC) Identifier (>= 32 bits, <= 15 * 32 bits). This field contains a list of SSRC identifiers. The length of the list is contained in the Contributing Source Count field. For example, the MP uses this field to tell the terminals the identifiers of those terminals whose voice streams are mixed in the payload.

Use of RTP in a Multi-Point Conference

The RTP header provides the information necessary to describe the payload in the multi-point conference. Table 4.3 shows the contents of voice packets between three endpoints (1, 2, 3) and ISP2-MP. The scenario from Figure 4.7 is used here; each endpoint sends voice packets to ISP2-MP. The ISP2-MP mixes the voice and provides each endpoint with its individual mix of voice. Each row in the first column of the table provides the following information about the endpoint and the voice packets being transmitted:

1. The direction of voice packets from and to a specific endpoint to and from the ISP2-MP. In the first row, voice packets are sent from Terminal 1 to ISP2-MP.
2. The unique H.245 terminalNumber assigned by ISP2-GK-MC to each terminal in the conference. The three endpoints are assigned 1, 2, and 3 as the terminal numbers by ISP2-GK-MC.
3. The NTP and the corresponding RTP timestamps are sent by all endpoints to all other endpoints in the RTCP reports. The ISP2-MP uses the

Table 4.3 Contents of Voice Packets in a Multi-Point Conference

Terminal↔MCU	Packet (y+5) SSRC; Timestamp; CC; CSRC; G723.1 Voice Frame	Packet (y+4)	Packet (y+3)	Packet (y+2)	Packet (y+1)	Packet y
Terminal 1→ISP2-MP terminal Number = 1 NTP Timestamp = t RTP Timestamp = 30	x01hex; 180; 0; ; V^1_6	x01hex; 150; 0; ; V^1_5	x01hex; 120; 0; ; V^1_4	x01hex; 90; 0; ; V^1_3	x01hex; 60; 0; ; V^1_2	x01hex; 30; 0; ; V^1_1
ISP2-GW→ISP2-MP terminal Number = 2 NTP Timestamp = t RTP Timestamp = 40	x02; 190; 0; ; V^2_{54}	←	Silence	→	x02hex; 70; 0; ; V^2_{53}	x02hex; 40; 0; ; V^2_{52}
Terminal 3→ISP2-MP terminal Number = 3 NTP Timestamp = t RTP Timestamp = 150	← Silence →	x03hex; 270; 0; ; V^3_{503}	x03hex; 240; 0; ; V^3_{502}	← Silence →	← Silence →	x03hex; 150; 0; ; V^3_{501}
ISP2-MP→Terminal 1 McuNumber = 0 NTP Timestamp = t RTP Timestamp = 2110	x00hex; 2260;1; x02hex; V^2_{54}	x00hex; 2230;1; x03hex; V^3_{503}	x00hex; 2200;1; x03hex; V^3_{502}	← Silence →	x00hex; 2140;1; x02hex; V^2_{53}	x00hex; 2110; 2; x02hex; x03hex; mix(V^2_{52},V^3_{501})
ISP2-MP↔ISP2-GW McuNumber = 0 NTP Timestamp = t RTP Timestamp = 4444	x00hex; 4594; 1; x01hex; V^1_6	x00hex; 4564; 2; x01hex; x03hex; mix(V^1_5,V^1_{503})	x00hex; 4534; 2; x01hex; x03hex; mix(V^1_4,V^3_{502})	x00hex; 4504; 1; x01hex;V^1_3	x00hex; 4474; 1; x01hex;V^1_2	x00hex; 4444; 2; x01hex; x03hex; mix(V^1_1,V^3_{501})
ISP2-MP→Terminal 3 McuNumber = 0 NTP Timestamp = t RTP Timestamp = 854	xC0hex; 1004; 2; x00hex; x01hex; mix(V^1_6,V^2_{54})	xC0hex; 974; 1; x01hex; V^1_5	xC0hex; 944; 1; x01hex;V^1_4	xC0hex; 914; 1; x01hex;V^1_3	xC0hex; 884; 2; x01hex; x02hex; mix(V^1_2,V^2_{53}))	xC0hex; 854; 2; x01hex; x02hex; mix(V^1_1,V^2_{52})

X = Don't Care V^n_m = M[th] G.723.1 voice frame from Terminal n

relationship between the NTP and the RTP timestamps to construct the absolute time when the received voice frame was captured. The MP then mixes voice frames belonging to the same absolute time but from separate terminals.

NOTE

RTCP is covered in "Large-Scale Conference using RTP/RTCP and SDP" later in this chapter. The design philosophies of RTP/RTCP and H.323 are different enough to be covered separately. RTCP is based on distributed control among peers on the multicast network; whereas H.323 has centralized control. Because RTP/RTCP was adopted without change in H.323, the functionality provided by RTCP was not duplicated in H.245. The NTP timestamp, provided through RTCP, is not duplicated in H.245.

Each of the remaining six columns in each row of the table show a voice packet sent between the endpoint and ISP2-MP. The six packets are sent consecutively in time with packet (y) sent first, and packet ($y + 5$) sent last. Each packet has the following information separated by semicolons:

- The SSRC field generated by each endpoint. The endpoints use their unique terminalNumber in the low order byte of the SSRC. The ISP2-MP picks a unique low byte in generating its own SSRC so that it does not conflict with any terminalNumber assigned.
- The RTP timestamp field whose initial value is a random number.
- The CC field consisting of the number of contributors to the voice streams mixed in the payload.
- The CSRC field listing the SSRCs of the contributors to the voice mixes.
- The voice payload consisting of one G.723.1 frame per packet. Each of the three endpoints transmits a stream of voice packets to ISP2-MP. The ISP2-MP mixes the voice streams received from the endpoints and transmits back a custom mix to each endpoint. At least three steps are involved in mixing voice streams:
  1. Generate comfort noise for the endpoint when it is not transmitting voice during periods of silence. An assumption is made that silence packets are not sent on the network. When the G.723.1 endpoint encoder detects silence, it transitions from voice to silence by generating a four-byte frame consisting of comfort noise parameters, which is sent on the network to the ISP2-MP decoder. During periods of silence, the ISP2-MP CNG uses the comfort noise parameters to generate comfort noise on behalf of the silent endpoint.
  2. If the level of gain in the voice streams from the endpoints or the comfort noise generated by the ISP2-MP is not controlled, it has to be adjusted by the Automatic Gain Control in ISP2-MP before mixing. A 20db discrepancy between the loudest and the quietest talker can make it hard for the listener to adjust to such a change.
  3. After level adjustment, only the loudest two or three streams should be mixed to avoid multiple streams introducing undesirable additive noise. This additive comfort noise degrades the listening experience when no one is talking and reduces the quality of the mixed voice when a single talker is active. At least two methods exist for mixing G.723.1 voice streams. One method is to integrate each stream of G.723.1 frames in their encoded state. This process is very complex and takes in code vectors and gain bits to determine a final mix without decoding to PCM samples. The second method is to first decode each stream of G.723.1 frames to PCM, add the PCM streams,

adjust the power level of the resultant stream to a comfortable playback level, and finally to encode the resultant stream back to a stream of G.723.1 frames for transmission on the network. This operation of first decoding and then encoding back to the same encoding is called *tandeming*. Although a single tandem may be acceptable, this process produces noticeable quality degradation every time voice goes through the tandem operation. A note on mixing levels: (a) Only one comfort noise stream should be mixed with speech to avoid the distracting gating of noise and silence while simultaneously avoiding unnecessary additive noise from multiple silent endpoints. (b) Gain management of the mix is very important. Adding speech signal strengths of two streams and dividing by 2 will reduce the signal strength inappropriately. Heuristics are often needed for optimal performance. A good rule of thumb is to maintain the RMS output signal level with at least one endpoint active at approximately 24db down from full-scale PCM.

Additions to Call Signaling Protocol

Because signaling is centralized at the MC, all slave endpoints in the conference are involved in a point-to-point call with the MC. As far as signaling is concerned, multipoint is just a simple extension of point-to-point. The extensions needed in the Setup message are described as follows:

conferenceID. It consists of a 128-bit globally unique identification number, which is unique in space and time for the conference. It is generated by the endpoint that creates the call, which may potentially expand to a conference. The procedure used to generate the unique number is the same as that used for the callIdentifier field described in Chapter 3. No two H.323 conferences have the same conferenceID. This field is used to globally differentiate one H.323 conference with another.

conferenceGoal. It is used to indicate the conference type. The choices are create, invite, and join. All point-to-point calls use the value of "create" because the calling endpoint is creating the call. The calling endpoint also generates the value of the conferenceID. When the point-to-point call expands to an ad hoc conference, the value of "invite" is used to invite another endpoint to the conference using the same value of conferenceID that was generated during the creation of the point-to-point call. The value of "join" is used when the calling endpoint is joining a meet-me conference. In this case, the value of conferenceID should be known because the conference is prearranged. In case the value of conferenceID is not known, a value of 0 (zero) should be used. If the MC in a meet-me conference invites an endpoint, the value of "invite" is used, and the value of conferenceID is that of the conference in which the endpoint is invited.

If the user has to enter the conferenceID to gain access to a conference, the 16-byte number is too long and random to be user-friendly. The conferenceID can be conveniently used among machines, but when users are involved, a short number or an identifiable string of characters provides a friendly user-interface. In conference types such as meet-me, it may not be necessary to use a globally unique conferenceID to identify the conference. Usually URLs and e-mail addresses can have sufficient information to uniquely identify the entity with the MC, and the name of the conference hosted by that MC. The name of the conference is also known as the conferenceAlias. This string of characters can be a URL, an e-mail address, or any other string. As an example, the URL of h323:\\mc.isp1.com\voice-chat-room1, or an e-mail address of voice-chat-room1@ mc.isp1.com have a conference alias of voice-chat-room1 and the domain name of mc.isp1.com, which resolves to the IP address of an entity consisting of an MC hosting the meet-me conference.

Scenarios

Let's consider scenarios based on Figure 4.7 (see page 154) to show how the meet-me and ad hoc conference types work. For the meet-me conference type, the centralized network configuration is described. The centralized meet-me conference is also known as the MCU-based conference. For the ad hoc conference type, both the decentralized and centralized network configurations are described. Only some of the fields are shown to illustrate their use in the messages. Assume Fast Connect and H.245 Tunneling are used.

MCU-Based Conference

Assume that ISP1 uses its MCU to host various voice-chat rooms and prearranged conferences. The chat rooms are accessed through URLs or e-mail addresses for users on the Internet, and through an E.164 phone number for users on the PSTN. Assume that Users 1, 2, and 3 are interested in joining a chat room with a URL of h323:\\mcu.isp1.com\voice-chat-room1, an e-mail address of voice-chat-room1@ mcu.isp1.com, and an E.164 phone number and conference alias of (+1) 503-253-5050 and 60604, respectively. The domain name of mcu.isp1.com and the phone number of (+1) 503-253-5050 resolves to the IP address of 184.40.60.99 (ISP1-MCU). The default H.323 port of 1720 is used for call setup. Each conference hosted by ISP1-MCU has a unique identification, so it can be distinguished from other conferences hosted by ISP1-MCU. Both voice-chat-room1 and 60604 are different names (conference aliases) of the same conference; other conferences hosted by ISP1-MCU do not have these names. The reason for having two conference aliases for the same conference is that it is easier for users to relate a conference with a name, but for a phone user it is easier to enter short numbers. The following steps and Figure 4.14 describe how an MCU-based conference works:

1. User 1uses Terminal 1 to connect to the voice-chat-room1 conference. Terminal 1 sends a Setup(remoteExtensionAddress = h323:\\mcu.isp1.com\voice-chat-room1, faststart(openLogicalChannel (G.711), openLogicalChannel(G.723.1))) message to its registered ISP1-GK. The ISP1-GK resolves the domain name in the URL of the Setup message to the IP address of 184.40.60.99 (ISP1-MC) and forwards Setup to ISP1-MC. This action establishes a voice channel from ISP1-MP to Terminal 1; ISP1-MP can send voice packets to Terminal 1. Note that conferenceID and conferenceGoal fields are not shown in the Setup message because their values are not useful to ISP1-MC in this scenario. The ISP1-MC and ISP1-MP are referred to as MC and MP, respectively.
2. The MC sends an Alerting(fastStart(openLogicalChannel(G.723.1))) message via ISP1-GK to Terminal 1. This message establishes a voice channel from Terminal 1 to MP; Terminal 1 can send voice packets to MP.
3. The MC sends a Connect message via ISP1-GK to complete the point-to-point connection with Terminal 1.
4. The MC sends the H.245 point-to-point messages described in (a) and the H.245 multi-point messages described in (b) in the same packet to Terminal 1:
    a. The MC sends TerminalCapabilitySet and MasterSlaveDetermination(x, 240). Because this MC is hosting the voice-chat-room1 conference, it declares itself as the active MC by using the terminalType of 240. The statusDeterminationNumber of *x* is a random number defined by the MasterSlaveDetermination message.
    b. The MC sends MultipointConference, terminalNumberAssign(1), enterH243TerminalID, and CommunicationModeCommand messages. It is important for the MC to send terminalNumberAssign as early as possible so the terminal can generate the SSRC field in the RTP header. If the elements in fastStart from the terminal are inconsistent with the modes in CommunicationModeCommand, the MC shall respond without fastStart in the Alerting and Connect messages. The terminal then opens the logical channels after receiving the CommunicationModeCommand. The CommunicationModeCommand specifies precisely the media the endpoints are allowed to transmit to the MP and the transport addresses of the MP used to receive the media.
5. Terminal 1 sends the H.245 point-to-point messages described in (a) and the H.245 multipoint messages described in (b) in the same packet to the MC via the ISP1-GK:

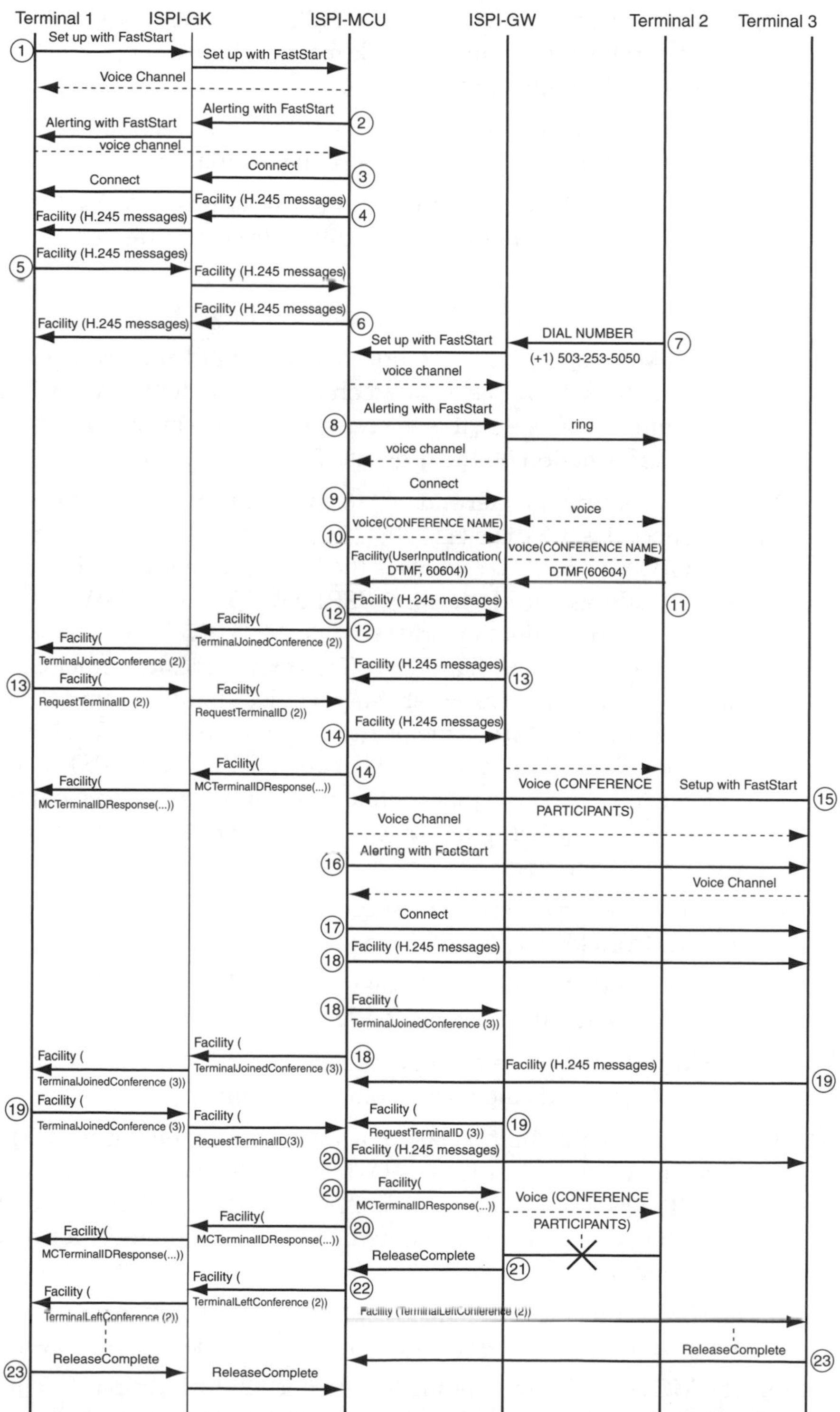

Figure 4.14 MCU-based conference.

   a. Terminal 1 responds with TerminalCapabilitySetAck and MasterSlaveDeterminationAck(master). It also sends TerminalCapabilitySet.
   b. Terminal 1 responds with TerminalIDResponse(1, John Doe, Iowa State University). It also sends requestAllTerminalIDs.

6. The MC sends the H.245 point-to-point messages described in (a) and the H.245 multi-point messages described in (b) in the same packet to Terminal 1:
   a. The MC responds with TerminalCapabilitySetAck.
   b. The MC responds with RequestAllTerminalIDsResponse(1, John Doe, Iowa State University). Based on RequestAllTerminalIDsResponse, the terminal knows that it is the only one in the conference. It provides this information on the user interface for its User 1.
7. User 2 uses a phone (Terminal 2) to connect to the voice-chat-room1 conference. User 2 dials (+1) 503-253-5050, and Terminal 2 connects to ISP1-GW. The ISP1-GW resolves the E.164 number from Terminal 2 to the IP address of 184.40.60.99 (ISP1-MC). The ISP1-GW sends a Setup(destinationAddress = (+1) 503-253-5050, faststart(openLogicalChannel (G.711), openLogicalChannel(G.723.1))) message to the MC. This establishes a voice channel from MP to ISP1-GW. Note that the fastStart elements in Setup include both G.711 and G.723.1 because ISP1-GW can transcode between G.711 on the PSTN and G.723.1 on the LAN. Also note that conferenceID and conferenceGoal fields are not shown in the Setup message because their values are not useful to the MC in this scenario.
8. The MC sends an Alerting message to ISP1-GW, which establishes a voice channel from ISP1-GW to MP. The ISP1-GW rings the phone.
9. The MC sends a Connect message to ISP1-GW. The ISP1-GW completes the connection with Terminal 2.
10. The MC sends a voice prompt requesting conference identification. The ISP1-GW forwards the voice prompt to Terminal 2.
11. User 2 enters the digits 60604. Terminal 2 sends the digits to ISP1-GW, which then sends the digits as DTMF signals in the UserInputIndication (DTMF, 60604) message to the MC. Because the conference identification is for the voice-chat-room1 conference, the MC connects Terminal 2 to that conference.

12a. The MC sends the H.245 messages shown in Step 4, except that the value of the Terminal number assigned is 2 in TerminalNumberAssign(2).

12b. The MC sends TerminalJoinedConference(2) to Terminal 1, which then tells its User 1 that someone has joined the conference.

13a. The ISP1-GW sends the messages shown in Step 5. The ISP1-GW does not request Terminal 2 for identification, and it does not provide an identification of User 2 in TerminalIDResponse(2, Phone user; identification unknown) to the MC.

13b. The Terminal 1 sends requestTerminalID(2) to the MC requesting identification of the user with a terminal label of 2.

14. The MC responds to ISP1-GW with the messages shown in Step 6. The list of users consists of RequestAllTerminalIDsResponse(1, John Doe, Iowa State University, 2, Phone user; identification unknown). The ISP1-GW can provide the list of conference participants through the voice message to Terminal 2.

    The MC responds to Terminal 1 with MCTerminalIDResponse(2, Phone user; identification unknown). The Terminal 1 can append to the displayed list of conference participants for User 1.

15. Terminal 3 does not have a gatekeeper, so it directly uses the DNS to resolve the domain name in the URL to the IP address of 184.40.60.99 (ISP1-MCU). Terminal 3 then sends Setup(remoteExtensionAddress = h323:\\mcu.isp1.com\voice-chat-room1, faststart(openLogicalChannel (G.711), openLogicalChannel(G.723.1))) to the MC. Note that conferenceID and conferenceGoal fields are not shown in the Setup message because their values are not useful to the MC in this scenario.

16. The MC responds to Terminal 3 with an Alerting(fastStart(openLogicalChannel(G.723.1))) message.

17. The MC sends a Connect message to complete the point-to-point connection with Terminal 3.

18a. The MC sends the H.245 messages shown in Step 4 to Terminal 2, except that the value of the terminal number assigned is 3 in terminalNumberAssign(3).

18b. The MC sends terminalJoinedConference(3) to Terminal 1 and ISP1-GW. The Terminal 1 and ISP1-GW tell their users that someone has joined the conference.

19a. The Terminal 3 responds with messages shown in Step 5. The User 3 provides the identification to Terminal 3, and Terminal 3 sends it in TerminalIDResponse(3, Bill Johnson, New York) to the MC.

19b. Both Terminal 1 and ISP1-GW send requestTerminalID(3) to the MC requesting identification of the user with a terminal label of 3.

20. The MC responds to Terminal 3 with the messages shown in Step 6. The list of users consists of RequestAllTerminalIDsResponse(1, John Doe, Iowa State University, 2, Phone user; identification unknown, 3, Bill Johnson, New York).

The MC responds to Terminal 1 and ISP1-GW with MCTerminalIDResponse(3, Bill Johnson, New York). Terminal 1 can append the identification of the new participant to the displayed list of conference participants. The ISP1-GW can convert the identification of the new participant from text to voice and provide the information to Terminal 2.

21. User 2 hangs up the phone, and the ISP1-GW sends ReleaseComplete to the MC.
22. The MC sends terminalLeftConference(2) to Terminals 1 and 3. The terminals update their list of participants for the user.
23. Terminals 1 and 3 leave the voice-chat-room1 conference by sending ReleaseComplete to the MC.

Decentralized ad hoc Conference

In this scenario, User 1 calls User 2. During their call, User 1 expands the call by inviting User 3 in the conference. The MC of Terminal 1 hosts the decentralized conference. An assumption is made that the three terminals involved are connected to a multicast network needed for a decentralized conference. User 1 is known though the URL h323://user1@isp1.com; User 2 is known through the E.164 number (+1) 503-400-5000, and User 3 is known through the e-mail address user3@isp3.com. The following steps and Figure 4.15 describe how a decentralized ad hoc conference works:

1. User 1 calls User 2. Terminal 1 sends a Setup(destinationAddress = (+1) 503-400-5000, faststart(openLogicalChannel (G.711), openLogicalChannel(G.723.1)), conferenceID = 7890, conferenceGoal = create) message to its registered ISP1-GK. The ISP1-GK resolves the E.164 address in the Setup message to the IP address of 179.6.8.20 (ISP2-GW) and forwards Setup to ISP2-GW. This establishes a voice channel from ISP2-GW to Terminal 1; ISP2-GW can send voice packets to Terminal 1.
2. The ISP2-GW rings Terminal 2 and sends Alerting(fastStart(OLC G.723.1)) to Terminal 1 via ISP1-GK. This establishes a voice channel from Terminal 1 to ISP2-GW; Terminal 1 can send voice packets to ISP2-GW.
3. When Terminal 2 goes off-hook, ISP2-GW sends Connect to Terminal 1 via ISP1-GK to establish a point-to-point connection with Terminal 1.
4. Terminal 1 sends TerminalCapabilitySet and MasterSlaveDetermination(5000, 70) to ISP2-GW, and ISP2-GW sends TerminalCapabilitySet and MasterSlaveDetermination(9000, 60) to Terminal 1. Note that ISP2-GW does not use its MC. This could be because the MC resources may have been exhausted due to other conferences that

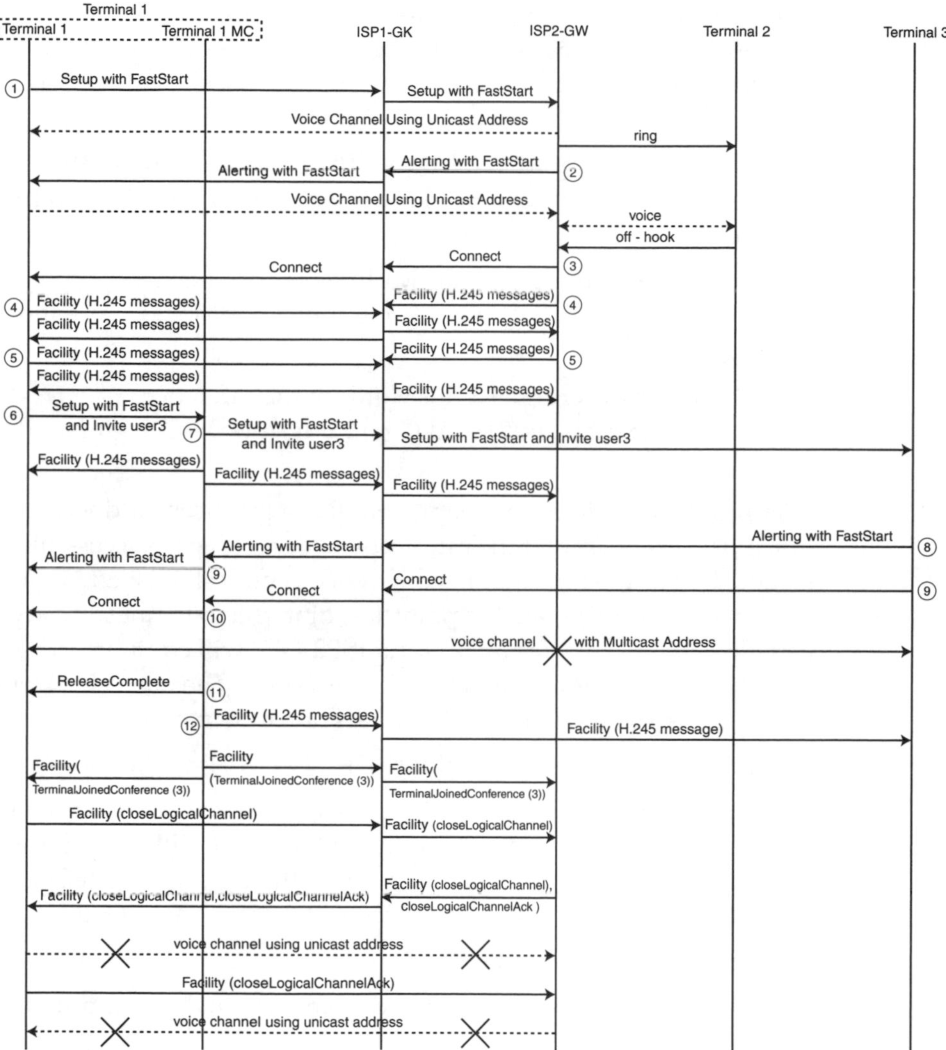

Figure 4.15 Decentralized ad hoc conference.

it may be hosting. Also note that Terminal 1 has an MC but not an MP, so it can establish only a decentralized multi-point conference.

5. ISP2-GW responds with TerminalCapabilitySetAck and MasterSlaveDeterminationAck(master) to Terminal 1, and Terminal 1 responds with TerminalCapabilitySetAck and MasterSlaveDeterminationAck(slave) to ISP2-GW. Based on the master-slave determination, the MC of Terminal 1 will be used if the point-to-point call is expanded to multi-point.

6. User 1 decides to invite User 3. Terminal 1 sends Setup(remoteExtensionAddress = user3@isp3.com, faststart(openLogicalChannel (G.711), openLogicalChannel(G.723.1)), conferenceID = 7890, conferenceGoal = invite) to the MC.
7. The MC forwards Setup to ISP1-GK. The ISP1-GK resolves the e-mail address in the Setup message to the IP address of 156.10.2.5 (Terminal 3) and forwards Setup to Terminal 3.

   The MC sends to Terminal 1 the MultipointConference, terminalNumberAssign(1), and CommunicationModeCommand messages.

   The MC sends to Terminal 2 the MultipointConference, terminalNumberAssign(2), and CommunicationModeCommand messages.

   CommunicationModeCommand contains a multicast address to which voice packets are sent if the multi-point conference is successfully established. If the multi-point conference is not established because User 3 does not answer the call, the point-to-point voice channel already established between Terminal 1 and ISP2-GW will continue to be used, and the multicast voice channel may be closed. The enterH243TerminalID message also may be included, but it is not shown here.
8. Terminal 3 sends Alerting(fastStart(OLC G.723.1)) to the MC.
9. The MC sends all H.225.0-Q.931 messages received from Terminal 3 to Terminal 1 because Terminal 1 initiated the call. In this way Terminal 1 is informed about the progress of the call with Terminal 3. The MC sends Alerting(fastStart(OLC G.723.1)) received from Terminal 3 to Terminal 1.

   Terminal 3 sends Connect to the MC.
10. The MC sends the Connect received from Terminal 3 to Terminal 1.
11. The MC sends ReleaseComplete to Terminal 1 to mark the end of the call, which Terminal 1 started with Terminal 3. Note that the call between the MC and Terminal 3 has not ended yet.
12. The state of the conference at this step is the same as that in Step 17 of the MCU-based conference except that the point-to-point voice channels exist between Terminal 1 and ISP2-GW. After Step 18 of the MCU-based conference is executed, Terminal 1 and the ISP2-GW know that Terminal 3 has joined the call and a multi-point conference has been established. Terminal 1 closes its point-to-point voice channel by sending a Closelogicalchannel message to ISP2-GW. Likewise ISP2-GW closes its point-to-point voice channel by sending a Closelogicalchannel message to Terminal 1. Both acknowledge each other's Closelogicalchannel message with CloselogicalchannelAck.

The remaining steps are similar to Steps 19 and onwards of the MCU-based conference. The reader is encouraged to go through these steps as an exercise to complete this scenario.

Centralized ad hoc Conference

In this scenario, User 1 calls User 2. During their call, User 1 expands the call by inviting User 3 in the conference. The MC of the gateway (ISP2-GW-MC) and the stand-alone MP (ISP2-MP) is used to host the centralized ad hoc conference. This scenario is quite similar to the decentralized ad hoc conference, except that the MC selected hosts a centralized ad hoc conference in conjunction with its standalone MP. User 1 is known though the URL h323://user1@isp1.com; User 2 is known through the E.164 number (+1) 503-400-5000; and User 3 is known through the e-mail address user3@isp3.com. The following steps describe how a centralized ad hoc conference works:

1–3. Steps 1–3 are the same as those shown in the decentralized ad hoc conference, except that the conferenceID has a value of 793277.

4. Terminal 1 sends TerminalCapabilitySet and MasterSlaveDetermination(3876, 70) to ISP2-GW, and ISP2-GW sends TerminalCapabilitySet and MasterSlaveDetermination(4637, 110) to Terminal 1. Note that ISP2-GW uses its MC and the standalone MP to host a centralized ad hoc conference. Even though the ISP2-GW is a proxy for a voice-only terminal, its MP is capable of voice/video/data conference with other multimedia terminals.

5. Terminal 1 responds with TerminalCapabilitySetAck and MasterSlaveDeterminationAck(master) to ISP2-GW, and ISP2-GW responds with TerminalCapabilitySetAck and MasterSlaveDeterminationAck(slave) to Terminal 1. Based on the master-slave determination, ISP2-GW-MC will be used if the point-to-point call is expanded to multi-point.

6. User 1 decides to invite User 3 in the call. Terminal 1 sends Setup (remoteExtensionAddress = user3@isp3.com, faststart(openLogicalChannel (G.711), openLogicalChannel(G.723.1)), conferenceID = 793277, conferenceGoal = invite) to ISP1-GK. Because Setup has the same conferenceID as the existing point-to-point call, the ISP1-GK forwards the Setup message to ISP2-GW-MC, also referred to as the MC.

7. The MC resolves the e-mail address in the Setup message to the IP address of 156.10.2.5 (Terminal 3) and forwards Setup to Terminal 3. It sends the H.245 multipoint messages shown in Step 7 of decentralized ad hoc conference to Terminal 1 and Terminal 2.

The remaining steps are similar to Steps 8 and onwards of the decentralized ad hoc conference. The reader is encouraged to go through these steps as an exercise to complete this scenario.

Scalability of Voice and Video on the Access Link

In this section, we reference Figure 4.7 to discuss issues involved in network bandwidth scalability of voice and video in conferences. Because the bandwidth on the access link is limited, the focus of the discussion is on the access side as opposed to the backbone network. In the centralized audio/video conference using ISP2-MC and ISP2-MP, the bandwidth limitation of 56 kbps for Terminal 1 is at the access link. The maximum bandwidth consumed on the access link includes a voice stream from Terminal 1 to ISP2-MP and the mixed voice stream from ISP2-MP to Terminal 1. The bandwidth used by a single 5.3 kbps G.723.1 stream consisting of one frame per RTP/UDP/IP/PPP packet is 17.1 kbps. The maximum bandwidth consumed on the access link by voice in a centralized conference is 34.2 kbps. Usually, either the participant at Terminal 1 is talking and the voice stream is flowing from Terminal 1 to ISP2-MP, or some other participant is talking and the voice stream is flowing from ISP2-MP to Terminal 1. If silence suppression is used, only one source of voice usually exists. Therefore, most of the time the bandwidth consumed by voice is 17.1 kbps. Once in a while, two or more participants talk simultaneously, but this lasts for a brief period of time. During this period of time, the bandwidth increases to 34.2 kbps on the access link when the participant at Terminal 1 is talking simultaneously with another participant.

In a decentralized conference, if silence suppression is not used, voice does not scale as the number of participating endpoints grows and as each endpoint sends voice packets. The voice bandwidth increases by 17.1 kbps as a new participant joins the conference. This limits the number of voice streams to three for Terminal 1. Therefore, for a decentralized conference, silence suppression is critical for the conference to scale. Even with silence suppression, the bandwidth used by voice can surge when two or more participants talk simultaneously.

In a centralized conference using silence suppression, if video is added the amount of bandwidth usually available on the 56 kbps link is 38.9 kbps (56 − 17.1). This means that Terminal 1 can transmit video to ISP2-MP at 19.45 kbps, and ISP2-MP can transmit mixed video to Terminal 1, also at 19.45 kbps. The content of mixed video depends on the policy of ISP2-MP. It usually includes the video of the talker, but also may include the video of multiple participants based on some criteria such as the last four talkers.

In a decentralized conference, video does not scale as the number of participating endpoints grows and as each endpoint sends video packets. A couple of methods of solving this problem exist. The video from each endpoint can be transmitted on a different multicast address. Then the endpoints can switch among multicast addresses based on the videos in which they are interested. This solution may have a problem with switching time if the multicast tree is torn down because receivers of some video do not exist and if the tree then needs to be built up when receivers for that video do exist. A solution to this problem may be to have all sources of video transmit on the same multicast address and to have the receivers use source pruning to get only the video streams they want. The endpoints can then switch among video sources based on their video selection policy.

When both voice and video streams are flowing on the same access link, the voice streams must have higher priority to video. Therefore, when multiple participants talk simultaneously and the voice bandwidth increases, the video packets can be dropped at the backbone to allow voice packets to go through on the link. This will degrade the quality of video, but all voices in the conference will be heard.

A conference usually has endpoints with varying link bandwidth and computational power. If the MP provides the same voice and video to all the participant endpoints, a less powerful endpoint on a low bandwidth network determines the quality of media for all the participating endpoints. However, an MP that provides custom media to all participating endpoints will provide higher quality media to higher bandwidth endpoints with higher computational power and lower quality media to lower bandwidth endpoints with lower computational power. The design of such an MP would be quite complex compared with a simple MP that provides the same media to all participating endpoints.

Large-Scale Conferences Using RTP/RTCP and SDP

H.323 was developed for telephony types of applications in which one party contacts another in real-time for the purpose of multimedia collaboration. A need for signaling exists so that the calling party can alert the called party. A need for endpoint capability exchange also exists to determine a common mode of operation when endpoints have varying capabilities. And, a need exists for exchanging addressing information to start the flow of media. The signaling and control required to set up a conference in real-time does not scale to large conferences consisting of hundreds and thousands of participants. The very nature of the procedures involved in setting up a real-time conference puts a limit to the scalability of participants in the telephony application. The centralized control in H.323 also limits the number of participants to the amount of hardware resources available at the centralized control entity.

Another set of applications does not require the real-time telephony procedures to set up a conference. These applications fall into the category of prearranged or presetup conferences. Such applications include Distance Learning, Town-Hall Meetings, Corporate Presentations, and so on. In these applications, the conference setup information can be disseminated before the conference begins. Then, at the time of the conference, the participants join that conference. The SDP protocol describes the information and the encoding needed to set up conferences ahead of time. The conference information can be delivered to the intended audiences through the use of e-mail, Web, and so on. When a conference starts, the RTP protocol carries the media, and the RTCP protocol carries the control information for that conference. The RTP/RTCP protocols were developed for large-scale distributed conferences using multicast. No centralized control exists; each endpoint involved is autonomous and independently executes the algorithms for the RTCP protocol.

Session Description Protocol (SDP)

SDP is a format for describing a conference/session to enable the recipient of the SDP announcement to learn about the session and to be able to join it. The SDP session description is divided into session, time, and media descriptions as follows:

1. The session-level description pertains to the whole session and includes information necessary for the recipient to learn about the session.
2. The time-level description also pertains to the whole session and includes information regarding the start and end time of the session.
3. The media-level description pertains only to that media and includes information necessary to transmit and receive that media.

The SDP description consists of multiple lines with each line consisting of a record of the form <type>=<value>, where <type> has a length of one character and <value> is a text string. The text string may be encoded in

US-ASCII subset of UTF-8, except in certain cases noted later in this section in which the ISO-10646 character set in UTF-8 encoding is used to allow most spoken languages to be represented. An example SDP session announcement is shown in Figure 4.16. The announcement is regarding a Distance Learning course in computer science on advanced topics in IP multimedia telephony. The details of the announcement are described as follows:

1. The protocol-version record specifies the version number of the SDP protocol used. This record has the syntax v=<protocol version>. The value

```
Session Description
Point 1
v=0
Point 2
o=joeb 7542158105 7542156815 IN IP4 140.50.16.4
Point 3
s=Computer Science 504, Iowa State University
Point 4
i=Advanced Topics In IP Multimedia Telephony
Point 5
u=http://www.cs.isu.edu/cs504/cs504syllabus.html
Point 6
e=joeb@isu.edu
Time Description
Point 7
t=(NTP(Monday, September 10, 2001 at 8 am)) (NTP(Friday, December 21,
2001 at 9am))
r=7d 1h 0 48h 96h
Point 8
t=(NTP(Tuesday, September 11, 2001 at 4 pm)) (NTP(Thursday, December
20, 2001 at 5:30 pm))
r=7d 90m 0 48h
Point 9
z=(NTP(October 31, 2001 at 2 am)) -1h
Media Description
Point 10
m=video 3620/3 RTP/AVP 110
a=rtpmap:110 H263-1998
c=IN IP4 234.4.6.112/127/3
Media Description
Point 11
m=audio 4010 RTP/AVP 4
c=IN IP4 231.40.200.3
```

Figure 4.16 An example SDP session announcement.

of 0 (zero) for the protocol-version field is assigned to the IETF RFC 2327 that describes SDP.

2. The origin record specifies a globally unique identifier for this version of the session announcement. A new globally unique identifier is generated if the announcement is modified. This record has the syntax o=<username> <session id> <version> <network type> <address type> <address>. The fields of this record are described as follows:
   - *username.* It consists of a text string to specify the user's login on the originating host. If unavailable, then "-" should be used instead.
   - *session id.* It consists of a numeric string to identify the session. The recommendation is to use the NTP timestamp.
   - *version.* It consists of a numeric string to specify the version number of the announcement. The recommendation is to use the NTP timestamp. If the announcement is modified, the version number should be increased.
   - *network type.* It consists of a text string to specify the network used. The only value currently allowed is "IN" for the Internet.
   - *address type.* It consists of a text string to specify the type of address used. The value can either be "IP4" for Internet Protocol version 4 or "IP6" for Internet Protocol version 6.
   - *address.* It consists of a text string to specify the address of the machine used in creating this session. If the address type is "IP4" or "IP6," the address should be a fully qualified domain name. If the domain name is unavailable, the dotted-decimal representation of the version 4 or version 6 IP address should be used for the "IP4" or "IP6" address type, respectively.
3. The session-name record specifies the title of the session. This record has the syntax s=<session name>, where the session-name field is a text string that must use the ISO 10646 character set in UTF-8 encoding to allow most spoken languages to be represented.
4. The information record describes the session. This record has the syntax i=<session description>, where the session description field is a text string that must use the ISO 10646 character set in UTF-8 encoding to allow most spoken languages to be represented.
5. The URI record provides an URI used to access a resource on the Web. This record has the syntax u=<URI>, where the URI field is a text string containing the URI used to access a Web page containing more information about this session.
6. The e-mail-address record specifies the e-mail address of the contact person for this session. This record has the syntax e=<email address>,

where the e-mail-address field is a text string containing the e-mail address.

7. The time record specifies the start and the stop time of this session. This record has the syntax t=<start time> <stop time>, where the start-time field and the stop-time field provide the start and stop time, respectively, of the session represented in NTP timestamp in seconds. From the announcement, the session starts on September 10, 2001, at 8 A.M. on Monday and stops on December 21, 2001, at 9 A.M. on Friday.

   The repeat record specifies repeat times of the session. This record has the syntax r=<repeat interval> <active duration> <list of offsets from start-time>, where the repeat-interval field provides the time in seconds when the session is repeated; the active-duration field provides the duration of the session in seconds; and the list-of-offsets-from-start-time field provides a list of offsets in seconds from the start-time field of the time record and then from the beginning of each repeat interval. In addition to using seconds as the unit, minutes (m), hours (h), and days (d) are also allowed. From the announcement, the repeat interval is seven days, so the session starts on September 10 at 8 A.M. on Monday and then repeats every seven days on Monday at 8 A.M. The duration of the session is one hour from 8 A.M. to 9 A.M. The list of offsets is 0, 48, and 96 hours from the start time and then from the beginning of each repeat-interval. Because the start time and the beginning of each repeat-interval are on Monday, the offsets are on Monday, Wednesday, and Friday at 8 A.M. In summary, the class is held three times a week on Monday, Wednesday, and Friday from 8 A.M. to 9 A.M. starting on September 10, 2001, and ending on December 21, 2001.

8. The time and repeat records are specified again because the class is also held two times a week on Tuesday and Thursday from 4 P.M. to 5:30 P.M. starting on September 11, 2001, and ending on December 20, 2001.

9. The zone record specifies adjustment in start time due to changes in time zone during the life of the session. This record has the syntax z=<adjustment time> <offset> < adjustment time> <offset> . . . , where the adjustment time field is the time in NTP when the start time is adjusted, and the offset field is the time that is added or subtracted from the start time field of the time record. From the announcement, at 2 A.M. on October 31, 2001, an hour will be subtracted from the start time due to the end of the daylight saving time.

10. The media record specifies the characteristics of the media. This record has the syntax m=<media> <port>[/<number of ports>] <transport> <fmt list>. The fields of this record are described as follows:

    - *media.* It specifies the type of media used. The values used are "audio," "video," "application," "data," and "control."

- *port*. It specifies the port on which the media streams are received. If media are transferred using RTP, an even-numbered RTP port is specified here, and the next higher odd number port is used for RTCP.
- *number of ports*. This optional field specifies multiple contiguous ports generally used for hierarchical encoded media, such as video. Each layer of video is sent on different ports. From the announcement, three (3620-3621, 3622-3623, 3624-3625) RTP-RTCP port pairs are allocated for this session.
- *transport*. It specifies the transport protocol used. Its value is dependent on the address type field of the connection record. If the address type in the connection record is "IP4" or "IP6," the values of the transport protocol are "RTP/AVP" or "UDP." The value of "RTP/AVP" refers to the RTP transport protocol using the Audio/Video Profile described in Chapter 2 and in RFC 1890.
- *fmt list*. It specifies a list of payload types used. The first payload type in the list is the default payload format, and the other formats also may be used in this session. If the transport field has a value of "RTP/AVP," the payload types are specified in RFC 1890. If the payload type is dynamic, as specified in the announcement, it has to be associated to the payload format. Because the media record did not originally have a mechanism to associate dynamic payload types to the payload format, the standard extension mechanism of a=<attribute>:<value> is used. The attribute field is encoded in US-ASCII, and the value field is encoded in ISO-10646.

The rtpmap record maps a dynamic payload type to the payload format. This record has the syntax a=rtpmap: <payload type> <encoding name>/<clock rate>[/<encoding parameters>], where the payload type field specifies the dynamic payload type, the encoding-name field specifies the name of the payload format, the clock-rate field specifies the clock rate for generating the RTP timestamp, and the encoding-parameters field is optional; it may be used to specify the number of audio channels. From the announcement, the dynamic payload type of 110 is mapped to the 1998 version of the H.263 payload format.

The connection record specifies information to enable a network connection to be established. This record has the syntax c=<network type> <address type> <connection address>.

- *network type*. It consists of a text string to specify the network used. The only value currently allowed is "IN" for the Internet.
- *address type*. It consists of a text string to specify the type of address used. The only value currently allowed is "IP4" for Internet Protocol version 4.

- *connection address.* It consists of a text string to specify the address for connecting to the media. If the address type field is "IP4" and the connection address is not a multicast address, the address should be a fully qualified domain name. If the domain name is unavailable, the dotted-decimal representation of the version 4 addresses should be used. If the address type field is "IP4" and the connection address is a multicast address, the connection address should consist of <base multicast address>/<ttl>[/<number of addresses>]. The base-multicast-address field consists of the dotted-decimal representation of the version 4 multicast addresses. The ttl field consists of the TTL value that sets an upper limit on the number of routers through which a packet passes. It has a value between 0 and 255. The number-of-addresses field specifies the number of contiguous addresses used above those specified by the base-multicast-address field. It usually is used to transmit different layers of the hierarchical encoded video on different multicast address. From the announcement, three multicast addresses (234.4.6.112, 234.4.6.113, 234.4.6.114) are allocated to this session. The first multicast address is associated with the first RTP-RTCP port pair specified in the number-of-ports field of the media record; the second multicast address is associated with the second port pair; and the third multicast address is associated with the third port pair.

11. The syntax for the media and connection records was already explained earlier. From the announcement, RTP is used to transport the static payload type of 4 on port 4010 and multicast address 231.40.200.3. From the RTP profile specified in RFC 1890, the static payload type of 4 corresponds to the G.723.1 payload format.

RTP Control Protocol (RTCP)

The main purpose of RTCP is to provide information regarding the quality of the received media to all the entities participating. This is done through the use of Sender Reports and Receiver Reports. The transmitters of media periodically send Sender Reports to provide information about the media being transmitted to the receiving terminals. The receivers of media periodically send Receiver Reports to provide feedback on the quality of the reception. The transmitters of media can use this feedback to modify their transmission by temporarily adding FEC to the media streams if packet loss rate is increasing. This feedback can also be used by network monitors to evaluate the network performance that may result in routing new RTP media flows and rerouting existing RTP media flows through less congested paths.

RTCP also provides minimal control information to allow participant rosters to be maintained. This is done through the use of Source Description reports.

Each participant periodically sends information, such as the participant's name, e-mail address, and phone number, in the Source Description reports to enable a roster of participants in the conference to be maintained. RTCP is designed for use with various applications consisting of conferencing, streaming, and so on. These applications provide the necessary control protocols. For example, the H.323 application provides the signaling and control protocol for conferencing and uses RTCP to provide the minimal control protocol tailored for the RTP media.

RTCP was designed especially for IP multicast networks in which the number of participant entities can range in thousands. The design is fully distributed with no centralized control. The distributed model has the inherent advantage of not having a single point of failure, but it also adds design complexity as compared to the centralized model.

RTP/RTCP-based conferencing is illustrated here in Figure 4.17. This conference is advertised through SDP as shown in Figure 4.16. The advertisement for the conference/session consists of a multicast audio session using G.723.1 and a multicast video session consisting of three hierarchical encoded layers of the 1998 version of H.263. The bandwidth

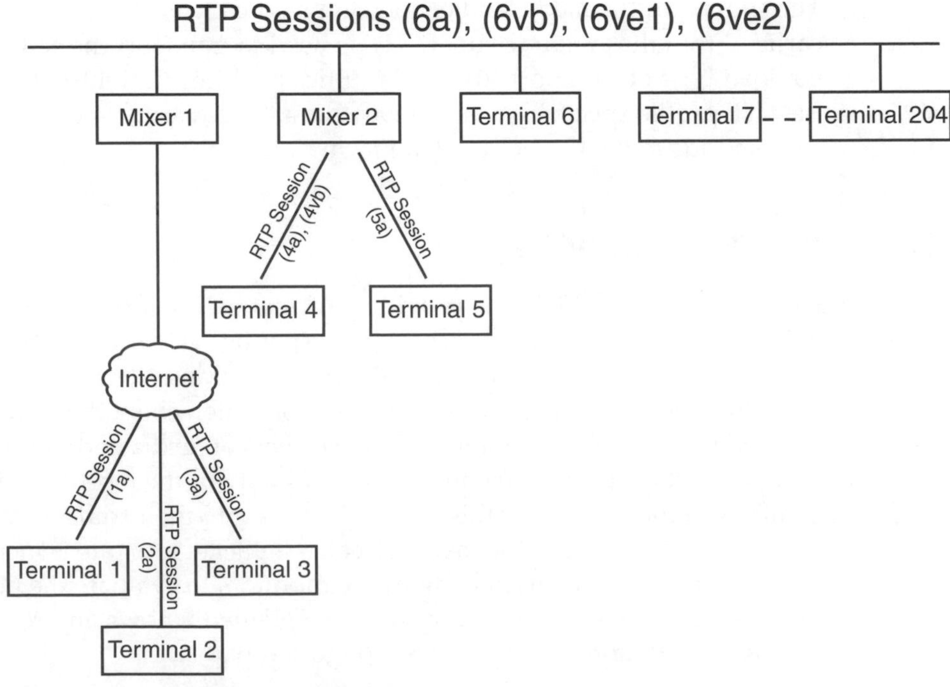

Figure 4.17 RTP/RTCP-based conference.

usage is not shown in the advertisement. The bandwidth used by a single 5.3 kbps G.723.1 stream consisting of one frame per RTP/UDP/IP packet is 16 kbps. The bandwidths used by the H.263 streams in the three layers starting with the base layer are 20, 30, and 50 kbps.

The entities used in the conference are Terminals 1 through 204, Mixer 1, and Mixer 2. Because this is a distance learning conference, let's assume that the teacher uses Terminal 6, and only Terminal 6 sends the video with all other entities as receivers of that video. The mixer in RTP/RTCP has the same functionality as the MP in H.323. In H.323, the MP is centralized in some H.323 entity. All terminals in a conference usually are connected to a single MP. In RTP the mixer can, unlike the MP, also be distributed on the network so that only a portion of the participant terminals in the conference is connected to the mixer. This conference has voice-only Terminals 1 through 3 on the nonmulticast Internet connected through Mixer 1 to the private multicast IP network. Terminals 1 through 3 each has one voice-only RTP session (1a) through (3a), respectively, with Mixer 1. Terminals 4 and 5 are connected to the private multicast IP network through Mixer 2 with a 56 kbps and 28.8 kbps connection, respectively. Terminal 4 has two RTP sessions with Mixer 2. The first RTP session (4a) consists of G.723.1 voice, and the second RTP session (4vb) consists of the base layer of H.263 video. Terminal 4 cannot use the enhancement layers of H.263 due to bandwidth constraints on its link. Terminal 5 has only one voice RTP session (5a) with Mixer 2. Terminal 5 cannot use video due to constraints in bandwidth on its link. Mixer 1, Mixer 2, and Terminals 6 through 204 have four multicast RTP sessions. The first RTP session (6a) consists of G.723.1 voice; the second RTP session (6vb) consists of the base layer of H.263 video; the third RTP session (6ve1) consists of the first enhancement layer of H.263 video; and the fourth RTP session (6ve2) consists of the second enhancement layer of H.263 video. The audio session consists of six related RTP sessions (1a) through (6a); the video session consists of four related RTP sessions (4vb, 6vb, 6ve1, and 6ve2); and the distance learning conference consists of the audio and the video sessions.

Unique SSRC identifiers identify all entities transmitting or receiving media stream of RTP packets in the RTP session. The convention used to specify the SSRC identifier generated by an entity within an RTP Session is $SSRC_{Entity\text{-}RTP\ Session}$. Thus, $SSRC_{M2\text{-}6ve2}$, is the SSRC identifier generated by Mixer 2 in the RTP Session (6ve2), and $SSRC_{T6\text{-}6a}$ is the SSRC identifier generated by Terminal 6 in the RTP Session (6a). The SSRC identifiers must be unique within the individual audio and video sessions. However, the SSRC identifiers may conflict between the audio and video sessions. The SSRC space for the audio session spans all RTP sessions related to voice in this conference. Similarly, the SSRC space for the video session spans all RTP sessions related to video in this conference.

In Figure 4.17 the audio session consists of 204 participant terminals. Because only one participant can talk at a time to have a meaningful dialogue, most of the time a single voice stream exists. On occasions two or more participants may talk together but only for a short period of time. During periods of silence, voice is not transmitted. Therefore, most of the time there is only one voice stream in the audio session. Figure 4.18 is an example of the snapshot of the audio RTP session (6a) and (4a). The following describes the periods in the RTP session (6a):

1. The teacher of the distance learning conference is speaking, and Terminal 6 is transmitting the voice.
2. The student on Terminal 4 interrupts the teacher. Both continue to talk for 4 seconds, and during this period, Mixer 2 and Terminal 6 transmit media streams simultaneously.
3. The teacher stops speaking, and the student continues to ask her questions for 400 seconds; only Mixer 2 transmits the voice during this period.
4. The student on Terminal 5 interrupts, and both students continue to step on each other's speech for 6 seconds; Mixer 2 mixes the voice from the two students during this period.
5. The student on Terminal 4 stops speaking, and the student on Terminal 5 continues for 180 seconds; Mixer 2 transmits the voice during this period.
6. There is silence for 3 seconds, so none of the entities are transmitting.
7. The teacher on Terminal 6 and two students on Terminals 43 and 197 speak for 6 seconds, transmitting a total of three voice streams simultaneously.
8. The teacher takes over and talks for 30 minutes; only Terminal 6 is transmitting.
9. A break follows for 10 minutes; during this period, none of the entities are transmitting.
10. Following the break, the teacher continues to speak, and Terminal 6 is transmitting.

The following describes the periods in the RTP session (4a):

1. The teacher on Terminal 6 is speaking, and Mixer 2 is transmitting her voice.
2. The student on Terminal 4 interrupts the teacher. Both continue to speak for 4 seconds, and during this period Mixer 2 and Terminal 4 transmit media streams simultaneously.
3. The teacher stops speaking, and the student continues to ask her questions for 400 seconds; only Terminal 4 transmits the voice during this period.

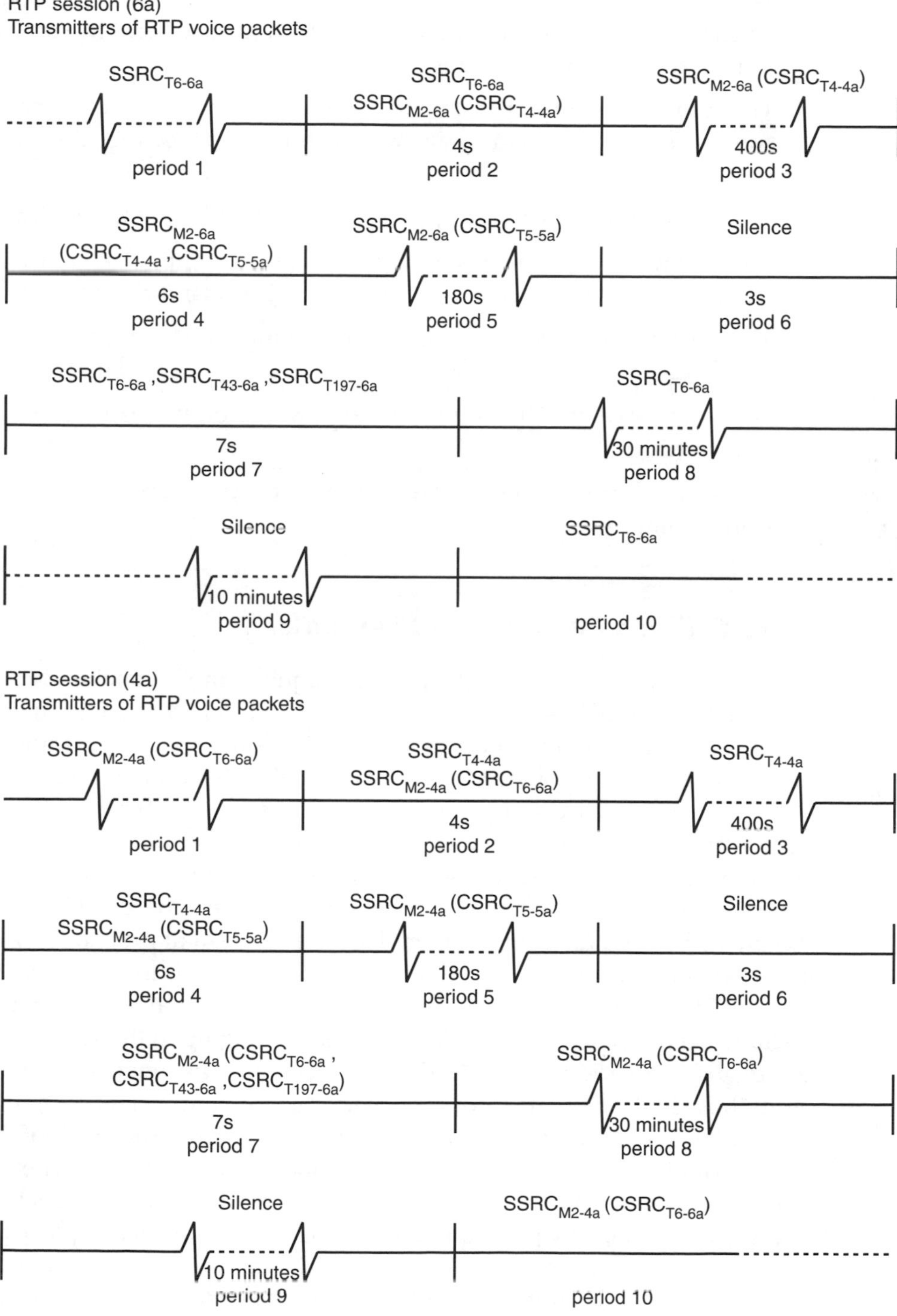

Figure 4.18 Snapshot of RTP sessions (6a) and (4a).

4. The student on Terminal 5 interrupts, and both students continue to step on each other's speech for 6 seconds; both Terminal 4 and Mixer 2 are transmitting voice during this period.
5. The student on Terminal 4 stops speaking, and the student on Terminal 5 continues for 180 seconds; only Mixer 2 transmits the voice during this period.
6. There is silence for 3 seconds, so none of the entities are transmitting.
7. The teacher on Terminal 6 and two students on Terminal 43 and 197 speak simultaneously for 6 seconds; only Mixer 2 is transmitting.
8. The teacher takes over and speaks for 30 minutes; Mixer 2 continues to transmit.
9. A break follows for 10 minutes; during this period none of the entities are transmitting.
10. Following the break, the teacher continues to speak, and Mixer 2 is transmitting.

SSRC Collision Detection and Resolution

In H.323, the centralized MC provides a unique terminalLabel to each participant terminal used to generate SSRC identifiers that are unique within the SSRC space consisting of all related RTP sessions. In an application that uses distributed control, however, the terminals must independently generate a 32-bit SSRC unique within its SSRC space. In this case, the 32-bit SSRC must be a random number to minimize the probability of having another terminal generate the same SSRC within their SSRC space. An algorithm to generate a 32-bit random number is described in [CAS96]. Because SSRC is a random number, there is a very small probability that SSRC identifiers will collide. All RTCP implementations must be able to detect SSRC collision and then resolve it. The detection algorithm may include keeping a list of all SSRC identifiers belonging to the same SSRC space and comparing the SSRC identifier generated by a new participant with those in the list. The resolution algorithm depends on whether the SSRC identifiers of other participants are colliding or whether the SSRC of this participant is colliding with another participant. If the collision is between other participants, this participant may drop the RTP and RTCP packets received from the new participant. If the collision involves this participant, then this participant must exit this RTP session and re-enter with a new random SSRC. Algorithms for SSRC collision detection and resolution are described in [CAS96].

Rules for RTCP Report Interval

Each participant entity independently maintains the state of the conference, so that if one or more participant entities are shut down, overall operation is not affected. The conference state associated with RTCP includes information about the media stream being transmitted, information on the quality of media being received, and information needed to maintain the roster. The participant entities should receive all state information sent in order to maintain a consistent state in those entities. Because packets may be lost on the Internet, there is no guarantee that information sent will be received by all the entities. Also, in conferencing, participant entities enter and leave the conference at different times. An entity entering the conference needs to synchronize its state with that of other participant entities. These problems, resulting in inconsistent state among participant entities of the conference, are solved by having senders periodically send the same or updated information. This solves the problem of eventually synchronizing the state information among entities, but it leads to a network bandwidth scalability problem as the number of participant entities increase to the thousands. Putting an upper limit on the network bandwidth used by the RTCP packets from all participant entities in the RTP session solves this scalability problem. The participant entities share this maximum RTCP bandwidth so that as the number of participant entities in the related RTP sessions increase, the share of bandwidth for each participant entity decreases. The algorithms used are described in [CAS96]. Participant entities use these algorithms to determine the RTCP report interval when they can send RTCP packets. Some of the features of the algorithms are enumerated as follows:

1. Bandwidth calculations include the transport and the network layers. The link layer is not included in the calculation, because it can change as the packet traverses from one network to another.
2. The RTCP bandwidth is suggested to be 5 percent of the RTP session bandwidth.
3. If the media senders add up to less than 25 percent of all participants in the RTP session, the senders get 25 percent, and the receivers get the remaining 75 percent of the RTCP bandwidth. Otherwise, both senders and receivers share the RTCP bandwidth equally.
4. The minimum theoretical report interval for multicast RTP sessions is 5 seconds. This interval is needed to avoid bursts of packets that occur when the report interval is small. For large report intervals, the network traffic is automatically smooth.
5. The minimum theoretical report interval of 5 seconds may be reduced to 360/(RTP session bandwidth in kbps) for active data senders.

6. The actual report interval is x * (theoretical report interval), where x is randomly changed over the range 0.5 to 1.5. This avoids the explosion of RTCP packets due to many participant entities unintentionally sending RTCP packets at the same time.

As shown in Figure 4.17, the amount of bandwidth used in the audio session is 16 kbps for one 5.3 kbps G.723.1 frame per RTP/UDP/IP packet. This calculation assumes that the RTP header is always 12 bytes in length, even though headers from mixers include CSRCs and are much larger. Also, a conservative calculation may include bandwidth for two voice streams to include those times when more than one participant is talking, but in this example bandwidth for one voice stream is allocated. Because the RTCP bandwidth is 5 percent of the RTP session bandwidth, the total bandwidth used by the audio session is about 16.84 kbps, where the 5 percent share of the RTCP bandwidth is 840 bps.

As shown in Figure 4.18, in RTP session (6a) the number of media transmitters is always less than 25 percent of the 201 participants that include Mixer 1, Mixer 2, and Terminals 6 through 204. Therefore, the senders get 210 bps, which is 25 percent of the RTCP bandwidth, and the receivers get the remaining 630 bps. In RTP session (4a) the number of media transmitters is always more than 25 percent of the two participants, so the RTCP bandwidth is divided equally with each one getting 420 bps.

The RTCP report interval will be calculated later in the next sections after the size of the RTCP packets is known.

RTCP Packets

RTCP consists of four major types of packets—Sender Report, Receiver Report, Source Description, and Goodbye. Multiple RTCP packets can be combined and transmitted as one compound RTCP packet to reduce the header overhead due to transport, network, and link layers. Individual packets in the compound packet can be processed in any order. These RTCP packets are described in detail in the following sections.

Source Description (SDES) RTCP Packet

The SSRC identifiers identify all participants in the RTP session. The SDES RTCP packet provides information—such as user's name, e-mail address, and telephone number—about the participants that are otherwise identified only through SSRC/CSRC. The format of SDES is shown in Figure 4.19. It consists of two parts. The first part consists of the packet header. The second part consists of one or more chunks, with each chunk describing the participant identified by SSRC/CSRC.

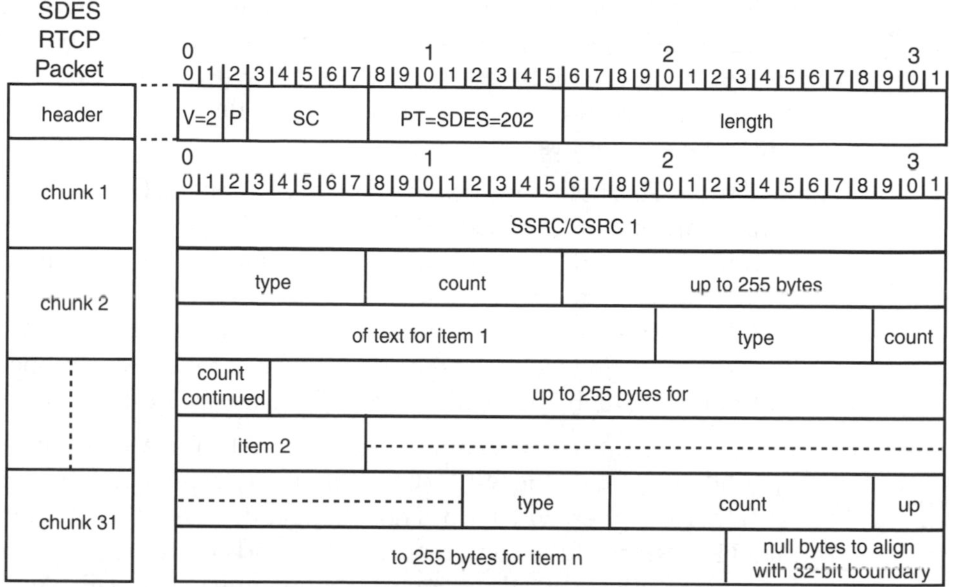

Figure 4.19 Format of Source Description RTCP packet.

The fields of the first part of the SDES packet containing the header are described as following:

version (V) (2 bits). This field specifies the version of the RTP/RTCP protocol used.

padding (P) (1 bit). This field, when set, specifies that the last byte of this RTCP packet contains the count of the number of redundant bytes at the end of this packet to be ignored. It aligns the RTCP packet to a boundary required by some applications.

source count (SC) (5 bits). This field specifies the number of chunks that are part of this SDES RTCP packet.

packet type (PT) (8 bits). This field specifies the type of the RTCP packet. It has a value of 202 assigned to the SDES RTCP packet, so it can be identified from the other types of RTCP packets.

length (16 bits). This field specifies the length of this RTCP packet in 32-bit words minus 1. The header and padding bytes are always included.

The second part of SDES consists of one or more chunks. Each chunk starts and ends on a 32-bit boundary and describes a single SSRC/CSRC. The fields of a chunk are described as follows:

SSRC/CSRC identifier (32 bits). This field contains an SSRC/CSRC identifier that will be described in the SDES items field.

SDES items. This field consists of a list of zero or more SDES items. An individual SDES item does not have to be aligned on a 32-bit boundary, but the SDES items combined shall be padded with NULL bytes so that this chunk is aligned on a 32-bit boundary. The fields of a single SDES item are described as follows:

type (8 bits). This field specifies the type of SDES item. Some of the types defined are end of SDES list (END) with a value of 0, canonical endpoint identifier (CNAME) with a value of 1, user name (NAME) with a value of 2, e-mail address (EMAIL) with a value of 3, and phone number (PHONE) with a value of 4. The last SDES item in the SDES list shall have a type of END to mark the end of the list, followed optionally by additional NULL bytes to align the SDES list to a 32-bit boundary.

The CNAME identifier is unique within related RTP sessions, and its use is mandatory. It binds the SSRC/CSRC that may change due to collision with this identifier, which does not change. If CNAME is unique across all RTP sessions of the conference, it also binds multiple sources of streams in different RTP sessions with the same participant. As shown in Figure 4.17, Terminal 6 should use the same CNAME to bind the voice stream from $SSRC_{T6\text{-}6a}$ in the audio session and the video streams from $SSRC_{T6\text{-}6vb}$, $SSRC_{T6\text{-}6ve1}$, and $SSRC_{T6\text{-}6ve2}$, in the video sessions.

The NAME identifier is the real name of the user. It is used in conferencing for display in the roster. The EMAIL identifier is the e-mail address of the user, and the PHONE identifier is the telephone number of the user. Because all five media streams from Terminal 6 can be associated through CNAME, the other non-CNAME SDES items can be sent in only one RTP session (6a), and the receivers can automatically associate them to the other RTP sessions (6vb), (6ve1), and (6ve2). The RTP session chosen must be the one used by all receivers; otherwise the SDES items will not be received by all receivers. If non-CNAME SDES items are sent only in the RTP session (6vb), the voice-only Terminal 5 will not get these items.

length (8 bits). This field specifies the length in bytes of the text that follows. If the SDES type is END, this length field is not present.

text (>= 0 bytes, <= 255 bytes). This field consists of up to 255 bytes of text that is relevant to the type of SDES item selected. The text is encoded in UTF-8 specified in [YERG98].

If the SDES type is END, this text field is not present.

If the SDES type is CNAME, the format of this text is suggested to be of the form "user@host" or "host," where "user" is the name of the user on the terminal, and "host" is either a fully qualified domain name or the dotted-decimal representation of the IP address of the terminal that is the source of the media stream.

If the SDES type is NAME, EMAIL, or PHONE, the text consists of the real name, e-mail address, or the phone number of the participant respectively.

Sender Report (SR) RTCP Packet

The senders of media periodically send Sender Reports to provide information about the media packets transmitted. The format of the Sender Report is shown in Figure 4.20. It consists of four parts. The first part consists of an 8-byte header. The second part consists of 20 bytes of sender information regarding the media stream being transmitted. The third part consists of zero or more 24-byte reception report blocks. Each reception report block consists of the quality of media received from a single source. The reason for putting the reception report blocks in the Sender Report is to reduce the overhead due to network headers. Otherwise, it makes more sense to include the reception report blocks only in the Receiver Report because it contains information about the quality of reception. This third part will be described later in the section on Receiver Report RTCP packet. The fourth part consists of provisions to extend the sender report with additional information specific to the RTCP profile being developed. To date, the

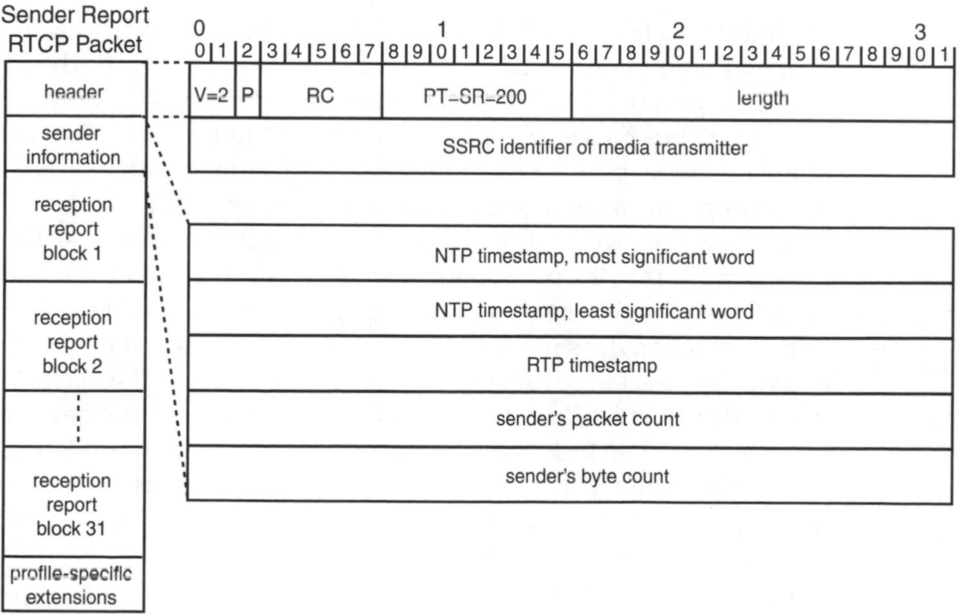

Figure 4.20 Format of the Sender Report RTCP packet.

authors are not aware of any extensions; therefore, no more information is provided on this part.

The fields of the first part of the sender report containing the header are described as following:

version (V) (2 bits). This field specifies the version of the RTP/RTCP protocol used.

padding (P) (1 bit). This field, when set, specifies that the last byte of this RTCP packet contains the count of the number of redundant bytes at the end of this packet to be ignored. It aligns the RTCP packet to a boundary required by some applications.

reception report count (RC) (5 bits). This field specifies the number of reception report blocks in the third part of this sender report.

packet type (PT) (8 bits). This field specifies the type of the RTCP packet. It has a value of 200 assigned for the Sender Report.

length (16 bits). This field specifies the length of this RTCP packet in 32-bit words minus 1. The header and padding bytes are always included.

SSRC Identifier (32 bits). This field consists of the SSRC identifier of the source of this RTCP packet.

The fields of the second part of the sender report containing the sender information are described as following:

NTP timestamp (64 bits). This field consists of the wallclock time (absolute date and time) represented in the timestamp format of NTP when this Sender Report is sent. NTP is a 64-bit unsigned fixed-point number with the high 32 bits consisting of the integer part and the low 32 bits consisting of the fractional part. It is assumed that the accuracy with which the NTP timestamp is measured is less than the resolution of NTP, so the figure on accuracy is not provided. The reason for periodically providing the NTP timestamp is that the participants join the conference at any time; the packet carrying the timestamp also can get lost in the network. If an implementation does not have access to wallclock time, it may use some other common clock or simply set this field to 0 (zero). If wallclock time is not used, and the different sources of media streams do not have access to some common clock, these streams cannot be synchronized. In a multipoint conference, the MP can mix voice streams generated from geographically scattered participants if all the sources of voice streams use some common clock; otherwise mixing cannot be done.

RTP timestamp (64 bits). This field consists of the RTP timestamp that corresponds to the NTP timestamp preceding. This RTP timestamp is from the same clock used to generate the RTP timestamps of the data packets, even though it may not correspond to one of the timestamps used in the data packets. The correspondence between the RTP and the NTP timestamp can be used to synchronize media streams from the same or from different sources.

sender's packet count (32 bits). This field consists of the total number of RTP data packets transmitted starting from the beginning of transmission to the time this Sender Report is sent. If the media source changes its SSRC identifier, this field should be reset to 0 (zero). This field can be used to calculate the average packet rate over a period of time.

sender's octet count (32 bits). This field consists of the total number of payload bytes transmitted starting from the beginning of transmission to the time this Sender Report is sent. The payload bytes do not include the headers or the padding bytes. If the media source changes its SSRC identifier, this field should be reset to 0 (zero). This field can be used to calculate the average payload data rate over a period of time.

Receiver Report (RR) RTCP Packet

The receivers of media periodically send Receiver Reports to provide feedback on the quality of media received. The format of the Receiver Report is shown in Figure 4.21. It consists of three parts. The first part consists of an 8-byte header. The fields in this header are the same as those in the header

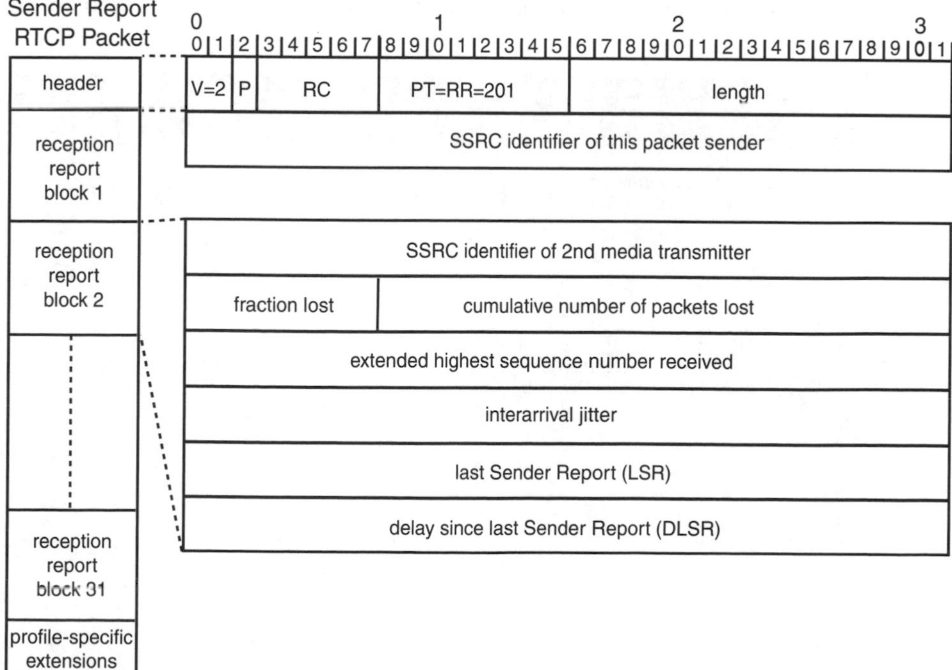

Figure 4.21 Format of the Receiver Report RTCP packet.

part of the Sender Report, except that the packet type field has a value of 201 assigned to the Receiver Report RTCP packet so it can be identified from the other types of RTCP packets. The second part consists of zero or more 24-byte reception report blocks. Each reception report block consists of data on the quality of media received from a single source. The receiver sends a Receiver Report without a reception report block if it did not receive any RTP media packets during the report interval. The third part consists of provisions to extend the sender report with additional information that is specific to the RTCP profile being developed. To date, the authors are not aware of any extensions; therefore, no more information is provided on this part.

The fields of the reception report block are explained by taking a snapshot of the beginning of the RTP Session (6a) in Figure 4.18, when Terminal 6 is transmitting and all other 200 participant terminals and mixers are receiving. This snapshot is taken over five consecutive report intervals (n — 4), (n − 3), (n − 2), (n − 1), and n when Mixer 2 is receiving RTP voice packets from Terminal 6 as shown in Table 4.4. The receivers are equally sharing an RTCP bandwidth of 630 bps with each receiver getting 3.15 bps. Each receiver must periodically send at every RTCP report interval a compound RTCP packet consisting of at least the Receiver Report and the CNAME SDES RTCP packets. The Receiver Report RTCP packet with one reception report block

Table 4.4 Reception Report Blocks for Four Consecutive RTCP Report Intervals

	RTCP Report Intervals →				
Fields of the Reception Report Block	**(n-4)**	**(n-3)**	**(n-2)**	**(n-1)**	**(n)**
RTCP report interval in seconds using random factors 1, 0.5, 1.5, 0.75, 1.25	254	127	381	190.5	317.5
Number of RTP voice packets expected during the report interval	8467	4233	12700	6350	10583
Highest RTP sequence number received in hexadecimal; sequence number of first RTP packet received is 0x41d5	0xff28		0x414d	0x5a1b	0x8372
EHSN in hexadecimal	0xff28		0x1414d	0x15a1b	0x18372
Total number of RTP voice packets expected (Ei)	48468		65401	71751	82334
Total number of RTP voice packets actually received (Ri)	48470		61170	64345	72282
CPL	0		4231	7406	10052
FPL			0.250	0.50	0.025

for $SSRC_{T6-6a}$ consists of 256 bits. If the CNAME is 30 bytes long, the SDES CNAME RTCP packet consists of 320 bits. With UDP/IP headers of 224 bits, the compound RTCP packet adds up to 800 bits. This means that the theoretical RTCP report interval is 254 seconds. This actual report interval is randomly changed by multiplying the theoretical report interval by a factor in the range of 0.5 to 1.5 to prevent participants from synchronizing their report intervals. In Table 4.4 the five report intervals in seconds for Mixer 2, starting with $(n - 4)$, are 254, 127, 381, 190.5, and 317.5 calculated by using the factors 1, 0.5, 1.5, 0.75, and 1.25, respectively. Note that these factors are not random and are picked for illustration purpose only. Because Terminal 6 is transmitting an RTP voice packet every 30 ms, the number of packets expected (not actually received) during the five report intervals, starting with $(n - 4)$, are 8467, 4233, 12700, 6350, and 10583. Assume that during the $(n - 3)$ report interval, all the 4233 voice packets are lost, so a Receiver Report will be issued without any reception report blocks for this interval. Also, assume that the RTP Sequence Number in hexadecimal of the first RTP voice packet received by Mixer 2 is 0x41d5, and the highest RTP Sequence Number in hexadecimal for the four report intervals $(n - 4)$, $(n - 2)$, $(n - 1)$, and n is 0xff28, 0x414d, ox5a1b, and 0x8372. The fields of the reception report block are described as follows:

SSRC Identifier (32 bits). This field consists of the SSRC identifier of the source of the media stream. All statistics in this reception report pertain to the media stream from this source. From Table 4.4, $SSRC_{T5-6a}$ is used in this field.

extended highest sequence number (EHSN) received (32 bits). This field consists of the highest sequence number generated from the last RTP data packet received. This field extends the 16-bit Sequence Number field of the RTP header by another 16 bits so that when the 16-bit RTP Sequence Number reaches the maximum count and wraps around to zero, the count is preserved by incrementing the high 16 bits of this field. From Table 4.4, the values of EHSN in hexadecimal calculated from the RTP Sequence Number field for the four report intervals starting from $(n - 4)$ are 0x0ff28, 0x1414d, 0x15a1b, and 0x18372.

cumulative number of packets lost (CPL) (32 bits). This field consists of the total number of RTP data packets lost since the beginning of reception. The CPL for the ith reception report block can be calculated using $CPL_i = E_i - R_i$, where E_i is the number of RTP data packets expected at the end of the ith report interval, and R_i is the number of RTP data packets received at the end of the ith report interval. If more packets are received than expected, due to duplicate packets, at the end of the ith report interval CPL_i is equal to zero. This means if $CPL_i < 0$, then $CPL_i = 0$. The E_i is calculated using $E_i = EHSI_i - SN_0 + 1$, where $EHSI_i$ is the EHSN of the last RTP data packet received, and SN_0 is the first RTP data packet received. The R_i is calculated by counting the RTP data packets as they are received. The count includes packets that arrive late and those that are duplicates. From Table 4.4, E_i for the four report intervals starting from (n—- 4) is 48468 (0x0ff28 – 0x041d5 + 1), 65401 (0x1414d – 0x041d5 + 1), 71751 (0x15a1b – 0x041d5 + 1), and 82334 (0x18372 – 0x041d5 + 1), respectively. The R_i for the four report intervals starting from (n – 4) is 48470, 61170, 64345, and 72282, respectively. Therefore, the CPL_i for the four report intervals starting from (n – 4) is 0 (48468 – 48470 = -2), 4231 (65401 – 61170), 7406 (71751 – 64345), and 10052 (82334 – 72282), respectively. Note that at the end of the (n – 4) report interval the number of packets actually received are higher than those expected due to duplicate packets generated by the IP network. The resultant negative packet loss is treated as equal to zero. Packet loss indicates congestion in the network, and the difference between the last two CPL values can be used to determine the recent quality of the reception.

fraction lost (FPL) (8 bits). This field consists of a fraction of RTP data packets lost since the last Sender Report or Receiver Report was sent. This fraction is a fixed-point number with the binary point to the left of this field. The FPL for the ith reception report block can be calculated using $FPL_i = ((E_i - E_{i-1}) - (R_i - R_{i-1}))/(E_i - E_{i-1})$, where the numerator provides the number of RTP data packets lost during the ith report interval, and $(E_i - E_{i-1})$ is the number of RTP data packets expected during the ith report interval. If packets are not received during the ith report interval, then FPL_i is equal to zero. This means if $(E_i - E_{i-1}) = 0$, then $FPL_i = 0$. Also, if more packets are received than expected, due to duplicate packets, during the ith report interval then FPL_i is equal to zero. This means if $((E_i - E_{i-1}) - (R_i - R_{i-1})) < 0$, then $FPL_i = 0$. From Table 4.4, $(E_i - E_{i-1})$ during the three intervals starting from (n – 2) is 16933, 6350, and 10583, and $(R_i - R_{i-1})$ during the three intervals starting from (n – 2) is 12700, 3175, and 7937. The FPL_i during the three report intervals starting from (n – 2) is 0.250, 0.50, and 0.025. Note that the numerator of FPL_i cannot be replaced with $(CPL_i - CPL_{i-1})$ because any negative packet loss in CPL_i is reported as equal to 0. The packet loss, during the (n – 2) interval, calculated using $((E_i - E_{i-1}) - (R_i - R_{i-1}))$ is 4233 whereas by using $(CPL_i - CPL_{i-1})$ it is 4231.

The FPL can be used to calculate the packet loss rate during the ith report interval by dividing FPL_i with the length in seconds of the ith report interval. The length in seconds of the ith report interval can be calculated through the use of the NTP and the RTP timestamps.

interarrival jitter (J) (32 bits). This field provides an estimate of the statistical variance of the difference in delay from packet to packet as packets are received. The J for the ith RTP data packet P_i is calculated using $J_i = J_{i-1} + (|(R_i - C_i) - (R_{i-1} - C_{i-1})| - J_{i-1})/16$, where C_i is the RTP timestamp of P_i, R_i

is the time expressed in RTP timestamp units when P_i is received, $|(R_i - C_i) - (R_{i-1} - C_{i-1})|$ is the absolute value of the jitter of P_i, and the initial value of J_{i-1} is zero when the first RTP data packet is received. Note that the received RTP data packets are ordered on the basis of their arrival time and not on the basis of their sequence. The *J* can be used to indicate impending congestion in the network. Increases in J over many consecutive report intervals indicate the arrival of congestion, which is marked by packet loss.

last Sender-Report timestamp (LSR) (32 bits). This field consists of the middle 32 bits of the 64-bit NTP timestamp in the last Sender Report received. The middle 32 bits of NTP consist of the low 16 bits of the 32-bit integer part and the high 16 bits of the 32-bit fractional part. This field is set to zero if the Sender Report has not yet been received. The transmitter can use the LSR along with DLSR to calculate the RTT between itself and this receiver of the media.

delay since last Sender-Report (DLSR) (32 bits). This field consists of the delay in 1/65536 seconds from the time the last Sender Report is received to the time this reception report block is sent. This field is set to zero if the Sender Report has not yet been received. The transmitter can use the LSR and DLSR to calculate the RTT between itself and this receiver of the media. This is done with the use of RTT = X − LSR − DLSR, where *X* is the NTP timestamp when this reception report block is received by the transmitter.

Goodbye (BYE) RTCP Packet

The BYE packet is sent to inform that one or more SSRC/CSRC identifiers are leaving the RTP session. This packet is sent as soon as the participant leaves the RTP session, instead of being sent at the next report interval. The format of BYE is shown in Figure 4.22. It consists of two parts. The first part consists of the packet header. The second part is optional and consists of text describing the reason for leaving. The header consists of the Version (V), Padding (P), Source Count (SC), Packet Type (PT), length, and one or more SSRC/CSRC identifiers. The V, P, and length fields have the same meaning as the corresponding fields in the Sender Report. The PT field has a value of 203 assigned to the BYE RTCP packet so it can be identified from the other types of RTCP packets. The remaining two fields of the first part are described as follows:

source count (SC) (5 bits). This field consists of the number of SSRC/CSRC identifiers that are part of this Goodbye RTCP packet. As shown in Figure 4.17, if Mixer 2 leaves the RTP session (6a), this field should contain a value of 3.

SSRC/CSRC identifiers (>= 0 bits, <= 31 * 32 bits). This field contains a list of SSRC/CSRC Identifiers that will no longer be participating in this RTP

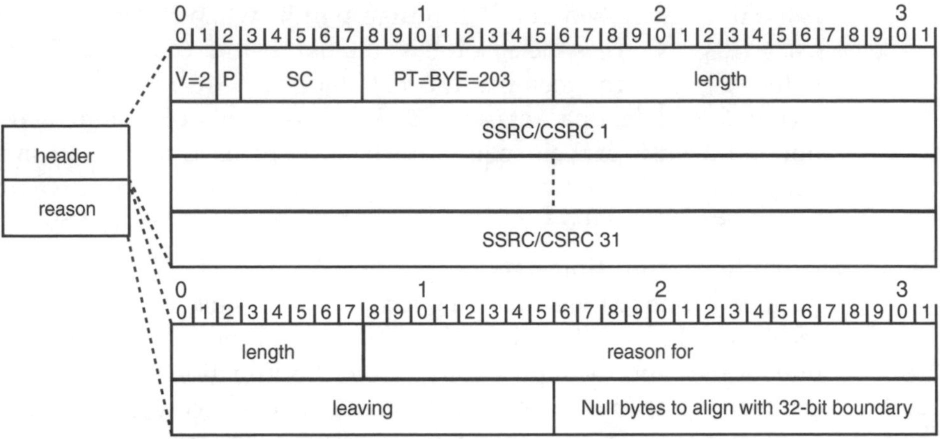

Figure 4.22 Format of the Goodbye RTCP packet.

session. The length of the list is contained in the Source Count field. As shown in Figure 4.17, if Mixer 2 leaves the RTP session (6a), this list will consist of $SSRC_{M2\text{-}6a}$, $CSRC_{T4\text{-}6a}$, and $CSRC_{T5\text{-}6a}$.

The fields of the second part of Goodbye are optional; these fields are described as follows:

length (8 bits). This field consists of the number of bytes of text. It does not include the number of NULL bytes, if any, used for padding.

reason for leaving (>= 0 bytes, <= 255 bytes). This field contains the text explaining the reason for leaving. The text is encoded in UTF-8 specified in RFC 2279. This field must be padded with NULL bytes if this BYE packet is not aligned on a 32-bit boundary.

Rules for Sending RTCP Packets

The following rules are specified in [CAS96] for sending RTCP packets and for determining the number of participants used for calculating the RTCP report interval:

1. The RTCP compound packet must contain the Sender or the Receiver Report. This is done to maximize the amount of statistics provided on the quality of media being received. If no media is sent or received, the Sender or the Receiver report will not contain any reception report blocks.
2. The RTCP compound packet must contain the SDES CNAME. This enables new receivers to resolve changes to SSRC due to collisions and quickly associate all media streams from the same participant.

3. No more than 20 percent of the participants' share of RTCP bandwidth in an RTP session can be used to transmit information other than Sender Report, Receiver Report, and SDES CNAME.
4. A new participant is added to the list of participants in an RTP session when multiple RTP data packets are received or a CNAME RTCP packet is received.
5. The initial theoretical delay before the participant sends the first RTCP packets is _ * (minimum theoretical report interval), which is 2.5 seconds. This provides sufficient time to the new participant entering the RTP session to estimate the report interval by gathering information about the approximate number of participants in that RTP session. This also provides a good tradeoff to the new participant to announce its presence so it is quickly added to the list of participants. The initial actual delay is x * (theoretical initial delay), where *x* is randomly changed over the range 0.5 to 1.5. This avoids the initial explosion of RTCP packets due to many participants joining the RTP session at the same time.
6. A participant is deleted from the list of participants when either a BYE RTCP packet is received or an RTCP packet is not received for 5 RTCP intervals.
7. In order to avoid the explosion of BYE RTCP packets due to many participants leaving the RTP session at the same time, the participant entity is allowed to send the BYE packet immediately only if the number of participants in the RTP session is less than 51. If the number of participants in the RTP session is more than 50, then the BYE packet is sent at the next report interval as described in the BYE back-off algorithm [CAS96]. The participant can also leave without sending BYE, and it will be timed out of the RTP session.

Use of RTCP Packets by MP/Mixer

The MP/mixer does not pass Sender Report packets between related RTP sessions because the characteristics of the mixed media are different from the individual media streams. The mixer must generate its own Sender Report packets for the RTP session in which it is sending the mixed media streams.

Just like Sender Reports, the mixer/MP does not pass Receiver Report packets between related RTP sessions because the characteristics of the mixed media are different from the individual media streams. The mixer must generate its own Receiver Report packets for the RTP session in which it is receiving the mixed media streams.

The mixer/MP forwards the SDES CNAME packet it receives from one RTP session to the other related RTP sessions. As shown in Figure 4.17, the SDES

CNAME packet from $SSRC_{T4-4a}$ is forwarded by Mixer 2 to the RTP sessions (5a) and (6a). The mixer/MP can combine the SDES chunks from the SSRC/CSRC identifiers in one or more related RTP sessions and send a single SDES RTCP packet in the other related RTP sessions. The SDES CNAME chunks can be extracted by Mixer 2 from the SDES packets from $SSRC_{T4-4a}$ and $SSRC_{T4-5a}$ and combined in a new SDES packet for the RTP session (6a). The mixer may filter out any SDES item except CNAME for any reason including constraints in bandwidth. The CNAME is forwarded unchanged to allow SSRC collision resolution to work. Assume Mixer 2 sends SDES packets in each of the RTP sessions (4a), (5a), and (6a). Then, in RTP session (4a) the SDES packets may contain chunks from $SSRC_{M2-4a}$, and up to 30 CSRCs from $CSRC_{T1-4a}$, through $CSRC_{T3-4a}$, and $CSRC_{T5-4a}$, through $CSRC_{T204-4a}$. Similarly, in RTP session (5a) the SDES packets may contain chunks from $SSRC_{M2-4a}$, and up to 30 CSRCs from $CSRC_{T1-4a}$, through $CSRC_{T4-4a}$, and $CSRC_{T6-4a}$, through $CSRC_{T204-4a}$. In RTP session (6a) the SDES packets may contain chunks from $SSRC_{M2-4a}$, $CSRC_{T4-4a}$, and $CSRC_{T5-4a}$.

The mixer/MP simply forwards the BYE packets received from its SSRC/CSRC identifiers to other related RTP sessions. As shown in Figure 4.17, Mixer 2 forwards the BYE packet from $SSRC_{T4-4a}$ to related RTP sessions (5a) and (6a). If the mixer/MP leaves the conference, it lists its SSRC and all CSRC identifiers it is handling. If Mixer 2 gracefully shuts down, it sends a BYE packet in all of the RTP sessions — (4a), (4b), (5a), (6a), (6vb), (6ve1), and (6ve2)—it is handling. In RTP session (4a), the BYE packet consists of $SSRC_{M2-4a}$ and up to 30 CSRCs from $CSRC_{T1-4a}$, through $CSRC_{T3-4a}$, and $CSRC_{T5-4a}$, through $CSRC_{T204-4a}$.

RTCP Report Interval Calculations

The calculations for the RTCP report interval are shown through the use of the examples illustrated in Figure 4.18. The RTCP report intervals are calculated for Mixer 2 for the RTP sessions (4a) and (6a). At every RTCP report interval, Mixer 2 sends a compound RTCP packet consisting of one Sender or Receiver Report packet, one SDES packet with one or more chunks of CNAME, and one chunk of NAME. The NAME should not take more than 20 percent of RTCP bandwidth allocated to the participant. The size in bits of the various components of the compound RTCP packet is shown as follows:

1. Sender Report with zero, one, two, and three reception report blocks is 224, 416, 608, and 800 bits, respectively.
2. Receiver Report with zero, one, two, and three reception report blocks is 64, 256, 448, and 640 bits, respectively.

3. Assume that the size of the text for CNAME and NAME is 240 bits and that the size of SDES packet with zero, one, two, and three chunks is 32, 320, 608, and 896 bits, respectively.
4. The UDP/IP header is 224 bits.

The RTCP report intervals calculated for $SSRC_{M2-6a}$ based on the periods of Figure 4.18 for RTP session (6a) are shown as follows:

1. During this period, $SSRC_{M2-6a}$ is the receiver of voice packets from $SSRC_{T6-6a}$. The 200 receivers ($SSRC_{M1-6a}$, $SSRC_{M2-6a}$, $SSRC_{T7-6a}$ through $SSRC_{T204-6a}$) equally share an RTCP bandwidth of 630 bps with each receiver getting 3.15 bps. The compound RTCP packet consisting of a Receiver Report packet from $SSRC_{M2-6a}$ with one reception report block for $SSRC_{T6-6a}$, an SDES packet with one CNAME chunk from $SSRC_{M2-6a}$, and UDP/IP headers occupies 800 bits. If the NAME chunk is added to the SDES packet and Mixer 2 alternates between sending the SDES NAME of $CSRC_{T5-5a}$ and $CSRC_{T4-4a}$, the compound RTCP packet occupies 1088 bits. If SDES NAME is sent in every other RTCP packet, the SDES NAME chunk occupies less than 20 percent of the RTCP bandwidth. This means that there are two theoretical RTCP report intervals of 254 seconds followed by 345.4 seconds, and this pair repeats. The actual report intervals are randomly changed by multiplying the theoretical report interval by a factor in the range of 0.5 to 1.5 to prevent participants from synchronizing their report intervals.

   Note that Mixer 2 does not send the SDES CNAME chunks from $CSRC_{T5-5a}$ and $CSRC_{T4-4a}$ until those terminals start transmitting media. This allows the mixer to keep the duration of the report interval to a minimum and the number of Receiver Reports sent to a maximum as the number of participants connected to the mixer in the RTP session increases. Otherwise, the solution is not scalable, because it will grow the compound RTCP packet as the number of participants connected to the mixer grows, even though most of the participants are receivers. By not sending all the CNAME items, collisions in SSRC identifiers will not be detected early on. Therefore, a tradeoff exists here between the scalability of compound RTCP packets and the early detection of SSRC collision.

   Note that the duration of the report interval is so high that it will take more than 33.8 hours for the last participant entering the RTP session to develop a complete roster of all the remaining 203 participants. This essentially makes the use of SDES items, other the CNAME, useless for large conferences in which the RTCP bandwidth is limited.

2. During this period $SSRC_{M2-6a}$ is the transmitter of voice packets from $CSRC_{T4-4a}$ and a receiver of voice packets from $SSRC_{T6-6a}$. This period with

a duration of 4 seconds is very short compared with the duration of the report interval. Therefore, it will end up being part of the report interval that includes period 1, period 3, or both. The two transmitters ($SSRC_{M2-6a}$, $SSRC_{T6-6a}$) equally share an RTCP bandwidth of 210 bps with each transmitter getting 105 bps. The compound RTCP packet consisting of a Sender Report packet from $SSRC_{M2-6a}$ with one reception report block for $SSRC_{T6-6a}$, an SDES packet with one CNAME chunk from $SSRC_{M2-6a}$ and the second CNAME chunk from $CSRC_{T4-4a}$, and UDP/IP headers occupies 1248 bits. If the NAME chunk is added to the SDES packet, the compound RTCP packet occupies 1536 bits. The SDES NAME is sent in every other RTCP packet. This means that two theoretical RTCP report intervals of 11.89 seconds followed by 14.63 seconds exist, and this pair repeats.

3. During this period $SSRC_{M2-6a}$ is the transmitter of voice packets from $CSRC_{T4-4a}$. Because it is the only transmitter, it gets an RTCP bandwidth of 210 bps. The compound RTCP packet consisting of a Sender Report packet from $SSRC_{M2-6a}$ with no reception report block, an SDES packet with one CNAME chunk from $SSRC_{M2-6a}$ and the second CNAME chunk from $CSRC_{T4-4a}$, and UDP/IP headers occupies 1056 bits. If the NAME chunk is added to the SDES packet, the compound RTCP packet occupies 1344 bits. The SDES NAME is sent in every other RTCP packet. This means that two theoretical RTCP report intervals of 5.03 seconds followed by 6.4 seconds exist, and this pair repeats.
4. During this period $SSRC_{M2-6a}$ is the transmitter of voice packets from $CSRC_{T4-4a}$ and $CSRC_{T5-5a}$. The only difference between this period and period 3 is that in this period the SDES packet has one extra CNAME chunk from $CSRC_{T5-5a}$, which gives the compound RTCP packet size of 1344 bits without the NAME chunk and 1638 bits with the NAME chunk. The NAME of $CSRC_{T4-4a}$ and $CSRC_{T5-5a}$ is alternated in the compound RTCP packet. The two theoretical RTCP report intervals are 6.4 seconds followed by 7.8 seconds, and this pair repeats.
5. During this period $SSRC_{M2-6a}$ is the transmitter of voice packets from $CSRC_{T5-5a}$. This period is like period 3, so it is not described here.
6. This period with a duration of 3 seconds of silence is too short. Therefore, it will end up being part of the report interval that includes period 5, period 6, or both.
7. During this period $SSRC_{M2-6a}$ is the receiver of voice packets from $SSRC_{T6-6a}$, $SSRC_{T43-6a}$, and $SSRC_{T197-6a}$. However, the position of the report interval at the beginning of this period will determine whether $SSRC_{M2-6a}$ sends Sender or Receiver Reports. If the last report interval of period 5 starts 1 second before the end of period 5, this report interval covers the end of period 5, the whole of period 6, and the beginning of period 7. Then the

compound RTCP packet consists of a Sender Report packet from $SSRC_{M2-6a}$ with three reception report blocks for $SSRC_{T6-6a}$, $SSRC_{T43-6a}$, and $SSRC_{T197-6a}$, and the SDES packet. However, if the last report interval of period 5 ends either at exactly the end of period 5 or in period 6, the next report interval covers period 6 and period 7. Then the compound RTCP packet consists of a Receiver Report packet from $SSRC_{M2-6a}$ with three reception report blocks for $SSRC_{T6-6a}$, $SSRC_{T43-6a}$, and $SSRC_{T197-6a}$, and the SDES packet. In the latter case, 198 receivers exist, and each equally shares an RTCP bandwidth of 3.18 bps. The compound RTCP packet size is 1184 bits without the NAME chunk and 1472 bits with the NAME chunk. The two theoretical RTCP report intervals are 372.33 seconds followed by 462.89 seconds, and this pair repeats.

8. During this period $SSRC_{M2-6a}$ is the receiver of voice packets from $SSRC_{T6-6a}$. This period is like period 1, so it is not described here.
9. During this period of silence all the participants send the compound RTCP packet consisting of a Receiver Report packet with no reception report blocks, and the SDES packet. The 201 receivers equally share an RTCP bandwidth of 840 bps with each receiver getting 4.18 bps. The compound RTCP packet size is 384 bits without the NAME chunk and 672 bits with the NAME chunk. The two theoretical RTCP report intervals are 91.87 seconds followed by 160.77 seconds, and this pair repeats.
10. During this period $SSRC_{M2-6a}$ is the receiver of voice packets from $SSRC_{T6-6a}$. This period is like period 1, so it is not described here.

The theoretical RTCP report intervals for $SSRC_{M2-4a}$ in Figure 4.18 for RTP session (4a) is always 5 seconds. There are two participants, so each gets an RTCP bandwidth of 420 bps. Because the minimum allowable theoretical RTCP report interval is 5 seconds, all compound RTCP packets less than 2100 bits will have the report interval of 5 seconds. The compound RTCP packets from $SSRC_{M2-4a}$ can be shown to always be less than 2100 bits, thus giving the theoretical RTCP report intervals of 5 seconds.

RTCP Scalability

In order to allow RTCP to scale to thousands of participants, two issues need to be considered: the scalability of network bandwidth, and the scalability of storage in the participant entity as the number of participants in the RTP session grows. The network bandwidth scalability issue is already solved by putting an upper limit on the usage of RTCP bandwidth per RTP session and by having the participant entities share this bandwidth. The storage scalability issue stems from having the participant entity store information about all SSRC identifiers of the RTP session. Using SSRC sampling can solve this issue; the details of this algorithm are given in [ROS00].

Large-Scale Conference Using H.332

H.323 is based on real-time, as opposed to prearranged, conferencing in which ad hoc conferences can be set up. The application targeted for H.323 is telephony in which single digit scalability of participants is sufficient. However, if H.323 is to be used for applications such as Distance Learning, Corporate Presentation, and Panel discussion with large audience, triple- or four-digit scalability of participants is required. The goal of H.332 is to scale H.323 to thousands of participant endpoints. Developed for telephony, H.323 requires a set of procedures for conference setup, capability negotiation, creation and control of media streams, and conference tear down. These procedures do not scale as the number of participant endpoints in the conference grows. Also, applications such as Distance Learning do not require these procedures to be handled in real-time. All information required to set up the conference can be disseminated well before the conference begins. These applications usually have one theme in common. There is a chairman—teacher in Distance Learning virtual classroom, president of a company in virtual auditorium, and chair of a panel in a panel discussion—with a wide audience. The chair is presenting most of the time, and the audiences intermittently ask questions. Discussions that last for a long time are usually confined to a small panel consisting of tens of participants either picked before the conference or created ad hoc from the audience of hundreds and thousands of participants.

The steps involved in setting up an H.332 conference consists of the following:

1. Encode the conference announcement in SDP and deliver the announcement information to the conference participants through any mechanism such as e-mail and Web.
2. The participants join the conference at some future time using the information in the announcement.

Conference Configuration

During the conference, the configuration of H.332 consists of a small panel and a large number of audiences as shown in Figure 4.23. The panel consists of an H.323 conference—centralized or decentralized—with H.323 endpoints. The audiences consist of RTP/RTCP terminals that receive only media, so they are listeners. To scale the audience, the media from the panel is multicast. A panel using a centralized conference must consist of an MP that can multicast media to the audience outside the panel. If the audiences are allowed to ask questions, they first join the panel. A panel has temporary and

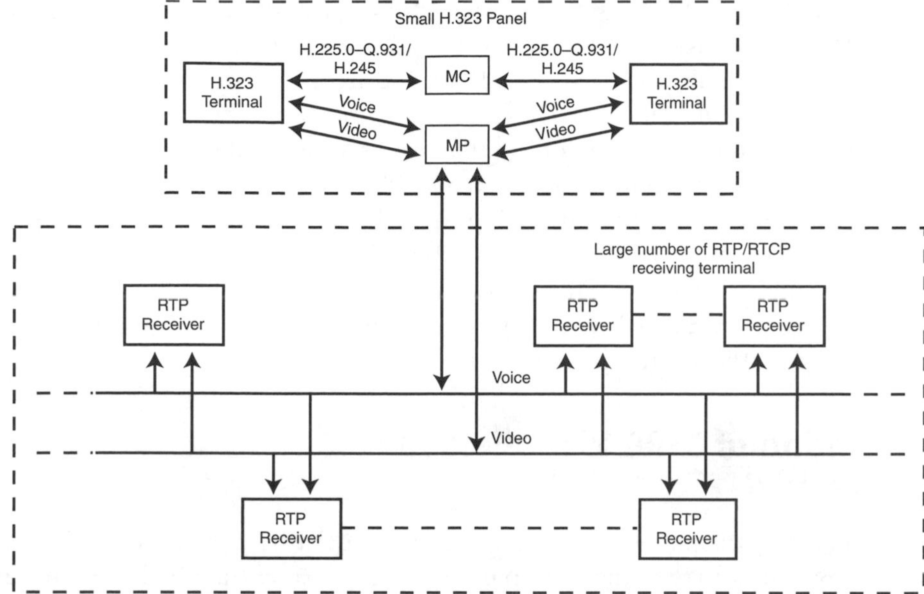

Figure 4.23 H.332-based conference.

permanent members. The permanent members are essential to the panel, so they are not forced to leave the panel. The temporary members come from the audience, and they can be forced to leave from the full panel to make room for a new temporary member. When the temporary member joins or gets invited to the panel, they switch from being an RTP receiving terminal to an H.323 terminal. When the temporary members leave the panel, they switch back from being an H.323 terminal to an RTP receiving terminal.

Extensions to SDP

SDP is extended to specify an H.332 conference by including "a=type:HLC" at the session level, which specifies that this announcement is for the H.332 conference. Also, the RTP terminals need to join the panel for discussion, so SDP is extended with "m=control <port>[/<number of ports>] H323 mc". Therefore, "m=control 3240 H323 mc" and "c=IN IP4 180.6.18.48" in the SDP announcement specify that the H.323 panel can be joined by making an H.323 connection at the IP address of 180.6.18.48 and port 3240.

Invitation from the Panel

The SDP announcement provides the address of the MC that enables the RTP receiving terminals to join the panel. However, during the conference, the panel also may invite a participant from the conference. This is equivalent to the teacher asking a question from a student. This is accomplished by having RTP terminals provide their callable addresses through the new RTCP SDES item CADDR. The CADDR can be an e-mail address, H.323 URL, dotted-decimal representation of the IP address, or any other address used to invite the RTP terminal to the H.323 panel. Those RTP terminals that cannot be called for any reason, including being behind the firewalls, shall not provide CADDR. By providing CADDR, the RTP terminal is advertising that it can be invited to the panel. The MC can invite the RTP terminal in the panel by sending an H.225.0-Q.931 Setup message with invite as the conferenceGoal to the callable address specified.

Generation of SSRC Identifiers in H.323 and RTP

Because the panel uses H.323, the SSRC identifiers are generated by using the low-order byte of the terminalLabel provided by the MC in low-order byte of the SSRC. This produces 256 SSRC identifiers that are unique within the conference. The RTP terminals outside the panel generate a 32-bit random SSRC. When the H.323 terminal detects the 32-bit SSRC collision with an RTP terminal, it should change its high 24 bits of SSRC so that its terminalLabel does not change. When the RTP terminal enters the panel as an H.323 terminal, it receives a terminalLabel that, most likely, changes its SSRC. H.323 terminals leaving the panel should not change their SSRC identifier unless they detect a collision.

Recommended Reading

Details on SDP can be found in the IETF RFC [HAN98]. The ITU-T recommendation H.332 for large-scale conferences is specified in [00H332]. The algorithm for SSRC sampling is provided in [ROS00].

The UTF-8 encoding for text is specified in [YERG98].

References

00H332 ITU-T Recommendation H.332. *H.323 extended for loosely-coupled conferences*. November 1998.

HAN98 Handley, M. and Jacobson, V. *SDP: Session Description Protocol*. RFC 2327, April 1998.

ROS00 Rosenberg, J. and Schulzrinne, H. *Sampling of the Group Membership in RTP.* RFC 2762, February 2000.

YERG98 Yergeau, F. *UTF-8, a transformation format of ISO 10646*. RFC 2279, January 1998.

Problems

1. What is the end-to-end delay experienced by G.723.1 voice in the multicast, multi-unicast, and the master-slave network configurations?
2. Give one scenario in which SSRC is not needed and one scenario in which it is needed by the MCU using centralized media.
3. Instead of SSRC, the receiver can use the network address of the sender to identify the source of the packet. So, how is SSRC useful?
4. In H.323, signaling is always centralized in the MC entity. The MC has the addresses of all the slave endpoints participating in the conference. A majority of ad hoc conferences are three-way calls. For three-way calls, the use of multi-unicast for media is quite effective. In this case, the MP is not needed, but the MC needs to provide the addresses of endpoints in the conference so endpoints can multi-unicast media. Develop additions to H.245 to enable multi-unicast of media by the endpoints. Test your design against cases in which endpoints join and leave an on-going conference.
5. In H.323, signaling is always centralized in the MC entity. Develop a distributed signaling protocol in which all endpoints in the conference are peers and a multicast address is used for signaling. Test your design against cases in which endpoints join and leave an ongoing conference. (Hint: Extend RTCP with functionality equivalent to a tightly controlled conference using H.245.)
6. The MCU-based conference scenario, described in this chapter, illustrates the enormous amount of signaling that is routed through the gatekeeper. What are some of the ways through which the gatekeeper-routed signaling can be preserved to allow the gatekeeper to monitor the call and route only those signals that provide useful information to the gatekeeper? List the H.225.0-Q.931 and H.245 messages that must be routed through the gatekeeper and the functionality they provide to the gatekeeper. Also, list the messages that do not have to be routed through the gatekeeper and give reasons for your decision.
7. Describe how the decentralized meet-me conference works. Assume the same scenario as the MCU-based conference described in this chapter, but have the voice chat room hosted at Terminal 1.
8. Compare centralized and decentralized meet-me conferences by listing their advantages and disadvantages.

9. Compare centralized and decentralized ad hoc conferences by listing their advantages and disadvantages.
10. If the SSRC field in the RTP header is used to identify the source of media stream, why is it not used to also identify the terminal instead of using the terminalLabel in H.245? Why is the CNAME in RTCP not used to replace the use of terminalLabel in H.245?
11. Develop an algorithm for a Decision Unit that processes RTCP provided reception quality information from network monitors and decides on routing/rerouting new/existing RTP data flows from congested to noncongested networks. The network monitors are placed at various points in the network to gather statistics from RTCP Sender and Receiver Reports.
12. RTCP requires that information about all SSRC identifiers in the RTP session be kept in each participant entity. This leads to the issue of storage scalability as the number of participants in the RTP session increases. Devise an SSRC sampling method that does not require that information about all SSRC identifiers be kept.

CHAPTER 5

Inter-Domain Communication

In this chapter, we describe the communication between administrative domains for address resolution, access authorization, and resource usage reporting in order to complete a call from the originating to the terminating administrative domain. In Chapter 4, "Multi-Point Conference," we did not describe the mechanics of resolving the URL, e-mail address, or an E.164 address to an IP address. In this chapter, we describe these mechanics by using the H.225.0 Annex G protocol and the *border element* (BE) functional entity. Figure 5.1 illustrates how H.225.0 Annex G works. This figure duplicates much of what Figure 4.7 shows and adds to the administrative domains of Telco1 and Clearinghouse1 and adds the use of border elements.

Address resolution occurs from the H.323 alias address to the transport address, which consists of IP address and port. Access authorization occurs at the terminating administrative domain in order to allow a specific call from the originating administrative domain to complete. Both the originating and the terminating administrative domains report resource usage for call settlement.

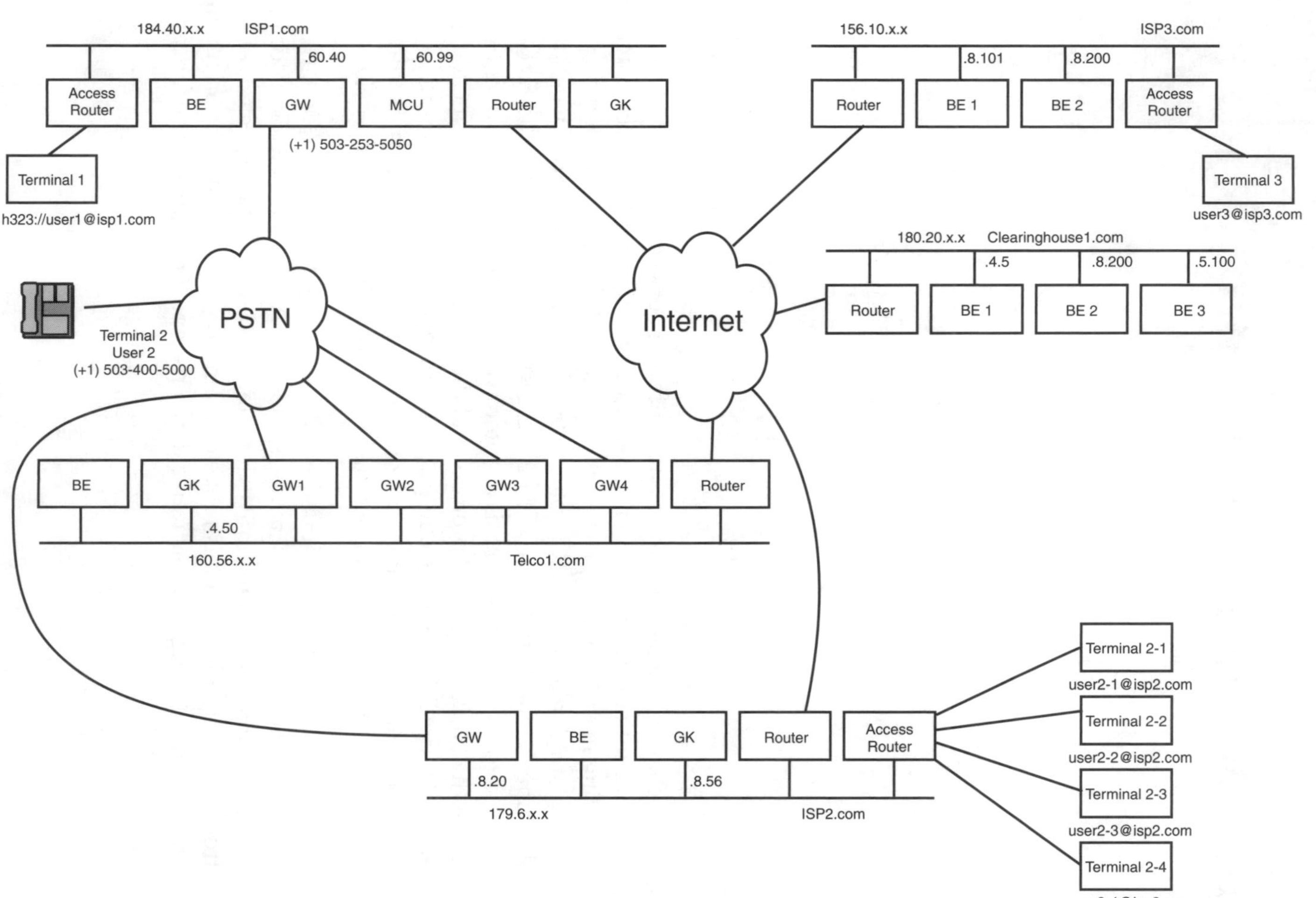

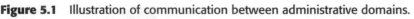

Figure 5.1 Illustration of communication between administrative domains.

Organization of Administrative Domains

The telephony service providers complete calls originating from their end users and terminating with end users anywhere in the world. A service provider cannot have a worldwide presence just so it can complete all the calls from its end users. Therefore, service providers and call brokers make agreements among themselves that enable them to complete calls anywhere in the world and give the appearance of a worldwide presence to their end users. As part of these agreements, the service providers share call routing information so that calls initiated by one service provider can be completed by another service provider. The H.225.0 Annex G protocol assumes that the service providers divide their networks into administrative domains. The administrative domains communicate routing information to each other through the use of the H.225.0 Annex G protocol. The administrative domains use one or more border elements to communicate such information. The BE is a functional entity that resides in a router or any other product. It can coexist with other H.323 functional entities, such as a gatekeeper or a gateway.

The H.225.0 Annex G protocol puts no restrictions on how the administrative domains are organized for resolving alias addresses. Figure 5.2 shows four approaches to organizing administrative domains. Figure 5.2(A) shows a hierarchical organization in which an administrative domain resolves all alias addresses that are an aggregation of the alias addresses resolved by the domains below it. The top-level administrative domain (AD), being the root of the tree, resolves all alias addresses handled by the administrative domains AD1–1 through AD1–N below it. The domain AD1–2 resolves all E.164 addresses that are an aggregation of the E.164 addresses resolved by the domains AD1–2–1 through AD1–2–9. The domain AD1–2–1 resolves E.164 addresses (+1) 5030* through (+1) 5031*; the domain AD1–2–2 resolves E.164 addresses (+1) 5032* through (+1) 5033*; and the last domain, AD1–2–9, resolves E.164 addresses (+1) 5038* through (+1) 5039*. Therefore, the domain AD1–2 resolves E.164 addresses (+1) 503*.

If an administrative domain cannot resolve an alias address, it requests the domain above it to resolve the address. If the higher domain cannot resolve the address, it goes to the next higher domain until the root domain is reached. Because the root domain has a complete list of all alias addresses, it goes to the appropriate domain below it for address resolution. The tree then is traversed downward to the next lower domain until the domain that can resolve the address is found. For example, if the administrative domain AD1–1–1 wants to resolve the E.164 address (+1) 503-100-4354, it requests AD1–1 to do it. Because AD1–1 cannot resolve this address, it requests AD for address

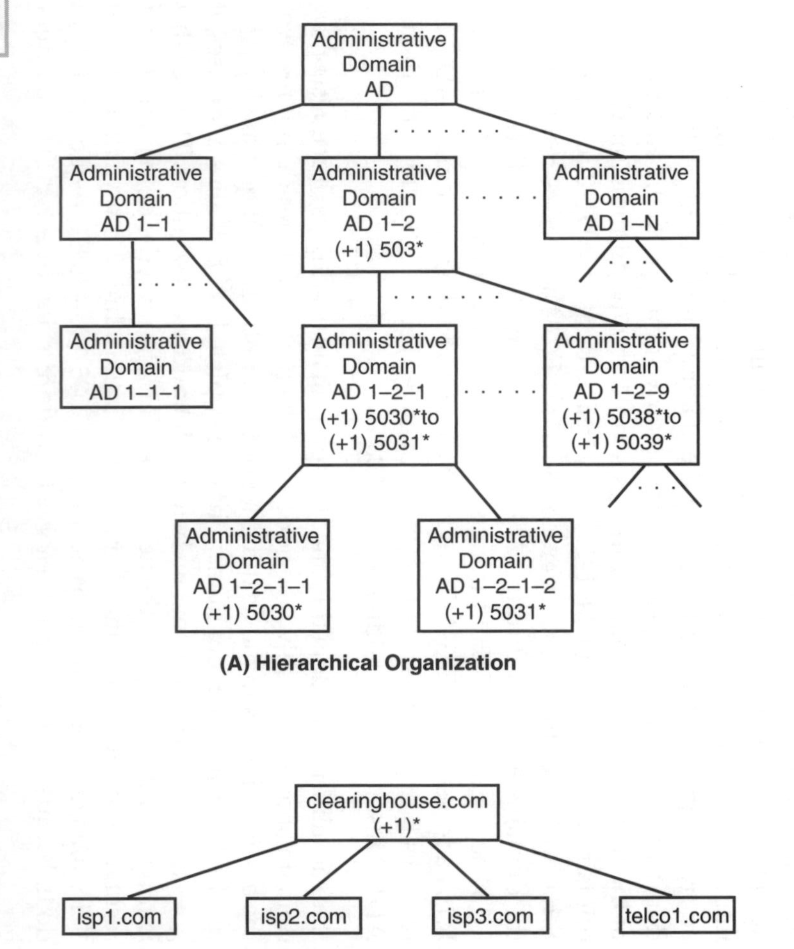

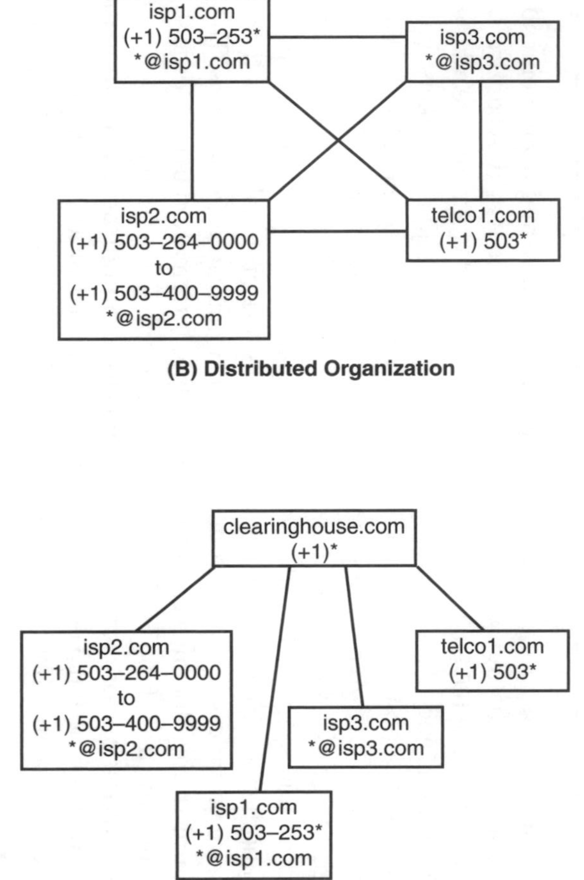

Figure 5.2 Organizations of administrative domains.

resolution. Because domain AD1–2 has advertised to AD that it can resolve (+1) 503*, AD requests that it do the resolution. AD1–2 in turn sends a request to AD1–2–1, which in turn sends a request to AD1–2–1–2. The domain AD1–2–1–2 resolves the E.164 address to the transport address consisting of, for example, an IP address of 160.56.4.50 and a port of 1766. The resolved address can be sent directly from AD1–2–1–2 to AD1–1–1, or it can traverse the same path back until it reaches AD1–1–1.

In a distributed organization of administrative domains, each domain has a list of all other administrative domains and the alias addresses they resolve. The administrative domain directly communicates with another domain, which can resolve the specific alias address. Figure 5.2(B) shows such an organization with four administrative domains: isp1.com, isp2.com, isp3.com, and telco1.com. Each domain has a bilateral agreement with the other three domains. The isp1.com domain resolves E.164 addresses that start with (+1) 503253* and e-mail addresses that end in *@isp1.com. The isp2.com domain resolves E.164 addresses between (+1) 503-264-0000 and (+1) 503-400-9999 and e-mail addresses that end in *@isp2.com. The isp3.com domain resolves e-mail addresses that end in *@isp3.com, and the telco1.com domain resolves E.164 addresses that start with (+1) 503*.

Figure 5.2(C) shows the clearinghouse organization of administrative domains. The clearinghouse.com administrative domain has bilateral agreements with each of the four administrative domains—isp1.com, isp2.com, isp3.com, and telco1.com. These four domains do not have an agreement among themselves. The clearinghouse acts as a middleman in bringing the two domains together so that they can complete a call originating from one administrative domain and terminating in the other domain. The clearinghouse also does the settlement for the call. Usually, the administrative domain that originated the call has to pay the domain that terminated the call. In that case, the originating domain pays the clearinghouse for the call; the clearinghouse keeps its commission and pays the terminating domain its share of money for the call.

Figure 5.2(D) shows a hybrid of the distributed and clearinghouse organizations. The four administrative domains—isp1.com, isp2.com, isp3.com, and telco1.com—have bilateral agreements with each other, and each of the four domains has a bilateral agreement with the clearinghouse administrative domain clearinghouse1.com. These five administrative domains are also shown in Figure 5.1. The border elements in these administrative domains can be identified by e-mail addresses, such as be-ID@be-admin-domain, or URLs, such as h2250-annex-g://be-ID@be-admin-domain or h2250-annex-g://be-admin domain/be-ID, where "h2250-annex-g" is the protocol used by the border element, "be-admin-domain" is the DNS domain name of the border elements, and "be-ID" is the identification of the border element in this "be-admin-domain". In Figure 5.1, the border elements in the administrative domains have the following URLs: h2250-annex-g://be1@be.clearinghouse1.com, h2250-annex-g://be2@be.clearinghouse1.com, h2250-annex-g://be3@be.clearinghouse1.com, h2250-annex-g://be@be.isp1.com, h2250-annex-g://beA@be.isp2.com, h2250-annex-g://be1@be.isp3.com, h2250-annex-g://be2@be.isp3.com, and h2250-annex-g://503@be.telco1.com. Note that an administrative domain can have one or more border elements based on the configuration of the network administrator.

H.225.0 Annex G Messages and Message-Flows

The H.225.0 Annex G protocol works on both the TCP and the UDP transport protocols. The messages are of the request-response type. The client BE sends the request message, and the serving BE responds with either a confirmation message if the request can be satisfied or a rejection message if the request cannot be satisfied. The messages fall into four categories; the first two categories are noncall related, and the next two category of messages are executed as a result of a call:

Service establishment. The messages used are ServiceRequest, ServiceConfirmation, ServiceRejection, and ServiceRelease.

Bulk address information exchange. The messages used are DescriptorRequest, DescriptorConfirmation, DescriptorRejection, DescriptorIDRequest, DescriptorIDConfirmation, DescriptorIDRejection, DescriptorUpdate, and DescriptorUpdateAck.

Authorization and address resolution. The messages used are AccessRequest, AccessConfirmation, and AccessRejection.

Exchange of resource usage information. The messages used are UsageRequest, UsageConfirmation, UsageRejection, UsageIndication, UsageIndicationConfirmation, and UsageIndicationRejection.

Figure 5.3 shows how the H.225.0 Annex G messages are used for service establishment, address information exchange, authorization and address resolution, and the exchange of resource usage information. Figure 5.3 shows how the client BE ISP1-BE gets configured with addressing information needed to route calls originating from the isp1.com administrative domain and terminating on a gateway in the clearinghouse1.com domain. The clearinghouse may have contracts with many H.323-PSTN gateway providers, which enables it to provide a nationwide or a worldwide service. The ISP1-BE first establishes a service relationship with the serving BE Clearinghouse1-BE2, by sending the ServiceRequest message. The

Clearinghouse1-BE2 responds with ServiceConfirmation if it can provide service; otherwise it responds with ServiceReject. Assuming the service relationship is established, ISP1-BE next sends a DescriptorIDRequest message to request a list of identifiers of descriptors. A descriptor consists of alias addresses that can be resolved by the serving administrative domain. The Clearinghouse1-BE2 responds with one or more identifiers of descriptors in DescriptorIDConfirmation; otherwise it responds with DescriptorIDRejection. Assuming the descriptor identifiers are received, the ISP1-BE uses DescriptorRequest to request for a descriptor with a specific identifier. The Clearinghouse1-BE2 responds with the requested descriptor in DescriptorConfirmation; otherwise it responds with DescriptorIDRejection. The ISP1-BE may send multiple DescriptorRequest messages—one for each descriptor—to request all descriptors from Clearinghouse1-BE2. Any changes to the descriptor are communicated by Clearinghouse1-BE2 to ISP1-BE with DescriptorUpdate. The ISP1-BE acknowledges the receipt of DescriptorUpdate with DescriptorUpdateAck. The ISP1-BE may then request the changed descriptor with the DescriptorRequest message. The ISP1-BE can establish service relationships with other administrative domains and obtain descriptors of alias addresses that can be resolved by those administrative domains. In this manner, ISP1-BE learns how to route calls that initiate from isp1.com and terminate in administrative domains with which it has service relationships.

After ISP1-BE has been configured with routing information, it should be able to route a call from Terminal 1 in isp1.com to Terminal 2 in isp2.com, as shown in Figure 5.1. Terminal 1 calls Terminal 2, as shown in Figure 5.3, by sending an H.225.0-Q.931 Setup for gatekeeper-routed calls or RAS ARQ message for direct-routed calls with the E.164 address of (+1) 503-400-5000 to ISP1-GK. Assume that ISP1-GK and ISP1-BE are collocated and that a descriptor from clearinghouse1.com can resolve this E.164 address. The ISP1-BE sends AccessRequest with (+1) 503-400-5000 to Clearinghouse1-BE2 to resolve the E.164 address. The Clearinghouse1-BE2 has contracts with many service providers. In this instance, it selects isp2.com and sends AccessRequest with (+1) 503-400-5000 to ISP2-BE.

If the alias address cannot be resolved because no capacity is left in ISP2-GW or for any other reason, ISP2-BE responds with AccessRejection to Clearinghouse1-BE2. In this case, Clearinghouse1-BE2 may select telco1. com and send AccessRequest to Telco1-BE. If Telco1-BE also responds with AccessRejection and if no other domain can resolve (+1) 503-400-5000, Clearinghouse1-BE2 responds with AccessRejection to ISP1-BE. The ISP1-GK will, in turn, respond with a H.225.0-Q.931 ReleaseComplete for gatekeeper-routed calls or RAS ARJ message for direct-routed calls to Terminal 1.

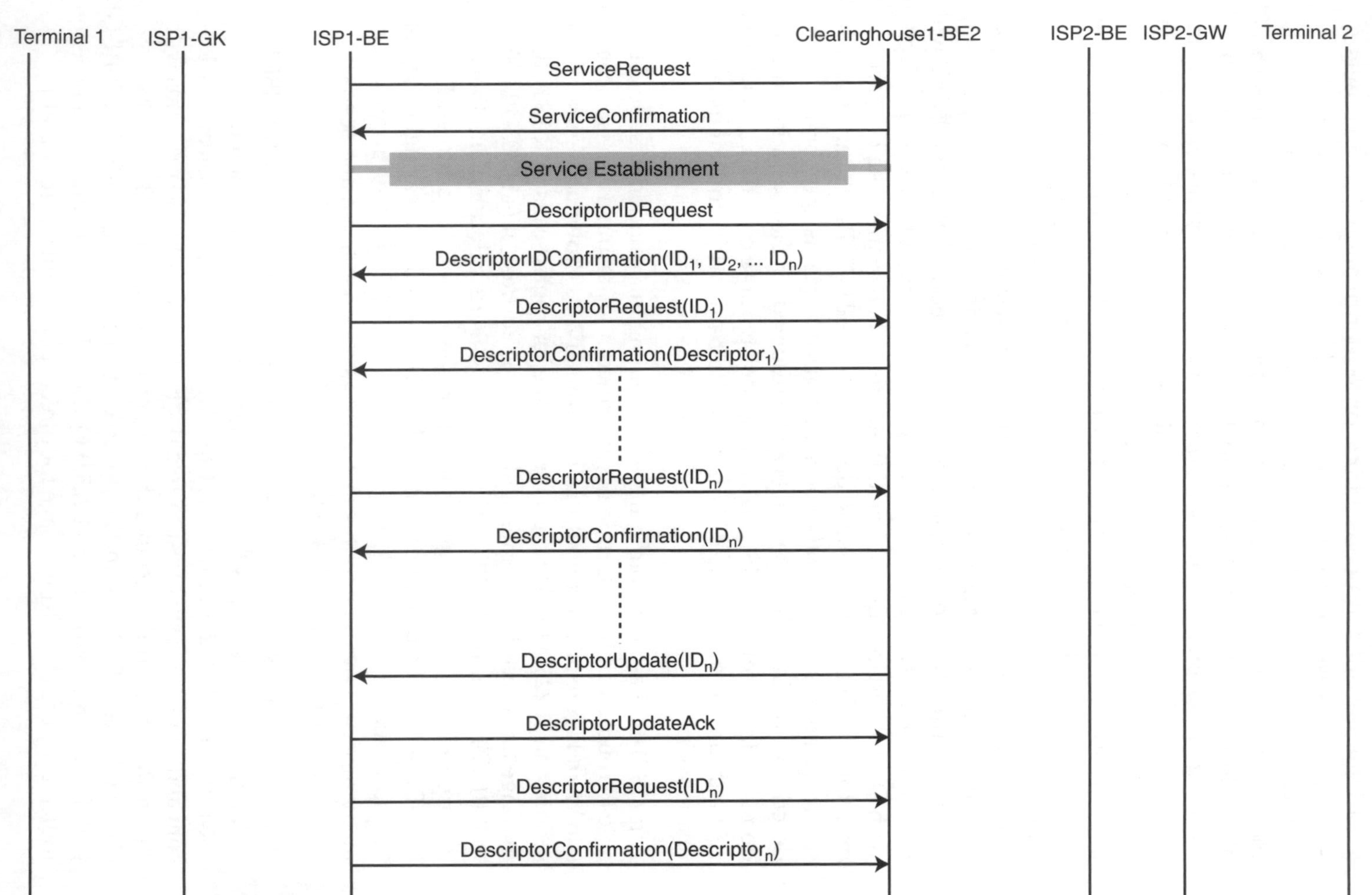

Figure 5.3 H.225.0 Annex G message-flows.

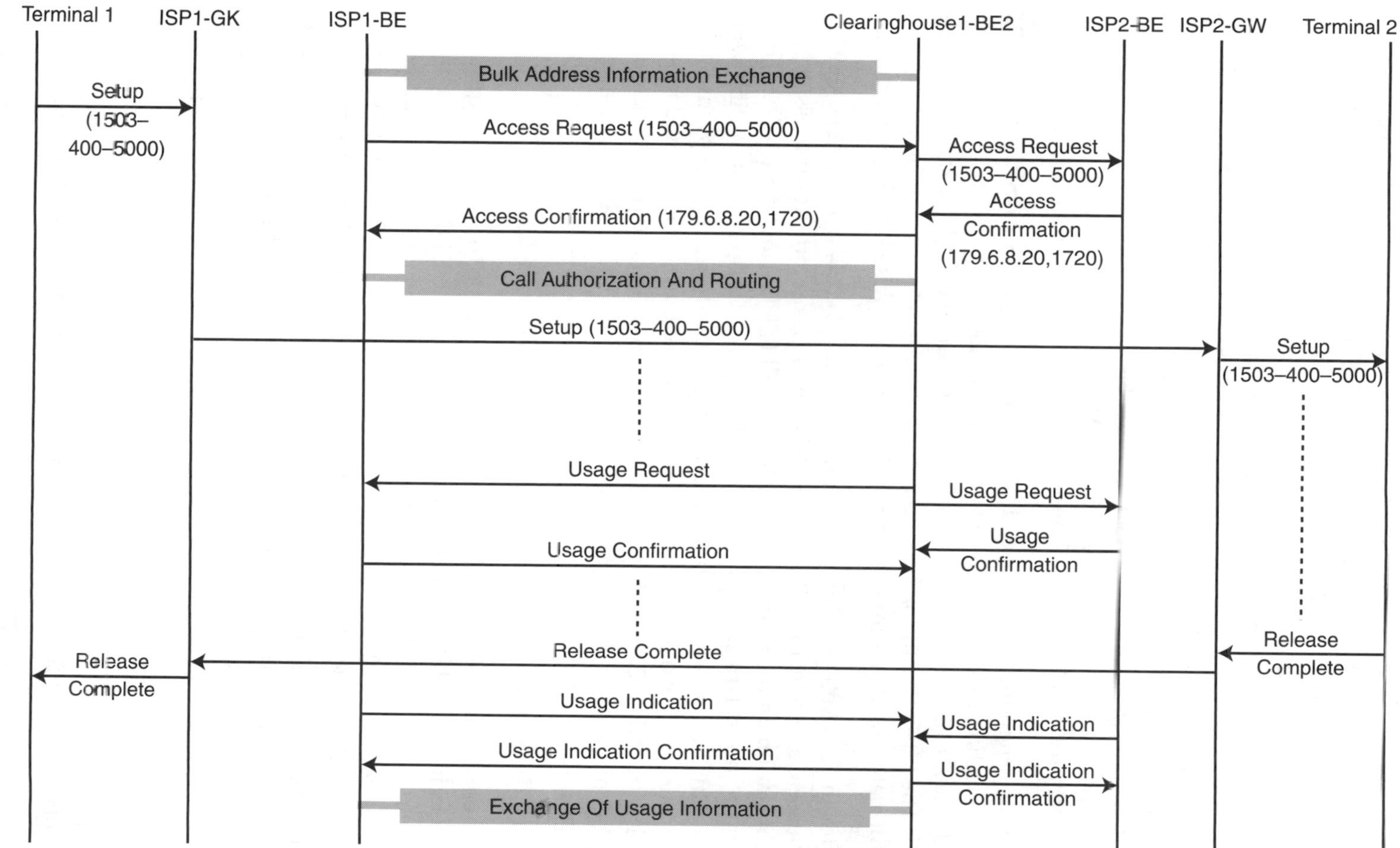

Figure 5.3 H.225.0 Annex G message-flows (Continued).

If the alias address of (+1) 503-400-5000 is resolved by ISP2-BE to the transport address of 179.6.8.20, 1720 (ISP2-GW), it returns the resolved transport address of ISP2-GW in AccessConfirmation to Clearinghouse1-BE2. The Clearinghouse1-BE2 responds with AccessConfirmation to ISP1-BE. Assuming that the alias address is resolved, the Clearinghouse1-BE2 sends AccessConfirmation with the transport address of ISP2-GW to ISP1-BE. The ISP1-GK then sends the H.225.0-Q.931 Setup message to ISP2-GW for gatekeeper-routed calls or a RAS ACF message to Terminal 1 for direct-routed calls. Terminal 1 then can send the H.225.0-Q.931 Setup message to ISP2-GW. Upon receiving the H.225.0-Q.931 Setup message, ISP2-GW then connects Terminal 1 on the IP network with Terminal 2 on the PSTN.

The Clearinghouse1-BE2 sends UsageRequest messages to ISP1-BE and ISP2-BE requesting that both provide information regarding resource usage at the end of the call. Resource usage information can be used to charge for the call. The ISP1-BE and ISP2-BE respond with UsageConfirmation if usage information will be sent in UsageIndication; otherwise UsageRejection is sent.

After the call between Terminal 1 and Terminal 2 ends with H.225.0-Q.931 Release Complete, ISP1-BE and ISP2-BE send UsageIndication messages with information on the resource usage in this call to Clearinghouse1-BE2. The Clearinghouse1-BE2 accepts or rejects UsageIndication by responding with UsageIndicationConfirmation or UsageIndicationRejection, respectively. The clearinghouse also does settlement between the two service providers—isp1.com and isp2.com. Because the calling party usually pays for the call, the isp1.com pays the clearinghouse.com for this call. The clearinghouse.com keeps its commission and pays the rest to isp2.com.

All H.225.0 Annex G messages have some common fields:

sequenceNumber. This field works the same way as the requestSeqNum field in all the H.225.0-RAS messages that use the UDP protocol. This field consists of an integer in the range of 0 to 65535. It is monotonically increased for a new request message, except that the retransmitted request message has the same sequenceNumber as the original message.

replyAddress. This field is present only in the request messages that use the UDP protocol. It consists of a transport address to which the response message is sent.

version. This field consists of the version of the H.225.0 Annex G protocol used by the message's sender.

hopCount. This field consists of an integer, in the range of 1 to 255, that specifies the maximum number of border elements through which this message can propagate. It stops a message from propagating forever. If the border element has to forward this message, it first decrements this field if it is not zero. If this field is zero, this message is dropped. If this is a request message, an appropriate response message is sent.

cryptoTokens. This field provides message authentication and integrity.

Address Templates for Routing Calls

The H.225.0 Annex G protocol divides up the service providers into administrative domains. Each administrative domain charges a price for terminating calls with certain destination addresses to the end users. The client administrative domain, from where the call originates, has an Address Resolution Table, shown in Figure 5.4. The Address Resolution Table has a list of serving administrative domains, which can terminate the calls. Each administrative domain consists of one or more descriptors. Each descriptor has one or more address templates. The template consists of the pattern of addresses and the routing information to resolve those addresses. The routing information consists of instructions on where to send the messages and the call's price.

Table 5.1 shows the Address Resolution Table of isp1.com in Figure 5.1. We've organized this table in a easy-to-understand manner; an actual address resolution table is organized differently for the quick retrieval of information. The isp1.com administrative domain has service relationships with isp2.com, isp3.com, telco1.com, and clearinghouse1.com administrative domains. The service providers are connected via the Internet, so the calls traverse the Internet unless they are routed to other networks, such as the PSTN or a managed IP network. The isp2.com can terminate calls with certain E.164 and users' e-mail addresses. The E.164 addresses are routed to the gateway, ISP2-GW, which then connects the calls to the users' telephones on the PSTN. The e-mail addresses are routed to the gatekeeper ISP2-GK, which resolves them to the IP address of the terminal on the Internet. The isp2.com can also route a call to its user's telephone or the IP terminal based on the user's pre-defined preferences. The isp3.com provides an address resolution service, whereby a call to a user in its domain is resolved to the IP address of the user's terminal.

The telco.com has PSTN gateways that terminate calls in the 503 area code within the USA. The clearinghouse1.com is a middleman between the administrative domain that initiates the call and the administrative domain that terminates the call. The clearinghouse provides two kinds of QoS for voice calls: best-effort QoS at a lower price by using the Internet and good

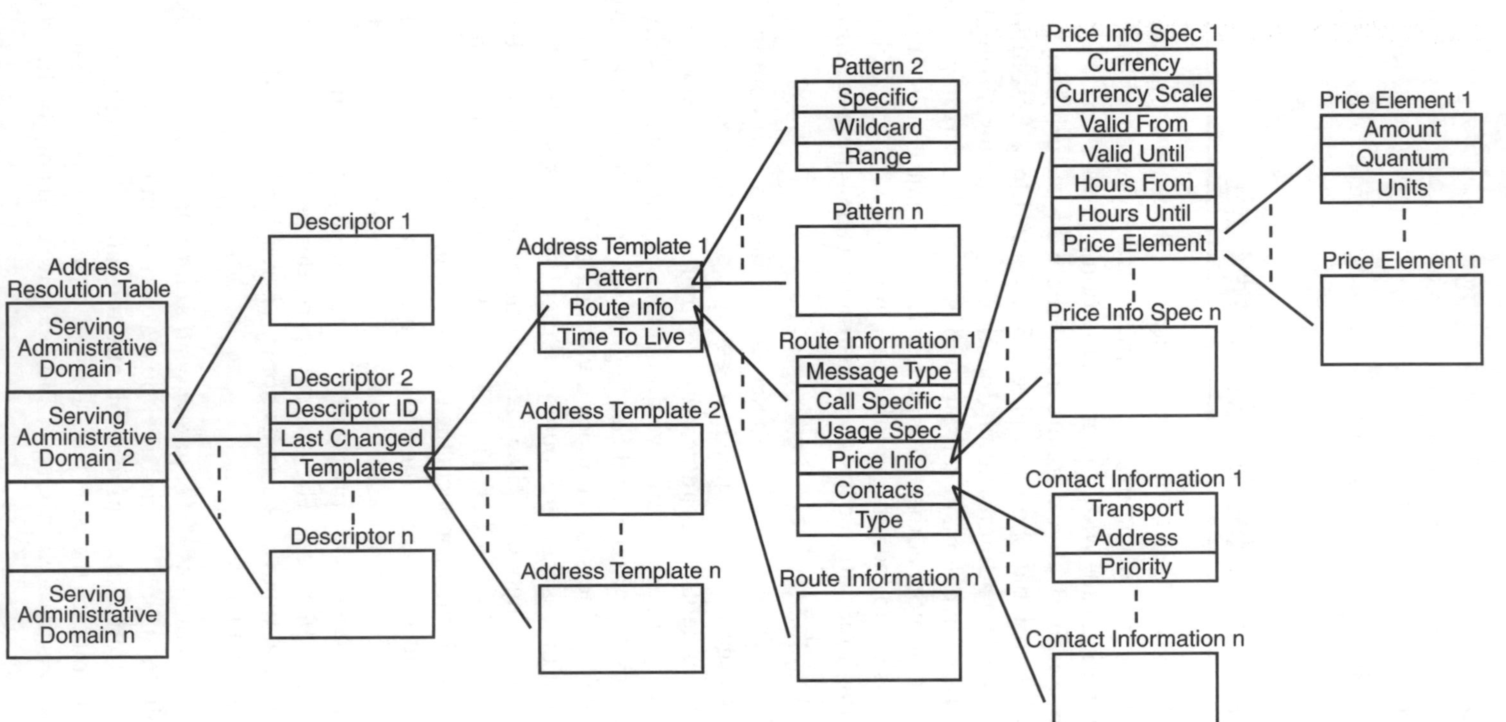

Figure 5.4 Address Resolution Table of a border element.

Table 5.1 Address Resolution Table for isp1.com

	ISP2.com Administrative Domain		ISP3.com Administrative Domain	Telco1.com Administrative Domain	Clearinghouse1.com Administrative Domain	
Descriptor ID	**Description ID$_0$**		**Description ID$_1$**	**Description ID$_2$**	**Description ID$_3$**	**Description ID$_4$**
last Changed	2001 02 14 09 41 06		2001 02 20 18 12 12	2000 11 18 23 10 52	2001 02 17 16 20 21	2000 04 21 23 50 21
template. pattern	range = (+1) 503–264–0000 To (+1) 503–400–9999	wildcard = *@isp2.com	wildcard = *@isp3.com	wildcard = (+1)503*	wildcard = (+1)*	wildcard = (+1)*
template. routeInfo. messageType	sendSetup	sendSetup	sendAccessRequest	sendSetup	sendAccessRequest	sendAccessRequest
template. routeInfo. callSpecific	False	False	False	False	False	True
template. routeInfo. usageSpec	sendTo = beA when = end			sendTo = 503 when = start, end	sendTo = be1 when = start, end, period 600	sendTo = be2 when = period 15
template. routeInfo. priceInfo	currency = USD currencyScale = 2	currency = USD currencyScale = 2	validUntil = 2001 04 30 22 00 00	currency = USD currencyScale = 2 hoursFrom = 080000 hoursUntil = 170000	currency = USD currencyScale = 2	currency = USD currencyScale = 3
template. route Info. Price Info. Price Element/ Price Formula	amount = 1 quantum = 60 units = seconds	amount = 1 quantum = 10000 units = Bytes	0.1 US cents per Access Request	amount = 2 quantum = 60 units = seconds	amount = 1 quantum = 60 units = seconds	amount = 5 quantum = 15 units = seconds
template. route Info. price Info.			valid = 2001 04 30 22 00 01	currency = USD currencyScale = 3 hoursFrom = 170001 hoursUntil = 075959		
template. route Info. price Info. price Element/ price Formula			0.2 US cents per Access Request	amount = 2 quantum = 30 units = seconds amount = 100 units = Initial amount = 200 units = minimum		
template. route Info. contacts	179.6.8.20, 1720; 0	179.6.8.56, 1720; 0	156.10.8.101, 2099; 0 156.10.8.200, 2099; 1	160.56.4.50 1766; 0	180.20.4.5, 2099; 0 180.20.8.2000, 2099; 1 180.20.5.100, 2099; 2	180.20.8.200, 1946; 0 180.20.5.100, 1946; 1 180.20.4.5, 1946; 2
template. route Info. type	Voice Gateway	Terminal	Terminal	Voice Gateway	Voice Gateway	Voice Gateway
template. time To Live	2952000	2952000	15552000	15552000	31104000	31104000

QoS at a higher price by using the PSTN. In both types of QoS, the calls originate from the Internet and terminate via the gateway on the PSTN to a telephone. The clearinghouse has contracts with one or more PSTN gateway providers. For the best-effort QoS, the clearinghouse uses a gateway closest to the called party so that most of the distance the call traverses is on the

Internet. For good QoS, the clearinghouse uses a gateway closest to the calling party so that most of the distance the call traverses is on the PSTN.

The details of Table 5.1 and some of the fields of the descriptor are as follows:

descriptorID. This field consists of a 128-bit globally unique identification number that is unique in space and time for the descriptor. It is generated through a procedure described in the H.225.0 recommendation. In Table 5.1, the isp2.com, isp3.com, and telco1.com administrative domains have one descriptor each with identifiers of $descID_0$, $descID_1$, and $descID_2$, respectively; whereas the clearinghouse1.com administrative domain has two descriptors with identifiers of $descID_3$, and $descID_4$.

lastChanged. This field is a global timestamp relative to *Coordinated Universal Time* (UTC) that consists of a character string of size 14 describing the date and time this descriptor was last changed. It's format is YYYYMMDDHHmmSS, where YYYY is the year in four digits, MM is the month in two digits, DD is the day in two digits, HH is the hour in two digits, mm is the minute in two digits, and SS is the second in two digits. In Table 5.1, the descriptor from isp2.com was last changed in the year 2001 on February 14 at 9:41 A.M. and 6 seconds.

templates. This field consists of one or more templates, with each template consisting of address resolution information for a range of alias addresses. Some of the fields are described as follows:

- *pattern*. This field consists of one or more alias addresses that can be resolved. The addresses are grouped as follows:
  - *specific*. This field consists of a single alias address resolved by this serving administrative domain. Note that an alias address can be a URL, e-mail address, E.164 address, a character string containing, for example, the name of the person, and so on. This field is used when the AccessRequest message is sent to the serving administrative domain to resolve a specific address.
  - *wildcard*. This field consists of a string of alias addresses resolved by this serving administrative domain. The string has a trailing wildcard for phone numbers and a leading wildcard for e-mail addresses.

    In Table 5.1, isp2.com can resolve the e-mail addresses whose domain name is isp2.com; isp3.com can resolve the e-mail addresses whose domain name is isp3.com; and telco1.com can resolve the E.164 addresses that start with 1503. The clearinghouse1.com domain has two descriptors. Both descriptors resolve the E.164 addresses that start with 1—all E.164 addresses in the USA. The first descriptor provides a gateway closest to the destination alias address of the called party so that most of the call traverses the Internet, which costs less but may have poor QoS. The second descriptor provides a gateway closest to the source alias address of the calling party so that most of the call traverses the PSTN, which costs more and has good QoS. This information is not explicitly specified in the descriptors.

- *range*. This field consists of one or more ranges of alias addresses resolved by this serving administrative domain. In Table 5.1, isp2.com can resolve the E.164 addresses between 1503-264-0000 and 1503-400-9999.

- *routeInfo*. This field consists of the following routing information to resolve the addresses specified in the pattern field:

  - *messageType*. This field specifies the type of message that should be sent to the destination specified in the contact field below in order to route the address specified in the pattern field above. This field consists of sendSetup or sendAccessRequest if the address is resolvable and nonExistent if the address is irresolvable. If sendSetup is used, the calling party sends an H.225.0-Q.931 Setup message to the alias address of the called party specified in the contact field below. If sendAccessRequest is used, the AccessRequest message first must be sent by the client border element to the alias address of the serving border element specified in the contact field below. This AccessRequest message introduces another message exchange to resolve the alias address in the pattern field before the calling party can send the Setup message. Resolving the address as quickly as possible speeds up the call setup time.

    In Table 5.1, isp2.com has two templates. The first template resolves its E.164 addresses (1503-264-0000 to 1503-400-9999) by having the calling party send the Setup message to the alias address of the called party specified in the contact field. The second template resolves its e-mail addresses (*@isp2.com) by having the calling party send the Setup message to the alias address of the called party specified in the contact field.

    The isp3.com domain does not have a gatekeeper that can resolve its e-mail addresses (*.isp3.com) to the IP addresses of its users at the time the call is made. If its terminals have dynamic IP addresses, they have to be resolved in real-time when the call is made. If its terminals have static IP addresses, the e-mail addresses can be resolved to their corresponding transport addresses before the call is made. This will create a huge number of templates, however—one for each e-mail address to transport address pair, so it is impractical. The only reasonable solution is to require that at the time of the call the specific called party's e-mail address is resolved to a transport address with an AccessRequest message sent by the client border element to the alias address of the serving border element specified in the contact field.

The telco1.com resolves its E.164 addresses (1503*) by having the calling party send the Setup message to the alias address of the called party specified in the contact field. The clearinghouse1.com domain has two descriptors. The E.164 addresses (1*) are resolved by having the client border element send the AccessRequest message to the serving border element specified in the contact field.

- *callSpecific*. This field is valid only when the messageType field is sendAccessRequest. If this field is set to TRUE, authorization is required before the call is made. Authorization consists of having the client border element provide the Call Identifier and Conference Identification of the call in the callInfo field of the AccessRequest message to the serving border element. The serving BE authorizes or rejects the call through AccessConfirmation or AccessRejection, respectively. In Table 5.1, clearinghouse1.com requires authorization for calls that hop onto the PSTN as quickly as possible and cost more. When the call is authorized, the serving administrative domain will allow only the call with matching Call Identifier and Conference Identification.
- *usageSpec*. If this field is present, it specifies to whom and when the UsageIndication message should be sent. The following fields are used:

  sentTo. This field specifies the BE through the element identifier of the serving administrative domain to which this UsageIndication message should be sent.

  when. This field specifies when the UsageIndication message should be sent and the period at which it should be sent. One or more of the following fields is used:

  never. This field specifies that the UsageIndication message should never be stopped.

  start. This field specifies that the UsageIndication message should be sent at the beginning of the call.

  end. This field specifies that the UsageIndication message should be sent at the end of the call.

  period. This field specifies the period, in seconds, at which the UsageIndication messages are sent. The allowable range for the period is between 1 and 65535.

failure. This field specifies that the failed call attempts should be reported.

In Table 5.1, isp2.com requires that for calls made to its E.164 addresses, the UsageIndication message be sent at the end of the call to its serving BE with an identification of *beA*. For calls to its e-mail addresses, the UsageIndication messages are not used. The isp3.com does not require the use of UsageIndication messages. The telco.com requires that the UsageIndication message be sent at the start and at the end of the call to its serving border element with an identification of *503*. The first descriptor in clearinghouse.com requires that the UsageIndication message be sent at the start and end of the call and every 600 seconds during the call to its serving border element with an identification of *be1*. The second descriptor in clearinghouse.com requires that the UsageIndication message be sent every 15 seconds during the call to its serving border element with an identification of *be2*.

- *priceInfo*. If this field is present, it specifies a list of pricing information for a call to an address specified in the *pattern* field. The following fields are used to specify pricing information:
  - *currency*. This field specifies the currency designator using ISO-4217 for the priceElement.*amount* field. For example, the currency designator for U.S. dollar is "USD."
  - *currencyScale*. This field specifies the number of places the decimal point in the *priceElement.amount* field should be shifted to the left. This field is an integer between −127 and 127. For example, if this field has a value of 2 for "USD," the value of *priceElement.amount* field is in U.S. cents.
  - *validFrom*. This field specifies the date and time when this pricing information is valid. The time is a string of 14 characters (YYYYMMDDHHmmSS) consisting of a global timestamp relative to UTC.
  - *validUntil*. This field specifies the date and time when this pricing information expires. The time is a string of 14 characters (YYYYMMDDHHmmSS) consisting of a global timestamp relative to UTC.
  - *hoursFrom*. This field specifies the starting time of the day when the price of the call specified in the *priceElement* field is valid. The time is a string of six characters (HHmmSS) consisting of the time of the day in hours, minutes, and seconds relative to UTC.
  - *hoursUntil*. This field specifies the ending time of the day when the price of the call specified in the *priceElement* field is valid. The

time is a string of six characters (HHmmSS) consisting of the time of the day in hours, minutes, and seconds relative to UTC.

- *priceElement.* This field specifies the price of the call in (amount per quantum units). For example, if the price of the call is 10 U.S. cents per minute, the fields of *priceInfo* are set as follows: amount = 10, currency = USD, currencyScale = 2, quantum = 60, and units = seconds. The following fields are used to express the price of the call:

  amount. This field indicates the amount of the call in the currency specified in the *currency* and *currencyScale* fields above. The value of this field is between 0 and ($2^{32} - 1$).

  unit. This field specifies the units to measure the duration of the call. Choices for units are

    seconds. This field measures the duration of the call by the amount of time elapsed in seconds.

    packets. This field measures the duration of the call by the number of packets transmitted and received.

    bytes. This field measures the duration of the call by the number of bytes transmitted and received.

    initial. This field specifies that the call has an initial connect charge.

    minimum. This field specifies that the call has a minimum charge.

    maximum. This field specifies that the call has a maximum charge.

  quantum. This field specifies the resolution of the call, and it is a multiplier for the *units* field. The value of this field is between 0 and ($2^{32} - 1$). As an example, if the duration of the call is measured on a per minute basis, the value of this field is 60 and the *units* field is in seconds.

- *PriceFormula.* This field is an alternative to the priceElement field and consists of up to 2048 characters to express the formula for call pricing. We use this field when the pricing structure is too complex to be expressed in the priceElement field.

  In Table 5.1, isp2.com charges 1 U.S. cent per minute for calls routed through its gateway (ISP2-GW) and 1 U.S. cent per 10000 bytes for calls that are routed through its gatekeeper (ISP2-GK). The isp3.com expresses its charges through the priceFormula field. It charges for resolving the e-mail addresses in its isp3.com domain to transport addresses. The charge is 0.1 U.S. cent per address resolution until the year 2001 on April 30 at 10:00 P.M.; the charge increases to 0.2 U.S. cent per address resolution starting from the year 2001 on April 30 at 10:00 P.M. and 1 second.

The telco1.com charges 2 U.S. cents per minute for a call during peak hours of 8 A.M. to 5 P.M. During off-peak hours from 1 second after 5 P.M. until 59 seconds after 7:59 A.M. it charges an initial amount of 10 U.S. cents for a connection fee, followed by 0.2 U.S. cents per 30 seconds, and a minimum charge of 20 U.S. cents if the parties have talked for at least 30 seconds. The clearinghouse.com charges 1 U.S. cent per minute when most of the call traverses the Internet and 0.5 U.S. cents per 15 seconds when most of the call traverses the PSTN.

- *contacts*. This field consists of a list of destination alias addresses and priorities. The priority is an integer in the range of 0 to 127, with 0 as the highest priority. The message specified in the messageType field is first sent to the alias address with the highest priority. If no response is received, the message is sent to the alias address with the next highest priority. This continues until a response occurs or the list is exhausted.

In Table 5.1, isp2.com specifies the static transport address of 179.6.8.20, 1720 (ISP2-GW) to resolve the E.164 addresses and the static transport address of 179.6.8.56, 1720 (ISP2-GK) to resolve the e-mail addresses. For example, when User 1 makes a call to User 2 on Terminal 2, Terminal 1 sends a Setup to ISP2-GW. The ISP2-GW extracts the destination E.164 address from the destinationAddress field of the Setup message and dials the E.164 number on the PSTN to connect to the called party on the telephone. When User 1 makes a call to User 2-1 on Terminal 2-1, Terminal 1 sends a Setup to ISP2-GK. The ISP2-GK extracts the destination e-mail address from the remoteExtensionAddress field of the Setup message and resolves it to the IP address of its user on Terminal 2-1. Note that even though some users of ISP2 may have both a telephone and an IP terminal, the ISP2 does not decide whether to route the call to the telephone or the IP terminal. The ISP2 routes the call to the telephone or the IP terminal based on the E.164 or the e-mail address, respectively, used by the calling party.

The isp3.com specifies the static transport address of 156.10.8.101, 2099 (ISP3-BE1) with the highest priority of 0 and the static transport address of 156.10.8.200, 2099 (ISP3-BE2) with the lower priority of 1 to resolve the e-mail addresses. The telco1.com specifies the static transport address of 160.56.4.50, 1720 (Telco1-GK) to resolve the E.164 addresses. The Telco1-GK acts as a demultiplexer by routing the incoming Setup message to the gateway least used, which balances the load among the four gateways.

The clearinghouse1.com has two descriptors. The first descriptor specifies the static transport address of 180.20.4.5, 2099 (Clearinghouse1-BE1) with the highest priority of 0, the static transport address of 180.20.8.200, 2099 (Clearinghouse1-BE2) with the lower priority of 1, and the static transport address of 180.20.5.100, 2099 (Clearinghouse1-BE3) with the lowest priority of 2. The second descriptor specifies the static transport address of 180.20.8.200, 1946 (Clearinghouse1-BE2) with the highest priority of 0, the static transport address of 180.20.5.100, 1946 (Clearinghouse1-BE3) with the lower priority of 1, and the static transport address of 180.20.4.5, 1946 (Clearinghouse1-BE1) with the lowest priority of 2. Note that the priorities of border elements in the two descriptors are different in order to somewhat balance the load among the descriptors.

- *type*. This field consists of the type of destination endpoint, such as a gateway (voice, h323, h320, and so on), terminal, or MCU, that serves the call. If the voice gateway serves the call, the only media used in the call is voice; whereas with the terminal or the MCU the call may involve multimedia. If the messageType field consists of sendSetup, this field will be filled with the appropriate endpoint.

  In Table 5.1, the voice gateways serve the E.164 addresses, and the H.323 terminals serve the e-mail addresses. Note that H.323 terminals can be represented with any alias addresses, including the E.164 addresses, even though they are not shown in this table.

- *timeToLive*. This field consists of time, in seconds, during which this template is valid. In Table 5.1, the two templates from isp2.com have an expiration of 30 days (2592000 seconds) from the date in its lastChanged field. The template from isp3.com has an expiration of 180 days (15552000 seconds), and the template from telco1.com has an expiration of 180 days (15552000 seconds) from the date in its lastChanged field. The two templates from clearinghouse1.com have expirations of 360 days (31104000 seconds) from the date in their lastChanged fields. Note that a template can be updated before its expiration date if we send an updated descriptor with the same identifier.

Pre-Call Population of Address Resolution Table

To resolve a nonroutable alias address to a routable address, the client administrative domain builds an address resolution table that provides routing instructions on how to complete a call to the serving administrative domain. To build this table, the client BE first discovers the serving BE. It then establishes a service relationship and retrieves the descriptors from the serving BE. The following sections describe how the client administrative domain uses H.225.0 Annex G to discover the serving BE, establish the service relationship, and retrieve the descriptors.

Border Element Discovery

We discover BEs manually through bilateral agreements among administrative domains of service providers. So far, an automatic method for discovering BEs has not been standardized in H.225.0 Annex G. Through bilateral agreements, we can configure a client BE with the DNS names of serving BEs. In Figure 5.1, ISP1-BE is preconfigured with the URLs of the following BEs: h2250-annex-g://be1@be.clearinghouse1.com, h2250-annex-g://be2@be.clearinghouse1.com, h2250-annex-g://be3@be.clearinghouse1.com, h2250-annex-g://beA@be.isp2.com, h2250-annex-g://be1@be.isp3.com, h2250-annex-g://be2@be.isp3.com, and h2250-annex-g://503@be.telco1.com.

When configured with the DNS name of the serving BE, the client BE has to obtain the transport address of the authorized serving BE before making contact. We do this through the use of the SRV [GUL00] or TXT [ROSE93] resource record query for the transport address of the serving BE. The SRV record query is made for the transport address of the "h2250-annex-g" service in the "be-admin-domain" of the h2250-annex-g://be-ID@be-admin-domain URL. Because the SRV resource record is not widely supported, it may fail. If so, we should use the TXT resource record query next. The TXT record response consists of the transport address or an A-record containing the fully qualified domain name. The A-record query then will yield the transport address in the response. If the resource record response consists only of the IP address and not the port, the well-known port of 2099 is used.

Service Relationship Establishment

The service relationship establishment is done through the use of ServiceRequest and ServiceConfirmation/ServiceRejection. After the transport address of the serving BE is known, the client BE unicasts the ServiceRequest message to the transport address of the discovered serving BE to establish a serving relationship. We can send the H.225.0 Annex G messages using the TCP or the UDP transport protocol. From Figure 5.3, ISP1-BE sends ServiceRequest to one of the three BEs, for example, Clearinghouse1-BE2. All the fields in ServiceRequest are optional; some of the fields are described as follows:

elementIdentifier. This field consists of a character string that identifies the client BE that sent this request. Per Figure 5.1, isp1.com identifies its BE through a URL *h2250-annex-g://be@be.isp1.com,* so an identification of *be* is used in this field.

domainIdentifier. This field consists of a character string that identifies the administrativedomain of the client BE that sent this request. Per Figure 5.1, isp1.com identifies its BE through a URL *h2250-annex-g://be@be. isp1.com,* so the administrative domain of *be.isp1.com* is used in this field.

timeToLive. This field consists of the suggested duration, in seconds, of this service relationship. If this field is absent, it implies a service relationship of infinite duration. Note that the actual duration of this service relationship is determined in the response message from the serving BE.

All serving BEs listen for ServiceRequest messages on both the TCP and the UDP ports of the transport addresses. When a serving BE receives ServiceRequest, it performs a series of checks. One check may be to determine whether it has a bilateral agreement with the client administrative domain specified in the domainIdentifier field. Another check could be to verify the crytoTokens field of the message for message authentication and integrity. If the checks pass, the BE responds with ServiceConfirmation; otherwise it responds with ServiceRejection.

Some of the fields in ServiceConfirmation are described as follows:

elementIdentifier. This field consists of a character string that identifies the serving BE that sent this response. From Figure 5.1, clearinghouse1.com identifies its BE through a URL *h2250-annex-g://be2@be.clearinghouse1.com,* so an identification of *be2* is used in this field.

alternates. This field consists of a list of alternate serving BEs in this administrative domain that can be used if this BE does not respond to queries in the future. The alternate BEs work the same way as alternate gatekeepers described in Chapter 3, "Point-to-Point Call: Signaling." For each alternate serving BE, this field provides its identifier, its priority in the list, and its transport address where the client border element will send the H.225.0 Annex G messages. When this serving BE fails, the client BE sends the H.225.0 Annex G messages to the transport address of the serving border element with the highest priority. If the highest priority serving BE is also unavailable, the client BE continues down the alternative serving BE list until some serving BE responds or until the list is exhausted. As shown in Figure 5.1, the alternate serving BEs in the *be.clearinghouse1.com* domain have identifications of *be1* and *be3* with priorities of 0 and 1 and transport addresses of 180.20.4.5, 2099 and 180.20.5.100, 2099 respectively.

domainIdentifier. This field consists of a character string that identifies the administrative domain of the serving BE that sent this response. As shown in Figure 5.1, clearinghouse1.com identifies its BE through a URL *h2250-annex-g://be2@be.clearinghouse1.com*, so the administrative domain of *be.clearinghouse1.com* is used in this field.

timeToLive. This field consists of the duration, in seconds, of this service relationship. If this field is absent, it implies a service relationship of infinite duration.

If a service relationship has a limited time to live, sending another ServiceRequest message can refresh it. Note that the exchange of ServiceRequest and ServiceConfirmation establishes a one-way relationship. As we can see in Figure 5.1, the ServiceRequest from ISP1-BE to Clearinghouse1-BE2 and the ServiceConfirmation from Clearinghouse1-BE2 to ISP1-BE establish a service relationship from ISP1 to Clearinghouse1, so Clearinghouse1 can terminate calls initiated from ISP1.

Populating the Address Resolution Table

We populate the address resolution table by using the following messages: DescriptorIDRequest, DescriptorIDConfirmation/ DescriptorIDRejection, DescriptorRequest, DescriptorConfirmation/ DescriptorRejection, DescriptorUpdate, and DescriptorUpdateAck.

The client administrative domain populates its address resolution table by retrieving the descriptors from each of the serving administrative domains in its address resolution table. The client BE sends a DescriptorIDRequest message to the serving BE requesting a list of descriptor identifiers. The serving BE responds with a DescriptorIDConfirmation message consisting of a list in which each entry consists of two items: descriptorID and the lastChanged fields of the descriptor. The client BE can request the specific descriptor by sending a DescriptorRequest with the appropriate descriptorID. The serving BE responds with the requested descriptor in DescriptorConfirmation. In this manner, the client administrative domain builds up its address resolution table. As shown in Figure 5.3 and Table 5.1, ISP1-BE sends the DescriptorIDRequest message. The Clearinghouse1-BE2 responds with a DescriptorIDConfirmation consisting of a list with two entries. The first entry is ($descID_3$, 20010217162021), and the second entry is ($descID_4$, 20000421235021). The ISP1-BE sends a DescriptorRequest ($descID_3$) message and a DescriptorRequest ($descID_4$) message. The Clearinghouse1-BE2 responds with two DescriptorConfirmation messages, each consisting of a corresponding descriptor. The isp1.com now has all the descriptors from clearinghouse1.com. Similarly, the isp1.com can retrieve descriptors from all the administrative domains with which it has a service relationship.

The serving administrative domain keeps a list of client administrative domains with its descriptor. If the descriptor changes, then the serving BE pushes this information to the client BEs through DescriptorUpdate. The fields of DescriptorUpdate are described as follows:

sender. This field consists of the alias address of the serving BE. The client BE should send the response message to this alias address. From Figure 5.3, Clearinghouse1-BE2 provides its URL h2250-annex-g://be2@be.clearinghouse1.com.

updateInfo. This field consists of a list of entries with two items. The first item is either the descriptorID or the descriptor. The second item specifies whether a new descriptor has been created, whether an old descriptor has been deleted and is not in use, or whether an old descriptor has been changed.

Upon receiving DescriptorUpdate, the client BE responds with a DescriptorUpdateAck message to acknowledge the receipt of DescriptorUpdate. As shown in Figure 5.3, if clearinghouse1.com has created a descriptor and if the DescriptorUpdate from Clearinghouse1-BE2 provides the descriptorID of $descID_5$, ISP1-BE can retrieve the new descriptor through DescriptorRequest($descID_5$). If a descriptor has been deleted and if the DescriptorUpdate from Clearinghouse1-BE2 provides the descriptorID of $descID_3$, ISP1-BE deletes the descriptor with an identification of $descID_3$ from its address resolution table. If a descriptor has been changed and if the DescriptorUpdate from Clearinghouse1-BE2 provides the descriptorID of $descID_4$, ISP1-BE can retrieve the changed descriptor through DescriptorRequest($descID_4$).

Address Resolution, Authorization, and Usage Reporting during the Call

When the user initiates the call, the called party's address may be in a nonroutable form. The client administrative domain resolves the nonroutable address to a routable address in order to complete the call. Before the call is routed, however, the serving administrative domain may require authorization. After authorization is granted and the call completes, one or both of the client and serving administrative domains may require a resource usage report for that call. The following sections describe how H.225.0 Annex G does address resolution, authorization, and resource usage reporting during the call.

Address Resolution and Authorization

AccessRequest and AccessConfirmation/AccessRejection provide address resolution and authorization. The serving administrative domain uses the callSpecific field in the address template to specify whether authorization for each call is required. At the time of the call, the route the call takes depends on the alias address and the level of QoS desired by the called party. In a call from Terminal 1 to Terminal 2 in Figure 5.3 and Table 5.1, the route taken depends on the alias address of the called party, and the QoS desired in the rsvpParameters field of the Setup message. The routing may also depend on the alias address of the calling party if good QoS is desired. Because Terminal 2 is addressed with an E.164 address, the call is routed via a PSTN gateway. The routing is based on whether best-effort or good QoS is desired as follows:

- If we want best-effort QoS, we can use four address templates—the E.164 address template of descriptor identifier $descID_0$, and the descriptor identifiers $descID_2$, $descID_3$, and $descID_4$—in the address resolution table of isp1.com to complete the call to the called party's E.164 address of (+1) 503-400-5000. In this case, the ISP1-BE picks the least expensive route. Both $descID_0$ and $descID_3$ advertise 1 U.S. cent per minute. The $descID_2$ advertises 2 U.S. cents per minute during peak hours. For off-peak hours, the rate is 10 cents if the parties talk for less than 30 seconds, and 0.4 U.S. cents per minute plus a minimum of 20 cents if the parties talk for at least 30 seconds. The route selected depends on the agreement that the isp1.com has with User 1. Assuming isp1.com charges User 1 a flat rate of 3 U.S. cents per minute for calls within the United State, ISP1-BE picks the route described in $descID_0$ or $descID_3$. Assuming that $descID_3$ is picked, this descriptor requires an AccessRequest message be sent to the transport address of 180.20.4.5, 2099 (Clearinghouse1-BE1) to resolve the called party's E.164 address.
- If we want good QoS, we can use one address template with the descriptor identifier of $descID_4$, which provides a PSTN gateway close to the calling party. As shown in Figure 5.1, isp1.com also has ISP1-GW, which can be used to hop onto the PSTN as soon as possible. Assuming that $descID_4$ is picked, this descriptor requires an AccessRequest message

be sent to the transport address of 180.20.8.200, 1496 (Clearinghouse1-BE2) to resolve the calling party's E.164 address.

The fields of AccessRequest are described as follows:

destinationInfo. This field consists of the alias address to be resolved. This information can be used to find a gateway closer to the called party in order to hop onto the PSTN as late as possible. Terminal 2's E.164 address of (+1) 503-400-5000 is provided in Figure 5.3.

sourceInfo. This optional field consists of the alias address of the calling party. This information can be used to find a gateway closer to the calling party in order to hop onto the PSTN as soon as possible to obtain good QoS. The H.225.0 Annex G protocol does not provide an explicit mechanism to specify that a gateway closer to the calling party is desired. So, use of this field may specify to the serving administrative domain that a gateway closest to the calling party is desired. Terminal 1, in Figure 5.1, is addressed with a URL that does not provide its geographical location; ISP1-BE can use an E.164 address (+1) 503-253-5050 of its ISP1-GW in this field.

callInfo. This optional field provides the Call Identifier and Conference Identifier of the call for which authorization is requested. This field is filled when the callSpecific field in the appropriate address template is set to TRUE. In this case, the serving administrative domain grants authorization on a per-call basis to a call whose Call Identifier and Conference Identifier is specified. From Table 5.1, the call with good QoS in $descID_4$ requires call specific information in this field. The ISP1-BE copies this information from the Setup message to this field.

Upon receiving an AccessRequest message, the serving BW provides to the client BE a list of address templates that can resolve the alias address in AccessConfirmation. If the callSpecific field in the address template is TRUE, the template is valid only for the call that has been authorized; otherwise the template is valid for all calls made within the time period provided in the timeToLive field of the template. The address template provided by Clearinghouse1-BE2, in Figure 5.3, for best-effort QoS consists of sending the Setup message to the transport address of ISP2-GW. Note that clearinghouse1.com has contractual agreements with many gateway providers, and isp2.com is one of them.

Resource Usage Reporting

Resource usage in a call is requested and reported through the use of the following messages: UsageRequest, UsageConfirmation/

UsageRejection, UsageIndication, and UsageIndicationConfirmation/ UsageIndicationRejection.

Resource usage by call, also known as the *Call Detail Record* (CDR), is reported through the use of UsageIndication. Some of the fields in UsageIndication are described as follows:

callInfo. This field provides the Call Identifier and Conference Identifier of the call whose resource usage is reported.

senderRole. This field specifies whether the sender of this message is the originator or the destination of the call.

usageCallStatus. This field provides the status of the call, which is one of the following: not started, in-progress, or ended.

srcInfo. This optional field provides the alias address of the calling party.

destAddress. This field provides the alias address of the called party.

startTime. This optional field provides the date and time when the call started. The time is a string of 14 characters (YYYYMMDDHHmmSS) consisting of a global timestamp relative to UTC.

endTime. This optional field provides the date and time when the call ended. The time is a string of 14 characters (YYYYMMDDHHmmSS) consisting of a global timestamp relative to UTC.

usageFields. This field consists of a list in which each entry consists of two items: object identifier and a character string. The object identifier specifies the format of the character string. As of this date, object identifiers have not been defined. Note that if the number of bytes measures the resource usage of the call transferred, this information can be provided in this field in a nonstandard manner.

A serving administrative domain may request UsageIndication during various stages of a call through the use of the usageSpec field in the address template of the descriptor. As shown in Table 5.3, the clearinghouse1.com requests UsageIndication for the best-effort QoS at the start of the call, every 10 minutes thereafter, and at the end of the call. For good QoS, the clearinghouse1.com requests UsageIndication every 15 seconds during the call. When UsageIndication is provided to Clearinghouse1-BE2, it responds with UsageIndicationConfirmation to accept the indication or UsageIndicationRejection to reject the indication.

An administrative domain may request another administrative domain to provide UsageIndication by sending a UsageRequest message. This request can be made anytime before, during, and after the call. The fields of UsageRequest consist of two subfields: callInfo to identify the call, and usageSpec to specify when UsageIndication should be sent. Both of these fields have been described previously in this chapter. If the administrative domain receiving UsageRequest accepts the request, it sends UsageConfirmation; otherwise it sends UsageRejection.

Recommended Reading

The ITU-T recommendation H.225.0 Annex G is specified in [H225G99].

Reference

H225G99 ITU-T Recommendation H.225.0 Annex G. *Communication between administrative domains*. May 1999.

Problems

1. Figure 5.2 shows four approaches to organizing administrative domains for the purpose of resolving alias addresses. List the advantages and disadvantages of one approach over another.
2. The descriptor from the administrative domain isp2.com requires that the E.164 addresses in the range 1503-264-0000 to 1503-400-9999 is resolved by sending the Setup message to the transport address of ISP2-GW. As the traffic grows, ISP2 installs two more gateways ISP2-GW1 and ISP2-GW2. Design a new descriptor that may change dynamically so that incoming Setup messages are somewhat equally distributed among the three gateways.
3. The descriptor from the administrative domain telco1.com requires that the E.164 addresses starting with 1503 are resolved by sending Setup messages to the transport address of TELCO1-GK. The TELCO1-GK essentially acts as a demultiplexer by taking the incoming Setup message and routing to the gateway that is least used, thus balancing the load among the four gateways. Develop a protocol between the gatekeeper and the gateways so that the gatekeeper can monitor the remaining capacity of the gateway and balance the load among the four gateways appropriately. Note that the Setup messages generated by the gateways as a result of calls originating from the PSTN are not routed through the gatekeeper.
4. The descriptor from the administrative domain isp2.com requires that the E.164 address is resolved by sending the Setup message to the gateway ISP2-GW, and the e-mail address is resolved by sending the Setup

message to the gatekeeper ISP2-GK. Develop a new descriptor for isp2.com so that the incoming call is routed to an H.323 terminal or a PSTN telephone of the same user, based on the availability and desires of the user and not on the type of the destination alias address—e-mail address or E.164 address. If user 2 in Figure 5.1 has a PSTN Terminal 2 and an H.323 Terminal 2-4, how can both of these devices be made to ring simultaneously if an incoming Setup message with either an e-mail address or the E.164 address of user 2 arrives?

5. Assume that a Clearinghouse has contracts with network providers so that it can provide nationwide private IP backbone network to bypass the Internet and provide QoS to H.323 multimedia calls. The users of this service are connected to the Internet. The calls hop onto the private IP network from the public Internet as early as possible and hop off of the private IP network to the public Internet as late as possible, so that the calls traverse the private IP network for most of the distance. Develop the descriptors for the clearinghouse to enable both ends of the call to hop on the private IP network as quickly as possible.

6. The H.225.0 Annex G protocol uses the push model in which address changes in the serving administrative domain are pushed to the client administrative domains. Show how the pull model would work where the client administrative domains would inquire from the serving administrative domain of any changes in its address information. List the merits and demerits of using the push model over the pull model.

CHAPTER 6

Supplementary Services: Overview and Approach

In Chapters 6 through 11 we describe how supplementary services available in traditional telephony networks are deployed in IP telephony for calls between two or more parties. In addition, we explore building blocks for new supplementary services that can be possible in IP telephony. Chapter 6 describes the architecture for the implementation of supplementary services in IP telephony networks. Subsequent chapters discuss the services, usage scenarios, and protocols in detail. Chapter 7 describes the three-party supplementary services; Chapter 8 describes call diversion services; Chapter 9 describes call completion services for unsuccessful calls; Chapter 10 describes stimulus signaling; and finally Chapter 11 describes HTTP-based transport services.

Chapters 7 through 9 of this book describe the supplementary services from the user's point of view. These descriptions are based on the service definitions of supplementary services in the ITU-T H.450 recommendations. These are generic and independent of the protocols, and their functions split between the telephones and the network. In other words, the end-to-end service functionality remains the same, regardless of the network signaling. The terminology used in these descriptions is based on the terminology used within the ITU-T and the ISO. In addition, commonly used synonyms are indicated, where necessary.

This chapter provides an architecture for the implementation of supplementary services in IP telephony networks. It includes an explanation of the purpose and origin of supplementary services from the perspective of a user, followed by a description of first- and third-party call control of supplementary services. In addition, an introduction to the signaling architecture of H.323 services is also provided—namely, H.450-based supplementary services, stimulus-services and HTTP-based services.

Purpose of Supplementary Services

Supplementary services encompass a wide range of services. Supplementary services provided within traditional circuit-switched telephone networks can be classified into two types:

- Functions such as consultation, call transfer, conferencing, and call waiting. These services were originally provided within private telephone networks (PBXs) and later migrated into various public networks such as ISDN and GSM as well.
- Functions such as leaving a message on an answering device or voice mail system, retrieving and listening to such messages, and sending a fax message.

IP telephony networks are, of course, not limited only to implementations of services known from the legacy telephone networks. Nevertheless, users of PBXs, Centrex services, and ISDN expect support for most of the current telephony features when they switch to IP telephony-based systems. Thus, IP telephony systems need to be designed such that they support most of the current telephony features in addition to having the flexibility for the creation of new services.

Adoption of services from the legacy networks has its advantages and disadvantages. The advantages include rapid creation and deployment of such services. This is because the knowledge gained from the standardization and deployment of such services within traditional telecommunication networks facilitates an ease of standardization and deployment of these same services within IP telephony systems. The disadvantages include understanding inherent differences between traditional circuit-switched networks and IP networks, which could make creation of the same service quite different on the two networks. Such differences include the following:

- In IP-based networks, the *Internet Protocol* (IP) acts as a glue or bond between disparate network technologies that may underlie these networks, thereby providing a transparent transport network. Such a transparent transport network when used in conjunction with intelligent end systems (say, PCs) facilitates a third-party creation of applications. On the other hand, in traditional circuit-switched networks such as ISDN, services may only be deployed by the network operator and are also bound to network elements such as telephone switches rather than the end systems.

- Many applications developed for IP-based networks can be installed in a "plug-and-play" fashion. Involvement of the service provider or any service personnel is not needed, and the application may be installed directly by the user. However, this is usually not the case in traditional circuit-switched networks such as the ISDN.

These differences make creation and deployment of services in IP-based networks quick and easy, while the deployment of similar services in circuit-switched networks is slow and difficult. This does not mean, however, that circuit-switched end systems such as desktop and wireless telephones will disappear. A more likely scenario is the use of a common IP-based network infrastructure and the use of both traditional—desktop and wireless phones—as well as intelligent end systems (IP phones) connecting to such networks.

In the following text, we discuss the architectural principles of call control by applications, which is followed by a discussion of the signaling architecture of feature control in H.323.

Categories of Call Control Applications

Call control applications are responsible for handling call control. The physical location where such an application runs can vary depending on the system being considered. In certain cases the application may run at the endpoints, while in others it may run within a centralized server in the network. In either case, a clear separation of the application and the call control itself has its advantages. When the design involves such a separation, the same design may be easily adopted to various systems irrespective of the physical location of the application.

Computer Telephony Integration (CTI) in traditional voice telephony deals with locating the call control application on the telephone switch. Thus, CTI involves the application running on a centralized server within the network, and an integration of computer applications and telephone switches. With H.323 multimedia telephony, on the other hand, the call control application is located at the H.323 endpoint rather than in a switch. The physical location of the call control application is thus different in a CTI system and in an H.323 system. However, due to the fundamental and architectural split between the application and call control within H.323 multimedia telephony systems as well as within CTI voice telephony systems, existing CTI call control applications can be used unchanged within the H.323 systems by running them at the H.323 endpoints over suitable application interfaces. Such reimplementation from an existing system to a new system facilitates cost reduction and faster deployment as well as a greater acceptance of services in new systems such as IP telephony systems.

Call control applications can be classified into the following three categories:

- *First-party call control applications.* The application (and its user) is a party in the call being controlled.
- *Third-party call control applications.* The application (and its user) is not a party in the call being controlled, but merely controls that call.
- *Call management applications.* The application only manages the databases that indirectly handle call control.

First-Party Call Control Applications

In a first-party call control scenario, the application which is responsible for call control is also a party in the call that is being controlled. First-party call control applications are usually single terminal applications. They operate locally for the controlled terminal when it is also one of the parties in the call. Figure 6.1 illustrates the scenario of a first-party call control. These applications are further split into functional components that represent the different possible roles (such as calling or a called party) in a call. All end-devices in a LAN environment that are parties in a call need to support first-party call control supplementary services. These devices can, for example, be desktop PCs, conference units, voice/multimedia response units or gateways to other networks.

First-party call control applications are usually created using first-party service provider software. This software offers its services to the application via standardized multimedia call control APIs such as Microsoft *Telephony API* (TAPI) and *Java Telephony API* (JTAPI). The network interface is controlled by the H.323/H.450 protocol. The call control applications do not directly interact with the network, but normally interact only via the Telephony APIs (such as TAPI or JTAPI) and signaling protocol (such as H.323). As shown in Figure 6.1, in certain situations such as within work groups, the client and server applications can also interact via an application layer protocol such as HTTP.

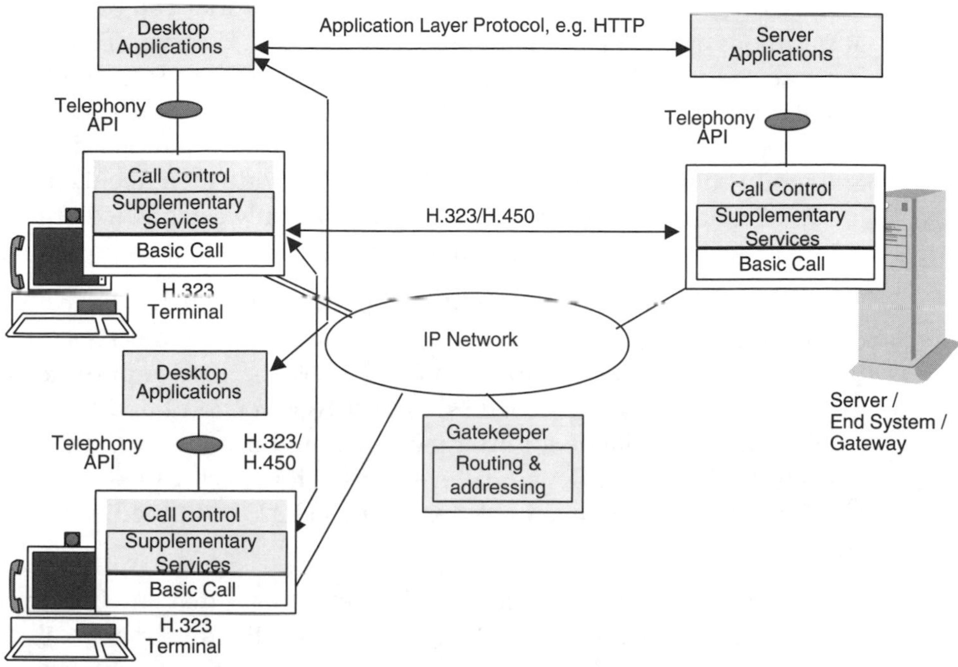

Figure 6.1 First-party call control in an H.323 multimedia environment.

Although the proposed standards for the networking protocol (H.450) and the call control APIs (TAPI, JTAPI) were originally specified for voice and voice-band services, most of their supported features and principles are also suitable for multimedia communication purposes. For multimedia call control, however, these protocols and APIs must be enhanced in order to meet specific media-handling requirements.

Third-Party Call Control Applications

Third-party call control applications perform actions on calls on other terminals remotely. Although the controlling application itself is not a party of the controlled call, it has the ability to perform all or most of the call control functions that a first-party application can do. These applications can run either on a server or on other terminals. Typical third-party call control applications are call center and group control applications. Third-party call control applications have become very attractive in their improvement of the voice communication processes in many private network business scenarios and are expected to become equally popular in emerging multimedia communication.

In the case of CTI within legacy private voice networks, call control applications are processed on a third party— the CTI server. The CTI server is connected to a PBX via a CTI link, which enables the server to remotely establish or answer calls and to monitor the connection or call states of the controlled terminal. Typical examples of CTI implementations are call center and group control applications. Call centers provide their agents (a specific group of controlled subscribers) with automatically established or received calls and also provide customer data related to the call, thus providing CTI.

The protocol between the call control application server and the call control is called *Computer Services Telephony Applications* (CSTA) and is standardized by the ISO. Although Version 1 and 2 of CSTA has specified support for voice and voice-band services only, most of the CSTA Version 1 and Version 2 services are also suitable for multimedia communication purposes. The current Version 3 of CSTA has been extended for specific media-handling requirements, making it suitable for use in a H.323 multimedia environment as well.

One major limitation within legacy PBX networks is that one CTI server can usually only be connected to a single PBX. Thus, the third-party call control application only has the ability to control those devices which are connected to that particular PBX. This limitation does not exist, however, when CTI is used in an H.323 multimedia environment. By using the CSTA standard as a CTI-link control protocol, third-party call control can be provided over the IP network to the H.323 endpoints (as shown in Figure 6.2). The CTI applications can be installed independently on different servers or even on an endpoint terminal. Moreover, each of the first-party call control service providers in the end-point devices can be connected to one (or more) CTI application.

Call Management Applications

Call management applications are call control applications that basically provide support for data-oriented services for registration, admission, address translation, and information retrieval (such as H.323 RAS gatekeeper services, or directory services). Thus, the application only manages the databases that indirectly handle call control.

These services typically run on a reliable centralized server. In such case, endpoints, such as IP telephones, only access the call management databases indirectly—for example, via the call management application located on the centralized server. However, these services can also run directly on endpoints. In this case, a direct interface is established from the endpoint to the database servers via application layer protocols such as HTTP or WAP.

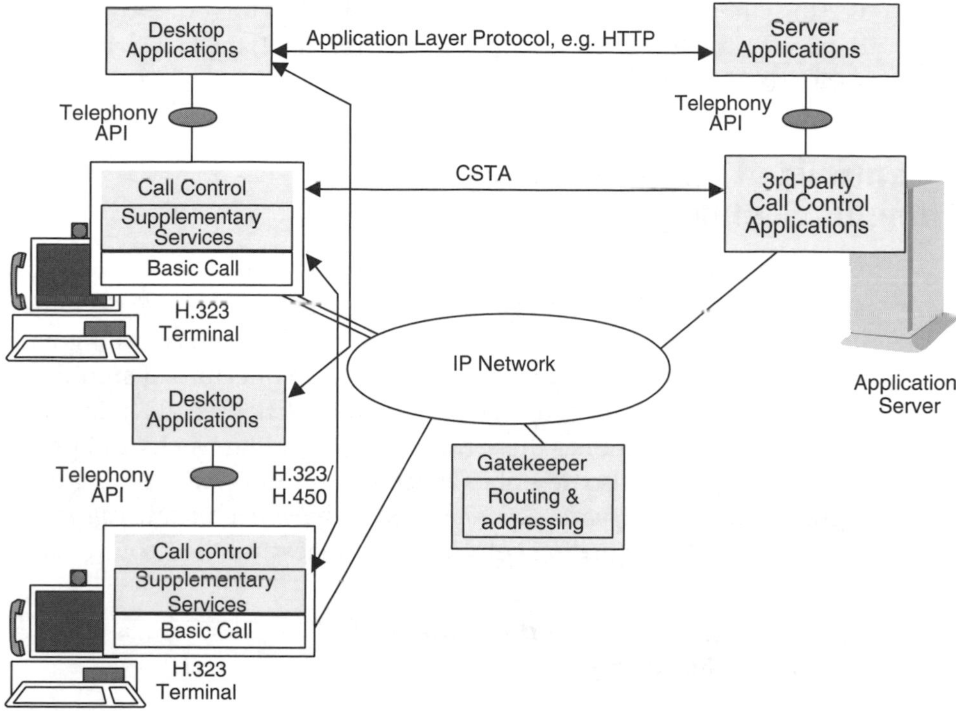

Figure 6.2 Third-party call control in a multimedia environment.

Signaling Architecture for Services in H.323

Based on the previous discussion of the architectural principles of call control, we can now begin to derive the basic distribution rules for the functions of supplementary services within multimedia systems and networks. Three possibilities exist for the function split:

1. Call control applications and supplementary services are *centralized* in the network, either behind the *gatekeeper* (GK) or in a separate feature server. This means that a *stimulus* protocol must be created between the terminal and the server. H.323/Annex L and H.248 telephony packages are examples of such stimulus protocols.
2. Call control and call management applications and supplementary services can be located anywhere in the network and are accessed via *HTTP-based service control*.
3. Call control applications and supplementary services are *distributed* in the endpoints and servers. This means that they interact with each other via a *peer-to-peer signaling* protocol, such as H.323/H.450.

Because the above methods are not exclusive but their deployment is dependent on the network and user environment, the H.323 standard supports all three methods.

A Centralized Approach Using Stimulus Signaling

This section describes what stimulus signaling is and why it is necessary and applicable in the IP telephony environment. Examples have been included of call scenarios involving stimulus services and their interworking with the H.450 series of supplementary services. The architecture of stimulus signaling will be discussed in greater detail in Chapter 10, "Stimulus Signaling," which defines the architecture's building blocks and programming model. Chapter 10 also describes stimulus protocols for handling the trunk signaling between a *media gateway* (MG) and a *media gateway controller* (MGC), as well as the line signaling between telephones and their controllers.

The Characteristics and Purpose of Stimulus Signaling

In stimulus signaling, the terminal does not execute any software applications for the features it supports. Such execution occurs in a feature server that can be either implemented in a standalone fashion or collocated with another entity such as a gatekeeper.

A feature key management protocol operates between the stimulus terminal and the feature server. The feature key management protocol does not directly control any supplementary service. It provides generic control services for the user interface functions (such as keys and indicators) of the stimulus terminal through specific supplementary service control entities in a gatekeeper. For example, when a key is pressed at the terminal, the terminal merely sends a signaling message containing the key identification to the feature server, which then executes the required feature actions. The actual meaning of the buttons and the related sequence of interactions with the user are controlled by the feature server. In the opposite direction, the stimulus protocol enables the feature server to write to the terminal display, change the state of the telephone's feature indicators, or switch audible guidance tones and announcements on and off. The main advantage of stimulus signaling is that terminals do not need to be changed or reloaded with new software, or when new features are assigned to feature buttons, feature indicators (e.g., LEDs) and/or to the display. The stimulus method enables the network service provider to implement new supplementary services for the terminals without remote downloads or local maintenance actions on the premises of the user. A typical example of the use of stimulus signaling is a LAN-attached business telephone which has a display, a few feature buttons (a call hold and a call transfer button), and the corresponding feature indicators, and its execution environment on a separate feature server.

A typical stimulus terminal is usually a simple one, such as the *Simple Endpoint Type* (SET) terminal, which does not perform H.450 supplementary services. Thus, the gatekeeper or the feature server is responsible for providing a proxy function for handling the H.450 procedures over the network on a terminal's behalf. The principle of stimulus signaling is shown in Figure 6.3.

H.323 Stimulus

Stimulus signaling (Annex L) was added to H.323 in version 3. The H.323 Annex L describes the stimulus signaling procedures (i.e., a feature key management protocol) between simple H.323 terminals and a gatekeeper or feature server. While Figure 6.3 illustrates the case where the protocol exists between the terminal and the gatekeeper, such a protocol also exists between the terminal and a standalone feature server.

H.323 Annex L extends the H.323 SET terminal procedures with feature key management. The H.323 procedures were extended in such a manner that the regular H.225.0 signaling is still used for basic call control. This extension provides for maximum backward compatibility with the earlier versions of H.323 (v1 and v2). In addition, it also implies that previously implemented basic call protocol stacks can be relatively easily enhanced with the stimulus functionality. The H.323 stimulus signaling uses the H.248 package definitions, which define the stimulus entities of terminals and the corresponding signaling. Thus duplicate definition of the stimulus protocol is avoided, and the

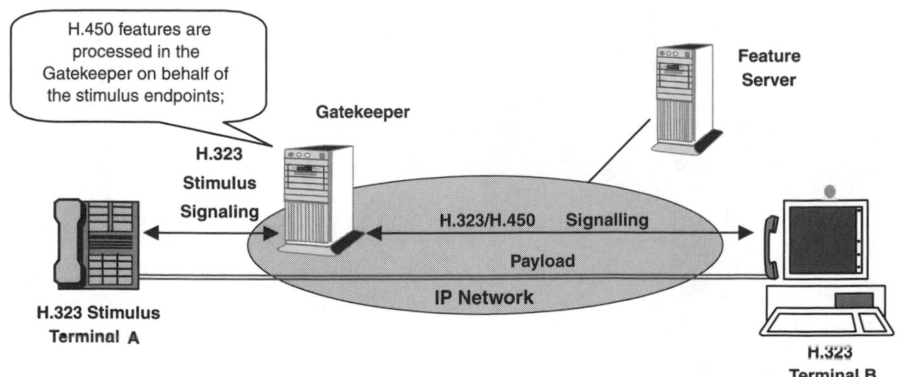

Figure 6.3. H.323 stimulus signaling entities.

implementation is simplified in cases where both an H.248 stimulus and an H.323 stimulus must be supported at the same time.

H.248 Stimulus

Stimulus control of terminals is also possible by means of the H.248 gateway control protocol (see Figure 6.4). The H.248 standard originally resulted from the decomposition of VoIP gateways into two components—*media gateway* (MG) and *media gateway controller* (MGC)—and is primarily used as the protocol between these two components. It was argued that small residential gateways and IP phones could be realized using a similar protocol. However, only a small portion of the H.248 gateway control signaling is actually usable for the subscriber line side, so additional packages were defined for the telephone line signaling. The architecture used for H.248 telephone line signaling is shown in.

The H.248 stimulus terminals and residential gateways are controlled by a gateway controller or call agent. It is this entity which performs all the line signaling, local feature control, and the interworking with H.323 and H.450 on behalf of the terminal. The H.248 terminals have a fixed association with their controller. Therefore, if an H.248 terminal is unplugged and moved elsewhere in its network domain, it is still associated with the same controller and is fully functional.

A Web-Based Approach Using HTTP

H.323 Annex K describes an application layer method based on HTTP for control of various features in H.323 entities. This essentially implies

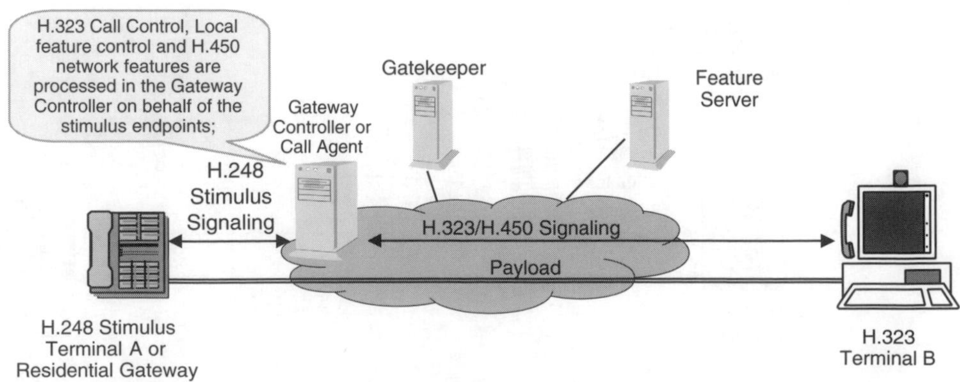

Figure 6.4 H.248 stimulus signaling entities.

third-party control, because the controlling entity is generally not an endpoint of the controlled call.

The method can be used either during a call or independently of a call. It not only permits access to the features of endpoints, unified messaging servers, gateways, and gatekeepers, but also enables access to directory information, call charge records, and at the very least, cost-routing databases. Annex K is optional in H.323 and can be utilized by any intelligent endpoint that supports an HTTP browser. The advantage of opening a separate HTTP connection that conveys a service independent control is that new services can be developed and deployed without updates to the H.323 endpoints. This service control channel is intended to be used for a wide range of services like those offered by H.323 unified messaging servers. It can also be used to create an easy-to-use user interface to the H.450 supplementary service, to upgrade software, or to push commercials to the clients.

Shown in Figure 6.5 is an example and a schematic view of an HTTP-based control of features that are provided by a gatekeeper for an H.323 stimulus terminal via a handheld wireless device. Figure 6.6 further illustrates the

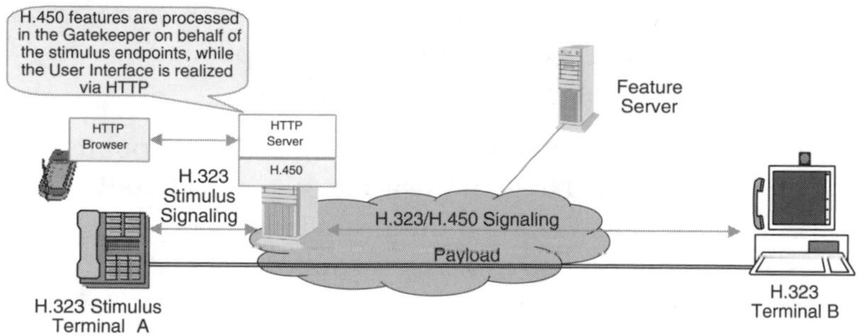

Figure 6.5 HTTP service control of a gatekeeper.

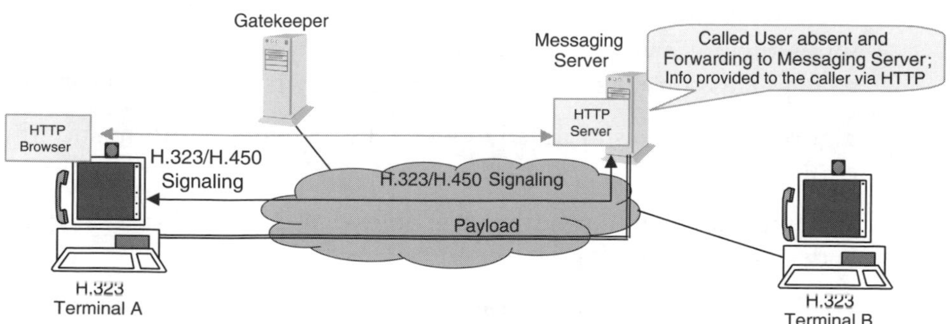

Figure 6.6 HTTP service control of a messaging server.

services provided to a calling H.323/H.450 multimedia terminal by a messaging server.

As seen in the last example, HTTP service control is an optional way of controlling supplementary services in an H.323 environment. It can be used as a supplement to the H.450 supplementary service control, or to nonstandard services. By opening a separate connection which conveys a service independent control protocol, new services can be developed and deployed without sending updates to the H.323 endpoints.

Distributed Peer-to-Peer Approach Using H.450

The models and architectures of H.323/H.450 supplementary services are based on 1) provisioning and 2) the distribution of functions between H.323 endpoints and servers. Thus, the supplementary service signaling is performed end-to-end between the multimedia terminals and is transparently sent through the network without requiring processing by any network entities. The network function of the gatekeeper is limited to admission control, address resolution, and call routing. It does not, of course, prevent the gatekeeper, or any other entities in the call signaling path, from becoming an endpoint for a given service. For example, a gatekeeper or a *gateway* (GW) can implement the call transfer requested by the user.

However, due to the distribution of functionality to the endpoints, mechanisms must be defined to guarantee a user's call is handled at the destination even if the called H.323 multimedia terminal is out of service. This requires a substitute (called proxy in the following text) to be nominated when the terminal goes out of service.

The architecture enables scalability, because clients and servers can be individually added to the network without mandating centralized provisioning entities. The cost of the required processing power and memory in the endpoints is unlikely to be a limiting factor. Uniform network infrastructure is very important for fast deployment of services, because it enables mass production of user equipment, which in turn lowers prices.

Figure 6.7 shows a simplified model of the network platform and functional entities.

The intelligence of the endpoints enables distribution of services across the endpoint, for example

- The IP Client contains the state of the calls that it is handling. Some of the services suitable for implementation in the client are Multiple Call

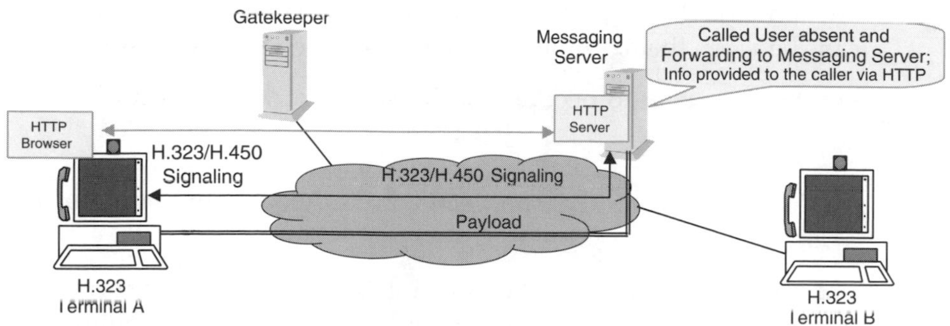

Figure 6.7 Peer-to-peer signaling entities.

Handling, Call Transfer, Call Forwarding, Call Hold, Call Waiting, Message Waiting, and N-way Conferencing.

- A Conference Server contains the state of the calls that it is handling. The service it provides is specifically N-way conferencing, i.e. conference with N participants.
- A feature server implements services that may not be suitable for client implementation. Services such as Call Park/Pickup are used in the Automatic Call Distribution environment where calls are not directed to a specific user/client yet can, for example, be directed to the first available agent with some specific skill. Such services are best implemented in a feature server, which then interfaces with a group of clients. A feature server can be collocated with a gatekeeper.

An example of a service easily implemented in the gatekeeper is calling card authorization. Once the call is authorized, the gatekeeper can reconnect the call to the specified client or user.

A feature server can be used as a proxy or secondary client for those clients that are nonoperational (i.e., powered-down). Upon detection of the operational failure of a primary client (e.g., it has been powered off), the gatekeeper notifies and routes all calls destined for the nonoperational client to a feature server. The feature server/proxy then has the ability to provide such services as Call Forwarding and Message Handling (voice, fax, and e-mail).

As IP-telephony networks emerge, they will consist of many subnetworks and domains. Examples of these are enterprise networks with many sites, where each site already consists of further domains and subdomains. Thus, the networks will consist of many independent *islands*. Considering such generic model, one of the most important requirements is that these *islands* are networked with each other, so that supplementary services are used on calls between them. Within the islands themselves it is possible to either use

- The same peer-to-peer or distributed networking concept

or

- Centralized control of supplementary services with a stimulus type of signaling

The architecture of IP telephony is suitable for use by both corporate networks and new generation telephone companies. The deployment of H.323 first began in corporate networks, mainly because many of their users could immediately utilize their existing PCs, workstations, and servers in their H.323 infrastructure. Additionally the QSIG-based core of H.450 enabled smooth migration from currently installed PBX networks to H.323 multimedia networks. Thus, the goal to lower short- and long-term costs and to enable easy, gradual growth of the network is reached.

In a similar manner, using H.323, new telcos can provide not only basic telephony and some related features, but also IP-based value-added services, such as unified messaging, call distribution, VPN, and one-number service. The H.450 supplementary services provide signaling methods and standard building blocks for such services. The H.323 gatekeeper-routed model enables any billing model of these network services. Existing analogue telephone and fax equipment can be connected to the H.323 network via terminal adapters and residential gateways.

Introduction to H.450 Supplementary Services

The main goal in the creation of the ITU-T H.450 series recommendations was to enable traditional telephony features over an IP network between any pair of endpoints, networks, and subdomains. This resulted in a set of the most common features—chosen from traditional telephony features— from which common protocol building blocks are defined. These building blocks are intended for use in the implementation of services such as IP PBXs, IP Centrexes, IP call centers, intelligent IP telephones, and feature servers.

Requirements for H.450

One of the main requirements for H.450 is that the functional entities must be able to communicate with their peer entities (servers, clients, MCUs, or gateways) directly without any network intervention. This requirement enables the building of H.323 network domains that are independent and tied with each other only via H.323/H.450. Additional requirements are as follows:

- Must have open and standardized protocol to enable vendor independence for the customer
- Must be independent of network configuration and topology
- Must easily interwork with existing QSIG-based PBX networks
- Must easily interwork with public ISDN networks such as E-DSS1 and National ISDN
- Must have an extensible protocol to enable manufacturer-specific supplementary services and additional network features to provide value-add when compared to competitors.
- Must have transparency for manufacturer-specific extensions and services
- Must easily use supplementary services, such as components accessed by applications via APIs

The protocol that comes closest to fulfilling these requirements is QSIG. QSIG is available as the worldwide standard ISO/IEC JTC1 for private ISDN telecommunication networks. In fact, no single protocol currently provides a functionality comparable to QSIG. Although QSIG was originally created mainly for support of voice telephony, it is logical to use it for other person-to-person multimedia communication as well. Moreover, some of the functions are applicable to other areas as well, such as access to servers. The choice of QSIG architectural elements also has the following further advantages:

- Standard QSIG feature support is required in any case—at least in the gateways in a heterogeneous (multivendor) network; that is, when equipment from different vendors is used for each end of the connection.
- Many QSIG features are specifically designed to interwork with the corresponding public network version of the feature. This gives the user a better QoS when communicating via an ISDN.

Thus, a full network transparency and a gradual migration for adoption of new multimedia supplementary services is guaranteed. Adoption of QSIG procedures for supplementary services enables easy interworking and migration from currently installed private networks to multimedia networks. This is especially important, because companies have high investments in private telecommunication networks and the network signaling of each of these networks is usually based on QSIG standards.

The Embedding of H.450 in H.323 System Architecture

The H.450 recommendations enhance the H.323 basic system model with additional functional entities that execute the supplementary service interactions. Figure 6.8 shows the embedding of H.450 in the H.323 system architecture.

The H.450 recommendations define functional components that are used directly by the applications for implementation of telephony features. Examples of such components are Near End Hold, Remote End Hold and Call Transfer. Figure 6.8 also shows compound services within H.450. Built with the help of existing functional components, these are supplementary services that do not require enhancement of the protocol with new data elements. Examples of such services are Consultation and Alternating, both of which make use of Call Hold and Basic Call as components. Another is the Consultation Transfer which uses Call Hold, Call Transfer, and Basic Call as components.

The H.450 functional entities are structured in a layered, modular manner. They do not have dependencies with each other, except via the messages exchanged for interaction purposes. These functional entities are systematically described in each of the H.450 supplementary service standards and can be used as the basis for implementation.

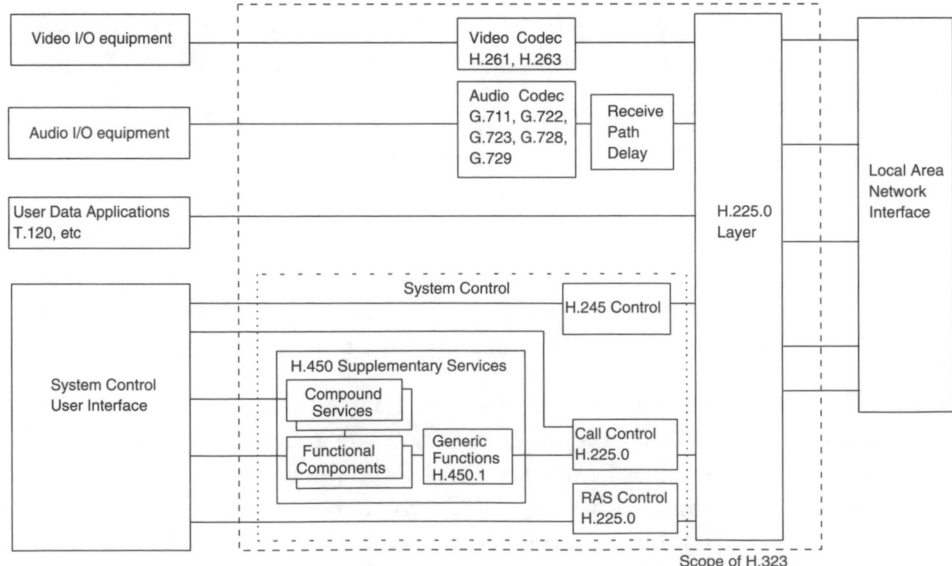

Figure 6.8 The embedding of H.450 in H.323 system architecture.

The Status of H.450 Recommendations

The ITU-T H.323/H.225.0/H.245 recommendations for basic multimedia already include a number of basic features that are often defined as supplementary services within the context of the ISDN. These include the following services and capabilities that we previously detailed in Chapters 2 through 5:

- Calling party number presentation and presentation restriction
- Connected party number presentation and presentation restriction
- Handling of numbering plans
- Addressing by aliases
- DTMF transport
- Limited user mobility due to the Gatekeeper concept
- Incoming call queuing and hunt groups via the gatekeeper
- Call detail recording by endpoint and gatekeeper
- Centralized and decentralized multimedia conference

However, there are many other supplementary services that can be useful in real-time multimedia communication. Most of them are known in one form or another in private and/or public network telephony.

Table 6.1 overviews the current status of the H.450 series of recommendations and provides references to the comparable ETSI and ISO standards, from which they were derived.

The following sections describe the signaling transport of supplementary service including transport of Common Information and Name Identification.

H.450.1 – Generic Functional Protocol

A key element of a powerful supplementary services control protocol is a mechanism that enables the protocol to be extensible, either by adding new standardized features or by adding manufacturer specific proprietary features. New features can also be agreed upon and added by multivendor consortia and other forums.

For this purpose H.450.1 describes the procedures and the signaling protocol between H.323 entities for the control of the supplementary services. The generic functional protocol operates in conjunction with the H.225.0 call signaling protocol and is common to all H.323 supplementary services. It

Table 6.1 H.450 Series of ITU-T Recommendations

SERVICE	LAN H.323 SERIES	PTN ISO QSIG (PSS1)	ISDN DSS1 (EURO-ISDN)
Basic Call	H.323, H.225, H.245	ISO 11572	ETS 300 102
-Including Conference		NA	ETS 300 185-1
Generic Functions	H.450.1 (2/98)	ISO 11582	EN 300 196-1, EN 301 061-1
ASN.1 Notation	X.680-X.683	X.208	X.208
ASN.1 Encoding	X.691 (PER)	X.209(BER)	X.209 (BER)
ROSE	X.880	X.229	X.229
Call Transfer	H.450.2 (2/98)	ISO/IEC 13860/13869	ETS 300 369-1
Call Diversion	H.450.3 (2/98)	ISO/IEC 13873/13873	ETS 300 207-1
Call Hold	H.450.4 (5/99)	included in ISO 11582	ETS 300 141-1
Call Park/Pickup	H.450.5 (5/99)	NA	NA
Call Waiting	H.450.6 (5/99)	Included in ISO 11582	ETS 300 058-1
Message Waiting	H.450.7 (5/99)	ISO/IEC 15506/15056	ETS 300 745-1, EN 300 899-1
Number Identification	H.225 (2/00)	Included in ISO 11572	ETS 300 092-1, ETS 300 093-1
Name Identification	H.450.8 (11/00)	ISO/IEC 13864/13868	ETS 300 097-1, ETS 300 098-1
CCBS/CCNR	H.450.9 (11/00)	ISO/IEC 13866/13870	EN 301 065-1
Call Offering	H.450.10 (4/01)	ISO/IEC 14841/14843	NA
Call Intrusion	H.450.11 (4/01)	ISO/IEC 14845/14846	NA
Common Information	H.450.12 (4/01)	ISO/IEC 15771	NA
Advice of Charge	NA	ISO/IEC 15049/15050	ETS 300 178- ETS 300 180
Recall	NA	ISO/IEC 15051/15052	NA
Call Interception	NA	ISO/IEC 15053/15054	NA
Do Not Disturb	NA	ISO/IEC 14842/14844	NA

does not control any supplementary service alone, however it does provide generic services to specific entities controlling the supplementary services. These mechanisms are common to standardized and manufacturer-specific services.

In order to be fully compatible and to interoperate with H.323s Version 1 and Version 2 endpoints, the H.450.1 generic functional protocol must be able to detect the supplementary service signaling capabilities of the remote endpoint and to adjust its operations accordingly. Therefore, the protocol may have to possibly revert back to basic call processing in the case of H.323 endpoints that do not support any supplementary services. Most of these endpoints do not even have H.450.1 capabilities (e.g., Microsoft NetMeeting 2.1 and 3.0).

H.450.1 Transport Connections

The H.450.1 generic functional protocol provides transport mechanisms, that 1) relate to the existing H.323 calls or 2) are entirely independent of any existing H.323 calls.

Supplementary service operations require an association between the respective peer supplementary service entities. This association is achieved implicitly by the transport connection and the call reference used for call signaling. Thus, for the *call-related transport* of H.450.1 Supplementary Service *Application Protocol Data Units* (APDUs), the call signaling channel and call reference of the call that the APDU relates to is used. *Call independent transport* means that a temporary signaling connection must be first established between the involved parties through corresponding H.225.0 procedures.

The Structure of H.450.1 APDUs

An *Application Protocol Data Unit* (APDU) is a sequence of data elements exchanged between peer application layer entities. The H.450.1 APDU can be repeated in a *User-User Information Element* (UUIE). Because the H.450.1 APDUs are exchanged between corresponding H.450 supplementary service entities, sending a FACILITY message does not change the underlying H.225.0 call state directly.

The H.450.1 data elements are encoded and sent using *Remote Operations Service* (ROS) APDUs. In accordance with Recommendation X.880, there are four types of ROS APDUs — 1) Invoke, 2) Return result, 3) Return error and 4) Reject. Invoke APDUs, return result APDUs, and return error APDUs when used in the context of a supplementary service are implicitly defined by the operations and errors used by that service. These operations and errors are defined in ASN.1— of the corresponding supplementary service specifications (standardized or manufacturer specific). Table 5 found in the ITU-T Recommendation H.450.1 also provides definitions of the problem codes for use in the reject APDUs.

The principal structure of the H.450.1 APDU is shown in Figure 6.9.

All H.450.1 Supplementary Service APDUs have the same basic structure and contain the following elements in the header part:

Network Facility Extension (NFE). Describes the intended receiver of the APDU. This intended receiver then looks to the Interpreter next. An entity, which is not a receiver, must pass on the APDU unchanged to the next signaling entity, unless it is an endpoint in which case the APDU is ignored.

Interpreter (I). Describes what the receiver must do if it cannot understand the contents of the APDU. The requested actions it replies with can be 1) Discard the APDU, 2) Clear the call, or 3) Reply with Reject message.

Manufacturer Specific Information (MSI). Permits the inclusion of nonstandardized information specific to a particular design of equipment or a particular network, and so on.

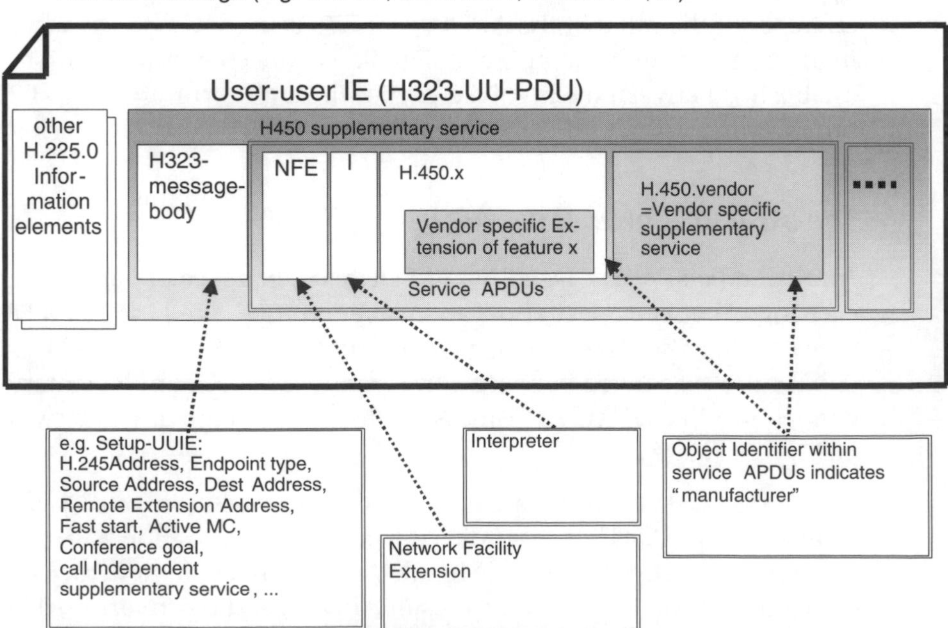

Figure 6.9 An H.450.1 supplementary service APDU.

The extensibility of the H.450.1 protocol is based on the correct handling of the H.450 APDU envelopes, which contains the NFE and Interpreter APDUs of the sending and receiving entities. The sender must set its contents to guarantee it receives a suitable response from the remote end to the APDU. If it is not supported or implemented, it is not understood by the H.323 protocol layer.

Valid Messages for H.450.1

The H.450.1 supplementary service APDU can be sent on the call signaling channel using a valid call control message at any time while a call reference exists. It is however, subject to the following conditions:

- If a call establishment (SETUP, CALL PROCEEDING, ALERTING, PROGRESS or CONNECT) or a call clearing message (RELEASE COMPLETE), which contains a H.450.1 supplementary service APDU, is to be sent in the context of a call or on a call independent signaling connection, the H.450.1 supplementary service APDU is included in that message. Otherwise, the H.450.1 supplementary service APDU is carried in a FACILITY message.
- If a SETUP message was previously sent or received and no response was received respectively sent, the FACILITY message is not to be sent.

The Sending Rules

The sending of the envelope (with NFE and I) is optional to the sender. If the sender wishes to include them to facilitate handling of unrecognized APDUs of the type Invoke at a destination entity, it can include an Interpretation APDU as the first APDU in the sequence of APDUs. The Interpretation APDU can be applied to all Invoke APDUs included in this H.450.1 APDU.

An NFE is included in the H.450.1 supplementary service APDU according to the following rules:

- If the remote endpoint is to be the destination entity of this information element, the NFE is included with destinationEntity set to 'endpoint' and with destinationEntityAddress being omitted.
- If no specific entity is to be the destination entity of this information element, the NFE is included with destinationEntity set to 'anyEntity' and with destinationEntityAddress being omitted.
- If a specific H.323 entity on the call signaling path to the remote endpoint is to be the destination entity of this information element, the NFE is included with destinationEntity set to 'anyEntity' and with destinationEntityAddress containing the address of the H.323 entity.

- If the next entity (e.g., a gatekeeper) on the call signaling path to a remote endpoint is the destination entity of this information element, the NFE is omitted.

The Reception Rules

An entity receiving a H.450.1 Supplementary Service APDU in a valid call clearing, a call establishment message, or a FACILITY message responds only to the APDU if it is the intended destination. A response is determined according to the following rules:

- If no NFE is present, the entity always becomes the destination entity.
- If the NFE is present with destinationEntity='endpoint', then the entity becomes the destination entity if it is an endpoint for this call or the independent signaling connection of this call. If destinationEntity= 'endpoint' is present, then a gatekeeper capable of acting as an endpoint for all the services indicated in the H.450.1 supplementary service APDU, becomes the destination entity for that H.450.1 APDU.
- If the NFE is present with destinationEntity='anyEntity' and a destinationEntityAddress is contained, the entity becomes the destination entity if that address matches one of its own.
- If the NFE is present with destinationEntity='anyEntity' and it does not have a destinationEntityAddress, the entity can become the destination entity if it understands the contents of the H.450.1 APDU.

If the receiving entity is the destination entity, the procedures of subclause 6.6 of the Recommendation H.450.1 are followed. This means that the H.450.1 APDU is processed by the supplementary service control of the receiver.

If the receiving entity is not the destination entity, the H.450.1 APDU is passed on if possible, otherwise the H.450.1 APDU is discarded. APDUs received in H.450.1 supplementary service APDUs are processed in the order in which they were received, following the normal ROS rules with the following exception: If the first APDU is an Interpretation APDU and any of the ROS APDUs are invoke APDUs of an unrecognized operation, then

- The Interpretation APDU indicates rejectUnrecognizedInvokePdu, and a reject APDU with InvokeProblem=unrecognizedOperation is sent to the source entity (see Note).

NOTE

This is the normal ROS procedure which also applies if no Interpretation APDU is present.

- The Interpretation APDU indicates clearCallIfAnyInvokePduNotRecognized, and a reject APDU with InvokeProblem=unrecognizedOperation is sent to the source entity. The call or signaling connection that was related to the invoke APDU is also cleared.
- The Interpretation APDU indicates discardAnyUnrecognizedInvokePDU and no reject APDU is sent to the source entity.

H.450.12–Common Information

H.450.12 is an additional network feature which enables the exchange of Common Information between H.323 or H.450 endpoints. This information is a collection of miscellaneous information which relates to the endpoint or equipment at one end of a connection and includes one or more Feature identifiers and Party category indicators. This information, when received by an H.323 or H.450 endpoint, can be used for any purpose—for example, as the basis for indications to the local user or to another network, or to filter feature requests.

A *solicited* and an *unsolicited service* can be offered to an H.323 or H.450 endpoint (which may be located at either end of a connection). The solicited service enables the H.323 or H.450 endpoint to request the Common Information from a peer endpoint. The unsolicited service enables an H.323 or H.450 endpoint to supply Common Information to a peer endpoint, without being requested to do so. These services can be combined and are not mutually exclusive.

In fact, H.450.12 makes use of the "Generic functional protocol for the support of supplementary services in H.323" as defined in the Recommendation H.450.1. The procedures and the signaling protocol are derived from the Common Information Additional Network Feature specified in the QSIG protocol by ISO/IEC 15771 and 15772.

The H.450.12 invoke APDUs are conveyed within H.450.1 supplementary service APDUs included in UUIE as specified in H.450.1. The destinationEntity data element of the NFE contains the value endpoint because the contents of the Common Information are exchanged directly between the endpoints with the intermediate entities transparent for the exchange of this information. However intermediate entities, such as a gatekeeper, can become an endpoint if it acts on its terminal's behalf, by performing a proxy function.

In a Facility information element conveying a Common Information request, the Interpretation APDU is included with the value rejectAnyUnrecognisedInvokePdu. This enables future implementations of

H.323 to keep adding new contents within Common Information, and to recognize whether the sent information was actually understood by the receiver. This is important to know, for example, in various kinds of interactions between the supplementary services. A Facility information element, which conveys a Common Information response, also contains an Interpretation APDU with the value discardAnyUnrecognisedInvokePdu for similar reasons.

The Feature Identifier List

Common Information contains feature identifiers and party category indicators which can be used in forward and/or backward direction. If the information is sent in a forward direction—from calling party to called party—it can include one or more of the elements listed in Table 6.2. If the information is sent in a backward direction—from called party to calling party—it may include one or more of the elements listed in Table 6.3.

H.450.8—Name Information

This supplementary service enhances H.323 systems with the Name delivery and display capability. The *Name* meant here is the real name, company

Table 6.2 Feature Identifiers in the Forward Direction

FEATURE IDENTIFIERS	VALUES	COMMENTS
SS-CF Call Forward rerouting available	Yes/No	Used in Call Forwarding: Originating endpoint supports Call Forwarding by rerouting.
SS-CT Call Transfer rerouting available	Yes/No	Used to detect H.450.2 Call Transfer capability: Endpoint supports Call Transfer rerouting.
SS-CT Call Transfer protection level	0 1 2 3	Used in Call Intrusion: Originating endpoint presents its protection level against Call Intrusion. Protection level 0 means either no protection or service is not supported.
ANF-CINT Can Intercept Calls—interception immediate ANF-CINT Can Intercept Calls—interception delayed	Yes/No Yes/No	Used in Call Interception.
SS-HOLD Near end call hold available SS-HOLD Remote end call hold available	Yes/No Yes/No	Used in Call Hold.

Table 6.3 Feature Identifiers in the Backward Direction

FEATURE IDENTIFIERS	VALUES	COMMENTS
SS-CT Call Transfer rerouting available	Yes/No	Used to detect H.450.2 Call Transfer capability: Endpoint supports Call Transfer rerouting.
SS-CCBS Call Completion on Busy available SS-CCNR Call Completion on No Reply available	Yes/No Yes/No	Terminating endpoint supports Call Completion on Busy Subscriber and on No Reply.
SS-CO Call Offering available	Yes/No	Terminating endpoint supports Call Offer.
SS-DNDO Do Not Disturb available SS-DNDO Do Not Disturb protection level	Yes/No 0 1 2 3	Used in Do Not Disturb Override by terminating endpoint. Protection level 0 means either no protection or SS is not supported.
SS-CI Call Intrusion available SS-CI Call Intrusion protection level Options: SS-CI Call Intrusion Forced Release available SS-CI Call Intrusion Isolation available SS-CI Call Intrusion Wait on Busy available	Yes/No 0 1 2 3 Yes/No Yes/No Yes/No	Used in Call Intrusion by terminating endpoint. Protection level 0 means either no protection or SS is not supported.
SS-HOLD Near End Call Hold available SS-HOLD Remote End Call Hold Available	Yes/No Yes/No	Used in Call Hold.

name, work group name, or other identification of the parties involved in the call. The name is distinct from the H.323 alias, which is an address information element. Even though it may often contain the whole name or part of it, the alias address is not intended for display purposes.

Name Information is transported along the H.323/H.225 basic call and contains the Name Presentation and Restriction for 1) Connected Party, 2) Alerting Party, and 3) Busy Party Name. The calling party name information can be provided by the calling endpoint or by the gatekeeper using the gatekeeper-routed call model. Connected party name information, alerting party name information, or busy party name information can be provided by the answering (connected) party, the alerting party, or the busy party, respectively, or by their gatekeeper if the gatekeeper-routed call model is used.

When the call is routed through the gatekeeper with the endpoint it is registered with, that gatekeeper may provide a screening service that assures the name provided is actually that of the party. The gatekeeper may also provide the name when no name is provided by the respective party, or it may overwrite the name when the party provides a false name. The method that a gatekeeper uses to obtain the name information is implementation dependent and outside the scope of the standard.

When a call originates in the switched-circuit network and enters the packet network through a *gateway*, the gateway will pass the calling party name information (provided by the switched circuit network) to the packet network.

Further individual characteristics of the subcategories of the name services are

- Calling Party Name Presentation is a feature that provides the name of the calling party to the called party.
- Calling Party Name Restriction is a feature which enables the calling user, or the calling user's gatekeeper, to restrict presentation of the calling party name to the called party. This feature can reside in either the endpoint or in the gatekeeper for the gatekeeper-routed calls. In some cases where Calling Party Name Restriction is indicated, there can exist certain situations where the restriction is overridden—for example, if the called party provides some emergency service.
- Connected Party Name Presentation is a feature that provides the name of the connected party to the calling party. It also includes the optional presentation to the calling party of the alerting party's name or of the name of the busy called party. The operation for alerting party name presentation and busy party name presentation is similar to connected party name presentation.
- Connected Party Name Restriction is a feature, which enables the connected user, or the connected user's gatekeeper, to restrict the presentation of the connected party name to the calling party. This feature can reside in the endpoint or in the gatekeeper for gatekeeper-routed calls. The operation for alerting party name restriction and busy party name restriction is similar to connected party name presentation.

The Calling Party Name information is sent within the H.450.1 information contained within the H.225.0 Setup message. The Connected Party Name information is sent in the H.225.0 Connect message; the Alerting Party Name information is sent in the H.225.0 Alerting message; and the Busy Party Name information is sent in the H.225.0 Release Complete message.

The following rules apply when a gateway generates the Name information:

- The party's name is obtained from the other network's available signaling and is transmitted in the H.323 environment as previously described.
- If no name can be obtained, then the Name element indicates nameNotAvailable.
- If the name can be obtained, but its presentation is marked as restricted, then the Name element indicates namePresentationRestricted.
- If the name can be obtained and no restrictions exist on its presentation, then the Name element indicates namePresentationAllowed.
- Name information available from the H.323 environment in an H.225.0 Setup Connect, Alerting, or Release message is converted to the signaling format of the other network and vice versa.

The following rules apply when a terminal or MCU generates the Name information:

- For calls originated on the packet network, the originating terminal or MCU can send a Setup message as previously described.
- If presentation of the name to the other party is desirable, the Name element indicates namePresentationAllowed.
- If presentation of the name to the other party is to be restricted, the Name element indicates namePresentationRestricted.
- A terminal or MCU in receipt of an H.225.0 Setup, Connect, Alerting, or Release Complete message containing the Name information cannot present its contents if the Name element indicates namePresentationRestricted.

In gatekeeper routed scenarios, the gatekeeper can provide the name information or a screening service. The services that are provided by a gatekeeper depend on the type of endpoint served in the following manner:

- If gateway is the endpoint that generated the Name information, a gatekeeper should not modify the information found in a message sent from the gateway, assuming that the telephone network has provided correct information.
- If a terminal or an MCU is the endpoint that generated the Name information, a gatekeeper can
  - Override the name information
  - Provide the name information if none is provided by the respective party, or if the gatekeeper determines the name is wrong

- Provide a presentation restriction by removing the name information from the H.225.0 message, or by replacing it with the nameNotAvailable indication in the Name element
- Override the presentation indication and, for example, change namePresentationRestricted to namePresentationAllowed if the originating endpoint presents the name information to the user (such as for a call from an emergency service).

Recommended Reading

The ITU-T Recommendations [H.450.1], [H.450.8], and [H.450.12] describe the H.450.1, H.450.8, and H.450.12 supplementary services, respectively. [X.680], [X.680/Amd.1], [X.681/Amd.1], and [X.691], are the relevant ITU-T recommendations that deal with ASN.1 coding. More information on ROSE may be obtained from [X.880].

References

H.225 ITU-T Recommendation H.225.0 Version 4, Call signaling protocols and media stream packetization for packet-based multimedia communications systems, H.225, November 2000.

H.245 ITU-T Recommendation H.245 Version 5, Control protocol for multimedia communication, H.245, February 2000.

H.323 ITU-T Recommendation H.323 Version 4, Packet-based multimedia communications systems, H.323, November 2000.

H.450.1 ITU-T Recommendation H.450.1 Generic functional protocol for the support of supplementary services in H.323, H.450.1, February 1998.

H.450.8ITU-T Recommendation H.450.8, Name Identification Supplementary Service for H.323, H.450.8, February 2000.

H.450.12 ITU-T Recommendation H.450.12, Common Information Additional Network Feature for H.323, H.450.12 (Work in progress) , 2001.

ISO11582 ISO/IEC 11582, Information technology—Telecommunications and information exchange between systems—Private Integrated Services Network—Generic functional protocol for the support of supplementary services—Inter-exchange signaling procedures and protocol, ISO11582 Edition 1, May 1995.

X.680 ITU-T Recommendation X.680 (1994) | ISO/IEC 8824–1:1996, Information technology—Abstract Syntax Notation One (ASN.1)—Specification of basic notation, X.680, 1994, 1996.

X.680/Amd.1 ITU-T Recommendation X.680/Amd.1 (1995) | ISO/IEC 8824-1/Amd.1:1995, Information technology—Abstract Syntax Notation One (ASN.1)—Specification of basic notation—Amendment 1: Rules of extensibility, X. .680/Amd.1, 1995.

X.681/Amd.1 ITU-T Recommendation X.681/Amd.1 (1995) | ISO/IEC 8824-2/Amd.1:1995, Information technology—Abstract Syntax Notation One (ASN.1)—Information Object Specification—Amendment 1: Rules of extensibility, X.681/Amd.1, 1995.

X.691 ITU-T Recommendation X.691 (1995) | ISO/IEC 8825-2:1995, Information technology—ASN.1 encoding rules—Specification of Packed Encoding Rules (PER), X.691, 1995.

X.880 ITU-T Recommendation X.880 (1994) | ISO/IEC 13712-1:1995, Information technology—Remote Operations: Concepts, model and notation, X.880,1994.

Problems

1. What distinguishes a supplementary service from any other service or feature provider by the H.323?

2. What advantages does the use of an IP network as a telecommunication network backbone offer, and what kinds of new services does it enable?

3. A LAN-attached multimedia PC is powered-off because the user left for vacation. How can one avoid calls to this terminal from being lost, if the LAN telephony system is based on H.323/H.450 protocol between all the endpoints?

4. Assume that an IP telephony software packet is implemented for a LAN-attached office PC using H.323 Annex L or H.248 stimulus protocols. What limitation do these protocols have for monitoring of calls that are received or initiated at that PC?

5. Describe a workgroup telephone system that uses H.323 Annex L stimulus protocol. Justify the use of H.323 Annex L stimulus protocol in the application.

6. Describe a LAN-based application that uses CSTA third-party call control protocol. Justify the use of CSTA in the application.

7. Describe a LAN-based application which uses HTTP service control in order to enable services to the user. Justify the use of HTTP in the application.

8. Describe a LAN-based application that uses H.450 protocol. Justify the use of H.450 in the application.

9. Describe the protocol and interface requirements for a QSIG/H.323 gateway, that would enable the LAN telephony users and QSIG PBX extension to use telephony features as if they belonged to the same PBX (single system image).
10. Describe at least five telephony applications that can be implemented in a multimedia PC locally without use of any server, but only through the use of the H.323/H.450 protocol.
11. Describe at least three telephony applications which are implemented in a multimedia PC, but require support by a H.323/H.450 server, using only H.323/H.450 protocol for communication.
12. Describe a software application for a H.323/H.450 multimedia PC that would provide personalized greetings to the caller and store the caller's message on the hard disk. Describe the IP telephony protocol functions that need to be accessed in the application.

CHAPTER 7

Three-Party Supplementary Services in H.450

In this chapter, we describe call scenarios involving three parties. Three-party services use the supplementary service protocol components defined in the ITU-T Recommendations H.450.4 Call Hold, H.450.2 Call Transfer, and H.323/H.225.0 Conference and Basic Call. Because each of the supplementary service standards contains reusable, functional components and compound supplementary services, we identify and describe both of these. We provide a summary of each service, the related protocols, and examples of call scenarios.

General

Three-party supplementary services consist of functions needed when a user manages calls with two parties simultaneously, for example when three parties are involved. These include functions such as the following:

Call Hold and Retrieve. The holding terminal stops sending multimedia information to the held terminal so that the parties cannot hear or see each other until the call is retrieved. Although call hold and retrieve may involve only two parties, we use it as a functional building block for most three-party supplementary services.

Consultation. While the first call is held, a second call is established to the consulted party, which is the third party.

Alternating. While the user has two calls—one being held and another being active—the user may swap between these two parties.

Single-step Call Transfer. The user can transfer an existing call to a third party without conversing with the transferred-to party. The transfer is executed only if the destination sends an alerting message or automatically answers the call; otherwise the original call remains in place.

Consultation Transfer. The user can transfer an existing call to a third party but has to have a conversation with that party.

Conference Out of Consultation. While the first call is held, the user establishes a second call to the consulted party and subsequently merges the two calls to a conference.

Call Hold

The Call Hold supplementary service is defined in the ITU-T Recommendation H.450.4 and enables the served User A to put User B (with whom User A has an active call) on hold and subsequently to retrieve User B. User A is the Holding Party and User B the Held Party. User B may be provided with music and/or video on hold. User A may also perform other actions while User B is being held, such as establishing and consulting with User C.

The H.450.4 Call Hold supplementary service was defined for voice and video calls, in which case it applies to the complete call (both audio and video streams). Theoretically, we can put a subset of media streams or a T.120 call on hold; the protocol does not forbid it, but the implementation will determine whether we use this option.

Only the served user for an active call may invoke Call Hold. When Call Hold is invoked, communication on the media channels is interrupted. The distant party is informed, and if appropriate, a specific *media on hold* (MOH) pattern (such as video and/or music) may be provided. The served user may originate or accept other calls or use other services without impacting the call on hold.

Unlike muting a call by closing the audio logical channel or closing the video logical channel, which is a video-off command in the ITU-T H.221 standard, Call Hold enables functional supplementary service control. This means that other features of an application may be useable only when a call is on hold or only when a call is not on hold. While a call is on hold, the served user and/or the held user may not be able to invoke other features. For example, someone on hold may be unable to put another person on hold (simultaneous hold forbidden).

Some implementations have realized near-end call hold (see "Near-End Hold Invocation and Operation.") by just interrupting the voice path, which causes the held party to hear silence. Even though this seems to work, the Call State has to be changed on the held side from "Talking" to "Held." If this does not happen, User B could, for example, put User A on hold, which usually is not the intention. For this reason, H.450 sends a notification message to the held side.

The served user uses the Retrieve procedure to terminate the held state of a call. The held party is informed of the retrieval, and communication on the media channels is re-established.

Implementations may also limit the amount of time that a call can remain on hold. A reminder that the distant user is still on hold may be provided to the served user (for example, providing a hold timeout notification).

Two scenarios are specified for Call Hold—near-end call hold and remote-end call hold. Although the application and implementation determine whether to invoke one or the other of the methods, a reason for deciding to use near-end call hold may be to advertise to the held party. A reason for invoking remote-end call hold may be to decrease network traffic.

Near-End Hold Invocation and Operation

The simplest form of hold is called *near-end hold*. In this form, the holding Endpoint A either sends media on hold information to Endpoint B or stops sending media, causing silence and frozen picture on the held Endpoint B. This is illustrated in Figure 7.1.

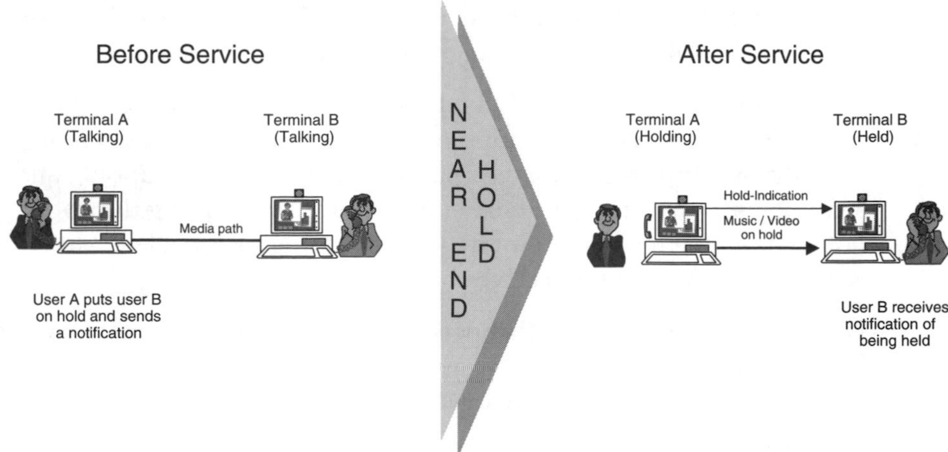

Figure 7.1 Near-end hold in H.450.4.

a) Near-End Call Hold

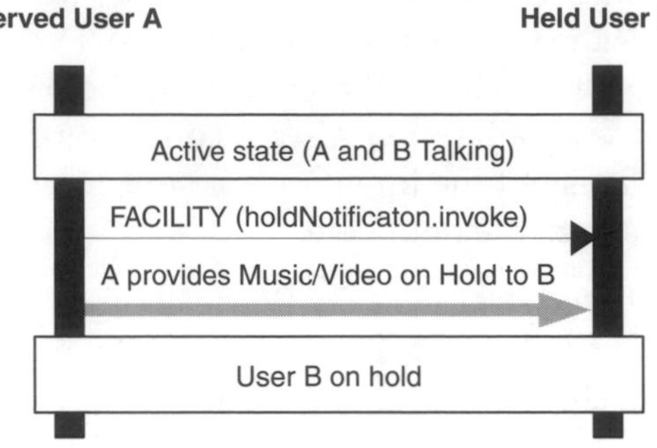

b) Retrieve from Near-End Hold

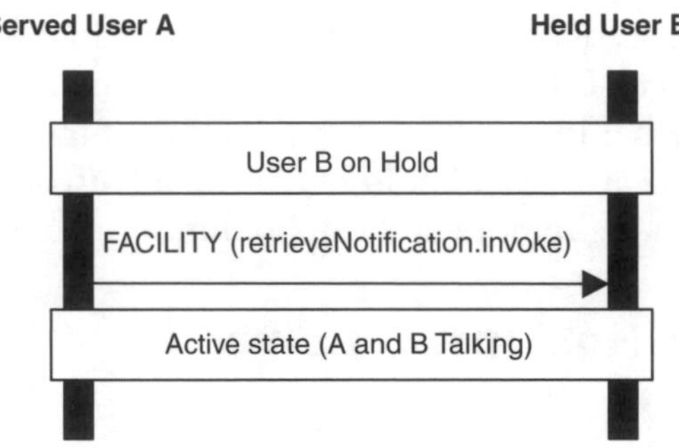

Figure 7.2 H.450.4 signaling flow for near-end hold and retrieve.

The signaling procedure of near-end hold and a subsequent retrieval from hold is shown in Figure 7.2. Near-end hold and retrieval signaling procedures are functional components of H.450.4, which can be reused in combination with other supplementary services and basic calls.

Hold is invoked at the holding endpoint as a local procedure. The holding endpoint informs the held endpoint of the hold condition by sending a hold notification, stops receiving user packets from the held endpoint, and stops sending user packets to the held endpoint. Upon receiving the hold notification, the held endpoint may stop sending user packets but will continue listening to the receive channel.

Depending on the opened channels and depending on the resources of the holding endpoint, the following MOH information may be provided from the holding endpoint to the held endpoint:

- Music/announcement in the audio logical channel
- Video in the video logical channel

- Video plus audio in the video and audio channels, respectively
- Freeze frame (still image) in the video channel plus music/announcement in the audio channel
- Other indications

Retrieval is also a local procedure at the holding endpoint. The holding user informs the held user that the hold condition is ending by sending a retrieve indication.

Remote-End Hold Invocation and Operation

The other form of hold is *remote-end hold* (see Figure 7.3). In this case, the holding Client A requests that the held Client B apply MOH information (often called *music/video/document on hold*).

The signaling procedure of remote-end hold and subsequent retrieval from hold is shown in Figure 7.4. Remote-end hold and retrieval signaling procedures are functional components of H.450.4, which can be reused in various contexts in combination with other supplementary services and basic calls.

The holding endpoint sends a hold request to the remote endpoint requiring that the held endpoint provides MOH to the held user. The held endpoint either accepts the request and returns an acknowledgement or rejects the request with an appropriate reason. If the request is rejected, the holding

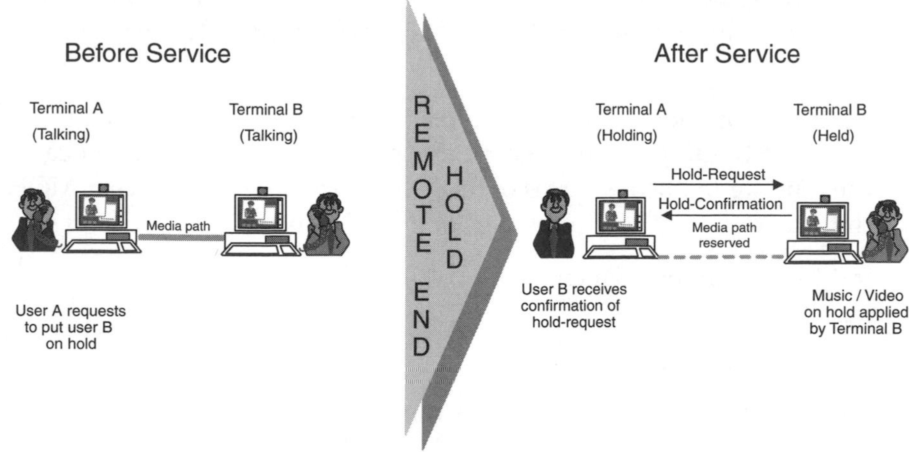

Figure 7.3 Remote-end hold in H.450.4.

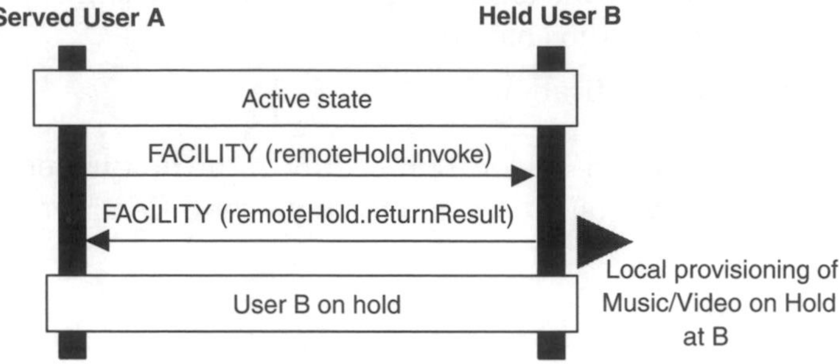

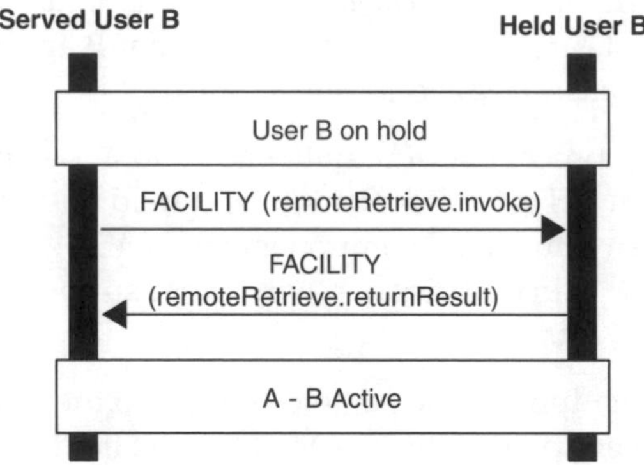

Figure 7.4 H.450.4 Signaling flow for remote-end hold and retrieve.

endpoint knows that the hold is not in effect, and Users A and B can continue communication based on the media types used prior to the Call Hold invocation.

If the remote-hold request is accepted, depending on the media types used between holding and held endpoints prior to the Call Hold invocation and depending on the resources of the held endpoint, the following MOH information may be provided from the held endpoint to the held user locally:

- Music/announcement
- Video
- Video plus audio
- Freeze frame (still image) plus music/announcement
- Other indications

The logical channels opened between the holding endpoint and the held endpoint prior to the invocation of the Call Hold are maintained. The holding endpoint sends silence and a blank freeze frame (when a video logical channel is in use) to the remote endpoint.

If the remote-hold request is rejected by the remote endpoint, the served user is informed.

The holding user may retrieve a held call by sending a retrieve request to the held endpoint. The held endpoint will terminate the hold state and send an acknowledgment or reject the retrieve request. If the retrieve request is rejected, the holding endpoint will clear the call.

After a successful remote retrieve request, Users A and B continue communication based on the media types used prior to the Call Hold invocation.

Near-End Hold/Retrieve Performed by Gatekeeper

A gatekeeper with which the holding endpoint is registered may act on the near-end call hold notification message and override the hold by providing its own MOH. For example, a simple endpoint may support only silence as MOH, and the gatekeeper may be able to provide music on behalf of the holding endpoint to the held endpoint. A near-end call hold notification message is in any case passed on to the held endpoint.

Because the gatekeeper cannot provide MOH, it has to reroute the logical channel(s) to a server that provides MOH. To do this, the gatekeeper uses the procedures for "Third-party-initiated pause and rerouting" [H.323, clause 8.4.6] for closing the old and opening the new logical channels when the hold and retrieve notification messages are received.

Remote-End Hold/Retrieve Performed by Gatekeeper

A gatekeeper on the call path between the holding and the held endpoint may act upon a received FACILITY message containing a remoteHold Invoke APDU. The gatekeeper acts in this case as a held endpoint toward the holding side and as a holding endpoint of near-end hold toward the held endpoint. As required by the near-end hold procedures, the gatekeeper has to provide MOH to the held endpoint. Because the gatekeeper cannot do this by itself, it has to reroute the logical channel(s) to a server that provides MOH. Logical channels between endpoints A and B are closed, and new channels are established between the MOH server and the held endpoint. Therefore,

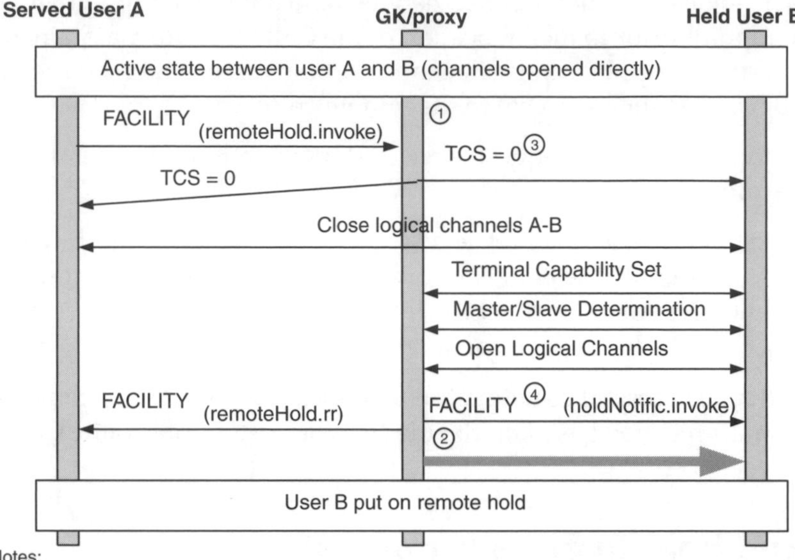

Notes:

① The GK/proxy acts upon the received remote end call hold invocation. Third party initiated pause and rerouting procedures according to H.323 clause 8.4.6 may be used for closing the channels between endpoints A and B as well as for establishing new channels for MOH provision between the GK/proxy and endpoint B. and B as well as for establishing new channels for MOH provision between the GK/proxy and endpoint B.

② Provision of MOH by GK/proxy server

③ TSC = 0 means Empty Terminal Capability Set

④ Optional

Figure 7.5 H.450.4 Signaling flow for a remote-end hold performed by a gatekeeper.

the procedures for "Third-party-initiated pause and rerouting" as described in [H.323, clause 8.4.6] are used here, too.

Figure 7.5 illustrates the resulting signaling flow for a remote-end hold performed by a gatekeeper

The gatekeeper that intercepts a FACILITY message with a remoteHold Invoke APDU must also intercept a subsequently received FACILITY message with a remoteRetrieve Invoke APDU. When the gatekeeper receives a remoteRetrieve Invoke APDU from the endpoint, it closes the logical channels between the server and Endpoint B establishes new channels between endpoint A and endpoint B. This happens again using the H.323 procedures for "Third-party-initiated pause and rerouting." Subsequently, a retrieveNotific Invoke APDU is sent to the held party.

Figure 7.6 illustrates the resulting signaling flow for a remote-end retrieve performed by the gatekeeper.

The gatekeeper is not the only possible place where the remote-end hold procedure can be executed. This procedure can be executed in any entity on

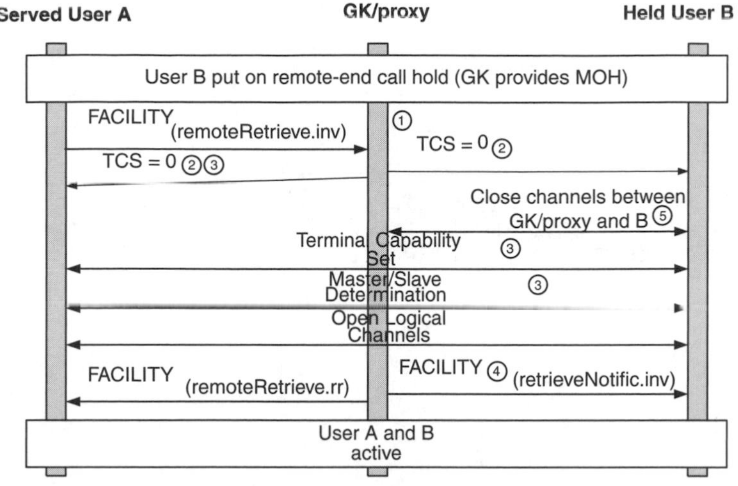

Notes:

① The GK/proxy acts on the received retrieve request for remote-end call hold. Third party initiated pause and re-routing procedures according to H.323 clause 8.4.6 may be used for closing the channels between the GK/proxy and endpoint B as well as for establishing new channels between endpoint A and endpoint B.

② TSC = 0 means Empty Terminal Capability Set

③ If applicable

④ Optional

⑤ Endpoint B may only have receive channels open at this time

Figure 7.6 H.450.4 Signaling flow for remote-end retrieve performed by the gatekeeper.

the call path that can process the signaling, for example in a gateway, in a border element, or in an H.323/H.450 proxy.

Consultation

Consultation is a feature that enables an initiating caller to put one call on hold and then to establish a second call to a third party, which is then the consulted party. This second call is established just as the first call—as a basic call.

A caller can invoke the consultation hold feature during an active, connected call involving two or more parties. Any one of the parties starts (becomes the consulting party) and establishes a consultation call to another party. This consultation may, for example, be used to prepare for a call transfer. The first connection is put on hold during consultation.

Typically, a caller invokes Consultation by pressing a feature key on the telephone or by a telephony application via a CTI interface (for example, by using the CSTA service "Consultation Call"). A party on consultation hold also may be able to hold the consulting party or place its own consultation call.

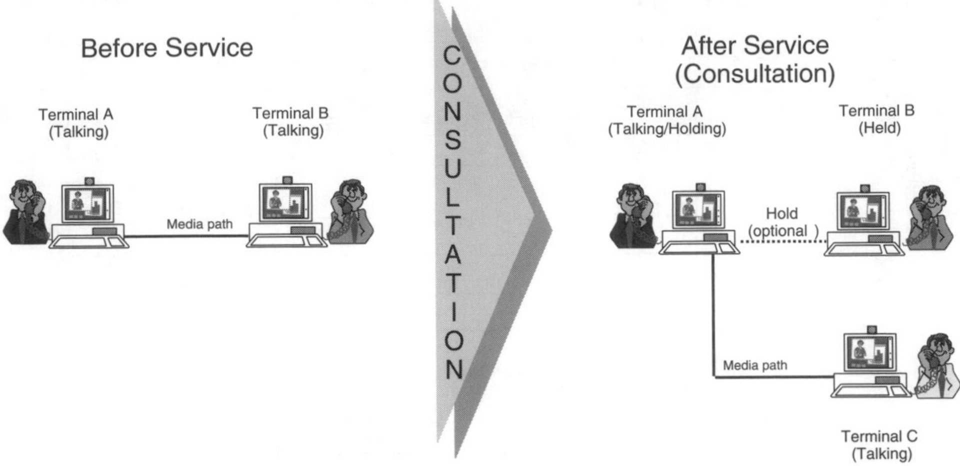

Figure 7.7 Consultation using H.450.4.

The Consultation scenario is illustrated by Figure 7.7.

When the consultation call is cleared (either by the consulting or the consulted party), the consulting party may retrieve the first connection that was put on hold for the duration of the consultation. If the consulting user wants to connect to the held call before the consultation call ends, that caller can use the alternate feature (see "Alternating").

Certain terminals or users cannot be placed on consultation hold. Setting a corresponding, preventing flag in the terminal's or the user's service profile will prevent this.

Note that the H.323/H.450 standards do not explicitly describe a consultation call. Consultation is a compound supplementary service that is achieved by using regular H.323 basic call setup procedures. Only the local application knows about the association of the original call that is held and the consultation call.

Alternating

Alternating is a feature that enables the user to swap between one call on hold and another active call; that is, the user can put the active call on hold and then retrieve a previously held call. See Figure 7.8.

A caller invokes alternating by pressing an Alternating button on the telephone or by a telephony application via a CTI interface (that is, by using the CSTA service "Alternate Call").

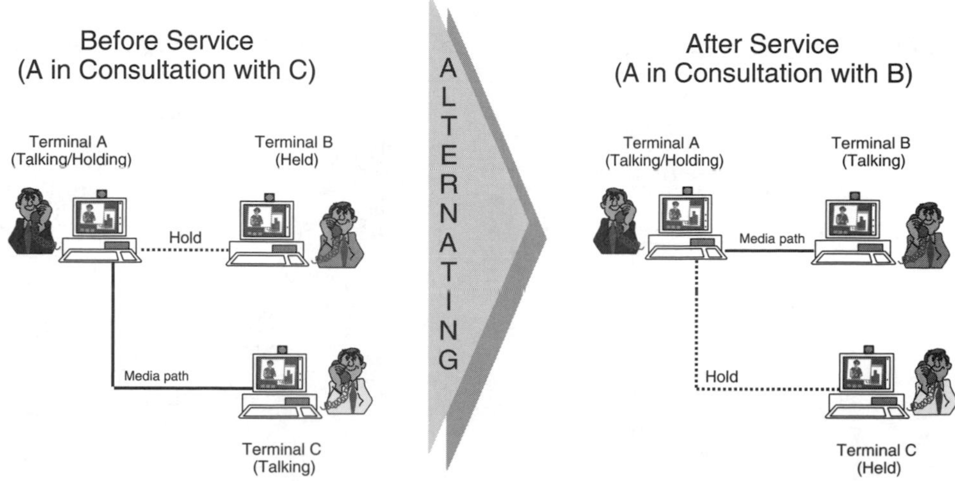

Figure 7.8 Alternating using H.450.4.

The H.323/H.450 standards do not describe Alternating. The feature is a compound supplementary service; only the local application knows about the association of the call currently held and the consultation call.

Certain terminals or users cannot use the alternating feature. Setting a corresponding, preventing flag in the terminal's or the user's service profile will prevent this.

Call Transfer

The basic form of the H.450.2 Call Transfer supplementary service is a single-step call transfer. Other names often used for this service are *supervised call transfer* or *blind call* transfer. This service enables a user to transfer an existing call (*primary call*) to a third terminal. The supervised call transfer requires that the transferred-to party answer the call. Attendants and call agents use this service often, because they usually do not need to talk to the transferred-to party. They just need to be involved in the transfer until the caller hears the requested party speaking.

Invocation and Operation

We perform this transfer in a single-step; the transferring terminal sends a signaling message to the transferred terminal requesting that a new connection be established directly from there to the transferred-to terminal.

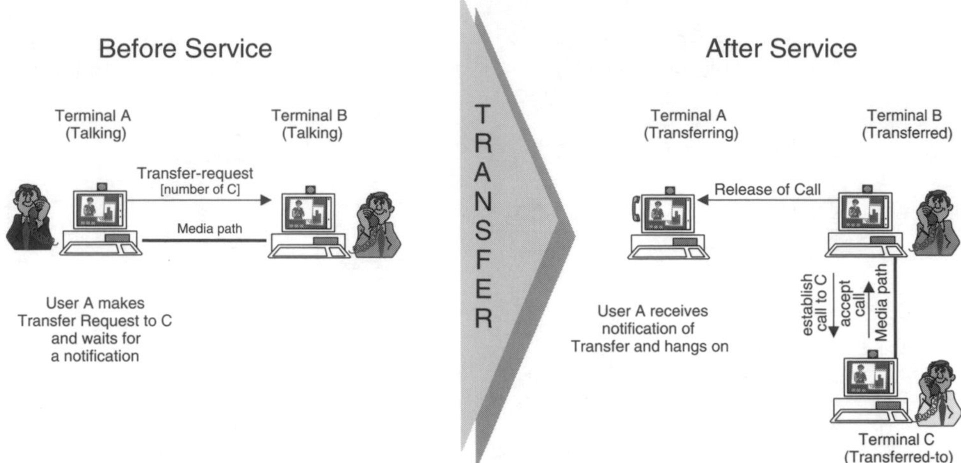

Figure 7.9 Single-step call transfer using H.450.2.

The transferred terminal then establishes an independent connection to the transferred-to terminal. Figure 7.9 shows the call transfer scenario. This scenario assumes that the conversation between User A and User B is not interrupted at the request of the transfer. However, it is an implementation option for Terminal A to provide alternate treatment and for example, to put Party B on hold during the transfer.

Signaling Protocol

The method of establishing the connection between User B and User C with a new call is *Call Transfer Rerouting*. The first call is dropped if the transfer is successful (Party C answers or is alerted). Figure 7.10 shows the information flow of call transfer.

The transferring endpoint (User A) requests that the transferred endpoint (User B) call the transferred-to endpoint (User C) by sending a FACILITY message with the *ctInitate.Invoke* APDU. This APDU contains the *callTransferInitiate* operation and the H.323 address of User C. Upon receipt of this message, the transferred endpoint establishes a call to the transferred-to endpoint. In Figure 7.10, the transferred endpoint is H.450.2 aware. If this is not the case, User B's gatekeeper has to handle the call transfer on behalf of its endpoint. This case is discussed in further detail later (see Figure 7.12).

The primary call is retained by the transferred endpoint (User B) until the CONNECT message has been received from the transferred-to endpoint (User C) and is then released by User B using the RELEASE COMPLETE message containing the ctInitiate.ReturnResult APDU. When an answer is

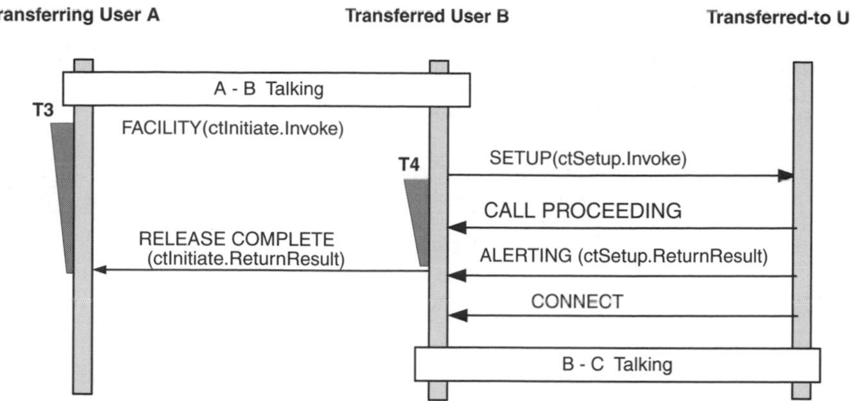

Figure 7.10 H.450.2 Signaling flow for single-step transfer.

received from User C, the transfer is completed, and User B and User C are connected. Timers T3 and T4 are used as protection timers.

Unsuccessful Transfers

If call transfer fails, for example, because User C is busy, the primary call remains in place. In such a case User A can return to the conversation with User B and explain the situation. User A can use some other means, for example paging, to try to reach User C.

Figure 7.11 shows the signaling flow if User C is busy when call transfer is attempted.

Applications and compound supplementary services can reuse and invoke call transfer rerouting in various scenarios. Its implementation is simple for intelligent terminals that are H.450 aware.

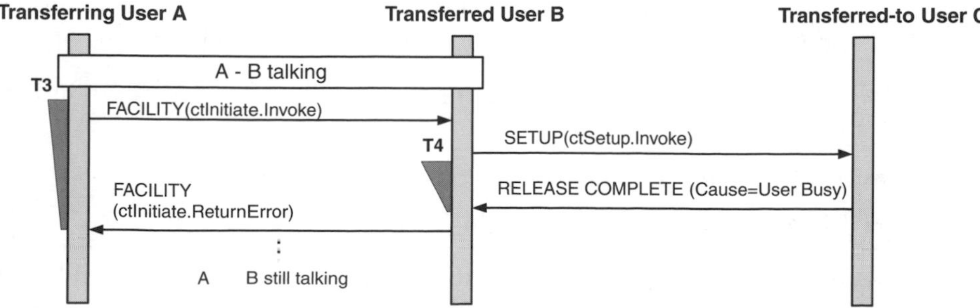

Figure 7.11 H.450.2 signaling flow for unsuccessful call transfer.

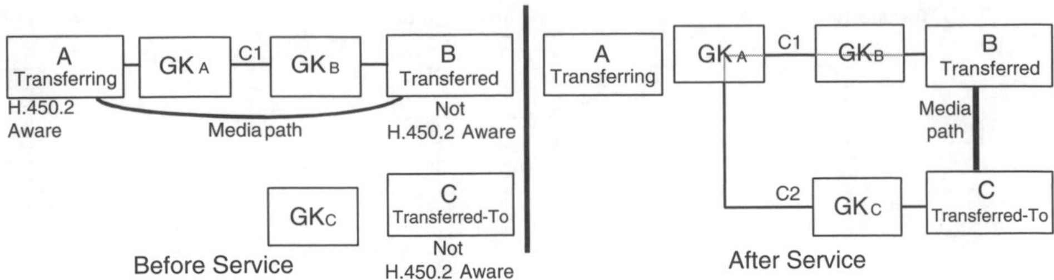

Figure 7.12 H.450.2 operational model for call transfers performed by a gatekeeper.

Call Transfer Performed by Gatekeeper

The Call Transfer signaling of H.450.2 works both in the direct signaling mode and in the gatekeeper routed signaling mode. In the latter case, the gatekeeper may either participate in the call transfer or be transparent for all call transfer operations. Implementing call transfer functions in the gatekeeper makes sense because the call transfer can be performed, even though some or all of the parties involved are not H.450 aware.

The general operational signaling model for gatekeeper call transfer is shown in Figure 7.12.

Figure 7.12 assumes that Endpoint A is H.450.2 aware. It could be, for example, a secretary's multimedia workstation. Neither Endpoint B nor C or their Gatekeepers GK_B and GK_C are H.450.2 aware. Therefore, a call transfer requested by Endpoint A has to be executed by the GK_A. Its task is to set up a basic call to User C and to instruct both Endpoint B and C to connect their media path with each other. After the transfer is completed, the signaling connections of the original call C1 and the new call leg C2 to Endpoint C remain joined through the Gatekeeper GK_A.

The supplementary service signaling between Gatekeeper GK_B and Endpoint B and Gatekeeper GK_C and Endpoint C is performed by means of

- The stimulus signaling as defined in H.323 Annex L (shown in Figure 9.14)
- HTTP-based control as defined in H323 Annex K
- H.248 Annex G-based stimulus protocol

As a result, the terminal Endpoints B and C do not need to be able to handle the H.450.10 Call Offering supplementary service or its components. Instead, the gatekeepers or feature servers act on behalf of Endpoints A and B.

Figure 7.13 illustrates the corresponding signaling information flow of call transfers when the gatekeeper performs the call rerouting function. For simplification, assume that all endpoints—A, B, and C—are registered in the same gatekeeper.

Because Gatekeeper GK_A can perform transfer rerouting, from the H.450.1 perspective it becomes the destination for a callTransferInitiate Invoke APDU message. Therefore, it must perform similar actions expected of a transferred H.450.2 endpoint. These steps are

1. Establish a call to User C by sending a SETUP message. Because Gatekeeper GK_A cannot know in this phase whether Endpoint C is H.405.2 aware, it includes the regular H.450.2 data elements in the SETUP message. These elements may be ignored by User B or its gatekeeper. The GK_A receives an ALERTING message and an H.245 message with the Terminal Capability Set of Endpoint C.
2. When Endpoint C is sending an alert, the GK_A closes the media path of the original call. This is possible in H.323, even though the media paths do not go through the gatekeeper. Because the H.245 connection is connected via the GK_A, it can insert its own messages to the H.245 channel and control the opening and closure of the logical channels. First, it sends to

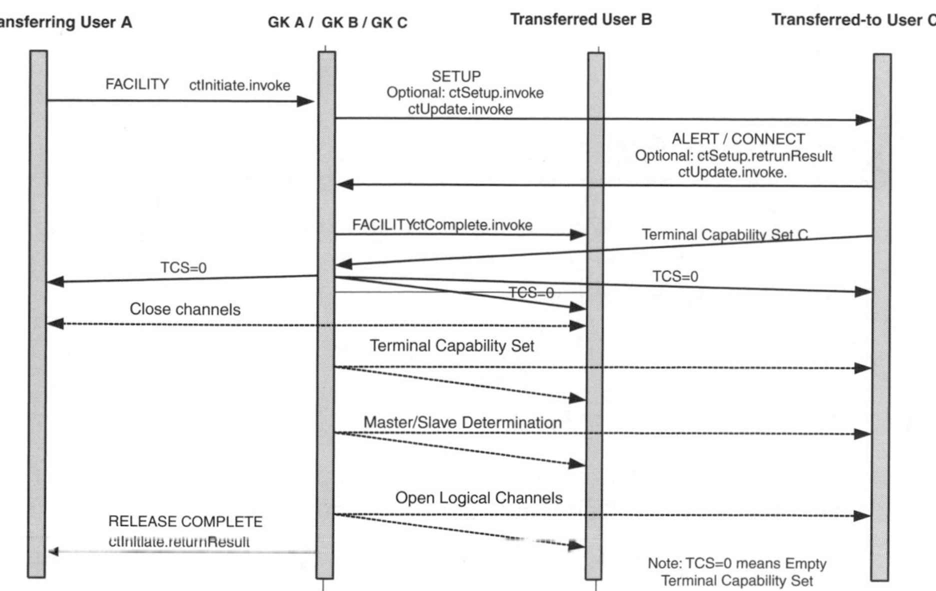

Figure 7.13 H.450.2 signaling for transfer rerouting performed by a gatekeeper.

all three endpoints a H.245 message with empty Terminal Capability Set, which causes the ports of all active logical channels to close.

3. Because Gatekeeper GK_A has received the Terminal Capability Set of Endpoint C and it plays the role of a matchmaker, GK_A relays this H.245 message to Endpoint B.
4. As Endpoint B receives the Terminal Capability Set of Endpoint C, it has no knowledge that this message actually did not come directly from Endpoint B. Therefore, Endpoint B continues the regular H.245 procedure, performs the master-slave determination, and reopens logical channels.

At this point, the call transfer is completed.

Endpoint A also can perform the actions described for the gatekeeper. The only disadvantage is that the resulting call signaling path goes through Endpoint A. If Endpoint A would be a desktop multimedia terminal or an H.323 telephone, the resulting joining of the signaling paths is not resided, because it consumes scarce resources of the terminal. Additionally, it would keep the terminal from being powered off if the transferred call is still active.

However, if Endpoint A is, for example, a call distribution server or a voice response unit, the implementation of a call transfer joining in the endpoint according to these procedures can be very useful.

The signaling procedure is called *third-party-initiated pause and rerouting* of logical channels in H.323. We can reuse this functional component of H.323 in various call contexts in combination with other supplementary services and basic calls.

Consultation Transfer

During consultation scenarios, the user may need to: (1) put a multimedia call on hold and retrieve it later; (2) call another person while keeping a call on hold; (3)alternate between the two calls; and (4) transfer a call to the party on hold.

Invocation and Operation

Figure 7.14 demonstrates the different steps in a consultation transfer scenario, namely: Call Hold, Consultation, Alternating, and Call Transfer.

The signaling procedure for Consultation Transfer is more complicated than the basic, unsupervised call transfer. When the transfer rerouting call arrives, Endpoint C will have two calls simultaneously. It has to recognize that these

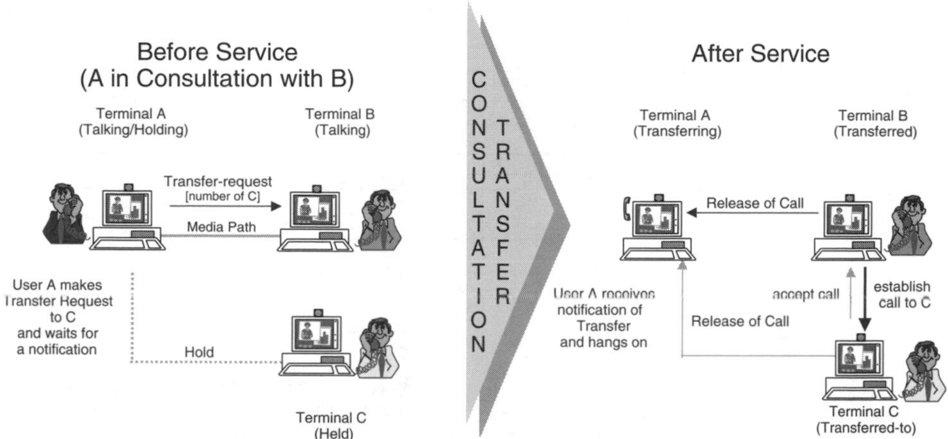

Figure 7.14 Consultation Transfer using H.450.2.

belong to the same call, switch over to the new call, and release the secondary call.

The initial call between User A and User B is called the primary call. On invocation of call transfer, if a call between User A and User C exists (a secondary call), the transferred-to endpoint (User C) is informed of the pending call transfer. Transfer proceeds only if this endpoint can participate. The transferred-to endpoint returns a temporary identifier to be used in the subsequent transfer procedure to identify the secondary call. The handling of the secondary call is described in further detail later in this chapter (see Figures 7.16 and 7.17).

Call transfer procedures do not demand a particular hold state for the primary or secondary call; User B or User C may or may not be put on hold prior to call transfer, depending on the capabilities of Terminal A and the specific implementation.

Signaling Protocol

The signaling flow of Consultation Transfer is shown in Figure 7.15. Consultation Transfer is a compound supplementary service that uses Call Hold, Supervised Call Transfer, and Basic H.323 Call as its components.

To prepare for a call transfer, transferring Endpoint A first sends a callTransferIdentify Invoke APDU in a FACILITY message to transferred-to Endpoint C. The call reference of the secondary call is used. Then the transferring endpoint starts a timer T1 and waits for the response. On receipt of a callTransferIdentify return result APDU on the secondary call,

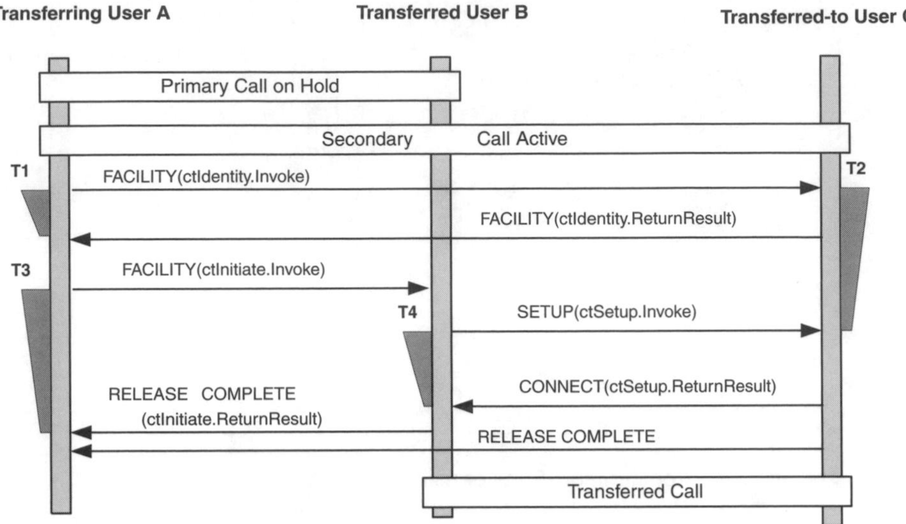

Figure 7.15 H.450.2 signaling for Consultation Transfer.

the transferring endpoint stops Timer T1. It then can send on to the primary call the actual call transfer request; send the callTransferInitiate Invoke APDU in a FACILITY message to transferred Endpoint B and wait for a response. The callTransferInitiate Invoke APDU on the primary call must now contain rerouteingNumber and callIdentity values as received in the callTransferIdentify return result received on the secondary call. As soon as a callTransferInitiate return result APDU is received on the primary call, the transferring endpoint clears both the primary and secondary call. At this point, the consultation transfer is completed and Party B and Party C are in a call.

Consultation Transfer Performed by Gatekeeper

As in the case of the basic call transfer, the consultation transfer signaling of H.450.2 works both in the direct signaling mode and in the gatekeeper-routed signaling mode. In the latter case, the gatekeeper may either participate in the call transfer or be transparent for all call transfer operations.

Implementing consultation transfer in the gatekeeper should be done for the same as in the basic call transfer, namely to be able to perform a call transfer, even though some or all of the parties are not H.450 aware. The operational signaling model for a gatekeeper call transfer is more complicated and shown in Figure 7.16.

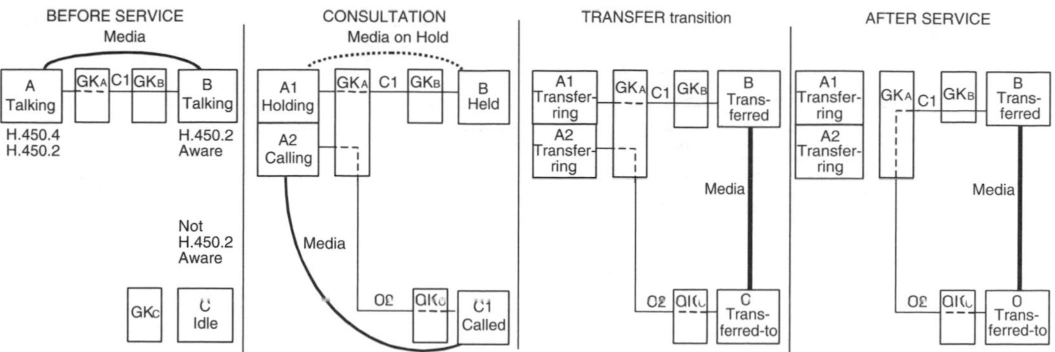

Figure 7.16 H.450.2 operational model for consultation transfer performed by a gatekeeper.

In the scenario shown in Figure 7.16, consider User A to be a secretary, User C to be the boss, and User B to be an external caller wanting to speak with the boss. Figure 7.16 assumes that Endpoint A is H.450.2 aware. Neither Endpoint B nor C is H.450.2 aware.

A call transfer requested by Endpoint A has to be executed by the GK_A. The gatekeeper's task is then to play the role of a transferred party toward Endpoint A, to set up a basic call to User C, and instruct both Endpoint B and Endpoint C to connect their media paths with each other. After the transfer is complete, the signaling connections of the original call C1 and the new call leg C2 to Endpoint C are joined through gatekeeper GK_A; whereas the resulting media path is directly between B and C.

Figure 7.17 illustrates the signaling information flow of a call transfer, when the gatekeeper performs the call rerouting function. The gatekeepers of Endpoint B and C are not shown, because they are transparent.

The call transfer procedure starts again from Endpoint A. To provide a correlation identifier for the consultation call, transferring Endpoint A has to fetch this identifier from transferred-to Endpoint C. It does this by sending a FACILITY message with callTransferIdentify Invoke APDU to Endpoint C. However, because GK_A acts as a transfer proxy, it intercepts the callTransferIdentify Invoke APDU and responds to it by generating a correlation identifier and sending back a FACILITY with callTransferIdentify returnResult APDU. No message is sent to the Endpoint C.

After receiving the correlation identifier from the secondary call, Endpoint A sends the call transfer reroute request along with the correlation identifier on the primary call toward Endpoint B. Endpoint A does this with a FACILITY message containing the callTransferInitiate Invoke APDU.

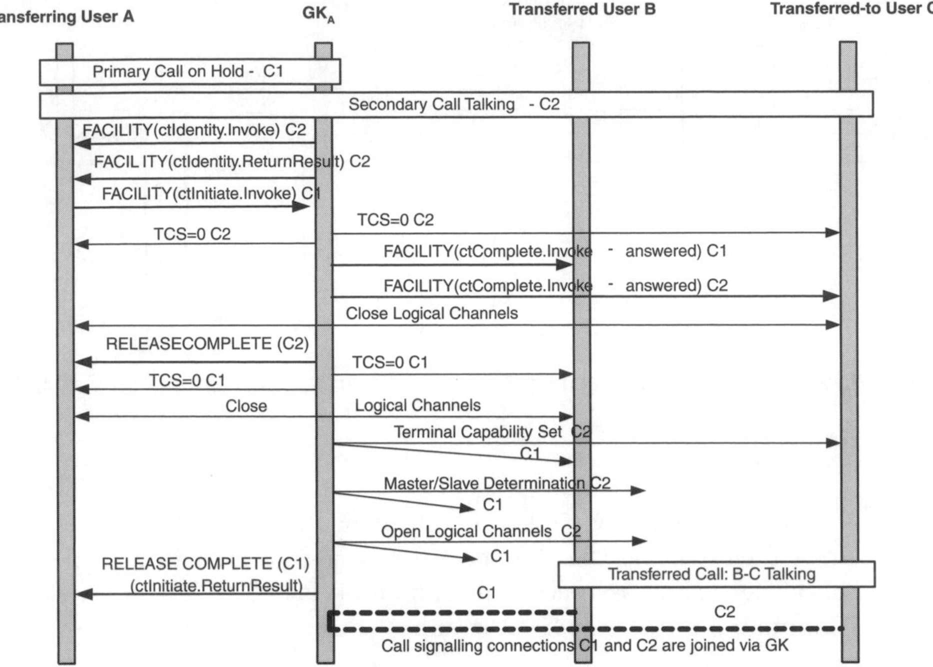

Figure 7.17 H.450.2 signaling for Consultation Transfer performed by a gatekeeper.

Gatekeeper GK_A now intercepts this Invoke APDU and processes the request, because it knows that Endpoint B cannot execute call transfer rerouting. This knowledge is derived from the endpoint profile. If Endpoint B is somewhere else in the network, the GK_A checks, whether the H.450.12 Common Information was received and whether it indicates that the call transfer rerouting is available. The Gatekeeper GK_A then becomes the call transfer rerouting point.

The subsequent signaling steps of the Gatekeeper GK_A are as follows:

1. Because media channels associated with the secondary call (C2) are already open, they need to be closed in case a transfer into active state occurs or in case of a transfer alert. For this purpose, gatekeeper GK_A instructs Endpoint C to close its media channels to Endpoint A using the H.323 procedures called "third-party-initiated pause and rerouting." This requires the gatekeeper to send an empty terminal capability set (TCS=0, which indicates that the remote entity has no receive capabilities) to Endpoints A and C, causing them to close their logical channels. Then the gatekeeper sends the H.245 command "end session" to Endpoint A and

releases the call signaling channel that still exists between Terminal A and Gatekeeper A using the RELEASE COMPLETE message containing callTransferInitiate return result APDU.

2. The media channels are closed on the primary call as well using the method already described.

3. The gatekeeper sends TerminalCapabilitySet representing Endpoint C's capabilities to Endpoint B and B's TerminalCapabilitySet to C. This causes Endpoints B and C to reset the H.245 state, as if H.245 had just completed the terminal capability set exchange; initiates master-slave determination; and opens appropriate logical channels between both endpoints.

4. The gatekeeper also may send a FACILITY message with a callTransferComplete Invoke APDU to Endpoints B and C to inform them that the call has been transferred (by means of joining in gatekeeper). Argument redirectionNumber contains the number of the transferred User C or B; argument endDesignation has the value "secondaryEnd"; and argument callStatus is set to "answered." These messages are ignored by the endpoints that are not H.450.2 aware.

5. Because the transfer is now completed, the gatekeeper closes the call to transferring Endpoint A by sending a RELEASE COMPLETE message to it on the primary call. The message must include a callTransferInitiate return result APDU.

The call has been successfully transferred, and the signaling connection C1 and C2 are joined in the Gatekeeper GK_A. The media is established directly between Endpoints B and C.

Conference Out of Consultation

To conduct a conference, the user needs to be able to do the following:

- Connect several persons to a multimedia conference call.
- Join an existing conference.

The capability to establish a multimedia conference is built into the H.323/H.225.0/H.245 signaling. We describe this capability in Chapter 5. Even though conference can be considered a supplementary service, a separate H.450 standard does not exist for it. In this section, we describe what the interactions are and when conference is established from a consultation situation. Conference Out of Consultation is a compound feature that uses H.323/H.225.0 Conference, H.450.4 Call Hold, and H.225.0 basic call as its components.

Invocation and Operation

The conference scenario is shown in Figure 7.18 from the user's perspective. Conference starts from the initial consultation situation, in which served User A, who is a conference master, has a call with User B and has User C on hold. User A also may have other parties waiting on consultation hold to be connected to the conference. After User A has invoked conference, the result is a conference conversation among users A, B, and C—or with more parties, if a multiparty conference was established.

It does not matter whether the original call was initiated by served User A or User B. The protocol is the same in both cases. What matters is that the user, who requests a conference, has to have conference capability in his terminal or be able to access a centralized conference server.

While in a conference conversation, served User A typically has certain capabilities. These include being able to

- Terminate the conference by dropping all calls.
- Drop (release) a conference member from the conference.
- Split from the conference (for example to establish a further consultation call).
- Add (invite) another user to the conference

During a conference conversation, any remote user can release its call from the conference conversation. A remote user also may invite further users to the conference.

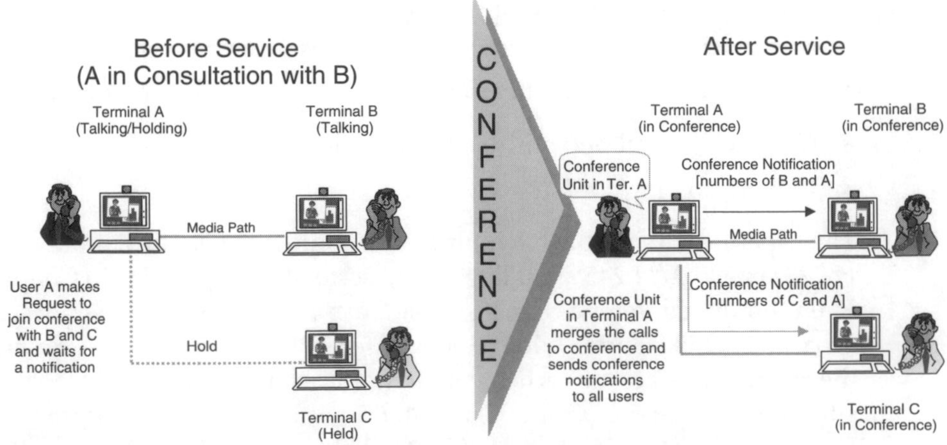

Figure 7.18 Conference Out of Consultation.

We describe additional capabilities in Chapter 5, but the ones we describe here show the main interactions with the consultation scenarios.

Signaling Protocol

Establishment of a conference call requires that a conference unit is present and accessible somewhere in the network. The served User A interacts with the conference unit and instructs it to set up the connections to the conference members and subsequently to merge them to a single conversation.

Location of conference unit. The conference unit providing the conference conversation may be located within the served terminal endpoint, within any server (for example, an MCU), in the network, or within the gatekeeper serving User A. The procedures defined are applicable for the gatekeeper-routed model as well as the direct-routed call model.

Conference unit in the endpoint. If the conference unit is located within the served terminal endpoint, no external MCU is required. An example of such a terminal is a high-end H.323 business telephone. The served user endpoint joins the existing calls to the remote users, and such joining happens within the served user endpoint. The remote endpoints continue having point-to-point calls with the served user endpoint and its conference unit. The served user provides the media mixing.

Figure 7.19 shows the signaling flow for a conference out of consultation. On receipt of a conference request from served User A while in consultation, the served user endpoint checks whether the local conference unit is available. If a conference unit is available and the conference request can be accepted, the served user endpoint retrieves the remote User(s) B from hold (if they are being held).

The conference unit establishes a conference conversation by the regular methods of H.245 (mcLocationIndication, terminalNumberAssign, multipointModeCommand, and communicationModeCommand). The conference unit mixes any audio and/or video channels. A conferenceIndication Invoke APDU is sent from the conference unit to the remote endpoints using a FACILITY message.

This procedure also applies if the conference master wants to establish a multiparty conference. In this case, the conference master will consult with several users and put them on hold. Subsequently, he will join them to a conference. Obviously, a multiparty conference bridge will need a more powerful *digital signal processor* (DSP) in the conference master's endpoint.

Conference unit in a server/MCU. If the served user endpoint does not have a conference unit, a conference unit, which may be located anywhere

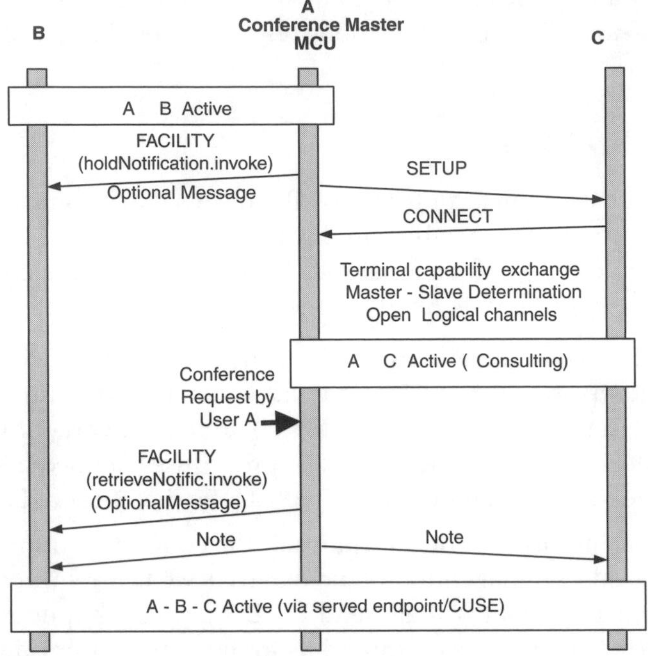

Note: H.245 messages are send as required for an H.323 conference (mcLocationIndication, terminalNumberAssign, multipointModeCommand, communicationModeCommand).

Figure 7.19 Signaling flow for Conference Out of Consultation.

in the network, needs to be called (for example, the served user and the conference unit may be in different zones). The existing calls between the served user endpoint and the remote endpoints need to be replaced by new point-to-point calls between the conference unit and the endpoints. The conference unit provides the media mixing.

The conference unit may be collocated with the gatekeeper (or may be accessible by the gatekeeper with the gatekeeper taking over some control). In this case, the gatekeeper serving served User A may provide the conference conversation, resulting in point-to-point calls (including media channels) between the gatekeeper/conference unit and the endpoints.

Recommended Reading

The ITU-T Recommendations [H.450.2] and [H.450.12] describe the H.450.2 and H.450.4 supplementary services, respectively.

References

H.225 ITU-T Recommendation H.225.0 Version 4, Call signalling protocols and media stream packetization for packet-based multimedia communications systems, H.225, November 2000.

H.245 ITU-T Recommendation H.245 Version 5, Control protocol for multimedia communication, H.245, February 2000.

H.323 ITU-T Recommendation H.323 Version 4, Packet-based multimedia communications systems, H.323, November 2000.

H.450.1 ITU-T Recommendation H.450.1, Generic functional protocol for the support of supplementary services in H.323, H.450.1, February 1998.

H.450.2 ITU-T Recommendation H.450.2., Call transfer supplementary service for H.323., H.450.2, February 1998.

H.450.4 ITU-T Recommendation H.450.4., Call hold supplementary service for H.323, H.450.4, May 1998.

I.112 ITU-T Recommendation I.112, Vocabulary of terms for ISDNs, I.112, 1993.

I.210 ITU-T Recommendation I.210, Principles of telecommunication services supported by an ISDN and the means to describe them, I.210, 1993.

ISO/IEC 13865 Information technology—Telecommunications and information exchange between systems—Private integrated services network—Specification, functional model, and information flows—Call transfer supplementary service, ISO/IEC 13865 Edition 1, November 1995.

ISO/IEC 13869 Information technology—Telecommunications and information exchange between systems—Private integrated services network—Interexchange signalling protocol—Call transfer supplementary service, ISO/IEC 13869, Edition 1, November 1995.

Problems

1. A common question is which of the commonly known supplementary services from voice telephony could be useful in multimedia? Prepare a list of at least 10 features that are not described in this book. Choose three features, write the feature description from the user's perspective, and draw the scenarios.
2. Draw the protocol information flows for the three features from problem 1.
3. Does it make sense to implement near-end call hold in the gatekeeper? Explain.
4. Because no hard limit exists on the number of H.323 calls a terminal can have simultaneously, the consultation procedure can be continued to the third party on hold as well and by establishing a call to a fourth party. Describe the associated signaling flows.

5. A party that is on consultation hold may be able to (1) hold the consulting party or (2) place its own consultation call. Describe the associated signaling flows.
6. Explain the advantages of all H.323 endpoints being able to execute H.450.2 transfer rerouting as transferred endpoints. How should the H.323 network manager take care of endpoints that do not have this capability?
7. Explain the advantages of all H.323 endpoints being able to execute H.450.2 call forward rerouting as forwarded endpoints. How should the H.323 network manager take care of endpoints that do not have this capability?
8. Because the standards process is time consuming, we can assume that within the next few years only a small amount of them will be standardized and that the rest will remain for proprietary implementation by the software and equipment vendors. For this reason, the supplementary service protocol has to contain generic functional protocol for treatments of supplementary service invocations that are not implemented everywhere in the network. Describe how you would use the capabilities of H.450.1 for definitions of signaling messages for the three features you invented in problem 1.
9. Describe the advantages of the execution of call transfer rerouting by the transferred endpoint.
10. Describe the tasks of an H.323 *voice response unit* (VRU) and describe how it would make use of the H.450 signaling. Be sure that your VRU can serve callers that use Microsoft NetMeeting Version 3.

CHAPTER 8

Call Diversion Services in H.450

In this chapter, we discuss the Call Diversion services of ITU-T Recommendation H.450.3. We provide a summary of each service and the related protocols. Because each of the supplementary service standards contains both reusable, functional components and compound supplementary services, we identify and describe each of these. We also provide a summary of each service, the related protocols, and examples of call scenarios.

General

Call Diversion is a supplementary service that enables the user to send all or specific incoming multimedia calls to another destination. The diversion can be made dependent on various circumstances, such as whether the called party has an ongoing call, whether the called party is absent, whether the called party replies to the call, who the calling party is, the time of day, and so on. Call Diversion consists of four services:

- *Call Forwarding Unconditional* (CFU) on all calls
- *Call Forwarding on Busy* (CFB)

- *Call Forwarding on No Answer* (CFNA)
- *Call Deflection* (CD)

An additional specific case is call diversion when the terminal is out of service. Each of the listed supplementary services is based on similar principles and functional components, and we describe them in more detail later in this chapter.

We define the previous call forwarding categories from the user's perspective, but we can make the functional grouping based on when call forwarding takes place. In this case, the categories are immediate call forwarding and delayed call forwarding.

The H.450.3 Call Diversion supplementary service consists of certain functional components:

- Call rerouting request
- Call forwarding notifications

These components are not limited to use in the Call Diversion supplementary service scenarios, but can be used in building new applications and services as well.

The paradigm of call forwarding is *not* the same as call rerouting. Rerouting of the call takes place by the network elements, such as a gatekeeper without user influence, and is executed by modifying the destination address of the call. No notifications are provided to the involved users. The call simply arrives at another destination. Call forwarding, on the other hand, is a service that enables a person, the *served user* to specify that another person, namely the *forwarded-to user* should receive his calls. When the forwarding is executed, appropriate notifications can be sent to the involved users.

The call forwarding service is not intended to be used as a means to reroute the call because the notifications that it provides to the users may be disturbing when the rerouting function is needed.

Common Characteristics of Call Diversion Services

The Call Diversion supplementary services apply during call establishment and provide the diversion of an incoming call to another H.323 destination address (for example, to a telephone number, IP address, or e-mail address). Any of the variants of call forwarding may operate on all calls or selectively on calls fulfilling specific conditions determined entered by the user. Such conditions include the state of the called party, the calling party number, the time of day, and so on.

The Call Diversion service does not limit the served user's ability to originate calls and is applicable only when the served user is the called party. After one or more of the diversion services have been activated, calls are forwarded independently of the status of the served endpoint.

A call that was already forwarded, can be forwarded again, but the number of diversions can be limited by the user's profile.

Each of the diversion services may be either permanently activated by the network manager, or the activation and deactivation may be under user control. A user can achieve activation and deactivation by one of the following methods:

- Local management procedures within the served endpoint
- H.450 remote activation and deactivation procedures by another endpoint
- Remote management procedures such as using a Web browser

Interrogation of the current status of call forwarding may be provided in a similar manner. With interrogation, the user can verify whether the supplementary service is active, for which service (for example, voice or fax) it is active, and with which parameters it is associated.

The Call Diversion services were defined for voice calls. However, the protocol permits its use for any type of call. It may be useful in some situations, for example, to forward fax calls to a unified messaging server at the same time the voice calls are forwarded to the secretary.

Remote Registration of Call Forwarding

Before a diversion can take place, a destination address must be programmed in the forwarding terminal. This address may be permanently stored, chosen by the user, or based on automatic, intelligent screening of the incoming call. Programming of the destination address can be done locally at the home terminal or by remote programming via a H.450.3 remote registration connection to the home endpoint.

Figure 8.1 shows the scenarios for activation of call forwarding.

Before the activation of call forwarding is accepted, the served endpoint should check whether the requested forwarding is possible. This checking procedure is called *restriction check*. It not only checks the validity of the

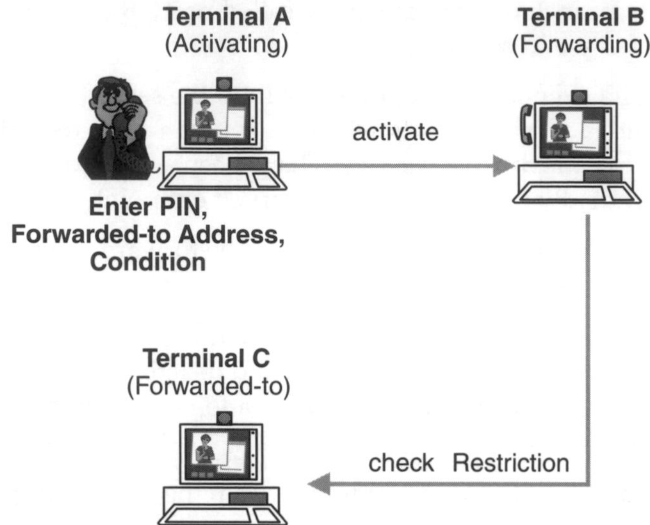

Figure 8.1 Remote registration of call diversion.

forwarded-to address, but also whether Terminal C will accept forwarded calls from Terminal B. If the restriction check fails, no call forwarding is activated, and an appropriate error message is given to the activating terminal.

Call Forwarding on All Calls and on Busy

Call Forwarding on All Calls is a supplementary service that causes calls to the served user to be forwarded to the address of another user. It can be used regardless of any condition. In other words, the call-state of the served user, the time of day, the calling party number, and so on, are irrelevant. However, it can also be invoked selectively only on calls that fulfill the user-defined rules.

Call Forwarding on Busy is, as the name indicates, conditional upon the served user being busy. We discuss the conditions under which the user is defined to be busy in more detail in the next chapter; note that this condition can be determined either by the served user's endpoint or by its gatekeeper based on consumed resources. In addition, the service may be invoked when the user has, for example, set his terminal to a Do-Not-Disturb state.

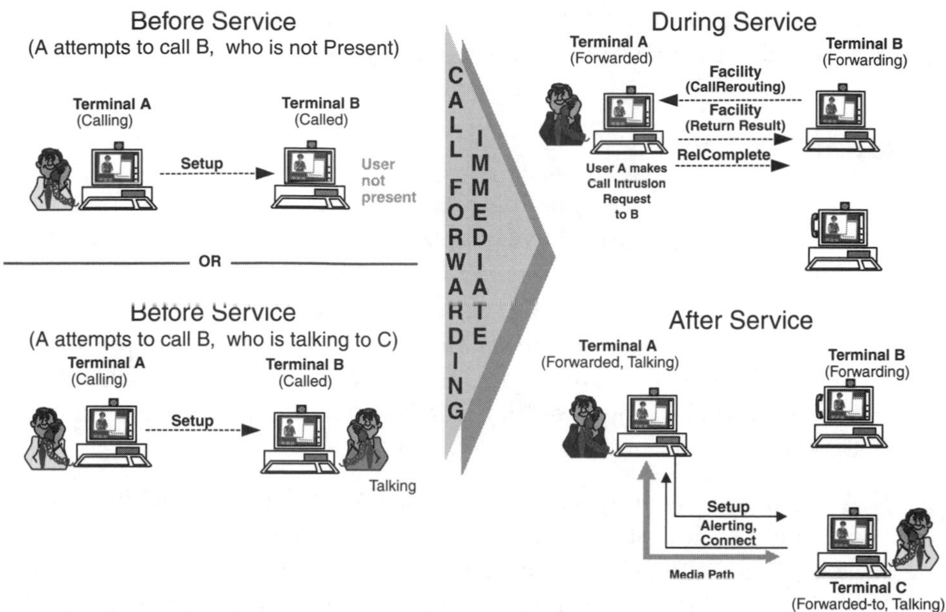

Figure 8.2 Call Forwarding Unconditional and on Busy.

Invocation and Operation

Figure 8.2 illustrates the user scenario and operation of Call Forwarding on All Calls and on Busy.

These services can take place unconditionally but may depend on various rules. Such rules can be defined by the user and may, for example, depend on the calling party address or time of day. After these rules are met, forwarding takes place. The called user is not alerted and not able to receive the call. Therefore, these services belong in the category of immediate forwarding, which means that call forwarding is performed automatically when the incoming call arrives at the destination. Even though the called user (who is the served user) is not alerted, a local notification that call forwarding is taking place may be provided.

The calling user (User A) may be informed that the call is being diverted visually via a display or by means of audible tones. Additionally, the name and number of the forwarded-to user and the diversion cause may be indicated. No further action is required from the calling party.

Also the forwarded-to user may be informed by the display that the call is being forwarded to him. The name and address of the forwarding and calling user is usually displayed. In the case of multiple call diversions, the name and address of the last forwarding user can be indicated.

Signaling Protocol

Figure 8.3 shows the signaling protocol for Call Forwarding on All Calls and on Busy. The signaling flows of both of these services are identical with differences only at the parameter level. Upon reception of a call attempt—immediately on arrival of the SETUP message—the served endpoint will detect the destination address of the call forwarding and reply with a FACILITY message containing a Call Rerouting Invoke APDU. The detection of a situation leading to a call diversion invoke request is a local procedure in the served endpoint.

After the calling endpoint receives the FACILITY message, it becomes the rerouting endpoint and will check whether the diversion request is valid. This check is done before the actual rerouting. If the plausibility check is positive, and the diversion request can be performed, an acknowledgement (returnResult APDU) is sent to the forwarding endpoint in a RELEASE COMPLETE message with a return result.

The data elements and information elements that were received in the rerouting request are now used in the establishment of a new call to the new

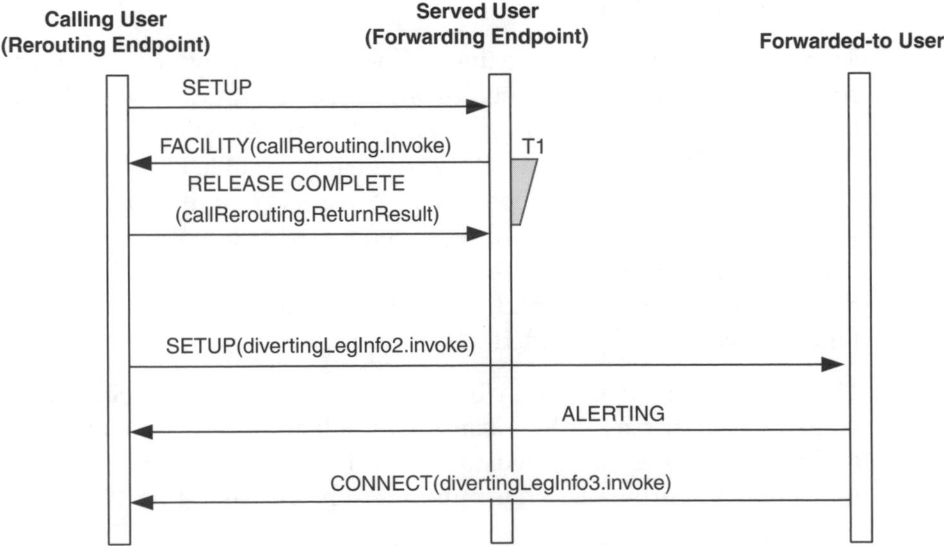

Figure 8.3 H.450.3 signaling flow for CFU and CFB.

destination (forwarded-to endpoint). Therefore, the SETUP message for the new call includes a divertingLegInformation2 Invoke APDU and the following call forwarding-specific elements:

- The rerouting address received in the callRerouting Invoke APDU is now used as the called party number in the SETUP message.
- The callingNumber of the callRerouting Invoke APDU is used as the calling party number in the SETUP message.
- The progress indicator and bearer capability information element (and high layer compatibility, low layer compatibility, and so on) are copied to the SETUP message, if received within the callRerouting Invoke APDU.
- All forwarding data elements are copied from the callRerouting Invoke APDU of the FACILITY message to the divertingLegInformation2 Invoke APDU of the SETUP message. These include typically diversionCounter, reroutingReason, originalReroutingReason, lastReroutingNr, redirectingInfo, originalCalledNr, and originalCalledInfo.

After the Forwarded-to endpoint has accepted the call, an ALERTING message is sent to the rerouting endpoint. This concludes the call forwarding procedure.

Call Forwarding on No Reply and Call Deflection

When Call Forwarding on No Reply is active for a given service, all incoming calls related to that service offered to the served extension. The incoming call sends the alert, and the normal call information is supplied to the served user. If the served extension does not answer within a certain time (that is configurable), the call is forwarded, and the served user will receive an appropriate notification.

When Call Deflection is active, the user is also alerted but can make a decision whether to receive or forward the call. Deflection can be done manually or semi-automatically. The only difference between Call Deflection and Call Forwarding on No Reply is that, in the former case, the user is involved in the decision making and selection of the call forwarding destination.

Invocation and Operation

Figure 8.4 illustrates the user scenario and operation of Call Forwarding on No Reply and Call Deflection services. The method of execution is called

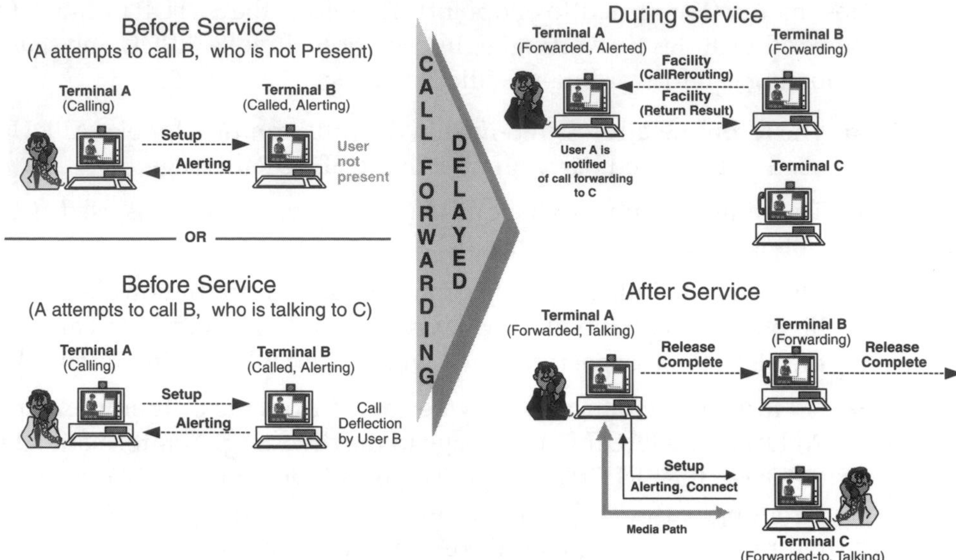

Figure 8.4 Call Forwarding on No Reply and Call Deflection.

delayed call forwarding, which means that the called user is alerted first and then, during ringing, forwarded. Otherwise, the operation is the same as for Call Forwarding on All Calls and on Busy discussed in the preceding section.

Call Forwarding on No Reply may also depend on various rules, which can be defined in a similar manner as discussed in the preceding section.

Signaling Protocol

Figure 8.5 shows the signaling protocol for Call Forwarding on No Reply and Call Deflection services. The signaling flows of these two services are identical with differences only in the parameter level.

The call forwarding is delayed because the served user is first rung, and the forwarding rerouting is initiated only after the call is not answered.

One further difference to the signaling flow of CFU and CFB in Figure 8.5 is that the forwarding endpoint continues ringing until an ALERTING message is received from the forwarded-to party. The calling party can invoke other supplementary services against the originally called party, if the forwarded-to endpoint is busy. An example would be to leave a callback request using the Message Waiting Callback service.

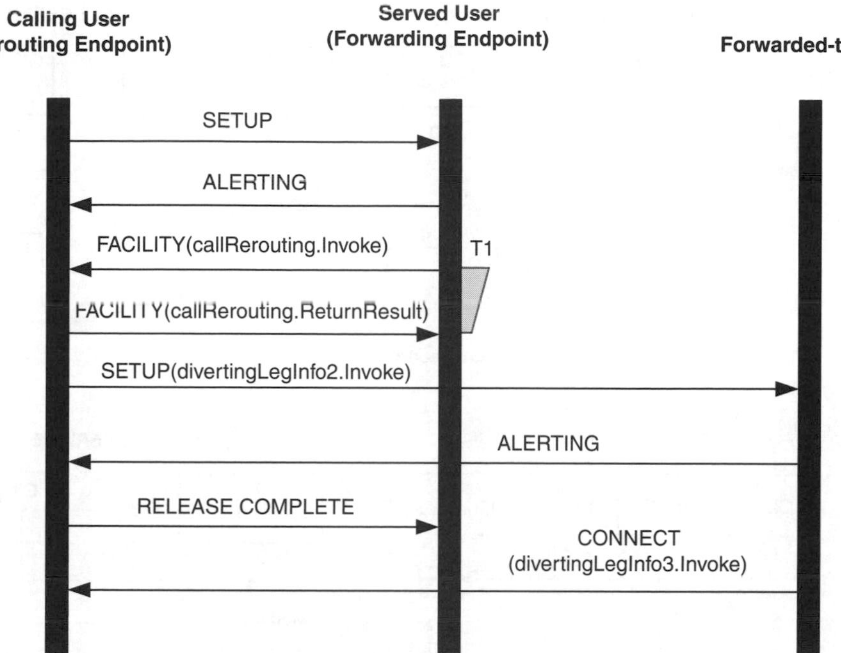

Figure 8.5 H.450.3 signaling flow for CFNR and CD.

Call Forwarding Performed in the Gatekeeper

The signaling of H.450.3 call forwarding works both in the direct signaling mode and in the gatekeeper routed signaling mode. In the latter case, the gatekeeper may either participate in the call forwarding or be transparent for all call forwarding operations.

We want to implement forwarding transfer in the gatekeeper to allow the use of the feature even if some or all of the parties are not H.450.3 aware. Two operational signaling models for gatekeeper-controlled call forwarding are shown in Figure 8.6: (1) in Gatekeeper A or (2) in Gatekeeper B.

A typical application of call forwarding in the called user's gatekeeper is when User B forwards calls to a mobile phone. Because the calls to mobile networks are usually charged higher than normal calls, the additional cost should be paid by User B. User A should pay only for the call from Endpoint A to Endpoint B. Even though the media path is established directly and is most optimal between A and C, the gatekeepers can determine the service-specific charges to their users.

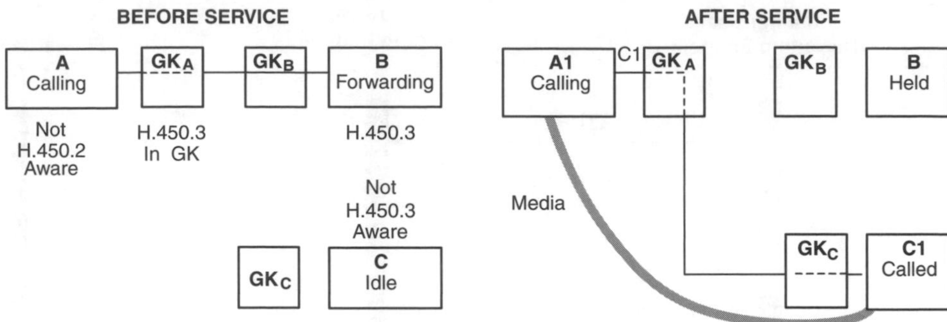

(a) Call Forward Rerouting in the Gatekeeper A

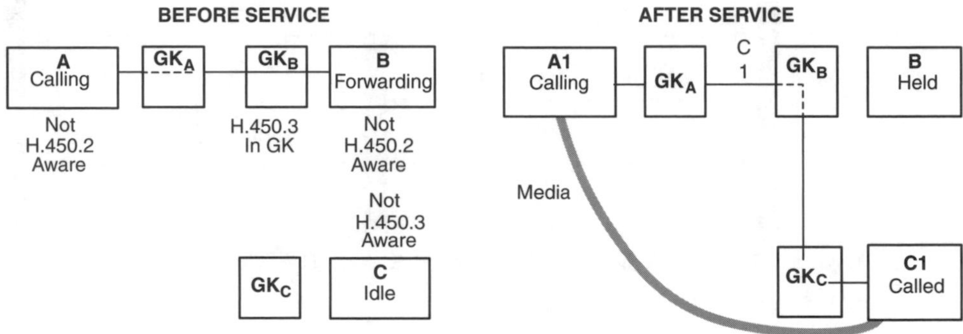

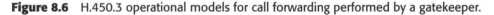

(b) Call Forward Rerouting by joining in the Gatekeeper B

Figure 8.6 H.450.3 operational models for call forwarding performed by a gatekeeper.

Figure 8.6(a) assumes that Endpoint A is H.450.3 aware, but Endpoint A is not, and its capabilities are not known. When Gatekeeper GK_A receives the rerouting request from Endpoint B, it performs the call-forward rerouting function on behalf of Endpoint A. The gatekeeper's task is then to play the role of a rerouting point toward Endpoint B and to set up a call ("diversion leg 2") to User C.

Figure 8.6(b) again assumes that neither Endpoint A nor its gatekeeper is H.450.3 aware, but that gatekeeper GK_B can perform call-forward rerouting. When Gatekeeper GK_B receives the rerouting request from Endpoint B, it becomes a rerouting point toward Endpoint B and establishes the call to Endpoint C by means of forward switching.

CFU and CFB Performed by Gatekeeper A

Figure 8.7 illustrates the signaling information flow of call forwarding on all calls and on busy, when gatekeeper GK_A performs the call-forward rerouting

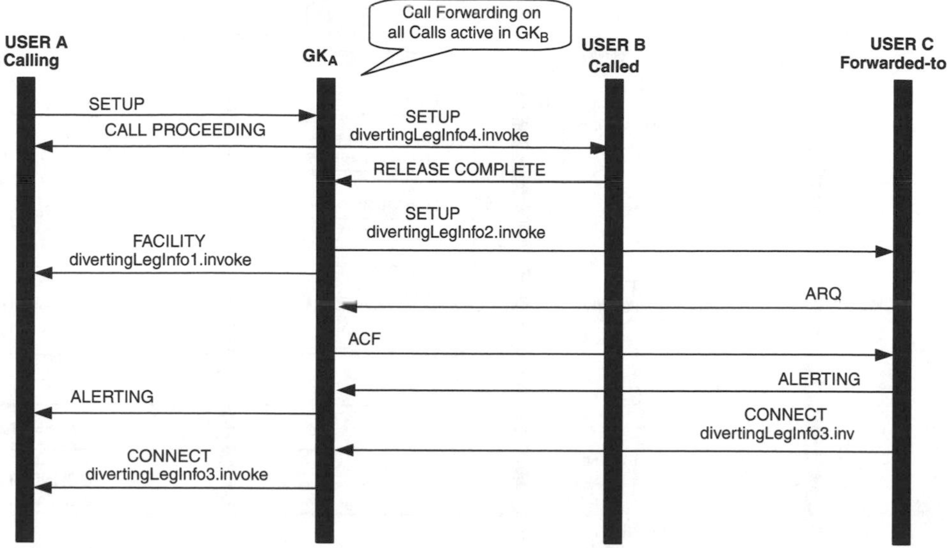

Figure 8.7 Signaling flow for CFU and CFB performed in Gatekeeper A.

function. The gatekeepers of Endpoints A and C are not shown because they are transparent.

In Figure 8.3, Endpoint A executes the rerouting function; whereas in Figure 8.7 this function was moved to Gatekeeper A. Therefore, an additional notification needs to be given by Gatekeeper A to Endpoint A about the progress of call forwarding. This is done when the SETUP message is sent to Endpoint C.

With regard to all other aspects, the signaling procedure is identical to Figure 8.3.

CFB Performed by Gatekeeper B

Figure 8.8 illustrates the signaling information flow of call forwarding on busy, when Gatekeeper GK_B performs the call-forward rerouting function. The gatekeepers of Endpoints B and C are not shown because they are transparent.

As the call arrives to Gatekeeper GK_B, it tries to establish the call to Endpoint B and finds it busy after receipt of the RELEASE COMPLETE message with Cause "User Busy." Because gatekeeper B plays the role of the Call-Forwarding point as well as the Call-Rerouting point, it establishes the call to User C and sends corresponding notifications to Endpoints B and A. Note that the notification to Endpoint B has to be sent using a call-independent signaling connection.

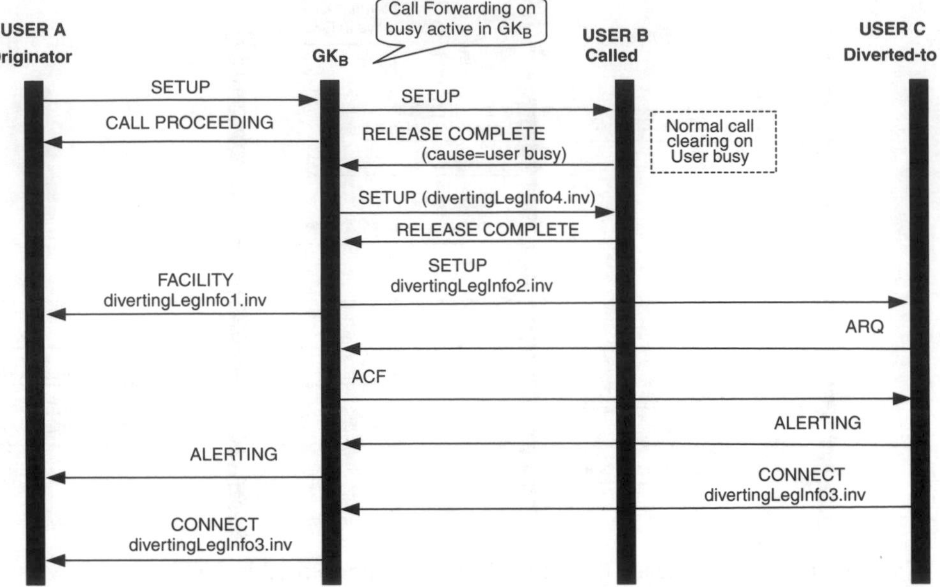

Figure 8.8 Signaling flow for CFB performed in Gatekeeper B.

Again the functional signaling components are the same regardless of the type of forwarding.

Call Diversion when Terminal Is Out of Service

When we discussed the scenarios in the preceding sections of this chapter, we assumed that the called terminal is in service when the calls arrive and is therefore able to execute call forwarding by itself. However, a multimedia terminal at a user's desktop is not always operational or may be powered down. Reasons for this include

- Desktop computers are powered down when the user is not present. This is done for power savings and/or for security reasons.
- Laptop computers are connected to docking stations and are removed when the user travels.
- Power failure occurs for desktops that do not have access to *Uninterruptable Power Sources* (UPS).
- Desktops may experience operational failure due to problems in applications and/or the operating systems.

If all information of its status, capabilities, and so on reside on the computer, the powering down of the computer has a serious effect on the operation of

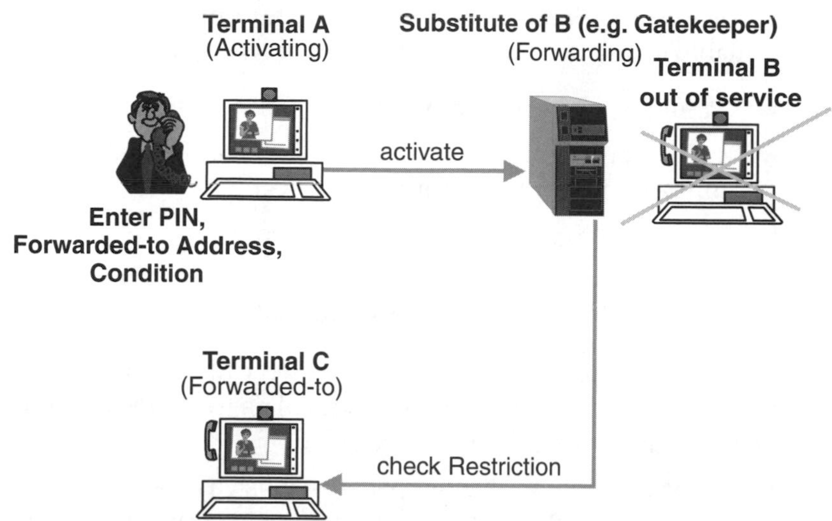

Figure 8.9 Remote activation of Call Forwarding, when a terminal is out of service.

the network. For example, supplementary services, such as call diversion, would not be operational.

The most important service that needs to be available for out-of-service endpoints is Call Forwarding. Because the terminal cannot execute forwarding, the service has to be done by its substitute. This substitute can be either the gatekeeper or another, secondary endpoint.

A substitute keeps track of the operational status of the desktop and acts on behalf of it whenever necessary. It has to detect that the user's terminal is out of service, announce itself to the gatekeeper, and start handling incoming calls for that user. The substitute may then perform most of the call diversion functions as the terminal itself. The procedures are the same as previously discussed.

A specific situation occurs when the endpoint goes out of service, but the call forwarding destination was not programmed before. Figure 8.9 shows how the H.450.3 remote activation procedures can be used in this situation for remote programming of call forwarding, that is, in the gatekeeper of the endpoint.

Interaction with Other Supplementary Services

The Call Forwarding service has many interactions with other supplementary services or basic functions of the H.225 basic call. The following lists some of them.

Identification services. The following name/number information has to be available to any user involved in a forwarded call:

- Calling party name and number
- Called party name and number (This is the original redirecting number if multiple call forwarding occurs.)
- Forwarded-to party name and number
- Connected party name and number (Exception: The forwarding endpoint does not receive this information.)

Consultation hold. A successfully forwarded call may be put on any variation of the Call Hold feature. The call is treated as a two-party call after the call forward feature is executed.

If a user involved in a call attempts to establish a consultation call to a user who has call diversion activated, the call is established to the diverted-to user.

Automatic recall. This feature activates, for example, when transfer fails and the call returns to the transferring user. These calls are not forwarded.

Message waiting call back. This service is activated against the called user, not the forwarded-to user. A message waiting callback call must not be forwarded.

Call waiting. When the called user is busy and has call forwarding unconditional activated, call forwarding takes precedence over call waiting. CFU can be activated while a call is waiting without changing the state of the waiting call.

Intrusion. If a call is forwarded to a destination that is found busy, the calling party may invoke Intrusion against the forwarded-to party.

References

H.225 ITU-T Recommendation H.225.0 Version 4, Call signalling protocols and media stream packetization for packet-based multimedia communications systems, H.225, November 2000.

H.245 ITU-T Recommendation H.245 Version 5, Control protocol for multimedia communication, H.245, February 2000.

H.323 ITU-T Recommendation H.323 Version 4, Packet-based multimedia communications systems, H.323, November 2000.

H.450.1 ITU-T Recommendation H.450.1., Generic functional protocol for the support of supplementary services in H.323, H.450.1, February 1998.

H.450.3 ITU-T Recommendation H.450.3., Call Diversion supplementary services for H.323, H.450.3, February 1998.

I.112 ITU-T Rec. I.112, Vocabulary of terms for ISDNs, I.112.

I.210 ITU-T Rec. I.210, Principles of telecommunication services supported by an ISDN and the means to describe them, I.210.

ISO/IEC 13872 Information technology—Telecommunications and information exchange between systems—Private integrated services network—Service capabilities and information flows—Diversion supplementary services, ISO/IEC 13872 Edition 1, December 1995.

ISO/IEC 13873 Information technology—Telecommunications and information exchange between systems—Private integrated services network—Interexchange signalling procedures and protocol—call diversion supplementary services, ISO/IEC 13873 Edition 1, December 1995.

Problems

1. Describe the interactions between attendant extension of calls and call forwarding. In other words, if the user to whom the attendant extended a call has Call Forwarding activated, what should happen to the call attempt made by the attendant? Describe different alternatives and their advantages and disadvantages.
2. Describe the interactions between call forwarding and Call Completion on No Reply and on Busy.
3. Describe the interactions between call forwarding and conference calls.
4. Describe how call forwarding can be used in connection with messaging servers.
5. Describe the interactions between call forwarding and call transfer.
6. Explain how your implementation of call forwarding would hinder call forwarding loops.
7. Policies are used to control users' rights to use various features. Describe how you would implement call forwarding policies (for example for different call types).

CHAPTER 9

Call Completion Services for Unsuccessful Calls in H.450

This chapter discusses features for calls that cannot be completed because the called user is either busy or does not answer the call. Call completion services for unsuccessful calls utilize the supplementary service protocol components defined in the ITU-T Recommendations H.450.6 Call Waiting, H.450.9 CCBS/CCNR, H.450.10 Call Offering, H.450.11 Call Intrusion, and the mechanisms of the H.323/H.225.0 Basic Call. Each of the supplementary service standards contains both reusable, functional components and compound supplementary services, which are each identified and described in this chapter. In addition, summaries of each service, their related protocols, and examples of call scenarios are given.

General Information

When a call is made to a party that is not reachable—for example when the called party does not answer or is busy—it is very helpful if the caller can immediately request the telephone system to automatically complete the call at the earliest possible time. The legacy telephone systems and networks—PBXs and Centrex services—are examples of such call completion services. In addition, these services are also obviously required for the IP-based multimedia telephony networks. Although the design experience of such legacy system features greatly benefits the design of IP telephony systems, inherent differences between the two systems enormously impact the functional split of the services.

Many call completion services are ideally simple for implementation in the terminals, which also simplifies the processing and signaling overhead. Examples of such services are *Call Waiting* (CW) and *Message Waiting* (MW). These services and others are discussed later in this chapter in more detail.

Unsuccessful call states. A call can be unsuccessful due to several reasons that involve the state of the called party. The called party can exist in one of the following states:

- The called party is on another call and is therefore busy.
- The called party is not at the terminal being called and does not know that he/she is being called and hence cannot answer.
- The called party is aware of being called, but decides not to answer the call (e.g., because the called party is in a meeting).
- The called party sets his/her profile to disallow certain calls (e.g., because he/she does not want to be disturbed).

Available services. The call completion services for unsuccessful calls exist to help both the calling and called party. These services are divided into the two following categories based on how the features are invoked:

- Functions that are activated by the called user and are automatically invoked, without any action from the calling party
- Functions that are available to the calling party, but require an explicit feature invocation from the calling party

In each of the previous categories, the corresponding actions are performed either manually or semi-automatically (e.g., by the software of the terminal or by the *gatekeeper* [GK]). The completion of an unsuccessful call can utilize one or more of the following capabilities:

- *Multiple Call Handling.* The calling party's terminal is able to receive and present several calls simultaneously to the user. The user then receives an alert of the incoming call and can choose to receive that call and place the other call on hold.
- *Call Waiting.* This feature is almost the same as multiple call handling, except that the arriving incoming multimedia call is automatically placed in Call Waiting mode. Either a regular or special ringback tone is used for this particular call.
- *Message Waiting.* A messaging server indicates to a called party that a message was delivered to the mailbox because the party was unreachable. There are several ways to leave a message: 1) by leaving it to an automatic

answering service, 2) by requesting a Message Waiting Callback, and 3) by sending an e-mail or short message to the mailbox.

- *Call Completion on Busy Subscriber (CCBS) and Completion on No Reply* (CCNR). Using these two features, a caller can automatically establish a call when the called party returns to his/her desk or whenever the called party is free.
- *Call Offering.* Using this feature, a caller can give a visual or audio indication to a busy called party that a call is waiting. The caller can then either request the called party to terminate the call or put the first call on hold to receive the incoming call.
- *Call Intrusion.* Using this feature, a caller can automatically enter (i.e., intrude) into a conference with the existing call, and then communicate directly with the called party. This can be done, for example, to deliver an urgent message to the called party.

The Treatment of Unsuccessful Calls

After failure to set up a call, the supplementary services mentioned previously are invoked to enable, an unsuccessful call to be turned into a successfully answered call. Depending on the service profile of the users involved and on the unsuccessful call condition itself, the original call is either retained or released and established again. If the original signaling transaction is released and the calling user requests a supplementary service, a new call is automatically established with the appropriate invocation of supplementary service.

Figure 9.1 shows a flow chart for the treatment of unsuccessful calls. An unsuccessful call attempt can result from the following states: 1) the called party is busy, 2) the called party does not answer, or 3) the call is automatically put into a waiting state or to a queue.

If the called party is busy, the calling party receives a busy signal (e.g., an audible or visual tone), and then can subsequently request one of the following features:

- Call Completion on Busy Subscriber
- Call Offering
- Call Intrusion
- Message Waiting callback

If none of these features are invoked, the called User B can continue the call undisturbed and the calling User A is released.

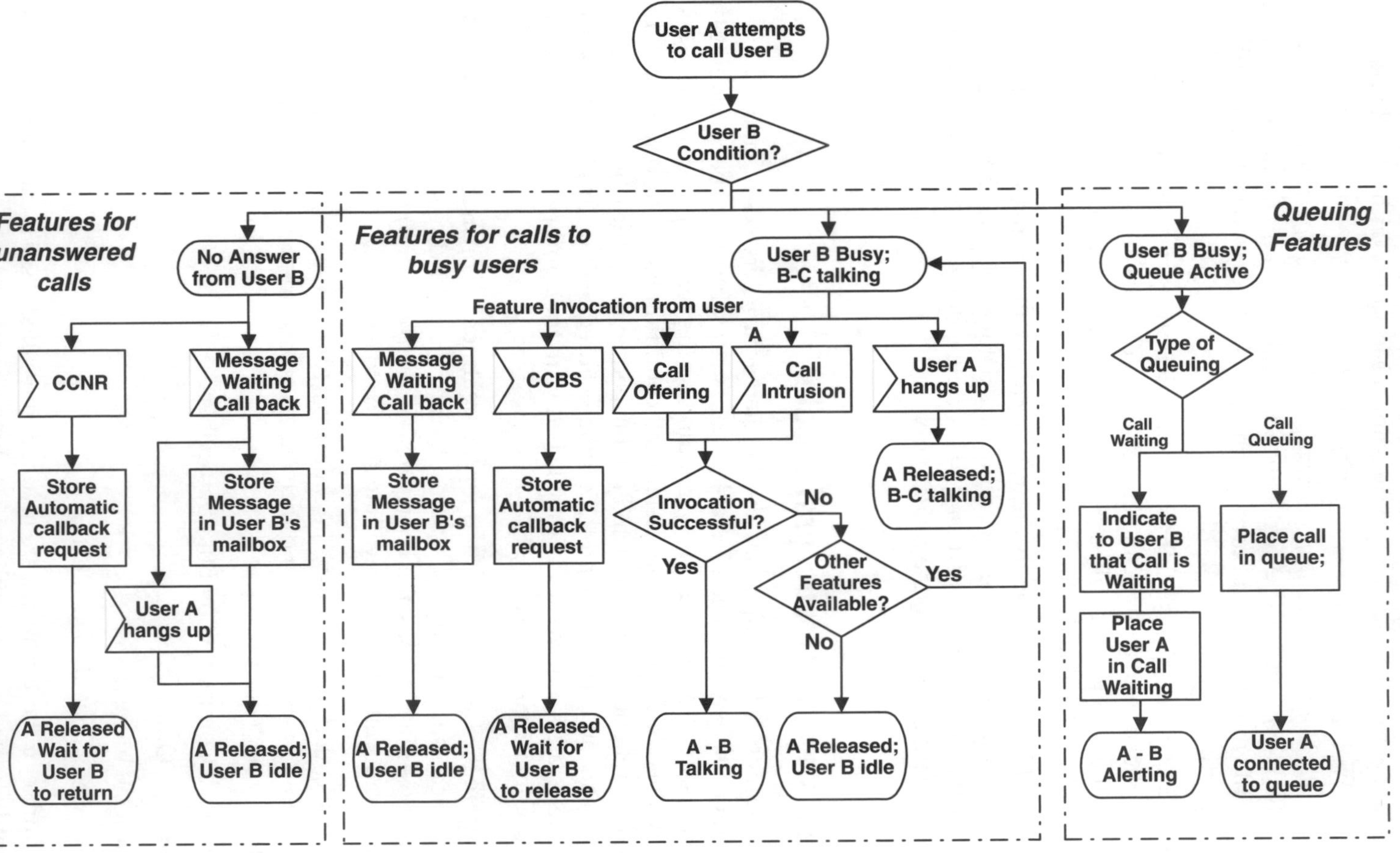

Figure 9.1 The treatment of unsuccessful call attempts.

If the called party does not reply, the calling user can then request the following features:

- Call Completion on No Reply
- Message Waiting callback

Finally, if the user is busy on another call, but has activated the call queuing or call waiting service, the call attempt receives a special treatment. From the calling user's perspective, the call does not reach a busy condition. If the call is placed into a CW state, the calling party receives a ringing tone and waits until the called party answers. The call can also be placed in a queue. In that case, the user is connected, for example, to an announcement server, and then given an appropriate message.

Note that neither Call Forwarding on Busy nor Call Forwarding on No Reply are included here as call completion services. This is because these features are rerouting functions configured by the called party and they cannot be influenced by the calling party. When these supplementary services are activated by the called user, the call never reaches a busy, no-answer, or CW state.

The Definition of Busy and the Handling of Multiple Calls

As discussed previously, certain supplementary services can only be invoked if a call attempt reaches a busy condition of a called user. Therefore it is important to understand the rules under which the user can be busy. If we compare the methods used in the legacy telephone networks and IP telephony networks to the methods that detect this condition, we will notice some important differences and also some commonalties.

If a user of an analog telephone line is using the line, it is clear that all addresses attached to it are busy—the line can be used for only one call at a time. The only way a caller does not reach a busy line is if these addresses are forwarded to another address. This busy condition is determined by the network.

In an ISDN, the user can have two calls at the same time on the two-channel basic access. Therefore, the network can only determine the busy condition if both channels are already in use, or if the called address has been configured to receive only one call at a time. In all other cases, the ISDN switch must attempt to establish the call anyway. As a result a busy condition can be reached. These two ways of determination are called:

- Network Determined User Busy
- User Determined User Busy

When an H.323 gatekeeper is attempting to place a call to an endpoint, it may be able to determine in advance that the destination is already busy—an endpoint and the associated address can be configured in such a way that enables it to receive only one call at a time. This is necessary, for example, with endpoints that cannot handle more than one call signaling transaction at a time. On the other hand, if the endpoint can handle multiple calls simultaneously, then the gatekeeper may already have in its database the maximum number of simultaneous calls, and it can determine if that destination is busy after reaching that limit. In all other cases, the gatekeeper attempts to establish the call, and it is up to the endpoint to determine whether resources are available and if it can handle the call.

In general, a *busy condition occurs whenever the resources associated with the destination address exist and are needed to successfully complete the call, yet are not available for that call.* In addition, if the resources are also incompatible, this condition cannot be fulfilled because the resources will probably still be incompatible when a second attempt is made. Therefore, the supplementary invocation to complete the call or to initiate a reattempt is useless.

If some of the network routing elements are unavailable, the call is not to be signaled as busy because these resources are not associated with the destination address. In the cases where network resources are unavailable or when such resources are out of service or are otherwise nonfunctional, other network internal unsuccessful call conditions apply. In these situations, none of the supplementary services for call completion help to establish the call because the destination was not reached at all.

Resources

When the destination gatekeeper detects whether the called address is reachable, it must determine the required resources involved and whether the configuration database of the endpoint shows that these resources are available. As long as the endpoint remains registered, the gatekeeper considers the H.225.0 signaling channel to be always available. An example of a situation where this is not true is a failure condition, which results in an initiation of recovery and restart procedures.

The gatekeeper can, for example, keep a record of the actual usage and maximum number of the following endpoint resources:

- Number of calls (N)
- Type of call (e.g., voice, fax, T.120, video, and so on)
- Available bandwidth
- Availability and number of codecs

If the endpoint itself determines the available resources for the call, it must be configured in the gatekeeper that it can handle signaling for more than one call simultaneously. Therefore, as a first step, if one call is already being established or active, it is required that this endpoint be sufficiently capable of handling the signaling for new calls.

From the perspective of the protocol, it is not significant, which extension resources are busy, how it is determined, or why. Any indication from the endpoint that some of the necessary extension resources are busy is sufficient. This indication can happen automatically or semi-automatically. The availability of fixed resources such as bandwidth and voice codecs can happen automatically without user influence, whereas the availability of the called party (i.e., the person) can be determined, for example, based on the calendar entries or by means of a call processing script.

Procedural Aspects

It is important to note that whenever supplementary services require the retaining of the calling user's original call, the user busy condition must not be signaled to the calling party by means of a RELEASE COMPLETE message. Instead a FACILITY message is used to indicate the call condition and the available features. This avoids the immediate release of the call, enabling the call to progress as soon as the calling user invokes one of the supplementary services.

Call Waiting—H.450.6

The Call Waiting supplementary service permits a busy User B to be informed of an incoming call while being engaged with one or more other calls (see Figures 9.1 and 9.2). In other words, Call Waiting operates on an incoming call when a busy condition within the endpoint is encountered. From the perspective of the protocol, it is insignificant how the busy condition is determined. It can also be encountered, for example, when the user is busy with workflow applications (e.g., writing e-mails).

When a User A (the calling user) attempts to call a busy User B, User B is given an appropriate indication of the waiting call. The calling User A receives either a regular ringing tone or a special ringing tone instead of busy tone. Some countries' data security regulations require that the calling User A is not informed about Call Waiting.

After receiving the Call Waiting indication, User B has the choice of accepting, rejecting, or ignoring the waiting call. Ignoring means that the

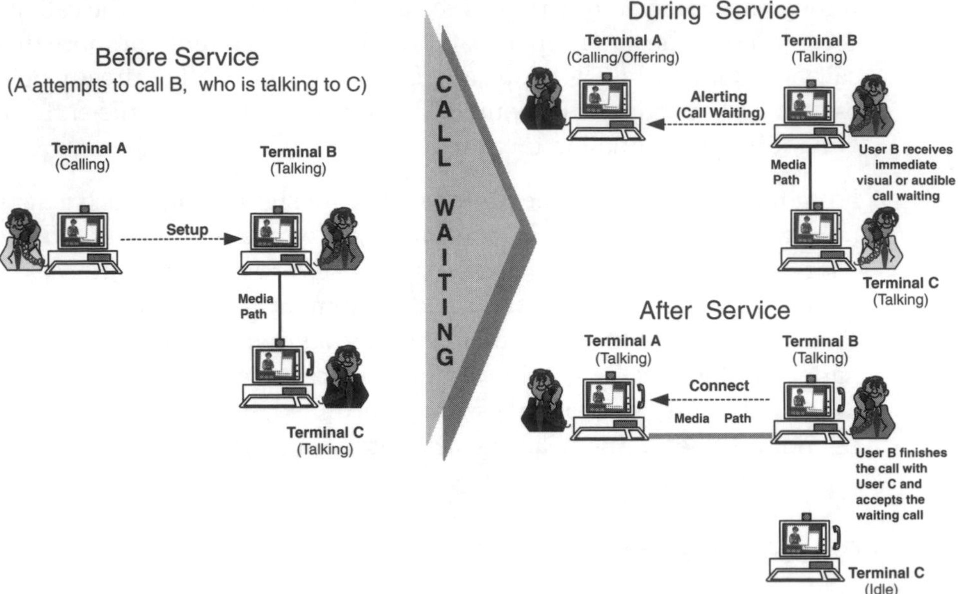

Figure 9.2 The H.450.6 Call Waiting supplementary service.

incoming call continues alerting User B until a forced release happens due to time expiry. Rejection means that the incoming call from User A is released by User B.

Invocation and Operation

Figure 9.2 illustrates the steps involved in invocation of the Call Waiting supplementary service which lead to the acceptance of the waiting call.

During the Call Waiting condition, the calling User A has the option to release the call or to invoke other supplementary services, such as Message Waiting Callback.

The maximum number of calls which can be handled (i.e., active, held, alerting, or waiting) for each endpoint is an implementation option. Call Waiting occurs only when an attempt is made to exceed these limits.

Signaling Protocol

Figure 9.3 shows the signaling flow for Call Waiting, including the acceptance of the waiting call.

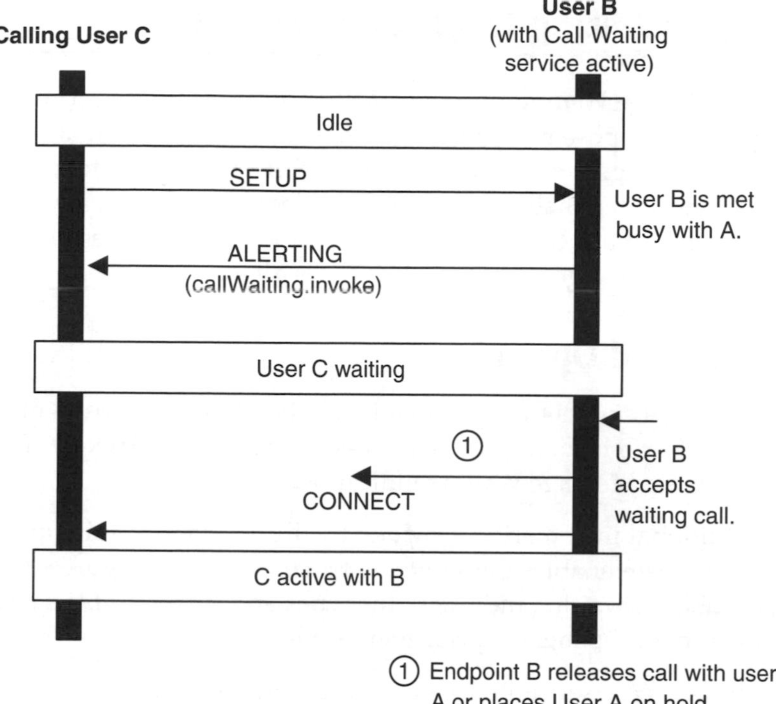

Figure 9.3 A signaling flow for Call Waiting.

Call Waiting applies to the complete call, including all logical channels related to the call. Although Call Waiting was originally developed for voice calls, the protocol can also be used for video calls. Its use in T.120 calls is also theoretically possible.

Conclusion of the H.450.6 Call Waiting Services

The Call Waiting supplementary service consists of a single functional component, namely the additional callWaiting.Invoke APDU in the ALERTING message. The procedures for the Call Wait invocation within the calling Terminal A are not visible at the protocol level and can therefore be implementation dependent.

Call Waiting is a perfect example of a supplementary service, which is ideally easy to implement in the endpoints, but which becomes as equally complicated as its near relative PBXs if it is implemented in the gatekeeper.

Message Waiting Indication—H.450.7

The *Message Waiting Indication* (MWI) supplementary service provides a general-purpose mechanism that tells users which available messages are their messages. A variety of message types are supported, such as voice mail, fax, and video mail. In one of its simplest forms, when a message is left for a user, a Message Server sends a notification to the served user's terminal, where a Message Waiting indication is given.

Invocation and Operation

Figure 9.4 shows the steps involved when User A leaves a message for User B after User B is forwarded to a messaging server. Subsequently, User B receives a Message Waiting indication.

Additional information provided by the Message Waiting notification mechanism enables the served user (i.e., User B in Figure 9.4) to know the number of waiting messages, the types and subjects of the messages, and the priority of the highest priority message.

The Served User can retrieve the messages in various ways from the server. In unified messaging systems, this retrieval can happen, for example, via e-mail or by calling the server via an interactive message retrieval interface.

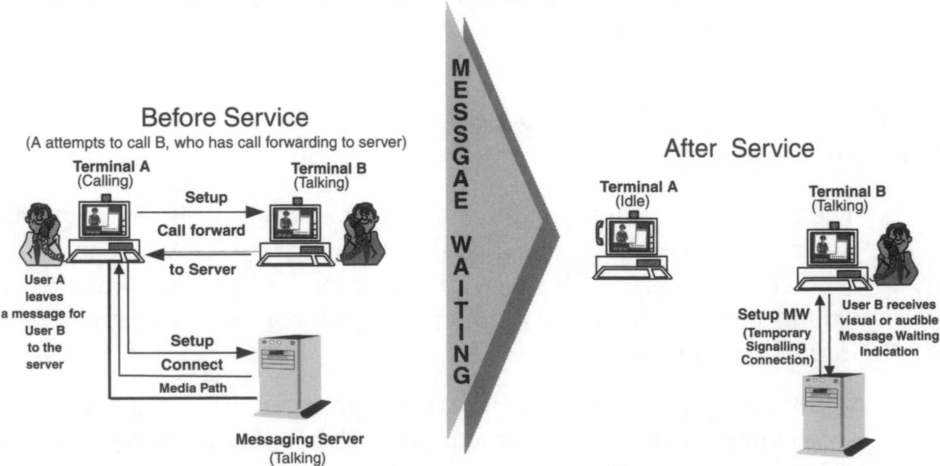

Figure 9.4 Forwarding to a server and the H.450.7 Message Waiting Indication.

Signaling Protocol

MWI Activation. As an example of the activation of MWI, Figure 9.5(a) shows the establishment of call independent signaling connection from the message server to the Served User. It also illustrates that the message server can use the same connection with multiple, subsequent FACILITY messages for the reporting of more than one message indication. This is particularly useful, for example, when different message classes need to be separately indicated.

MWI Deactivation. As soon as the messages have been read and retrieved from the server, the *Message Waiting Indication* (MWI) is switched off by means of a MWI deactivation message. Figure 9.5(b) shows an example of the deactivation of an MWI. Only the server, which sent the corresponding MWI message, can perform this action. Otherwise, the status of an MWI indicator in the terminal and in the server would not be consistent.

The MWI activation and deactivation requests are carried in a mwiActivate and mwiDeactivate Invoke APDU, respectively. The message server is responsible for clearing the call-independent signaling connection toward the Served User. The message center can release the connection immediately after the receipt of a mwiActivate or mwiDeactivate Return Result APDU. Or, the signaling connection can also be alternatively retained so that it can be used to subsequently send an MWI without re-establishing the connection every time.

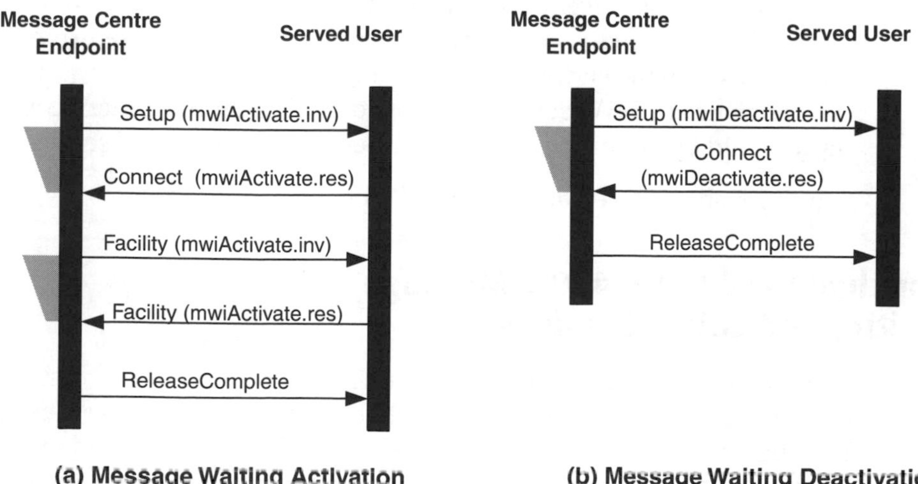

Figure 9.5 The signaling flow for the (a) activation and (b) deactivation of a Message Waiting Indication.

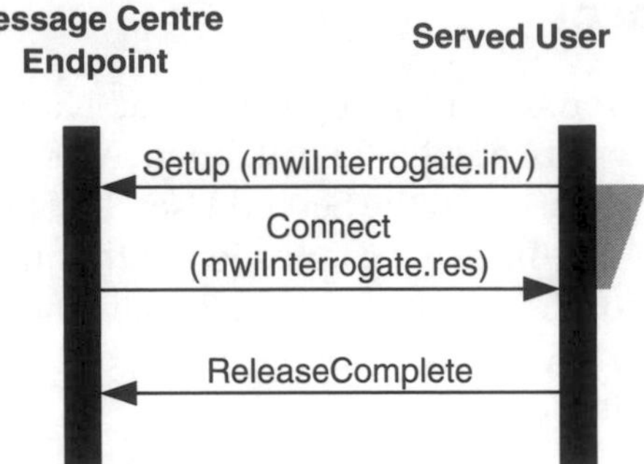

Figure 9.6 A signaling flow for the interrogation of a Message Waiting Indication.

The Message Server can include in the mwiActivate Invoke APDU any of the following additional information:

- An identifier of the Message Server, in the element msgCentreId
- The number of messages waiting in the server for the Served User in the element nbOfMessages
- An H.323 address of the user who left a message in the element originatingNr
- The time a message was left in the element timestamp
- The priority of the highest priority message for the Served User in the element priority

The *interrogation mechanism* enables a Served User to query Message Centers, whether a MWI is currently activated to it or not. A typical use of this mechanism is when the endpoint has been restarted and is returning to service or when the endpoint is a roaming terminal. In this case, the Served User recreates its MWI status by means of interrogation. Otherwise, the status could be lost or change while the endpoint was out of service.

Figure 9.6 shows an example of an MWI interrogation.

Conclusion of the H.450.7 Message Waiting Indication Services

The Message Waiting Indication is a functional component consisting of a temporary signaling connection which is used to transport the Message Waiting activation and deactivation APDUs. This method is independent of the server characteristics and can be used even when several servers work for the same user.

Message Waiting Callback—H.450.7

Message Waiting Callback permits a user to leave a request for a callback on the terminal of another user. The request can be stored in the same mailbox where the Message Waiting indications from other servers are stored. The receiver of the request can then select a message and ask for establishment of the call without manually dialing the address of the party. This mechanism is included in the H.450.7 supplementary service.

Whereas the CCBS and CCNR services complete the call automatically without the user interaction, the Message Waiting Callback feature enables the receiver of the message (the server user) to decide when to initiate the callback. Another difference is that in CCBS/CCNR the call is established from the side of the party that made the call completion request, whereas in case of Message Waiting Callback, the receiver of the callback request establishes the call. This, of course, has implications on the charging of the call as well.

If the receiver of the callback request does not want to make the call, the receiver simply deletes the Message Waiting Callback message.

Invocation and Operation

Figure 9.7 shows the Message Waiting Callback scenario and the steps involved.

The MWI callback request makes use of the MWI activation mechanism defined in H.450.7. In this instance, the calling terminal becomes the message source and server for the sent message. Because leaving a callback request does not require message content storage, only an originator's callable address must be present for the served user to establish a callback to this address. The callback request can also be cancelled by a MWI deactivation message.

Signaling Protocol

Figure 9.8 shows the signaling flow for the Message Waiting Callback. The Message Waiting Callback request is sent using the same mwiActivate Invoke APDU and any of the additional information previously described for the regular MWI. The only exception is that the nbOfMessages element is set to zero, and the msgCentreId element contains the H.323 endpoint address destination, in which the callback should be made.

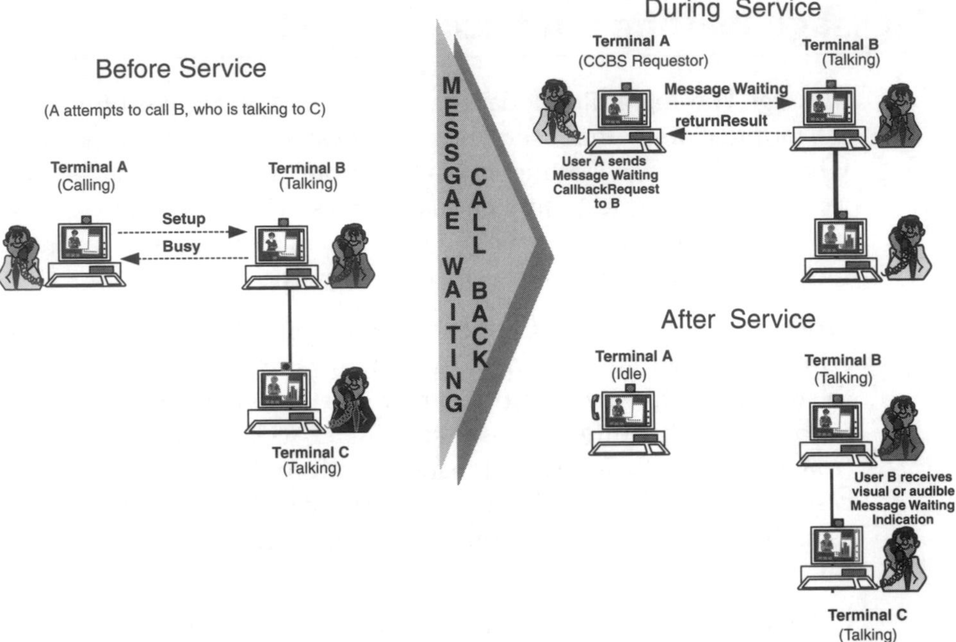

Figure 9.7 An H.450 Message Waiting Callback.

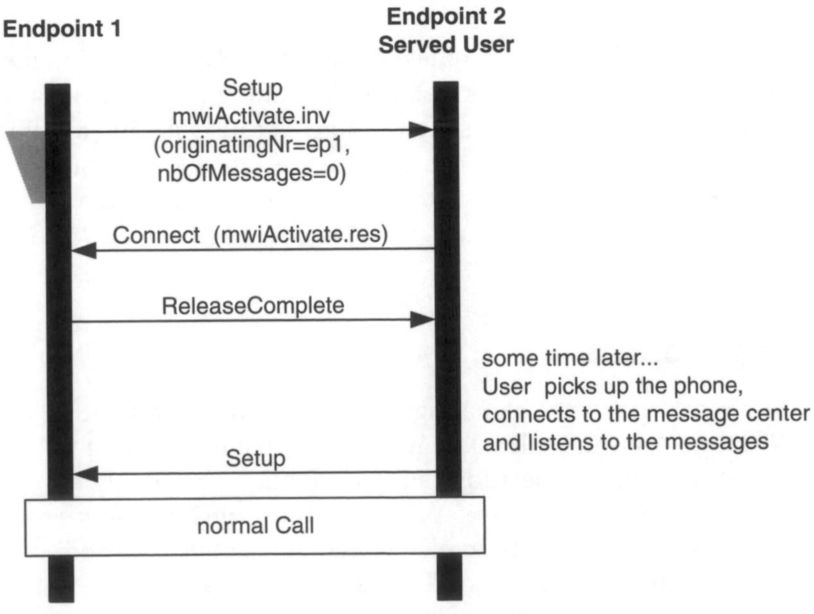

Figure 9.8 A signaling flow for a Message Waiting Callback.

Conclusion of the H.450.7 Message Waiting Callback Services

The Message Waiting Callback is contained in the Message Waiting functional component. It consists of a temporary signaling connection that is used to transport the Message Waiting Callback activation and deactivation APDUs. It can also be used directly between endpoints without help of a server as a mediator.

Call Completion Services—H.450.9

The Call Completion supplementary services consist of separate, yet related capabilities—*Completion of Calls to Busy Subscribers* (CCBS) and *Completion of Calls on No Reply* (CCNR).

CCBS enables a calling User A to complete a call to a busy User B. In this situation, User A places a call to a busy User B. CCBS then automatically initiates and completes the call when User B is free.

CCNR similarly enables a calling User A to complete a call to a busy User B. In this situation, User B is alerted, but does not answer. CCNR then automatically initiates and completes the call when User B becomes free after an active period.

Invocation and Operation

Figure 9.9 illustrates the different steps in the invocation of the CCBS service from the perspective of the user. Figure 9.10 shows the same steps for the invocation of the CCNR service. As shown by the figures, the procedures for these two services are very similar and have several common parts. The only difference between CCBS and CCNR is the detection of the user's activity, which initiates the callback establishment.

Whereas CCBS is normally executed immediately after the user finishes the call, the detection of user activities which trigger the execution of CCNR is more complex. The following examples are activities that can trigger CCNR:

- Lifting the handset of the telephone
- Hitting a key of the keyboard
- Moving the mouse

Automatic call completion means that the user does not need to keep attempting to make a new call until the call succeeds. Instead, the

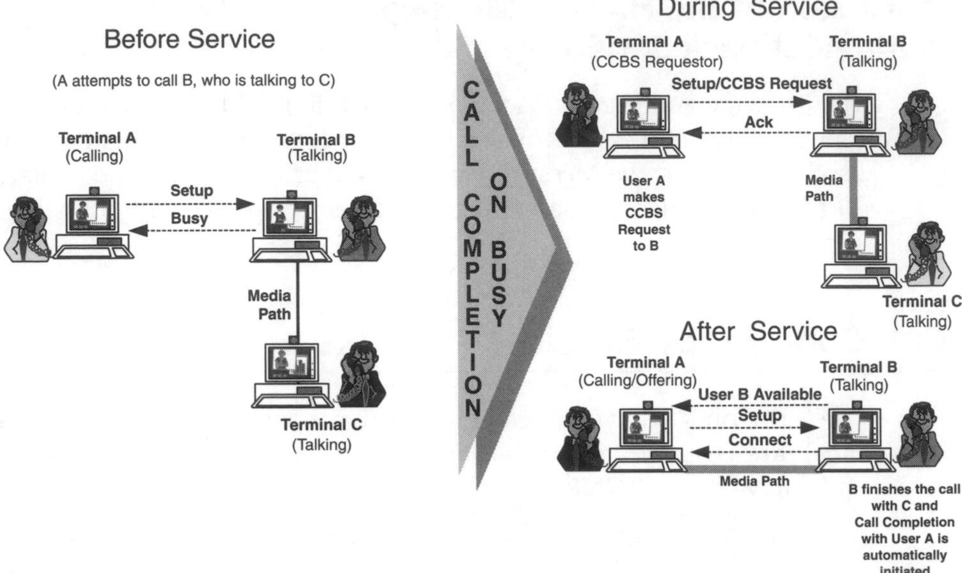

Figure 9.9 The H.450 Call Completion on Busy supplementary service.

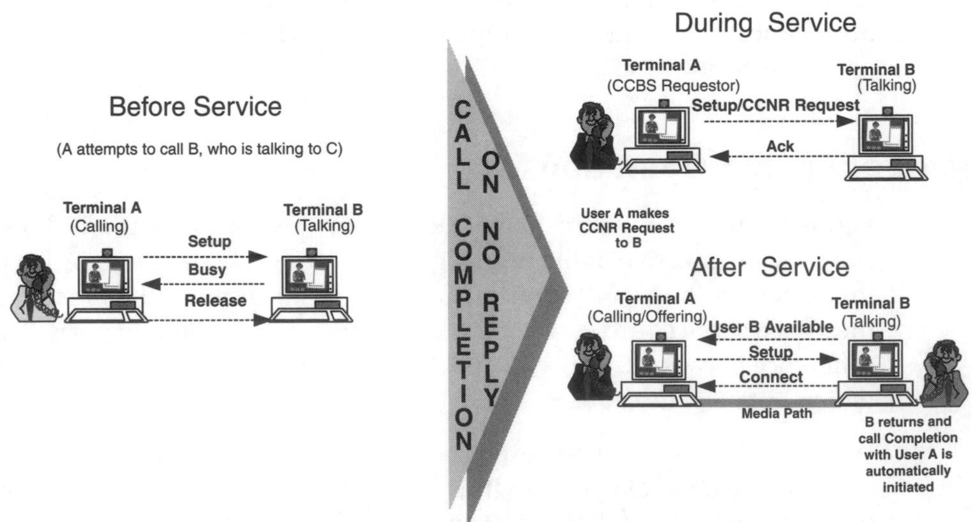

Figure 9.10 The H.450 Call Completion on No Reply supplementary service.

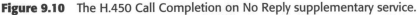

call-processing software of both of the endpoints does the supervision and call establishment for the user.

Some products implement the Call Completion service simply by repeatedly trying to call the destination. In most cases, this is not a good solution, however, because it creates an additional load on the network. In fact, any unsuccessful call attempt creates almost the same amount of load on the gatekeepers as a regular call establishment. Therefore, CCBS and CCNR services provide an obviously better solution with the optimized monitoring and reporting of called party availability.

The H.323 endpoint implementations enable the user to invoke a call completion in several different ways. The following are a few examples:

Upon user request. Telephone User A dials a call completion access code or presses a feature key, while busy tone (in the case of CCBS) or ringing tone (in the case of CCNR) is received. A PC user can similarly click a menu button to request call completion.

Automatically by the endpoint after a timeout. User A remains off the hook and a busy tone is generated until an endpoint's automatic invocation is executed and an audible indication is given (e.g., a different tone).

After having placed a CCBS/CCNR request, User A can receive and originate other calls.

After the request has been accepted, Destination B is monitored by the terminating Endpoint B for availability again for User A. Endpoint B keeps information about the CCBS/CCNR requests placed against it—by storing the H.323 address of User A and all other necessary callback information, such as the time of service invocation. If several users have placed a CCBS/CCNR request against the same User B, this information is used to identify the different requests for their sequential execution.

Endpoint A also keeps information about callbacks invoked by its user—for example, for the local interrogation and cancellation of invoked call completion requests, dependability checking, supervision of service duration, and so on.

Signaling Protocol

The signaling flow for CCBS is shown in Figure 9.11(a) and for CCNR in Figure 9.11(b). In both cases, the original call is released. If the user requests call completion, a corresponding invocation is sent to Terminal B by means of a temporary signaling connection within a ccbsRequest.Invoke or ccnrRequest.Invoke APDU respectively in a SETUP message. If the invocation is accepted by the Terminal B, a ccbsRequest.returnResult or ccnrRequest. returnResult is returned in the CONNECT message. The signaling connection now remains connected, and the monitoring of User B begins. From this point on the signaling procedures for CCBS and CCNR are identical.

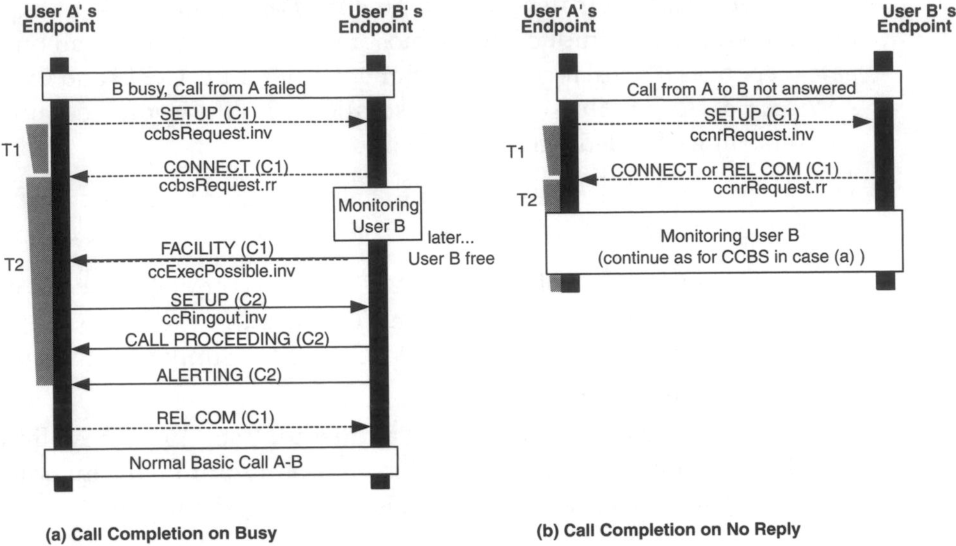

Figure 9.11 A signaling flow of the H.450.9 CCBS and CCNR.

When User B becomes available, a FACILITY message is sent from Endpoint B to Endpoint A, informing that the call can be placed. The message contains the ccExecPossible.Invoke APDU. But before B is called, Endpoint A must first verify that User A is still present, and then give an appropriate notification. To User A, this notification can again be implemented in various ways. For example, if the endpoint is a telephone, then a recall is normally initiated.

On receipt of such notification, User A has the following choices:

- Accept the recall.
- Ignore the notification, thereby causing the recall and the call completion request to be cancelled by Endpoint A as soon as the recall timer expires. (A useful timer value is in the range of 10–30 seconds.)
- Cancel the CCBS request.

As soon as the calling party answers the recall by going off hook, a new call setup is initiated to User B.

In addition, it can also happen that User B is not available anymore when a call attempt is made. If this happens, the monitoring connection is kept and the supervision of User B begins again. If User B accepts the call, the call completion service has performed its task, and the monitoring connection is released.

The intermediate entities involved in the connection only need to support the H.450.1 transparent transport in order to provide an end-to-end path for these supplementary services.

Additional Implementation Aspects

On receipt of a request for CCBS or CCNR, User B's endpoint will check whether it is possible to initiate the service. If it is, an acknowledgment to User A's endpoint is sent and monitoring of User B begins. On receipt of the acknowledgment, User A's endpoint starts the CCBS service duration timer. Acknowledgment means that User A expects to receive a *Call Completion* (CC) Recall if User B becomes free within the period of the CCBS service duration timer.

In the process of executing the CC request, the involved entities must be especially careful in the following situations:

- Although User B is already being monitored as a result of a CC request from another user, it should not cause User A to reject the request. The handling of multiple requests against the same User B is an implementation matter; typically involving some sort of queue arranged in chronological or priority order.
- The fact that User A has already invoked call completion against another user should not cause rejection of any further CC requests from User A. The handling of multiple requests by the same User A is an implementation matter.
- CCBS can be invoked after the notification that User B is busy. The recommended value of the CCBS service duration timer is 1 to 60 minutes. A suitable default value could be 15 minutes.
- The selective operation of CCBS on calls associated with a specific address or call type is also possible in the H.450.9 protocol. This enables a more sophisticated application to be implemented.

Conclusion of the H.450.9 Call Completion Services

CCBS and CCNR are relatively complex supplementary services consisting of several steps and functional components that are executed by the cooperating Endpoints A and B.

The functional components of CCBS and CCNR services are

- Call completion service requests, which result in the monitoring of User B
- Notification of User B availability, which causes User A to be recalled
- Cancellation of the service request
- Actual call completion with an association of the original call

The use of these components is not limited in the CCBS and CCNR supplementary services only. They can also be powerful tools used in the building of various new applications and are also ideal for implementation within intelligent endpoints.

In addition, it is, of course, also possible to implement call completion services in the gatekeeper. In this case, it is assumed that the protocol between the gatekeeper and the endpoint is either stimulus- or HTTP-based. In fact, such an implementation would be quite comparable to PBX and ISDN implementations.

Call Offering—H.450.10

Call Offering is a supplementary service which, on request from the calling user, enables a call to be offered to a busy user and enables the calling user to wait until the call is accepted.

Because the called user is involved in another call, an indication of the offered call is given. The called user can then do one of the following:

- Accept the call after making the necessary resources available—for example, by releasing the other call or placing it on hold
- Reject and disconnect the offered call
- Ignore the offered call

After the necessary resources become available, the call is connected normally to the called user.

Invocation and Operation

Figure 9.12 shows the steps involved in the invocation of the Call Offering supplementary service.

If the called User B is involved in another call, a call attempt from User A is immediately released because User B is busy. However, if both Endpoints A

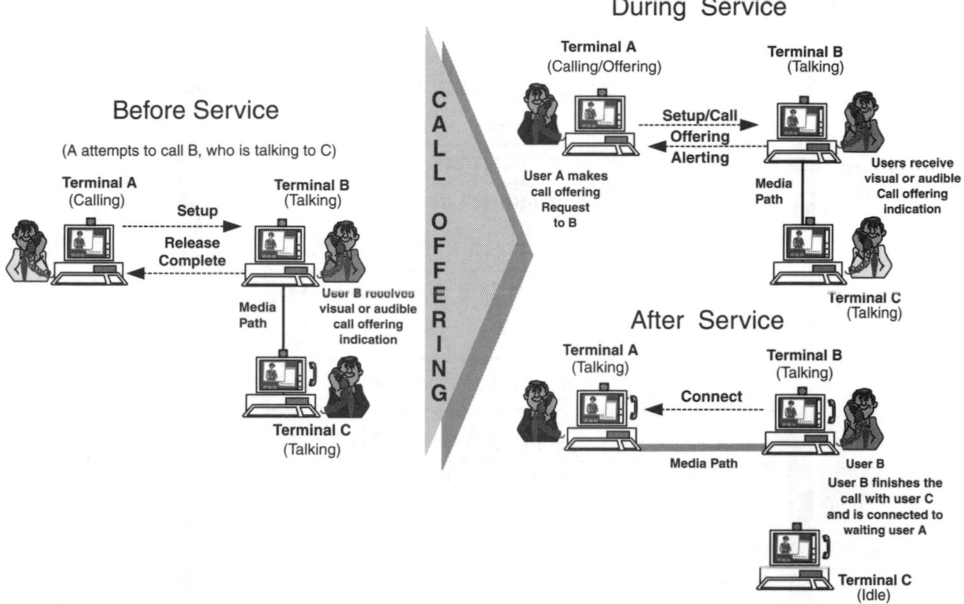

Figure 9.12 An H.450.10 Call Offering supplementary service.

and B support call offering and the calling User A is authorized to use this feature, then User A can invoke call offering.

There are several methods of invoking Call Offering depending on the implementation of the calling endpoint (and its gatekeeper):

- A calling user can invoke Call Offering manually after entering a busy condition. This can happen, for example, by pressing a feature key on a telephone.
- The calling endpoint will, after informing the calling User A about the busy condition, automatically invoke Call Offering unless the calling user clears the call within a certain time period.
- The calling user can request a Call Offering invocation as part of the initial call setup, assuming that the user manual acts before the call initiation.
- The calling Endpoint A can request a Call Offering invocation as part of the initial call setup on either all or specific calls.

Signaling Protocol

The Call Offering supplementary service as previously described can be invoked manually by the user or automatically by Endpoint A on behalf of

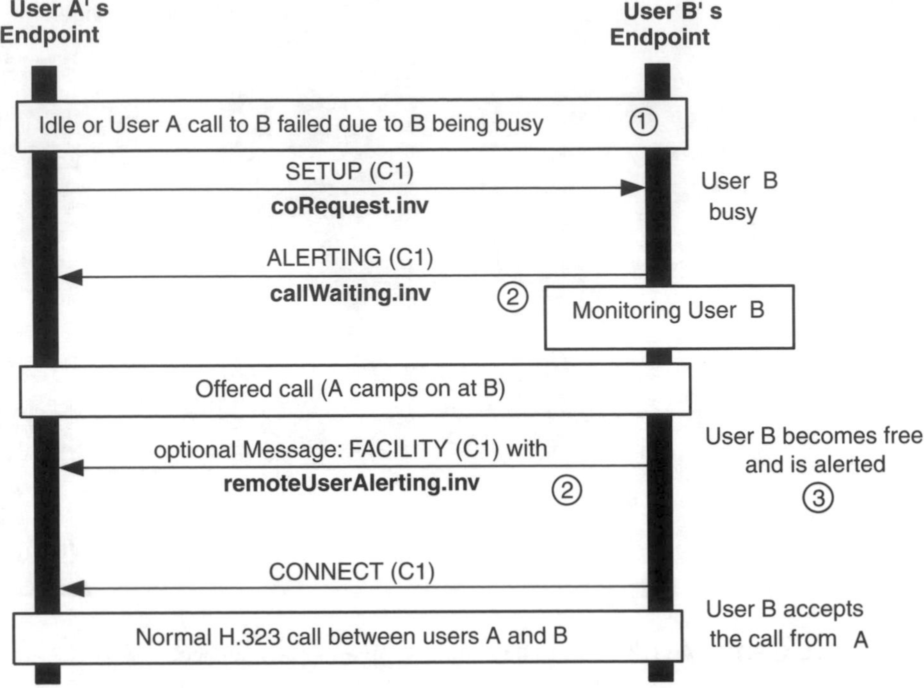

Note ① RELEASE COMPLETE received
- with Cause #17 user busy
- or with releaseCompleteReason *inConference*

Note ② In case of Call Offering (H.450.6), callWaiting.invoke may also be sent in a PROGRESS message (e.g., due to interworking). In such a case, a normal ALERTING message is sent instead of the FACILITY.

Note ③ User B becomes free, for example, by releasing another call or by putting another call on hold.

Figure 9.13 The signaling flow of the H.450.10 Call Offering supplementary service.

the user. Automatic invocation is often used, for example, when an attendant extends a call to a busy station or if a station transfers a call to a busy station. The signaling protocol remains the same in all of these cases. The only difference is whether or not a call attempt was previously made.

Figure 9.13 shows the signaling flow of the Call Offering supplementary service.

A Call Offering request is sent in the SETUP message using the coRequest.Invoke APDU. This causes Endpoint B to place the incoming call in a call waiting state. Therefore, the call does not enter a busy state, but is alerted. Consequently, an ALERTING message containing the callWaiting.Invoke APDU is sent.

Upon a successful Call Offering invocation, the called user receives an indication of the offered call (e.g., a call offering tone in the audio channel). The calling user is then advised that Call Offering has been invoked. Additional information that normally accompanies an incoming H.323 call indication can be optionally provided to the called user.

Logical channels are established the same as in a basic call and are available from B to A after the ALERTING message is received. This enables the calling party to receive an audible announcement from User B while in waiting state. The presence of an announcement or audible tone is indicated by a progress indicator information element in the ALERTING message. It directs Endpoint A to connect the B-to-A logical channel to User A instead of giving local tones.

Call Offering is completed when any of the following occurs:

- The called user starts alerting.
- The called user accepts the call.
- The calling user releases the offered call.
- The called user rejects (i.e., releases) the offered call.

As soon as the called user accepts the waiting call and starts alerting, a FACILITY message containing the remoteUserAlerting.Invoke APDU is sent to Endpoint A. As a result, User A is given an appropriate indication. The procedure continues as a normal basic call, and when User B answers the alerting call, a CONNECT message is then sent to User A.

Call Offering Performed by Gatekeeper

Figure 9.14 shows the signaling flow when the gatekeepers of the calling and called party perform Call Offering on behalf of the endpoints.

It is assumed that the supplementary service signaling between the gatekeeper and the endpoint can only be performed by one of the following:

- By means of the stimulus signaling as defined in H.323 Annex L (as shown in Figure 9.14)
- By means of HTTP-based service control as defined in H.323 Annex K
- By means of H.248 Annex G-based stimulus protocol

As a result, the terminal Endpoints A and B do not need to be able to handle the H.450.10 Call Offering supplementary service or its components. The gatekeepers or feature servers instead act on behalf of Endpoints A and B.

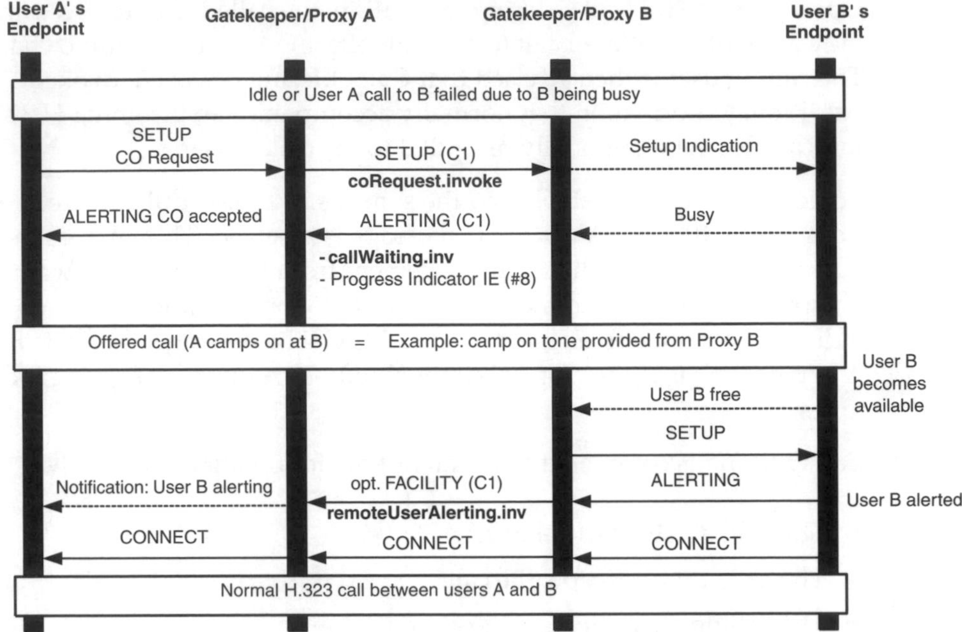

Figure 9.14 The H.450 Call Offering performed by Gatekeeper.

Conclusion of the H.450.10 Call Offering Services

The H.450.10 Call Offering supplementary service consists of three functional components:

- A Call Offering service request, which results in the call entering a CW state at the called User B
- A notification in the ALERTING message that the call is in a waiting state
- A notification that User B is available and is being alerted

However, these components are not used only in the Call Offering supplementary service scenario. They are also used in building new applications and services. Due to their simplicity, they are ideal for implementation in intelligent endpoints.

Call Intrusion—H.450.11

Call Intrusion (CI) is a supplementary service which, on request from the served User A, enables the served user to establish communication with a busy called User B by breaking into an established call between User B and a third user named User C. It can be requested by a served user which has the appropriate authorization.

Call Intrusion includes the following three modes of invocation:

- *Normal Call Intrusion.* On successful intrusion, the calling User A is connected with User B, and the third User C is either 1) put automatically on hold, or 2) connected in an intrusion conference with both A and B. Whether a hold or conference mode is invoked depends on the implementation options supported by Endpoint B.
- *Call Intrusion by Forced Release.* On successful intrusion, the calling User A is connected with User B, and the third User C is automatically released.
- *Call Intrusion by Silent Monitoring.* This type of intrusion enables User A to enter and listen to the call between both B and C.

Invocation and Operation

The different modes of Call Intrusion supplementary service operate in the following ways:

Normal Call Intrusion by Hold. In this case, User B is automatically connected with User A, and User C is split from User B. For this reason, the endpoint of User B automatically invokes Call Hold against User C prior to the establishment of communication between User B and the served user. In addition, User C can be provided with an indication that Call Intrusion has been invoked.

Normal Call Intrusion by Conference. User A automatically enters into a conference with Users B and C. Upon successful invocation of Call Intrusion, the served User A, User B, and User C are merged into a conference. As an option, B and C can be provided with a Call Intrusion warning notification and/or a warning tone for a short time period before the conference connection type is established. *Note:* This requires three-party conferencing capability within Endpoint B.

Call Intrusion by Silent Monitoring. User A enters Silent Monitoring of the call between Users B and C, whom are not informed about Call Intrusion taking place. *Note:* This feature also requires three-party conferencing capability within Endpoint B.

Call Intrusion by Forced Release of User C. This intrusion type can be requested by a served user, who is authorized appropriately. A served User A can request and cause a Forced Release of the established call at the busy called User B. A Forced Release may either be invoked initially or after a conference or held type of Call Intrusion has been successfully invoked.

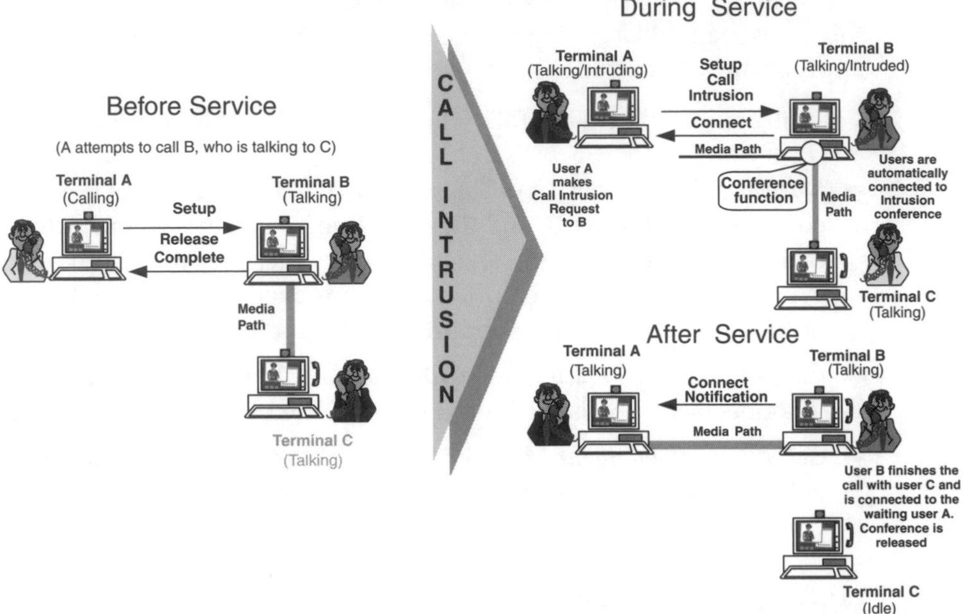

Figure 9.15 The H.450.11 Call Intrusion supplementary service.

Call Intrusion Levels. An intrusion request is accepted if only the served user has a higher *Call Intrusion Capability Level (CICL)* than the *Call Intrusion Protection Level (CIPL)* of both Users B and C. The CICL is assigned a value ranging from one (lowest capability) to three (highest capability) and CIPL is assigned a value ranging from zero (no protection) to three (total protection).

Figure 9.15 shows the steps involved in the invocation of the Call Intrusion supplementary service by means of a conference.

In the same way as Call Offering, Call Intrusion supplementary service can also be invoked manually by the user or automatically by Endpoint A on the user's behalf. Automatic invocation is often used, for example, when an attendant extends a call to a busy station in order to announce an important incoming call. The signaling protocol remains in all these cases the same. The only difference is whether or not a call attempt was previously made.

Signaling Protocol

Figure 9.16 shows the signaling flow of a Call Intrusion supplementary service for a case where the intrusion phase executes as conference.

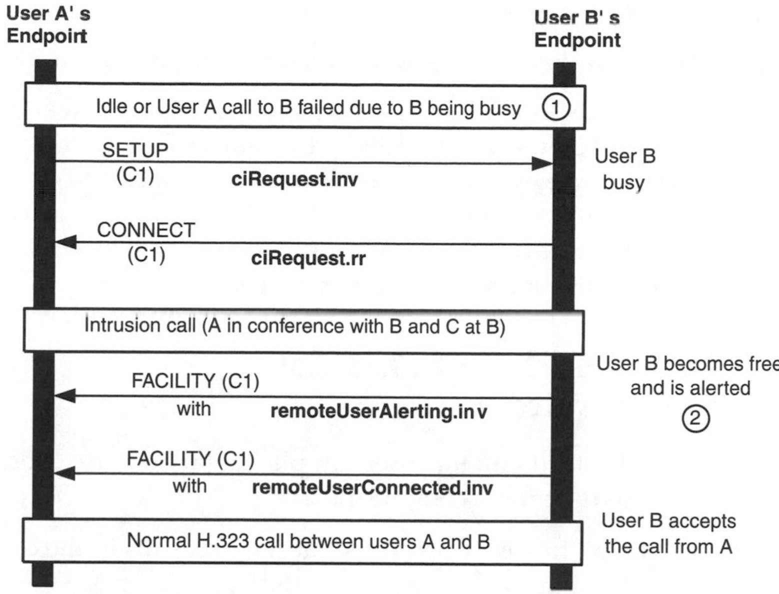

Note ① RELEASE COMPLETE received
- with Cause #17 user busy
- or with releaseCompleteReason inConference

Note ② User B becomes free, for example, by releasing another call or by putting another call on hold.

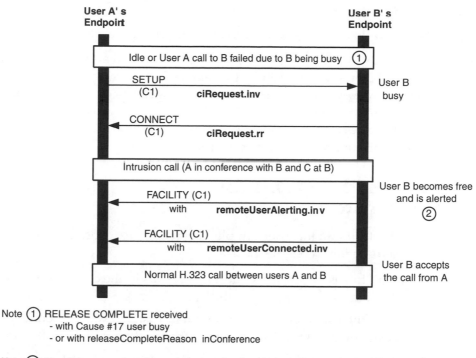

Figure 9.16 A signaling flow of an H.450.11 Call Intrusion.

The Call Intrusion request is sent in the SETUP message using the ciRequest.Invoke APDU, which causes Endpoint B to place the incoming call into call waiting state. Therefore, the call will not enter a busy state, but it enters into conference with the existing call.

On successful invocation of Call Intrusion, the Users B and C receive an indication of the intruding call (e.g., a call intrusion tone in the audio channel). The calling user receives a CONNECT message with the ciRequest.returnResult APDU as an indication that Call Intrusion has been invoked. Additional information that normally accompanies an incoming H.323 call indication can optionally be provided to the called user.

Logical channels are established the same way as in a basic call and are available between Users B and A after the CONNECT message is received.

Call Intrusion is completed when any of the following occurs:

- The called user starts alerting.
- The called user accepts the call.

- The calling user releases the call.
- The called user rejects (i.e., releases) the intruding call.

As soon as the called user accepts the intruding call and starts alerting, a FACILITY message containing the remoteUserAlerting.Invoke APDU is sent to Endpoint A. User A, as a result, is given an appropriate indication. When User B answers the alerting call, a FACILITY message containing the remoteUserConnected.Invoke APDU is sent to User A. After this point, the procedure continues as a normal basic call.

Conclusion of the H.450.11 Call Intrusion Service

The H.450.10 Call Intrusion supplementary service consists of the following several functional components:

- A Call Intrusion service request that results in the call entering a Call Intrusion conference state at the called User B
- A Call Intrusion service request with intrusion levels that enable a Forced Release of User C and an immediate connection with User B
- A notification that the call is in a intrusion state in the CONNECT message
- A notification that User B is available and is being alerted
- A notification that User B has answered the call

These components are not only used in the Call Offering supplementary service scenario, they can also be used in building new applications and services. Due to their simplicity they are ideal for implementation in intelligent endpoints.

References

H.225 ITU-T Recommendation H.225.0 Version 4, *Call signalling protocols and media stream packetization for packet-based multimedia communications systems*, H. 225, November 2000.

H.245 ITU-T Recommendation H.245 Version 5, *Control protocol for multimedia communication*, H.245, February 2000.

H.323 ITU-T Recommendation H.323 Version 4, *Packet-based multimedia communications systems*, H.323, November 2000.

H.323 Annex L ITU-T Recommendation H.323 Annex L, *Stimulus Protocol for H.323*, H.323 Annex L (Work in progress), November 2000.

H.450.1 ITU-T Recommendation H.450.1, *Generic functional protocol for the support of supplementary services in H.323*, H.450.1, February 1998.

H.450.4 ITU-T Recommendation H.450.4, *Call Hold Supplementary Service for H.323*, H.450.4, May 1999.

H.450.6 ITU-T Recommendation H.450.6, *Call Waiting Supplementary Service for H.323*, H.450.6, May 1999.

H.450.7 ITU-T Recommendation H.450.7, *Message Waiting Supplementary Service for H.323*, H.450.7, May 1999.

H.450.9 ITU-T Recommendation H.450.9, *Call Completion on Busy and No Reply Supplementary Service for H.323*, H.450.9, November 1999.

H.450.10 ITU-T Recommendation H.450.10, *Call Offering Supplementary Service for H.323*, H.450.10 (Work in progress), 2001.

H.450.11 ITU-T Recommendation H.450.11, *Call Intrusion Supplementary Service for H.323*, H.450.11 (Work in progress), 2001.

ISO/IEC 11582 ISO/IEC 11582, *Information technology—Telecommunications and information exchange between systems—Private Integrated Services Network—Specification, functional model and information flows—Generic functional protocol for the support of supplementary services*, ISO/IEC 11582 Edition 1, June 1995.

ISO/IEC 13870 ISO/IEC 13870, *Information technology—Telecommunications and information exchange between systems— Private Integrated Services Network—Specification, functional model and information flows— Call Completion on Busy and No Reply supplementary service*, ISO/IEC 13870 Edition 1, November 1995.

ISO/IEC 14841 ISO/IEC 14841, *Information technology—Telecommunications and information exchange between systems—Private Integrated Services Network—Specification, functional model and information flows—Call Offering supplementary service*, ISO/IEC 14841 Edition 1, September 1996.

ISO/IEC 14845 ISO/IEC 14845, *Information technology—Telecommunications and information exchange between systems—Private Integrated Services Network—Interexchange signaling protocol—Call Intrusion supplementary service*, 1995, ISO/IEC 14845 Edition 1, October 1996.

ISO/IEC 15505 SO/IEC 15505, *Information Technology—Private Integrated Services Network (PISN)—Specification, Functional Model and Information Flows—Message Waiting Indication Supplementary Service (MWISD)*, ISO/IEC 15505 Edition 2, March 2000.

ISO/IEC 15506—ISO/IEC 15506, *Information Technology—Private Integrated Services Network (PISN)—Interexchange Signaling Protocol—Message Waiting Indication Supplementary Service (QSIG-MWI)*, ISO/IEC 15506 Edition 2, March 2000.

Problems

1. Add Do-Not-Disturb features to Figure 9.1
2. Describe how Call Waiting supplementary service can be implemented in the gatekeeper. Explain the required function split (i.e., the tasks of the gatekeeper and the endpoints), and the resulting protocol information flows.
3. Explain why the MWI deactivation must be done by the same server that sent the corresponding MWI activation message.
4. Call completion services for unsuccessful calls contain several functional components. Describe three new applications that make use of these components.
5. Describe protocol requirements and signaling flow diagrams for implementation of CCBS service in the gatekeeper. Handle the originating and terminating sides separately.
6. Describe a hunting group process in a gatekeeper by means of a flow chart diagram.

CHAPTER 10

Stimulus Signaling

This chapter describes stimulus signaling and why it is necessary and applicable in the IP telephony environment. We discuss the architecture of stimulus signaling by defining the building blocks and the programming model. We focus not only on the H.323 Annex L stimulus signaling between telephones and their feature server, but also on the H.248 stimulus protocols for the handling of stimulus signaling between a *media gateway* and its *media gateway controllers* (MGCs). Finally, examples are given of call scenarios involving stimulus services.

General Information

Stimulus signaling is a term most often used in telephony systems, although it is a general mechanism that can be applied to many kinds of systems. The goal of stimulus signaling is to define the terminal's functionality in such a manner that the terminal's software does not have to be changed when features are added to the system controlling that particular terminal. Thus, the terminal must have a rich set of user interface functions supporting various types of input and output methods. These functions should support in such a manner that the system does not know how the information was actually entered—by the user or indicated to them. A telephony feature then could be accessed several ways—by pressing a button labeled with its meaning, by touching a soft display key, by entering a key sequence, or by speaking a command to the system via its voice recognition capabilities. In the same manner, the system can also provide information to the user by means of a display, visual indicators, audible tone signals, voice recording, or other means.

For example, some protocol variants simply transmit to the system the coordinates of the depressed keys, letting the system decide their meanings. Thus, the key maps are required to be defined in the system software. Although it is very simple to use, this method requires the system programmer to know the terminal key layout in advance. The same applies to displays and indicators. For this reason, a stimulus protocol, which is going to be used in various types of terminals made by many manufacturers, needs to contain a sufficiently high level of definition and handling of the user interface elements and actions. One terminal type from one manufacturer can then interoperate with a system made by another without any changes on either side.

A common characteristic of stimulus signaling is that the terminal is not aware of the semantics of the features it is used for. Instead, the controlling system executes the software functions for the features.

The main advantage of the stimulus signaling is that terminals do not need to be changed or reloaded with new software when new features are assigned to feature buttons, feature indicators (e.g., LEDs), and to the display. In telephony applications, the stimulus method enables the network service provider to implement new supplementary services for the terminals without remote software downloads or local maintenance actions on the user's premises. This feature can be implemented in a feature server which can be collocated, for example, in a *gatekeeper* (GK).

Variants of Stimulus Signaling

Because there are several ways of splitting the functions between the terminal and the network side of the system, there are also many flavors of stimulus signaling. We discuss briefly the following three main categories:

- *Keypad Stimulus.* All key depressions are sent to the system as characters or character strings. Display is usually treated as one line. Function keys are just programmed with key strings. For example, a keypad stimulus protocol is used in the European variant of the ISDN DSS1 protocol.
- *Pure Stimulus.* Key depressions are sent as key coordinates to the system and the system modifies the status of the indicators by directly addressing the indicator coordinates. None of the keys or indicators, consequently, have any meaning, but must be assigned a function by the system. Many PBX manufacturers use this method in the protocol of digital phones.

- *Feature Key Management.* The terminal has predefined functions or function blocks, such as Keypad, Display, Feature Keys, and Feature Indicators. Thus, it contains the Keypad stimulus as a subset, but additionally enables a functional definition of input and output actions. In the simplest variant of feature key management, the functions of the keys and indicators as well as the size and capabilities of the display are fixed. However, the functions can also be downloaded by the system. The beauty of feature key management is that it enables individual customization by means of the system software, and it also takes advantage of the mass production of the terminals.

Centralized versus Distributed Stimulus Call Control

Stimulus signaling can be implemented in various ways depending on the amount of functions executed locally in the terminal and in a centralized server. A good example is handling of a line.

Opening of the line. In ordinary telephones the line is automatically opened when the handset is lifted or when the speaker key is pressed. The line is similarly released when the handset is laid down or when the speaker key released. On the protocol level, this is typically realized in two quite different ways:

- The handset and speaker key positions are transmitted to the system using the stimulus protocol after the system performs the subsequent actions toward the terminal. The terminal is a full slave of the system. The plain old telephones systems (POTS) operate in this manner. Consequently, the terminals can only implement very few features independently of the telephone system. Examples of such features are speed-dial keys, local clock, and answering machine. The rest of the features, such as call forwarding and call transfer, are functions of the switching system.
- The terminal independently opens and closes the line towards the system (or the network) and consequently provides for its own call control. This requires a functional protocol for the attachment of the terminal to the network. Examples are Q.931 in the ISDN and H.323 in IP telephony.

Provisioning of features. In each of the previous cases, the telephone sends a signaling message containing the key identification to the feature server, which then executes the required feature actions. The actual meaning of the buttons and the subsequent series of interactions with the user are controlled by the feature server. The stimulus protocol enables the feature server to write to the display of the terminal, change the state of the telephone's feature indicators, or switch audible guidance tones and announcements on and off.

H.323 Stimulus Signaling

The essential requirement for an H.323-based stimulus protocol is to provide a set of capabilities that allow supporting endpoints access to a potentially unlimited set of supplementary services. There are many benefits to such a protocol, such as allowing endpoints to remain relatively lightweight in terms of CPU processing power and memory requirements. The ability to support a large variety of supplementary services and features is a requirement for many telephony service providers. It enables them to implement services that can be accessed from any of the stimulus terminals, regardless of the underlying technology vendor.

An associated requirement is a high level of interoperability between equipment from different vendors, which requires a versatile standards-based solution.

At the same time, equipment vendors require that the standard enable them to support *Value Added Services* (VAS) highlighting their own products. This can be achieved using a proprietary means, but then the interoperability between vendors is compromised. In some cases, such a penalty is acceptable or even desirable, yet this is often not the case, especially from the perspective of the service providers.

The goal, therefore, is to define a standard that is sufficiently flexible enough to support all (or most) of the services that a vendor wishes to supply.

The Goals

The goals of the stimulus protocol are

- To have support for arbitrary (standard- and manufacturer-specific) supplementary services.
- To support feature provisioning from different service providers simultaneously to the same users.
- To have interoperability of services between a Feature Server and any stimulus-based endpoint.
- To have backwards compatibility with the endpoints using H.323 (version 2 or later).

This protocol achieves these goals by incorporating significant portions of the protocol described in Recommendation H.248. Whereas H.248 describes a *pure stimulus* model of endpoint control with one and only one controller per endpoint, the H.323 stimulus is an add-on to the H.225 basic call. The result is a hybrid of both stimulus and functional call control of H.225.

These stimulus services are typically controlled by a functional entity that is collocated in a gatekeeper, a proxy, or other network entity. In the following text, the term *Feature Server* generically designates any network entity providing stimulus-based features for the endpoints.

Relationship of H.323 stimulus to H.248. H.248 was developed for control of media gateways, implying a tight relationship between the controller and the media gateways. Endpoints (e.g., telephones and residential gateways) can be included as controlled devices and are treated as single line media gateways. However, they are tied to exactly one controller, which provides all connection control, features, and services to the H.248 endpoints. In H.248, a user subscribes to features from only one controller at a time.

Relationship of H.323 stimulus to HTTP. H.323 Annex K enables third party control of an H.323 call based on a separate hypertext connection (using HTTP) for user interaction. There is no fixed capability set for the user interface—various types of text formats, images, and sounds are utilized dynamically as registered MIME types. The service provider (the HTTP server) is responsible for the mapping between HTTP events and call control actions (H.450 or other messages) for supplementary services, so the H.323 endpoint is unaware of the HTTP application. The service provider can be associated with the local gatekeeper, the remote endpoint, or remote gatekeeper within a call.

Relationship of H.323 stimulus to H.450. Because a stimulus terminal does not perform H.450 supplementary services, the feature server or gatekeeper is responsible for providing a proxy function for the handling of the H.450 procedures over the network on the terminal's behalf. In this case, the feature server becomes an endpoint for all H.450 operations and implements all supplementary services and the state machines involved. The interaction with the user happens in the telephone user interface, which the gatekeeper can control via H.323 stimulus signaling.

Programming Model

The feature key management extensions operate in conjunction with the call signaling protocol as defined in Recommendation H.225.0. Therefore, the media control happens using the existing means defined for H.323 terminals.

For example, the gatekeeper-initiated pause and reroute procedure can be used to mute media channels or to reconfigure media channels (e.g., to cease transmission to one address and resume transmission to another).

The H.323 stimulus signaling can be used in conjunction with both the direct and gatekeeper-routed signaling model of H.323. Figures 10.1 and 10.2 are examples of corresponding H.323 stimulus terminal network scenarios.

The feature key management extensions provide mechanisms for the support of supplementary services that relate to existing H.323 calls or are independent of any existing H.323 calls. In performing a supplementary service function, whether using call independent- or call related-mechanisms, the terminal and a feature server use the feature key management procedures which are described next.

Annex L describes a framework that enables delivery of services to both H.323- and H.248-based systems, by permitting a high degree of commonality between an Annex L Feature Server and an H.248 *Media Gateway Controller* (MGC). This framework enables the reuse of H.248-based packages in H.323-based systems and enables a Feature Server to control the user interface capabilities of a stimulus terminal, such as the following:

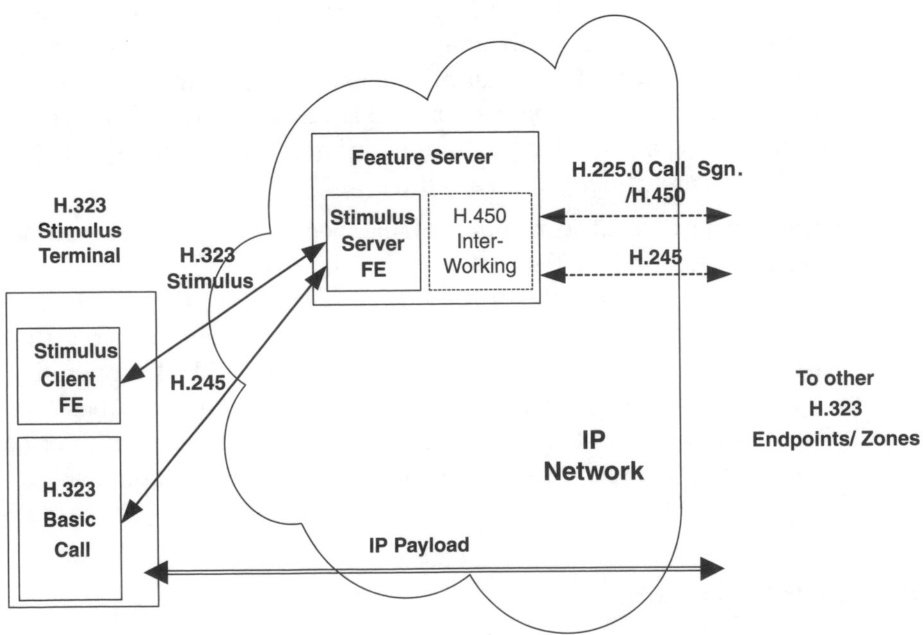

Figure 10.1 Stimulus signaling in conjunction with a direct signaling model.

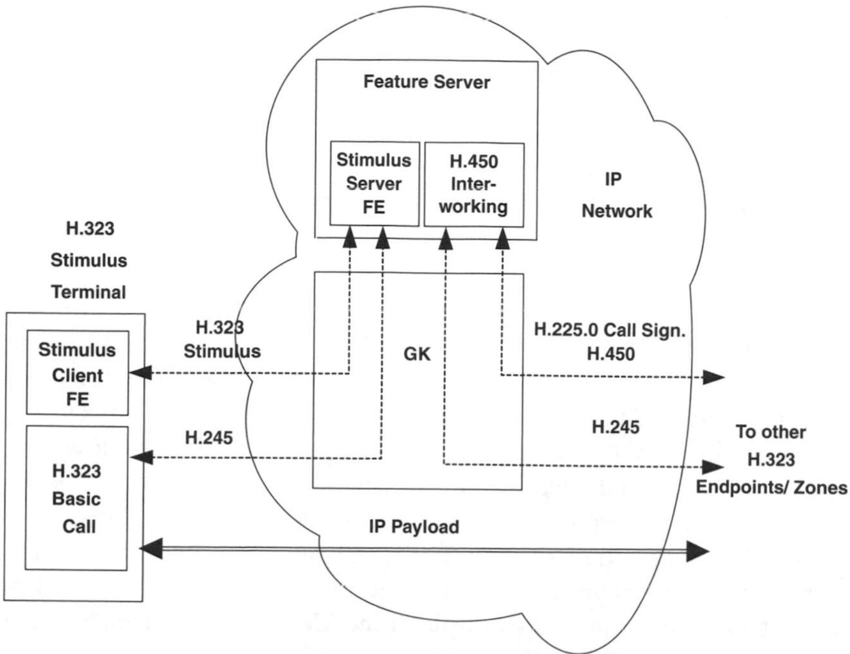

Figure 10.2 Stimulus signaling in conjunction with a gatekeeper-routed signaling model.

- Write to a text display
- Provide hardware-independent indications to the endpoint, enabling the endpoint to control its own indicators, such as message waiting or line lamps
- Receive user input such as digits, text, and special keys (e.g., hookswitch and function keys)
- Assign functions to soft keys and into an endpoint resident directory
- Request an application of specific tones
- Specify tones dynamically

Annex L terminals have the previous control capabilities in common with H.248 terminals. These two types of terminals differ only by how they manage the media streams and the association of one or more calls. In H.248, the calls exist only as stimulus *contexts*, whereas in H.323 Annex L, each call is established using the normal call establishment procedures of H.225.0.

H.323 Annex L stimulus protocol is suggested for, but is not restricted to, the H.323 Annex F *Simple Endpoint Types* (SET).

Functional Units

An H.323 stimulus terminal can support some or all of the following functional units:

- *Audio unit* consisting of a handset, a hands-free unit, a headset, or a microphone and speaker. Associated with the audio unit are also transducers, codecs, DTMF tone generators, and a key feedback tone generators cadences list.
- *Function keys* may be assigned a function based on their administration or by some other means, yet the feature server holds the meaning of those feature keys. Events associated with common telephone function keys are defined in a generic manner to allow, for example, line keys to be implemented without specific knowledge of the physical layout in a stimulus terminal's feature server l. Function keys have well known names—for example, Hookswitch, Hold, or Handsfree. Function keys can also be assigned an identifier by a feature server and returned by a terminal as key events. Function keys with an associated indicator share the same identifier. For example, if the identifier for a function key is "Call Forward," then the indicator identifier is also "Call Forward."
- *Indicators* could be, for example, status lamps associated with the feature key, or could use some other method to indicate the indicator state. They are defined in a generic manner, so a feature server does not need to know the physical layout of the stimulus terminal. Indicators can have well known identifiers, such as message waiting, hold, line active, and so on, and are as alterable as the Function Keys.
- *Text Display* has the following characteristics: 1) it is character-oriented, 2) it supports UTF-8 and Unicode character sets for multiple languages, 3) the text display can be written and controlled by such messages as Write a string, Move the cursor, Clear the display, and so on.
- *Soft keys,* a combination of a function key and a display element that shares some behavior of each. Soft keys are dynamically configured—based on the current call state and application context controlling the stimulus terminal—by a feature server.
- *Keypad* is used to represent a standard ten digit telephone keypad plus the *, #, A, B, C, and D keys.

Messages and Actions

The functional units of a stimulus terminal are controlled by stimulus *information elements* (IE) which are contained in the H.225.0 call control messages (e.g., SETUP, ALERTING, CONNECT, INFORMATION, and

RELEASE COMPLETE). Each message performs specific actions for each of these units.

The feature key management extensions include the following elements:

Expression of device capabilities. The endpoint describes its capabilities for display, length, and character sets; fixed feature keys, for example, transfer, conference, drop, hold, and mute; flexible feature keys (a gatekeeper holds the meaning of the feature key) and soft keys, which may be assigned a function based on administration or some other means; feature indicators, which can be status lamps associated with the feature key or some other method to indicate the state of the indicator; "switch hook," speakerphone; and call progress indicator, for example, a ringer.

Function assignment. Includes labels for feature indicators and feature keys.

Feature activation. Indicates the function selected (e.g., switch hook flash or fixed function).

Feature indication. Includes providing call progress indication. This could include blink rates or colors for status lamps.

Audit capabilities. The endpoint provides the current state of selectors and indicators, open media channels, and so on.

Bulk updates. The gatekeeper/gateway orders an endpoint to place the resources into a specified state.

Protocol Framework

Annex L terminals use the standard H.323 mechanisms for registration and signaling channel establishment. Normal H.225.0 call signaling is used for call establishment and termination. Media control can use the H.323 fast connect procedures, which include repeated fastStart, or can optionally use H.245 signaling, which uses the procedures described in H.245, H.323, and its Annexes.

Stimulus signaling capabilities of Annex L Endpoints are specified in packages as in H.248. For example, an Annex L terminal can be described by a basic set package, a keypad package, an alerting package, a key package, and a display package. Additional packages can be included, permitting the modification of operational parameters and/or the collection of performance statistics.

H.225.0 Call Signaling is the most suitable transport for the stimulus protocol. It enables a Feature Server to be placed in any H.323 endpoint, but can also collocate it with a gatekeeper.

In the special case where a Feature Server is collocated with a gatekeeper and provides access to certain call-independent services, it can be argued that the stimulus protocol should use H.225.0 RAS messaging for transport. However, use of RAS signaling for transport is not suitable because it lacks reliable transport mechanisms. Additionally, it would limit the provisioning of features to GK. Annex L consequently uses only H.225.0 call signaling. It provides the same functionality as RAS, yet has the additional benefits of reliability of signaling and location independence for the Feature Server.

Annex L entities encapsulate the H.248 messages in the StimulusControl field, which can be carried in any H.225.0 call signaling message.

When an endpoint registers with a gatekeeper, the gatekeeper can indicate an alias for the Feature Server in the featureServerAlias field of the RCF message. This alias is used by the endpoint as the destinationInfo in an ARQ and as the destinationAddress in a SETUP message, when originating a call where no other destination information exists. Otherwise, normal H.323 rules for specifying these fields apply. Use of this alias address enables the gatekeeper to associate or route the call to the Feature Server. The Feature Server can then coordinate overlap dialing, or other activities, as required.

This enables the two following models of interaction between a Feature Server and an Annex L Endpoint:

- The Feature Server is present in the call signaling path of all H.225.0 call signaling messages for all calls originating and terminating on an Annex L Endpoint.
- A separate call signaling connection between the Annex L Endpoint and the Feature Server is established only when a feature is invoked.

For gatekeeper-routed calls, the gatekeeper is between the Feature Server and the endpoint.

The Use of Call Reference

A feature server can respond to the feature activation request in several, specific service ways. The stimulus terminal can handle one or more active connections at a time (transactions identified by a call reference). H.248 capabilities, which are used to control the H.248 stimulus context, do not apply to the H.323 calls. Instead, stimulus transactions, which are initiated by a feature server and are related to an existing call, are exchanged using the call reference of any existing call between the endpoint and the Feature Server (for example, to invoke a consultation hold).

If no such call reference exists, a temporary signaling connection is created by using the H.323 call establishment procedures with the H.225.0 Setup-UUIE conferenceGoal specified as create, and a Q.931 *call reference value* (CRV) and a H.225.0 conferenceId chosen according to the rules of H.225.0. Both the terminal and the feature server can initiate the connection. Once established, the connection can be kept for a longer time period or can be released if no activity exists.

For stimulus activities associated with an active call with the desired Feature Server in the call signaling path, any appropriate H.225.0 call signaling message can be used to communicate between a Feature Server and an endpoint. If no call establishment or release message is due to be sent, an INFORMATION message is used.

Table 10.1 shows the *Call References* (CR) chosen to be used, and their preferred choice of stimulus service.

Encapsulation of H.248

Annex L encapsulation can include any commands defined in H.248.

Use of the following H.248 descriptors is not applicable to Annex L entities—ModemDescriptor, MuxDescriptor, MediaDescriptor, TerminationStateDescriptor, StreamDescriptor, TopologyDescriptor. Use of other descriptors is application-specific and can be limited through the definition of appropriate packages.

All Annex L-related signaling uses the StimulusControl field in the H323-UU-PDU element. Use of Annex L by an endpoint is inferred from this structure's presence in the first call signaling message sent by the endpoint to the feature server. If no H.248 message is encapsulated in this structure, then all of its optional contained fields can be omitted.

H.248 signaling is either binary- (H.248 Annex A) or text-based (H.248 Annex B). The default is binary encoding. The presence of the isText field indicates that text encoding is used for the H.248 descriptors in the StimulusControl

Table 10.1 The Use of Call Reference

TYPE OF STIMULUS SERVICE	NO CALL EXISTS	CALL EXISTS
Call independent	Non-Call-related SETUP with the new CR	Non-Call-related SETUP with the new CR (or active CR)
Call related	(Error)	Active CR
Indeterminate	Non-Call-related SETUP with the new CR	Active CR

structure. Because Annex L endpoints can pick up the form of encoding they want to support, the Feature Servers must be capable of supporting both forms of encoding.

The H.248 message is encapsulated in the h248Message field of the following ASN.1 structure:

```
StimulusControl ::= SEQUENCE
{
   nonStandard     NonStandardParameter OPTIONAL,
   isText          NULL OPTIONAL,
   h248Message     OCTET STRING OPTIONAL,
   ...
}
```

An overview of the H.248 message contents and structure is provided later in the H.248 section of this chapter.

Guidelines for the Use of Stimulus Protocol

Due to the nature of the stimulus protocol, there are no strict procedures and message sequences one must follow. Instead, the terminal is controlled by messages which comprise a "toolbox" by means of the desired transaction sequence that the terminal user created. Nevertheless, there are a number of rules and restrictions which must be taken into consideration. These rules and restrictions and some additional, helpful hints are described in the following text.

Handling of feature keys and local keys. When supplementary services are controlled in H.323 terminals by the stimulus procedures, they do not need to retain knowledge of feature states. For example, a *hold key* does not directly cause mute function in the terminal. Each feature key depression results in a message being sent to the feature server. It is, of course, allowed that the terminal has additionally local functions and related keys, such as redial keys. These must be fully implemented locally in the terminal and they do not cause stimulus message transactions.

Return of feature indication. A feature server can return one or more feature indications in an INFORMATION message or any other call control message. The feature indicator may or may not have the same function key value as the value present in the original feature activation request.

Prompting for further information. A feature server can prompt the user for more information. This prompting may be done via the display, audible tones, or announcements.

Acknowledgments. Due to the nature of the stimulus protocol, there are no explicit acknowledgements of the requested features. An activation of a specific feature key (such as a Hold key or a Call Forwarding key) often causes the related feature indicator (e.g., an LED next to the key) to be turned on. However, no rule states that such indicators exist for all features or that they can be used as an acknowledgment for successful service invocation. In many cases the response is implicit, such as the audible tone inherently caused by the execution of the requested service.

Return of audible tones or display. Other network elements (gatekeepers, servers, gateways, remote endpoints, and so on) along the call path can also return any combination of audible tones or displays, in addition to the responses provided by the feature server.

Responses during error conditions. When an error condition exists, for example, in the execution of the requested supplementary service, a feature server can do the following:

Respond with one or more of the following actions:

- Return a feature indication
- Prompt for further information via audible tones and/or display
- Provide an implicit response

Ignore the feature activation request (not respond at all).

Clear the appropriate existing calls in conjunction with the previous actions and send an appropriate Cause information element in the RELEASE COMPLETE message.

Feature indications independent of a feature request. A feature server can choose to send feature indication information at any time independent of the call status. If more than one indicator is to be updated, multiple feature indications can be included in any message. An example of this use is an update of a Message Waiting Lamp when a message is received in a server.

Deactivation procedures. When the feature server is explicitly deactivating a feature, either of the following two methods may be used:

- Sending a feature activation request with the same feature identifier—some features may be toggled on and off
- Sending a feature activation request with a different feature identifier as a deactivator for that service

Sending multiple feature activation requests. If a sequence of feature activation requests is received rapidly in a single or in multiple messages, the feature server will process all the feature activation requests in the order they are received.

Sending multiple feature indication requests. If a sequence of feature indication requests is received rapidly in a single or in multiple messages, the stimulus terminal processes all the feature indication requests in the order they are received.

Feature interworking. When the terminal makes a connection over the network to a feature server, the feature server performs the interworking functions for the interaction of the stimulus procedures with other protocols. For example, this can include the following tasks:

- Interworking with H.450 functional supplementary service protocol. Because a stimulus terminal does not perform H.450 supplementary services, the feature server is responsible for providing a proxy function to handle the H.450 procedures over the network on behalf of the terminal.
- Interworking with gateways controlled by H.248 media gateway control protocol.
- Providing the interworking with SCN telephony protocols (such as those used by analog and ISDN networks) when the feature server is integrated with a gateway to it.

Examples of Stimulus Signaling

The following procedures represent stimulus signaling scenarios and functionally illustrate some of the possible usages and applications. They do not, of course, have to be implemented in full in all systems and terminals. Due to the nature of stimulus signaling, the message flows shown should be perceived as examples of how a feature could be implemented. These examples are intended to support a reader's understanding of how feature key management signaling procedures for control of supplementary services work and can also be extended to include other features. It is not required for the network server/gatekeeper designer to implement the features exactly in the manner shown. A terminal designer cannot assume that a given feature always uses the sequences described in these examples.

Figure 10.3 shows how the stimulus procedures can be applied to the implementation of Call Waiting in a feature server. In this figure, the endpoint is involved in an existing call as another arrives in the Feature Server. The Feature Server does not attempt to set up another call to Endpoint B, but instead sends the endpoint an INFORMATION message. This message, containing a feature indication, indicates that a call is waiting. Additionally, a Display information element, which contains further information about the call—for example, the number and name of the person trying to call—is also sent. This feature indication can also include an audible alert. We assume here that User B is willing to take the waiting call and therefore subsequently terminates the original call by hanging up. User B

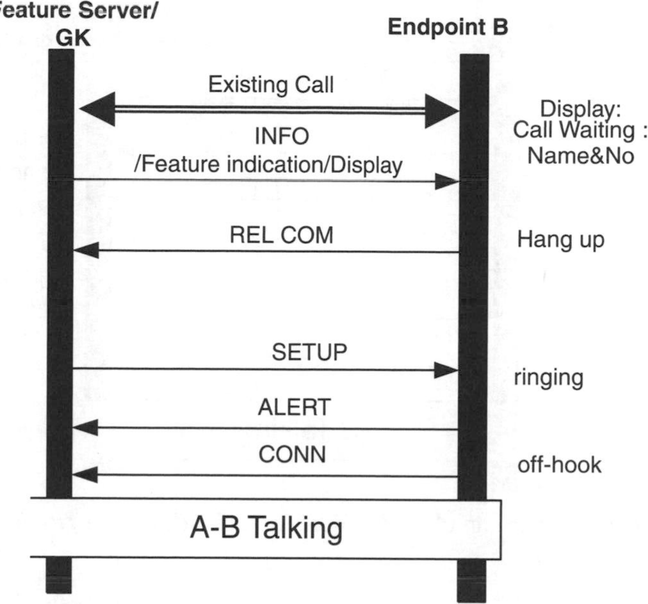

Figure 10.3 The stimulus procedure for Call Waiting.

could also put the existing call on hold instead of hanging-up, although this is not shown in the example. After User B hangs up, the Feature Server connects the waiting caller to Endpoint B by a regular H.225 call setup.

Figure 10.4 shows an example of a Call Pickup scenario. In this case, a call arrives at the Feature Server, and the called User B is alerted by it. Additionally, the pickup group members are alerted by the Feature Server, which sends an INFORMATION message to each of the group members containing a Call Pickup feature indication and the name and number of the calling party.

We assume that the person called is at Endpoint N as the call arrives. The person answers the call by picking up the phone and pressing the pickup key. As they lift the handset, the phone automatically reserves a line to the feature server by a regular H.225 call setup, yet it is not connected to the call that is ringing. Only after the pickup key is pressed and the INFORMATION message containing Call Pickup feature activation is sent, will the Feature Server connect the two calls using the procedures defined in H.323 for gatekeeper-initiated pause and reroute.

Using the same Call Pickup scenario as Figure 10.4, Figure 10.5 adds an applicaton where the pickup happens by a single key depression. In this example, a call arrives again in the Feature Server and the called User B is alerted by it. The pickup group members are also alerted by the Feature

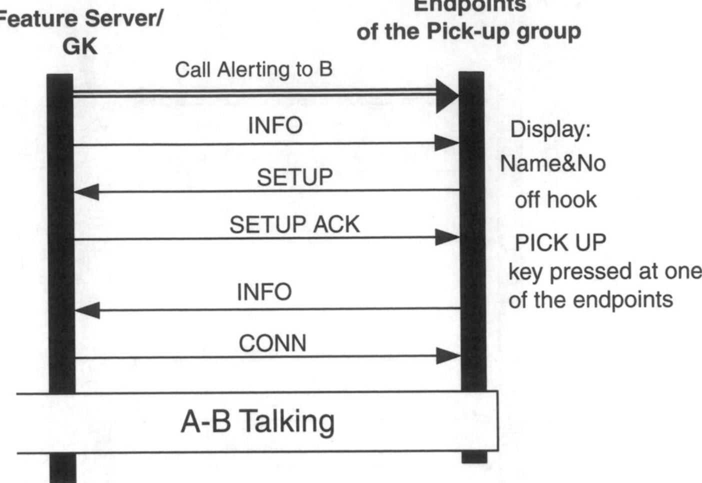

Figure 10.4 The stimulus procedure for Call Pickup by a group member.

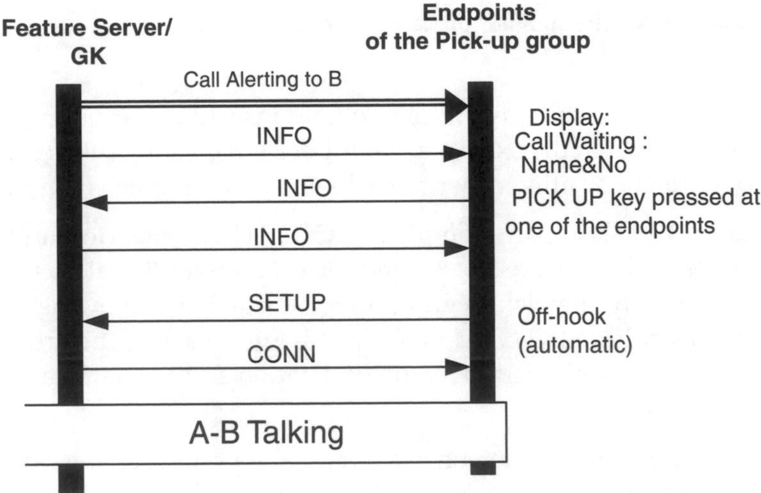

Figure 10.5 The stimulus procedure for a Single Button Call Pickup.

Server which sends an INFORMATION message containing a Call Pickup feature indication and the name and number of the caller.

In this example, the call is received by pressing the pickup key at Endpoint N, which causes an INFORMATION message containing Call Pickup feature activation to be sent to the Feature Server. Because the user has not picked up the phone yet, the Feature Server will force the phone to switch to the hands-free mode. This automatically establishes a connection to the Feature Server, which then connects the two calls.

The examples of Call Pickup illustrate how an H.225 call is established from the terminal side. This call can also be established from the Feature Server side towards the terminal. This variant avoids the re-establishment of the logical channels. The construction of the corresponding procedures is left to the reader as an exercise.

Stimulus Signaling Protocol in H.248

H.248 is a generic gateway control protocol not expressly designed for H.323. It is intended for applications where all gateway control is maintained in a central entity—the Media Gateway Controller. Packet network interfaces can include IP, ATM, and possibly others. These interfaces support a variety of SCN signaling systems, including tone signaling, ISDN, ISUP, QSIG, GSM, and their national variants. To achieve greater scalability, the ITU-T Recommendation H.248 decomposes the H.323 gateway function defined in H.246 into functional subcomponents and specifies protocols that these components use for communication. This enables implementations of H.323 gateways to be highly scalable and encourages leverage of widely-deployed circuit-switched network capabilities such as SS7 exchanges. It also enables H.323 gateways to be composed of components from multiple vendors that are distributed across multiple physical platforms.

From the viewpoint of a system, no functional differences exist between a decomposed gateway—with distributed subcomponents potentially on more than one physical device—and a monolithic gateway as described in H.246. H.248 does not define how voice gateways, fax gateways, multi-point control units, or Interactive Voice Response (IVR) units work. Instead, it creates a general framework that is suitable for these applications.

The H.248 protocol is designed to be easily extendable by the packages using it to support a specific service. The services supported by an H.248-based system are only limited by the packages which are supported by MGC, or media gateway, or both, depending on the specific service.

The H.248 Connection Model

The connection model for the H.248 protocol describes the logical entities, or objects, within the media gateway that can be controlled by the MGC. In H.248, only the MGC is aware of the actual calls between the media gateways and performs call control for them. Because the MGC uses a stimulus protocol to control the media gateways, a new abstraction which does not require call control awareness had to be introduced for the media gateways. The main abstractions used in the connection model are *Terminations* and *Contexts*.

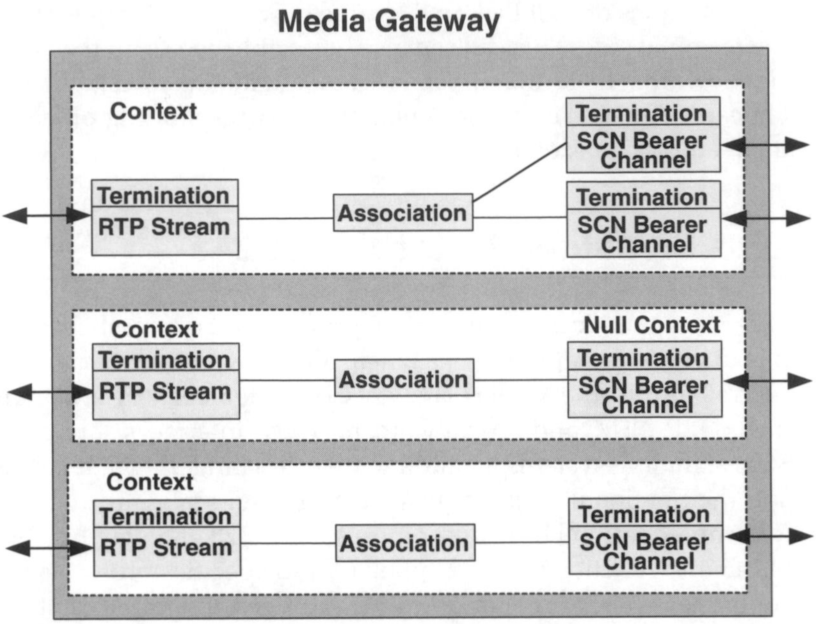

Media Gateway

Context		Termination / SCN Bearer Channel
Termination / RTP Stream	Association	Termination / SCN Bearer Channel

Figure 10.6 An example of an H.248 Connection Model.

Figure 10.6 is a graphical depiction of these concepts from the H.248 standard. It shows several examples and is not meant to be an all-inclusive illustration. The association box in each Context represents the logical association of Terminations implied by that Context. This association also has the capability to cross-connect the streams with each other and includes all the necessary code conversion. Note the streams do not necessarily need to be on opposite sides of the gateway.

Terminations

A *Termination* is a source and/or a sink for one or more streams. In a multimedia conference, a Termination can be the source or sink of multiple media streams. In other words, multiple media streams can terminate at the same Termination. Multimedia gateways can also process multiplexed media streams. The media stream parameters, as well as the modem and bearer parameters, are encapsulated within the Termination.

Context

A *Context* is an association between a collection of Terminations. The Context describes the topology (who hears/sees whom) and the media-mixing and/or switching parameters when more than two Terminations are involved in the association. There is a special type of Context—the null

Context—which contains all the Terminations that are not associated with any other Termination. For instance, in a decomposed access gateway, all idle lines are represented by Terminations in the null Context. Terminations in the null Context can have their parameters examined or modified and can also have events detected on them.

The maximum number of Terminations in a Context is an implementation-specific media gateway property. *Media gateways,* which offer only point-to-point connectivity, may allow at most two Terminations per Context. Media gateways supporting multi-point conferences may allow three or more Terminations per Context.

Commands, Signals, and Events

In general, an *Add command* is used to add Terminations to Contexts. If the MGC does not specify an existing Context to which the Termination is to be added, the media gateway then creates a new Context. A Termination can be removed from a Context with a *Subtract command,* and moved from one Context to another with a *Move command.* A Termination exists in only one Context at a time.

Terminations may have *Signals* applied to them. Signals are media gateway-generated media streams, such as *tones* and *announcements,* as well as *line signals* such as hook switch. Terminations can be programmed to detect *Events;* their occurrence can trigger notification messages to the MGC or an action by the media gateway. Statistics can be accumulated on a Termination. Statistics are reported to the MGC upon request (using the Audit commands) and when the Termination is removed from its call.

Packages

Different types of gateways can implement Terminations that have widely differing characteristics. Variations in Terminations are accommodated in the protocol by enabling the Terminations to have optional Properties, Events, Signals, and Statistics that are implemented by the media gateways.

In order to achieve MG/MGC interoperability, such options are grouped into Packages, and a Termination realizes a set of such Packages. An MGC can audit a Termination to determine which Packages it realizes.

Termination Properties and Descriptors

Terminations have properties that have unique PropertyIDs. Most properties have default values that are explicitly defined in this standard or in a package or are set by provisioning. If the properties are not provisioned otherwise, all descriptors except TerminationState and LocalControl default to empty/"no value" when a Termination is first created or returned to the null Context.

There are a number of common properties for Terminations and properties specific to media streams. The common properties are also called the termination state properties. For each media stream, there are local properties and properties of the received and transmitted flows.

Properties not included in the base protocol are defined in Packages. These properties are referred to by a name consisting of the PackageName and a PropertyId. Most properties have default values which are described in the description of the Package. Properties are read-only or read/write. The possible property values and their current values can be audited. For properties that are read/write, the MGC can set their values. A property may be declared *Global*—it has a single value shared by all terminations realizing the package. Related properties are grouped into descriptors for convenience.

When a Termination is *Add*ed to a Context, the value of its read/write properties can be set by including the appropriate descriptors as the parameters to the Add command. Properties not mentioned in the command will retain their prior values. A Termination property in a Context can have its value similarly changed by the Modify command. Properties not mentioned in the Modify command will retain their prior values. Properties can also have their values changed when a Termination is moved from one Context to another as a result of a Move command. In some cases, descriptors are returned as the output from a command.

Table 10.2 lists all of the possible Descriptors and their uses. Not every descriptor can be legal as an input or an output parameter to every command.

Commands

The protocol provides commands for manipulating the logical entities of the protocol connection model, Contexts, and Terminations. Commands provide control at the finest level of granularity supported by the protocol. For example, Commands exist to add Terminations to a Context, to modify Terminations, to subtract Terminations from a Context, and to audit properties of Contexts or Terminations. Commands provide complete control of the properties of Contexts and Terminations. This control includes specifying the Context's topology (who hears/sees whom), and specifies which events a Termination must report to and the signals or actions that are applied to a Termination.

Table 10.2 Descriptors

DESCRIPTOR NAME	DESCRIPTION
Modem	Identifies modem type and properties when applicable
Mux	Describes multiplex type for multimedia terminations (e.g., H.221, H.223, and H.225.0) and the Terminations forming the input mux
Media	A list of media stream specifications
TerminationState	Properties of a Termination, which can be defined in Packages, that are not stream-specific
Stream	A list of remote/local/localControl descriptors for a single stream
Local	Contains properties, which specify the media flows, that the media gateway receives from the remote entity
Remote	Contains properties, which specify the media flows, that the media gateway sends to the remote entity
LocalControl	Contains properties, which can be defined in packages, that are of interest to the media gateway and the MGC
Events	Describes events to be detected by the media gateway and what to do when an event is detected
EventBuffer	Describes events to be detected by the media gateway when Event Buffering is active
Signals	Describes signals and/or actions to be applied (for example, Busy Tone) to the Terminations
Audit	Identifies which information is desired
Packages	Returns a list of Packages realized by Termination in AuditValue
DigitMap	Defines patterns to which sequences of a specified set of events are matched so they can be reported as a group rather than one at a time
ServiceChange	Reports what and why service change occurred, and so on
ObservedEvents	Reports the events observed in Notify or AuditValue
Statistics	Provides a Report of Statistics kept on a Termination in Subtract and Audit

Most commands are used specifically by the MGC as the command initiator in controlling media gateways as command responders. The exceptions are the *Notify* and *ServiceChange* commands. Notify is sent from the media gateway to the MGC, and ServiceChange can be sent by either entity. The following is an overview of the commands.

Add. The Add command adds a Termination to a Context. The Add command on the first Termination in a Context is used to create a Context.

Modify. The Modify command modifies the properties, events, and signals of a termination.

Subtract. The Subtract command disconnects a Termination from its Context and returns statistics on the Termination's participation in the Context. The Subtract command on the last Termination in a Context deletes the Context.

Move. The Move command automatically moves a Termination to another context.

AuditValue. The AuditValue command returns the current state of the properties, events, signals, and statistics of Terminations.

AuditCapabilities. The AuditCapabilities command returns all the possible values for Termination properties, events, and signals allowed by the media gateway.

Notify. The Notify command enables the media gateway to inform the MGC of the occurrence of events in the media gateway.

ServiceChange. The *ServiceChange* command enables the media gateway to notify the MGC that a Termination or group of Terminations is about to be taken out of service or has just been returned to service. ServiceChange is also used by the media gateway to announce its availability to an MGC (registration), and to notify the MGC of an impending or completed restart of the media gateway. The MGC can also announce a handover to the media gateway by sending it a ServiceChange command. The MGC also uses ServiceChange to instruct the media gateway to take a Termination or group of Terminations in or out of service.

Recommended Reading

The authoritative references for the H.323 Annex L protocol and the H.248 stimulus protocols can be found at H.323 Annex L and H.248 respectively. Annex L is expected to become an ITU-T recommendation in 2001. Other recommendations that may be needed for understanding this chapter are H.225.0, H.245, and H.323. In addition, the H.450 Recommendations and the *Simple Endpoint Type* (SET), which are specified in H.450.1 and H.323 Annex F, are also useful.

A description of HTTP 1.1 can be found at RFC2616, while a description of MIME can be obtained from RFC2045, RFC2046, RFC2047, and [RFC2048].

References

H.225.0 ITU-T Recommendation H.225.0 version 4, *Call Signaling Protocols and Media Stream Packetization for Packet Based Multimedia Communications Systems*, H.225.0, November 2000.

H.245 ITU-T Recommendation H.245 version 7, *Control Protocol for Multimedia Communication*, H.245, November 2000.

H.248 ITU-T Recommendation H.248, *Gateway Control Protocol*, H.248, 2000.

H.323 ITU-T Recommendation H.323 version 4, *Packet Based Multimedia Communication Systems*, H.323, November 2000.

H.323 Annex F ITU-T Recommendation H.323 Annex F, *Simple Endpoint Type*, H.323 Annex F, May 1999.

H.323 Annex L ITU-T Draft Recommendation H.323 Annex L, *Stimulus signaling procedures for H.323*, H.323 Annex L (Work in progress), November 2000.

H.450.1 ITU-T Recommendation H.450.1, *Generic functional protocol for the support of supplementary services in H.323*, H.450.1, February 1998.

RFC2045 Freed, N., and Borenstein, N., *Multipurpose Internet Mail Extensions (MIME) Part One: Format of Internet Message Bodies*, RFC 2045, November 1996.

RFC2046 Freed, N., and Borenstein, N. *Multipurpose Internet Mail Extensions (MIME) Part Two: Media Types*, RFC 2046, November 1996.

RFC2047 Moore, K. *Multipurpose Internet Mail Extensions (MIME) Part Three: Message Header Extensions for Non-ASCII Text*, RFC 2047, November 1996.

RFC2048 Freed, N., Klensin, J., and Postel, J. *Multipurpose Internet Mail Extensions (MIME) Part Four: Registration Procedures*, RFC 2048, November 1996.

RFC2616 Fielding, R., Gettys, J., Mogul, J., Frystyk, H., Masinter, L., Leach, P., and Berners-Lee, T. *Hypertext Transfer Protocol - HTTP/1.1*, RFC-2616, IETF, June 1999.

Problems

1. What distinguishes a stimulus supplementary service from H.450 supplementary services?
2. What distinguishes a stimulus supplementary service from the services provided by HTTP?
3. Describe a workgroup telephone system that uses H.323 Annex L stimulus protocol. Justify the use of H.323 Annex L stimulus protocol in the application.

4. Assume that one implements an IP telephony software packet for a LAN-attached office PC using H.323 Annex L or H.248 stimulus protocols. What limitation of call monitoring do these protocols have if they are received or initiated at that PC?
5. Describe Annex L stimulus message flows for Call Forwarding including Registration. Show the interworking with H.450.
6. Describe Annex L stimulus message flows for *Call Completion on Busy Signal* (CCBS) and on *Call Completion on No Reply* (CCNR). Show the interworking with H.450.
7. Describe Annex L stimulus message flows for Call Transfer and Consultation. Show the interworking with H.450.
8. Describe Annex L stimulus message flows for conference. Show the interworking with H.323 Conference.
9. Describe Annex L stimulus message flows for Call Offering. Show the interworking with H.323 Conference.
10. Describe Annex L stimulus message flows for *Call Intrusion* (CI). Show the interworking with H.323 Conference.
11. Describe five new supplementary services which have no H.450 protocol defined for them. Describe their stimulus signaling procedures.
12. How would one use stimulus procedures in a unified messaging server for provision services to callers and mailbox owners? Describe the corresponding Annex L stimulus message flows.
13. What kinds of problems would an endpoint application confront when using stimulus procedures? How would H.450 solve the problems?
14. Describe how to use the stimulus protocol in order to make a LAN telephony feature server out of a PBX.

CHAPTER 11

Service-Independent Transport by Using HTTP

In this chapter we describe how you can use the *Hypertext Transfer Protocol* (HTTP), which is widely used on the Internet, to control as well as provide enhanced value to H.323-based calls. We will discuss the mechanisms that you can use to achieve such HTTP-based call control and will explore their use within both servers and terminals. Finally, we will provide examples of call scenarios involving HTTP-based services and interworking with the H.450 series of supplementary services.

Characteristics and Purpose

HTTP is a generic mechanism that you can use to access various kinds of services on the Web. For some time, people have already deployed HTTP (for example, in unified messaging systems in order to provide remote access to the mailbox via the Web). The utilization of *Internet Protocol* (IP) networks for telephony makes it possible to utilize HTTP-based methods for accessing services on the network, and this usage is what the H.323 Annex K "Service-Independent Transport by Using HTTP" means.

You can use the method either during a call or independently of a call. This method not only permits access to endpoint features, unified messaging servers, and gateways and gatekeepers, but it also enables access to directory information, *Call Detail Records* (CDRs), and least-cost routing databases. Annex K is optional in H.323. You can utilize Annex K by any intelligent endpoint that supports an HTTP browser. The advantage of opening a separate HTTP connection conveying a service-independent control is that you can develop new services and deploy them without updates to the H.323 endpoints. This service control channel is intended for a wide range of services, such as those that H.323 unified messaging servers offer. You can also use this channel for the creation of easy-to-use user interfaces for the H.450 supplementary service and for software upgrades or for pushing commercials to the clients.

Figure 11.1 shows the system overview of HTTP service control as described in Annex K of the H.323 recommendation. Any entity through which the H.323 call is routed can provide Annex K services, including H.323 endpoints, gatekeepers, gateways, border elements, firewall proxies, databases, and other network elements. Because the access to the service happens through HTTP, the controlled entity must contain an HTTP proxy and must implement an HTTP application that enables the user to gain access to the features. Note that because the HTTP link is separate from the H.225.0 signaling, it does not necessarily have to lead to the same terminal as the H.225.0 signaling.

We can consider the browser and the Web servers as belonging to the service control plane, and the call control of the endpoint and the gatekeeper as belonging to the control plane.

Comparison to Stimulus Signaling

In the previous chapter, we discussed how you can deploy stimulus signaling for first-party call control of supplementary services. We saw that the stimulus signaling is carried via the signaling channel to the endpoint, which makes use of it. In other words, the party that is using the supplementary

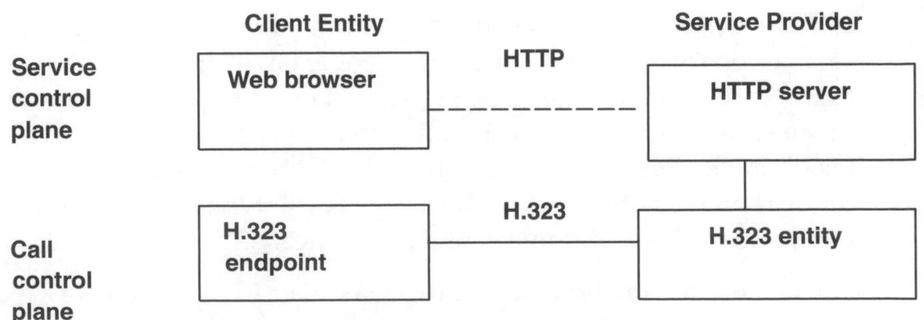

Figure 11.1 System overview of HTTP-based service control.

services is also a party to the call. The main difference between the Annex K HTTP-based solution and the Annex L stimulus protocol is that the latter does not require the terminal to have a Web browser. The stimulus protocol also enables the call control application to tightly control the user interface hardware, which is useful in the case of telephones. On the other hand, the service control method introduced in the H.323 Annex K is essentially a third-party control of an H.323 call.

Supported Features

No fixed set of capabilities exists for the user interface because various types of text formats, images, and sounds are utilized dynamically as registered *Multi-Purpose Internet Mail Extensions* (MIME) types. The service provider (the HTTP server) is responsible for the mapping between HTTP events and the call control actions (H.450 or other messages) for supplementary services, so the controlling entity is unaware of the HTTP application. Features are limited by the capabilities of the HTTP browser and the associated client device. For example, some might have sufficient audio capabilities to provide a ringing tone, but others might not.

You can use this service control channel for a wide range of services, some of which require the use of H.450 or proxy signaling for invocation/execution. Because this channel is service independent, no specific services are defined or advocated. The data that are exchanged on this channel are meant to be informative (user control) and should be followed by appropriate actions (for example, H.450 invocations) in the call-signaling plane when needed.

You can use the service control channel for both call-related and non-call-related services. This channel might be opened, for example, between the terminal and the network or between two endpoints in the call.

While the normal use of the Annex K service control channel is for the control of supplementary services, you could also use it for software upgrades or for advertising new features to clients, for example.

Application Scenarios

Because the HTTP service control channel is generic, no specific services are defined or advocated in the H.323 Annex K recommendation. The channel might be utilized for both call-related and non-call-related services. The channel might be opened between the terminal and any H.323 network entity or between two endpoints in the call. Here are a few potential application scenarios:

- The called party's gatekeeper/feature server provides services to the calling party.
- The calling party's gatekeeper/feature server provides services to the called party.
- The messaging server provides services to callers.
- The messaging server provides mailbox management services to the mailbox owner.
- Conference services (such as add-on conferences, meet-me conferences, and so on) for conference master and conference members exist.
- The outgoing gateway provides network access services to the calling party.
- The incoming gateway provides call reception services to the called party.

Figure 11.2 illustrates an example scenario where a gatekeeper provides features for a simple H.323 endpoint via a hand-held wireless device. The features are executed in the gatekeeper on behalf of the endpoint while the user interface occurs via HTTP. By using this method, you can provide sophisticated features (such as conference control) for endpoints that do not have supplementary service control capabilities. Examples of such endpoints are analog telephones that are connected to an H.323 terminal adapter.

Figure 11.3 illustrates the services provided by a messaging server for a calling H.323/H.450 multimedia terminal.

As you can see in the last example, HTTP service control is an optional way of controlling supplementary services in an H.323 environment. You can use

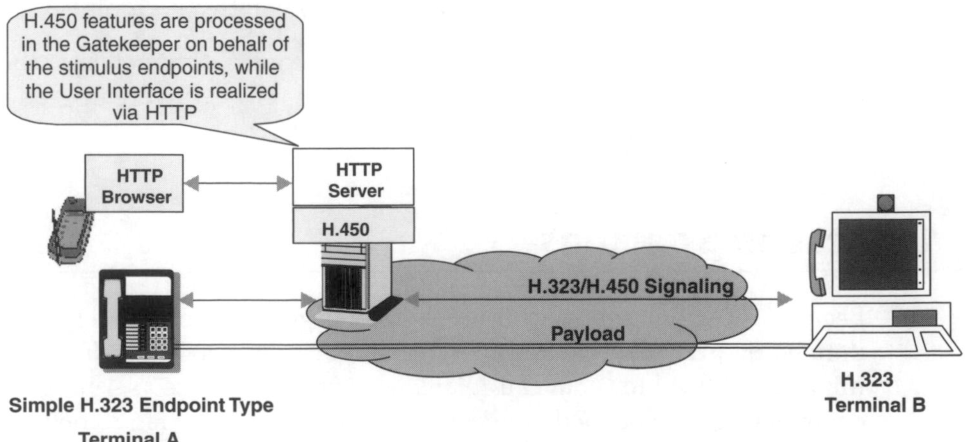

Figure 11.2 HTTP service control of a gatekeeper.

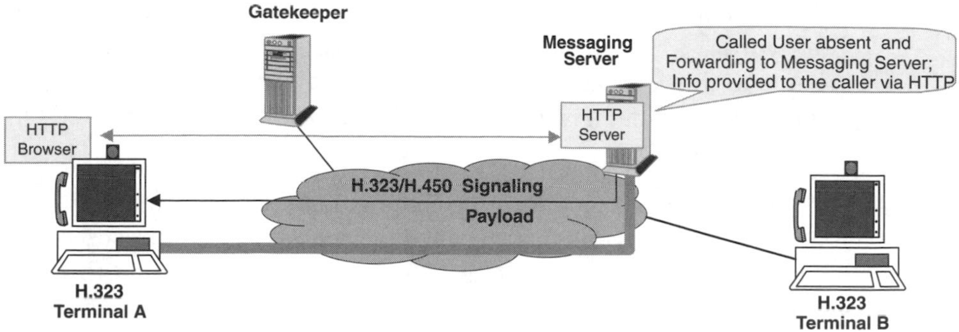

Figure 11.3 HTTP service control of a messaging server.

this control as a supplement to the H.450 supplementary service control or for non-standard services. By opening a separate connection conveying a service-independent control protocol, you can develop and deploy new services without updates to the H.323 endpoints.

Protocol Mechanisms

The feature's key management extensions operate in conjunction with the call-signaling protocol defined in Recommendation H.225.0, and you can use them in conjunction with both direct and gatekeeper-routed signaling models of H.323. The media control occurs via existing means that are defined for H.323 terminals. For example, the server can use the gatekeeper-initiated pause and reroute procedure in order to mute media channels or to reconfigure media channels (for example, to cease transmission to one address and resume transmission to another address).

While you might use several protocols, Annex K describes the use of HTTP. The reason is because HTTP is a widely known and used protocol that is open, flexible, and firewall-friendly. The actual service application protocol is dynamic (indicated by using MIME types in HTTP signaling). Example applications can include *Extensible Markup Language* (XML) pages possibly including Java and JavaScript, the download of tones and announcements to be played to the client, the upload of CPL from the client to a gatekeeper, and so on.

The Annex K protocol simply defines how any H.323 entity involved in a call can send its URL by using the ServiceControlSession structure to the endpoint so that it automatically fires a browser window for access to the offered services. You can send the URL by using either the *Registration, Admission, and Status* (RAS) or the H.225.0 call control messages. The URL should be complete in terms of defining the protocol, server, and resource (in other words, <protocol>://<server-address>/<resource>). The endpoint might load this URL and display the services and service control functions as provided by the data given by this URL (for example, a Web page with menus and links).

The data exchanged on the HTTP channel is used, for example, for the creation of graphics and feature selection menus and to directly control the display and user input functions. If the selected features lead to invocations of network-wide features, such as holding a call or call transfer, the HTTP server side will execute the appropriate H.450 signaling actions and perform rerouting or re-establish the logical channels. The network signaling between the entities involved in the call still requires the use of H.450 signaling.

You can open the HTTP service control channel for both non-call-related and call-related purposes. The following examples illustrate some practical uses.

Non-Call-Related Service Control

The provisioning of services outside a call context means that either the service is requested when no call exists or that the service requested is not related to the call that exists. You can initiate service in one of two ways: by pull, where the endpoint requests a service from a server, or by push, where the server delivers a service to an endpoint without the endpoint explicitly making a request. The server entity can typically be located in the gatekeeper, but it can also be located elsewhere on the network.

Service delivery by pull. In this case, there is no call and therefore no reference between the endpoint and the server. The URL that we need for opening a new HTTP session must be made available to the endpoint by other means, namely either by making the URL known to the endpoint via RAS signaling or by entering it manually.

Service delivery by push. If the network needs to notify the endpoint about service-related events (during a call or as part of the registration), it can send an H.225.0 *Information Request* (IRQ) message with a URL to this endpoint. In order to indicate that this URL relates to the non-call-related service control session (that is possibly already active), we will set the field callReferenceValue to 0 and the field callIdentifier to a sequence of zeros. The endpoint can then load this URL, which provides updated services and service control functions. An endpoint that receives such an IRQ message responds as usual with an *Information Request Response* (IRR) message.

In order to provide services relating to the registration session, the gatekeeper sends a URL in the H.225.0 RCF message.

Example 1: Access to the Network-Based Phone Book Application

The scenario that we describe here is one in which a user's personal phone book is located on a server and the user can access and possibly edit (add, delete, and modify) his or her phone book entries. The user's client device has a Web browser, and the server on which the phone book is stored is a Web server—thereby facilitating the use of HTTP between the client and the server. Figure 11.4 shows the sequence of operations and associated signaling. As you can see in the figure, Endpoint A first registers with gatekeeper GKA and receives a URL that references a phone book. Upon receiving this URL, Endpoint A automatically opens a Web browser with the phone book URL. Assuming that the User A wants to call User B but User B is not listed in the phone book, he or she first adds User B to the phone book.

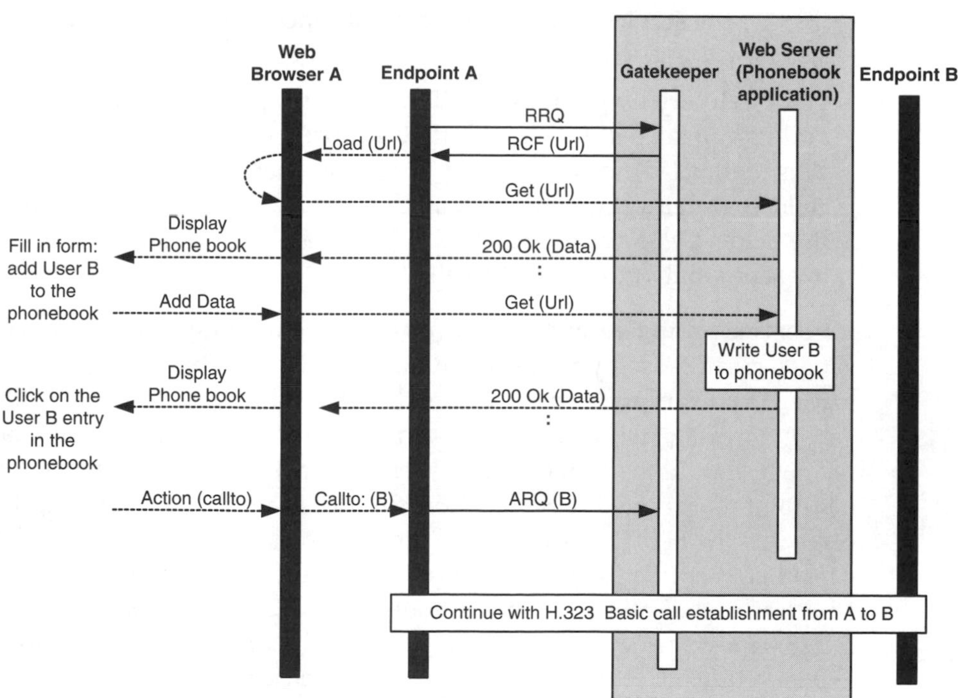

Figure 11.4. Non-call-related service provided by the gatekeeper.

After the phone book is refreshed, User A clicks the name of User B, which causes Endpoint A to establish a call to Endpoint B.

The interface between the browser and the call control on the client or the service provider is not within the scope of Annex K itself. This interface could include HTML or XML tags (such as callto links).

Call-Related Service Control

You can deliver the call-related services by using one of two methods: pull or push. The call-related session does not have an effect on the non-call-related service control session. If such a session is already active, the user simply sees two simultaneously active service windows.

Service delivery by pull. Because a call (and therefore, a reference) exists between the endpoint and the server, the URL that we need in order to open a new HTTP session is made available to the endpoint via the H.225.0 call signaling channel. Subsequently, the HTTP session is opened between an endpoint and a gatekeeper or between two endpoints with a URL in the call control messages. The endpoint can load this URL and display the services and service control functions as provided by the data given by this URL.

Service delivery by push. An HTTP session is opened between an endpoint and its gatekeeper with a URL that is carried in the H.225.0 IRQ message. This method is useful especially for gatekeepers that use direct routed calls. In order to signal which call this service control channel is relating to, the field's *Call Reference Value* (CRV) and call identifier of the IRQ message are set to that of the targeted call.

If a service provider needs to notify an endpoint about new services or events, it can do so by refreshing data on a URL that has been previously loaded (for example, applet/servlet dialogues) or by issuing an H.225.0 Facility message with a new URL. An endpoint that receives such a facility message should load this URL and render the data that it presents. An endpoint that receives a ServiceControlAddress with a URL of length 0 considers the HTTP session closed and has to close any resources, such as *Graphical User Interfaces* (GUIs) and so on. You can reopen a new session at any time in the call with a present non-null URL in any H.225.0 message. Any H.225.0 messages without the ServiceControlAddress present do not influence the HTTP session at all (except Release Complete). If Release Complete is received without a URL, the session ends. On the other hand, if a Release Complete message is received with a URL, it means that the call-related session is closed (if any existed), but a new call-unrelated session is opened.

Example 2: Call Waiting

Figure 11.5 illustrates a variant of the Call Waiting supplementary service, where the calling party can influence the execution of the service via interactions with a Web server by using an HTTP link. The gatekeeper of the called party detects that User B is busy and provides a URL to the calling party in the H.225.0 alerting message. The URL references a Web page that contains a set of options for further processing of the call. The options could be to divert to voice mail, e-mail, or the operator. User A can then select voice-mail, for example, in order to leave a message. This selection is signaled to the HTTP application, which instructs the gatekeeper to execute call diversion. After the diversion is successfully completed, the gatekeeper informs the HTTP application about the successful diversion and the HTTP application sends a new Web page to Endpoint A, notifying it that diversion

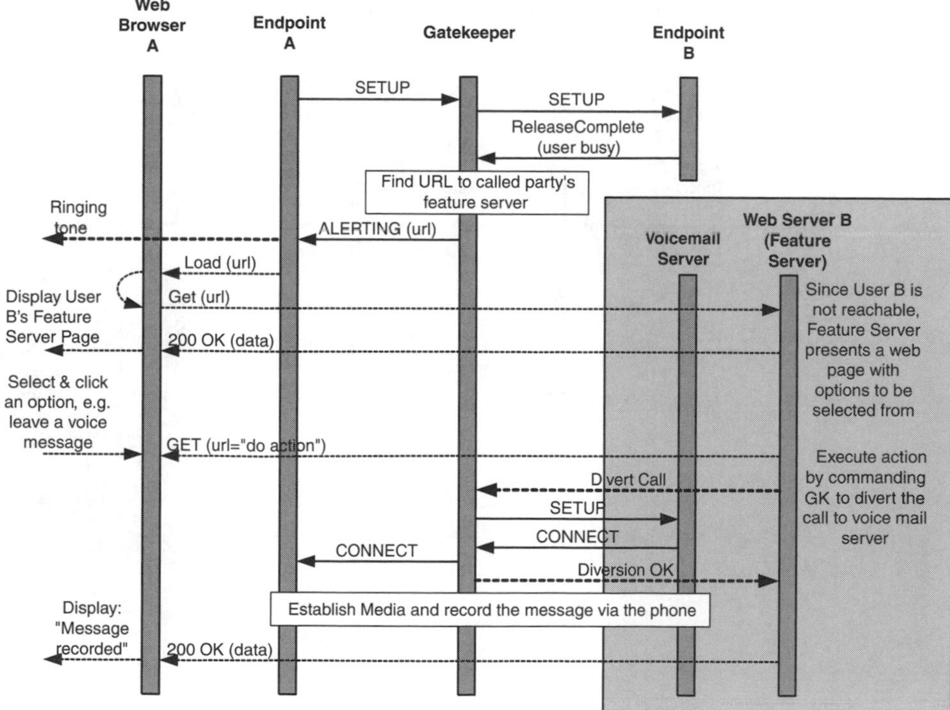

Figure 11.5 Call-related service by the gatekeeper.

was completed successfully. Additionally, Endpoint A can obtain new options for the invocation of further features.

Example 3: Call-Related Service Control (Non-Gatekeeper-Routed Call)

Figure 11.6 illustrates a service similar to Example 2, but the HTTP service control entity is this time at the called endpoint. The called endpoint is again busy in a call and returns a URL to the calling party. The URL references a Web page that contains a set of options for the invocation of more features.

The user hears the audio alert, and at the same time a Web page with options is automatically presented to the user. The options might include features to choose between a) diverting to voice mail, b) sending an e-mail, or c) diverting to an operator or secretary. In this example, the user subsequently chooses to leave a voice mail, and this selection is signaled to the HTTP server. The endpoint executes the feature by sending a diversion request to the gatekeeper. The HTTP server is informed about the successful diversion. The HTTP server then responds to the browser with a new Web page by displaying a message that the diversion was completed successfully and by possibly providing the user with more options.

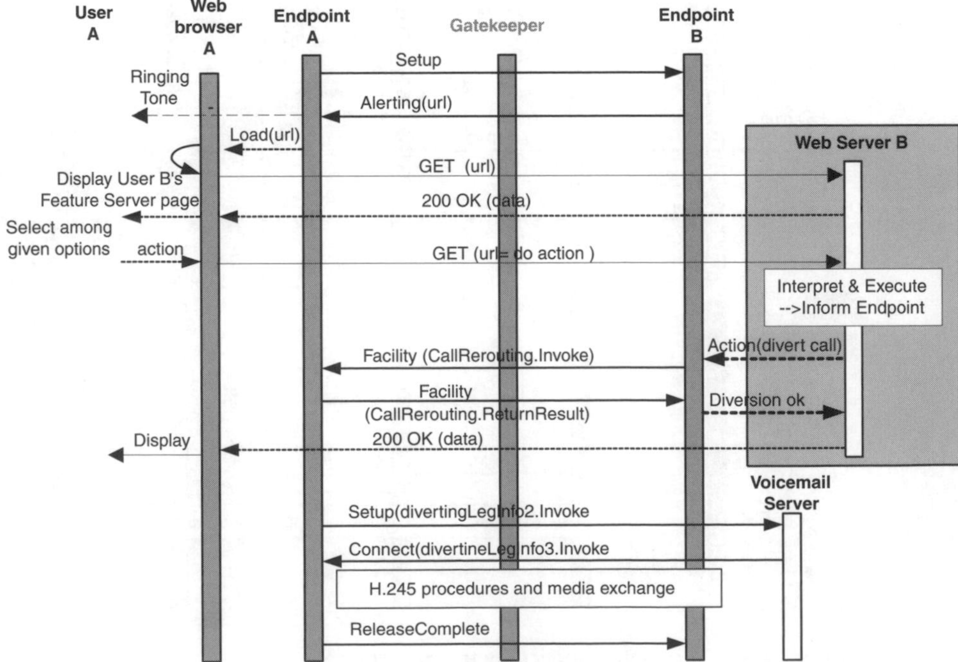

Figure 11.6. Call-related service by the gatekeeper.

Example 4: Non-Call-Related Service Control and Script Upload

Call-processing scripts are also a form of service control. One example is CPL. Because CPL is based on XML/SGML, HTTP is a natural carrier. The example shows a terminal uploading this script after registration (see Figure 11.7). The user prepares the script by using a graphical builder in the endpoint or by other means and decides to upload this information to the server.

In this case, the endpoint notes that the returned URL contains a CPL tag. Hence, when the user decides to upload the script, it must utilize the POST scheme. The details of the script and the impact that it has on further call signaling depends on the contents of the script.

Service Interactions

Because the HTTP service control channel is stateless and unaware of the execution of the services in the underlying layers, it does not take service interaction problems (with supplementary services, for example) into account. An application that utilizes this service control channel should, however, consider this situation carefully.

For example, gatekeeper applications that utilize the HTTP service control should be careful not to interact with end-to-end service control. This

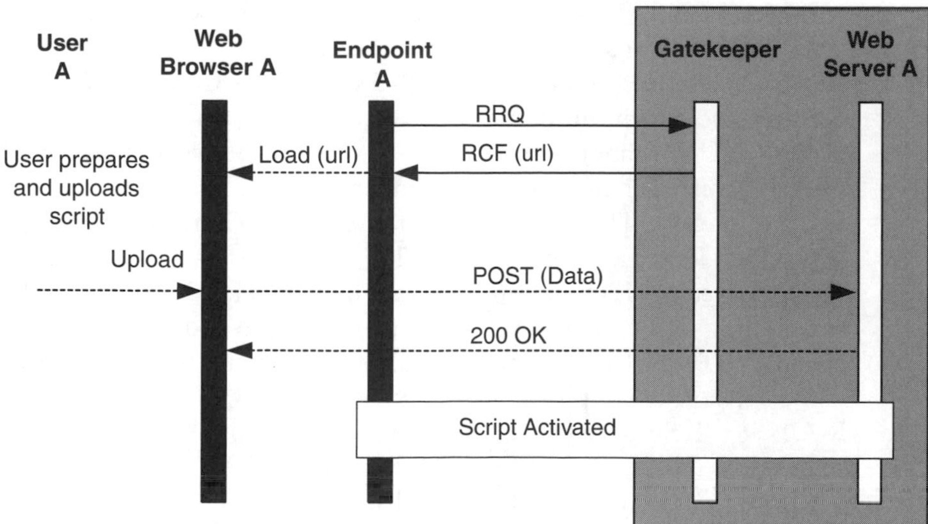

Figure 11.7. Non-Call-Related Service, script upload.

situation is the case in particular for non-gatekeeper-routed calls where the gatekeepers are unaware of the call control messages and states.

Recommended Reading

H.323 Annex K [H.323 Annex K] is the standard that describes service-independent transport by using HTTP and is the authoritative reference for this chapter. [H.225.0], [H.245], [H.323], [H.323 Annex L], and [H.450.1] are other *International Telecommunications Union—Telecommunications* (ITU-T) recommendations that might be needed in order to understand the contents of the chapter.

The HTTP protocol itself is described in [RFC2616] while the markup languages HTML, XML, and CPL are specified in [RFC1866], [XML], and [RFC2824], respectively. URLs and MIME are explained in [RFC1738] and [RFC2045], respectively.

References

XML T. Bray et al, "Extensible Markup Language (XML) 1.0," W3C Recommendation February 1998.

WAP Wireless Application Protocol, Architecture Specification, version 1.2, WAP Forum, April 1998.

H.225.0 ITU-T Recommendation H.225.0 version 4, "Call Signaling Protocols and Media Stream Packetization for Packet Based Multimedia Communications Systems," November 2000.

H.245 ITU-T Recommendation H.245 version 7, "Control Protocol for Multimedia Communication," November 2000.

H.323 ITU-T Recommendation H.323 version 4, "Packet Based Multimedia Communication Systems," November 2000.

H.323 Annex K ITU-T Recommendation H.323 Annex K, "Service Independent Transport Using HTTP," 2000.

H.323 Annex L ITU-T Draft Recommendation H.323 Annex L, "Stimulus signaling procedures for H.323," 2000. (work in progress)

H.450.1 ITU-T Recommendation H.450.1, "Generic functional protocol for the support of supplementary services in H.323," 1998.

RFC1738 T. Berners-Lee, L. Masinter, M. McCahill, "Uniform Resource Locators (URL)," RFC 1738, IETF, December 1994.

RFC1866 T. Berners-Lee, D. Connolly, "Hypertext Markup Language - 2.0 (HTML)," RFC 1866, IETF, November 1995.

RFC2045 N. Freed, N. Borenstein, "Multipurpose Internet Mail Extensions (MIME), Part One: Format of Internet Message Bodies," RFC 2045, IETF, November 1996.

RFC2616 R. Fielding, J. Gettys, J. Mogul, H. Frystyk, L. Masinter, P. Leach, T. Berners-Lee, "Hypertext Transfer Protocol—HTTP/1.1," RFC-2616, IETF, June 1999.

RFC2660 T. Rescorla, A. Schiffman, "The Secure HyperText Transfer Protocol (S-HTTP)," RFC 2660, IETF, August 1999.

RFC2824 J. Lennox, H. Schulzrinne, "Call Processing Language Framework and Requirements," RFC-2824, IETF, May 2000.

Problems

1. Describe a workgroup telephone system that uses an H.323 Annex K-based method of service control. Justify the use of the H.323 Annex K protocol in your application.
2. Assume that you would implement an IP telephony software packet for your *Local Area Network* (LAN)-attached office PC by using H.323 Annex K protocols. What kind of limitations does this usage cause for the monitoring of calls that are received or initiated at that PC?
3. Describe Annex K message flows for Call Forwarding (including registration).
4. Describe Annex K message flows for Call Completion on Busy and on No Reply.
5. Describe Annex K message flows for Call Transfer and Consultation.
6. Describe Annex K message flows for conference.
7. Describe Annex K message flows for Call Offering.
8. Describe Annex K message flows for Call Intrusion.
9. Describe five new supplementary services for which there is no H.450 protocol defined. Describe the Annex K signaling procedures for two of them.
10. How would you use Annex K procedures on a gateway to a circuit-switched network for provisioning calling-card services? Describe the corresponding Annex K message flows.

CHAPTER 12

Principles of Interworking

This chapter describes the system architecture of gateways and the scenarios in which you can deploy them. We also explain the use of trunking gateways and network-access gateways in public and private networks.

As carriers, service providers, and business users start to deploy *Internet Protocol* (IP) multimedia telephony, they must adapt new systems to existing communication networks—and these systems have to interwork with legacy communication equipment that is attached to the IP network. The result is a hybrid communication network, as shown in Figure 12.1.

From Figure 12.1, we can derive some of the network requirements for interworking and the operation of supplementary services from a corporate network and carrier network perspective. For example, we can make native H.323 calls for voice, facsimile, and other media among users of a corporate H.323 network without the involvement of a gateway. For these calls, supplementary services are available if both endpoints support the H.450 protocols and if the users have subscribed to the services. The service provider might charge for the use of supplementary services or block the use of services to which the user does not subscribe. We could control this situation by a gatekeeper that has access to back-end services containing a service subscription database.

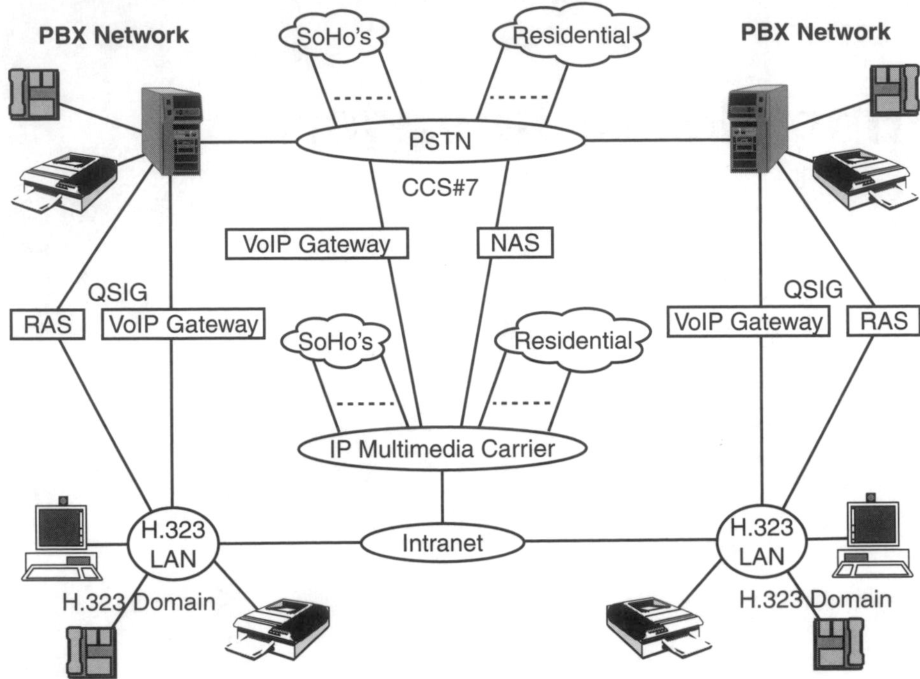

Figure 12.1 A hybrid communication network.

LEGEND:

SOHO = SMALL-OFFICE/HOME-OFFICE
PSTN = PUBLIC-SWITCHED TELEPHONE NETWORK
RAS/NAS = REMOTE ACCESS SERVER/NETWORK ACCESS SERVER
CCS NO.7 = COMMON CHANNEL SIGNALING SYSTEM 7
QSIG = D-CHANNEL PROTOCOL AT Q REFERENCE POINT FOR *Private Branch Exchange* (PBX) NETWORKING

Supplementary service functionality and availability on calls between legacy systems within the *Switched-Circuit Network* (SCN) and an H.323 multimedia network depends on the capabilities of the entities and gateways that are involved with the call signaling along the path of the call. Again, the gateway service provider can charge not only for the call duration, but also for supplementary service usage.

You can use terminal adapters for the attachment of one or more legacy fax and telephone devices to an H.323 network. Their structure is analogous to the H.323/SCN gateway except that the SCN side of the protocol stack is replaced with an appropriate analog signaling scheme. H.450 supplementary services that are necessary for the operation of the analog devices can be implemented within the terminal adapter. You perform the invocation of features between the analog device and the terminal adapter over the analog interface by using *Dual-Tone Multi-Frequency* (DTMF) tones.

Because gateways are endpoints on the two attached networks, they have to perform call-control functions (including supplementary services on both sides). In other words, the supplementary services signaling must be translated from one side to the other.

On an IP network that provides *Quality of Service* (QoS), the H.323 endpoints communicate directly with the others without involving a gateway. If the terminals are on different domains, however, and QoS is not guaranteed if they communicate by using regular packet routing, then QoS can be provided by routing the call through gateways in order to bypass a router or a low-bandwidth link. Gateways that are configured between two IP networks are called border elements.

QSIG Interworking with H.323

The deployment of IP telephony systems begins quite often as small islands within a larger *Private-Branch Exchange* (PBX) network. Companies hope to gain experience first and then move on with larger-scale subnetworks. In such situations, the H.323 IP telephony systems are attached to the existing PBX networks via gateways. The task of the gateway is to convert the circuit-switched calls of legacy PBXs to H.323 (and vice-versa). Because the standard protocol for PBX networking is QSIG, we discuss in the following section the tasks of the gateway in more detail.

This standard specifies signaling interworking between QSIG and H.323 in support of generic, functional procedures for supplementary services within a *Corporate Network* (CN).

QSIG is a signaling protocol that is used for networking PBXs. In the terminology of the standards, it operates at the Q reference point between *Private Integrated Services Exchanges* (PINX) within a *Private Integrated Services Network* (PISN). PINX can be a PBX (or, for example, a messaging server). For short, we will use the term PBX in the following chapters.
The Q reference point is defined in ECMA-133 and in the corresponding *International Standards Organization* (ISO) standards. A PBX network provides circuit-switched, basic services and supplementary services to its users. QSIG is specified in other ECMA and ISO standards—in particular, ECMA-143 (call control in support of basic services), ECMA-165 (generic functional protocol for the support of supplementary services), and a number of standards specifying individual supplementary services.

The following discussion of H.323 interworking with QSIG is based on ECMA Technical Report ECMA TR-73 and ECMA Standards ECMA-302, ECMA-308, and ECMA-309.

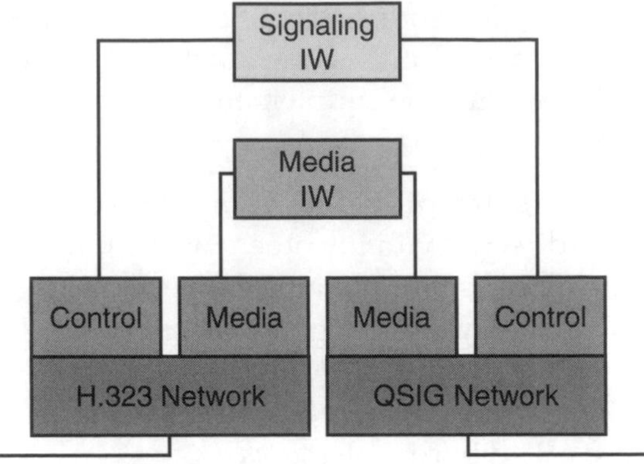

Figure 12.2 QSIG/H.323 interworking scenario.

Figure 12.2 shows a simplified scenario of H.323 interworking with QSIG PBXs and networks.

The QSIG gateway is a piece of equipment that belongs to two networks and has to fulfill two requirements of those two networks: 1) on the IP network side, it has to behave like an endpoint of the H.323 network, and 2) on the PBX network side, it must behave like a PBX.

With regard to the handling of voice steams, the QSIG gateway behaves like any other IP telephony gateway. The QSIG gateway has to digitize and compress voice calls from the PBX trunks into IP packets for routing to another gateway or to an H.323 endpoint. The media interworking function (Media IW) performs this task and involves encoding and decoding as well as packetization and sequencing of voice streams.

QSIG Gateway-Layer Architecture

Figure 12.3 shows the protocol stack architecture for transcoding between ISDN bearer channels and voice streams over IP.

With regard to signaling, the QSIG gateway terminates the H.225.0 basic call signaling on the H.323 side and the QSIG basic call signaling on the PBX side.

Figure 12.4 shows the protocol stack architecture for the mapping of QSIG signaling to H.323/H.450 (and vice-versa).

Because the H.225.0 signaling protocol was developed from ISDN Q.931 signaling (as was QSIG), the interworking of basic calls is straightforward. This situation reflects a minimum implementation of a QSIG gateway. Simple gateways support only basic call interworking and do not enable the use of supplementary services on these calls. Their behavior is very similar to a

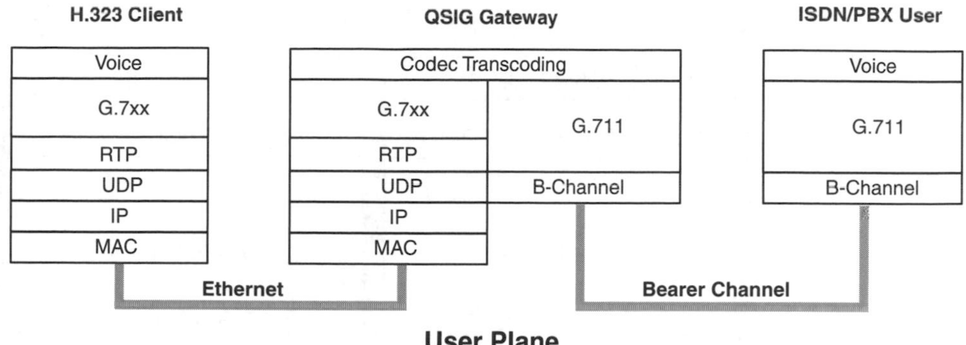

Figure 12.3 Transcoding of voice in a QSIG gateway.

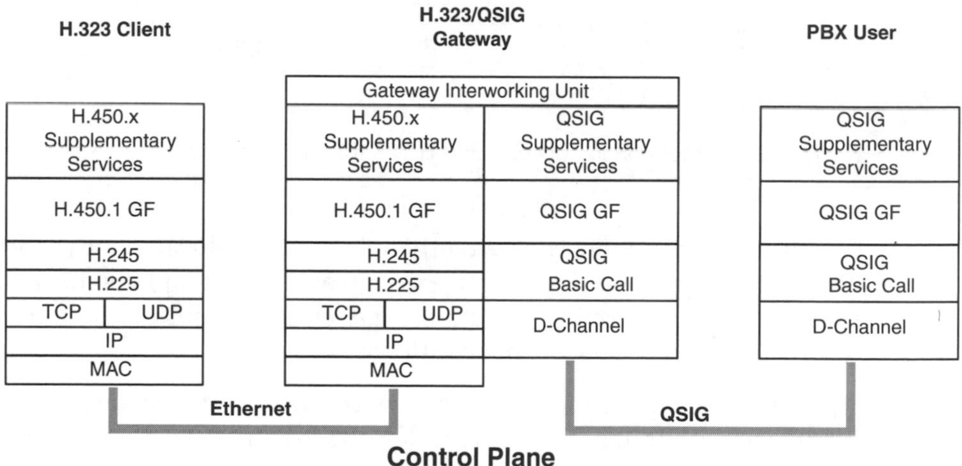

Figure 12.4 Architecture of QSIG/H.323 signaling interworking.

simple PBX in that when connected to form a network, they only enable basic call functionalities between the PBXs.

Gateway Signaling

Figure 12.5 summarizes the mapping of signaling messages from QSIG and H.323/H.225 and vice-versa. The mapping of the basic call control messages is straightforward.

Table 12.1 compares the capabilities of QSIG-GF and H.450.1 and gives a summary of the functional mapping between the two.

Table 12.1 shows that the capabilities that are currently used by standardized supplementary services are supported in both environments (with one

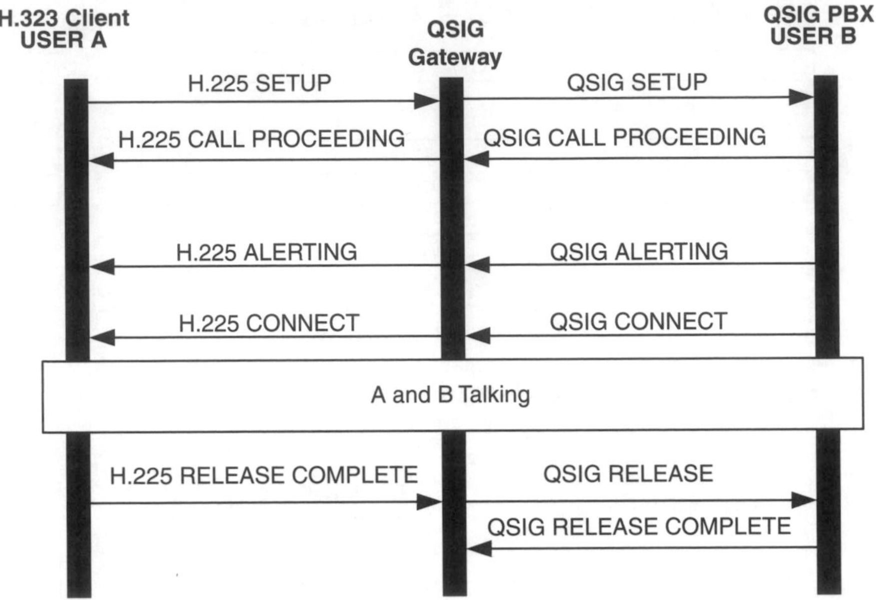

Figure 12.5 Interworking of QSIG and H.323 for a basic call.

exception: Notifications are currently not used in H.450. In many cases, however, an equivalent operation exists in an H.450 supplementary service). Interworking or mapping, therefore, is generally possible (although detailed coding of the messages might be different).

You can implement supplementary services in the gateway one by one. Because H.450 protocols have been derived from the corresponding QSIG specifications, the interworking for supplementary services is straightforward. The implementers have to take into account that there are many different kinds of PBXs from various manufacturers, however, and their QSIG implementations might contain different, more or less overlapping subsets of QSIG supplementary services. This situation results because none of them are mandatory to implement, although many PBXs implement the basic QSIG supplementary services (such as calling and called-party name, call transfer, consultation, and call diversion). Therefore, the gateway has to take into account that the particular QSIG feature invocation might not be implemented in the destination PBX of the call. In the same manner, the gateway has to take into account that a particular H.450 feature invocation is not implemented in the H.323 destination of the call.

Interworking of Consultation Transfer

In order to understand the functionality of the gateway better, we discuss the interworking of Consultation Transfer supplementary service in more depth

Table 12.1 Capabilities

CAPABILITY	QSIG-GF	H.450.1	REMARKS
Call-related transport	✔	✔	
Call-independent, connection-oriented transport	✔	✔	
Call-independent, connectionless transport	✔	-	Currently not used by standardized QSIG supplementary services
Network Facility Extension (NFE)	✔	✔	Extended addressing capabilities in H.450.1
Interpretation APDU	✔	✔	
ROSE APDUs and procedures	X.219/229	X.880 series	In practice no relevant difference.
Other APDUs and procedures: DSE (dialogue procedures), ACSE	✔	-	Currently not used by standardized QSIG supplementary services
Manufacturer-specific information	✔	✔	Two alternative containers in H.450.1
Notifications	✔	-	
Messages	ALERTING CONNECT DISCONNECT	ALERTING CALL PROC. CONNECT	These QSIG messages are defined in ECMA-143 and in the corresponding ISO standard.
	PROGRESS	PROGRESS	All messages for H.450.1 transport are defined in H.225.0.
	RELEASE REL. COMP. SETUP FACILITY NOTIFY	REL. COMP. SETUP FACILITY	These QSIG messages are defined in ECMA-165 and in the corresponding ISO standard.
Information elements	Facility; Notification indicator	User-user information	Element H 450.1 Supplementary Service APDU within User-user information is the equivalent of information element Facility.
ASN.1 encoding rules	X.208 X.209 BER	X.680 series X.691 PER (BAV)	BER—Basic Encoding Rules PER—Packed Encoding Rules BAV—basic aligned variant

in the following section. Call Transfer and Consultation are relatively simple supplementary services from the signaling point of view. The PBXs and H.323 endpoints do not necessarily implement all functions of the standard, however, but only subsets. For this reason, the gateway has to cope with the different call scenarios caused by the difference in implementations.

In Figures 12.6 to 12.15, Entity A is always the transferring party; Entity B is the transferred party; and Entity C is the transferred-to party. Each figure shows the location of these entities on the PBX and H.323 networks. The locations of Entities B and C are as follows.

If User A (and therefore, Entity A) are on the QSIG network at PBX A and PBX A only implements transfer by join or chooses to perform transfer by join, Entities B and C will be located at PBX A. Interworking will occur on Leg B and/or on Leg C, depending on the location of Users B and C. Figure 12.6 shows this example.

If User A (and therefore, Entity A) are on the QSIG network at PBX A and PBX A performs transfer by rerouting, if User B is on the H.323 network, the gateway between User A's network and User B's network can choose, upon receipt of a transfer request from PBX A, whether to provide Entity B (in which case interworking occurs on Leg B) or to instruct the H.323 network to provide Entity B (in which case interworking occurs on Leg AB).

Similarly, if User C is on the H.323 network, the gateway between User A's network and User B's network can choose, upon receipt of a transfer identify

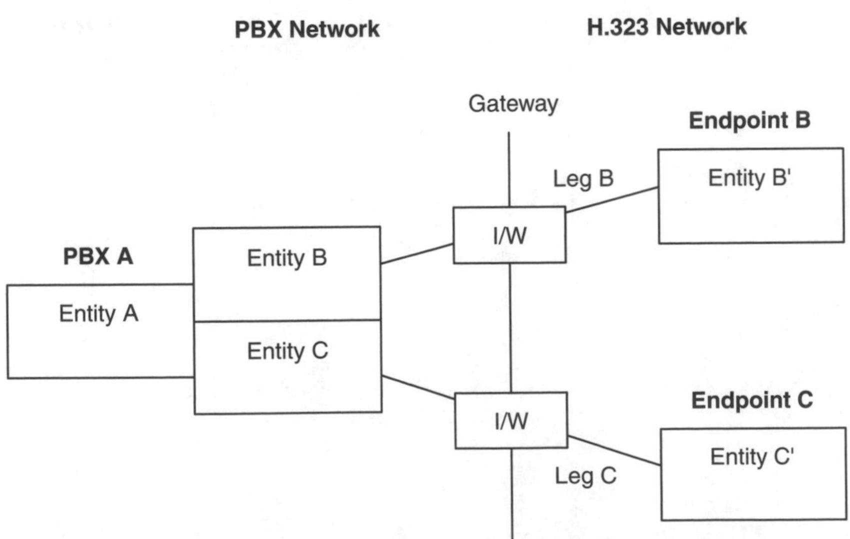

Figure 12.6 QSIG interworking: transfer by join on a PBX network.

request from PBX A, whether to provide Entity C (in which case interworking occurs on Leg C) or to instruct the H.323 network to provide Entity C (in which case interworking occurs on Leg AC).

Figures 12.7 and 12.8 show the two cases where the two gateways make the same decision. If the two gateways make different decisions, interworking

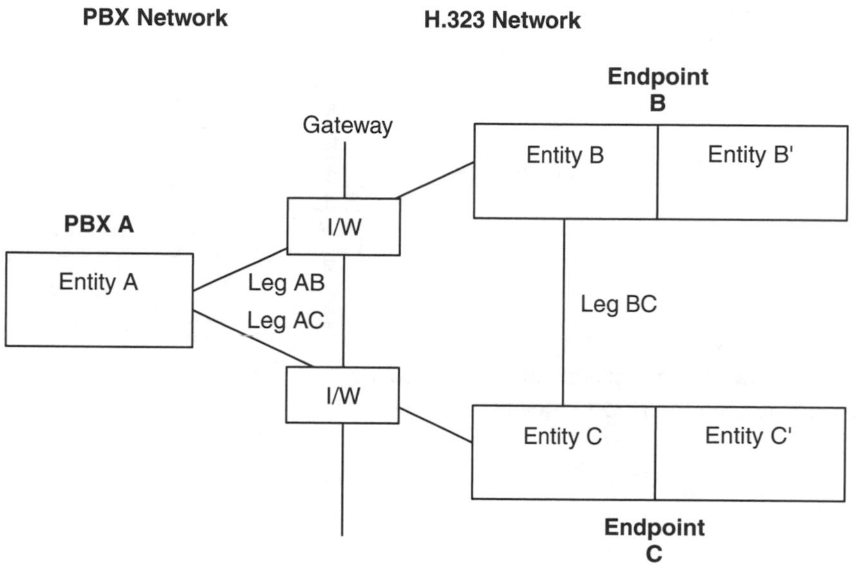

Figure 12.7 Interworking: transfer by rerouting between PBX A and Endpoints B and C on the H.323 network.

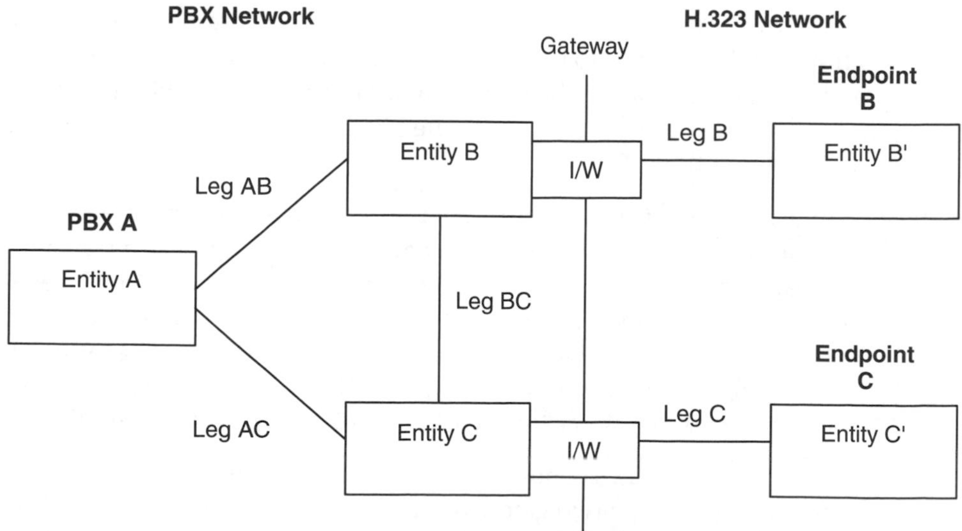

Figure 12.8 Interworking: transfer by rerouting between PBX A and two gateways.

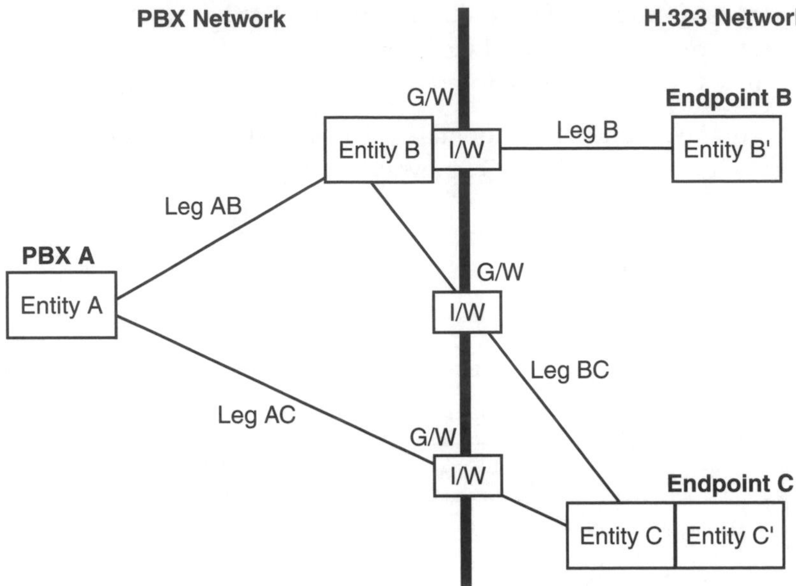

Figure 12.9 Interworking: transfer by rerouting between PBX A, Entity B on a gateway, and Entity C on the H.323 network.

will also occur on Leg BC. The case where Entity B is on the PBX network and Entity C is on the H.323 network appears in Figure 12.9. We do not show the reverse situation.

If User A (and therefore, Entity A) are on the H.323 network at Endpoint A, and if User B is on the PBX network, the gateway between User A's network and User B's network can choose, upon receipt of a transfer request from Endpoint A, whether to provide Entity B (in which case interworking occurs on Leg B) or to instruct the PBX network to provide Entity B (in which case interworking occurs on Leg AB). The latter requires support for transfer by rerouting on the PBX network.

Similarly, if User C is on the PBX network, the gateway between User A's network and User C's network can choose, upon receipt of a transfer identify request from Endpoint A, whether to provide Entity C (in which case interworking occurs on Leg C) or to instruct the PBX network to provide Entity C (in which case interworking occurs on Leg AC). The latter requires support for transfer by rerouting on the PBX network. If the two gateways make different decisions, interworking will also occur on Leg BC.

Figures 12.10 and 12.11 show the two cases where the two gateways make the same decision. If the two gateways make different decisions (not shown), interworking will also occur on Leg BC.

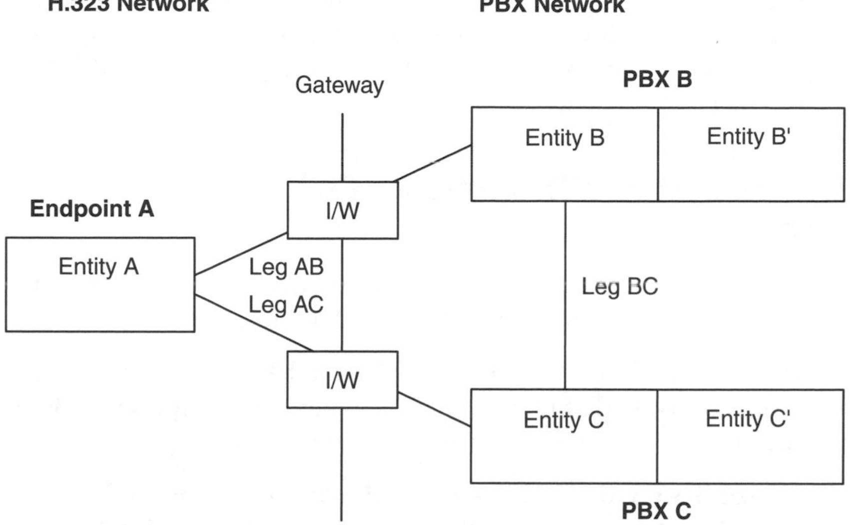

Figure 12.10 Interworking: transfer by rerouting between Endpoint A on the H.323 network and PBXs B and C.

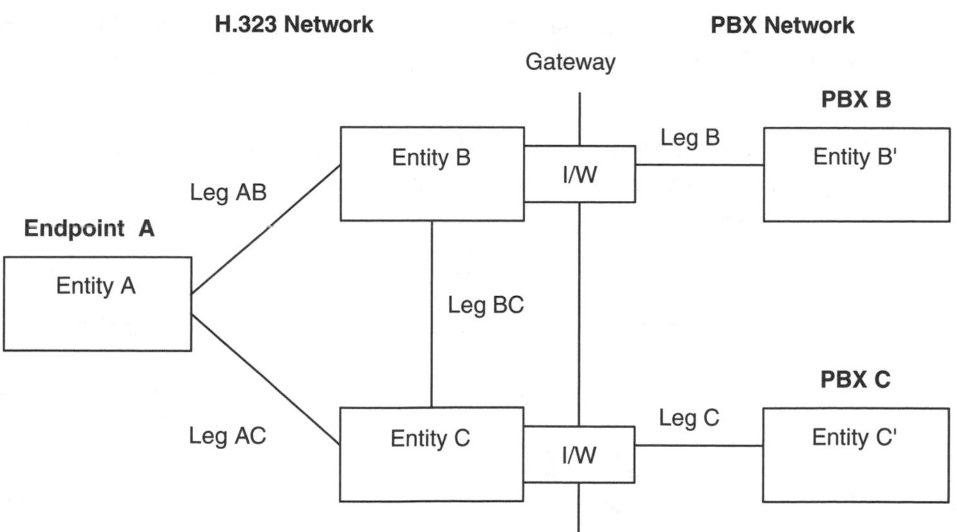

Figure 12.11 Interworking: transfer by rerouting between Endpoint A on the H.323 network and two gateways.

In cases where a gateway can choose whether to provide Entity B or Entity C functionality, the gateway's decision is an implementation matter. This decision can, but is not required to, take account of User C or User B, respectively. The behavior of Entity B or Entity C, if provided at the gateway, is outside the scope of this standard and is assumed to be in accordance with the requirements of QSIG Call Transfer (when Entity A is on the PBX network) or in accordance with the requirements of H.450.2 (when Entity A is on the H.323 network).

The Interworking of Single-Step Call Transfer

Entities A*, B′, C*, and C′ are always located on the network of the user in question. The location of Entity B* is determined as follows:

If User A (and therefore, Entity A*) is on the QSIG network at PBX A, Entity B* can be located at PBX A. Interworking will occur on Leg B* and/or on Leg BC*, depending on the location of Users B and C.

If User B is on the H.323 network, the gateway between User A's network and User B's network can choose, upon receipt of a transfer request from PBX A, whether to provide Entity B* (in which case interworking occurs on Leg B*) or to instruct the H.323 network to provide Entity B* (in which case interworking occurs on Leg AB*).

Figure 12.12 shows the situation where Entity B* is provided by the gateway. Figure 12.13 shows the situation where Entity B* is provided by the H.323 network.

Also, in the case where Entity B* is provided by the H.323 network and User C is on the PBX network, interworking will also occur on Leg BC*. We do not show this situation.

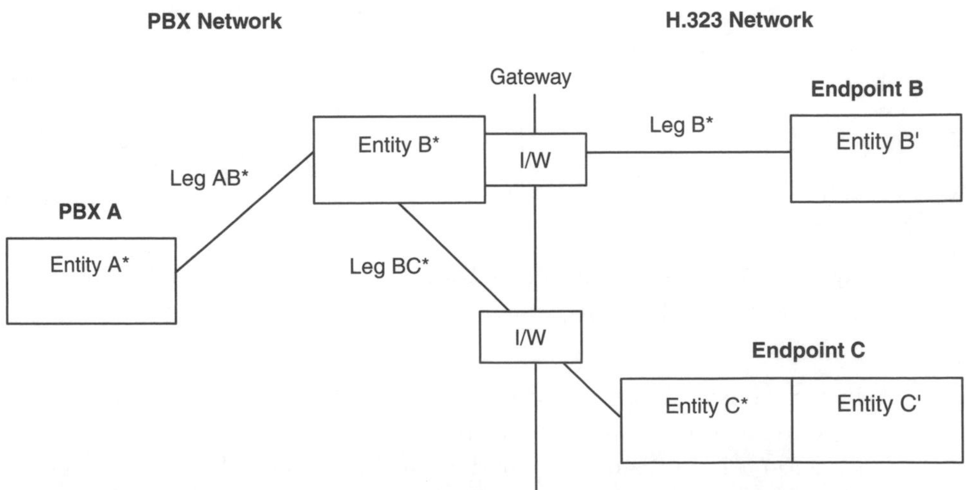

Figure 12.12 Interworking: single-step call transfer on a PBX network.

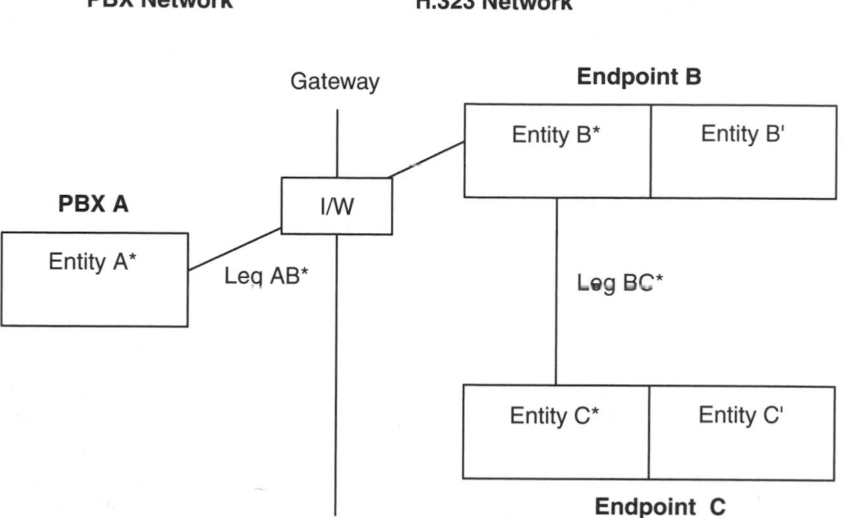

Figure 12.13 Interworking: single-step call transfer between PBX A and Endpoints B and C on the IP network.

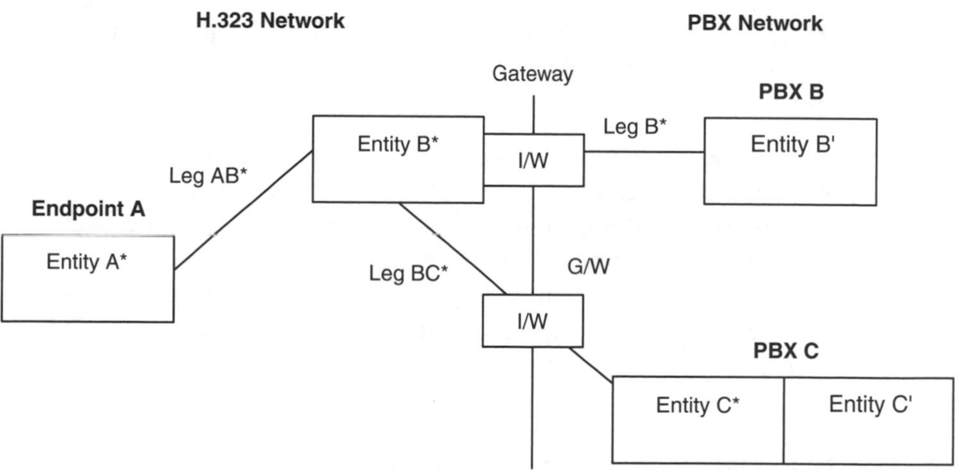

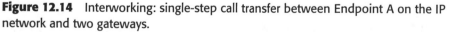

Figure 12.14 Interworking: single-step call transfer between Endpoint A on the IP network and two gateways.

If User A (and therefore, Entity A*) is on the H.323 network at Endpoint A, and if User B is on the PBX network, the gateway between User A's network and User B's network can choose, upon receipt of a transfer request from Endpoint A, whether to provide Entity B* (in which case interworking occurs on Leg B*) or to instruct the PBX network to provide Entity B* (in which case interworking occurs on Leg AB*). Figures 12.14 and 12.15 show these situations.

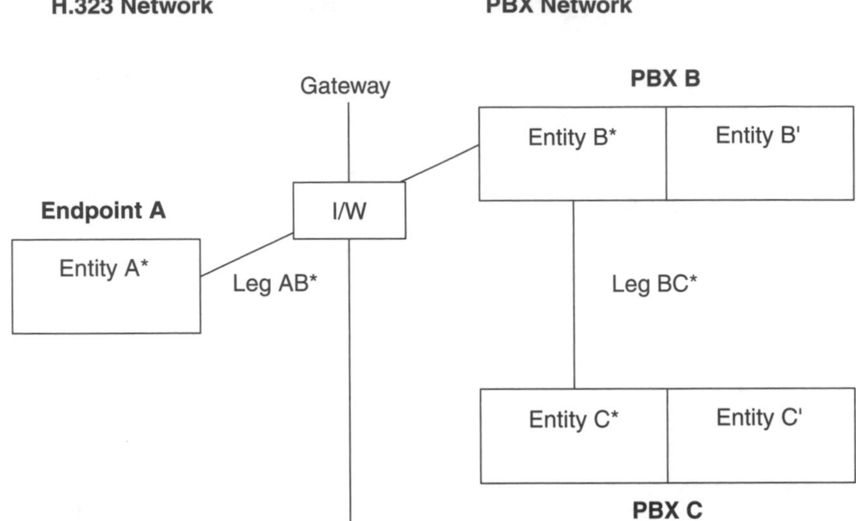

Figure 12.15 Interworking: single-step call transfer between Endpoint A on the IP network and PBXs B and C.

Also, in the case where Entity B* is provided by the PBX network and User C is on the IP network, interworking will also occur on Leg BC*. We do not show this situation.

In cases where a gateway can choose whether to provide Entity B* functionality, the gateway's decision is an implementation matter. This decision can, but does not need to, take into account the location of User C. The behavior of Entity B*, if provided at the gateway, is assumed to be in accordance with the requirements of QSIG Call Transfer (when Entity A* is on the PBX network) or in accordance with the requirements of H.450.2 (when Entity A* is on the H.323 network).

ISUP Interworking with H.323

H.246 Annex C describes the interworking between CCS No.7 *ISDN User Parts* (ISUP) of Signaling System 7 (SS7) and the H.225.0 Multimedia Call Control protocol. This annex specifies the necessary mapping that an interworking function would utilize in order to achieve connectivity and functionality between an H.323 network and an ISUP network.

H.246 Annex C describes an interworking function when it is in an H.323 to PSTN gateway. The mapping described in Annex C relates to a H.323 call to a telephone that is located on a circuit-switched network. We assume that the gateway has an ISDN Q.931 type of interface to the PSTN. H.246 Annex C does not attempt to define functionality in ISUP or Q.931 networks but instead seeks to show how the ISUP services and functions would interwork with H.225.0.

ISUP Gateway-Layer Architecture

Figure 12.16 shows the protocol stack architecture for the transcoding between ISDN bearer channels and voice streams over IP.

With regard to signaling, the ISUP gateway terminates the H.225.0 basic call signaling on the H.323 side and the ISUP basic call signaling on the PBX side.

Figure 12.17 shows the protocol stack architecture for the mapping of ISUP signaling to H.323/H.450 and vice-versa.

Although the H.225.0 signaling protocol was developed from ISDN Q.931 signaling instead of ISUP, the interworking of basic call is straightforward. This situation reflects a minimum implementation of an ISUP gateway. Simple gateways support only basic call interworking and do not permit the use of supplementary services on these calls.

Gateway Signaling

Figure 12.18 summarizes the mapping of signaling messages from ISUP and H.323/H.225 and vice-versa.

You can implement supplementary services in the gateway one by one. Because H.450 protocols were derived from the corresponding QSIG specifications, the interworking for supplementary services is straightforward. Also, however, in case of ISUP, the implementers have to

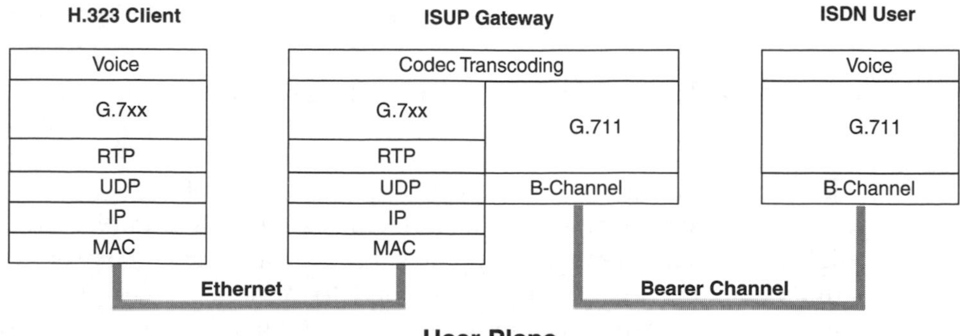

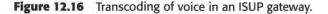

Figure 12.16 Transcoding of voice in an ISUP gateway.

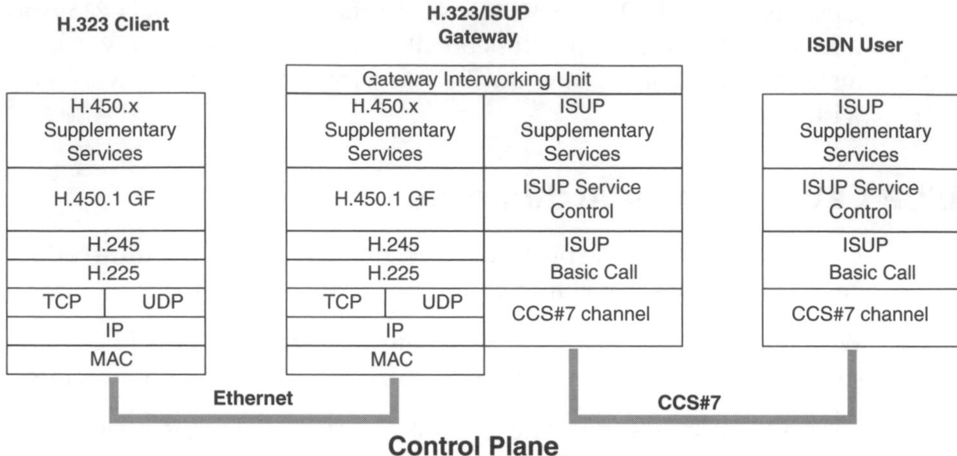

Figure 12.17 Architecture of ISUP/H.323 signaling interworking.

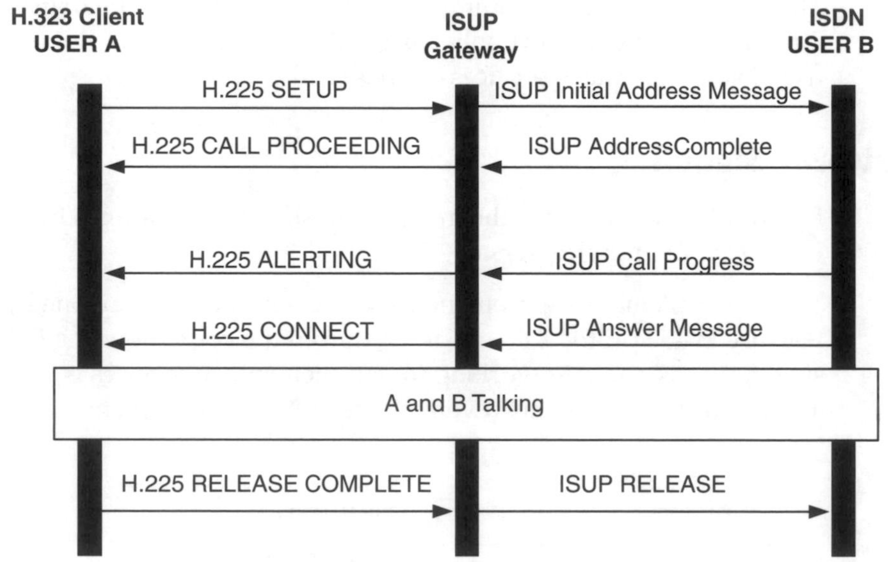

Figure 12.18 Interworking of ISUP and H.323 for a basic call.

take into account that there are many different kinds of ISUP implementations from various manufacturers—and their implementations might contain different, overlapping subsets of supplementary services. This situation results because they are optional to implement. Therefore, the gateway has to take into account that the particular feature invocation might not be implemented in the destination of the call. In the same manner, the gateway has to take into account that a particular H.450 feature invocation is not implemented in the H.323 destination of the call.

Trunking Gateways

H.323 has the capability to support the encapsulation and transport of foreign signaling information elements between native signaling entities. This process is also known as tunneling of the circuit-switched network signaling over H.323. You can determine whether or not to allow a tunnel on a per-call basis, depending on the administrative policy within the terminating domain.

QSIG Trunking

Figure 12.19 shows the principle of QSIG trunking over H.323. In the trunking scenario, all of the calls originating from a QSIG gateway terminate in another QSIG gateway, so there is no need to convert the supplementary service signaling protocol from QSIG to H.450 and vice-versa. Instead, the QSIG supplementary services signaling information is packed into envelopes and is transported transparently over H.323. Therefore, the implementation of the gateway is simpler. H.323 Annex M1 describes the method of QSIG tunneling.

ISUP Trunking

ISUP trunking over H.323 is similar to QSIG trunking. Figure 12.20 shows the principle. In the ISUP trunking scenario, all of the calls originating from an ISUP gateway also terminate in another ISUP gateway, so there is no need to convert the supplementary service signaling protocol from ISUP to H.450 and vice-versa. Instead, the ISUP supplementary services signaling information is packed into envelopes and is transported transparently over H.323. Again, the implementation of the gateway becomes much simpler.

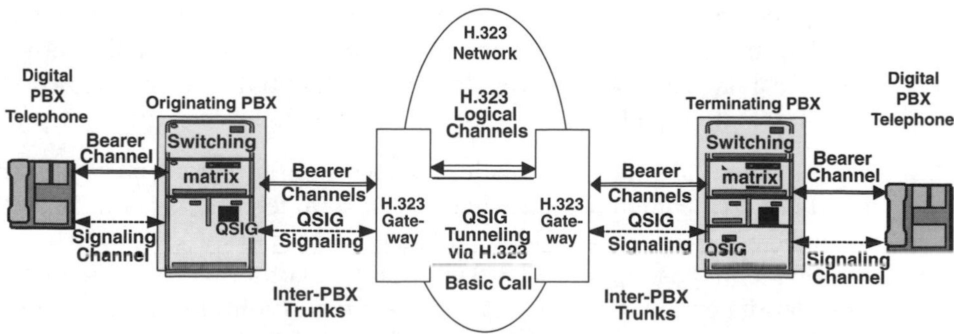

Figure 12.19 QSIG trunking over H.323.

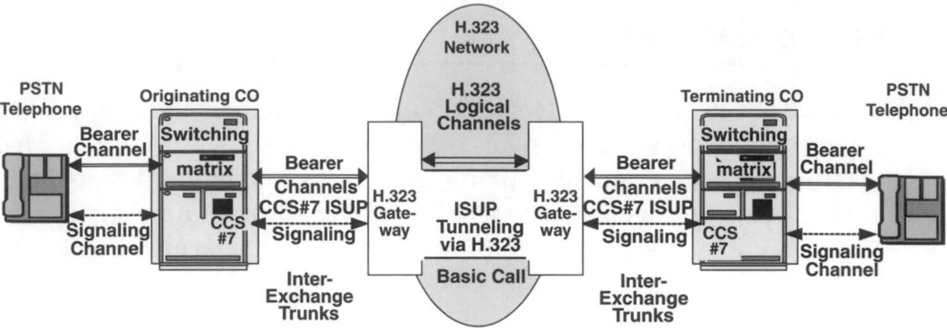

Figure 12.20 ISUP trunking over H.323.

BICC Interworking

The *Bearer Independent Call Control* (BICC) protocol was defined by the ITU-T Study Group 11 for the purpose of ISUP trunking over IP networks. BICC is defined in ITU-T Recommendations Q.1902.1 to Q.1902.4 and ISUP in ITU-T Recommendations Q.761 to Q.764. Figure 12.21 shows the BICC architecture. If you compare it with Figure 12.20, you can see that the ultimate goals are the same—but the protocols are different. In practical terms, the BICC defines yet another IP telephony call control protocol that specifically makes the tunneling of ISUP one step easier (because it is limited only to basic voice calls).

You can also implement a gateway that performs interworking between H.323 and BICC. Figure 12.22 shows this architecture.

Residential H.323 Gateways

The task of residential H.323 gateways is to connect standard analog telephone and facsimile equipment to the H.323 network. For this reason, each of the attached devices becomes an endpoint of the H.323 network as if it were a native H.323 device. Thus, the residential gateway is not simply a smaller gateway. (The name *gateway* is somewhat misleading.)

The residential gateway provides interworking functions on a subscriber line and not on a trunk line. Particularly, if several telephones or fax devices are connected to the same residential gateway, each of these have to be implemented as separate H.323 endpoints. In other words, it is not the residential gateway that is registered as an endpoint in the gatekeeper, but each of the connected analog devices.

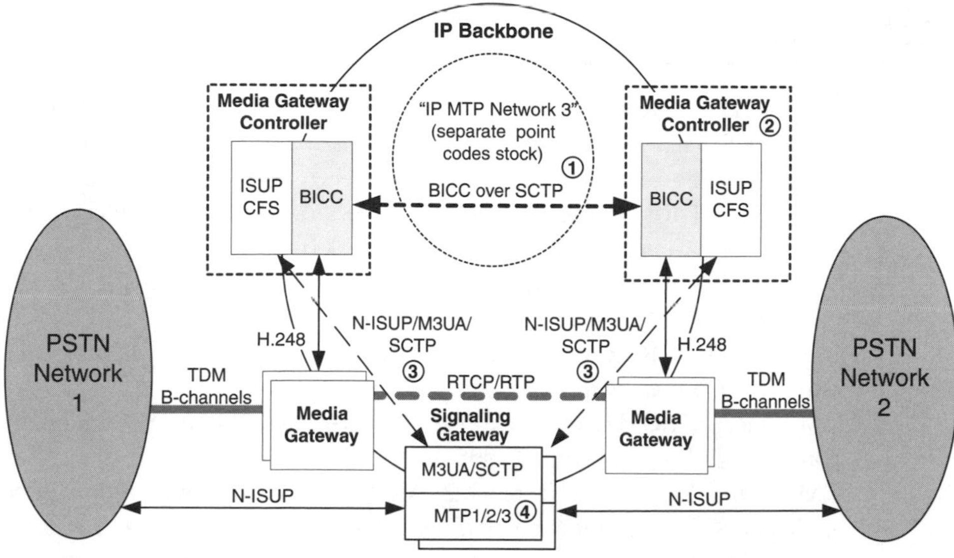
IP Backbone
Media Gateway Controller
ISUP CFS
BICC
"IP MTP Network 3" (separate point codes stock)
①
BICC over SCTP
Media Gateway Controller ②
BICC
ISUP CFS
PSTN Network 1
H.248
N-ISUP/M3UA/ SCTP
③
N-ISUP/M3UA/ SCTP
③
H.248
PSTN Network 2
TDM B-channels
Media Gateway
RTCP/RTP
Signaling Gateway
Media Gateway
TDM B-channels
M3UA/SCTP
N-ISUP
MTP1/2/3 ④
N-ISUP
Notes:
① BICC contains M3UA and is transported using Signaling Control Transfer Protocol (SCTP) as transport protocol over IP
② Media Gateway Controller (MGC) encapsulates ISUP into BICC and controls the Media Gateway
③ Signaling Gateway (SG) transports the ISUP signaling to the MGC using SCTP over IP MTP Level 3 User Adaptation (M3UA) is used for establishment of signaling connections to each MGC.
④ Signaling Gateway behaves as a STP toward the attached ISUP network. Each SG may have multiple CCS#7 Point Codes for each of the connected ISUP Networks

Figure 12.21 ISUP trunking via IP by using BICC.

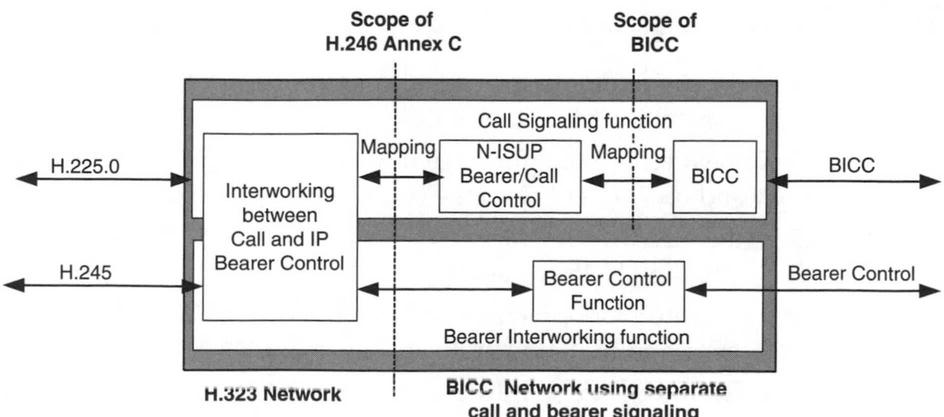
Scope of H.246 Annex C
Scope of BICC
Call Signaling function
H.225.0
Interworking between Call and IP Bearer Control
Mapping
N-ISUP Bearer/Call Control
Mapping
BICC
BICC
H.245
Bearer Control Function
Bearer Control
Bearer Interworking function
H.323 Network
BICC Network using separate call and bearer signaling

Figure 12.22 ISUP/BICC interworking.

References

H.225.0 ITU-T Recommendation H.225.0 Version 4, *Call Signaling Protocols and Media Stream Packetization for Packet-Based Multimedia Communications Systems*, November 2000.

H.245 ITU-T Recommendation H.245 Version 7, *Control Protocol for Multimedia Communication*, November 2000.

H.323 ITU-T Recommendation H.323 Version 4, *Packet-Based Multimedia Communication Systems*, November 2000.

H.450.1 ITU-T Recommendation H.450.1, *Generic functional protocol for the support of supplementary services in H.323*, January 1998.

ECMA TR73 ECMA Technical Report TR-73, *H.323 / B-ISDN Signalling Interoperability*, December 1998

ECMA-307 ECMA standard ECMA-307, *Corporate telecommunication networks–Signalling interworking between QSIG and H.323–Generic functional protocol for the support of supplementary services*, June 2000.

ECMA-308 ECMA standard ECMA-308, *Corporate telecommunication networks–Signalling interworking between QSIG and H.323–Call transfer supplementary services*, June 2000.

ECMA-309 ECMA standard ECMA-309, *Corporate telecommunication networks—Signalling interworking between QSIG and H.323—Call Diversion supplementary services*, June 2000.

ISUP ITU-T Recommendations Q.761 to Q.764 *Specifications of Signalling System* No.7 ISDN User Part (ISUP), 2000.

BICC ITU-T Recommendations Q.1902.1 to Q.1902.4 *Specifications of the Bearer Independent Call Control Protocol* (BICC), 2001.

Problems

1. Describe interworking message flows between QSIG Call Forwarding and the corresponding H.450 protocol.
2. Describe interworking message flows between QSIG Call Completion on Busy and on No Reply and the corresponding H.450 protocol.
3. Describe interworking message flows between QSIG Call Offering and the corresponding H.450 protocol.
4. Describe interworking message flows between QSIG Call Intrusion and the corresponding H.450 protocol.
5. Describe interworking message flows for ISUP Call Completion on Busy and on No Reply and the corresponding H.450 protocol.
6. Describe interworking message flows for ISUP Call Transfer and Consultation and the corresponding H.450 protocol.

CHAPTER 13

H.323 Security

This chapter describes aspects of the H.235 standard, which deals with the security services that H.323-based *Internet Protocol* (IP) telephony systems offer, and the mechanisms for achieving such security services. The next chapter provides a more detailed description of some of the generic security protocols (for example, IPSec and IKE), and that chapter also covers issues relating to firewalls, private addressing and RADIUS servers.

Security Services for H.323 Systems

Generally speaking, in any system we consider five fundamental security services:

1. *Authentication*. This term refers to verification of the claimed identity of an entity, such as a terminal or a user.
2. *Integrity*. Integrity of a received message ensures that the message is identical to that which the sender transmitted and that the message is not tampered with in transit.
3. *Confidentiality*. The presence of message confidentiality implies that the specific message is intelligible only to the intended recipients.

4. *Non-repudiation*. This term implies that usage of a service or receipt of a message by an entity is provable.
5. *Authorization*. This service ensures that only those entities that are authorized to use a certain resource can gain access to the resource.

In the context of security for H.323 systems, we must consider the following two categories separately:

- Security services for signaling messages (RAS, H.225.0, and H.245). These services include one or more of the following components:
  - User-authentication mechanisms. These mechanisms support three techniques: (1) encrypting certain fields with a secret key, (2) using a keyed hash technique, and (3) using digital signatures.
  - Generation of a secret key, either from an *a priori* shared password or by using the *Diffie-Hellman* (DH) technique. You can use this secret key for user authentication or for message authentication/integrity.
  - Securing the entire H.225.0/H.245 channel by using mechanisms such as IPSec/TLS. This helps provide security services that can be obtained by using IPSec/TLS—authentication, integrity, non-repudiation, and so on.
  - Security capability exchange between communicating endpoints by using H.245 capability exchange procedures so that a resource-constrained endpoint is not overwhelmed.
  - A receiver requesting a certain security mode from the transmitter.
  - Anonymity, where only an alias address is known to the other endpoint but the physical address is not known.
- Security services for the media streams, which include the following components:
  - Opening logical channels with media stream confidentiality.
  - Key generation, distribution, and refresh for media-stream encryption.
  - Media-stream confidentiality techniques: RTP-level encryption, IPSec, and so on.

In this chapter, we will discuss the mechanisms that we use to achieve these security services.

Generation of a Secret Key

You can use a secret key shared between a pair of communicating entities in order to achieve security services (such as user authentication and message authentication/integrity). Because secret key-based mechanisms are faster than public key-based mechanisms, they are usually preferred when message authentication/integrity is desired—because in this case, each message might need to be authenticated and/or integrity-checked. Public key-based mechanisms might be too slow and/or computationally intensive for this purpose, however.

Here, we describe two cases of generating a secret key in the H.235 standard:

- A password (known *a priori* by the communicating entities) generates the secret key.
- The DH technique generates the secret key. Because the DH key exchange itself needs to be authenticated, either a secure channel or public key-based authentication mechanisms are used to achieve authentication.

Key Generation from a Password

Often, the communicating entities share a password/passphrase *a priori*, and the secret key is generated dynamically from this password when needed. This situation is usually the case when human users are involved, because it is more convenient to remember a password rather than to remember a non-mnemonic secret key. You can generate secret keys from passwords by using several different methods. The mechanism mandated by H.323 is based on ISO 9798-2:

Let the required length of the secret key be n bytes. The key generating mechanism is as follows:

- If password length = n bytes, key = password.
- If password length < n bytes, key = password padded with zeros.
- If password length > n bytes, key = initially assign first n bytes of password to key, then the $(n + M)^{th}$ byte of the password is XORed with the $(M \bmod (n))^{th}$ byte of the key (for all password bytes beyond n).

As an illustration, let us consider the case where the password is abcdEF56 and derive the secret key for three cases when the desired key length is (1) 24 bits, (2) 128 bits, and (3) 160 bits. Because the H.323 standard uses the *Universal Character Set* (UCS), or in other words, the ISO/IEC 10646 standard (an international standard to encode various characters), we will use this encoding method. We should note that any representation that follows the Unicode standard of character representation is also ISO/IEC 10646-compliant. Looking up the Unicode 16-bit representation of the characters in the password, we find them to be the following:

a = 00000000 01100001; b = 00000000 01100010; c = 00000000 01100011; d = 00000000 01100100; E = 00000000 01000101; F = 00000000 01000110; 5 = 00000000 00110101; 6 = 00000000 00110110

It is seen that the password length is 128 bits. The three cases are as follows:

1. When the desired key length is 24 bits, the size of the password exceeds the desired key size. Hence,

	00000000 01100001 00000000
XOR	01100010 00000000 01100011
XOR	00000000 01100100 00000000
XOR	01000101 00000000 01000110
XOR	00000000 00110101 00000000
XOR	00110110

   equals 00010001 00110000 00100101, which is the key.

2. When the desired key length is 128 bits, the size of the password equals the desired key size. Hence, the key is identical to the password: 00000000 01100001 00000000 01100010 00000000 01100011 00000000 01100100 00000000 01000101 00000000 01000110 00000000 00110101 00000000 00110110.

3. When the desired key length is 160 bits, the size of the password is less than the desired key size. Hence, the key is merely the password appended with the appropriate number of zeroes, resulting in: 00000000 01100001 00000000 01100010 00000000 01100011 00000000 01100100 00000000 01000101 00000000 01000110 00000000 00110101 00000000 00110110 00000000 00000000 00000000 00000000.

Key Generation by Using Diffie-Hellman

An endpoint pair can use the DH key-generation technique in order to generate a secret key. The dhkey field in a ClearToken carries the DH parameters. Figure 13.1(a) illustrates the exchange of the DH parameters (denoted as $dhkey_A$ and $dhkey_B$). In addition, a random number and timestamp are included in order to combat replay attacks; and the sender's ID (denoted as $sendersID_A$ and $sendersID_B$) and receiver's globally unique ID (denoted as $generalID_B$ and $generalID_A$) are included as well.

If the channel on which the DH parameters are exchanged is an insecure one, an endpoint cannot ascertain with certainty the identity of the other endpoint

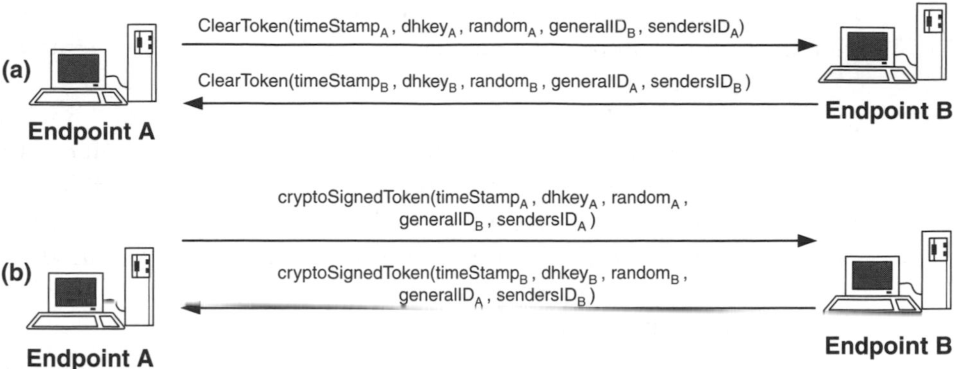

Figure 13.1 DH-based secret key generation by (a) using a secure channel and (b) using an insecure channel.

(the identity with which the secret key is established). In order to authenticate the communicating endpoints, a signature is included as well, as shown in Figure 13.1(b). You achieve this task by using the cryptoSignedToken within a CryptoToken instead of a ClearToken. The toBeSigned field of the token of the cryptoSignedToken, as seen in Figure 13.2, contains ClearToken (timestamp, dhkey, random, generalID, and sendersID) while the signature field contains the corresponding signature of this ClearToken. AlgorithmOID of the token denotes the signing algorithm while the params field contains any run-time parameters that are needed for the signing algorithm.

DH Technique

The DH key-generation technique, as indicated, involves the exchange of DH parameters through the dhkey field. This process involves two well-known

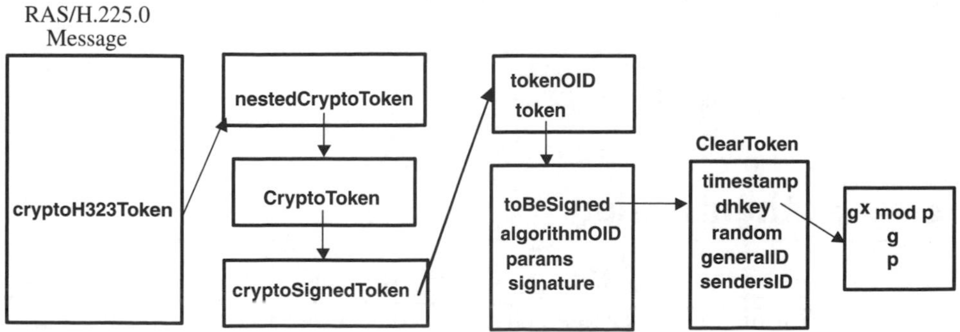

Figure 13.2 Illustrating cryptoSignedToken usage for DH-based key generation.

parameters: the generator (g) and a prime number (p). Each endpoint generates a random number, denoted as rand, and sends $g^{(rand)}$ (mod) p to the other endpoint. If Endpoint A generates random number x and Endpoint B generates y, then g^x (mod) p is sent by Endpoint A to Endpoint B while g^y (mod) p is sent by Endpoint B to Endpoint A. Each endpoint can then compute g^{xy} (mod) p, which is the secret key. We should note that all exchanges are sent in the clear and are hence accessible to any eavesdropper. Because the eavesdropper cannot determine rand from $g^{(rand)}$ (mod) p, he or she cannot compute the secret key with only the knowledge of g, p, g^x (mod) p, and g^y (mod) p.

The parameter set (g,p) is usually referred to as a DH group. Two DH groups, one using a 768-bit prime number and the other a 1,024-bit prime number, appear as follows:

$$\text{Prime (p)} = 2^{768} - 2^{704} - 1 + 2^{64} * \{ 2^{638} \pi] + 149686 \}$$

$$= (1552518092300708935130918131258481755631334049434514313202351194902966239949102107258669453876591642442910007680288864229150803718918046342632727613031282983744380820890196288509170691316593175367469551763119843371637221007210577919)_{10}$$

Generator (g) = 2

$$\text{Prime (p)} = 2^{1024} - 2^{960} - 1 + 2^{64} * \{ [2^{894} \pi] + 129093 \}$$

$$= (179769313486231590770839156793787453197860296048756011706444423684197180216158519368947833795864925541502180565485980503646440548199239100050792877003355816639229553136239076508735759914822574862575007425302077447712589550957937778424442426617334727629299387668709205606050270810842907692932019128194467627007)_{10}$$

Generator (g) = 2

User Authentication

User authentication refers to the situation where the identity of a communicating user needs to be verified. User authentication is conceptually different from message authentication, where the recipient of a message needs to ensure that the message came from the claimed transmitter. While message authentication also results in user authentication, user authentication can be performed more infrequently than the number of messages that is exchanged. The mechanisms that are used to achieve user authentication and message authentication are quite similar. We will discuss user authentication in this section and explore message authentication in the next section.

Two broad techniques exist for user authentication, and H.323 supports both of them:

- *Shared/secret key mechanisms*. These mechanisms are based on the two communicating entities sharing a common secret key. You can then use this key in one of several ways in order to authenticate either user. Two of these mechanisms that H.323 supports are as follows:
  - Encryption of certain fields—including a timestamp or random field—with the secret key
  - Generating a hash of certain fields, one of which is the secret key

  You should note that shared-key mechanisms do not provide non-repudiation, because either party that is in possession of the secret key could produce the authenticating material.

- *Public-key mechanisms*. These mechanisms rely on the entity that wishes to authenticate itself, possessing a public key pair—a private key that is known only to this entity, and a public key that is known to the entity that wishes to authenticate it. The public key is usually made accessible through a certificate issued by a certification authority. Authentication occurs by generating a digital signature, which is produced by encryption of certain fields (including a timestamp/random field) by using the private key. We should note that public-key mechanisms provide non-repudiation because only the party that is in possession of the private key could have produced the authenticating material. The verifying party only possesses the public key and hence could not have generated the digital signature.

Authentication by Shared Secret-Based Encryption

Figure 13.3 depicts the mechanism for achieving authentication by using shared secret-based encryption. Figure 13.3(a) illustrates the situation of one-way authentication while Figure 13.3(b) illustrates two-way authentication. In Figure 13.3(a), Endpoint B authenticates Endpoint A, whereas in Figure 13.3(b), Endpoint A authenticates Endpoint B as well. We assume that the unique generalID of each Endpoint is known to the other Endpoint. Other than the secret key, no other fields need to be kept secret. When the shared

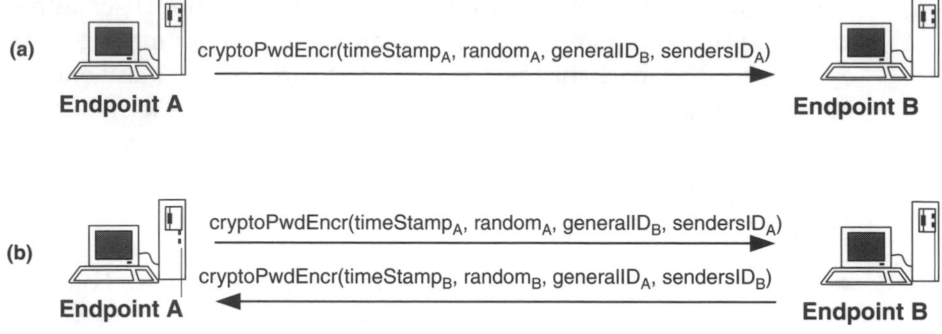

Figure 13.3 Shared-secret encryption for (a) one-way authentication (b) bidirectional authentication.

secret is a password (and not a secret key), then the secret key is derived from the password based on the mechanism described in the previous section.

The entity that wishes to be authenticated (Endpoint A in Figure 13.3(a)) encrypts generalID$_B$, the current timestamp, a random number, and Endpoint A's ID with the secret key that it shares with Endpoint B and sends the result to Endpoint B in a CryptoToken. The CryptoToken choice is cryptoPwdEncr, which uses a PwdCertToken (a ClearToken with mandatory components of generalID and timeStamp). In our case, the PwdCertToken additionally includes random and sendersID.

For the case of bidirectional authentication, Endpoint B additionally authenticates itself to Endpoint A by encrypting generalID$_A$ and the current timestamp with the same secret key and sending it in a CryptoToken to Endpoint A.

No new messages are defined for authentication. User authentication may be achieved using either RAS, H.225.0, or H.245 messages. As seen in Figure 13.4, the CryptoToken is sent within the cryptoH323Token of existing RAS and H.225.0 messages. Because H.245 messages do not contain a field to carry

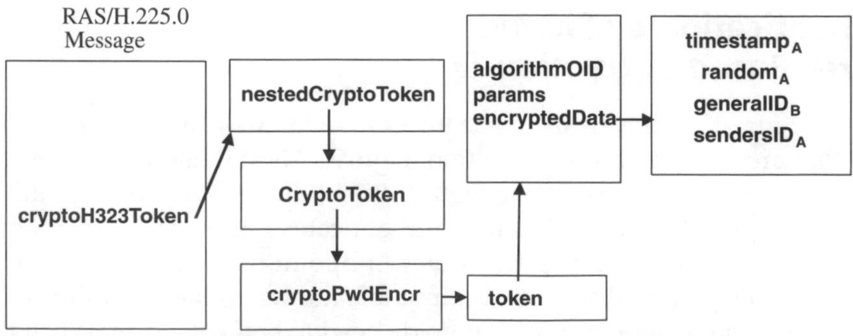

Figure 13.4 Use of cryptoPwdEncr.

a cryptoH323Token, in order to use H.245 messages for user authentication, these messages are tunneled within H.225.0 messages. You can then use the cryptoH323Token field of the H.225.0 message.

Computation of cryptoPwdEncr

The shared secret-based encryption method, as illustrated in Figure 13.4, uses the cryptoPwdEncr choice within CryptoToken, which is present within the nestedCryptoToken field of cryptoH323Token. The cryptoH323Token field is present in each RAS and H.225.0 message. The token field within cryptoPwdEncr contains encryptedData, which represents the generalID and timestamp fields that are encrypted by using the secret key. The algorithmOID field is set to denote the encryption mechanism used (such as DES, 3-DES, and so on), and params is set to any run-time parameters that are needed for the encrypting algorithm.

Authentication by Shared Secret-Based Hash

Authentication by shared secret-based hash is similar to that of shared secret-based encryption, with the difference being that the CryptoToken contains a hash of the generalID of the authenticating entity, the shared secret between the two entities, and the current timestamp. Figure 13.5(a) and Figure 13.5(b) show this diagram for one-way and two-way authentication, respectively.

Computation of cryptoHashedtoken

The shared secret-based hash method, as illustrated in Figure 13.6, uses the cryptoHashedToken field within CryptoToken, which is present within the nestedCryptoToken field of cryptoH323Token. The cryptoH323Token field is

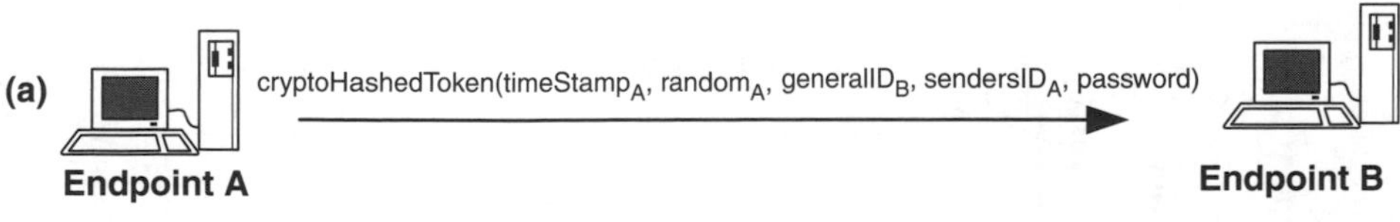

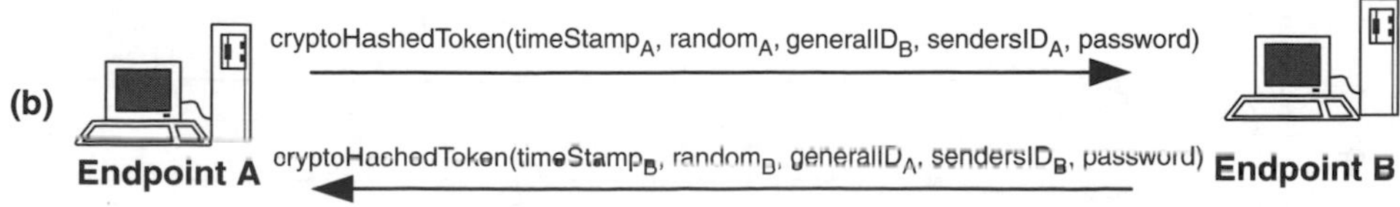

Figure 13.5 Shared secret hash-based (a) one-way authentication, and (b) bidirectional authentication.

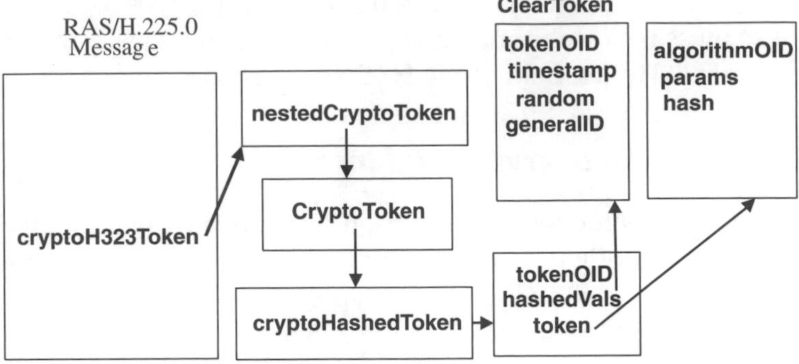

Figure 13.6 Use of cryptoHashedToken.

present in each RAS and H.225.0 message. The hashedVals field contains a ClearToken that carries fields that are used in computing the hash while the hash itself is included in the token field. The algorithmOID field is set to denote the hash mechanism used (such as MD5, SHA-1, and so on), and params is set to NULL. The tokenOID within cryptoHashedToken identifies which fields of the RAS/H.225.0 message are being authenticated. The tokenOID within ClearToken identifies the ClearToken as being used for the purpose of authentication, and the generalID carries the unique identifier of the recipient.

Authentication by Using a Digital Signature

Authentication by using digital signatures is similar to shared secret-based encryption—with the exception that the key that is used is the private key of the entity that wishes to be authenticated. The choice of the CryptoToken in this case is the cryptoSignedToken. Figure 13.7 illustrates the usage of the

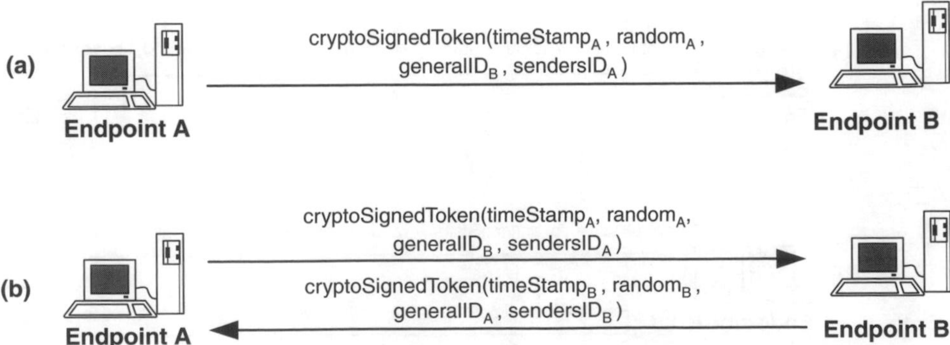

Figure 13.7 Digital signature-based (a) one-way authentication, and (b) bidirectional authentication.

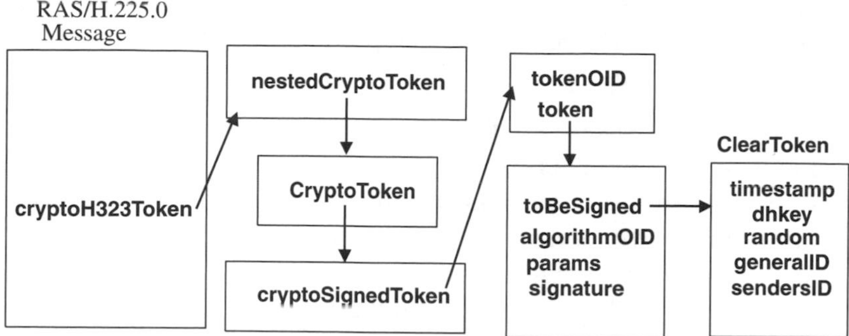

Figure 13.8 Computation of cryptoSignedToken.

cryptoSignedToken for one-way and two-way authentication and shows the fields that are signed.

Computation of cryptoSignedToken

The digital signature-based method, as illustrated in Figures 13.7 and 13.8, uses the cryptoSignedToken field within CryptoToken, which is present within the nestedCryptoToken field of cryptoH323Token.

For instance, when the *Elliptic Curve Digital-Signature Algorithm* (ECDSA) is used to compute the digital signature, the algorithmOID denotes that the ECDSA algorithm is being used. The signature contains the ECDSAlikeSignature structure containing the two ECDSA parameters—r and s—that are ASN.1 encoded.

Message Authentication/Integrity

In addition to user authentication, message authentication and integrity might also be desirable for select/all RAS/H.225.0/H.245 signaling messages. With minor modifications, the techniques that are used for user authentication can be used to achieve message authentication and integrity. When you use public key-based mechanisms, you can achieve non-repudiation as well.

In order to merely authenticate a message without providing integrity, you can use the techniques for user authentication. In other words, you can only use selective fields of the message in order to compute either a *Message Authentication Code* (MAC) based on encrypting certain fields or a keyed hash or a digital signature. Usually, these fields are not modified by intermediate application-level entities such as proxies; hence, they have an end-to-end significance. Such techniques also provide integrity for the fields that are used to compute the MAC/digital signature.

When you must provide message integrity in addition to authentication, all fields of the message need to be protected against tampering. Such a service is usually provided on an application-level hop-by-hop level as against an application-level end-to-end level. Integrity of all fields on an end-to-end level is not relevant because intermediate application-level entities such as proxies can modify certain fields. Figure 13.9 illustrates hop-by-hop and end-to-end security services.

Mechanisms to Achieve Message Integrity

At least two mechanisms are possible for achieving message integrity. These are (1) the use of CryptoH323Token for all signaling messages—RAS, H.225.0 and H.245—and (2) the use of the IntegrityCheckValue field for RAS messages.

Use of CryptoH323Token for RAS/H.225.0/H.245 Messages

The mechanism that is used to achieve message authentication/integrity by using CryptoH323Token is similar to what is used to achieve user authentication. The difference is that for message authentication/integrity, the tokenOID of the CryptoToken (either cryptoEncryptedToken, cryptoHashedToken, or cryptoSignedToken, as the case might be) is set to a value that is used to indicate that all fields of the message are used to compute the MAC/digital signature. For user authentication, as we discussed earlier, the tokenOID of the CryptoToken is set to a value that depicts the small set of fields that are used to compute the MAC/digital signature.

Figure 13.9 Illustrating hop-by-hop and end-to-end security services.

Use of IntegrityCheckValue for RAS Messages

An alternative mechanism for achieving integrity that is only applicable to RAS messages is the use of the *IntegrityCheckValue* (ICV) field. The ICV field was introduced only in RAS messages and not in H.225.0 or H.245 messages, because the desire for the unreliable transport-based RAS message integrity (such as when UDP is used) was seen as critical. They carried H.225.0 and H.245 messages by using a reliable transport mechanism such as the *Transmission Control Protocol* (TCP). (Note that the use of UDP for H.225.0 message transport was specified only much later.) The capability to carry cryptoH323Token within RAS (as well as H.225.0) was introduced later, and with integrity being possible by the use of cryptoH323Token, the ICV mechanism is not seen as a popular method any more. All security profiles that have been specified to date make use of cryptoH323Token for RAS message integrity rather than the ICV field.

Figure 13.10 shows the relevant ASN.1 for achieving RAS message integrity by using the ICV field.

Securing H.225.0 and H.245 Channels

In the previous section, we saw how message authentication can be achieved. The mechanisms described there did not require a secure communication channel. Alternatively, you can secure an H.225.0 (or H.245) channel, and then send H.225.0 (or H.245) messages through this channel. The advantage of using a secure communication channel is that security services such as authentication need not be provided on a per-message basis.

Securing the H.225.0 Channel

In order to secure the H.225.0 channel, you can use mechanisms such as TLS or IPSec. Because each H.225.0 message needs to be secured and H.225.0 messages are the first that are exchanged between the communicating endpoints, negotiation of the security mechanism cannot be performed by using H.323/H.225.0. The channel has to be secured prior to any message exchange using techniques such as TLS or IPSec. A TLS-secured H.225.0 channel employs well-known port 1300, and all H.225.0 messages that are sent to this port will be protected by TLS. Currently, no well-known port exists for H.225.0 channels that are secured by using IPSec.

Securing the H.245 Channel

The communicating endpoints can negotiate the mechanism by which you secure the H.245 channel by using the H.225.0 message exchanges. The optional

```
GatekeeperRequest     ::= SEQUENCE
{
      ...,
      integrity   SEQUENCE OF   IntegrityMechanism OPTIONAL,
      integrityCheckValue       ICV OPTIONAL,
      ...,
}

AdmissionRequest ::= SEQUENCE
{
      ...,
      integrityCheckValue       ICV OPTIONAL,
      ...,
}

IntegrityMechanism      ::= CHOICE
{
      nonStandard   NonStandardParameter,
      digSig        NULL,
      iso9797       OBJECT IDENTIFIER,
      nonIsoIM      NonIsoIntegrityMechanism ,
      ...
}

NonIsoIntegrityMechanism      ::= CHOICE
{
      hMAC-MD5    NULL,
      hMAC-iso10118-2-s   EncryptIntAlg,
      hMAC-iso10118-2-1   EncryptIntAlg,
      hMAC-iso10118-3     OBJECT IDENTIFIER,
      ...
}

EncryptIntAlg     ::= CHOICE
{
      nonstandard           NonStandardParameter,
      isoAlgorithm          OBJECT IDENTIFIER,
      ...
}

ICV ::= SEQUENCE
{
      algorithmOID    OBJECT IDENTIFIER,
      icv             BIT STRING
}
```

Figure 13.10 Relevant ASN.1 for RAS message integrity by using the ICV field.

h245SecurityCapability field within the H.225.0 Setup-*User-User Information Element* (UUIE) lists the possible methods of securing the H.245 channel that the calling endpoint supports. The called endpoint (which receives the Setup-UUIE) can then choose one possible mechanism and return it in the h245SecurityMode field of the Alerting-UUIE, CallProceeding-UUIE, and Connect-UUIE. The currently provided secure mechanisms are TLS, IPSec, any nonstandard mechanism, and no security. If the mechanisms that the calling endpoint offers are not supported by the called endpoint, it might send a ReleaseComplete-UUIE with the ReleaseCompleteReason field set to securityDenied. If the called endpoint sends a Connect-UUIE but sends it with a h245SecurityMode that is not compatible with the set that the calling endpoint sent, the calling endpoint might send a ReleaseComplete-UUIE with the undefinedReason field (thereby terminating the call). The relevant ASN.1 is shown in Figure 13.11.

Secure H.235 Control Channel

Instead of securing the H.245 control channel, you can also use an insecure H.245 control channel in conjunction with a secure H.235 control channel. The secure H.235 control channel is a logical channel that is opened by using standard H.245 logical channel procedures. As indicated in Figure 13.12, the dataType field for the H.245 OpenLogicalChannel message is set to h235Control. This logical channel is secured by using mechanisms such as IPSec or TLS. The secure h235Control channel can then be used to perform authentication, to generate shared secrets, and/or to transfer the shared secret by using the EncryptionSync field. In a later section, we explain the procedure for the generation and transfer of shared secrets.

Security Capability Exchange

In Chapter 3, we described the H.245 capability exchange mechanism and procedures. In this section, we will describe how security capability exchange makes use of these procedures.

Security capabilities (transmit and receive) need to be exchanged between endpoints so that a resource-constrained endpoint is not overwhelmed due to required security processing. As you can see in Figure 13.13, the h235SecurityCapability choice within the Capability structure describes each security capability. Because the security capability is associated with some media processing capability, the associated media processing CapabilityTableEntryNumber is indicated as well. For instance, a (simplistic) security capability of DES encryption for H.263 video transmission is associated with the capability of H.263 video transmission (which has a CapabilityTableEntryNumber).

```
Setup-UUIE ::= SEQUENCE
{
    ...
    h245SecurityCapability  SEQUENCE OF H245Security  OPTIONAL,
    ...
}

Connect-UUIE ::= SEQUENCE
{
    ...
    h245SecurityMode  H245Security  OPTIONAL,
    ...
}

CallProceeding-UUIE ::= SEQUENCE
{
    ...
    h245SecurityMode  H245Security  OPTIONAL,
    ...
}

Alerting-UUIE ::= SEQUENCE
{
    ...
    h245SecurityMode  H245Security  OPTIONAL,
    ...
}

H245Security ::=CHOICE
{
    nonstandard       NonstandardParameter,
    noSecurity        NULL,
    tls               SecurityCapabilities,
    ipsec             SecurityCapabilities,
    ...
}

ReleaseCompleteReason ::= CHOICE
{
    ...
    securityDenied      NULL
    ...
}
```

Figure 13.11 ASN.1 for negotiating the H.245 channel-securing mechanism.

```
OpenLogicalChannel      ::=SEQUENCE
{
        ...
        forwardLogicalChannelParameters     SEQUENCE
        {
                ...
                dataType     DataType,
                ...
        }
}

DataType ::= CHOICE
{
        ...
        h235Control           NonStandardParameter,
        ...
}
```

Figure 13.12 ASN.1 for opening the H.235 control logical channel.

Receiver Requesting a Security Mode

As we discussed in the Chapter 3, a receiver can provide the transmitter with a set of modes—in the order of the receiver's preference with the most preferred first—that the receiver would like the transmitter to transmit to it. This action takes place by using the RequestMode message. The transmitter can then either acknowledge the request with a RequestModeAck message or reject it with a RequestModeReject message.

The ModeDescription that a receiver provides the transmitter in the RequestMode message contains a set of ModeElements. One type of ModeElement is the h235Mode, which is a media mode (such as AudioMode, VideoMode, and so on) in conjunction with a set of security parameters described in the encryptionAuthenticationAndIntegrity field. Figure 13.14 shows the relevant ASN.1 for a receiver requesting a security mode.

Media-Stream Encryption

From an end-user's perspective, one of the important security services is media-stream confidentiality. This service occurs by encrypting the media stream, which involves two issues:

```
Capability  ::= CHOICE
{
     ...
     h235SecurityCapability  H235SecurityCapability,
     ...
}

H235SecurityCapability  ::= SEQUENCE
{
  encryptionAuthenticationAndIntegrity     EncryptionAuthenticationAndIntegrity,
  mediaCapability                          CapabilityTableEntryNumber
  ...
}

EncryptionAuthenticationAndIntegrity         ::= SEQUENCE
{
  encryptionCapability        EncryptionCapability        OPTIONAL,
  authenticationCapability    AuthenticationCapability    OPTIONAL,
  integrityCapability         IntegrityCapability         OPTIONAL,
  ...
}

EncryptionCapability  ::=SEQUENCE SIZE(1..256) of MediaEncryptionAlgorithm

MediaEncryptionAlgorithm      ::= CHOICE
{
     nonstandard   NonStandardParameter,
     algorithm     OBJECT IDENTIFIER,
     ...
}

AuthenticationCapability      ::= SEQUENCE
{
     nonstandard NonStandardParameter    OPTIONAL,
}

IntegrityCapability      ::= SEQUENCE
{
     nonstandard NonStandardParameter    OPTIONAL,
}
```

Figure 13.13 ASN.1 for security capability exchange.

```
RequestMode          ::= SEQUENCE
{
      requestedModes    SEQUENCE  SIZE (1..256) of  ModeDescription,
      ...
}

ModeDescription       ::= SET SIZE (1..256) of  ModeElement

ModeElement       ::= SEQUENCE
{
      type              CHOICE
      {
                  ...,
                  h235Mode     H235Mode,
      }
      ...
}

H235Mode::= SEQUENCE
{
      encryptionAuthenticationAndIntegrity     EncryptionAuthenticationAndI ntegrity,
      mediaMode     CHOICE
      {
                  ...,
                  videoMode     VideoMode,
                  audioMode     AudioMode,
                  ...,
      }
}
```

Figure 13.14 ASN.1 for the receiver that is requesting a security mode.

- In the OpenLogicalChannel message, the transmitter indicates to the receiver that the media stream is encrypted.
- The media encryption key needs to be generated and distributed to all parties that are involved in the conference.

Opening a Logical Channel for the Encrypted Media Stream

After the capability exchange phase, a transmitting endpoint is aware of the security capabilities of the receiver. The endpoint can then open a logical channel with the supported security capabilities of the receiver. We illustrate this concept in Figure 13.15.

```
OpenLogicalChannel     ::= SEQUENCE
{
        ...,
        forwardLogicalChannelParameters     SEQUENCE
        {
                ...,
                dataType    DataType,
                ...
        }
        ...
}

DataType     ::= CHOICE
{
        ...
        h235Media          H235Media,
        ...
}

H235Media     ::= SEQUENCE
{
        encryptionAuthenticationAndIntegrity
        EncryptionAuthenticationAndIntegrity,
        mediaType     CHOICE
        {
                ...,
                videoData   VideoCapability,
                audioData   AudioCapability,
                ...,
        }
}
```

Figure 13.15 Illustrating ASN.1 for the H.235Media OpenLogicalChannel procedure.

Encryption Key Generation, Distribution, and Refresh

We now describe three aspects dealing with session media encryption keys:

- How you can generate them
- How they are distributed initially to the communicating endpoints
- How refreshed keys are distributed subsequently to the communicating endpoints

Session Media Encryption Key Generation

The master always generates the session media encryption key (both initial and subsequent keys) and distributes the key to the slave(s). The length of the key depends on the encryption algorithm that you use. For instance, if you use DES, then a 56-bit key is generated. You need a good random number generator for this purpose.

Initial Session Media Encryption Key Distribution

After generating the session key, the master needs to distribute it to the slave(s). For the initial session media encryption key (in other words, the session key that is distributed along with opening the logical channel), you perform this task by using the optional encryptionSync field within H.245 logical channel messages. The encryptionSync field is present within both the *OpenLogicalChannel* (OLC) and the *OpenLogicalChannelAck* (OLCAck) messages. If the master opens the logical channel, then the encryptionSync field of the OpenLogicalChannel message is used. If the slave opens the logical channel, however, then the encryptionSync field of the OpenLogicalChannelAck message is used. In other words, the encryptionSync field of the relevant message (OLC or OLCAck) that the master sends to the slave is used for initial key distribution because it is the master that distributes the key to the slave.

Figure 13.16 shows the relevant ASN.1 for this purpose. EncryptionSync includes the h235Key field (which contains the key material) and the SynchFlag field (which contains the RTP dynamic payload number that matches the key). By using the pair (key and RTP payload number), the receiver can determine the key to be used for the decryption of received RTP packets. Because the distribution of the key needs to be performed in a secure manner, the actual distribution of the key within the h235Key field uses one of three possible methods.

- When the H.245 channel is secure (with confidentiality provided), any OLC or OLCAck messages that carry the EncryptionSync field automatically receive confidentiality. Consequently, no extra protection is necessary for the key material. This information is indicated by the secureChannel choice of the h235Key field.
- You can encrypt the key by using a shared secret that has been established between the communicating endpoints. You specify this secret by using the sharedSecret choice of the h235Key field. The key material and the general identifier of the slave are encrypted by using the shared secret and are transmitted along with the algorithm *Object Identifier* (OID) of the encrypting algorithm and any run-time parameters that the algorithm might require.

```
OpenLogicalChannel   ::= SEQUENCE -- (OLC)
{
      ...
      encryptionSync   EncryptionSync   OPTIONAL,
      ...
}

OpenLogicalChannelAck   ::= SEQUENCE  -- (OLC)
{
      ...
      encryptionSync   EncryptionSync   OPTIONAL,
      ...
}

EncryptionSync   ::= SEQUENCE  -- (OLC)
{
      ...
      synchFlag    INTEGER(0..255),
      h235Key      OCTET STRING(SIZE(1..65535)),
      ...
}

H235Key  ::= CHOICE
{
      secureChannel      KeyMaterial,
      sharedSecret       ENCRYPTED{EncodedKeySyncMaterial},
      certProtectedKey   SIGNED(EncodedKeySignedMaterial),
      ...
}

KeySignedMaterial   ::= SEQUENCE
{
      generalID    Identifier,
      mrandom      RandomVal,
      srandom      RandomVal     OPTIONAL,
      timeStamp    TimeStamp     OPTIONAL,
      encrptval    ENCRYPTED {EncodedKeySyncMaterial},
}
KeySyncMaterial   ::= SEQUENCE
{
      generalID    Identifier,
      keyMaterial  KeyMaterial,
      ...
}

ENCRYPTED { ToBeEncrypted}   ::= SEQUENCE
{
      algorithmOID     OBJECT IDENTIFIER,
      paramS           Params,
      encryptedData    OCTET STRING
}
SIGNED {ToBeSigned}    ::= SEQUENCE
{
      toBeSigned     ToBeSigned,
      algorithmOID   OBJECT IDENTIFIER,
      paramS         Params,
      signature      BIT STRING
}
```

Figure 13.16 ASN.1 for initial session media encryption key distribution.

- You can encrypt the session key by using the public key of the slave. Because the public key is usually obtained from a certificate, this mechanism is indicated by the certProtectedKey choice of the h235Key field. In this case, as in the previous situation, the key material and slave general ID are encrypted but use the public key of the slave (instead of the shared secret), and the algorithm ID of the public key algorithm and any run-time parameters are included as well. In addition, a signature of this result is also computed.

Subsequent Session Media Encryption Key Distribution

You might need to generate a new session media encryption key and distribute it after the logical channel has been opened. This situation can happen, for instance, if (1) no media encryption was provided at the beginning and media encryption was required at a later time; (2) if the original key needs to be refreshed for security reasons; or (3) if the encrypting algorithm is changed. In any case, because the OLC/OLCAck messages cannot be used during this time (because the logical channel is already open), an alternative mechanism is needed to distribute the new session key.

In the case of a two-point conference, the encryptionUpdateRequest message is sent by a slave to the master in order to request a new media encryption key if the slave is the transmitter (in other words, the one who opened the logical channel). The master then uses the encryptionUpdate message in order to send the new key to the slave. The master can also asynchronously (without a request from a slave) decide to generate a new key and transmit it to the slave by using the encryptionUpdate message (if the master is the transmitter).

In the case of a multi-point conference, the slave that is the transmitter can request the MC for a new media encryption key by sending it an encryptionUpdateRequest message. The MC (master) then generates the new encryption key and transmits it to all conference participants (slaves) except for the transmitter (slave), after which it transmits it to the transmitter. The encryptionUpdate message is used for this purpose. The transmitter can begin using the new key any time after receiving it.

Figure 13.17 shows the relevant ASN.1 for this purpose. Both encryptionUpdate and encryptionUpdateRequest are miscellaneous commands, and the logicalChannelNumber is used to identify the logical channel to which the command pertains. The encryptionUpdate message is identical to EncryptionSync, which we discussed in the previous section. The encryptionUpdateRequest message optionally lists how the new key needs to be protected by the master while distributing it.

```
MiscellaneousCommand      ::= SEQUENCE
{
    logicalChannelNumber  LogicalChannelNumber
    type                  CHOICE
    {
        ...
        encryptionUpdate          EncryptionSync,
        encryptionUpdateRequest   EncryptionUpdateRequest,
        ...
    }
    ...
}

EncryptionUpdateRequest     ::= SEQUENCE
{
    keyProtectionMethod    KeyProtectionMethod    OPTIONAL,
    ...
}

KeyProtectionMethod     ::= SEQUENCE
{
    secureChannel       BOOLEAN,
    sharedSecret        BOOLEAN,
    certProtectedKey    BOOLEAN,
    ...
}
```

Figure 13.17 ASN.1 for subsequent media encryption key distribution.

Use of RTP-Based Techniques for Media-Stream Encryption

Because RTP is used for H.323 media stream packetization, the H.323 media stream encryption procedure follows that which the RTP standard describes. We now describe three aspects dealing with RTP-based techniques for media stream encryption:

- Which fields are encrypted
- How the Initialization Vector (IV) is computed
- Ciphertext stealing and padding techniques

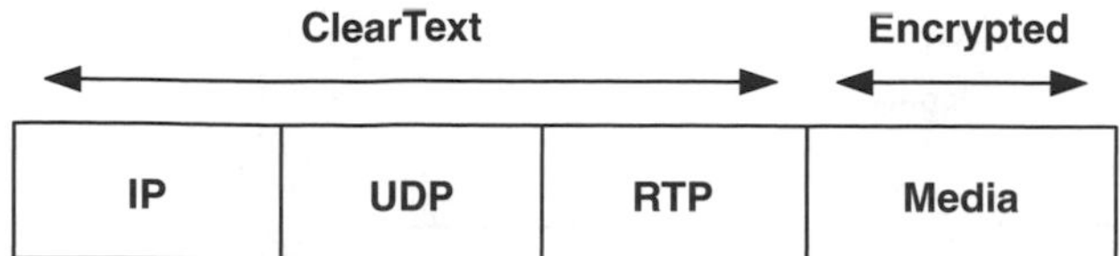

Figure 13.18 Illustrating fields that are encrypted by using RTP-level encryption.

Encrypted Fields

The RTP header as well as any higher layer headers (such as IP and UDP headers) are sent unencrypted. Only the RTP payload is encrypted, as we can see in Figure 13.18. As we described previously, when a media encryption key is distributed by the master to the slave (either in the encryptionSync or encryptionUpdate fields), the associated RTP dynamic payload number is included in the synchFlag field. When the receiver receives a packet with this RTP payload number, it uses this media encryption key to decrypt the packet. Because the receiver needs to inspect the dynamic payload number of the RTP header, the RTP header needs to be sent unencrypted.

Another important aspect with the media stream encryption is that each RTP packet is encrypted independently of other RTP packets belonging to the same stream. In other words, *Initialization Vector* (IV) computation and padding (which we explain next) are determined on an individual RTP packet basis. The advantage of performing encryption of one RTP packet independent of other RTP packets is that the mechanism can tolerate RTP packet losses. If dependencies existed in the encryption of RTP packets, then the loss of one RTP packet would mean that all other RTP packets that rely on this lost RTP packet for their successful decryption cannot be decrypted (and therefore have to be discarded).

IV Computation

Block ciphers operate on plain-text inputs that are equal to the block size. Hence, an RTP payload has to be broken into units equaling the block size so that you can input each block into the cipher. The encryption of each individual block can be referred to as occurring in a cycle, and the different cycles might (or might not) be chained/linked. The way in which this chaining/linking occurs is referred to as the mode. Four common modes of operation exist for block ciphers: *Electronic Code Book* (ECB), *Cipher Block Chaining* (CBC), *Output FeedBack* (OFB), and *Cipher FeedBack* (CFB). Except for ECB, the other three modes involve feeding information from one encryption cycle to the next.

Because CBC, OFB, and CFB modes operate by chaining/linking data from one encrypting cycle to other cycles, the first encryption cycle requires an IV.

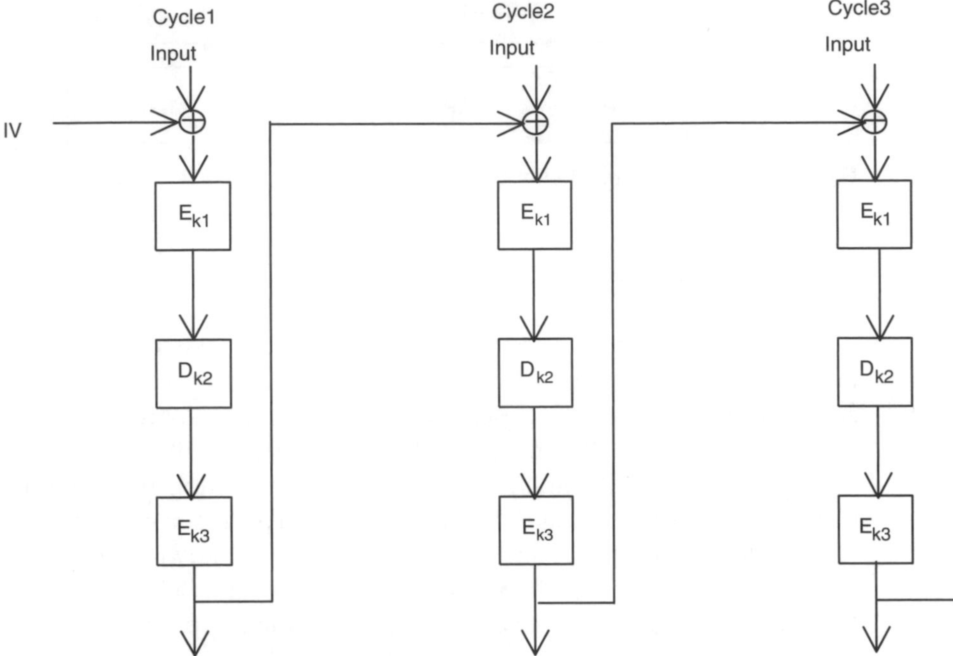

Figure 13.19 Triple-DES in CBC mode.

For instance, Figure 13.19 illustrates the triple-DES encryption algorithm in CBC mode with the IV shown for the first cycle. The H.323 standard specifies how this IV is computed, taking into consideration the mode of operation. In each case, the IV is a function of the RTP sequence number and/or timestamp, which permits the scalability of operation and resynchronization in the face of lost RTP packets. The size of the IV equals the block size (B) and is generated as follows:

- For CBC mode: IV = First B octets of RTP (Sequence Number + Timestamp) fields, repeated so that enough bytes are present. Here, + denotes concatenation. Note that the RTP Sequence Number field is 16 bits long while the Timestamp field is 32 bits long.
- For CFB and OFB modes: IV = (Base IV) XOR (Counter Value). Base IV is supplied along with the key material. The counter is initialized to the initial RTP Sequence Number field and is incremented subsequently so that the low-order 16 bits are in synchronization with the RTP Sequence Number field.

As an illustration, consider the case where the DES encrypting algorithm, which uses a block size of 64 bits, is used. Let's determine the IV for the following cases:

A. CBC mode is used, and the RTP packet has a Sequence Number of 0x3A72 and a Timestamp of 0xE1846B4A. Because the block size is 64 bits, whereas Sequence Number + Timestamp (which equals 0x3A72E1846B4A) is only 48 bits long, the (Sequence Number + Timestamp) fields are repeated in order to obtain 0x3A72E1846B4A3A72E1846B4A. The first 64 bits of this 96-bit string then give us the IV of 0x3A72E1846B4A3A72.

B. Eight-bit CFB mode is used, and the RTP packet has a Sequence Number of 0x3A72. Assume that the leading 16 bits of the counter have 0x0001 and that the Base IV is 0x0123456789ABCDEF. Because the counter has a value of 0x00013A72, the (Base IV) XOR (Counter Value) gives a value of 0x0123456789AAFE9D, which is the IV for blocks of this RTP packet.

C. Eight-bit OFB mode is used, and the RTP packet has a sequence number of 0x3A72. As in the previous case, assume that the leading 16 bits of the counter have 0x0001 and that the Base IV is 0x0123456789ABCDEF. Because the IV computation is identical for CFB and OFB modes, the IV for this case is identical to that for the previous case.

Ciphertext Stealing and Padding

The input in each encryption cycle usually needs to equal the block size. If the payload size is an integral multiple of the block size, then the payload is split into block-sized fragments. Each fragment is sent as an input to an encryption cycle. If the payload size is not an integral multiple of the block size, however, then a mechanism is needed to handle the last fragment (which does not equal a block size). We commonly employ two techniques:

- *Ciphertext stealing*. In this method, the output of the last encryption cycle is less than the block size.
- *Padding (as specified in the RTP standard)*. When the payload is padded so that the resulting size is an integral number of blocks, the *padding bit* (P bit) in the RTP header is set to one. The last octet of the payload denotes the number of padding bytes including this last octet. The value of the pad depends on the encryption algorithm. In this method, the output of the last encryption cycle equals the block size.

The receiver can independently determine whether the initial payload size is an integral multiple of the block size. If it is not, it can determine whether ciphertext stealing or padding was used. A three-step process completes this task:

1. If the encrypted RTP payload is an integral multiple of the block size—and if the RTP header has P = 0—then the receiver concludes that the original payload was an integral multiple of the block size.
2. If the encrypted RTP payload is an integral multiple of the block size—and if the RTP header has P = 1—then the receiver concludes that the original payload was not an integral multiple of the block size and that padding was used.

3. If the encrypted RTP payload is not an integral multiple of the block size, then ciphertext stealing was used. In this case, the RTP header must have P = 0.

Use of IPSec for Media-Stream Encryption

So far, we have discussed the use of application-level techniques for media-stream encryption. Here, we will see how we can use IPSec for this purpose. Figure 13.20 illustrates the headers that are encrypted when IPSec is used for encryption. IPSec introduces a header termed the *Encapsulating Security Payload* (ESP) for the purpose of achieving encryption.

The RAS and H.225.0 connection establishment phase are unchanged. During the H.245 capability exchange phase, endpoints indicate their capability of using IPSec with specific codecs. In other words, as we described previously, the MediaEncryptionAlgorithm field within encryptionCapability of encryptionAuthenticationAndIntegrity field of the H235SecurityCapability field contains an object identifier that denotes IPSec capability. This situation implies that IPSec can be used with the codecs that are specified in the associated mediaCapability of the same H235SecurityCapability field. When a logical channel is opened, the use of the suitable codec with IPSec-based security is indicated. Subsequently, an IPSec *Security Association* (SA) can be established between the two media channel transport addresses. This action might involve the use of the *Internet Key Exchange* (IKE) protocol.

Anonymity

Anonymity is an important service that needs to be offered to subscribers who desire to use it. With such a service, either (1) the physical address of the caller can be hidden from the callee, or (2) the physical address of the callee can be hidden from the caller. You achieve this task by using tokens suitably, as we illustrate here. A user's profile indicating a desire for anonymity—for called and/or received calls—is present at its gatekeeper. You can use several

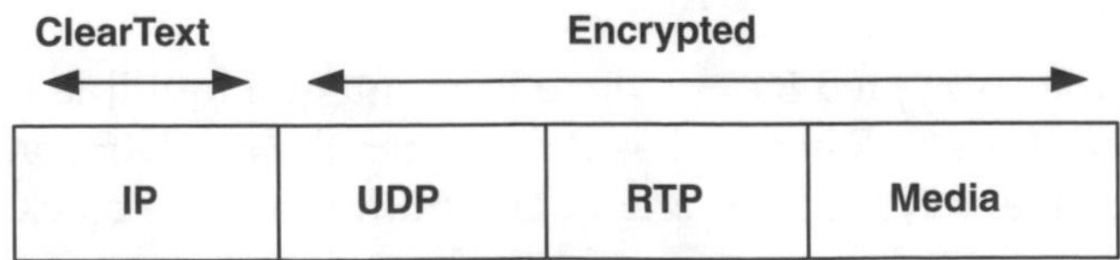

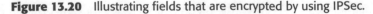

Figure 13.20 Illustrating fields that are encrypted by using IPSec.

mechanisms by which an endpoint can convey its desired call-processing profile to its gatekeeper. One possible mechanism is that the user interface at the endpoint supports this functionality, and the *Call Processing Language* (CPL) syntax is used as a standard format to transfer this user profile to the gatekeeper. You might also resort to simpler non-automated mechanisms, such as speaking with a human representative or mailing the desired profile to a processing center.

Figure 13.21 illustrates the situation where Endpoint A initiates communication with Endpoint B. Consider the case where Endpoint B wishes to keep its physical address hidden from Endpoint A. Endpoint A sends an ARQ to Gatekeeper A with the alias address of Endpoint B included in the destinationInfo field of the ARQ message. Note that neither Endpoint A nor Gatekeeper A are aware of the transport address of Endpoint B but merely have knowledge of the alias address. Upon receiving the ARQ, Gatekeeper A sends an LRQ to Gatekeeper B, and the destinationInfo field of the LRQ message contains the alias address of Endpoint B. Gatekeeper B, upon looking up the profile of Endpoint B, realizes that anonymity needs to be provided for this session. This situation implies that the transport address of Endpoint B needs to be hidden both for the signaling and for the media channels. For the signaling channel, you achieve this goal by using gatekeeper-routed call signaling (H.225.0) and call control (H.245) channels. For the media stream, you achieve this task by using a media proxy (or an RTP proxy) in order to route the media stream from Endpoint A to Endpoint B. The OLCAck that Endpoint B sends Gatekeeper B contains the transport address of Endpoint B in order to receive the media stream in the

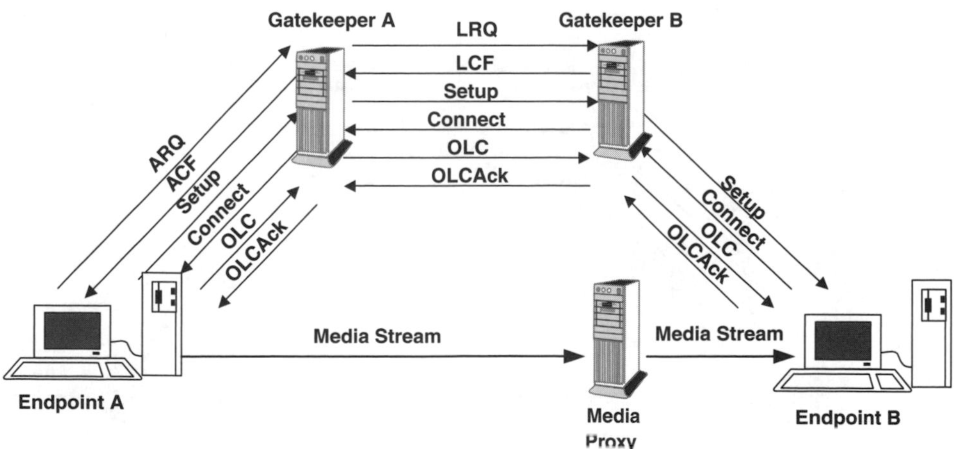

Figure 13.21 Illustrating anonymity by using gatekeeper-routed signaling/control channels and a proxy-routed media stream.

mediaChannel field of the H2250LogicalChannelParameters field of the OLCAck. The OLCAck that Gatekeeper B sends to Gatekeeper A as well as the OLCAck that Gatekeeper A sends to Endpoint A contains the transport address of the media proxy that receives the media stream in the mediaChannel field of the H2250LogicalChannelParameters field of the OLCAck.

Figure 13.22 illustrates the case where Endpoint B is a *Plain Old Telephone Service* (POTS) phone (in other words, a legacy analog telephone whose physical address needs to be hidden when called by Endpoint A). As in the previous scenario, Gatekeeper B prevents the call signaling and control addresses of Endpoint B from being exposed to Endpoint A or Gatekeeper A while the gateway prevents the media channel address of Endpoint B from being exposed. This scenario requires a gatekeeper-routed call-signaling and call-control model. The setup message from Endpoint A to Gatekeeper A, as well as that going from Gatekeeper A to Gatekeeper B, contains the alias address of the POTS phone in the destinationAddress field (without indicating the physical address, such as the E.164 number associated with it). Gatekeeper B replaces the alias address with the actual physical address (E.164 number) and sends the resulting setup message to the gateway, which then calls the POTS phone.

If the gatekeeper that is associated with the gateway is to translate the alias address that is associated with the POTS phone to the E.164 number, a gatekeeper-routed model is necessary (as we saw in Figure 13.22). Anonymity can also be provided without the need for a gatekeeper-routed model, however. Figure 13.23 illustrates this situation and makes use of

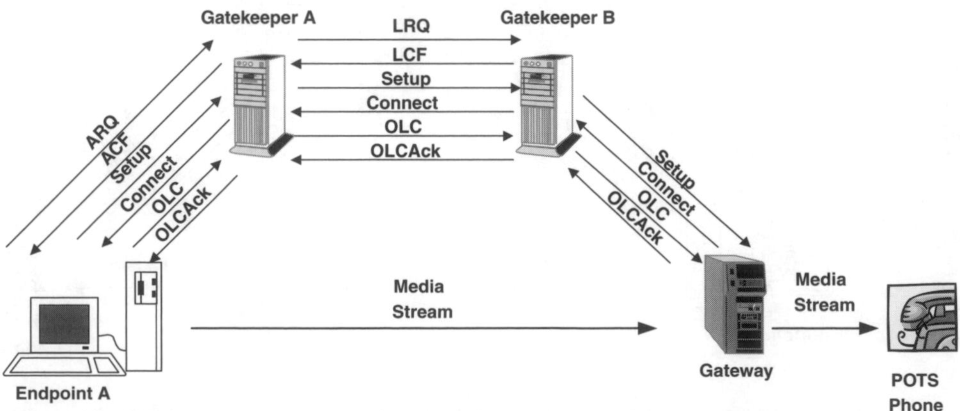

Figure 13.22 Illustrating anonymity for a POTS phone with a gatekeeper-routed call.

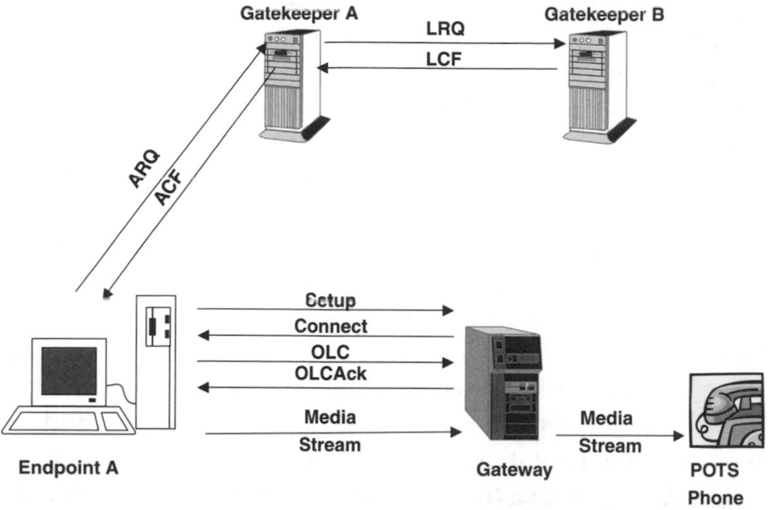

Figure 13.23 Illustrating anonymity for a POTS phone with a direct-routed call by the use of tokens.

tokens in order to achieve anonymity. When the LRQ message containing the alias address of the POTS phone is received at Gatekeeper B, it includes an encrypted token in the resulting LCF that is sent back to Gatekeeper A. This token contains the E.164 address of the POTS phone and is encrypted by using a secret that is shared between Gatekeeper B and the gateway. The opaque token is transferred transparently in the ACF from Gatekeeper A to Endpoint A and in the setup message from Endpoint A to the gateway. The gateway can decrypt the token and use the resulting E.164 number to place a call to the POTS phone.

An alternative scenario of token usage could use a local secret at Gatekeeper B (which is not known to the gateway) in order to encrypt the E.164 number and transmit it in the token. In this case, when the gateway receives the opaque token in the setup message, it sends it transparently to Gatekeeper B in the ARQ message, and Gatekeeper B returns the decrypted E.164 number in the ACF message. The gateway can then place a call to the POTS phone.

Security Profiles

As we can see from the discussions in previous sections of this chapter, H.235 —the security standard for H.323—provides several security services, and usually more than one mechanism exists in order to achieve the same security service. Moreover, given a certain security service and mechanism to achieve the service, the specific cryptographic algorithms that are chosen can vary. The H.235 standard does not mandate any security service or algorithm, although when given a service, the mechanism that is used to achieve the service might be fixed in certain situations. This flexibility in the choice of security services, mechanisms, and algorithms that an implementer can implement (and still be considered H.235-compliant) can result in non-interoperable implementations. For instance, if one implementation only supports the DES algorithm while another only supports the RC2 algorithm for media-stream encryption, then these two implementations (while each being H.235-compliant) will not interoperate. Hence, security profiles—which mandate specific security services, mechanisms, and algorithms—are needed. Implementations that are compliant with a particular security profile will be interoperable. In this section, we briefly discuss two security profiles that are specified within the H.235 standard.

Baseline Security Profile

The H.235 standard specifies a baseline security profile, based on work that was carried out within the *International Multimedia Telecommunications Consortium* (IMTC) and the *European Telecommunications Standards Institute* (ETSI) *Telecommunications and Internet Protocol Harmonization Over Networks* (TIPHON) project. The profile provides the following security services:

- Authentication and integrity for all RAS, H.225.0, and H.245 messages
- Optionally, confidentiality for media streams

Authentication and Integrity for Signaling Messages

In the section describing the mechanisms to achieve message authentication/integrity, we listed three possible mechanisms for this purpose: shared secret-based encryption, shared secret-based hash, and digital signatures. The baseline security profile uses the shared secret-based hash mechanism by using an *a priori* password in order to provide authentication and integrity for all RAS, H.225.0, and H.245 messages.

The baseline security profile assumes that communicating entities share an *a priori* password and that gatekeeper-routed call signaling is mandated. The reason for mandating a gatekeeper-routed model is that it makes the most sense in an *a priori* password situation. It is possible or even likely for an endpoint to share a password with its gatekeeper and also for gatekeepers to share a password with other gatekeepers, but it is unlikely for communicating endpoints to share a password with each other. The profile also mandates H.245 tunneling so that the CryptoTokens within the encapsulating H.225.0 message can be used to carry the authenticating data (MAC). Although not connected with security functionality, the profile also mandates Fast Connect.

The algorithm that we use to create the MAC is HMAC-SHA1-96. The resulting MAC using this algorithm is 96 bits long. Table 13.1 provides a snapshot of the security services and the mechanisms/algorithms that are used (i.e., the functions that are called-denoted as "call functions") within the baseline security profile.

Media-Stream Encryption

Encryption of the media stream is optional in the baseline security profile. In the section detailing media-stream encryption procedures, we mentioned that the master always generates the session key for media-stream encryption. Three mechanisms exist for distributing this session key to the slave within the h235Key field: using a secure H.245 channel, encrypting by using a shared secret, and encrypting by using the recipient's public key. The baseline security profile relies on encryption by using a shared secret, and an unauthenticated *Diffie-Hellman* (DH) key exchange generates the shared secret itself. The actual encryption algorithm used can either be 56-bit RC2, 56-bit DES, or 168-bit triple DES. Table 13.2 provides a snapshot of the security services provided by this optional part of the baseline profile and the mechanisms/algorithms that are used to achieve these services. The mechanism to achieve session key generation, distribution, and refresh is collectively referred to as integrated H.235 session key management in the table.

Signature Security Profile

The H.235 standard also specifies an optional signature security profile that provides the following security services:

- Authentication, integrity, and non-repudiation for all RAS, H.225.0, and H.245 messages
- Optionally, confidentiality for media streams

The basic difference between this profile and the baseline profile is that digital signatures are used in this profile while the baseline profile used MACs (in other words, shared secret-based hash). You create digital signatures by using public-key mechanisms; hence, non-repudiation is provided in addition to authentication and integrity. The actual algorithm that you use to create the digital signature is either RSA-SHA1 or RSA-MD5.

Table 13.1 A Snapshot of the Baseline Security Profile

SECURITY SERVICES	CALL FUNCTIONS			
	RAS	H.225.0	H.245	RTP
Authentication and integrity	HMAC-SHA1-96	HMAC-SHA1-96	HMAC-SHA1-96	
Key Management	*a priori* password	*a priori* password		

Table 13.2 A Snapshot of Optional Media Encryption for the Baseline/Signature Security Profile

SECURITY SERVICES	CALL FUNCTIONS			
	RAS	H.225.0	H.245	RTP
Confidentiality				56-bit DES or RC2/ 168-bit triple DES
Key management		Authenticated D-H key exchange	Integrated H.235 session key management	

Table 13.3 A Snapshot of the Signature Security Profile

SECURITY SERVICES	CALL FUNCTIONS			
	RAS	H.225.0	H.245	RTP
Authentication, integrity, and non-repudiation	RSA-SHA1 or RSA-MD5	RSA-SHA1 or RSA-MD5	RSA-SHA1 or RSA-MD5	
Key Management	Certificates	Certificates		

Thus, the SHA1 or MD5 algorithm is used to create a hash, which is then signed by using the sender's RSA private key. Table 13.3 provides a snapshot of the signature security profile.

The signature security profile can also be used in conjunction with the optional media stream encryption profile that we specified previously.

Recommended Reading

Stallings and Schneier are good books for readers who are not familiar with security and need to gain a better understanding of security principles. For an easier understanding of concepts such as the different security protocols and algorithms (DH, DES, triple-DES SHA-1, MD5, and so on), the different modes of operation of block ciphers, and so on, the reader should consult these books rather than the original references.

The authoritative reference for security for H.323 systems is the ITU-T H.235 standard H.235v3. The reference section of the H.235 standard points to several useful references as well. The H.225.0, H.245, and H.323 standards need to be referred to for various aspects described in this chapter. They are found in H.225.0, H.245, and H.323, respectively.

ISO 9798-2 describes the technique for generating a key from a password, and this technique is the basis for this functionality within H.235. The *Universal Character Set* (UCS), which is used for encoding characters, is specified in ISO/IEC 10646. Although elliptic curve mechanisms are only mentioned briefly, their popularity is growing. You can find more information about them at ISO/IEC 15946 and ISO/IEC 15946-2. The RTP standard RFC1889 describes encryption techniques that are used for media-stream encryption.

Much of the initial work on security profiles was carried out within the IMTC and ETSI TIPHON, and references for this work include IMTC-SP1, IMTC-iNOW, and TIPHON-Sec.

References

H.225.0 ITU-T Recommendation H.225.0 Version 4, *Call Signaling Protocols and Media Stream Packetization for Packet Based Multimedia Communications Systems*, November 2000.

H.235v3 ITU-T Recommendation H.235 Version 3, *Security and Encryption for H-series (H.323 and other H.245-based) multimedia terminals*, November 2000.

H.245 ITU-T Recommendation H.245 Version 7, *Control Protocol for Multimedia Communication*, November 2000.

H.323 ITU-T Recommendation H.323 Version 4, *Packet Based Multimedia Communication Systems*, November 2000.

IMTC-SP1 IMTC Service Profile 1 (SP1), 2000.

IMTC-iNOW IMTC iNOW profiles, 2000.

ISO 9798-2 ISO/IEC 9798-2, *Information Technology—Security Techniques—Entity Authentication—Part 2: Mechanisms Using Symmetric Encipherment Algorithms*, 1994.

ISO/IEC 10646 ISO/IEC 10646

ISO/IEC 15946 ISO/IEC 15946-1, *Information Technology—Security Techniques—Cryptographic Techniques based on Elliptic Curves, Part 1: General*, 2000.

ISO/IEC 15946-2 ISO/IEC 15946-2, *Information Technology—Security Techniques—Cryptographic Techniques based on Elliptic Curves, Part 2: Digital Signatures*, 2000.

RFC1889 H. Schulzrinne, S. Casner, R. Frederick, V. Jacobson, *RTP: A Transport Protocol for Real-Time Applications*, RFC-1889, IETF, January 1996.

Schneier B. Schneier, *Applied Cryptography*, Second Edition, John Wiley & Sons.

Stallings W. Stallings, *Cryptography and Network Security*, Second Edition, Prentice Hall, 1999.

TIPHON-Sec ETSI TIPHON Security Profiles.

Problems

1. Consider the case where a secret key needs to be generated from a password by using the technique specified in the H.235 standard. If the password is "password" (which incidentally is one of the most common passwords used), determine the secret key if the desired key length is (a) 5 bytes, (b) 16 bytes, and (c) 24 bytes. Assume that 16-bit Unicode encoding is used for character representation (hint: the Unicode representation for ASCII characters is merely the seven-bit ASCII representation prepended with nine zeros).
2. Discuss the different techniques that you can use in order to achieve user authentication. How can you combine message integrity with message authentication?
3. The SynchFlag field within EncryptionSync contains the RTP dynamic payload number that matches the encryption key. Consider the case where an MPEG media stream containing I, P, and B frames is sent in a logical channel. Each of the frames is sent in a separate RTP packet. Let I frames alone be encrypted while the P and B frames are sent in the clear. If dynamic payload numbers 10 and 11 are used for I frame and P/B frame RTP packets, respectively, discuss the content of the SynchFlag field.
4. The use of IPSec for media-stream encryption was described. Can TLS/SSL be used for the same? If so, how? If not, why not?

5. The Rijndael algorithm was selected as the *Advanced Encryption Standard* (AES) by the United States *National Institute of Standards and Technology* (NIST) in October 2000. With Rijndael, the block length can be either 128, 192, or 256 bits long. Assume that Rijndael is used for media-stream encryption.

   a. Determine the IV for an RTP packet with a sequence number of 0xA253 and a timestamp of 0x1428D9E2 if Rijndael is used in CBC mode with a 192-bit block size.

   b. Let Rijndael be used in eight-bit CFB mode for a 128-bit block size. If the current counter value is 0x00001234 and if the received RTP packet has a sequence number of 0x1237, determine the new counter value. Determine the IV to be used for this RTP packet, assuming that the base IV is 0x12345678123456781234567812345678.

6. Assume that a block encryption algorithm in ECB mode is used to encrypt media streams. Describe how a "cut and paste" attack can possibly be launched. Based on this situation, discuss why CBC mode is preferable to ECB mode. Also, compare the processing time for ECB and CBC modes.

7. We mentioned that each RTP packet is encrypted separately. Discuss the usefulness of this feature under the following situations:

   a. No packets are lost or in error, but packets might be delivered out of sequence.

   b. No packets are lost or in error, and packets are always delivered in sequence.

8. The optional media-encryption profile mandates the use of 56-bit DES while 168-bit triple DES is optional. One of the advantages of implementing 168-bit triple DES is that such an implementation subsumes (includes) the implementation of 56-bit DES. Discuss why this situation is the case.

9. The signature security profile relies on certificates for key exchange. One of the issues with widespread use of such techniques is the need for a global *Public-Key Infrastructure* (PKI). Discuss some of the issues that need to be considered in the deployment of a global PKI and why this task is not trivial.

10. Specify a security profile other than the ones that were specified in this chapter. Discuss the relative merits and demerits of your specified profile with the ones specified here.

CHAPTER 14

H.323, Generic Security Protocols, and Firewalls

In the previous chapter, we described many of the salient features of securing H.323 systems. The content of this chapter is three-fold:

- To provide a more detailed description of some of the generic *Internet Protocol* (IP)-based security protocols (such as IPSec, TLS, IKE, and so on) as well as security algorithms such as DES, SHA-1, and so on. The intention is that this information would provide the reader with greater insight into the operation of these protocols as well as describe their use within H.323 systems.
- To discuss issues dealing with firewall traversal.
- To discuss the use and interaction of certain other security systems such as RADIUS servers within H.323 systems.

Generic IP Security Protocols and Algorithms

In the previous chapter, we mentioned several security protocols and algorithms that have been standardized for generic secure IP communications. These include protocols such as the *Internet Key Exchange* (IKE), *IP Security* (IPSec), *Transport Layer Security* (TLS), and so on and algorithms such as the *Digital Encryption Standard* (DES), *Secure Hash*

Algorithm (SHA), *Message Digest 5* (MD5), and so on These protocols and algorithms are used widely within IP-based communications, and H.323 systems also utilize them where possible. In this section, we give a more detailed description of some of these security protocols and algorithms.

Security Protocols

The security protocols that we will discuss here are IPSec, TLS, and IKE. While IPSec and TLS are protocols that are used to obtain certain security services such as authentication, encryption, and so on, IKE is a protocol that is used for secure key exchange.

IPSec

IPSec is a protocol that is standardized within the *Internet Engineering Task Force* (IETF) and provides security services at the network layer (in other words, the IP layer) for IP-based communications. IPSec offers two security protocols: the *Authentication Header* (AH) and the *Encapsulating Security Payload* (ESP)—each of which provides certain security services. The security services provided by AH are connection-less integrity, data origin authentication, optional antireplay service, and access control. The security services provided by ESP are message confidentiality, connectionless integrity (optional), data origin authentication, antireplay service, and access control. While the security services offered by ESP include all of those that are offered by AH, the set of fields that the services are applicable over varies in the two cases. AH and ESP are defined as separate headers that are carried within the IP datagram.

AH

IPSec AH provides connectionless integrity, data origin authentication, optional antireplay service, and access control. With IPSec AH, an AH is inserted between the IP header and the UDP/TCP header. The format of this header appears in Figure 14.1(a). The actual authenticator (such as the MAC or the digital signature) goes in the last field labeled authentication data. The sequence number field is provided in order to combat replay attacks. The *Security Parameters Index* (SPI), which is an arbitrary 32-bit value assigned by the destination, in conjunction with the destination IP address and the security protocol (which is AH in this case), uniquely identifies the *Security Association* (SA).

IPSec AH can exist in two modes—transport mode and tunnel mode—and these appear in Figure 14.1(b) and 14.1(c). Transport mode is used when the security association exists between the two communicating endpoints.

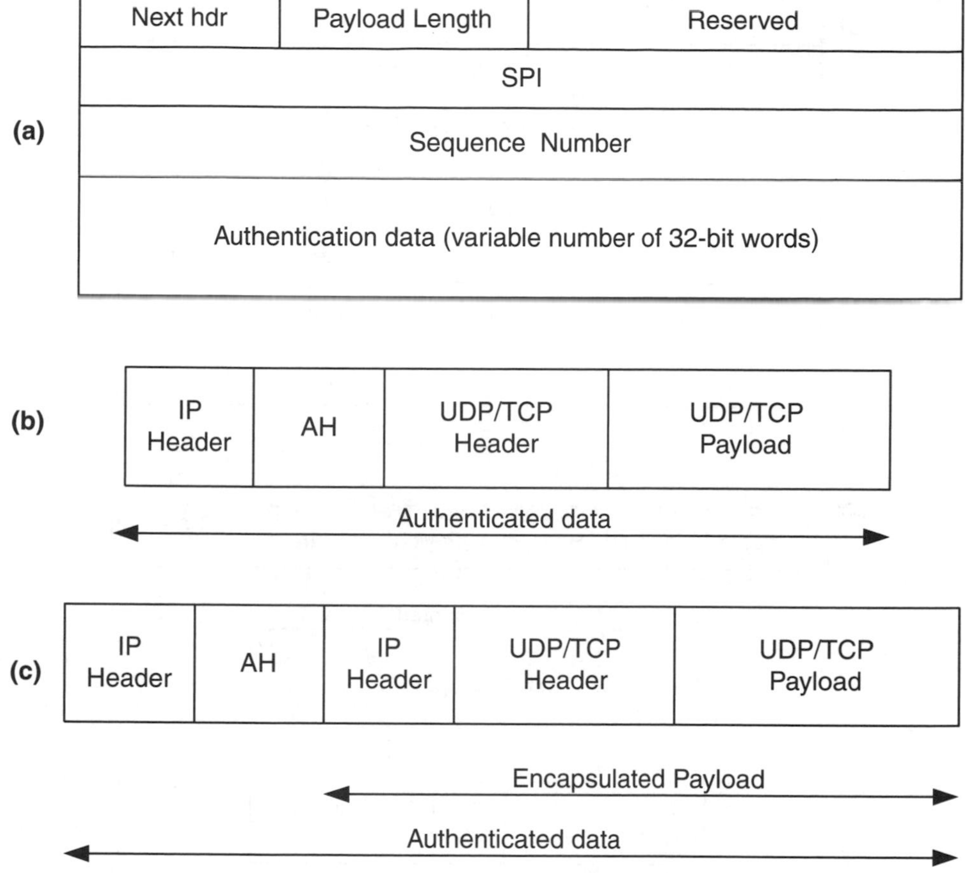

Figure 14.1 Packet format for (a) AH, (b) AH in transport mode, and (c) AH in tunnel mode.

Tunnel mode, which uses IP in IP encapsulation, is used when at least one of the terminating points of the security association is at a security gateway instead of the communicating endpoint. In either case, the entire IP datagram is authenticated.

Encapsulating Security Payload (ESP)

IPSec ESP provides message confidentiality, connectionless integrity (optional), data origin authentication, antireplay service, and access control. With IPSec ESP, an ESP header is inserted between the IP header and the UDP/TCP header. In addition, an ESP trailer is inserted after the UDP/TCP payload. The format of the ESP header and trailer appears in Figure 14.2(a). As in the case of AH, the three-tuple of destination IP address, ESP, and SPI is used to identify the ESP security association. Similarly, the sequence number field is used to combat replay attacks. Because several encryption algorithms

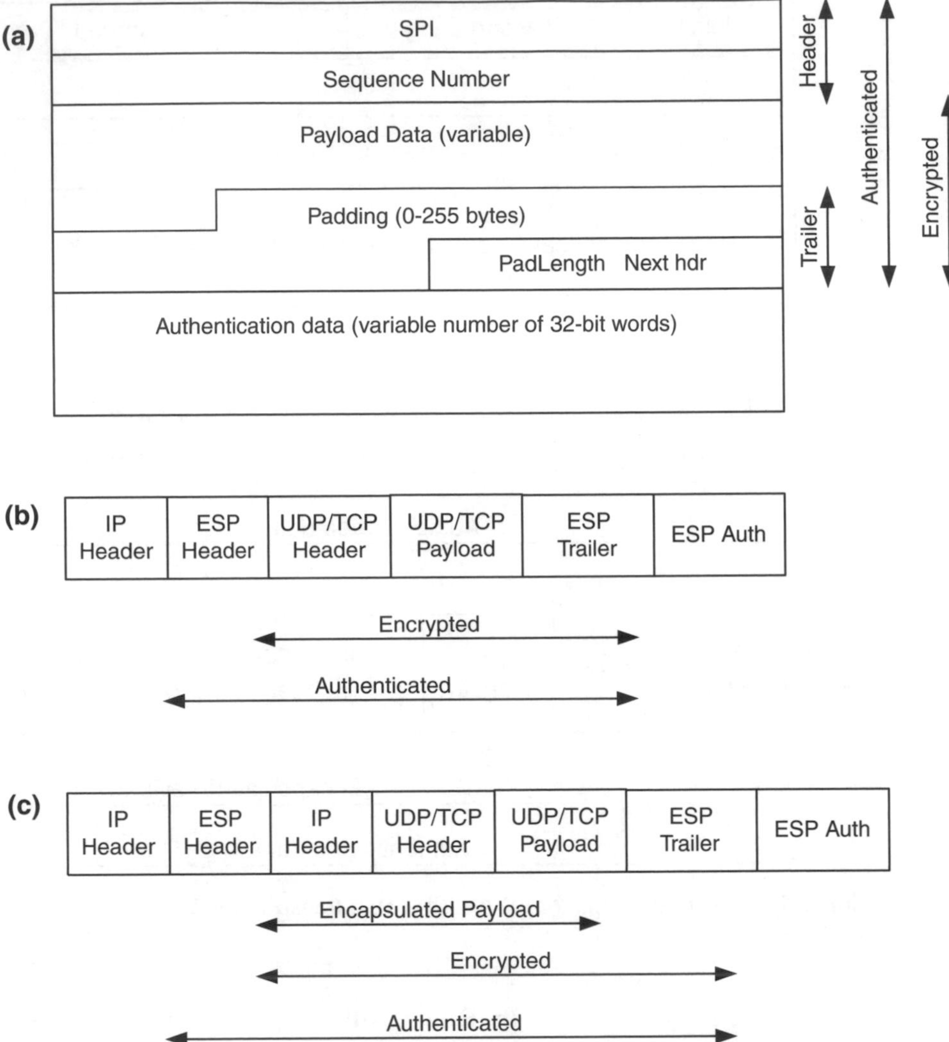

Figure 14.2 Packet format for (a) ESP, (b) ESP in transport mode, and (c) ESP in tunnel mode.

are block algorithms (in other words, they operate on blocks of fixed size), the UDP/TCP payload might have to be padded to an integral multiple of the block size. As in the case of AH, ESP can be used either in transport or tunnel mode. ESP also provides optional authentication, and the authenticator (MAC or digital signature) is carried in the Authentication data field. When you compare Figures 14.1 and 14.2, however, you see that while IPSec AH authenticates the entire IP datagram, authentication within IPSec ESP does not cover the IP header.

In addition to being used separately, IPSec AH and ESP can also be used in conjunction on the same packet.

Illustrating IPSec Processing

Consider the case where a media stream flows from Endpoint A to Endpoint B and IPSec ESP encrypts the traffic by using the DES algorithm. We assume that an ESP security association has already been established between the two endpoints (say, by using IKE). Let the IP address of Endpoint A be 192.100.70.10, that of Endpoint B be 185.25.35.6, the source port at Endpoint A for the media stream be 1355, and the destination port at Endpoint B be 1656. Let the SPI (which Endpoint B chooses during security association establishment) associated with this security association be 35. Figure 14.3 illustrates the outbound security processing that occurs at Endpoint A while Figure 14.4 illustrates the inbound security processing that occurs at Endpoint B.

As you can see in Figure 14.3, each IP datagram at Endpoint A is sent to an IPSec control unit that consults a *Security Policy Database* (SPD) in order to determine what action, if any, needs to be applied to the packet. Upon consulting the SPD, we see that packets with source IP address 192.100.70.10, destination IP address 185.25.35.6, source port number 1355, destination port number 1656, and a protocol field of UDP need to be processed by using a certain security association. The security association that is used to process the packet is described in the *Security Association Database* (SAD), and a pointer to the entry in the SAD exists in the SPD. The packet is suitably processed by using this security association (which happens to be DES with Key2) and is sent out of the outbound interface.

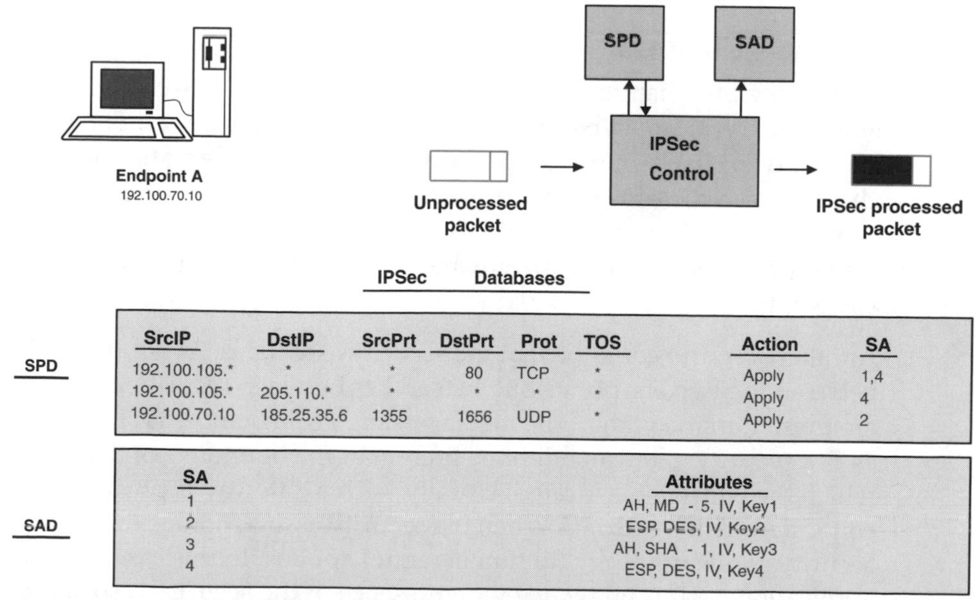

SrcIP	DstIP	SrcPrt	DstPrt	Prot	TOS	Action	SA
192.100.105.*	*	*	80	TCP	*	Apply	1,4
192.100.105.*	205.110.*	*	*	*	*	Apply	4
192.100.70.10	185.25.35.6	1355	1656	UDP	*	Apply	2

SA	Attributes
1	AH, MD - 5, IV, Key1
2	ESP, DES, IV, Key2
3	AH, SHA - 1, IV, Key3
4	ESP, DES, IV, Key4

Figure 14.3 Illustrating IPSec outbound processing at Endpoint A.

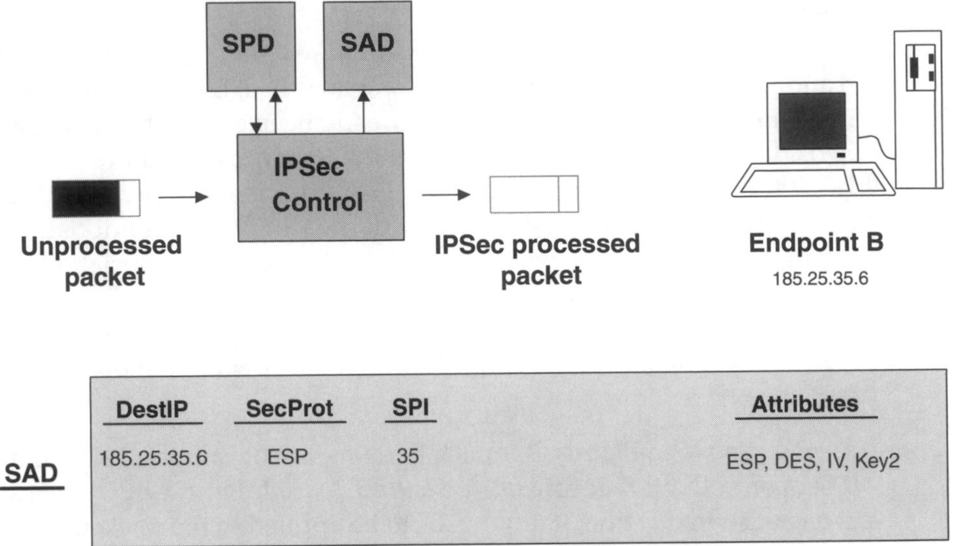

Figure 14.4 Illustrating IPSec inbound processing at Endpoint B.

As we can see in Figure 14.4, upon receiving the packet, Endpoint B looks up the three-tuple of destination IP address, security protocol, and SPI based on which the security association is ascertained by using the SAD. In this example, the three-tuple of 185.25.35.6, ESP, and 35 points to the appropriate security association in the SAD at Endpoint B. The attributes of this security association (which include the key) are used to suitably decrypt the packet.

IPSec Usage in H.323

In the previous chapter, we described how the use of IPSec ESP for media-stream encryption can be signaled by using H.245 messages. The H.245 capability exchange messages indicate support for IPSec, and the logical channel procedures are used to signal the use of IPSec when a media channel is opened. In this case, IPSec ESP is used in transport mode. In other words, the security association is directly between the two communicating endpoints.

Another scenario could be that the security association is not directly between the two endpoints but instead lies between security gateways that are present in the path of the media stream. For instance, as shown in Figure 14.5, a security gateway might be present at the boundary of the domain in which the endpoint is located. Usually, such a gateway is physically collocated with a firewall. When the security association exists between security gateways, IPSec (in tunnel mode) applies. In this case, the H.323 application itself is unaware of the presence of the security association, and no H.323 signaling is applied in order to handle the security association.

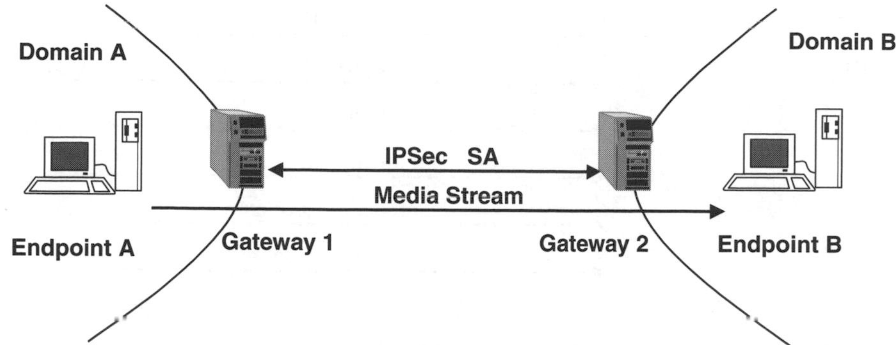

Figure 14.5 Illustrating IPSec tunnel mode for H.323 media streams.

In addition to the encryption of media streams by using IPSec ESP (as described in the previous chapter), you can also use IPSec to secure the H.225.0 or H.245 channels.

Transport Layer Security (TLS)

The most commonly used security protocol on IP networks today (specifically, the Internet) is probably the *Secure Socket Layer* (SSL) protocol. SSL is a proprietary protocol that has not been standardized by any organization (but is an industry de facto standard). The TLS protocol is based on SSL and has been standardized by the IETF. TLS has a mode where it can fall back to SSL.

TLS contains two main layers:

1. A handshake layer that negotiates the secure connection.
2. A record layer that provides the security services by using the security association that is created by the handshake layer.

One-way or two-way authentication by using public key mechanisms is used during the handshake layer. The security services provided by the record layer are primarily 1) confidentiality by using symmetric key encryption (DES, RC4, and so on) and 2) message integrity by using keyed MAC (keyed SHA, keyed MD5, and so on). The TLS record protocol requires a reliable transport layer, such as TCP, for its operation. When UDP is used for transport, as is the case with real-time media streams, you cannot use TLS.

Two modes of handshakes exist:

1. A full handshake, as illustrated in Figure 14.6: The ClientHello and ServerHello messages are used to exchange security capabilities of the TLS client and server, and at the end of the exchange, the following attributes are established: protocol version, session ID, cipher suite,

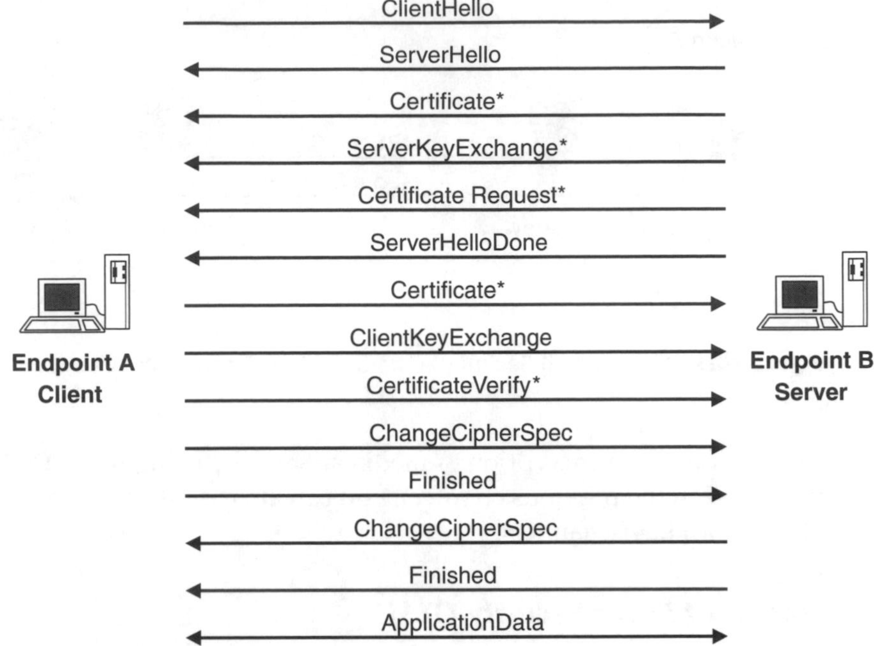

Figure 14.6 TLS full handshake.

compression method, and random numbers. The messages that follow are used for key exchange purposes. A ChangeCipherSpec and a Finished message are sent in order to indicate that the security attributes that were established as part of this handshake will be used to secure the message exchanges. The asterisks in the figure imply that the message is optional.

2. An abbreviated handshake, as illustrated in Figure 14.7. You can use this type of handshake when the client wishes to resume or duplicate an existing session that is identified by the session ID.

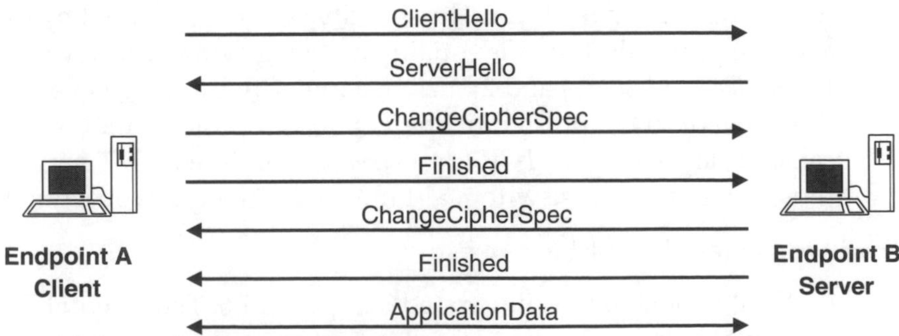

Figure 14.7 TLS abbreviated handshake.

H.323 and TLS

TLS can be used to secure H.225.0 or H.245 channels. Because these channels use TCP, TLS can protect them. H.225.0 also has an optional UDP-based transport and if used, H.225.0 cannot rely on TLS for its protection. The previous chapter described how we can use TLS to secure the H.225.0 or H.245 channels.

You cannot protect RAS messages or the media streams by using TLS because these channels use UDP for their transport. TLS requires a reliable transport mechanism such as TCP.

Internet Security Association and Key Management Protocol (ISAKMP)

ISAKMP provides a framework for authentication and key management. You can use several key exchanges within the ISAKMP framework. OAKLEY describes several key exchanges (or modes), and SKEME describes one key exchange that you can use within ISAKMP. Depending on the nature of the key exchange protocol, one or more of certain security services are provided for the *security association* (SA).

ISAKMP provides several payload types: Security Association, Proposal, Transform, Key Exchange, Identification, Certificate, Certificate Request, Hash, Signature, Nonce, Notification, Delete, and Vendor ID. Figure 14.8 shows the structure of some of these payload types along with the generic ISAKMP message header. One or more payload types can be present in an ISAKMP message, and the Exchange Type field within the ISAKMP header determines the presence and ordering of the payloads. The exchange types that have been defined within ISAKMP include Base, Identity Protection, Authentication Only, Aggressive, and Informational. Protocols using the ISAKMP framework, such as IKE, can define additional key exchanges for their purpose.

Figure 14.9 provides an example of usage of these payload types for the purpose of establishing a security association. The ISAKMP message on the left is sent by Endpoint 1 to Endpoint 2, offering a set of security capabilities. The ISAKMP message shown on the right is subsequently sent by Endpoint 2 to Endpoint 1 and conveys the security context that Endpoint 2 chooses. The ISAKMP message sent by Endpoint 1 to Endpoint 2 contains two proposals denoted as Proposal #1 and Proposal #2. Proposal #1 is a proposal for IPSec ESP and IPSec AH. With IPSec ESP, you can use one of two security transforms—one being the DES encryption algorithm with specified attributes and the other being the 3-DES algorithm with specified attributes. With IPSec AH, only one security transform is offered: the HMAC-MD5 that

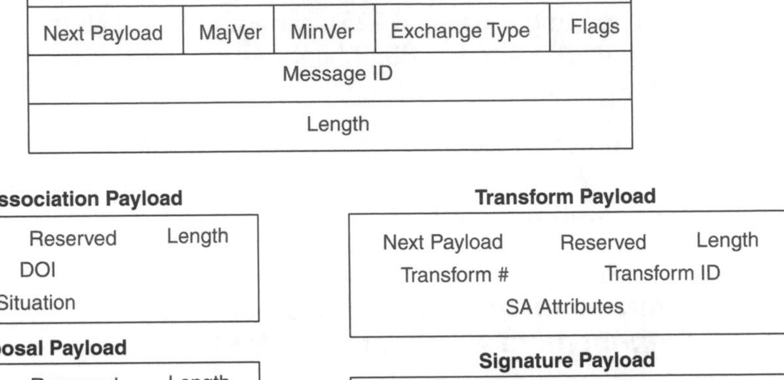

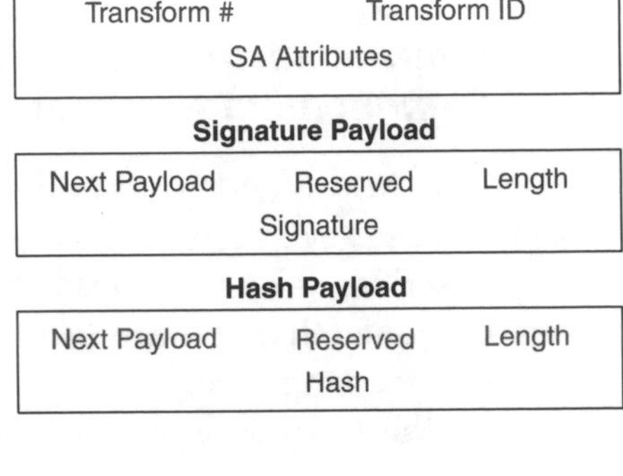

Figure 14.8 ISAKMP payload types.

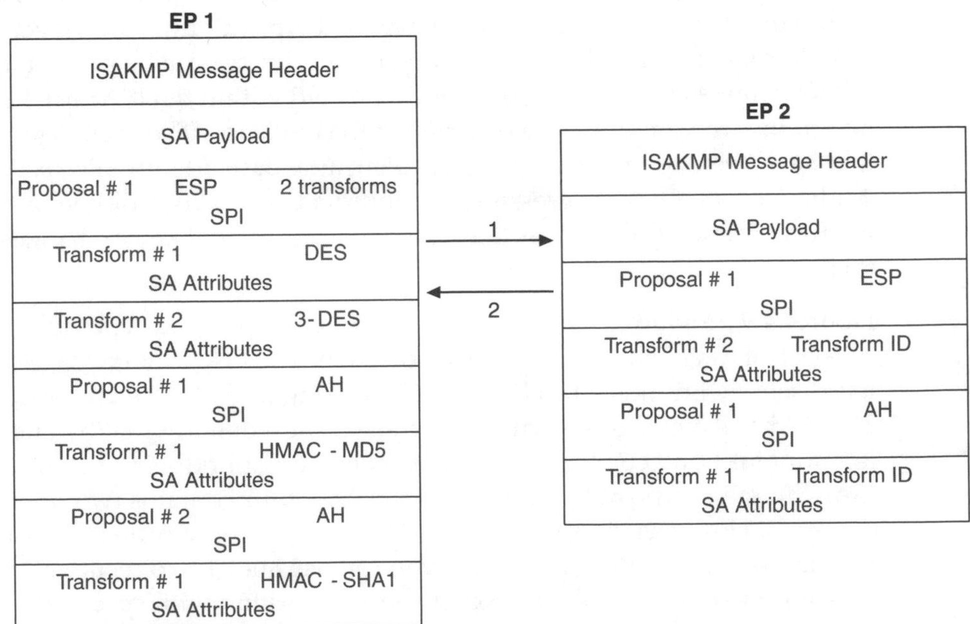

Figure 14.9 Security association establishment example.

has certain specified attributes. Proposal #2, on the other hand, is a proposal for IPSec AH only. This IPSec AH proposal offers only one security transform: HMAC-SHA that has certain specified attributes.

Upon receiving these two proposals, Endpoint 2 chooses one of the two offered proposals (assuming that at least one of the two is supported by Endpoint 2). In the example, Endpoint 2 chooses Proposal #1, which implies that IPSec ESP along with IPSec AH is being chosen. Because two transforms were offered with IPSec ESP, Endpoint 2 needs to choose one of the two—and in this case, the 3-DES encryption algorithm is chosen rather than the DES algorithm.

You must note that a complete exchange is not presented in Figure 14.9. Instead, we only present an illustrative one (which is incomplete).

Internet Key Exchange (IKE)

While ISAKMP provides a framework for authentication and key exchange, the *Internet Key Exchange* (IKE) protocol makes use of this framework. IKE utilizes parts of the OAKLEY and SKEME key exchange mechanisms within the ISAKMP framework in order to define a robust key exchange mechanism.

IKE operates in two phases. Phase 1 establishes the general IKE SA while Phase 2 establishes specific protocol security associations (SA) (such as IPSec AH SA, IPSec ESP SA, TLS SA, and so on). The advantage of a two-phase approach is that a common IKE SA can be used to create multiple Phase 2 security associations, thereby presenting a faster and more efficient mechanism for creating security associations. Certain modes have been specified within IKE, and the security services vary depending on the specific mode that is used. For instance, the establishment of a Phase 1 security association (in other words, a general IKE SA) can use one of two modes: main mode or aggressive mode. While the main mode is more robust, the aggressive mode is achieved with fewer message exchanges at the expense of compromising identity protection. Main mode is an instantiation of the ISAKMP Identity Protect exchange while the aggressive mode is an instantiation of the ISAKMP Aggressive exchange. Similarly, a quick mode has been defined for use in creating Phase 2 security associations. Quick mode is not an instantiation of any of the predefined exchanges within ISAKMP and is specified only within IKE.

H.323 and ISAKMP/IKE

As we mentioned previously, IKE (which uses the ISAKMP framework) can be used to create security associations for IPSec and TLS. Although TLS has its own handshake protocol in order to create the security association, it is also possible to use IKE to create the security association. Thus, when an IPSec or a TLS SA needs to be created for the protection of H.323 channels, IKE can be used to create the security association. Examples include the use of IKE for creation of an IPSec security association in order to protect either the H.225.0, H.245 or media channels.

Security Algorithms

The choice and use of security algorithms are at the heart of the security of any system. We now describe various encryption, hash and signature algorithms, that might be used for achieving one or more security services.

Encryption Algorithms

You employ encryption algorithms within protocols such as IPSec or TLS in order to provide confidentiality service. Such algorithms are one of two kinds: block ciphers and stream ciphers. Block ciphers, which include DES, 3-DES, Blowfish, Rijndael, RC2, and RC5, operate on input blocks of certain sizes in order to produce ciphertext (encrypted text) of the same size. The size of the block depends on the encryption algorithm (in other words, cipher) that is used. A block size of 64, 128, 196, 256 bits, and so on is typical. Stream ciphers, on the other hand, which include RC4, operate on a single bit or a single byte at a time.

Operation Modes

Because block ciphers operate one block at a time, you can chain or feed information that is performed in one block-ciphering operation to that in the subsequent block-ciphering operation. Depending on whether and how you perform this task, four modes of operation are commonly defined: *Electronic Code Book* (ECB), *Cipher Block Chaining* (CBC), *Cipher Feedback* (CFB), and *Output Feedback* (OFB).

In ECB mode, each block of data is encrypted independently of any other block of data, as shown in Figure 14.10(a). In the figure, the input blocks are represented as P_1 for plain text while the cipher output blocks are represented as C_1 for ciphertext. In CBC, the ciphertext of one cycle is XORed with the plain text of the next before feeding it to the cipher algorithm. For the first cycle, we use an *Initialization Vector* (IV). We show this depiction in Figure 14.10(b). CFB and OFB modes are a way of approximating the behavior of stream ciphers by using block ciphers. J-bit CFB or OFB mode operates on j-bits (where j does not exceed the block size) of plain text in each cycle in order to produce j-bits of ciphertext. In CFB, for the first cycle, the leading j-bits of the output of the ciphering operation is XORed with the j-bit

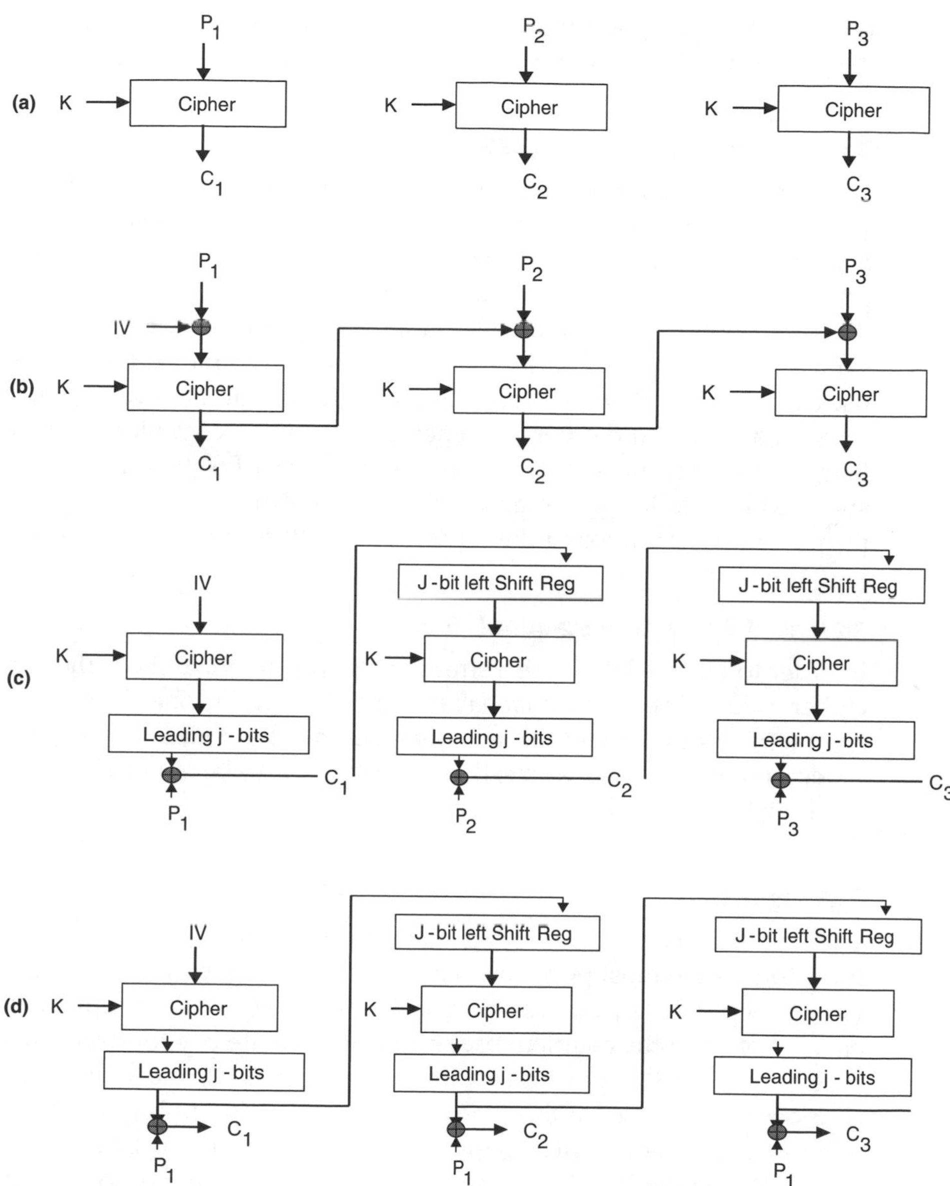

Figure 14.10 Illustrating (a) ECB, (b) CBC, (c) j-bit CFB, and (d) j-bit OFB modes for block ciphers.

plaintext (P_1) in order to produce the j-bit ciphertext (C_1). C_1 is also fed to rightmost j-bits of a left-shift register, which is initialized to IV. The contents of this shift register along with the key K constitute the input to the next ciphering operation. The process continues, as illustrated in Figures 14.10(c) and 14.10(d). OFB is similar to CFB with the difference that in OFB, the j-bit output from the ciphering operation in one cycle is fed into the next cycle instead of the j-bit ciphertext that is fed in the case of CFB.

Data Encryption Standard (DES)

DES is the most widely used encryption algorithm to date. The algorithm was standardized by the United States government's *National Institute of Standards and Technology* (NIST) in 1977 and has experienced widespread popularity since then. DES is a symmetric block cipher, which implies that the same key is used for encryption and decryption. Generally speaking, symmetric ciphers are considerably faster than asymmetric ciphers (which use a different key for encryption and decryption) and hence are widely used for media stream and other bulk encryption. DES takes a block input of 64-bit length and, by using a 56-bit key, outputs a block of 64 bits. The key length specified is actually 64 bits, although every eighth bit is used for parity purposes (thereby making the actual key length 56 bits).

Advanced Encryption Standard (AES)

In order to replace DES with a stronger algorithm, NIST chose the Rijndael cipher as its *Advanced Encryption Standard* (AES) in October 2000. AES is a symmetric block cipher that can operate on blocks of size 128, 196, or 256 bits. Independent of the block size, the key size can also be either 128, 196, or 256 bits long.

RSA Algorithm

The *Rivest, Shamir, Adleman* (RSA) algorithm, which was named after its three inventors, is the most popular asymmetric cipher. Asymmetric ciphers, also known as public key algorithms, use the public key of the recipient for encryption, and the recipient uses his or her private key for decryption. The patent for the RSA algorithm expired in October 2000, and we will likely see an increase in its use for this reason. Because RSA is a public key algorithm, it is considerably slower than symmetric algorithms such as DES, 3-DES, and so on. Consequently, it is not used for media-stream encryption but instead is usually used for operations such as key exchanges. The algorithm is straightforward and is as follows:

$C = P^e \mod n$, is the encryption algorithm

$P = C^d \mod n$, is the decryption algorithm

P is the binary representation of the plaintext, and C is the corresponding cipher text. The private key is the two-tuple (d, n), and the public key is the two-tuple (e, n). The strength of the algorithm lies in the difficulty of factoring a product of two large prime numbers.

Hash and Signature Algorithms

One-way hash functions (commonly referred to simply as hash functions) are the core of authentication and integrity services. A hash function takes an input of arbitrary size and creates an output of fixed size (called the message digest). This output, which is quite small, acts as a fingerprint of the input. In other words, if two different inputs are provided to a hash function, the likelihood of getting the same output should be small. This desirable functionality of hash functions is referred to as collision avoidance. The one-way nature of hash functions implies that it is extremely unlikely to determine the input when given the output of the hash function.

You can use hash functions in several ways in order to provide authentication/integrity services. For instance, in conjunction with a secret key, they are used to generate *Message Authentication Codes* (MACs). Two popular mechanisms exist for this purpose: keyed MAC and *Hashed MAC* (HMAC). When used in conjunction with a private key, they are used to generate digital signatures. Two popular digital signature algorithms are the RSA algorithm and the *Digital Signature Algorithm* (DSA).

When the output of a hash function along with a user's private key is input into a suitable signing algorithm, a digital signature is obtained. This digital signature can be used for authentication, integrity, and non-repudiation purposes. Authentication is provided because only the holder of the private key could have produced the digital signature. Nonrepudiation is provided for a similar reason (and because the recipient does not possess the private key). Message integrity is provided because any alteration of the message in transit would result in a mismatch between the included and the computed message digest at the receiver.

Message Digest 5 (MD5)

Message Digest 5 (MD5) is probably the most widely used hash function. MD5 takes an input of arbitrary size and produces a message digest of 128 bits. The MD5 algorithm internally operates with inputs of size 512 bits, but the algorithm itself (or you can also view it as a wrapper to the core algorithm) has the functionality to break an arbitrary input into 512-bit blocks. Padding and length-indication functionality is also included within the algorithm specification. Recently, certain security attacks (brute force and other forms of cryptanalysis) have been mounted successfully upon the MD5 algorithm, due to which its use in certain applications is being replaced by the SHA-1 hash function.

Secure Hash Algorithm 1 (SHA-1)

NIST standardized the *Secure Hash Algorithm 1* (SHA-1) in 1995. SHA-1 takes inputs of arbitrary length and creates a message digest of 160 bits. As with MD5, SHA-1 internally takes inputs of blocks of 512 bits. As with MD5, SHA-1 itself has the functionality to break an arbitrary-sized input into blocks of 512 bits, to append any padding and length fields, and so on. Compared to MD5, SHA-1 is more resistant to brute force and to other forms of cryptanalysis.

RSA Algorithm

You can use the RSA algorithm to compute a digital signature. The hash of the original message is signed by using the sender's RSA private key in order to create the digital signature. The digital signature is concatenated with the original message and is sent to the recipient. The recipient recomputes the hash from the message and compares this computation with the output that is obtained when the digital signature is processed by using the sender's RSA public key. If these two match, then the integrity of the message is intact.

Digital Signature Algorithm (DSA)

The DSA was standardized by NIST within the *Digital Signature Standard* (DSS) in 1991 with revisions in 1993 and 1996. The hash of the original message, a random number, the sender's private key, and a set of global parameters is input into a signature algorithm that outputs two parameters s and r (which are concatenated with the original message and are sent to the receiver). The receiver computes the hash of the message and sends this hash along with the parameters s and r, the sender's public key, and the set of global parameters to a verifier, which should output r if the integrity of the message is not compromised.

Firewall Traversal

Firewalls are commonly used at the edge of a protected domain in order to regulate access (by allowing or denying access) to flows that cross the boundary of this domain. We will begin the discussion of firewalls by detailing certain scenarios of firewall usage and the requirements for H.323 streams to traverse firewalls. We will then describe the various kinds of firewalls and discuss their advantages and disadvantages concerning H.323 stream traversal.

Issues Surrounding Firewall Traversal of H.323 Streams

RAS Channel and Firewalls

Two cases exist concerning the RAS channel and firewalls:

- The endpoint and the gatekeeper are on the same side of the firewall, as illustrated in Figure 14.11(a). In this case, the RAS messages do not traverse the firewall, and we do not discuss this nontrivial case here because the firewall is not involved.
- The endpoint and the gatekeeper are on opposite sides of the firewall, as illustrated in Figure 14.11(b). In this case, the RAS messages traverse the firewall. The firewall needs to be suitably configured in order to allow

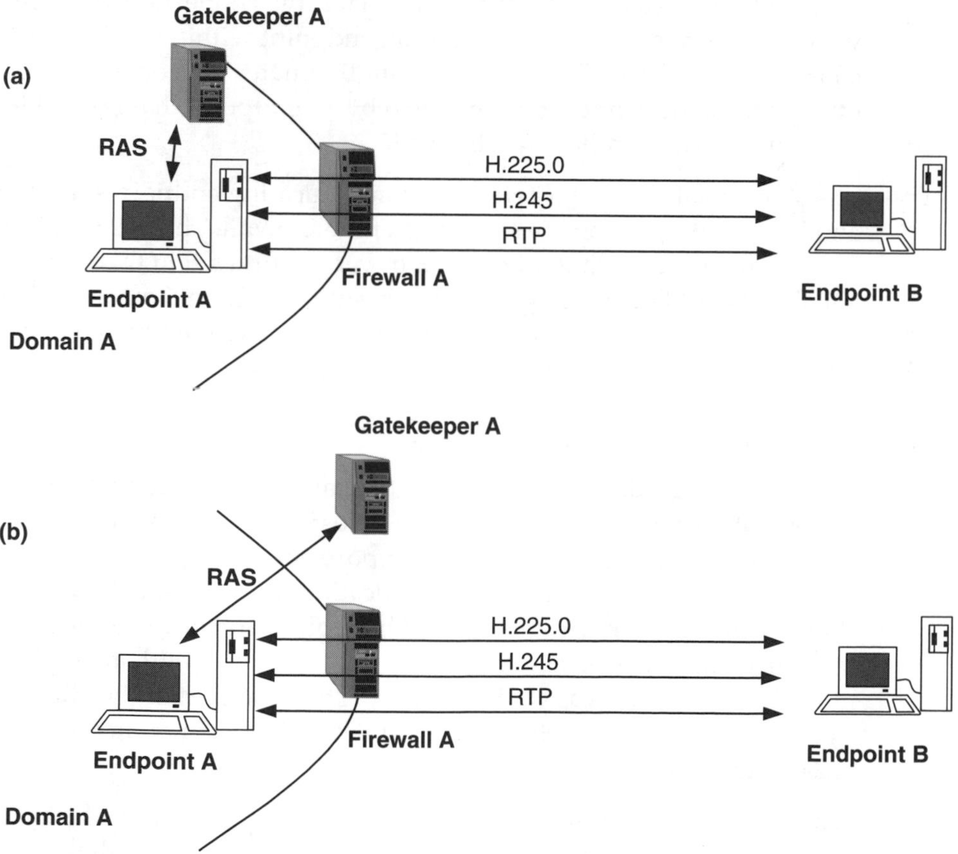

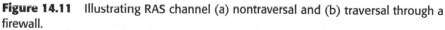

Figure 14.11 Illustrating RAS channel (a) nontraversal and (b) traversal through a firewall.

only legitimate RAS messages to flow through, keeping in mind that RAS messages are UDP messages. You need to consider two specific cases: 1) RAS messages are sent by Endpoint A to Gatekeeper A, and b) RAS messages are sent by Gatekeeper A to Endpoint A.

H.225.0/H.245/RTP Channels and Firewalls

Figure 14.11 illustrates the case where the H.323 streams—call signaling, call control, and media—traverse a firewall when flowing from Endpoint A to Endpoint B. The figure shows a direct point-to-point connection between two endpoints—Endpoint A and Endpoint B—through Firewall A, which is the firewall controlling Endpoint A. The firewall configuration needs to take into consideration the fact that the H.225.0 channel can use either UDP or TCP, that the H.245 channel uses TCP, and that media streams use UDP. You need to consider two cases: 1) Endpoint A initiates the connection, or in other words, the connection is initiated by an endpoint within the domain that is controlled by a firewall, and 2) Endpoint B initiates the connection, or in other words, the connection is initiated by an endpoint that is outside the domain that is controlled by a firewall.

The scenario also exists where both communicating endpoints (Endpoint A and Endpoint B) are on the same side of the firewall. The H.225.0, H.245, and media streams, consequently, do not traverse a firewall in this case. This situation would be the case when Endpoint B is within Domain A, in Figure 14.11. Because this situation is the trivial case where the firewall does not play a role, we do not consider it in this discussion.

Handling Dynamic/Ephemeral Ports

Packet filtering rules within firewalls typically use the destination port (among other fields) in a packet in order to determine how the packet is to be treated. When well-known destination ports are used, packet filters can associate the streams with known applications and suitably treat the packets. When well-known ports are not used but ephemeral or dynamic ports are used instead, however, associating the stream/packet with an application is more difficult. In the case of H.323, the destination port of the H.225.0 call signaling channel is a well-known port while the destination ports for the H.245 and media channels are dynamic.

When you use dynamic ports, the destination transport address that an endpoint uses for receiving a certain channel is indicated to the sending endpoint in a message on a different channel. This process enables the sending endpoint to determine the transport address to which a message can

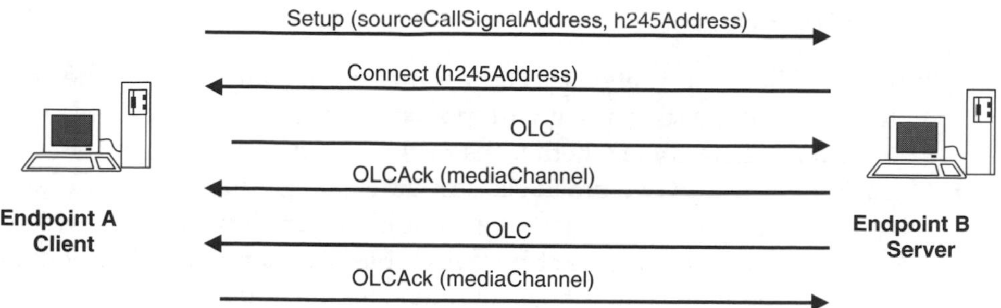

Figure 14.12 Receiver notifying the sender of the transport addresses to be used.

be sent. We illustrate this situation in Figure 14.12, which shows the relevant fields that are used for this purpose. The H.225.0 messages are sent to a well-known port from Endpoint A to Endpoint B. The sourceCallSignalAddress field within the H.225.0 Setup message indicates to Endpoint B the transport address used by Endpoint A for receiving H.225.0 messages. H.225.0 messages that are sent by Endpoint B to Endpoint A have their transport address set to the value indicated in this sourceCallSignalAddress field. The Setup and Connect messages each have an h245Address field that carries the transport address on which H.245 messages will be received by Endpoint A and Endpoint B, respectively. H.245 messages, such as the OLC and OLCAck messages, are destined to this transport address. The OLCAck message contains the mediaChannel field, which denotes the transport address that is used for receiving the RTP media stream. The figure depicts the case where two logical channels are opened: the first being directed from Endpoint A to Endpoint B and the second in the other direction.

In the presence of dynamic ports, firewalls need to be application aware so that they can determine the ports that have been assigned for various channels during the call. In other words, we need an H.323 proxy (or application-level gateway) that is capable of extracting the transport addresses from the appropriate fields. Because the H.225.0 and H.245 messages are ASN.1 encoded, the address fields are not at fixed-byte offsets—thereby making the H.323 proxy more complex.

Types of Firewalls

Firewalls generally fall into three broad categories: packet filters, circuit gateways (such as SOCKS), and application level gateways (ALG, also known as proxies). We will now discuss each of these in some detail.

Packet Filters

Packet filters use a set of selectors, which are usually fields in the header of the traversing packet along with possibly some state stored at the firewall, in order to determine whether the packet can pass or not. You can classify packet filters into two broad classes: static packet filters and stateful packet filters. Static packet filters have a static configuration based on which packets are, on an individual packet-by-packet basis, either allowed or denied access through the filter. Stateful packet filters, on the other hand, maintain the state of a flow and utilize this state along with the packet headers in order to determine packet access/denial.

Static Packet Filters

Static packet filters have a static configuration based on which packets are either allowed or denied access through the filter. Certain selectors within the IP and transport header are used to ascertain packet traversal or access denial. The selectors that the configuration is based on are usually the source and destination IP address, source and destination ports, and the status of certain flags (such as the ACK flag in TCP.) Such filters operate on a packet-by-packet basis without maintaining any state about the flow.

Table 14.1 shows an illustrative packet filter. The first six columns (Source/Destination IP Address/Port Number, Transport Protocol, and Flags) denote the parameters that are used to select packets, and the last column (Action) determines whether the packet can pass or not. Assume that the (sub)network with addresses a.b.*.* is under consideration and the packet filter resides on the edge of this network. Note that port number 25 is the well-known port for the *Simple Mail Transfer Protocol* (SMTP) while port number 1720 is the well-known port for H.225.0 messages.

While specifying rules for packet filters, you will find that the order of the different rules is critical. The first row of the rule set that matches the packet's parameter values determines the packet treatment. For instance, when a packet with source IP address of a.b.c.1 and destination port of 25 is received, both rows 1 and 2 of the packet filter match the packet's parameter values. The action to be performed on the packet is determined by the first such matching row, however, which happens to be Row 1 in our case.

Going through the rules of the packet filter in Table 14.1, we see that the first row states that mail cannot be sent from host a.b.c.1 to any other host. The second row (in conjunction with the first) states that all hosts a.b.*.* other than a.b.c.1 can send mail to any other host. The third row ensures that acknowledgements, for the establishment of the TCP session for the purpose of sending e-mails, can pass through. Rows 4, 5, and 6 are similar to Rows 1, 2, and 3 with the difference being that the well-known port number is 1720,

Table 14.1 Illustrating Static Packet Filtering

SOURCE IP ADDRESS	DESTINATION IP ADDRESS	SOURCE PORT	DESTINATION PORT	TRANSPORT PROTOCOL	FLAGS	ACTION
a.b.c.1	*	*	25	TCP		Deny
a.b.*.*	*	*	25	TCP		Allow
*	a.b.*.*	25	*	TCP	ACK	Allow
a.b.c.1	*	*	1720	TCP/UDP		Deny
a.b.*.*	*	*	1720	TCP/UDP		Allow
*	a.b.*.*	1720	*	TCP	ACK	Allow
x.y.z.*	a.b.*.*	*	25	TCP		Allow
x.y.z.*	a.b.*.*	*	1720	TCP/UDP		Allow
..*.*	*.*.*.*	*	*			Deny

implying that call setup of H.323 is being considered. Such call setup can take place either over TCP or UDP. Rows 7 and 8 imply that e-mail can be sent and calls can be initiated from the subnet x.y.z.* to any host a.b.*.*. The last row, although explicitly specified here, is usually implicit and states that if a packet does not match any of the previous rules, then the packet is discarded.

Although packet filters have been used for a long time (specifically, in the early deployment of firewalls), they suffer from two major disadvantages: 1) the configuration for access/denial is static, and 2) they deny access to most UDP traffic.

Let's examine why static packet filters are not very friendly to UDP traffic. The static configuration of the filters is such that they maintain no state and determine the fate of each packet independently. If access for a packet is to be determined independently, there needs to be a way to ascertain whether a packet entering the firewall is in reply to a previous request that originated from behind the firewall. If this situation is the case, the packet needs to be let through. If not, the packet needs to be let through only if the destination port is a well-known port (such as port 25 for SMTP.) In the case of TCP, the ACK flag determines whether the packet entering a firewall is in reply to a request from behind the firewall or not. The initial connection request packet does not have its ACK flag set, whereas (almost all) other packets in the connection have their ACK flag set. Hence, a packet that is entering the firewall and that is destined to an arbitrary port can be allowed access if the ACK flag is set. In the case of UDP, however, there exists no way of determining whether a packet entering the firewall is in reply to a request behind the firewall or not. Hence, UDP traffic entering the firewall and destined to arbitrary ports is usually filtered.

Packet filters are not suitable for H.323 traffic in the following areas:

- All incoming UDP traffic will be filtered because the packet filter cannot be statically configured with the destination UDP port address of legitimate incoming packets. Thus, if an RAS message is sent from Endpoint A within a firewall to Gatekeeper A that lies outside the firewall by using the source port of 1564 (for example) within the UDP header, then the RAS message from Gatekeeper A back to Endpoint A uses a destination port of 1564 within the UDP header. Because no state is maintained at the packet filter, however, upon inspecting the incoming packet, the packet filter cannot correlate this packet to the original outgoing RAS message. Hence, the message is likely to be filtered. We can demonstrate similar scenarios for other UDP streams (such as media streams).
- All outgoing TCP connection initiations need to be allowed for successful H.245 connection establishment. Incoming TCP traffic can be allowed if

the ACK flag is set, with the assumption that the packet is a legitimate response packet. If the packet is not legitimate, the TCP application that receives the spurious packet will discard the packet upon receiving it. When the initiating Endpoint A is behind the firewall and the receiving Endpoint B is outside, the initial call signaling setup message is sent by Endpoint A to the well-known port 1720 of Endpoint B; hence, the firewall can be configured in order to let it through. H.225.0 signaling messages such as Alerting, Proceeding, Connect, and so on that flow from Endpoint B to Endpoint A can be allowed access by the firewall upon noticing the ACK flag set. Upon establishing the H.245 channel, the port at Endpoint B for this purpose is not a well-known port. In order to successfully establish an H.245 channel, the static packet filter needs to be configured in order to enable all TCP connection initiation from behind the firewall.

- Setting up a TCP connection for the H.245 channel is problematic when the endpoint that is initiating the connection is outside the firewall. The destination port on the endpoint behind the firewall is not a well-known port for H.245 channels. When Endpoint A outside the firewall sends a H.225.0 Setup message to Endpoint B behind the firewall, the firewall enables access because the destination port of the packet is the well-known port of 1720. Subsequently, when Endpoint A wishes to establish a H.245 channel, because the TCP connection establishment message does not go to a well-known port on Endpoint B, the static packet filter cannot be configured to grant access to this message without granting access to all incoming TCP connection establishment messages.

Stateful Packet Filters

Stateful packet filters overcome some of the limitations of static packet filters that we discussed previously. With stateful packet filters, enhanced functionality is provided because the filter configuration is dynamically adjusted based on information about the flow. Specifically, such filters (which perform filtering on the basis of a state-based dynamic configuration) can better handle dynamic ports as well as UDP traffic (compared to their static counterparts). Stateful packet filters maintain the state of the TCP or UDP connection, thereby providing an added level of security.

Consider the case where an H.323 Endpoint A behind a firewall (in other words, within the domain under the firewall's control) initiates a call to Endpoint B on the outside (in other words, within a domain that is not under the firewall's control). Because the H.323 standard permits the use of UDP for connection initiation, assume that UDP is used for the purpose of sending the H.225.0 Setup message. The UDP datagram from Endpoint A to Endpoint B would have the source address set to the IP address of Endpoint A, the destination address set to the IP address of Endpoint B, the source port set to some arbitrary high-numbered port chosen by Endpoint A, and the destination port set to the well-known port for UDP-based call signaling. This UDP datagram establishes a connection state in the firewall, which includes the IP address and port numbers of Endpoint A and Endpoint B. A packet from Endpoint B back to Endpoint A (such as a H.225.0 Connect message) would have the source and destination IP addresses interchanged as well as the source and destination ports interchanged, compared to a packet that was sent from Endpoint A to Endpoint B. This UDP datagram would be distinguished from an arbitrary datagram that is sent to a high-numbered port behind the firewall by the existence of the connection state, however. The connection state in the case of UDP usually has a timeout value (packets received after which are not permitted access). (For TCP applications, however, the connection state is deleted upon receipt of the FIN packet.) Thus, we see that stateful packet filters can handle UDP traffic better than stateless packet filters.

Circuit Gateways (SOCKS)

With circuit gateway-type firewalls, a TCP connection (in other words, circuit) is established between Endpoint A within the domain of the circuit gateway and the circuit gateway. A subsequent circuit is established between the circuit gateway and Endpoint B (which lies outside the domain of the gateway). The circuit gateway firewall then relays the connection from Endpoint A to Endpoint B.

The most popular circuit gateway is the SOCKS server, with SOCKS Version 5 being the latest version. In this case, as shown in Figure 14.13, Endpoint A is the SOCKS client. The SOCKS client establishes a TCP connection to the well-

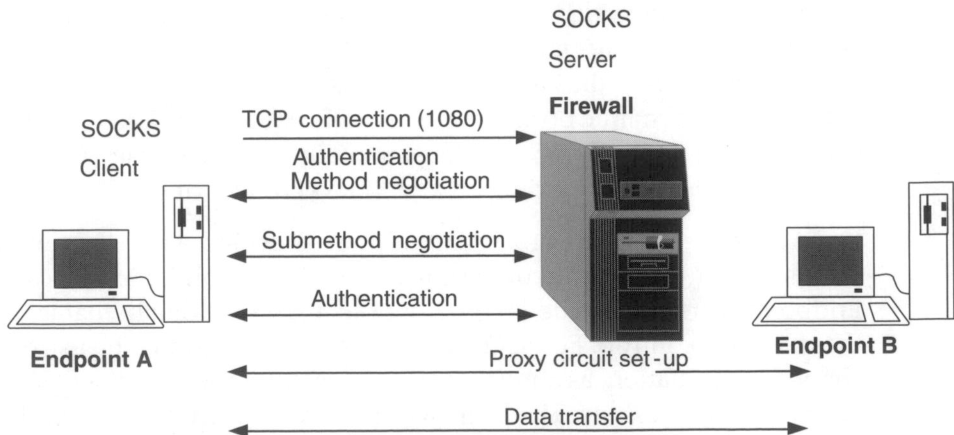

Figure 14.13 Illustrating the SOCKS v5 operation.

known port 1080 on which the SOCKS server is listening. An authentication method and submethod are negotiated between the SOCKS client and server, after which the client authenticates itself to the server. Optionally, an encryption mechanism can be agreed upon, as well. The Endpoint A client then sends a connection request to the SOCKS server, indicating that communication needs to be established with Endpoint B. The server then authorizes the client, after which a connection accept message is sent back to the client. This message contains an IP address and port number (usually belonging to the SOCKS server) to which the client needs to send data. The SOCKS server then sets up a TCP connection to Endpoint B, thereby establishing a proxy circuit between Endpoint A and Endpoint B with the SOCKS server acting as the relay in the middle.

You can implement SOCKS within a client in one of two ways. You can either integrate it with the H.323 application or provide it as a shim layer at the client. The latter method facilitates the use of SOCKS for existing H.323 applications that might not have a SOCKS client integrated with them.

Compared to packet filters, SOCKS is more complex but also more secure. SOCKS might also be suitable for certain UDP datagram traversal where the UDP datagram is sent within the established virtual circuit. One of the disadvantages of SOCKS is that the client needs to be aware of the presence and location (IP address) of the SOCKS server. Although some mechanisms for automatic discovery of such gateways exist, none of them is mature.

Application Level Gateways or Proxies

Application Level Gateways (ALGs), also known as proxies, function at the application layer. This characteristic is in contrast to packet filters and circuit-level gateways that operate at lower layers of the protocol stack. A proxy is, therefore, specific to a particular application while packet filters and circuit-level gateways are more generic in nature. For H.323 systems, a H.323 proxy needs to be installed at the gateway/firewall.

Because H.323 proxies can parse H.323 messages, you can achieve several sophisticated functionalities. Specifically, H.323 proxies have the capability to detect the dynamic TSAP address (in other words, IP address and port number) that is assigned to any channel—H.245, media stream, and so on. Let's examine how we can accomplish this task in two typical scenarios: one in which the endpoint behind the firewall initiates the connection and the other in which the endpoint outside the firewall initiates the connection.

Figure 14.14 illustrates the case where Endpoint A behind a firewall initiates a connection to Endpoint B that is outside the firewall. The figure is similar to Figure 14.12 that we described previously, with the difference being that

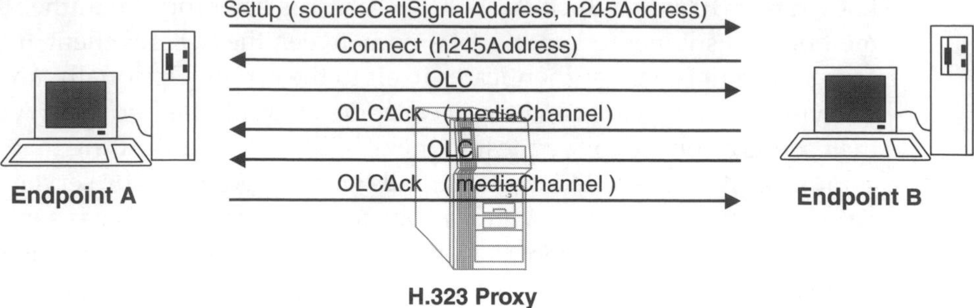

Figure 14.14 H.323 proxy operation.

we show the H.323 proxy for clarity. Endpoint A sends an H.225.0 Setup message to the well-known port 1720 of Endpoint B. The H.323 proxy inspects the message and stores the value of the sourceCallSignalAddress field. The sourceCallSignalAddress indicates the transport address (IP address and port number) used by Endpoint A for receiving H.225.0 messages. When H.225.0 messages such as Alerting, Proceeding, Connect, and so on are sent by Endpoint B to Endpoint A, the H.323 proxy matches the destination transport address of the packet with the value in the sourceCallSignalAddress field in the Setup message (that it had stored). If there is a match, the packet is given access. The H.323 proxy also stores the h245Address field within the Setup, Alerting, Connect, and so on messages. The h245Address field within the Setup message indicates the transport address on which H.245 messages will be received by Endpoint A while the h245Address field within the Alerting, Connect, and so on messages indicates the transport address on which H.245 messages will be received by Endpoint B. Thus, when H.245 messages—such as those for logical channel signaling, master-slave determination, capability set exchange, and so on—are sent either by Endpoint A or Endpoint B, the proxy compares the transport address of the packet with the corresponding value of the h245Address field stored within the proxy. If there is a match, then the packet is allowed access. During logical channel signaling, the H.245 OLCAck message carries the transport address for receiving the RTP media stream within the mediaChannel field. The H.323 proxy stores such transport addresses as well; hence, any media stream that is destined to a transport address that matches a stored value within the proxy is allowed access by the proxy.

The second scenario where Endpoint B initiates the connection to Endpoint A is similar to the first scenario. The H.323 proxy enables the setup message from Endpoint B to Endpoint A, which is destined to the well-known port of 1720, to pass through. The sourceCallSignalAddress and h245Address fields are stored within the proxy, which enables the H.225.0 messages from Endpoint A to Endpoint B (as well as the H.245 messages from Endpoint A to Endpoint B) to have access by the proxy. Similarly, the h245Address within Connect and the mediaChannel within OLCAck are also stored within the proxy (similar to the previous scenario).

Some advantages of H.323 proxies are as follows:

- They are generally more secure than packet filters.
- Compared to packet filters and circuit gateways, in the presence of *Network Address Translators* (NATs), only a proxy-based solution works. We will explain this concept in greater detail when we discuss NATs.

Some disadvantages of H.323 proxies are as follows:

- They create a process for each connection that they manage and hence suffer from a scalability problem.
- They are slow compared to packet filters.
- In the presence of end-to-end encryption (using, for example, IPSec or TLS), an H.323 proxy is rendered ineffective. All application layer fields are encrypted and are therefore unavailable to the proxy.

Network Topology and Firewall Placement

While the nature and configuration of firewalls is important, the physical network topology and the placement of firewalls is equally important in order to design a secure system. Often, networks are logically subdivided into subnetworks on the basis of certain common functionalities. Each department in a corporate environment might consist of a separate subnetwork, and these subnetworks might possibly be secured by firewalls from users of other subnetworks within the same corporation. Firewalls that are located at the edges of the entire network protect all interior subnetworks from users belonging to other networks. This situation results in a hierarchical structure of firewalls, as shown for Net 2 or Net 3 in Figure 14.15. In the figure, Net 2 is protected by Firewalls F_1, F_2, and F_3 while Net 3 is protected by Firewalls F_7 and F_8. Three subnets within Net 2 are protected by F_4, F_5, and F_6, and one subnet within Net 3 is protected by F_9 while the other subnet is not protected by a firewall.

The physical location of the firewalls should be such that all traffic from outside the protected zone that enters the protected zone should go through the firewall. The purpose of a firewall is beaten if an outsider can circumvent it. For instance, in Figure 14.15, if a route exists from A_1 to B_1 without

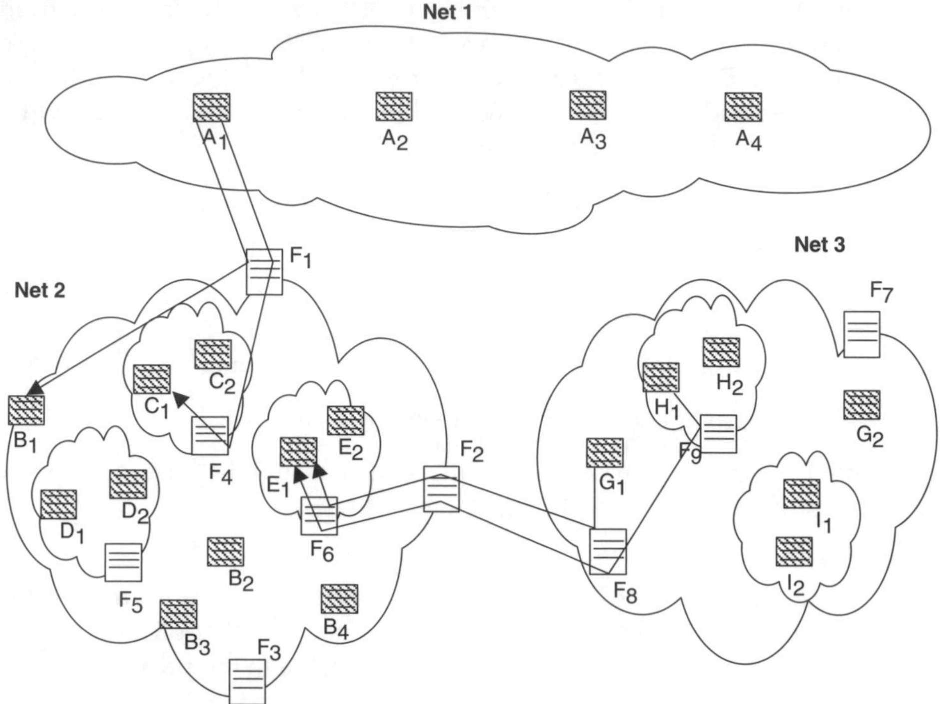

Figure 14.15 Network topology illustrating firewall placement.

traversing any of the firewalls F_1, F_2, or F_3 that are protecting Net 2, then a malicious host A_1 might be capable of launching attacks against B_1. Packet-filtering rules within the firewalls that are protecting Net 2 might forbid A_1 from initiating an H.323 call to any host within Net 2. This situation is the case when A_1 has an IP address other than x.y.z.* for the set of rules specified in Table 14.1. If a route exists for the H.225.0 call signaling Setup message (destined to port 1720) from A_1 to B_1 without traversing F_1, F_2, or F_3, however, then the security policy is not enforced.

Similarly, traffic that is flowing out of the protected zone needs to be routed through a firewall as well. As in the case of calls originating from the outside, policies can be specified for calls originating from the inside. If you can bypass firewalls, then it might not be possible to enforce such security policies.

Depending on the specific type of firewall that is being used, it might be necessary to route incoming and outgoing packets of the same session through the same firewall or through a set of cooperating firewalls. This function is necessary, for instance, in the case of stateful packet filters that populate the state for the incoming traffic based on outgoing traffic. Also, generally speaking, a multi-homed firewall is more secure than a single-homed firewall. The address of the network behind the firewall is usually hidden in a multi-homed configuration, but in a single-homed configuration, the network addresses are exposed.

Private Addressing

In order to conserve the limited IPv4 address space, private addressing is commonly used within enterprises and within other administrative domains. Private addresses are those that fall within the address ranges 10.0.0.0 to 10.255.255.255, 172.16.0.0 to 172.31.255.255, and 192.168.0.0 to 192.168.255.255. Administrative domains such as enterprises are free to use these private addresses for IP hosts within their domains as long as these addresses are not visible outside the administrative domain.

In the presence of private addressing, when the communication extends beyond the administrative domain, the private address needs to be hidden. Two approaches are possible in this case:

- *Network Address Translation* (NAT). This approach has commonly been used and involves changing the private transport address of IP packets into a public one at the NAT. The NAT is usually present at the boundary of the private network. H.323 systems in the presence of NATs require an H.323 proxy.
- *Realm Specific IP* (RSIP). This effort was recently proposed and has received considerable support from the Internet community for its advantages over NATs. A client-server approach—with the host acting as an RSIP client and an RSIP server containing a pool of public addresses—is used. Hosts within a private administrative domain that wish to communicate with hosts outside the private domain lease a public address from the RSIP server. This public address is then used by the host within the private domain for communicating with the host in the public domain.

We will discuss these two approaches in the context of H.323 systems and their impact on firewalls in this section.

Network Address Translation

Several flavors of NATs exist, and the functionality depends on the particular flavor that is in use. Some NAT flavors are as follows:

- *Traditional NAT*. Typically, sessions here originate within the private network. Two variations exist:
  - *Basic NAT*. A basic NAT replaces the private source IP address (and related checksums) of packets that are flowing out of the private domain with a public IP address. Similarly, it replaces the public destination IP address (and related checksums) of packets that are flowing into the private domain with the corresponding private IP address. The binding between the private and public IP addresses is usually established at session establishment.
  - *Network Address Port Translator* (NAPT). With NAPT, the private IP address of each host in the private domain is mapped to the same public IP address. Different sessions are distinguished by mapping the source port numbers of outbound packets to distinct port numbers and destination port numbers of inbound packets to the corresponding original port numbers. NAPTs, thus, change both the IP address and port numbers (and related checksums) of transiting packets.
- *Two-way NAT or bidirectional NAT*. Such NATs permit session establishment from both inside and outside the private domain. In order to establish sessions from the public domain to a host in the private domain, the addressing space to address the private host needs to be globally unique. For instance, you can use *Fully Qualified Domain Names* (FQDNs) or *Uniform Resource Identifiers* (URI). A static or dynamic mapping at the NAT then permits the address translation of traversing packets.
- *Twice NAT*. Such NATs translate both the source and destination IP address of traversing packets. A typical usage scenario is when the private domain also uses addresses from the public address space, but these addresses are not advertised outside the private domain.
- *Multi-homed NAT*. Such a NAT is primarily used for reliability purposes under the event of a NAT or link failure. A typical scenario can have one primary NAT box and one secondary/backup NAT box, and the backup NAT would only be used in the event that the primary NAT fails. Coordination and synchronization of state information between the primary and backup NAT is needed in order to maintain transparency under failure. Another scenario, which protects under link failures, is to have multiple links/interfaces for a single NAT.

Issues with H.323 Operation with NAT

Let's now discuss certain issues that surface when H.323 systems operate in the presence of private addressing and NATs.

Consider the scenario shown in Figure 14.11(a) on page 459 and assume that private addressing is used within the administrative domain A. Let Firewall A—located at the boundary of domain A and the public domain—perform traditional NAT. Specifically, basic NAT functionality is incorporated into the firewall. Let the private IP address assigned to Endpoint A be 10.0.0.1 and the public IP address that is mapped to at the NAT be 195.0.0.1. When a H.225.0 Setup message is sent from Endpoint A to Endpoint B, the sourceCallSignalingAddress field is set to the transport address of Endpoint A, which contains the IP address of 10.0.0.1. In addition, the IP header of the IP datagram transporting this message contains a source IP address of 10.0.0.1. When the datagram reaches the NAT, the NAT replaces the source IP address within the IP header to 195.0.0.1. Because the NAT does not inspect any application fields, the sourceCallSignalingAddress field within the setup message is left untouched. The IP datagram arriving at Endpoint B then contains the value of 10.0.0.1 within the sourceCallSignalingAddress field. Because Endpoint B uses this address for the IP address of Endpoint B, and because 10.0.0.1 is a private address that cannot be used within the domain of Endpoint B for routing packets to Endpoint A, there is a problem. The same situation exists when NAPT traditional NATs, twice NATs, or multi-homed NATs are used.

Using the H.323 Proxy to Solve the Problem

In order to solve this problem that H.323 systems face in the presence of NATs, you can use an H.323 proxy. When an H.323 proxy is used in conjunction with a NAT, the proxy can replace the value of the sourceCallSignalingAddress field within the setup message with the public IP address that the NAT assigns. For the example discussed in the previous section, the proxy would replace the IP address of 10.0.0.1 within the sourceCallSignalingAddress field with the IP address of 195.0.0.1. Upon reaching Endpoint B, Endpoint B then uses an IP address of 195.0.0.1 (and not 10.0.0.1) in order to address Endpoint A.

Because H.323 proxies would be rendered ineffective if end-to-end encryption using, say, IPSec or TLS were performed, the problem with NATs would continue to exist.

Realm Specific IP

RSIP uses a different approach compared to NATs when dealing with private addressing. The approach with RSIP is that when an Endpoint A that is assigned a private address needs to communicate with an Endpoint B that lies outside this private addressing domain, then Endpoint A leases a public address from an RSIP server for the purpose of this communication. Because

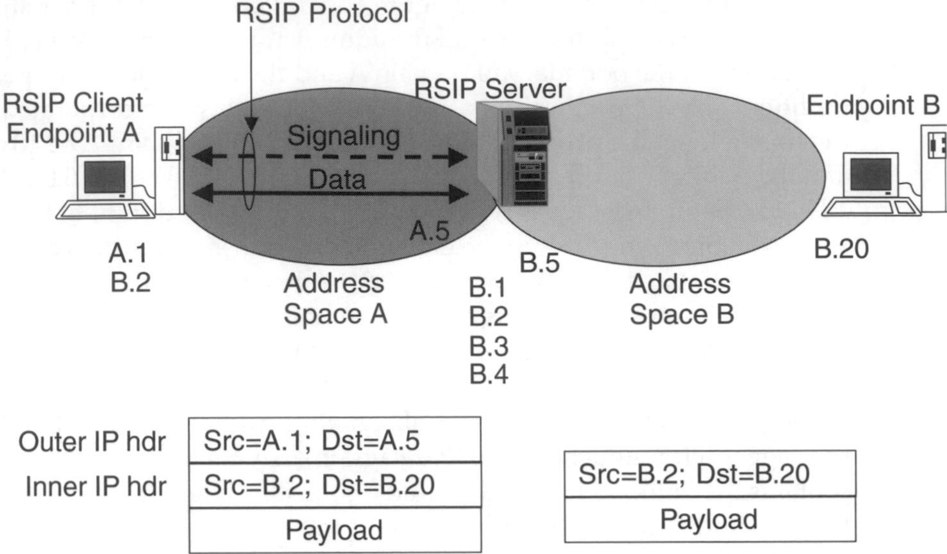

Figure 14.16 RSIP operation.

this public IP address is then used by the H.323 application, the problem that NATs face is not encountered here.

Figure 14.16 illustrates the operation of RSIP, which we will describe in the specific context of H.323 systems. As you can see in the figure, Endpoint A (which is located within a private addressing domain called Address Space A) initiates communication with Endpoint B (which is located in a public addressing domain called Address Space B). We denote certain IP addresses in the figure, and for illustration, let's assume that IP address A.x represents the private address 10.0.0.x while IP address B.x represents the public address 195.0.0.x. We can see that Endpoint A has a private address of 10.0.0.1 assigned to it while Endpoint B has a public address of 195.0.0.20 assigned to it. The RSIP server that resides at the boundary of the private and public domains has two interfaces: the private domain has an IP address 10.0.0.5 while the public domain has an IP address of 195.0.0.5. The RSIP server also has a pool of four public IP addresses—195.0.0.1 through 195.0.0.4—that it can lease to its clients within the private domain.

Because Endpoint A wishes to communicate with Endpoint B, which is a host in the public addressing domain, Endpoint A (which is an RSIP client) leases the public IP address 195.0.0.2 from the RSIP server by using the RSIP protocol. Certain criteria can be associated with this lease, such as the duration of the lease and whether the leased IP address can be used for communication only with Endpoint B or with other endpoints as well (and so on). Now, the IP address that the H.323 application at Endpoint A is aware of is 195.0.0.2 and not 10.0.0.1. When a H.225.0 Setup message is sent by Endpoint A to Endpoint B, the sourceCallSignalingAddress field contains a value of 195.0.0.2. Similarly, the source IP address of the IP datagram created at Endpoint A also contains 195.0.0.2. In order to transport this IP datagram from Endpoint A to Endpoint B, the datagram is tunneled through another IP datagram from Endpoint A to the RSIP server. This outer IP datagram, which has a source IP address of 10.0.0.1 and a destination IP address of 10.0.0.5, is necessary because the inner IP datagram cannot be routed within the private domain. Upon reaching the RSIP server, the outer IP header is stripped and the original IP datagram is routed through the public domain to Endpoint B.

Because the only address that Endpoint B sees for Endpoint A is 195.0.0.2, this address is used for Endpoint A. Messages that Endpoint B sends to Endpoint A, such as the H.225.0 Connect message, are subsequently tunneled to Endpoint A when they reach the RSIP server. Thus, we can see that with the use of RSIP, you do not require an H.323 proxy in the presence of private addressing. With NATs, on the other hand, you need an H.323 proxy.

Using RADIUS within H.323 Systems

The *Remote Authentication Dial-In User Service* (RADIUS) is a client-server protocol (standardized by the IETF) that is used for *Authentication, Authorization, and Accounting* (AAA) services. RADIUS servers have been widely deployed within enterprises in order to facilitate remote user dial-in. H.323 systems can leverage existing RADIUS deployments in order to obtain the security services that they provide.

RADIUS Overview

Three entities are involved in the RADIUS protocol: a user, a RADIUS client, and a RADIUS server. Essentially, the user provides identity (username) and authenticating information (password) to the RADIUS client, which then passes them on to the RADIUS server that uses the messages that are defined within the RADIUS protocol. Using an a priori shared secret that exists between the two protects communication between a RADIUS client and server. Figure 14.17 illustrates the protocol operation. The first Access Request message contains the username and password information while the second Access Request message contains the response to the challenge that was sent in the Access Challenge message.

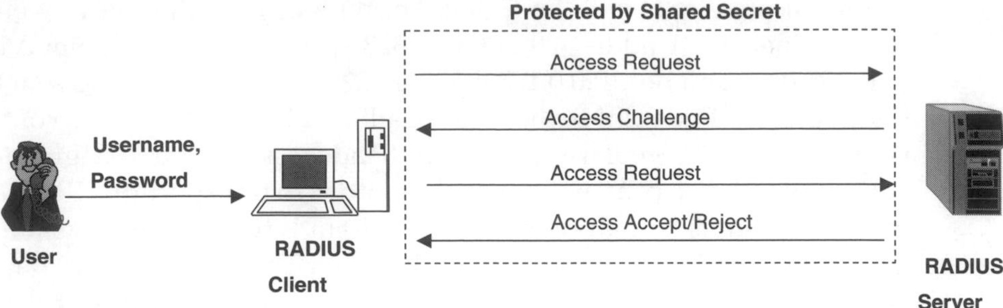

Figure 14.17 The RADIUS protocol.

H.323 and RADIUS

H.323 systems can use the RADIUS protocol as a back-end service in order to obtain certain AAA services. They achieve this goal by using the gatekeeper as a RADIUS client that communicates with a RADIUS server, which is a *Back-End Server* (BES) as far as the H.323 system is concerned. Two different topologies/configurations exist:

1. The endpoint is not aware of the existence of the RADIUS server. In this case, the gatekeeper acts as a trusted entity between the endpoint and the RADIUS server, and all fields that are sent between the endpoint and the RADIUS server are accessible to the gatekeeper.
2. The endpoint is aware of the existence of the RADIUS server. In this case, the gatekeeper is not necessarily a trusted entity between the endpoint and the RADIUS server. The endpoint shares a secret with the RADIUS server. Certain fields that are exchanged between the endpoint and the RADIUS server, although they transit the gatekeeper, might not be decipherable by the gatekeeper.

The Endpoint Is Unaware of the RADIUS Server

User authentication information that is sent by an endpoint to its gatekeeper can also be transparently sent by the gatekeeper (acting as a RADIUS client) to a RADIUS server in order to authenticate the user. In the previous chapter, we examined three possible mechanisms for user authentication: shared secret-based encryption, shared secret-based hash, and digital signatures. With each of these mechanisms, instead of the gatekeeper locally determining whether authentication succeeded or failed, the gatekeeper can transparently formulate an Access Request message containing the appropriate user identification and authentication information and send this message to the

RADIUS server. The RADIUS server then performs the authentication and notifies the gatekeeper of authentication success or failure. In each of these cases, the endpoint might be totally unaware of the use of the RADIUS protocol between the gatekeeper and the RADIUS server. Moreover, the endpoint does not have a security association (in other words, does not share a secret) with the RADIUS server.

In addition, the H.235 standard defines an additional mechanism by which an endpoint can send authenticating information to its gatekeeper while being totally unaware that the RADIUS protocol is used by the gatekeeper to communicate with a RADIUS server. Figure 14.18 illustrates this situation. The endpoint sends authenticating information to its gatekeeper by using the cryptoH323Token field of any RAS/H.225.0 message. The cryptoH323Token field contains a nestedCryptoToken field that contains a CryptoToken (which is of type cryptoEncryptedToken). The tokenOID within the cryptoEncryptedToken has an OID denoting a defaultBES mode. (In other words, the endpoint is unaware of the use of the RADIUS protocol between the gatekeeper and the RADIUS server.) The token itself contains three fields: the algorithmOID containing an OID denoting the encryption algorithm used; the params containing any run-time parameters that are needed for the

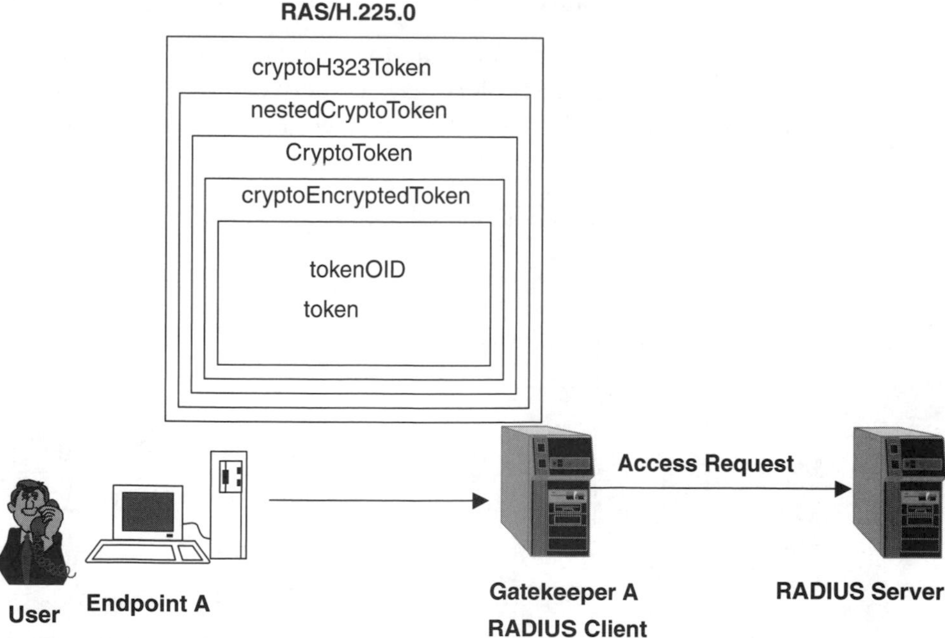

Figure 14.18 A scenario where the endpoint has no direct association with the RADIUS server.

encryption algorithm; and the encryptedData field containing the actual encrypted data that is used as the authenticating information. We should note that the secret here is shared between the endpoint and the gatekeeper. Using this decrypted authenticating information, the endpoint can compute an Access Request message to the RADIUS server.

We saw that the mechanism described previously uses the cryptoEncryptedToken choice of the CryptoToken. The reader might observe that the three user-authentication mechanisms discussed in the previous chapter used the remaining three choices for the CryptoToken: cryptoSignedToken, cryptoHashedToken, and cryptoPwdEncr. Upon closer examination, the reader will note that the cryptoEncryptedToken is very similar to the cryptoPwdEncr choice. The difference is that in the former situation, a clearToken is provided without any constraints on which fields are mandatory, and in the latter situation, some fields of the clearToken are mandatory.

The Endpoint Is Aware of the RADIUS Server

In this scenario, the endpoint is aware of the existence of a RADIUS server beyond the gatekeeper, and the gatekeeper merely forwards the relevant fields between the endpoint and the RADIUS server. The endpoint does not necessarily trust the gatekeeper.

Figure 14.19 illustrates the procedure that we use in this case. As you can see in the figure, the RADIUS protocol is used between the gatekeeper and the RADIUS server while RAS/H.225.0 messages are exchanged between the

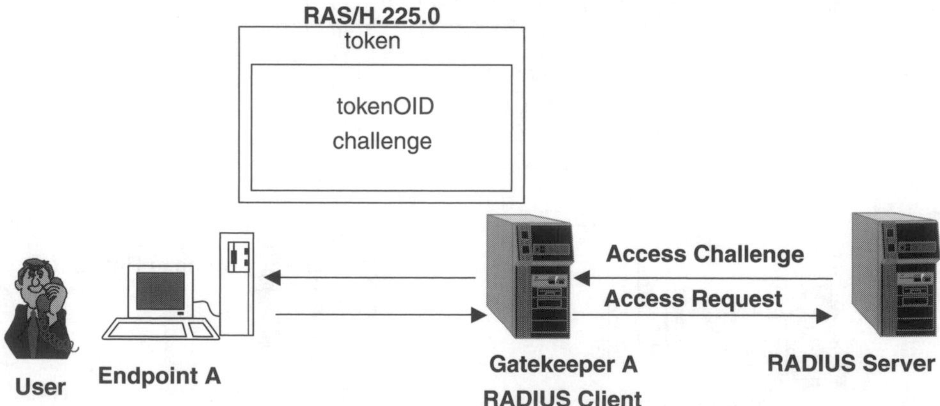

Figure 14.19 A scenario where the endpoint has direct association with the RADIUS server.

endpoint and the gatekeeper. The relevant fields that are used within the RAS/H.225.0 messages in either direction are also indicated in the figure.

When a RADIUS server passes a challenge to the RADIUS client (which is the gatekeeper) by using the Access Challenge message, the gatekeeper forwards the challenge on to the endpoint within a RAS or H.225.0 message. The challenge field of the token within a RAS/H.225.0 message (as seen in the figure) is used to carry the challenge. The tokenOID field has an OID indicating the use of RADIUS; hence, the endpoint can determine that the RADIUS challenge is being carried within the challenge field. Upon reception of the challenge, the endpoint computes the response and includes it within the same challenge field of a RAS/H.225.0 message that is sent back to the gatekeeper. Several methods that are outside the scope of the H.323 standard itself can be used to compute the response to the challenge. For instance, one possible mechanism is that the user has a smart card into which he or she enters the challenge and a *Personal Identification Number* (PIN), and the smart card computes the response. Regardless of the method that you use to compute the response from a challenge, the RADIUS server can also compute the same response for any user within its database. The RAS/H.225.0 message that is sent from the endpoint to the gatekeeper and contains the response within the challenge field has the OID within the tokenOID field as the RAS message carrying the challenge from the gatekeeper to the endpoint. The gatekeeper, upon seeing this OID, can ascertain that the challenge field contains a RADIUS response. Therefore, the gatekeeper inserts this response into an Access Request message that it sends to the RADIUS server.

Recommended Reading

ITU-T Recommendation H.235 H.235v3 is the security standard for H.323 systems. The H.225.0, H.245, and H.323 standards need to be referred to for various aspects that we described in this chapter. They are found in H.225.0, H.245, and H.323, respectively.

For aspects dealing with generic security protocols and algorithms, Stallings and Schneier are very good books. The most authoritative references on IPSec, TLS, ISAKMP, and IKE protocols are the relevant RFCs that are freely available from the IETF's Web site at www.ietf.org. RFC2402 and RFC2406 describe IPSec AH and ESP, respectively, while RFC2408, RFC2412, and RFC2409 describe the ISAKMP, OAKLEY, and IKE protocols (respectively). Prior to reading these RFCs, you will find it useful to read RFC2401, which provides an overview of the security architecture for Internet protocols.

Information about DES, AES, MD-5, and SHA-1 algorithms exists at FIPS-81, AES, RFC1321, and FIPS-180-1, respectively. You can find a description of *Hashed MACs* (HMAC) at RFC2104.

You can find a good introduction to firewalls in Cheswick. The SOCKS protocol is described in RFC1928, and there is ongoing work within the IETF to revise this protocol. You can obtain a good overview of the concepts of NAT and RSIP from RFC2663. Other Internet drafts in the area of NAT and RSIP appear on the IETF's Web site www.ietf.org. The RADIUS protocol is described in RFC2138.

References

AES J. Daemen, V. Rijmen, *The Rijndael Block Cipher*, http://csrc.nist.gov/encryption/aes/, 2000.

Cheswick W. R. Cheswick, S. M. Bellovin, *Firewalls and Internet Security*, Addison-Wesley, 1994.

FIPS-81 NIST, FIPS PUB 81: DES Modes of Operation, December 1980, http://www.itl.nist.gov/div897/pubs/fip81.htm

FIPS-180-1 NIST, FIPS PUB 180-1: Secure Hash Standard, April 1995, http://csrc.nist.gov/fips/fip180-1.ps

H.225.0 ITU-T Recommendation H.225.0 version 4, *Call Signaling Protocols and Media Stream Packetization for Packet Based Multimedia Communications Systems*, November 2000.

H.235v3 ITU-T Recommendation H.235 version 3, *Security and Encryption for H-series (H.323 and other H.245-based) multimedia terminals*, November 2000.

H.245 ITU-T Recommendation H.245 version 7, *Control Protocol for Multimedia Communication*, November 2000.

H.323 ITU-T Recommendation H.323 version 4, *Packet Based Multimedia Communication Systems*, November 2000.

RFC1321 R. Rivest, *The MD-5 Message Digest Algorithm*, RFC-1321, IETF, April 1992.

RFC1928 M. Leech, M. Ganis, Y. Lee, R. Kuris, D. Koblas, L. Jones, *SOCKS Protocol Version 5*, RFC-1928, IETF, March 1996.

RFC2104 H. Krawczyk, M. Bellare, R. Canetti, HMAC: *Keyed-Hashing for Message Authentication*, RFC-2104, IETF, February 1997.

RFC2138 C. Rigney, A. Rubens, W. Simpson, S. Willens, *Remote Authentication Dial-In User Service (RADIUS)*, RFC-2138, IETF, April 1997.

RFC2246 T. Dierks, C. Allen, *The TLS Protocol Version 1.0*, RFC-2246, January 1999.

RFC2401 S. Kent, R. Atkinson, *Security Architecture for the Internet Protocol*, RFC-2401, IETF, November 1998.

RFC2402 S. Kent, R. Atkinson, *IP Authentication Header*, RFC-2402, IETF, November 1998.

RFC2406 S. Kent, R. Atkinson, *IP Encapsulating Security Payload*, RFC-2406, IETF, November 1998.

RFC2408 D. Maughan, M. Schertler, M. Schneider, J. Turner, *Internet Security Association and Key Management Potocol (ISAKMP)*, RFC-2408, IETF, November 1998.

RFC2409 D. Harkins, D. Carrel, *The Internet Key Exchange (IKE)*, RFC-2409, IETF, November 1998.

RFC2412 H. Orman, *The OAKLEY Key Determination Protocol*, RFC-2412, IETF, November 1998.

RFC2663 P. Srisuresh, M. Holdrege, *IP Network Address Translator (NAT) Terminology and Considerations*, RFC-2663, IETF, August 1999.

Schneier B. Schneier, *Applied Cryptography*, Second Edition, John Wiley & Sons.

Stallings W. Stallings, *Cryptography and Network Security*, Second Edition, Prentice Hall, 1999.

Problems

1. Assume that both authentication and encryption need to be provided for a certain H.323 channel and that you would like to use IPSec for this purpose. Discuss the tradeoffs between using a) IPSec ESP in conjunction with IPSec AH and b) IPSec ESP with the optional authentication.
2. Look up the description of the Rijndael algorithm (which is the AES standard) at http://csrc.nist.gov/encryption/aes/. Look up the latest H.235 recommendation and determine if support for AES is provided. If so, how? If not, describe how support can be provided.
3. Discuss the tradeoffs between the four modes of operation for block ciphers. Specifically, discuss how much precomputation might be possible for each mode in order to enhance the speed of operation.
4. Describe the various kinds of firewalls and the operation of H.323 systems with these. Describe why the operation of UDP traffic through firewalls is harder than TCP traffic.
5. The text provided a numerical illustration of the problem that we face when a basic NAT operates in conjunction with H.323 systems. Describe a similar numerical illustration for other kinds of NATs as well, specifically

demonstrating how they create problems for H.323 systems. How can you solve this problem?

6. What is the impact of end-to-end IPSec encryption between two communicating endpoints on an intermediate H.323 proxy?
7. The DIAMETER framework protocol (the name is not an acronym but instead originates from the fact that the diameter is twice the radius) has been proposed as a replacement for RADIUS AAA servers. Study the relevant Internet drafts from www.ietf.org in this area, and determine how this framework might be applicable within H.323 systems for AAA services.

CHAPTER 15

H.323 Mobility

In this chapter, we discuss three topics dealing with mobility, each of which is covered in a separate Annex within the H.323 specifications:

- User, terminal and service mobility issues are covered in the H.323 Annex H specification.
- *Interworking Function* (IWF) facilitating user mobility between PLMNs and H.323 systems is covered, as specified in the H.246 Annex E specifications.
- Wireless issues—specifically error correction—are covered in the H.323 Annex I specification.

As of mid-2001, H.323 Annex H and H.323 Annex I specifications have not been frozen by ITU-T. So, there may be some variation between the discussion here and the final specification of these Annexes.

Types of Mobility

Mobility can be classified into three types:

- *User Mobility*. This refers to the ability of a user who is capable of utilizing different devices, which are possibly connected to different network types, in order to access their account/subscription. A typical example of user mobility is one where a user can log on from a desktop at work at a certain time, while at a different time the user can log on and access an account from a laptop at home or in a hotel room. Although the same user is able to access the account from several types of devices and networks, the services obtained could be different in each case. In user mobility, the mobility takes place in an off-line fashion or between sessions.

- *Terminal Mobility*. This refers to the ability of a user who is currently in a session (i.e., online or connected) using a certain device, moving geographically using the same device, retaining session connectivity. Terminal mobility consists of two types—continuous and discrete. A typical example of continuous terminal mobility is one where a user on a laptop with Wireless LAN (for example, 802.11) connectivity is moving around the room, or the case where a user using a cellular phone is traveling in a car during conversation. A typical example of discrete terminal mobility is one where a user who is logged in to his/her account at work using Ethernet connectivity removes the Ethernet cable thereby temporarily suspending connectivity, and is able to resume the session by using a different Ethernet cable in the conference room after moving to that room.
- *Service Mobility*. This refers to the ability of the user to obtain similar services, irrespective of the user or terminal mobility. Depending on the constraints of the device and the network being utilized, there can be some limitations to the service set that a user receives. Service mobility, thus, is a user profile and interface which the user always can access.

User Mobility

Figure 15.1 is an example of user mobility. Four different types of user mobility are presented. In move 1, the user does not change the type of terminal or network being used, but merely changes his geographical location. For example, this is the case when a user logs into an account from one *Personal Computer* (PC) at one point in time, but uses another PC to log in at a different point in time. In move 2, the user changes the type of terminal being used, yet the network type remains unchanged. For example, this is the case when a user logs into an account from a PC with an Ethernet connection to a network at one point in time, and then uses a *Personal Digital Assistant* (PDA) with an Ethernet connection to the same network at another point in time. In move 3, the user changes both terminal and network types during the move. For example, this is the case when the user utilizing a PC with an Ethernet connection subsequently utilizes a *Wireless Application Protocol* (WAP) phone to connect to data network. Move 4 depicts the case where the service provider of the local network, in which a user is connected, is different.

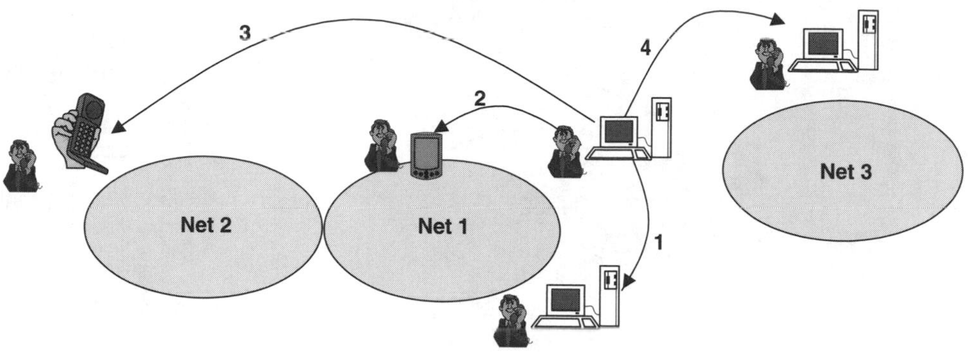

Figure 15.1 Example of user mobility.

Terminal Mobility

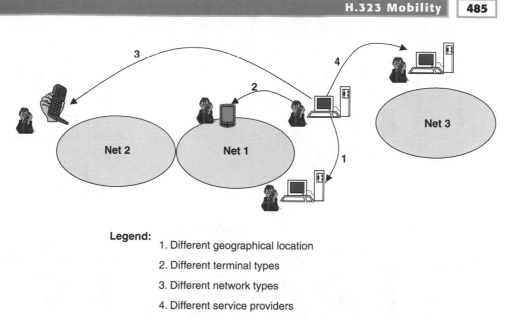

Figure 15.2 is an example of terminal mobility. Figure 15.2(a) illustrates discrete terminal mobility which implies that the user is off-line while the terminal is moved. For example, this is the case when a user takes a laptop to a different location and connects it to the network from that location. Figure 15.2(b) illustrates continuous terminal mobility which implies that the user is on-line while the terminal changes physical location. For example, this is the case when a user with a wireless LAN connection on a laptop changes geographical locations while connected to the network. In each case, a link level and network level mobility are shown. Link-level mobility exists when the connectivity changes only at the link level—there is no change at the network level (i.e., no change in the IP domains, assuming usage of a TCP/IP network). With network-level mobility however, the IP domain changes as well.

Service Mobility

Three possible mechanisms exist to achieve service mobility:

- *The user's entire service set is present within the visited network.* This is the case when a user carries a service profile (for example, within a *Subscriber Identity Module* [SIM]); or when the user's entire service set is downloaded

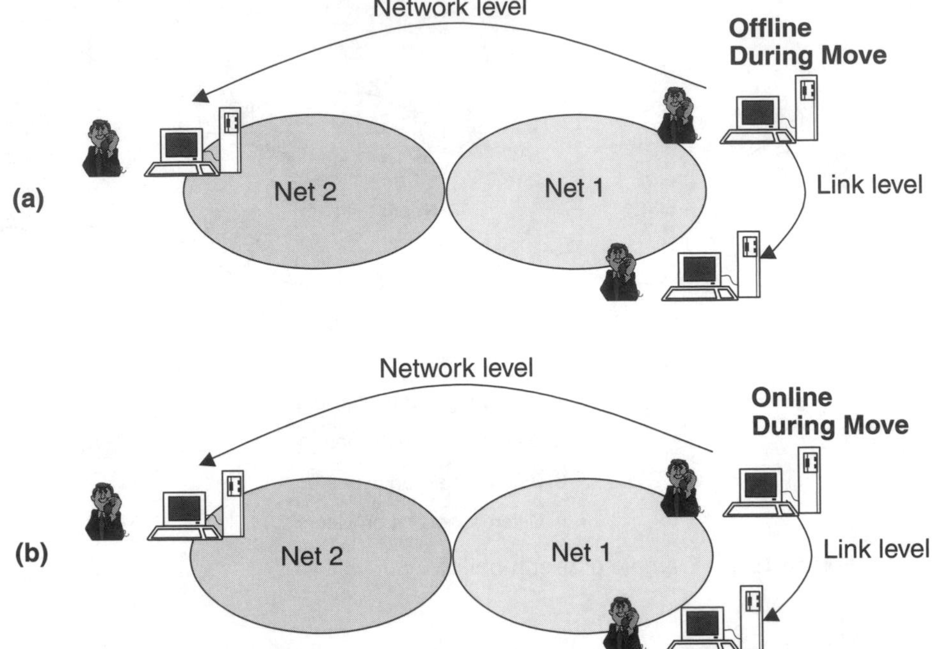

Figure 15.2 Example of (a) discrete and (b) continuous terminal mobility.

from the home network (i.e., home gatekeeper) to the visited network upon registering with that network. A combination of the two—where a part of the user's service profile is carried by a SIM, and the rest is downloaded from the home network upon registration—is also possible, as shown in Figure 15.3(a).

- *The user's service set is not downloaded within a visited network.* Instead, each time the user wishes to access a certain service, the home network is contacted, as shown in Figure 15.3(b).
- *A hybrid case in which a portion of the user's service set is downloaded in a visited network.* To access any of the remaining services, the home network must be contacted.

There are trade-offs between downloading and not downloading the user's service profile. Downloading is preferred when a user is relatively static; when the home gatekeeper trusts the visited gatekeeper sufficiently to transfer a user's set of services to it; and when optimized routing for call signaling is desired. No downloading is preferred when the home gatekeeper wants to control the calls made by its subscribers and when the home gatekeeper does not want to download a subscriber's service set to a visited gatekeeper.

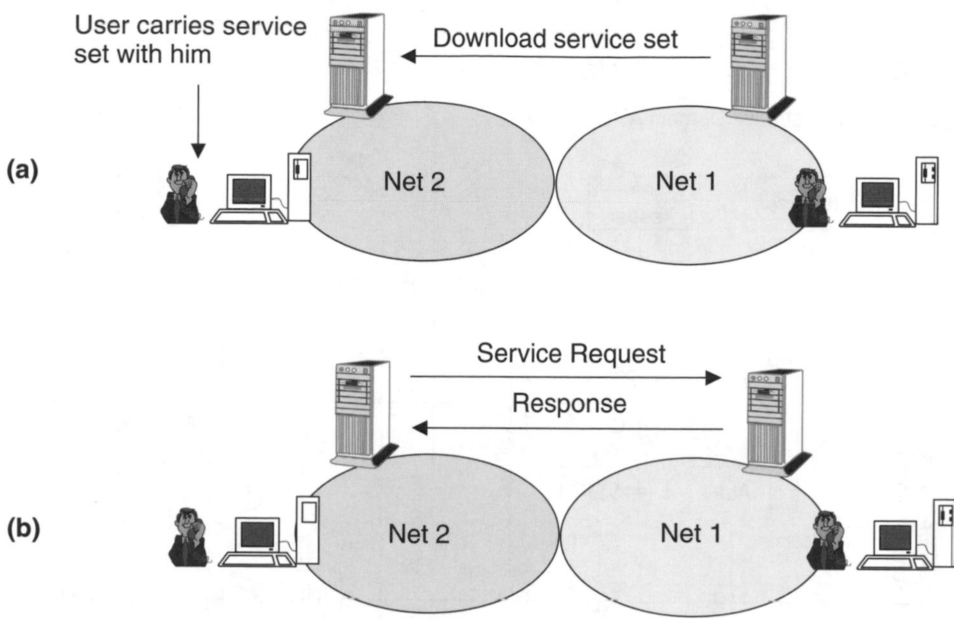

Figure 15.3 Example of service mobility.

H.323 Mobility Architecture

In order to provide user, terminal, and service mobility within an H.323 system, the following functional entities are introduced:

- *Home Location Function* (HLF)
- *Visitor Location Function* (VLF)
- *Authentication Function* (AuF)
- *Interworking Function* (IWF)

Figure 15.4 shows how these various functional entities fit within the H.323 model, and their interconnecting reference points.

Initial Gatekeeper Discovery and Registration

In Chapter 2, we discussed that an H.323 endpoint first must initialize itself by performing a gatekeeper discovery process, and if a suitable gatekeeper exists, then the endpoint must register with the gatekeeper. Every gatekeeper has a VLF associated with it, and the gatekeeper informs the VLF that the endpoint is registered with it. The VLF then subsequently contacts the HLF of the endpoint to inform it that the endpoint is within the service zone of the VLF.

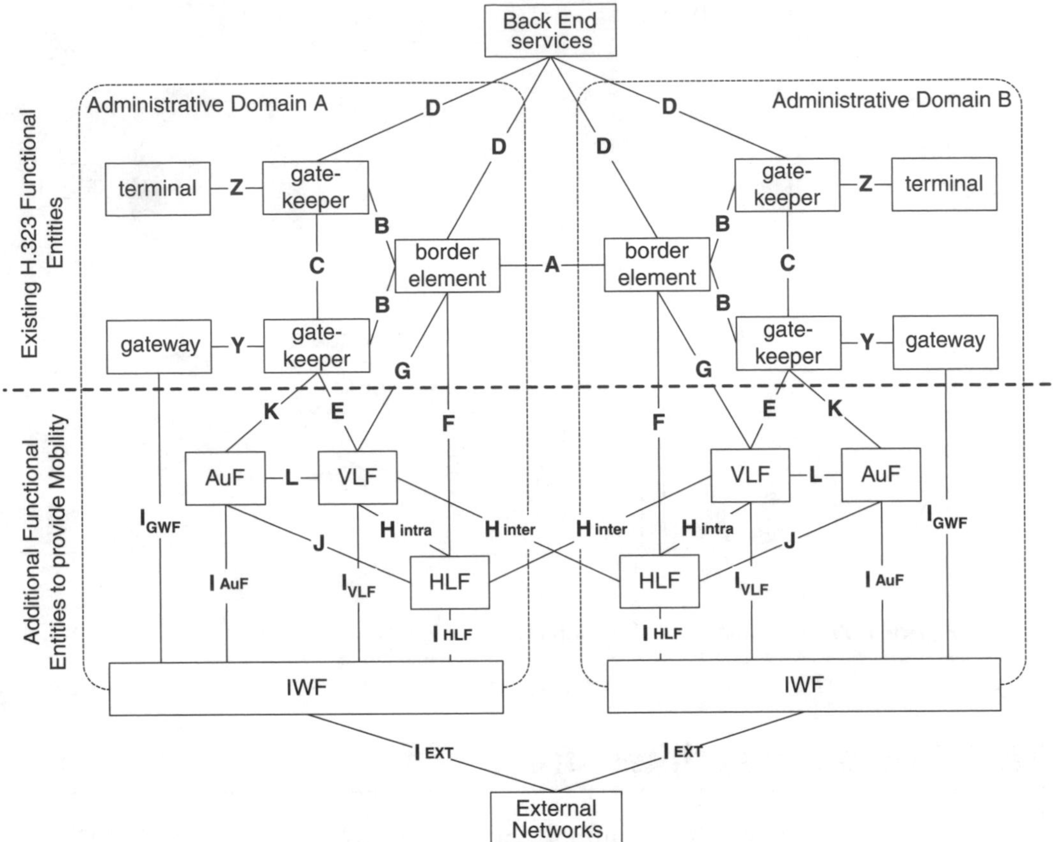

Figure 15.4 A draft H.323 Annex H functional architecture diagram with interface points.
Source: ITU.

The interfaces that exist between the relevant functional entities are shown in Figure 15.4. No direct interface exists between the endpoint and the VLF/HLF, and the only way for an endpoint to communicate with either one is via its gatekeeper. Nor can a gatekeeper similarly communicate directly with an HLF. However, it can always communicate via a VLF. This interface path exists regardless of whether the endpoint is within its home or a visiting *Administrative Domain* (AD). When the endpoint is within its home AD, the VLF in Figure 15.4 is a VLF which belongs to the home AD. On the other hand, when an endpoint is within a visiting AD unlike the home AD, the VLF belongs to the visiting AD.

The gatekeeper discovery procedure is identical to the explanation in Chapter 3. When the endpoint is within a visiting AD, a multicast gatekeeper discovery query can be received by a suitable gatekeeper in the visiting AD, which then responds with a confirm message (GCF). If a unicast GRQ message is sent to a gatekeeper in the home AD that the endpoint is statically configured with, then the gatekeeper responds with a GRJ message which contains a list of gatekeepers within the visiting AD with whom the endpoint can try to register.

Location Update

When an endpoint moves, a location update is needed. The following three cases are considered in this regard:

- *Intra-zone mobility.* As illustrated in Figure 15.5, this term refers to the case when a gatekeeper (where the endpoint is registered) does not change as a result of the mobility. Because the gatekeeper does not change, the VLF remains unchanged as well. The broken line in the figure indicates the endpoint's original location, while the solid line indicates the endpoint's current location. In this example, the VLF and HLF are both unaware of the move.
- *Inter-zone and Intra-VLF mobility.* As illustrated in Figure 15.6, these terms refer to the case when a gatekeeper (where the endpoint is registered) changes as a result of the mobility. However, the VLF associated with each of the two gatekeepers (Gatekeeper A and Gatekeeper B) is the same. In this example, the endpoint needs to discover and register with the new

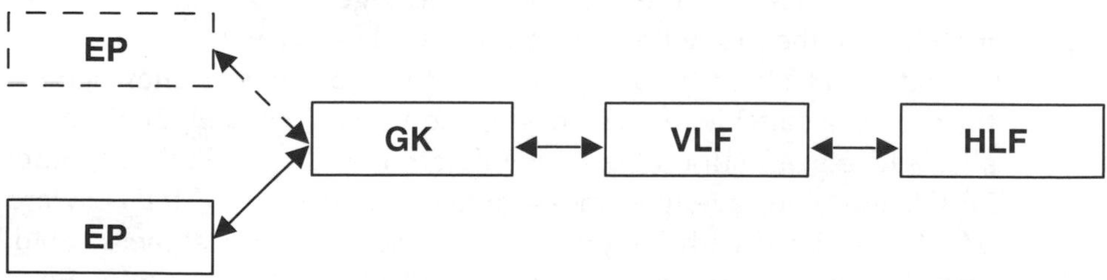

Figure 15.5 Intra-zone mobility.

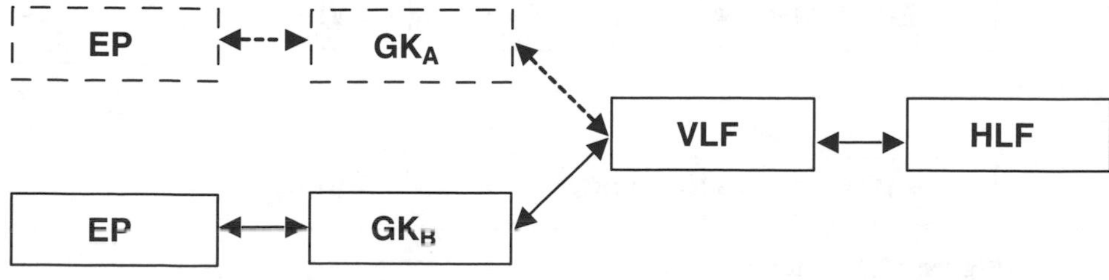

Figure 15.6 Intra-VLF mobility.

gatekeeper, Gatekeeper B, at the new location. Gatekeeper B then informs the VLF of the new registration, and the VLF notifies the old gatekeeper, Gatekeeper A, that the endpoint is no longer registered with it. In addition, the registration of the endpoint at Gatekeeper A can also simply time out. Because the VLF does not change, the HLF does not need to be notified about the move. In this example, the VLF is aware of the change, while the HLF is unaware of the endpoint's move.

- *Inter-VLF mobility*. As illustrated in Figure 15.7, this term refers to the case when both the gatekeeper and the VLF change as a result of the endpoint's mobility, and each are aware of the endpoint's move. The endpoint discovers and then registers with Gatekeeper B, which notifies its new VLF (VLF B) of the registration. VLF B then informs the endpoint's HLF about the registration, which notifies the old VLF (VLF A) that the endpoint is no longer associated with it. VLF A can then subsequently notify Gatekeeper A that the endpoint is no longer registered with it.

Call Signaling to an Endpoint

Consider the case where Endpoint A wishes to call Endpoint B. We previously discussed the signaling flows using H.225.0 messages in Chapter 2. We now briefly mention enhancements which facilitate this in the context of mobility.

Figure 15.8 illustrates the sequence of message flows in the context of mobility for the case where Endpoint A wishes to call Endpoint B. Endpoint A sends an H.225.0 Call Setup message to Gatekeeper A (message 1), which then sends a suitable request message to VLF A (message 2). Based on the alias address of Endpoint B, VLF A determines the HLF of Endpoint B to be HLF B and sends a request message to it (message 3). HLF B is aware of the VLF B associated with Endpoint B, and it sends a request message to VLF B (message 4). The response message from VLF B, which contains Endpoint Bs

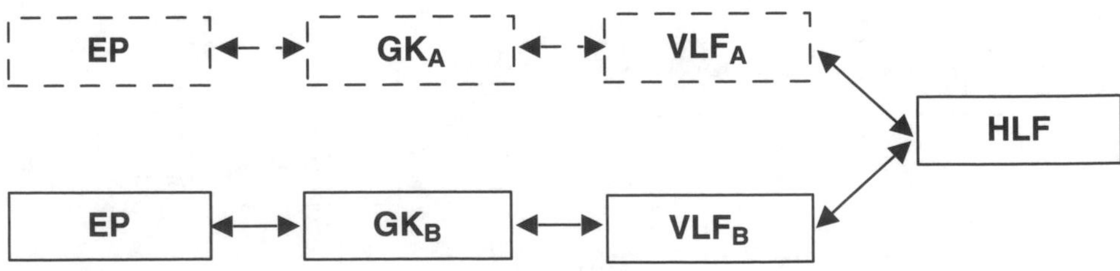

Figure 15.7 Inter-VLF mobility.

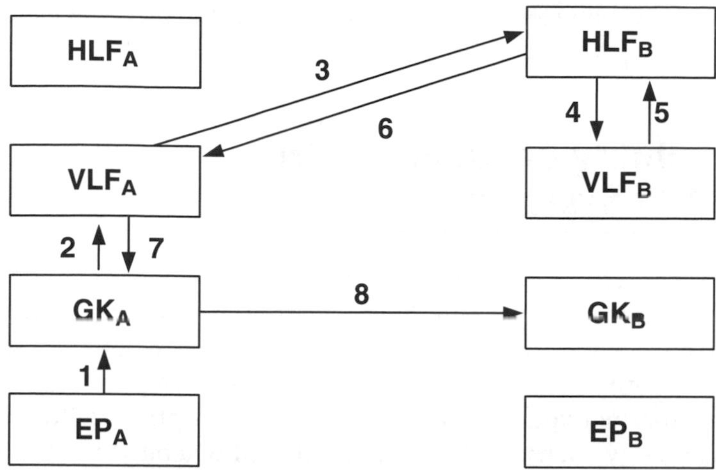

Figure 15.8 Example of the message flows during call establishment.

registered Gatekeeper B, then flows from VLF B to HLF B (message 5) and to Gatekeeper A (message 7) via a VLF A (message 6). Upon receiving this response (message 7), Gatekeeper A is aware that Gatekeeper B is the gatekeeper registered with Endpoint B, and it consequently sends an H.225.0 setup message to Gatekeeper B.

Authenticating Function (AuF)

The AuF, which is associated with an HLF, stores the authenticating information of subscribers who are associated with that HLF. Such authenticating information is usually a shared secret known only to the AuF and to the endpoint. This shared secret is used for the following primary purposes:

- To ascertain the authenticity of a subscriber using mechanisms such as a challenge-response mechanism.
- To generate a session key which may be used for secure communication between the endpoint and its gatekeeper.

Interworking Function (IWF)

An IWF, as shown in Figure 15.4, is present at the boundary of two different networks—the H.323 network and another network such as PSTN, ISDN, *Public Land Mobile Network* (PLMN), and so on. The IWF acts as a protocol translator between the H.323 protocol and the protocol used within the other network.

User Mobility between PLMN and H.323 Systems

User mobility was defined earlier as the ability of a user to use different devices, which are possibly connected to different networks, in order to access an account. A specific example of user mobility is when the user is able to access an account on a cellular network as well as on a packet network. When on a cellular network, the user utilizes the appropriate cellular network technology such as GSM or ANSI-41; and when the user is on a packet network, H.323 technology is utilized.

Currently there are several million subscribers using first- and second-generation cellular networks. Such networks include GSM, ANSI-41, and the Japanese Personal Digital Cellular (PDC) network. Third-generation cellular networks are likely to be deployed in the next few years. Such networks, which are referred to as *Public Land Mobile Networks* (PLMN), use a unique identifier to identify a subscriber. When H.323 systems utilize this same identifier in conjunction with a suitable interworking unit, the following advantages are obtained:

- The existing infrastructure of PLMNs for authentication, billing, and other actions can be utilized.
- A subscriber of a PLMN can use the same telephone number to receive calls on a H.323 phone when registered on a H.323 endpoint.

Subscriber Identifiers

Subscribers are assigned unique identifiers within a system, so that they may be distinguished from other subscribers. Different systems have different ways of identifying their subscribers. We now describe subscriber identifiers that are used in a PLMN and in H.323 networks.

Subscriber Identifier in a PLMN

A subscriber in a PLMN is identified using a specific identifier, which includes the following information:

- An *International Mobile Subscriber Identity* (IMSI) for GSM networks
- A *Mobile Identification Number* (MIN) for ANSI-41 networks

```
AliasAddress ::= CHOICE
{
     dialedDigits     IA5String (SIZE (1..128)) (FROM ("0123456789#*,")),
     h323-ID          BMPString(SIZE (1..256)),  -- Basic ISO/IEC 10646-1 (Unicode)
     ...,
     url-ID           IA5String (SIZE(1..512)),  -- URL style address
     transportID      TransportAddress,
     email-ID         IA5String (SIZE(1..512)),  -- rfc822-compliant email address
     partyNumber      PartyNumber,
     mobileUIM        MobileUIM
}

MobileUIM ::= CHOICE
{
     ansi-41-uim ANSI-41-UIM,     -- Americas standards Wireless Networks
     gsm-uim GSM-UIM,             -- European standards Wireless Networks
     pdc-uim PDC-UIM,             -- Japanese standards Wireless Networks
     ...
}
```

Figure 15.9 H.225.0 AliasAddress structure depicting a MobileUIM field.

Subscriber Identifier in H.323

In an H.323 system, a subscriber is identified using an alias address. The structure of an alias address, as specified within the H.225.0 standard, is shown in Figure 15.9. In order to facilitate user mobility between PLMNs and H.323-based systems, the mobileUIM field has been introduced within the AliasAddress structure. Depending on the type of PLMN desired by user mobility, an appropriate *User Identity Module* (UIM) is used. Three types of PLMNs are considered by H.323—ANSI-41, GSM, and PDC. The details of the UIM structure for these three popular PLMNs are shown in Figure 15.10.

Achieving User Mobility with IWF

We will now describe how user mobility may be achieved with the IWF. After providing an overview of mobility in PLMNs, we will describe the generic IWF functionality and its location within an H.323 system. While discussing the IWF functionality, we will examine several scenarios of operation.

Overview of Mobility in PLMNs

Before we discuss a description of the IWF, a high-level understanding of mobility management in PLMNs (such as GSM, ANSI-41, and PDC networks) is useful. As shown in Figure 15.11, several *Base Stations* (BS) or cell sites comprise a *Routing Area* (RA), and one or more RAs are associated with

```
ANSI-41-UIM ::= SEQUENCE
{
        imsi   TBCD-STRING      (SIZE (3..16)) OPTIONAL,
        min    TBCD-STRING      (SIZE (3..16)) OPTIONAL,
        mdn    TBCD-STRING      (SIZE (3..16)) OPTIONAL,
        msisdn TBCD-STRING      (SIZE (3..16)) OPTIONAL,
        esn    TBCD-STRING      (SIZE (16))    OPTIONAL,
        mscid  TBCD-STRING      (SIZE (3..16)) OPTIONAL,
        system-id CHOICE
        {
               sid TBCD-STRING (SIZE (1..4)),
               mid TBCD-STRING (SIZE (1..4)),
               ...
        },
        systemMyTypeCode OCTET STRING (SIZE (1))     OPTIONAL,
        systemAccessType OCTET STRING (SIZE (1))     OPTIONAL,
        qualificationInformationCode  OCTET STRING (SIZE (1)) OPTIONAL,
        sesn   TBCD-STRING             (SIZE (16))    OPTIONAL,
        soc    TBCD-STRING             (SIZE (3..16)) OPTIONAL,
        ...
}

GSM-UIM ::= SEQUENCE
{
        imsi   TBCD-STRING      (SIZE (3..16)) OPTIONAL,
        tmsi   TBCD-STRING      (SIZE (3..16)) OPTIONAL,
        msisdn TBCD-STRING      (SIZE (3..16)) OPTIONAL,
        imei   TBCD-STRING      (SIZE (16))    OPTIONAL,
        hplmn  TBCD-STRING      (SIZE (1..4))  OPTIONAL,
        vplmn  TBCD-STRING      (SIZE (1..4))  OPTIONAL,
        ...
}

PDC-UIM::= SEQUENCE
{
        imsi   TBCD-STRING      (SIZE (3..16)) OPTIONAL,
        tmsi   TBCD-STRING      (SIZE (3..16)) OPTIONAL,
        msisdn TBCD-STRING      (SIZE (3..16)) OPTIONAL,
        imei   TBCD-STRING      (SIZE (16))    OPTIONAL,
        hplmn  TBCD-STRING      (SIZE (1..4))  OPTIONAL,
        vplmn  TBCD-STRING      (SIZE (1..4))  OPTIONAL,
...
}

TBCD-STRING ::= OCTET STRING (FROM ("0123456789#*abc"))
```

Figure 15.10 UIM structures for different cellular networks.

a *Mobile Switching Center / Visitor Location Register* (MSC/VLR). When a *Mobile Station* (MS) is in a visiting PLMN, the HLR associated with the station in the Home PLMN is aware of the MSC/VLR associated with the station in

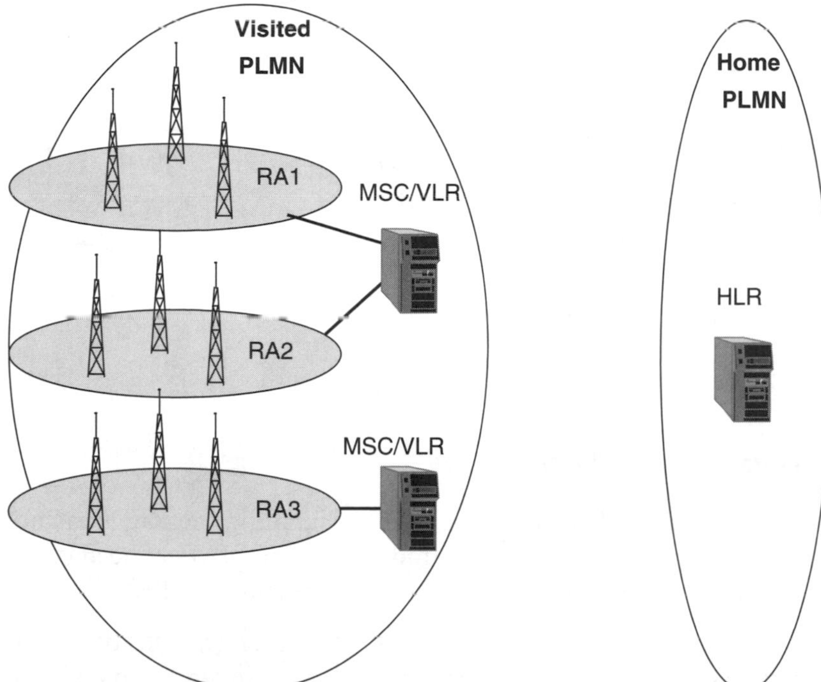

Figure 15.11 Mobility management in PLMNs.

the visiting PLMN. When the MS changes cell sites within the one or more RAs associated with the same MSC/VLR, the entry within the HLR is not updated. However, when the MS changes cell sites which are in RAs associated with different MSC/VLRs, then the HLR is updated to point to the new MSC/VLR.

The Location and Appearance of The IWF

User mobility between a PLMN and an H.323-based system is achieved by the presence of an *Interworking Function* (IWF) within a gatekeeper. A gatekeeper containing such an IWF is termed a *H.246 Annex E Gatekeeper*. Figure 15.12 illustrates the IWF being collocated with the gatekeeper. From the perspective of the H.323 system, the GK/IWF looks like a regular gatekeeper. However, from the perspective of the PLMN, the GK/IWF looks like the serving MSC/VLR. A subscriber's HLR has a pointer to the serving MSC/VLR of the subscriber (i.e., the MSC/VLR within the visiting PLMN). In other words, the H.323 system containing the IWF/GK appears as a visited PLMN to the home PLMN.

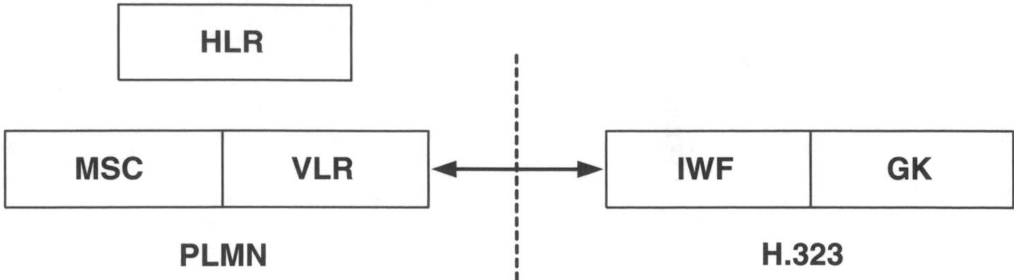

Figure 15.12 An IWF collocated with a gatekeeper.

Generic IWF Functionality

The role of the IWF is to map H.225.0 signaling messages to and from PLMN *Mobile Application Part* (MAP) messages. The MAP is the signaling portion of PLMNs, just as H.225.0 is the signaling portion of H.323 systems.

Consider Figure 15.12. Let the HLR (shown on the left) be the HLR associated with a certain subscriber. This subscriber is currently on an H.323-based system, and the endpoint that the subscriber is using registers with the gatekeeper (shown on the right of figure). As mentioned previously, the GK/IWF is seen as an MSC/VLR from the perspective of the PLMN. Because the HLR keeps a record of the MSC/VLR that the MS is associated with currently, appropriate MAP signaling messages are sent from the GK/IWF to the HLR to ensure that the record within the HLR is accurate.

We now present a typical deployment example from a GSM subscriber's perspective. A GSM subscriber is provided with a *Subscriber Identity Module* (SIM) card, which is used to uniquely identify the GSM subscriber (using an identifier called the IMSI), irregardless of the *Mobile Equipment* (ME) that the subscriber uses. In other words, when a GSM subscriber inserts a SIM card into a compatible ME (i.e., phone), then the subscriber is uniquely identified. Similarly, a *Personal Computer Memory Card International Association* (PCMCIA) card with a slot to hold a SIM card can be provided so that the same subscriber can use a H.323-based system. The subscriber's identity is determined by reading the IMSI from the SIM card located on the PCMCIA card.

Registration

The sequence of message flows involved when a UIM-enabled H.323 terminal registers with an AnnexE_GK is shown in Figure 15.13. The figure represents the specific case of ANSI-41 networks, where the IWF from Figure 15.12 is shown as an MSC/VLR. The GRQ, GCF, RRQ, and RCF messages are

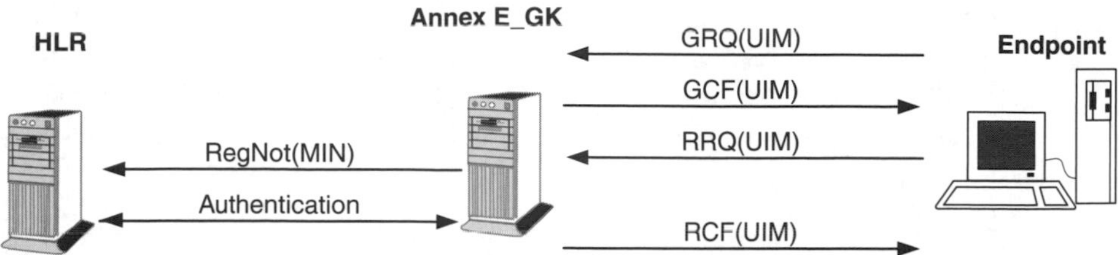

Figure 15.13 H.323_UIM terminal registration and authentication messages flow.

the relevant H.225.0 RAS messages, while the Registration_Negotiation and Authentication messages are the relevant ANSI-41 messages. The interworking between these two sets of messages is also illustrated in the Figure 15.13. The GRQ message from the H.323 endpoint to the gatekeeper contains one or more alias addresses, one of which is the UIM. When the AnnexE_GK responds with a GCF message, the endpoint then sends an RRQ message containing the same UIM. Receipt of this RRQ message triggers the Registration_Negotiation sequence within the PLMN, where the AnnexE_GK acts as the serving MSC/VLR and the operations are directed toward the subscriber's home PLMN. Authentication procedures using the Authentication_Request message take place before an RCF is sent by the AnnexE_GK to the endpoint.

Call Setup for Call Reception

Figure 15.14 illustrates the case where a call is made from a subscriber on the PSTN/PLMN to a mobile subscriber currently registered with an H.323 network. Following the ANSI-41 specifications, a LocReq message is sent by the serving MSC (when the caller is on a PLMN) or the gateway MSC (when the caller is on the PSTN) to the HLR of the called subscriber. Because the called subscriber's HLR has a pointer to the serving MSC/VLR of the called subscriber (AnnexE_GK in this case), a RoutReq message is sent

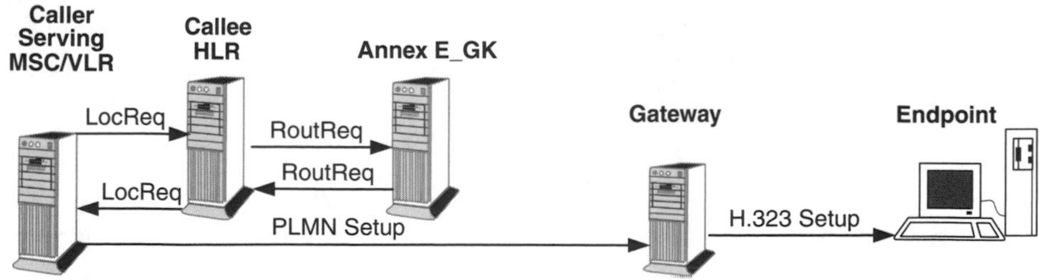

Figure 15.14 Call delivery to ANSI-41 subscriber roaming in H.323 network with a PSTN/PLMN subscriber originating the call.

to the AnnexE_GK, requesting the GW location to also send the Setup message. Upon receiving the GWs address through the RoutReq and LocReq messages, the serving MSC/VLR of the calling subscriber sends a PLMN Setup message to the GW, which sends an H.323 Setup message to the called endpoint.

Figure 15.15 illustrates the case where a mobile subscriber (Endpoint B) currently registered with an H.323 network receives a call made by another H.323 endpoint (Endpoint A). As shown in this figure, this case is treated identically to a normal H.323 call.

Call Setup for Call Origination

A mobile subscriber currently registered with an H.323 network initiates a call to a subscriber on a PLMN (as shown in Figure 15.16). Usage of an integrated Annex E GK/GW is assumed in this example. The calling H.323 endpoint sends an H.225.0 Setup message to the Annex E GK/GW. Because the Annex E GK/GW behaves as an MSC/VLR on the interface toward the PLMN, it sends a LocReq message to the called subscriber's HLR (the callee), which sends a RoutReq message to the serving MSC/VLR of the callee. Upon

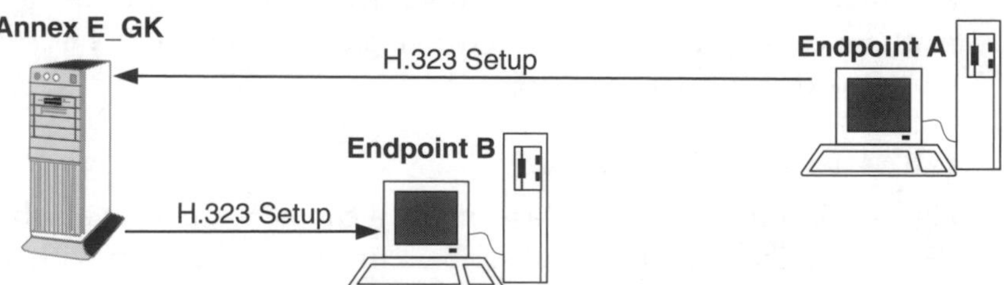

Figure 15.15 Call delivery to ANSI-41 subscriber roaming in H.323 network with an H.323 endpoint originating the call.

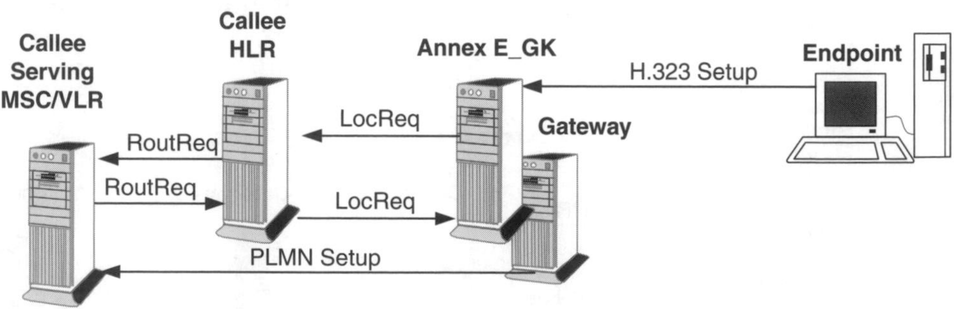

Figure 15.16 Call origination from an ANSI-41 subscriber roaming in an H.323 network to a PLMN subscriber.

obtaining a suitable response indicating the location (routing number) of the callee, a PLMN setup message is originated by the Annex E GK/GW toward the PLMN.

A mobile subscriber (Endpoint A) registered with an H.323 network initiates a call to another H.323 endpoint (Endpoint B) is shown in Figure 15.17. Because both endpoints are on the H.323 network, the call is placed as a normal H.323 call.

Other Services

We have discussed so far subscriber registration, call reception, and call initiation for the case where a PLMN subscriber roams into an H.323 network. In addition, this subscriber can also receive benefits of service mobility. Some services that this subscriber can continue to receive while on the H.323 network include *Short Message Service* (SMS) and *Message Waiting Indication* (MWI).

Non-Application Layer Wireless Issues

We have discussed so far only mobility-related issues at the application layer. In this section, we briefly discuss some of the issues at layers below the application layer—the link layer and network layer.

Error Correction

The rate of errors in communication varies according to the nature of the communication link/channel. Error correction schemes, which are suitable for the communication link utilized, are needed. With wireless channels, their error-prone nature makes the task of devising suitable error-correction

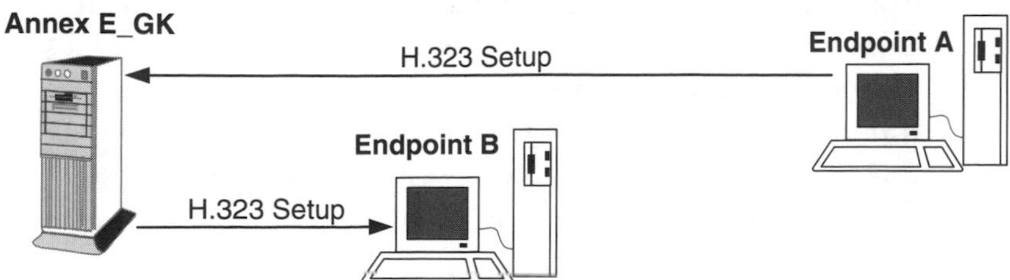

Figure 15.17 Call origination from an ANSI-41 subscriber roaming in an H.323 network to an H.323 Endpoint.

schemes more relevant. When mobility is added to a wireless channel, the characteristics of the channel can change dynamically, thus making error-correction schemes even more challenging.

A host of techniques for achieving error correction in the presence of mobile wireless channels is available. H.323 Annex I discusses the techniques which are relevant in the context of H.323 systems. We briefly discuss one of these techniques—the generic *Uneven Level Protection* (ULP) mechanism.

Uneven Level Protection (ULP)

ULP is an error-correction mechanism which is transparent to the specific codec used to encode the media stream. The idea here is that a secondary logical channel is opened alongside the logical channel transporting the media stream, and this secondary logical channel transports the *Forward Error Correction* (FEC) packets. The mechanism allows for variable protection level values for the specific data packets which need protection.

Link and Network Layer Handoff

Handoff—sometimes referred to as handover—is the term that is used to represent the handing over of an existing wireless connection from one wireless access point to another. Handoff is a challenging task for any wireless system involving terminal mobility. We can classify handoff along two dimensions:

- Hard handoff versus soft handoff. Hard handoff refers to the case where a mobile station communicates with only one access point at any given time. Soft handoff refers to the case where a mobile station can communicate with more than one access point at any given time.
- Intra-wireless technology handoff versus inter-wireless technology handoff. Intra-wireless technology handoff refers to the case where the handoff occurs between wireless technologies of the same kind. For example, this is the case when a mobile station hands off from one digital GSM system access point to another. On the other hand, by inter-wireless technology handoff, we refer to the case where the handoff occurs across different wireless technologies. For example, this is the case when a mobile station hands off from a digital GSM system access point to an 802.11 wireless LAN access point.

With efficient handoff schemes at link and network layers, we can pave the way for seamless mobility at the application layer—such as the H.323 application layer.

Recommended Reading

Several good books are available which describe the general concepts of mobility within cellular networks, and the concepts of identifiers such as IMSI. Goodman is one such book which gives an overview of a host of cellular technologies, while Mehrotra describes the GSM system in good detail.

The ITU-T Recommendation H.323 Annex H (H.323 Annex H) is the definitive reference for user, terminal, and service mobility in H.323 systems. For more information, the H.225.0, H.245, and H.323 standards can be used as references for the various aspects previously described in this chapter. They are found in H.225.0, H.245, and H.323 respectively.

The ITU-T Recommendation H.246 Annex E is the definitive reference for the IWF between H.323 systems and the MAP of PLMNs. This is described in a set of four documents—H.246 Annex E.1 discusses the general concepts, H.246 Annex E.2 discusses the specific case of ANSI-41, H.246 Annex E.3 discusses the specific case of GSM, and H.246 Annex E.4 deals with PDC.

Recommendation H.323 Annex I (H.323 Annex I) is the ITU-T standard for mobile and wireless issues, and it focuses on those layers which exist below the application layer.

References

Goodman Goodman, D. J., *Wireless Personal Communications Systems*, Addison-Wesley, September 1997.

H.225.0 ITU-T Recommendation H.225.0 Version 4, *Call Signaling Protocols and Media Stream Packetization for Packet Based Multimedia Communications Systems*, H.225.0, November 2000.

H.245 ITU-T Recommendation H.245 Version 7, *Control Protocol for Multimedia Communication*, H.245, November 2000.

H.246 Annex E.1 ITU-T Recommendation H.246 Annex E.1, *General Inter-Working Function (IWF) between Mobile Application Part and H.225.0*, H.246 Annex E.1, November 2000.

H.246 Annex E.2 ITU-T Recommendation H.246 Annex E.2, *Inter-Working Function (IWF) between ANSI-41 Mobile Application Part and H.225.0*, H.246 Annex E.2, November 2000.

H.246 Annex E.3 ITU-T Recommendation H.246 Annex E.3, *Inter-Working Function (IWF) between GSM Mobile Application Part and H.225.0*, H.246 Annex E.3, November 2000.

H.246 Annex E.4 ITU-T Recommendation H.246 Annex E.4, *Inter-Working Function (IWF) between PDC Mobile Application Part and H.225.0*, H.246 Annex E.4, November 2000.

H.323 ITU-T Recommendation H.323 Version 4, *Packet Based Multimedia Communication Systems*, H.323, November 2000.

H.323 Annex H ITU-T Draft Recommendation H.323 Annex H, *User, Terminal and Service Mobility*, H.323 Annex H, November 2000.

H.323 Annex I ITU-T Recommendation H.323 Annex I, *Wireless Issues*, work in progress.

Mehrotra Mehrotra, A. *GSM System Engineering*, Artech House Publishers, 1997.

Problems

1. List the three kinds of mobility and the differences between them.
2. Which kind of mobility is achieved by H.246 Annex E? Discuss how it is achieved.
3. Why does H.246 Annex E require H.323 Version 4 or later? Specify how the version number is known when a gatekeeper receives a GRQ message?
4. H.246 Annex B and H.246 Annex C deal with H.323 gateways for PSTN and ISDN systems respectively. Specify the distinction between the roles played by these annexes and H.246 Annex E. Discuss how these roles are complementary and not contradictory.
5. H.323 Annex I deals with error correction schemes such as the ULP scheme. Specify why the schemes discussed are mainly FEC-based schemes and not schemes based on retransmission of the lost/erroneous packets.

CHAPTER 16

QoS Principles and Application Level QoS

In this chapter, we look at some of the governing principles of QoS and some models that can be used for gauging QoS. Factors affecting the QoS of a H.323 system are also discussed and a description of the application level techniques used to improve QoS is also provided.

Motivation and Drivers

Generally speaking, a service provider provides one or more services to its customers. In the specific case where the service provider is an *IP telephony service provider* (ITSP), the services are divided into two types—basic services and supplementary services. Basic services include point-to-point or point-to-multi-point calls. Supplementary services include call waiting, call forwarding, calling party identification, multimedia mail, instant messaging, and so on. Associated with each of these basic or supplementary services is a certain quality, which is referred to as the *Quality of Service* (QoS) of that particular service.

Metrics are needed to assess the QoS of these services. The QoS of the media transfer portion of a point-point or point-to-multi-point call is usually quantified by parameters such as one-way delay, jitter, and packet loss. The quality of connection establishment usually depends on factors such as call completion probability, connection establishment time, and accuracy of call completion. Similarly, the QoS of supplementary services can be assessed by metrics such as service completion time, accuracy of service, the underlying security, and so on.

In order for an ITSP to provide suitable service to its customers, an ITSP may solely rely on other entities such as network providers, clearinghouses, and other ITSPs. A network provider is responsible for the actual transport of packets over the network. Therefore, it is responsible for the control of parameters such as packet loss, delay, jitter, and so on. Thus, an ITSP may rely on a network provider to transport packets belonging to its customers with a certain QoS. The services provided to an ITSP by a clearinghouse include address resolution, billing, and settlement services. Clearinghouses themselves may rely on other clearinghouses in order to deliver services to an ITSP that is its customer. A pair of ITSPs can have a peering relationship in which each ITSP provides services such as roaming support to the other. Thus, in order to provide its customers with a certain QoS, an ITSP must exclusively obtain the services of network providers, clearinghouses, and other ITSPs. The dependency of the ITSPs on these other entities is shown in Figure 16.1.

When ITSPs need to utilize the services of other ITSPs or clearinghouses, a contract is signed between the two entities. The portion of the contract that deals with the set of services provided—the associated service quality, the service monitoring procedures, and the recourse mechanisms—is referred to as a *Service Level Agreement* (SLA).

While service differentiation is considered important by ITSPs, traditional circuit-switched *Telephony Service Providers* (TSP) usually do not resort to such service differentiation as a means of revenue generation. Traditional TSPs do not offer different qualities for the same basic or supplementary service. Subscribers of traditional TSPs do not have the capability to choose a certain quality for the (voice) conversation or a certain call completion rate for dialed calls. All subscribers to the same TSP are provided the same QoS for basic as well as supplementary services. Some of the reasons for this interest in service differentiation between ITSPs and traditional TSPs are as follows:

- There has been a larger concentration of monopolies and oligopolies within the traditional TSP market compared to that within the ITSP market. In the presence of a monopoly or oligopoly, the overhead involved in providing and managing service differentiation among subscribers may not be cost beneficial.
- Interoperator service differentiation is increasingly being seen among traditional TSPs. Interoperator service differentiation refers to the case

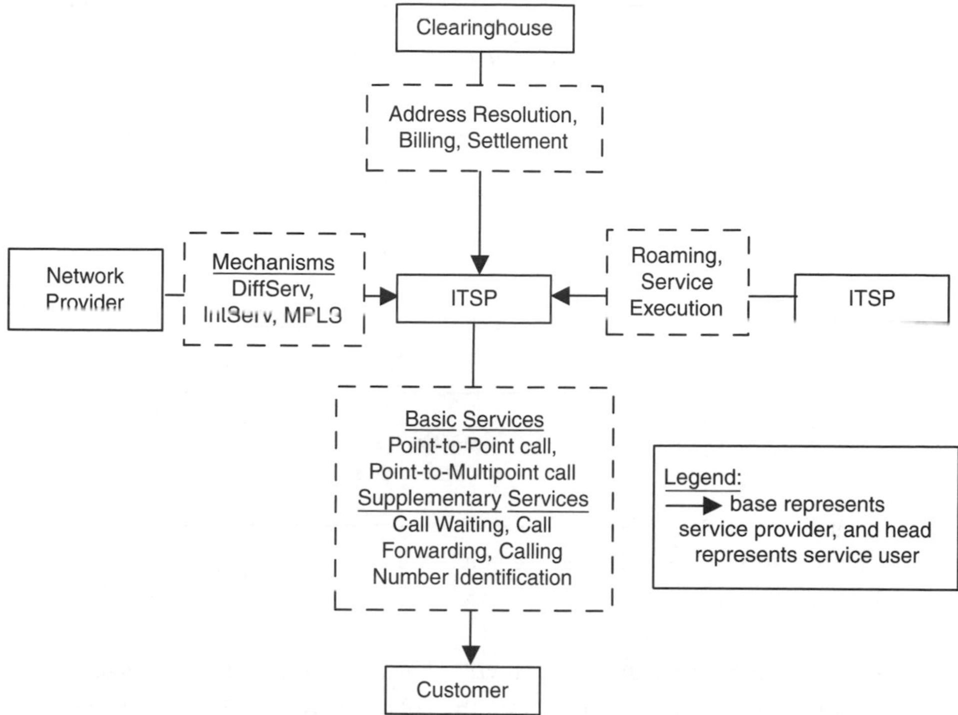

Figure 16.1 An example of the services an ITSP provides its customers and the services it receives from other entities.

where the QoS offered by one TSP is different from another. A single TSP might not offer different levels of QoS to its subscribers, but a TSP may differentiate itself from another TSP by offering a different QoS level. The QoS offered by a traditional TSP usually depends on the provisioning of the network used by the TSP. Sufficient provisioning (or over-provisioning) of the network results in a good QoS for subscribers, while under-provisioning results in a poorer quality.

- The large number of competing ITSPs and the lack of regulation is paving the way for service differentiation among subscribers of the same ITSPs.

The service differentiation that an ITSP offers its subscribers can come in several flavors. For instance, the quality of a certain service can be fixed at subscription time. Alternatively, the subscriber can request the quality desired for any service prior to invoking the service. In any case, it is likely that the ITSP offers these different service levels to the subscriber in the form of categories such as gold, silver, and bronze service. The subscriber may be unaware of the QoS parameter values (such as delay, jitter, loss) associated with these classes, and the specific mechanisms (such as diffserv and intserv)

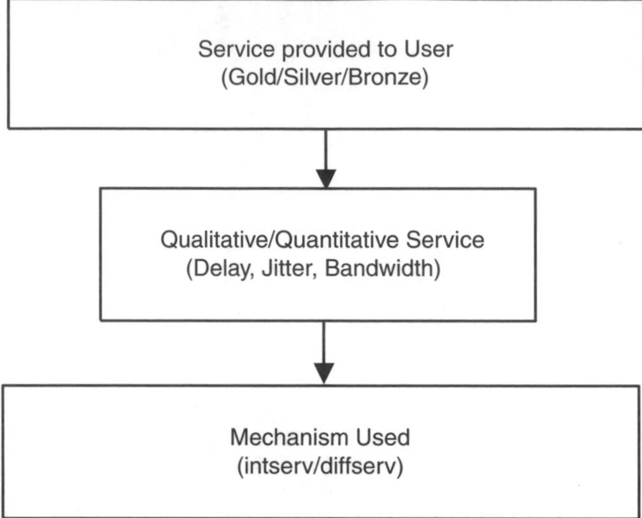

Figure 16.2 QoS and its service interfaces.

used to realize such service levels. The mapping between these service levels that are seen by the subscriber, the corresponding parameters associated with them, and the mechanisms used to achieve such service levels are shown in Figure 16.2.

An example of service level classification is shown in Table 16.1. Four service levels—best, high, medium, and best effort—are defined, and their associated qualitative and quantitative values are specified as well. The conditions under which these service levels can be achieved are specified using a combination of terminal type (Class A, B, and C) and network type (high, medium, and low bandwidth).

The mappings shown in Table 16.1, which correlate a user's subjective assessment of service quality to objective (or quantitative) values are obtained using one of the following techniques: (1) Mean Opinion Scores (commonly known as MOS scores) and (2) Comparison with a known signal.

Factors Affecting H.323 System Quality

An H.323 system generally has four distinct channels—RAS, call signaling (H.225.0), call control (H.245), and media flow. From an end-user's perspective, the quality of an H.323 system is determined by the quality associated with the operations involved in each of these channels. This

Table 16.1 QoS Classification by ETSI TIPHON

SERVICES PROVIDED TO USER		Best	High	Medium	Best Effort
QUALITATIVE VALUES					
One-Way NonInteractive Speech Quality		Similar to G.711	Similar to G.726 at 32 kbps	Similar to GSM EFR	
QUANTITATIVE VALUES					
End-to-End Delay		< 150 ms	< 250 ms	< 450 ms	
Call Setup Delay	Direct IP Addressing	< 1.5 sec	< 4 sec	< 7 sec	
	E.164–IP Translation	< 2 sec	< 5 sec	< 10 sec	
	E.164–IP Translation via Clearinghouse	< 3 sec	< 8 sec	< 15 sec	
	E-mail alias–IP translation	< 4 sec	< 13 sec	< 25 sec	
MECHANISMS					
		Class A terminal, High bandwidth network (LAN)	Class A terminal, High bandwidth network (LAN)	Class B terminal, Medium bandwidth network (< 64 kbps)	Class C terminal, Limited bandwidth network (< 28 kbps)

depends on several factors—the system's availability; the granularity that requests the operation; the admission or blocking of that requested operation; the completion accuracy of the requested operation; the delay or latency in completion of the operation; and the ease of use for the customer.

Quality in the RAS, H.225.0, and H.245 Channels

The RAS channel is primarily used for *gatekeeper* discovery and registration, call admission, bandwidth negotiation, and call disengagement. If the suitable gatekeeper has failed during any of these operations, the system may not be available. The system availability or uptime can be increased by the presence of alternate gatekeepers capable of handling operations that a failed gatekeeper would have handled otherwise. Failure of backend servers, such as databases that store address resolution or security information, has a similar effect on system availability.

The latency involved in the RAS discovery, admission, and bandwidth negotiation processes depends on several factors. The factors affecting the latency during gatekeeper discovery include the discovery mechanism used (e.g., multicast or unicast), and the processing delay within the gatekeeper that is receiving the request. When pre-granted ARQ is not used, there is a delay in the resulting admission phase. This depends on the following factors: the latency in location determination and in authenticating and authorizing the local endpoint; the availability of the remote endpoint; and the determination of the availability of resources (e.g., bandwidth) for the call. While caching certain address and security information at the gatekeeper can result in a decrease in latency during the admission phase, care must be taken to ensure the current accuracy of the information.

If users are assigned priorities, then the availability of resources for a call—either during the admission or bandwidth negotiation phase—can vary depending on the assigned priority. For example, users in a zone can be assigned one of two priorities and the zone can be provisioned in such a manner that a certain amount of bandwidth is always reserved for high-priority users who are not currently in a call. While this can increase the call blocking probability of a low-priority user, the call blocking probability of a high-priority user improves. The system can similarly allow for pre-emption of low-priority user bandwidth by high-priority users. In this case, a low-priority user who has been granted admission to a call at a certain bandwidth may be requested by the gatekeeper at a later time—when a high-priority user requests admission or a bandwidth increase—to decrease the bandwidth.

The H.225.0 channel is used to set up and tear down a call. From a quality viewpoint, the delay and accuracy of call setup—the connection to the correct remote party—must be considered. The call setup delay depends on whether a reliable channel (such as TCP) or an unreliable channel (such as UDP) is used for call establishment. The two endpoints involved in a TCP connection must exchange a series of messages prior to connection establishment, and this procedure is referred to as a handshake. Due to the lack of handshake in UDP, the usage of UDP for call establishment results in a lower call establishment time when compared to the usage of TCP.

The H.245 channel is used to exchange capability sets and open channels for media flow, and to indicate any changes in the media stream processing. From an end-user's perspective, the delay involved in these operations needs to be minimized.

Quality in the Media Stream

Factors that affect the quality of a media stream—audio or video—include one-way delay, jitter, and packet loss. Because jitter is the variation of delay and the packet arrivals beyond a certain delay value are considered lost, the critical parameter for media stream quality is a one-way packet delay. In order to tolerate more jitter, a larger receiver buffer is required which, in turn, results in a larger playback delay at the receiver. Note that a packet loss is mathematically equivalent to a packet arrival with an infinite delay. The effect of one-way speech delay on human interaction quality is shown in Table 16.2 .

Several factors contribute to the end-to-end delay of a media stream that flows from a sender to a receiver: the retrieval delay of digital media samples from the buffer, the packetization delay, the transmission delay, the propagation delay, the queuing delay, and the delay at the receiver to account for jitter. These delays are tabulated in Table 16.3 in time sequential

Table 16.2 Tabulating the Effect of One-Way Speech Delay on Human Interaction Quality

DELAY RANGE	EFFECT OF DELAY
10-15 ms	No effect on human ear
< 150 ms	Good Human Interaction possible
200-300 ms	Compromised but acceptable human interaction
> 300 ms	Difficult for human interaction

Table 16.3 The Illustrating Factors Contributing to Delay in an End-to-End Media Flow

OPERATION PERFORMED	REASON FOR DELAY	MECHANISMS TO REDUCE DELAY
1. Analog media is digitized and buffered at the sender.		
2. Digitized media samples are retrieved from the buffer and entered into the codec.	Presence of a nonreal-time *Operating System* (OS) implies that the interrupts generated by the OS for data retrieval from the buffer may be at a limited rate.	Use a real-time OS. Use special purpose hardware or *Application Specific Integrated Circuits* (ASIC) for a sample acquisition and compression, so the OS is not involved.
3. Codec compresses the media samples.	Frame-based codecs wait for a certain number of media samples before compressing.	A codec which uses fewer samples per frame may be employed. (This can result in a lower compression efficiency though.)
4. Output of codec is sent to an RTP for packetization.	A certain number of codec frames may be needed for packing the payload of an RTP packet.	Reduce the number of frames sent as payload of one RTP packet.
5. RTP packets are sent to the UDP and IP layers for packetization.	Packetization delay.	Efficient TCP/IP stack implementation.
6. The IP datagram is transmitted.	Transmission delay.	Increase the transmission capacity (i.e., the output link rate) of the sender.
7. The IP datagram traverses various routers before arriving at the receiver.	Propagation or Queuing delay.	Propagation delay: Lower the actual distance traversed from sender to receiver. (This delay reduction is usually negligible.) Queuing delay: Over-provision the network; Use mechanisms such as diffserv and intserv; Reduce network congestion.
8. IP datagram is depacketized at the receiver.		
9. It is then sent to the codec.	Artificial delay may be introduced to account for jitter.	Reduce jitter.
10. The codec output is played at the receiver.		

(i.e., chronological) order along with the mechanisms employed to counter or minimize them.

If the delay in media stream reception were constant, the buffer required at the receiver could be minimal because the arriving media packets could be played back promptly. The playback offset—which is the time offset between the start of packet transmission at the sender and its playback at the receiver —is easily determined when the delay is constant. On the other hand, the introduction of jitter in media stream reception warrants determining the buffer amount required at the receiver. The amount of receiver buffer usually directly affects the playback offset at the receiver. Traditional circuit-switched telephony usually results in constant reception delay, while packet-switched telephony (such as the telephony in H.323) usually results in the introduction of jitter in reception. This is one of the fundamental differences that exist between these two systems.

Figure 16.3 illustrates the impact of jitter on the playback quality. Figure 16.3(a) represents the case of constant delay, while Figure 16.3(b) represents the case with jitter. For the sake of simplicity, we assume that uniformly sized packets are transmitted continuously from the sender to the receiver and that the packet playback order is identical to the packet transmission order. (Note that for MPEG streams, the packet transmission order is different from the playback order.) In Figure 16.3(a), the playback offset is set to the constant delay. In Figure 16.3(b), the playback offset is a design parameter whose value depends on the delay bounds (i.e., maximum and minimum delay), the tolerable latency of playback, and the tolerable loss of packets. For the value of the playback offset chosen in Figure 16.3(b), Packet 4 is essentially a lost packet because it arrives after its playback point. If a larger value of playback offset had been chosen, then Packet 4 would have arrived before its playback point and could have been used for playback. On the other hand, early packet arrival (i.e., with a delay less than the anticipated minimum delay) places a constraint on the buffer. A resulting lack of buffer storage requires packets to be dropped in this case. Hence, there is a trade-off between the playback offset and the tolerated packet loss. Note that if the playback offset can be dynamically adjusted, then the delayed packet can still be used for playback—however, this causes distortion.

Such considerations apply in the design of H.323 systems. Knowledge of the available buffer and desired playback offset at the receiving H.323 endpoint translates into a requirement of delay bounds. Using suitable network QoS mechanisms, which are described in a later chapter, it is then possible to achieve such bounds.

In addition to delay considerations in QoS, reduction of echo improves the QoS of audio streams. Talker echo is the echo that the talker hears when his

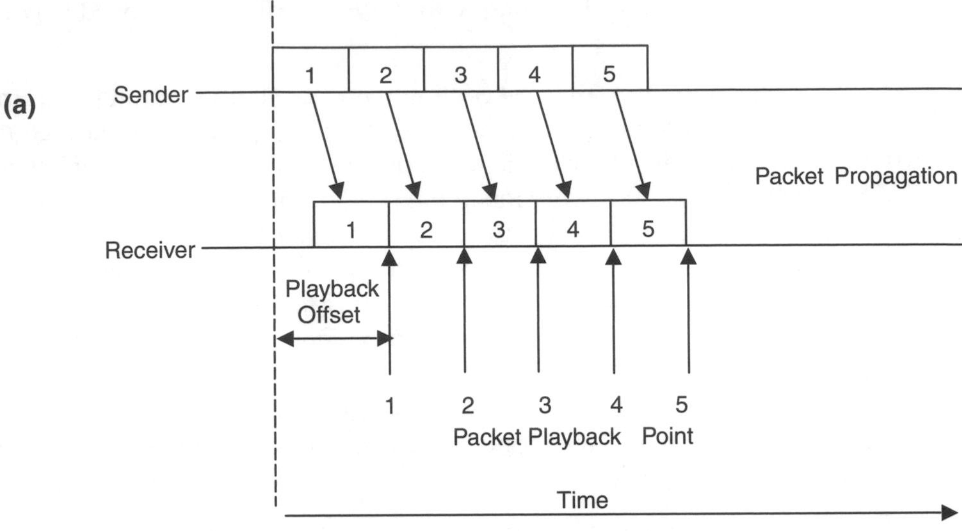

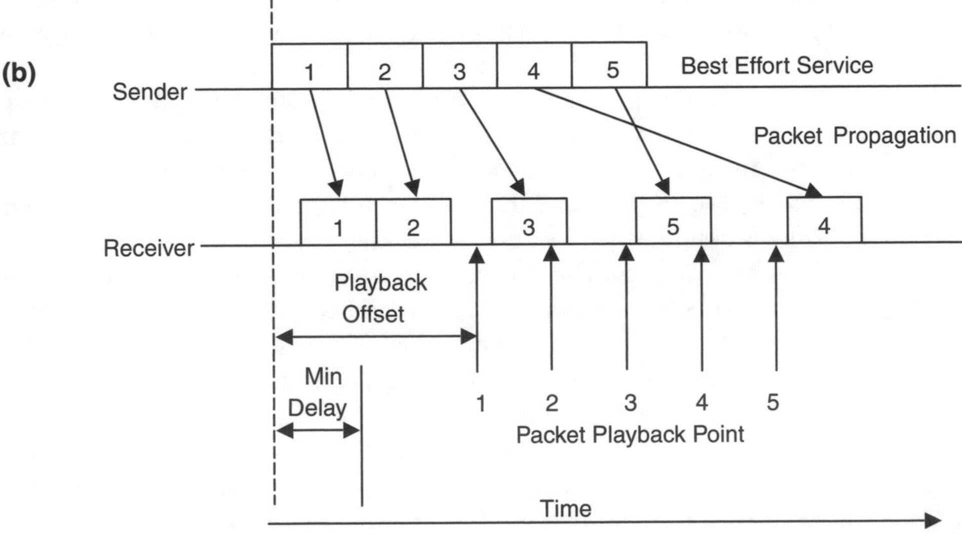

Figure 16.3 The impact of jitter on playback quality in (a) the case without jitter and (b) the case with jitter.

speech signals are reflected back from the receiver. Listener echo is the echo that the listener hears of a transmitted signal due to a double reflection. In Figure 16. 4, the original audio stream flows from the microphone of the

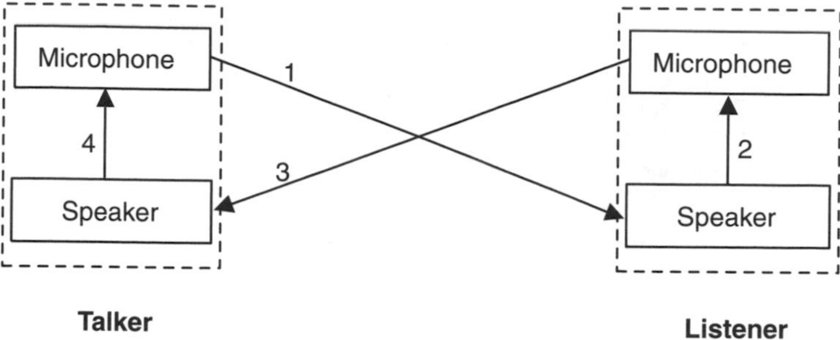

Figure 16.4 Talker and listener echo.

Talker to the Listener's speaker (Flow 1). This signal is fed back into the Listener's microphone (Flow 2), and is thus heard at the Talker's speaker (Flow 3). When the flow sequence of 1,2,3 occurs, a talker echo results. In addition, the talker echo can be further fed back to the Talker's microphone (Flow 4) and can again be fed to the receiver (Flow 1). When the flow sequence of 1,2,3,4,1 occurs, listener echo results and this sequence of operation can continue. Thus, the flows (1,2,3), (1,2,3,4,1,2,3), (1,2,3,4,1,2,3,4,1,2,3) and so on represent talker echoes, while flows (1,2,3,4,1), (1,2,3,4,1,2,3,4,1), (1,2,3,4,1,2,3,4,1,2,3,4,1) and so on represent listener echoes. Suitable echo cancellation and echo suppression techniques can be employed to counter the effects of echo.

Application Level QoS

Application level QoS refers to the mechanisms incorporated into the application layer which enable a desired end-to-end QoS to be obtained. This usually applies to media streams, although some techniques can be employed for signaling channels as well.

Feedback Mechanisms

In application level QoS techniques, there is usually some feedback—either from the receiver or from the network—back to the source and it is based on how the source suitably adjusts its transmission parameters. While the feedback from the network may come from a layer lower than the application layer, the application layer at the source will act on this feedback. In Figure 16.5, the media flow from the source to the receiver traverses a network, which is represented by the solid line, while the dotted lines represent the

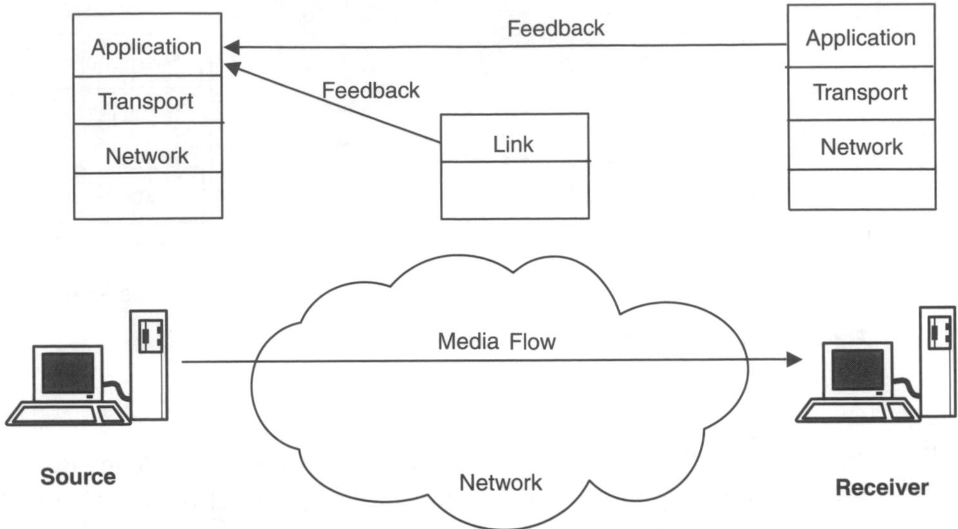

Figure 16.5 Feedback in application level QoS.

Table 16.4 Feedback Mechanisms for QoS in H.323

QOS FEEDBACK MECHANISM	NODE PROVIDING FEEDBACK	DESCRIPTION IN H.323
H.245 messages	Receiver	Usage described in H.323
RTCP messages	Receiver	Usage described in H.323
Link layer mechanisms	Network node	Usage not described in H.323, yet not prohibited

feedback from the network (at the link layer) and the receiver (from the application layer) back to the source.

As shown in Table 16.4, there are at least three possible feedback mechanisms that can be employed:

1. Using H.245 messages, a receiver can inform the source to use certain values for transmission parameters. This is especially relevant for point-to-point calls and tightly coupled point-to-multi-point calls—those that go through an MP and are thus essentially multiple point-to-point calls from the MP to the receivers—than for loosely coupled point-to-multi-point calls. In point-to-point and tightly coupled point-to-multi-point calls, the receiver can inform the source or the MP (whatever the case may be) to alter the transmission parameters. This is not suitable, however, in a loosely coupled conference where multicast mechanisms are used because the media stream from the source is intended for all receivers (although

mixers/translators can modify them in transit). An example of a H.245 message used for this purpose is the flowControlCommand message.

2. In the case of RTCP, which was primarily designed with a multicast environment in mind, the receiver provides feedback information of the cumulative number of packets lost, the inter-arrival jitter, and delay since the last feedback. The report block in Receiver Report RTCP packet is used to carry this information. In the case of point-to-point calls, the source gets this information from one receiver; while in the case of point-to-multi-point calls, the source gets feedback information from several receivers. Because the receivers only provide feedback information but do not inform the source about which transmission parameters to use, it is then up to the source to select suitable transmission parameters based on the feedback information.
3. While the use of H.245 or RTCP messages for feedback implies that the feedback comes from the receiver, it is also possible to employ mechanisms which provide feedback from an intermediate network node. For instance, in the case of wireless interfaces it is possible to use a link layer feedback for the quality of the wireless channel. However, such usage is not explicitly discussed in the standard.

Source Acting on the Feedback

Once the source receives feedback information, it can suitably adjust its transmission parameters. In certain networks such as the public best-effort Internet, it has been determined that when several sources do not react suitably to feedback information indicating network congestion, they can seriously degrade the network congestion situation. It is important for sources to back off (i.e., decrease their transmission rate) in a controlled fashion in the presence of congestion. Such a back-off mechanism has been built into the functionality of TCP. However, no such mechanism exists for UDP, which is the protocol used for media stream transport. Hence, if suitable back-off mechanisms are not implemented within the application, such an application could cause serious network congestion.

As previously discussed in the case of H.245 messages, the information that is fed back to the source indicates values for the transmission parameters. Yet, in the case of RTCP, the information that is fed back to the source contains the reception quality parameters. Some mechanisms that the source can use to adjust its transmission parameters are as follows:

- *The source can adjust the bandwidth used for transmission of the media stream.* Permission needs to be granted by the gatekeeper of the source (using the BRQ/BCF RAS message sequence) prior to exceeding the cumulative bandwidth of the call. When multi-rate codecs such as the G.723.1 or *Adaptive Multi-Rate* (AMR) speech codecs are used, it is possible to change the output rate of the codec. The source can also be alternatively switched to another codec supported by the receiver.

- *If a layered-source codec is being used, the number of layers transmitted can be suitably adjusted.* A layered source codec, such as the H.263 video codec, generates a stream comprising a base layer and additional enhancement layers. The capability to handle media layering is indicated during the H.245 capability exchange phase, and one or more logical channels are opened afterward to carry one or more media layers in each of them. The number of enhancement layers generated at the source and transmitted to the receiver can be adjusted according to the feedback information. A source can also close and open logical channels containing enhancement layers in a suitable fashion.
- Forward Error Correction *(FEC) with the appropriate parameters can be employed.* FEC techniques result in a decrease in the number of discarded packets at the receiver (due to bit errors), thereby improving the QoS. Because the media streams require a real-time transport, the latency involved in the use of retransmission techniques renders them unsuitable. Hence, FEC is more appropriate. FEC can be provided either at the output of the codec—for example, H.263 and AMR provide FEC—or at the RTP layer.
- *Application level retransmission techniques can be employed to ensure the reliability of the signaling message reception using UDP.* Signaling messages such as RAS, H.225.0, and H.245 messages do not have a hard real-time constraint. When the H.225.0 and H.245 messages are transmitted over TCP, the detection of losses and retransmission is built into the TCP. However, when RAS and H.225.0 messages are transmitted over the UDP, detection of losses and retransmission must be provided at the application layer.

Most of these techniques are optional and sometimes not explicitly described in the standard. The H.323 standard also forbids the use of certain techniques under certain conditions. For instance, the use of the *Bose, Chaudhuri, and Hocquenghem* (BCH) error correction or error correction framing is not permitted when the H.261 or H.263 video codecs are used.

The use of layered source coding is further illustrated in Figure 16.6. Layered source coding is particularly useful in a multicast scenario with heterogeneous receivers. A receiver connected via a low-bandwidth link (or which has a limited processing power) can choose to receive fewer layers compared to one that is connected via a high-bandwidth link (or which has a higher processing power). With layered source coding, a resource-constrained

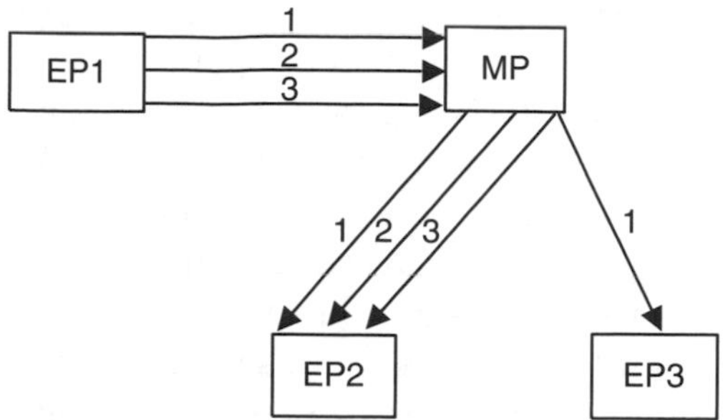

Figure 16.6 Use of layered media in a heterogeneous multicast example.

receiver does not have a negative impact on more capable receivers. Thus, in Figure 16.6, the two receivers named Endpoint 2 and Endpoint 3 have different processing capabilities. Endpoint 1, which is the source, encodes the media stream in a layered fashion containing three layers: a base layer 1 and the two enhancement layers 2 and 3. Each of these layers is transmitted as a separate logical channel from Endpoint 1 to MP. While Endpoint 2 elects to receive all three channels, the processing-constrained Endpoint 3 elects to receive only the base channel 1.

The possible use of layered source coding under changing network conditions—such as when the terminal is a mobile terminal with a wireless link—is shown in Figure 16.7. In Figure 16.7(a), Endpoint 3 is a mobile terminal which is connected to the MP by a wireless link. There can be intermediate nodes between Endpoint 3 and MP, and Endpoint 3 can be connected to the first such node by a wireless link. The wireless link in Figure 16.7(a) is a bandwidth-constrained link, which results in Endpoint 3 receiving only the base channel. As Endpoint 3 moves during the call, the wireless link

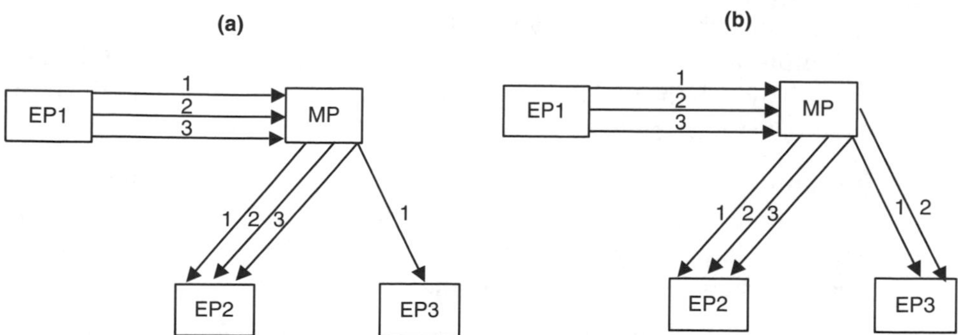

Figure 16.7 Use of layered source coding under changing network conditions: (a) Endpoint 3-MP is a low-bandwidth network and (b) Endpoint 3-MP is a high-bandwidth network.

conditions change and there can be an increase in bandwidth over the new link. This could be the case when Endpoint 3 has, for instance, both a low-bandwidth cellular interface as well as a high-bandwidth wireless LAN interface and Endpoint 3 roams into the wireless LAN coverage area. An additional logical channel can then be opened between MP and Endpoint 3 to transport the enhancement layer 2 to Endpoint 3, which is shown in Figure 16.7(b). Although it is illustrated in a multicast environment, the discussion holds for a point-to-point example as well. Figure 16.7 could then be modified as follows—Endpoint 2 does not exist and MP is replaced by an H.323 proxy or *Application Level Gateway* (ALG).

We now discuss the possible usage of error correction and retransmission techniques for RAS messages. Consider the case where an endpoint wishes to register with a gatekeeper using an RRQ message. Because the RRQ message is a RAS message, it is transmitted using the unreliable UDP channel. Although not explicitly discussed in the standard, reliability can be built into RAS messages using a combination of FEC and retransmission techniques. One possible way to handle packet loss is to use a technique called diversity. Diversity relies on sending more than one packet containing the same message in quick succession with the hope that at least one of the packets arrives error-free at the receiver. Diversity is a kind of FEC technique. Another possible mechanism is to retransmit the RAS message if no response —RCF or RRJ in our case—is received within a certain timeout period. If an RCF/RRJ is not received by the sending endpoint within a timeout period, then either the RRQ or the RCF/RRJ was lost in transit.

Similar techniques can be applied to H.225.0 messages using UDP. For H.225.0 messages using TCP or H.245 messages (which always use TCP), the TCP layer provides reliability. Hence, these H.323 channels rely on the dependability of the TCP transport mechanism, and there is no need to provide any additional reliability mechanism at the application layer. If TCP determines that it cannot deliver the packet to the destination after several attempts, a notification is sent to the appropriate H.323 layer (H.225.0 or H.245), which then takes corrective measures such as closing the transport channel and possibly re-opening a new one for example.

We now discuss the change of codecs during a call. When the source changes to a different codec, the seven bit *Payload Type* (PT) field in the RTP header is suitably changed. When the receiver receives packets with the new PT value, these packets are decoded using the new codec.

The *Sequence Number* (SN) field is a 16-bit field whose value is monotonically increasing (i.e., by increments of one) for each RTP packet sent. It is used by the receiver to detect any lost RTP packets as well as to resequence RTP packets which arrive out of sequence. The ability to detect lost and out-of-sequence packets is extremely important for a playback of good quality. The

32-bit timestamp field carries the time at which the first data byte being carried in the RTP packet is sampled. This is used for synchronization purposes and to determine the interarrival jitter.

Overhead Reduction Techniques

In the previous section, we discussed some mechanisms in which the source can change its transmission rate: (1) by changing codecs and (2) by changing the output codec rate when multi-rate, adaptive, or layered codecs are used. The output of the codec undergoes several layers of packetization (such as RTP, UDP, IP, and link layer) before being transmitted. Decreasing such packetization overhead is very desirable because it increases the actual link utilization. In this section, we explore two mechanisms which can decrease the packetization overhead: (1) IP/UDP/RTP header compression and (2) multi-frame packetization.

IP/UDP/RTP Header Compression

When a media frame is packetized using IP/UDP/RTP, the total overhead equals forty bytes (as shown in Figure 16.8). Very often, especially in the case of audio codecs, the size of the media frame is quite small. For instance, a G.723.1 audio codec packet size is 20 bytes and a G.729 audio codec is 10 bytes. If one audio frame is encapsulated by IP/UDP/RTP, the overhead is 66.7 percent and 80 percent respectively. In order to decrease this overhead, the 40-byte IP/UDP/RTP header is compressed.

Multi-frame packets

Another technique used to decrease the overhead is to concatenate several media frames (i.e., output of the media codec) before encapsulating them in a single IP/UDP/RTP packet. This technique is shown in Figure 16.9.

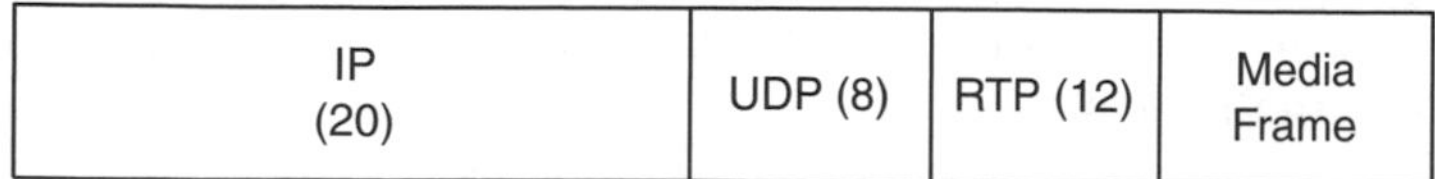

Figure 16.8 Packetization overhead for IPv4.

IP (20)	UDP (8)	RTP (12)	Media Frame	Media Frame	Media Frame

Figure 16.9 Multi-frame packets.

Recommended Reading

Verma gives an excellent treatment of the service level agreements on IP networks—what they are and how they may be realized. The book also provides useful references to other books and articles which deal with various aspects of SLAs—such as Hiles and Hallows.

TIPHON 101329-1 describes ETSI TIPHON's QoS architecture. Precise definitions and practical measurement techniques for several Internet QoS metrics— one-way delay, round-trip delay, and packet loss for example— are currently being formulated within the *IP Performance Metrics* (IPPM) *working group* (WG) within the IETF. More information on the IETF IPPM WG is available at http://www.ietf.org/html.charters/ippm-charter.html. To learn more about QoS measurement techniques, P.800 describes *Mean Opinion Scores* (MOS) and P.861 discusses objective measurement mechanisms. Echo cancellation techniques are described in P.310 and G.168.

More information on IP/UDP/RTP header compression techniques is provided in RFC 2508. Recent work within the IETF has also resulted in several Internet Drafts which deal with header compression over wireless links.

References

AMR1 GSM 06.90, *Adaptive Multi-Rate speech transcoding*, ETSI Technical Specification, AMR1.

AMR2 GSM 05.09, *Adaptive Multi-Rate inband control and link adaptation*, ETSI Technical Specification, AMR2.

Bolot Bolot, J-C. *End-to-end packet delay and loss behavior in the Internet*, Proc. of ACM SIGCOMM '93, pp. 289, 1993.

Busse Busse, I., Deffner, B., and Schulzrinne, H. *Dynamic QoS Control of multimedia applications based on RTP*, Computer Communications, January 1996.

Fig Figueiredo, D. R., and E. de Souza e Silva, *Efficient mechanisms for recovering voice packets in the Internet*, Proc. of IEEE Globecom 1999, pp. 1830, 1999.

G.168 ITU-T Recommendation G.168, Digital Network Echo Cancellers, G.168, 1997.

H.263 ITU-T Recommendation H.263, *Video coding for low bitrate communication*, H.263, 1996

Hagsand Hagsand, O., Hanson, K., and Marsh, I. *Measuring Internet telephony quality: Where are we today?*, Proc. of IEEE Globecom 1999, pp. 1838, 1999.

Hallows Hallows, R. T., *Service Management in Computing and Telecommunications*, Artech House, Boston, 1995.

Hiles Hiles, A. *Service Level Agreements: Measuring Cost and Quality of Service Relationships*, Chapman & Hall, 1993.

P.310 ITU-T Recommendation P.310,*Transmission characteristics for telephone band (300–3400 Hz) digital telephones*, P.310, 1996.

Paxson Paxson, V. Measurements and Analysis of End-to-End Internet Dynamics. Ph.D. thesis, University of California, Berkeley, 1997.

RFC 2508 Casner, S., and V. Jacobson, V. *Compressing IP/UDP/RTP headers for low-speed serial links*, RFC 2508, February 1999.

TR 101 329-1 ETSI Technical Recommendation TR 101 329-1, *Telecommunications and Internet Protocol Harmonization over Networks (TIPHON); End-to-End Quality of Service in TIPHON Systems; Part 1: General Aspects of Quality of Service (QoS)*. ETSI, July 2000.

Problems

1. Discuss the different services that a clearinghouse provides an ITSP.
2. Describe a QoS classification mechanism similar to ETSI TIPHON (as shown in Table 6.1) that one may have to devise in order to satisfy the requirements of a corporate intranet. Base the assumptions on the corporate intranet itself.
3. Consider the case where two zones—Zone A and Zone B—are identically configured. There are two classes of users in each zone—high-priority and low-priority users. At any given time in a zone, the ratio of the number of high-priority users not in a call to the bandwidth which can be made available to them is constant. The only difference between the two zones is that Gatekeeper A in Zone A can request its low-priority users who are currently in a call to decrease their bandwidth usage; whereas Gatekeeper B in Zone B cannot do this. Determine which of the two zones has a lower initial call blocking probability and why.
4. An H.323 source capable of generating four audio layers sends four OLC messages to the receiver—one for each layer. Due to current bandwidth constraints in the radio link, the receiver is only capable of receiving two audio layers. The receiver then sends an OLCAck for the first two layers and an OLCRej for the last two. Describe why this scenario is unlikely to occur in an H.323 system. 5. The jitter for packet transmission between two communicating Endpoints A (sender) and B (receiver) equals 400 ms. Assuming that each packet is 200 bytes long and packets are transmitted continuously from A at the rate of 1 Mbps, determine the buffer required at B if the packets are played back in order.

CHAPTER 17

Network Provided QoS for H.323

While in the previous chapter we discussed application-level techniques for improving the QoS in H.323 systems, in this chapter we discuss network-level techniques for the same purpose. Network-level techniques are considerably more powerful and can go much farther than application-level QoS techniques. After a discussion of the building blocks for network-level QoS, we then discuss the *Resource reSerVation Protocol* (RSVP), the *Integrated services* (intserv) architecture and the *differentiated services* (diffserv) architecture and illustrate their use within the H.323 framework. In addition, H.323 RAS messages that play a role in QoS are discussed as well. Finally, the role of policy and resource management is also explained.

Motivation

Having discussed application-level QoS techniques in the previous chapter, one may wonder if network support for QoS is needed to obtain a desired quality. While application-level QoS techniques only improve the QoS perceived by the receiver to a certain extent, QoS improvement beyond a certain point can only be achieved by network-level techniques. This is because application-level techniques only play a role at the two endpoints and possibly at some intermediate application-level gateways, and have no influence on the way packets are treated at the intermediate network routers.

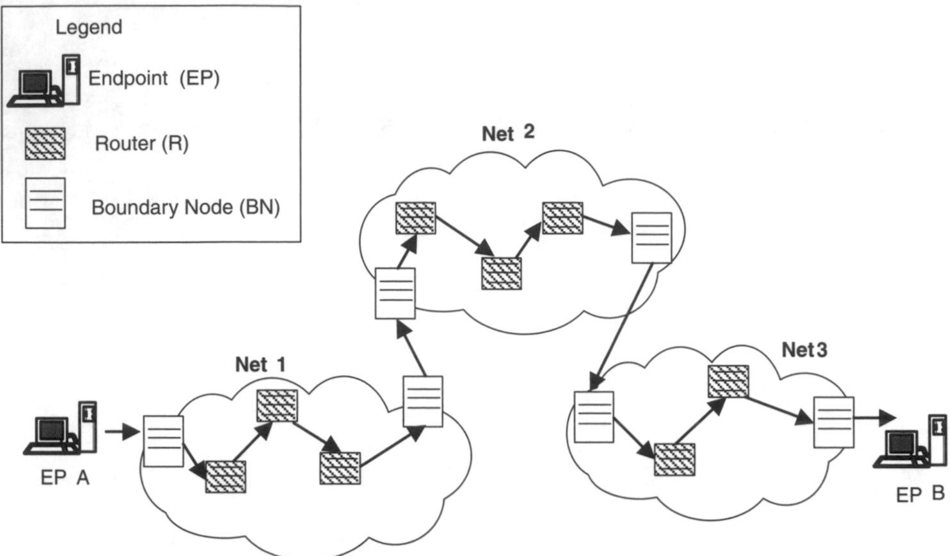

Figure 17.1 A media flow through several routers.

In order to be able to control packet handling at routers, network-level QoS techniques are needed.

Consider the example in Figure 17.1 where a media stream opened using H.323 logical channel procedures flows from Endpoint A to Endpoint B. The media stream traverses three administrative domains (Net 1, Net 2 and Net 3), six boundary nodes (BN) and eight interior routers (R). Along with this media stream, traffic generated by other flows (not shown in the figure) also traverses these networks. When these three networks do not provide QoS, each of the routers (BN and R) do not discriminate between packets and will usually forward them on a *First In First Out* (FIFO) basis. Different packets belonging to the media stream (as well as packets belonging to other flows) are treated identically at those routers. Therefore, while application-provided QoS techniques can improve the overall end-to-end quality that the user perceives at Endpoint B, the extent of the improvement is limited. In order to achieve QoS improvement beyond a certain point, network-level techniques are required. For instance, using network-level QoS techniques it is possible to specify delay and packet loss bounds for the media stream, which is impossible to do using application-level QoS techniques alone.

When the network is capable of providing QoS, the routers (BN and R) can discriminate between packets, consequently giving preferential treatment to certain packets. When packets belonging to a media stream flowing from endpoint A to endpoint B are given preferential treatment over packets belonging to other flows, it results in an improvement in quality. In addition, certain packets belonging to the media stream may also be treated preferentially compared to other packets in the same media stream. In order for the routers to be able to differentiate between packets and to preferentially treat certain packets, suitable functionality must be incorporated into the routers as shown in Figure 17.2.

In the case where the network does not provide QoS, the routers (BN and R) in Figure 17.1 are as shown in Figure 17.2(a). No packet discrimination occurs and packets are usually treated on a FIFO basis. In the case where the network provides QoS, the routers in Figure 17.1 are as shown in Figure 17.2(b). Packet discrimination and preferential packet treatment is made possible by the packet classifier and packet scheduler functions respectively. In addition, an admission control function may be present to regulate the number of flows within the network and a rate control function may be present to ensure that the admitted flows conform to their specified traffic

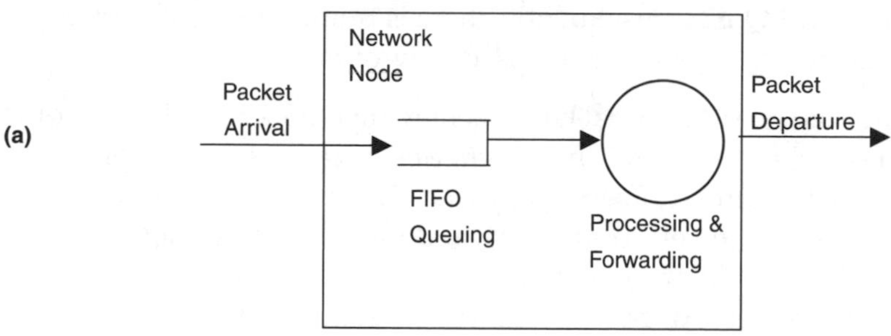

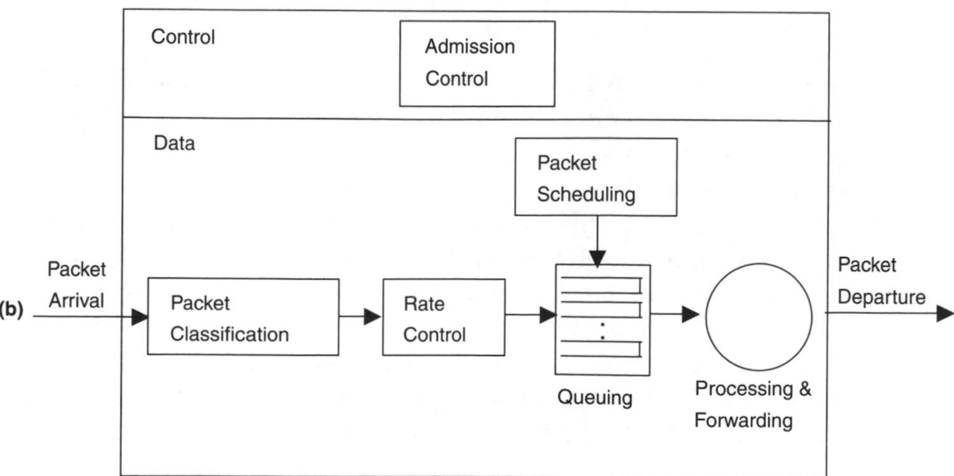

Figure 17.2 Block diagram of (a) non-QoS enabled routers and (b) QoS enabled routers.

profiles. While the packet classification and scheduling functions are present in all routers (BN and R), the admission and rate control functions are usually only present in the BN (and not R).

It is sometimes argued that network-provided QoS is not necessary if bandwidth becomes excessive and packet processing/forwarding within routers can be quickly completed. Sufficient bandwidth and extremely fast forwarding within routers can result in a negligible packet delay at the router, and consequently in a good end-to-end QoS. However, the availability of low-cost bandwidth sufficient for traffic generated by all applications is not a current reality and is unlikely to be available in the near future. Cost of bandwidth will remain high enough for several years that network operators will continue to look for better means to utilize a given amount of network bandwidth. Even if bandwidth became abundantly cheap due to massive fiber optic trunk deployment, there will still remain segments in the system where bandwidth is scarce—for instance, wireless links and other congested links. These bottlenecks can cause packet queuing and loss thereby impacting the end-to-end QoS. Consequently, there is tremendous interest in providing QoS at the network level for IP-based networks.

There are two broad approaches to achieving QoS within IP networks using network-level techniques—the *Integrated services* (intserv) approach and the *Differentiated services* (diffserv) approach. These approaches are sometimes referred to as the intserv framework and the diffserv framework. An intserv framework means that routers in the network support the Integrated services architecture, while a diffserv framework means that the routers in the network support the differentiated services architecture. Networks (i.e., routers in the network) may support only intserv, only diffserv, both or neither. The likely scenario of deployment is to use diffserv within the network core and intserv or diffserv at the network edges.

Applications such as H.323-based IP telephony applications (which are QoS aware) are able to suitably utilize the QoS capabilities offered by IP networks. QoS-aware applications are capable of specifying the desired QoS and will respond suitably if the desired QoS cannot be obtained. An H.323 application can, for instance, specify the total bandwidth required for all transmitting and receiving media streams within a call prior to placing it. When such a request is made to the *gatekeeper* of the requesting H.323 endpoint, the endpoint may decide not to place the call if the bandwidth is not granted by the gatekeeper. A non-QoS-aware application is not able to directly invoke the QoS capabilities of the underlying network, although such an application may still receive QoS by the network upon a third entity request.

In the remainder of this chapter, we examine the various QoS building blocks as well as the two main techniques that can provide QoS in IP networks—

Integrated services (intserv) using RSVP signaling and *Differentiated Services* (diffserv). Furthermore, a specific description of how H.323-based applications utilize such services—from the viewpoint of a system as well as a protocol—will also be provided.

Basic Network QoS Building Blocks

Regardless of which kind of QoS mechanism is used in the IP network (RSVP/intserv or diffserv) or the QoS-aware application running atop the IP network (H.323-based IP telephony or another application), there exists a core set of network QoS building blocks that is used to provide the QoS. As seen in Figure 17.2(b), this includes admission controllers in the control path; and rate controllers, packet classifiers and packet schedulers in the data path. In addition, mechanisms for representing a traffic stream and specifying a traffic profile are also needed.

Traffic Characterization Using Token Bucket

When a QoS-aware application requests a certain QoS from the network, the application often needs to specify the traffic which it would generate. When a H.323-based application opens a media stream and requires the network to provide a certain QoS for that stream, a specification of the traffic generated by the media stream is required. The traffic specification could include parameters such as the average rate of flow, the burstiness of the flow, the duration of burst, etc. Based on such a traffic specification, admission controllers can then determine whether sufficient resources exist to admit the media flow.

After the network is provided with a certain traffic specification for a generated media stream and the desired QoS has been granted, it is possible for a rogue H.323 application to generate excessive traffic which does not conform to its specified profile. If the network is unable to detect and suitably react to such nonconformance, it could result in quality degradation of other media streams as well. To prevent this from occurring, traffic policers check the application's actual traffic generated for conformance to its original specified profile when a media flow is admitted.

Thus, from a QoS perspective, formal traffic characterization is needed for at least the following two reasons:

1. Applications can specify the nature of precisely generated traffic so that admission controllers may determine whether to admit the flow into the network.
2. Rate controllers (or policers) can validate conformance of an admitted flow to its traffic specification.

It is not often necessary to exactly characterize the traffic, although it is sufficient to determine if the actual traffic fits a certain profile. The most commonly used profile is referred to as a token bucket whose parameters can be suitably adjusted to represent any traffic. The most commonly implemented model to represent traffic—and one that has been adopted by the H.323 standard— is based on a token bucket. A token bucket (r,b) means that the token arrival rate is r and the bucket depth is b. The traffic is further constrained by a peak data rate p and a maximum datagram size M. For policing purposes, a minimum datagram size m is also specified. Packets of a size less than m are thought to be size m when the traffic is policed for conformance. This set of five parameters (r,b,p,M,m) specifies the traffic flow. We will now examine what this means.

As shown in Figure 17.3, a token bucket (r,b), implies that tokens enter the bucket (of depth b) at a rate r and if the bucket is full, the arriving token is discarded. As traffic flows, tokens are removed from the bucket and the token removal rate is proportional to the rate of traffic flow. Traffic specified by a token bucket (r,b,p,M,m) implies that the average traffic flow rate is r and that the traffic may burst at a rate bounded by p as long as there are

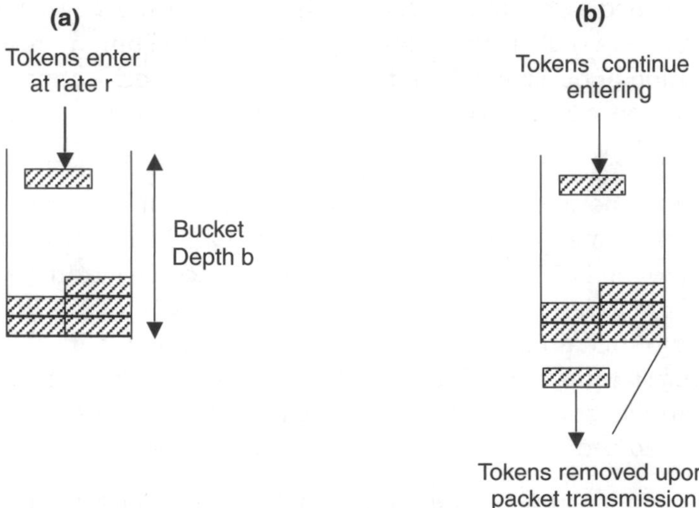

Figure 17.3 An example of a token bucket operation.

tokens left in the bucket. If there are no tokens in the bucket during traffic flow, then the traffic is not in conformance with the token bucket. The specific requirements to be satisfied by the flow conforming to a token bucket (r,b,p,M,m) are

$$\text{Data Sent} \leq M + pt, \quad \forall t \qquad \text{(Condition 1)}$$

$$\text{Data Sent} \leq b + rt, \quad \forall t \qquad \text{(Condition 2)}$$

It is also assumed that $p \geq r$ and that all values are non-negative.

Figure 17.4 shows the ASN.1 code from the H.245 specification where the traffic is characterized using a token bucket (r,b,p,M,m). Once the call has been established between two communicating endpoints and a media stream (logical channel) is opened with a certain desired QoS, the transmitting endpoint includes the traffic specification within the *OpenLogicalChannel* (OLC) message as shown in Figure 17.4. As we will see later, RSVP messages use token bucket parameters for traffic specification and hence these parameters have been labeled as RSVPParameters although a more appropriate name would have been token bucket parameters.

For example, an H.323 application opens a logical channel for transmitting a video stream. In this example, the sender specifies that the bursty video it transmits conform to a token bucket traffic profile specified as follows: r = 7000 bytes/sec, b = 42000 bytes, p = 20000 bytes/sec, M = 1000 bytes, m = 100 bytes. In other words, these values have been included within the RSVPParameters structure of the H.245 OLC message as indicated in Figure 17.4. If the actual flow is as shown in Figure 17.5, you must determine if the flow conforms to the specifications for the period [0,2T] under the following five situations:

a. R = 14,000 bytes/sec; T = 6 seconds; packet size [100,1000]

b. R = 21,000 bytes/sec; T = 1 second; packet size [100,1000]

```
RSVPParameters ::= SEQUENCE
{
     ...
     tokenRate      INTEGER      OPTIONAL,
     bucketSize     INTEGER      OPTIONAL,
     peakRate       INTEGER      OPTIONAL,
     minPoliced     INTEGER      OPTIONAL,
     maxPktSize     INTEGER      OPTIONAL,
     ...
}
```

Figure 17.4 ASN.1 code from H.245 which uses a token bucket to characterize traffic.

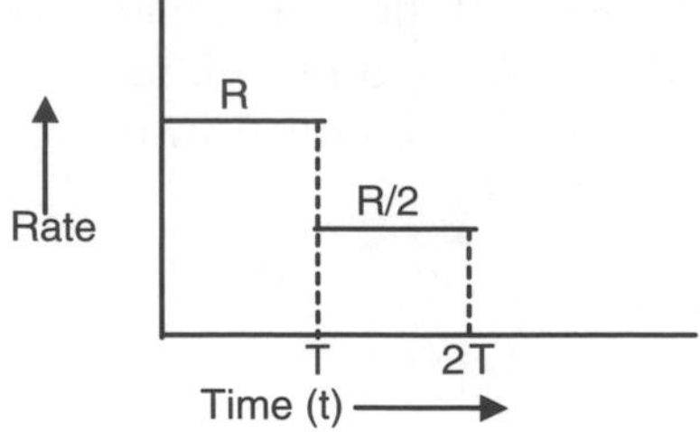

Figure 17.5 Example of the traffic flow of a media stream.

c. R = 5,000 bytes/sec; T = 6 seconds; all packets are of 50 bytes

d. R = 10,000 bytes/sec; T = 6 seconds; all packets are of 50 bytes

e. R = 5,000 bytes/sec; T = 6 seconds; first packet is 2000 bytes long, all others are 100 bytes long

We assume that at time t = 0, the token bucket is full. In order to check for conformance, we need to see if the two conditions previously specified are satisfied. Upon doing so, we see that cases a, b, and c represent conforming flows, while cases d and e represent nonconforming flows (which are described later).

For case (a)

Testing condition 1:	Data Sent $\leq$ M + pt, $\forall$ t
At t = T = 6s:	Left Hand Side (LHS) = RT= 14000*6 = 84,000 bytes
	Right Hand Side (RHS) = 1000 + 20000*6 = 121,000 bytes.
	Hence, LHS < RHS.
At t = 2T = 12s:	LHS = RT + (R/2)T = 126,000 bytes
	RHS = 1000 + 20000*12 = 241,000 bytes. Hence, LHS < RHS.

Similarly, for other values of t, it can be seen that LHS < RHS.

Testing condition 2:	Data Sent $\leq$ b + rt, $\forall$ t
At t = T = 6s:	LHS = 84,000 bytes
	RHS = 42,000 + 7000*6 = 84,000 bytes. Hence, LHS = RHS.
At t = 2T = 12s:	LHS = 126,000 bytes
	RHS = 42,000 + 7000*12 = 126,000 bytes. Hence, LHS = RHS.

Similarly, for other values of t, it can be seen that LHS $\leq$ RHS

For case (b)

Testing condition 1: Data Sent $\leq$ M + pt, $\forall$ t

At t = T = 1s: Left Hand Side (LHS) = RT = 21000* 1 = 21,000 bytes

Right Hand Side (RHS) = 1000 + 20000*1 = 21,000 bytes.

Hence, LHS = RHS.

At t = 2T = 2s: LHS = RT + (R/2)T = 31,500 bytes

RHS = 1000 + 20000*2 = 41,000 bytes. Hence, LHS < RHS.

Similarly, for other values of t, it can be seen that LHS $\leq$ RHS.

Testing condition 2: Data Sent $\leq$ b + rt, $\forall$ t

At t = T = 1s: LHS = 21,000 bytes

RHS = 42,000 + 7000*1 = 49,000 bytes. Hence, LHS < RHS.

At t = 2T = 2s: LHS = 31,500 bytes

RHS = 42,000 + 7000*2 = 56,000 bytes. Hence, LHS < RHS.

Similarly, for other values of t, it can be seen that LHS $\leq$ RHS.

For case (c)

In this case, the size of transmitted packets is 50 bytes, but the minimum packet size for policing purposes (m) equals 100 bytes. Hence, the rate of transmission needs to be effectively doubled for checking conformance. Thus, although R = 5,000 bytes, it is effectively regarded to be 10,000 bytes while testing for conformance.

Testing condition 1: Data Sent $\leq$ M + pt, $\forall$ t

At t = T = 6s: Left Hand Side (LHS) = RT = 10000* 6 = 60,000 bytes

Right Hand Side (RHS) = 50 + 20000*6 = 120,050 bytes.

Hence, LHS < RHS.

At t = 2T =12s: LHS = RT + (R/2)T = 90,000 bytes

RHS = 50 + 20000*12 = 240,050 bytes. Hence, LHS < RHS.

Similarly, for other values of t, it can be seen that LHS ≤ RHS.

Testing condition 2: Data Sent ≤ b + rt, ∀ t

At t = T = 6s: LHS = 60,000 bytes

RHS = 42,000 + 7000*6 = 84,000 bytes.
Hence, LHS < RHS.

At t = 2T = 12s: LHS = 90,000 bytes

RHS = 42,000 + 7000*12 = 126,000 bytes.
Hence, LHS < RHS.

Similarly, for other values of t, it can be seen that LHS ≤ RHS.

For case (d)

In this case, the size of transmitted packets is 50 bytes but, the minimum packet size for policing purposes (m) equals 100 bytes. Hence, the rate of transmission needs to be effectively doubled for checking conformance. Thus, although R = 10,000 bytes, it is effectively regarded to be 20,000 bytes while testing for conformance.

Testing condition 1: Data Sent ≤ M + pt, ∀ t

At t = T = 6s: Left Hand Side (LHS) = RT=20000* 6 = 120,000 bytes

Right Hand Side (RHS) = 50 + 20000*6 = 120,050 bytes.

Hence, LHS < RHS.

At t = 2T = 12s: LHS = RT + (R/2)T = 180,000 bytes

RHS = 50 + 20000*12 = 240,050 bytes.
Hence, LHS < RHS.

Similarly, for other values of t, it can be seen that LHS ≤ RHS.

Testing condition 2: Data Sent ≤ b + rt, ∀ t

At t = T = 6s: LHS = 120,000 bytes

RHS = 42,000 + 7000*6 = 84,000 bytes.
Hence, LHS > RHS.

At t = 2T = 12s: LHS = 180,000 bytes

RHS = 42,000 + 7000*12 = 126,000 bytes.
Hence, LHS < RHS.

Since LHS > RHS for condition 2 at t = T = 6s, condition 2 is violated at this point. Hence, the traffic does not conform to the specified profile.

For case (e)

The maximum datagram size specified in the profile was M = 1000 bytes, but a packet of size 2000 bytes was transmitted. Hence, the flow violates the specified profile.

Packet Classifiers

Packet classification is needed to determine the suitable flow or *Behavior Aggregate* (BA) in which a packet belongs. A Border or an Interior router needs to determine the flow or behavior aggregate which a packet belongs to so that the packet may receive the appropriate treatment at the router. A behavior aggregate represents a collection of flows that are indistinguishable from the perspective of a router's classification and treatment. For instance, if packets belonging to two audio streams could be treated identically at each router, then it would not be necessary to distinguish between them, and they could be considered to belong to a behavior aggregate. Determination of the flow or behavior aggregate that a packet belongs to is termed packet classification.

There are two kinds of IP packet classifiers—*Multi-Field* (MF) classifiers and *Behavior Aggregate* (BA) classifiers. Multi-field classifiers base their classification on one or more fields in the IP and transport (TCP/UDP) header. The commonly used fields are the source IP address, the destination IP address, the protocol ID, the source port and the destination port. BA classifiers, on the other hand, base their classification on the codepoint (i.e., value) in the *Differentiated Services* (diffserv) field of the IP header. The diffserv field is the *Type of Service* (TOS) byte within an IPv4 header and the Traffic Class byte in the IPv6 header. While a finer granularity of classification may be achieved using multi-field classification, behavior aggregate classification is simpler, faster and requires less storage. When packets have to be classified down to the granularity of individual flows, multi-field classification needs to be used. When packet classification down to the granularity of behavior aggregates is sufficient, behavior aggregate classification is preferred.

As we will discuss later, the RSVP/intserv approach to providing QoS relies on multi-field classification to determine how packets are treated. Diffserv approach, on the other hand, only relies on multi-field classification at the network boundaries and relies on behavior aggregate classification within the network itself.

As an example let us look at Figure 17. 1 again where Endpoint A has established a call to Endpoint B. Let the source IP address (i.e., the IP address of Endpoint A) be 105.10.52.1, and let the destination IP address (i.e., the IP address of Endpoint B) be 215.46.104.78. (Note: Although we are assuming IPv4 is being used here, the principle of the discussion holds for IPv6 as well.) Let the source port be 1459 and the destination port 2104. Because media flows use the *User Datagram Protocol* (UDP), the protocol field within the IP header has a value of 17,which is the decimal value assigned by the *Internet Assigned Numbers Authority* (IANA) for UDP, denoting UDP as the transport layer.

- When multi-field classification based on the tuple (src IP addr, dest IP addr, src port, dest port, protocol) is done by each router in the media path, the routers examine one or more of the five fields in the tuple. Upon matching them to 105.10.52.1, 215.46.104.78, 1459, 2104 and 17 respectively, the routers associate the packet to the particular media flow and suitably treat the packet.
- It is possible for Endpoint A to include a diffserv codepoint within the TOS byte in the IPv4 header. When this is done, multi-field classification may be done at the network edges while behavior aggregate classification may be done within the network. When multi-field classification is done at the network edges and behavior aggregate classification is done within the network itself, the edge routers base their classification on the five-tuple (105.10.52.1, 215.46.104.78, 1459, 2104 and 17) while the interior routers base it merely on the diffserv codepoint.

The use of transport (TCP/UDP) header fields in multi-field classification has two issues that warrant mention. First, if the IP datagram is fragmented, then the transport headers are not carried by any fragment other than the first one. In this case, since intermediate routers do not maintain any state relating one fragment to another, multi-field classification cannot be done on any packet other than the first one. This issue is resolved by keeping the IP datagram size smaller than the network's *Maximum Transmission Unit* (MTU) between the source and destination, thus resulting in no packet fragmentation. Second, if the IP datagram is encrypted using IPSec *Encapsulating Security Payload* (ESP), then the transport headers are not visible to the routers because they are encrypted. In this case, either behavior aggregate or multi-field classification is usually resorted to as long as it does not utilize transport header fields.

Rate Controllers

Rate controllers may be used either to shape or police the traffic, which is generated at the egress of a node. To ensure that the generated traffic conforms to a certain profile, traffic shaping can occur at the egress points. When traffic arrives at the ingress of a node, the traffic needs to be checked for conformity to a certain profile. Hence, traffic policing may also be completed at node ingress points.

Usually, traffic shaping and policing occurs at the network boundaries rather than at each node within the network. Traffic shaping occurs so the flow of packets fits a desired profile. Traffic may also be policed by a receiving entity to check if an injecting entity has conformed the traffic according to a certain predetermined profile. Thus, traffic policing checks to see if the profile is being violated. If this is the case, the packet flow then may be reshaped by suitably delaying or dropping packets. Two commonly used rate controllers are the token bucket rate controller and the timestamp-driven rate controller.

We now discuss what it means when a token bucket rate controller of parameters (r,b,p,M,m) is used as a traffic shaper and/or a traffic policer. Earlier, we discussed how a traffic flow may be characterized by the token bucket parameters (r,b,p,M,m). A token bucket rate controller (r,b,p,M,m) used as a traffic shaper/policer implies that the generated traffic is characterized by the token bucket (r,b,p,M,m). For traffic shaping, such traffic characterization may be obtained by passing an arbitrary traffic stream through a token bucket traffic shaper of parameters (r,b,p,M). For traffic policing, a token bucket traffic policer of parameters (r,b,p,M,m) may be used to determine if a traffic flow adheres to the characterization (r,b,p,M,m).

Timestamp-driven rate controllers, on the other hand, rely on packet arrival timestamps and the available application flow rate to determine the packet transmission instants. When the packet transmission instants are determined and the packet is transmitted accordingly, the resulting traffic can then be suitably shaped or policed.

As an example, look at Figure 17. 6 which shows three media streams—one between each H.323 endpoint pair (A, B), (C, D) and (E, F). The media

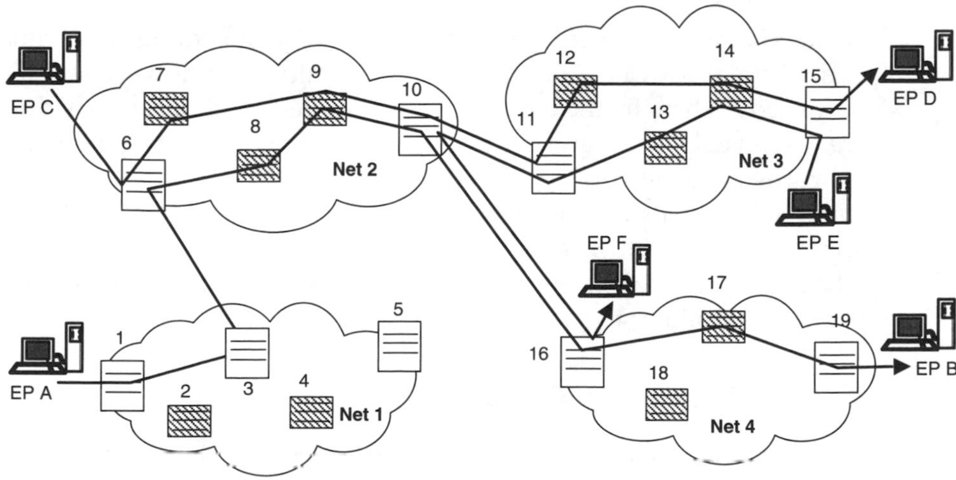

Figure 17.6 Scenario with multiple streams traversing common network nodes.

streams traverse several routers prior to arriving at their destination. It is already known that certain routers process packets belonging to two or more media streams. We discussed earlier that multi-field packet classification likely occurs at the network boundaries while behavior aggregate classification likely occurs at the network interior. Therefore, node 1 may perform multi-field classification on the media stream (A, B), while node 3 also performs behavior aggregate classification on the same media stream as well. Node 6 may perform multi-field classification on the media stream (C, D) while it may also perform behavior aggregate classification on the media stream (A, B).

Let the media stream flowing between the endpoint pairs (A, B), (C, D) and (E, F) be characterized by the token bucket parameters (r1,b1,p1,M1,m1), (r2,b2,p2,M2,m2) and (r3,b3,p3,M3,m3) respectively. Traffic policing/shaping at network nodes may also be either flow- or behavior aggregate-based. Network node 1 may police the traffic (A, B) for conformance to the specification (r1,b1,p1,M1,m1), and if the traffic is nonconformant, suitable shaping may be resorted to at Node 1.

Packet Schedulers and Queue Management

So far, we have discussed the need for traffic characterization and rate controllers. Traffic characterization is necessary so that applications (such as H.323) can specify their generated traffic to the network (and possibly the remote endpoint as well). Rate controllers, which may be used as traffic policers or shapers, are needed to ensure that the generated traffic conforms to its specification.

Packets belonging to conforming as well as nonconforming flows must be treated suitably by network nodes so that conforming flows obtain the QoS promised to them by the network. This is achieved by packet schedulers that are responsible for determining the order in which packets are processed/forwarded at a network node. Network operators, whom are responsible for suitably dimensioning the network to handle the requirements of supported applications, need to be concerned about the use of appropriate packet schedulers within their network. Next, we discuss some of the popular packet-scheduling schemes.

First In First Out (FIFO) Queue

A FIFO queue packet scheduler processes packets in the order in which they arrive. Packets enter a single queue, and the packet at the head of the queue is processed first. Such a mechanism is extremely simple and is the most widely used within (non-QoS enabled) routers today. When an FIFO queue is used under heavily loaded traffic conditions, real-time streams such as an H.323 media stream may experience severe quality degradation due to large queuing delays and loss. Thus, an FIFO queue within network nodes is not suitable for use if the network must provide QoS to H.323 media streams. However, it may be possible to obtain a certain QoS level using FIFO queuing within some network nodes while other nodes use a more sophisticated queuing discipline such as those discussed next.

Static Priority Scheduler

A static priority scheduling scheme contains multiple FIFO queues—each which has a priority assigned to it. Packets belonging to a higher priority queue are processed prior to processing packets belonging to a lower priority queue. There are two kinds of static priority schedulers—one that is pre-emptive and the other that is not. A pre-emptive static priority scheduler is one that aborts (or pre-empts) a lower priority packet transmission upon the arrival of a higher priority packet. A static priority scheduler that is not preemptive, on the other hand, completes (does not pre-empt) the transmission of a lower priority packet before transmitting a higher priority packet which arrived during the lower priority packet's transmission.

For example, a router implements static priority scheduling with eight priority levels—0 through 7—where a smaller number denotes a higher priority. At t= 0, let the number of packets in each of the eight FIFO queues be as follows: 3,1,0,2,4,1,0,2; implying that queue 0 has 3 packets, queue 1 has 1 packet, and so on. Assuming that the packets are of uniform size and that the packet transmission time is T, determine the delay incurred before the start of transmission of a complete Queue 5 packet under the following conditions:

a. *If no other packets arrive after t= 0.* Because static priority scheduling is used, packets in Queue 0 are processed prior to those in Queue 1, which are processed prior to those in Queue 2, and so on. Because packets do not arrive after t = 0, it is immaterial whether pre-emptive or not pre-emptive scheduling is used. Because the 10packets in Queues 0 through 4 have to be transmitted prior to transmitting a packet in Queue 5 and the time taken to transmit each packet is T, the delay before transmission start time of a complete Queue 5 packet is 10T.

b. *If two packets arrive at Queue 6 at t = 3T.* Because Queue 6 has a lower priority compared to Queue 5 and the arrival of the two Queue 6 packets occurs at t = 3T (which is when Queue 2 processing started), the packets in Queue 6 do not affect the packet transmission of in Queue 5. Hence, the transmission start time of a complete Queue 5 packet is the same as case a., which is 10T.

c. *If one packet arrives at Queue 1 at t* = T. In this case, there are two packets in Queue 2 when Queue 2 processing starts. Because 11 packets are also present in Queues 0 through 4 and must be transmitted prior to transmission of a Queue 5 packet, it takes a time of 11T prior to the transmission start time of a Queue 5 packet.

d. *If one packet arrives at Queue 0 at t* = 5T, and one arrives at Queue 1 at t = 6T. At t =5T, one of the two packets in Queue 3 have been processed. Because a packet arrives into Queue 0 at this time, the packet is processed by t = 6T. Then, the newly arrived packet in Queue 1 is processed by t = 7T. Next, the second packet in Queue 3 and the four packets in Queue 4 are processed, with the packet in Queue 5 being processed afterward. Thus, at t = 12T, processing of the packet in Queue 5 begins.

e. *If one packet arrives at Queue 1 at t* = 1.5T. Because packets in Queue 0 are still being processed at t = 1.5T, it does not matter whether pre-emptive or not pre-emptive scheduling is used. By t = 3T, packets in Queue 0 are processed; by t = 5T the packets in Queue 1 are processed; by t = 7T the packets in Queue 3 are processed; and by t = 11T, the packets in Queue 4 are processed. Thus, the processing start time of a Queue 5 packet is t = 11T.

f. *If one packet arrives at Queue 1 at t* = 10.5T assuming pre-emptive scheduling. At t = 10.5T, the packet in Queue 5 is being processed. Because pre-emptive scheduling is used, processing of this packet is aborted upon arrival of the higher priority Queue 1 packet. Processing of this higher priority Queue 1 packet takes place by t = 11.5T, and then the processing of the Queue 5 packet starts again (completing this time). Thus, at 11.5T, the processing start time of a complete Queue 5 packet begins.

g. *If one packet arrives at Queue 1 at t* = 10.5T assuming the scheduling is not pre-emptive. Since not pre-emptive scheduling is used in this case, processing of the Queue 5 packet, which began at t = 10T, is not aborted upon arrival of the higher priority Queue 1 packet. Thus, at t = 10T, the processing start time of a complete Queue 5 packet transmission begins.

Weighted Fair Queuing (WFQ)

A *Weighted Fair Queuing* (WFQ) scheduling scheme contains multiple FIFO queues that each have an assigned weight. In the simplest case, the queues are serviced in a round-robin fashion, and the number of packets that are processed when a queue is serviced is proportional to the weight assigned to the queue.

For example, a router implements WFQ scheduling with four FIFO queues of weights 2,1,2,3; where Queue 0 has weight of 2, Queue 1 has a weight of 1, and so on. At t=0, let the number of packets in each of the queues be set as 3,4,2,2. Assuming that the packets are of uniform size and that the packet transmission time is T, determine

a. *The time in which all packet transmissions are completed if no other packet arrives after t=0.* Because there is a total of 11 packets, it takes a time of 11T before the completion of all packet transmission.
b. *The time in which transmission of the third packet of Queue 1 starts if no other packet arrives after t=0.* The queue weights of 2,1,2,3 implies that the two packets of Queue 0 are processed, one packet of Queue 1 is processed next, followed by the two packets of Queue 2, and then the two packets of Queue 3 by t=7T. Then, the remaining packet of Queue 0 is processed by t=8T . During this time Queue 1 has the only remaining two packets and the other queues are empty of packets. Therefore, the processing of the third packet of Queue 3 starts at t=9T.
c. *The time in which transmission of the third packet of Queue 1 ends if one packet arrives at Queue 2 by t=7T.* The queue weights of 2,1,2,3 implies that the two packets of Queue 0 are processed, one packet of Queue 1 is processed next, followed by the two packets of Queue 2, and then the two packets of Queue 3 by t=7T. At this time, the new packet comes into Queue 2. By t=9T, the remaining two packets of Queue 0 are transmitted, leaving only packets in Queue 1. Thus, complete transmission of the third packet in Queue 1 occurs by 11T.

With WFQ, output link bandwidth is apportioned to packets belonging to different queues according to the queue weights under heavy load. Under lightly loaded conditions, packets belonging to any queue can utilize the full link bandwidth. WFQ is commonly implemented in routers, and it is well suited to handle QoS requirements of media streams generated by H.323 applications.

Class-Based Queuing (CBQ)

A *Class-Based Queuing* (CBQ) scheduling scheme is similar to a WFQ scheduling scheme—it contains multiple FIFO queues with weights assigned to each queue. In CBQ, traffic is categorized into different classes (based on some criteria) and each class is assigned its own queue in the network node. Therefore, one way of interpreting CBQ is as a specific case of WFQ where the number of queues equals the number of traffic classes.

For example, a media stream flows between the pair of communicating H.323 endpoints, Endpoint A and Endpoint B (as shown in Figure 17. 6). Let the arrival rate of the media stream into node 10 for the period [0,2T] be the same as the cumulative arrival rate of all other traffic at node 10 for period [0,2T]. Let each of these rates be set as shown in Figure 17. 5, and let the rate of traffic departure from node 10 be R. We now must determine the time instant when the H.323 video stream [0,2T] completes transmission for each of the following cases. We must assume that T is much larger than the packet transmission time to approximate a fluid model of flow, and that the buffers are large enough so that packets are not dropped. The buffer is empty at t=0, and no traffic arrives after 2T.

a. *FIFO queuing is used.* At the end of T, a cumulative traffic of 2RT has arrived at node 10, 1RT of which belongs each to the H.323 video stream and the remaining traffic. Out of this 2T traffic, only RT has been serviced by t=2T, half of which belongs to the H.323 video stream. Thus, there is a traffic buildup of RT at t=T, with RT/2 belonging to the H.323 video stream. Transmission of this traffic will complete at t=2T, after the arrival of additional cumulative traffic of RT at the node, with RT/2 of it belonging to the H.323 video stream. Thus, all traffic belonging to the H.323 video stream is serviced by t=3T.
b. *Static priority scheduling is used with the H.323 video stream which is assigned a higher priority.* In this case, the RT traffic belonging to the H.323 video stream is transmitted at t=T while none of the other traffic has been serviced. Between [T,2T], an equal amount of traffic belonging to the H.323 video stream and the other traffic is serviced. Thus, transmission of the H.323 video stream is completed at t=2T.
c. *Static priority scheduling is used with the H.323 video stream which is assigned a lower priority.* In this case, the RT traffic belonging to the other streams is serviced at t=T while none of the H.323 video stream has been transmitted. By t=2T, all traffic belonging to the other stream has been transmitted while only RT/2 of the H.323 video stream has been transmitted. The remaining RT of the H.323 video stream takes another T for transmission. Thus, by t=3T all the H.323 video traffic is transmitted.
d. *CBQ where the H.323 video stream is assigned to a class of weight 2 and the remaining traffic is assigned to a class of weight 1.* By t=T, (2/3)(RT) of the H.323 video stream is transmitted while only (1/3)(RT) of the other streams has been transmitted. By t=2T another (2/3)(RT) of the H.323 video stream will be transmitted, leaving an additional (1/6)(RT) of the

H.323 traffic in the buffer. This traffic takes an additional (1/4)T to transmit. Thus, by t=2.25T, all the H.323 video traffic is transmitted.

RAS Operations for H.323 QoS

At the RAS phase, there is no indication of the actual mechanisms—such as RSVP/intserv or diffserv—that are employed to achieve QoS for individual media streams. Instead, this phase deals with issues such as determining the H.323 entity responsible for QoS control, negotiating the total bandwidth available for all media streams in the call, and so on.

H.323 Entity Controlling QoS

The H.323 entity responsible for QoS control may either be the *endpoint* (EP) or the gatekeeper. In the former case, the endpoint handles QoS control without any assistance from the gatekeeper. However, in the latter case, the endpoint's gatekeeper handles QoS control on its behalf. This decision may be made either at registration time—where it would apply to all endpoint-involved calls—or it may be made on a call-by-call basis at the call admission time.

As we can see in Figure 17.7, the endpoint's preference of a QoS controlling H.323 entity is indicated by using the transportQoS field within the RRQ or ARQ RAS message. When the endpoint sets the value of the transportQoS field to endpointControlled, it means that the endpoint prefers to control the QoS. When the endpoint sets the value of the transportQoS field to gatekeeperControlled, it means that the endpoint prefers that its gatekeeper would control the QoS on its behalf. Finally, when the endpoint sets the value of the transportQoS field to noControl, it means that there is no QoS control.

If the endpoint prefers that all calls it is involved in be controlled by the same H.323 entity—either the endpoint itself or the gatekeeper—then the transportQoS field is included in the RRQ message. If this is not the case, then it is included in the ARQ message.

Once the gatekeeper processes the transportQoS field in the RRQ/ARQ message and is aware which QoS control entity the endpoint prefers, the gatekeeper provides its response which indicates its choice of the QoS control entity within the transportQoS field of the RCF/RRJ/ACF/ARJ message. The five specific scenarios following detail this further:

1. The endpoint includes the transportQoS field in the RRQ message to indicate its preference of the H.323 QoS control entity for all calls involving the endpoint, and upon processing this message, the gatekeeper decides to accept the endpoint's preference. The gatekeeper then indicates

```
RegistrationRequest ::= SEQUENCE --(RRQ)
{
      ...
      transportQOS             TransportQOS OPTIONAL,
      ...
}

RegistrationConfirm ::= SEQUENCE --(RCF)
{
      ...
      transportQOS             TransportQOS OPTIONAL,
      ...
}

RegistrationRejectReason ::= CHOICE
{
      ...
      transportQOSNotSupported    NULL, -- endpoint QoS not supported
      ...
}

AdmissionRequest ::= SEQUENCE --(ARQ)
{
      ...
      transportQOS             TransportQOS OPTIONAL,
      ...
}

AdmissionConfirm ::= SEQUENCE --(ACF)
{
      ...
      transportQOS             TransportQOS OPTIONAL,
      ...
}

AdmissionReject ::= SEQUENCE --(ARJ)
{
      ...
      rejectReason             AdmissionRejectReason,
      ...
}

AdmissionRejectReason ::= CHOICE
{
      ...
      qosControlNotSupported        NULL,
      ...
}

TransportQOS ::= CHOICE
{
      endpointControlled     NULL,
      gatekeeperControlled   NULL,
      noControl              NULL,
      ...
}
```

Figure 17.7 RAS message support that determines the H.323 entity controlling QoS.

its decision to the endpoint by including the transportQoS field in the RCF message—the value contained in this field matches the endpoint's preference in the transportQoS field of the RRQ message.

2. The endpoint includes the transportQoS field in the RRQ message to indicate its preference of the H.323 QoS control entity for all calls involving the endpoint. However, the gatekeeper, upon processing this message, decides that although a single QoS control entity is present for all endpoint-involved calls, this entity is different from the endpoint's preference. The gatekeeper indicates this difference to the endpoint by including the transportQoS field in the RCF message—the value contained in this field equals the gatekeeper's choice of the QoS control entity which is different from the endpoint's preference.
3. The endpoint includes the transportQoS field in the RRQ message to indicate its preference of the H.323 QoS control entity for all calls involving the endpoint. However, this time the gatekeeper decides that the QoS control entity should be chosen on a per-call basis. The gatekeeper indicates its decision by returning an RCF message which does not include the transportQoS field.
4. The endpoint prefers that the QoS control entity be determined on a call-by-call basis, which is acceptable to the gatekeeper. In this case, the endpoint does not include the transportQoS field in the RRQ message. Because this decision is acceptable, the gatekeeper returns an RCF message which does not include the transportQoS field. During an admission request for a call, the endpoint includes the transportQoS field in the ARQ message with a value indicating the endpoint's preference of the QoS control entity. If the endpoint's preference is acceptable to the gatekeeper, then the gatekeeper returns an ACF message with the transportQoS field with the same value as the ARQ message. However, if the gatekeeper decides that the QoS control entity should be different from the endpoint's preference, then the gatekeeper returns an ACF message with the transportQoS field containing the gatekeepers choice of the QoS control entity.
5. The endpoint prefers that the QoS control entity be determined on a call-by-call basis, but the gatekeeper decides that the same QoS control entity is to be used for all calls involving the endpoint. The endpoint does not include the transportQoS field in the RRQ message, indicating that it prefers to handle the choice of QoS control entity on a call-by-call basis. Upon receiving the RRQ message without the transportQoS field, the gatekeeper returns an RCF message with the transportQoS field included and set to the gatekeeper's choice of the QoS control entity.

It is likely that the gatekeeper would decide to have the same entity (endpoint or gatekeeper) control QoS for all calls dealing with the same endpoint because this decision largely depends on the endpoint capability and on the administrative domain policy. In addition, a gatekeeper may also return an RRJ or an ARJ message because the QoS control requested by the endpoint is not supported by the gatekeeper (as shown in Figure 17. 7).

So far, we discussed how an endpoint might use the transportQoS field to indicate to its gatekeeper its preference for the entity that controls QoS. In addition, certain messages exchanged between Border Elements in inter-domain communications for H.323 systems also carry the transportQoS field. The transportQoS field has been provided in these messages so that QoS control can be achieved between administrative domains.

Call Bandwidth

During the call admission phase, an endpoint must indicate to its gatekeeper the maximum bandwidth that can be used by all transmitted and received media streams involved in the call. This information is indicated by using the bandwidth field in the ARQ message. When the gatekeeper does not have enough resources to grant admission with the requested bandwidth, it sends an ARJ message back to the endpoint with the AdmissionRejectReason set to requestDenied. This message implies that the admission request is being rejected because the requested bandwidth cannot be granted by the gatekeeper. The endpoint may then decide to initiate a new ARQ message with a lower value of requested bandwidth. Once admission has been granted for a call, an endpoint may request that the gatekeeper either increase or decrease the call's cumulative bandwidth. This request is transmitted by the BandwidthRequest (BRQ) message. The BRQ message can also be used by the gatekeeper to request the endpoint to decrease its cumulative call bandwidth. The BRQ message contains the BandwidthDetails field in addition to the Bandwidth field. As seen in Figure 17.8, using the BandwidthDetails field, finer details of the requested bandwidth usage can be specified. For instance, it is possible to specify the bandwidth being used by one media stream, whether that bandwidth is being used for transmission or reception purposes, and whether the stream is a multicast or a unicast stream.

RSVP/Intserv Based QoS for H.323 Systems

In this section, we discuss the RSVP and intserv models, and their applicability to H.323 systems. While intserv was originally conceived to be an end-to-end QoS model, it is more likely to see deployment only at

```
BandWidth ::= INTEGER (0.. 4294967295)
            -- in 100s of bits

BandwidthDetails ::= SEQUENCE
{
   sender                        BOOLEAN,
                                 -- TRUE=sender, FALSE=receiver
   multicast                     BOOLEAN,
                                 -- TRUE if stream is multicast
   bandwidth                     BandWidth,
                                 -- Bandwidth used for stream
   rtcpAddresses                 TransportChannelInfo,
                                 -- RTCP addresses for media stream
   ...
}
```

Figure 17.8 RAS message support that determines bandwidth usage.

network edges. In order to provide QoS within the core network, mechanisms such as diffserv—discussed in the next section—are likely to be used. RSVP is a generic signaling protocol that may be used to provision intserv and diffserv networks. After a discussion of the intserv framework and RSVP, we will discuss how they may be invoked by H.323 systems.

Integrated Services (Intserv)

The Integrated services (intserv) framework was the first comprehensive QoS framework proposed for IP networks. Support for the intserv framework is provided within the H.323 standard. An H.323 application may be able to invoke suitable requests for intserv-based QoS. Thus, if the network is intserv capable, then the H.323 application can receive suitable QoS.

The intserv architecture defines two kinds of services—the Guaranteed service and the Controlled-Load service. The Guaranteed service provides an assured bandwidth, bounded end-to-end delay and zero queuing loss to conforming flows. The Controlled-Load service provides a quality similar to that provided under a lightly loaded network using a best-effort service. When a media flow is established between two communicating H.323 endpoints, the flow may be provided by a service defined by intserv—Guaranteed or Controlled-Load service. Therefore, the end-to-end QoS parameters of the flow will suitably be affected due to its chosen service. It is possible for different flows between the same communicating H.323 endpoint pair to obtain different QoS services. Thus, an audio stream flowing between an H.323 endpoint pair could be given Guaranteed service, while a video stream flowing between the same pair could be given a Controlled-Load service, and a second video stream flowing between the same endpoint pair

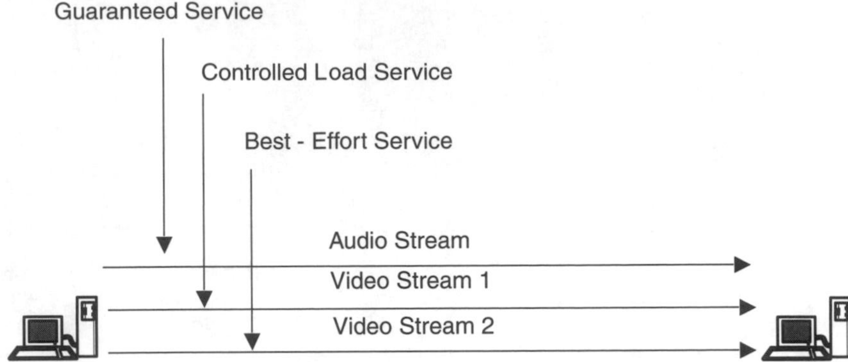

Figure 17.9 Example of an Integrated Services Architecture.

could be given neither service. When neither Guaranteed nor Controlled-Load service is given to a media stream, it uses the default best effort service. This scenario is illustrated in Figure 17.9.

Due to the guarantees which Guaranteed service provides to flows that consequently impact network provisioning and reservation, it is more likely that H.323-based IP telephony deployments utilizing the Integrated Services architecture would utilize the Controlled-Load service rather than the Guaranteed service.

Guaranteed Service

The Guaranteed service provides a quantitative upper bound on the end-to-end queuing delay. Because a packet loss is equivalent to a packet with an infinite delay, an upper bound on the end-to-end queuing delay automatically implies zero packet loss.

For example, let the traffic be characterized by the token bucket parameters (r,b,p,M,m), and let the reserved bandwidth for this flow be R. In a fluid model—where the source and receiver are assumed to be connected by a pipe of bandwidth R—the end-to-end queuing delay is $(b-M)/R * (p-R)/(p-r)$ when the pipe bandwidth R is less than the traffic peak rate p. When R equals or exceeds p, the end-to-end queuing delay is zero. In a realistic case that does not conform to the fluid model, the maximum deviation from the fluid model is captured in the term (M + Ctot)/R + Dtot. Here, Ctot is the cumulative rate-dependent queuing delay along the path, while Dtot is the cumulative rate-independent queuing delay along the path. The end-to-end queuing delay bound specified by the Guaranteed service is given in the following equation:

$$\frac{(b - M)}{R} \times \frac{(p - R)}{(p - r)} + \frac{(M + Ctot)}{R} + Dtot \quad \forall \quad r \leq R < p$$

$$\frac{(M + Ctot)}{R} + Dtot \quad \forall \quad R \geq p$$

Applications such as H.323 that wish to use the Guaranteed service to bound the end-to-end delay for a media stream can control the end-to-end queuing delay bound by varying the parameters b,p,M or R in a suitable fashion. For a given traffic flow characterization, an increase in the reserved bandwidth R results in a decrease in the end-to-end queuing delay bound. For a given reserved bandwidth R, you can adjust the traffic flow parameters b,p,M to suitably adjust the end-to-end queuing delay bound. An increase in b and/or an increase in p results in an increase in the end-to-end queuing delay bound; while an increase in M can either increase or decrease the end-to-end queuing delay bound depending on the value of other parameters. The smallest bound is Dtot.

Although, the Guaranteed service merely bounds the end-to-end queuing delay, it provides no information on other delay metrics such as the average delay, minimum delay, or delay jitter. While Guaranteed service provides an upper bound for the packet delay, it is likely that the majority of packets will experience a delay which is significantly lower than this bound. Most packets need to be buffered for a longer period of time than in the case where some packet loss is tolerated. An increase in buffering time means that larger buffers are needed and the playback time increases. Applications that are able to tolerate some packet loss may be able to decrease buffer size and playback times while utilizing the Guaranteed service. However, a better alternative for this situation would be to use the Controlled-Load service. Another advantage of the Controlled Load Service is that network utilization is higher in the presence of flows given Controlled-Load service compared to the case where flows are given Guaranteed service.

In the following example, a pair of communicating H.323 applications use the Guaranteed service to bound the end-to-end delay experienced by a video stream which is flowing between the two. The bound on the maximum delay is computed to be 400ms, thus the playout offset is 400ms at the receiver. This implies that no packet loss occurs and that all packets will be processed at an offset of 400ms. However, if the receiving H.323 application can tolerate a small packet loss, then it may be possible to obtain a smaller playback offset as well as decrease the amount of required buffer. Let the distribution of packet delay for the flow duration be as shown in Figure 17.10. Assuming that the video quality is not compromised with a two percent packet loss, it is shown that the suitable playout offset which could be chosen is 150 ms.

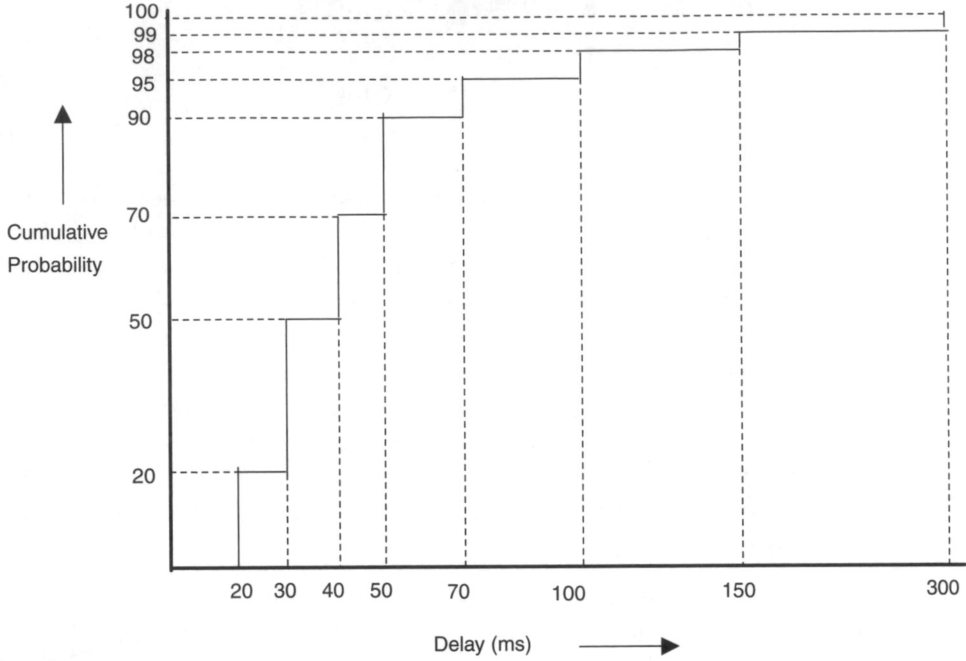

Figure 17.10 Delay distribution.

Similarly, if the application is willing to tolerate a three percent packet loss, then the playout offset could be 100 ms.

Controlled-Load Service

The Controlled-Load service defined within the intserv framework provides a quality (end-to-end delay and packet loss) similar to what is provided under a lightly loaded network using best-effort service. In order to request a Controlled-Load service, an application (such as H.323) only needs to provide the traffic specification. Each network node needs to determine (i.e., perform admission control) whether sufficient resources exist to provide Controlled-Load service for the traffic.

For example, an H.323 media stream (r,b,p,M,m) requires Controlled-Load service. Let R and B (which could each be dynamically changing) be the bandwidth and buffer respectively that one of the network nodes allocates for the flow. The flow burst time is defined as b/R. Controlled-Load service requires that the end-to-end delay is not significantly larger than the delay in a lightly loaded network for timescales, which are much larger than the burst time. Therefore, a Controlled-Load service cannot be provided if R = r constantly. (When the flow bursts initially and then transmits at rate r throughout, the burst can never clear if R = r.) Another requirement of

Controlled-Load service is that the packet loss due to buffer overflow (i.e., congestion) must be minor when the flow conforms to its specification. Based on the knowledge that network nodes providing Controlled-Load service do not reshape traffic to its original specification, setting B = b constantly at a network node will not suffice. In the absence of reshaping, bursts from intermediate nodes will be larger than b, thus having the potential for significant loss.

The Controlled-Load service specification has been kept slightly vague because the quality obtained under a lightly loaded network using best-effort service itself is not quantified.

RSVP

The *Resource Reservation Protocol* (RSVP) is a signaling protocol originally designed to establish reservations for services based on the intserv framework. RSVP was developed as a general purpose signaling protocol that could easily extend to set up reservations for services based on other frameworks as well. For instance, it is possible to use RSVP for provisioning diffserv networks as well.

Operational Overview

In RSVP, the sender of a media stream sends PATH messages to the receiver, who then sends RESV messages that retrace their way back to the sender. A PATH message creates a path state within each RSVP compliant network node it traverses. Such path state includes, among other things, the IP address of the previous hop router from which the PATH message was received. This path state is then used to forward a message specifying the reservation parameters—termed the RESV message—to the appropriate upstream router. The PATH message includes a mandatory sender template and sender *traffic specification* (Tspec) as well as an optional *advertising specification* (Adspec). The sender template includes information such as the source IP address and port number which may be used to identify the flow. The Tspec contains a traffic specification that the sender originates and is desired for reservation. Each network node along the data path advertises its QoS characteristics to the receiver using the Adspec. The Adspec carries two types of information—information independent of any particular QoS such as Guaranteed service or Controlled-Load service, and information that pertains to a particular QoS. Based on QoS reservation feedback (or advertisements), the receiver may decide to modify subsequent RESV messages.

As shown in Figure 17.11, an RSVP reservation request message or a RESV message contains a *filter specification* (filter spec) and a *flow specification* (flowspec). The filter spec specifies which packets are afforded QoS, and

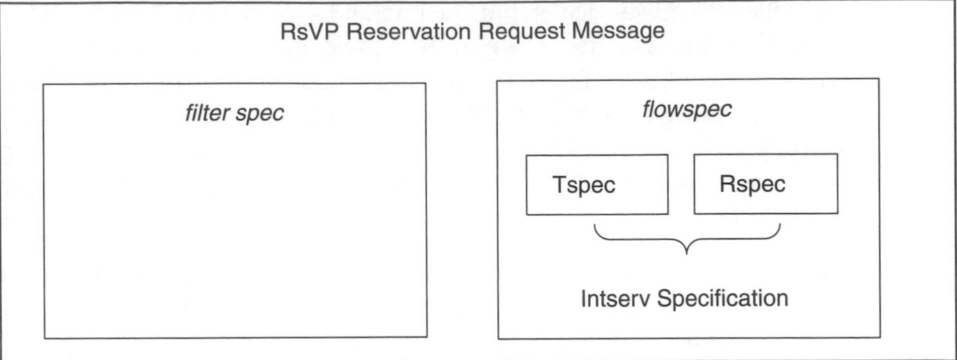

Figure 17.11 An RSVP RESV message.

hence is used as an input to the packet classifier. The flowspec specifies the QoS desired for a flow, and hence is used as an input to the packet scheduler. When intserv is used for QoS, the flowspec contains two intserv parameters —the *traffic specification* (Tspec) and the *reservation specification* (Rspec). The Tspec describes the traffic flow, while the Rspec describes the desired QoS. These parameters are carried opaquely by the RESV message.

Filter Spec

A filter spec is used to select the packets in an RSVP session that are afforded a certain QoS. An RSVP session is usually identified by the receiver's transport address (IP address and port number) and transport protocol (TCP/UDP). Filter specs may base their classification on application, transport or IP header information, as we illustrate in the following text describing two possible scenarios.

Filter Spec Scenario 1

Consider the example of a point-to-point H.323 system, where a layered media stream flows from Endpoint A to Endpoint B via two intermediate routers (R1 and R2) as shown in Figure 17.12. Different reservations can be made for the different layers, and an inspection of the application headers

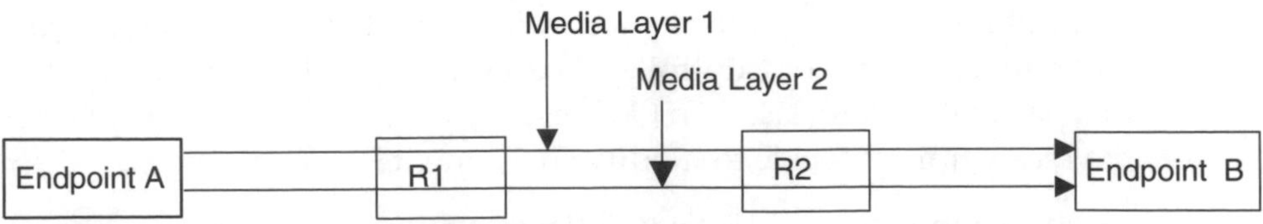

Figure 17.12 A scenario with layered source coding.

can determine on what layer a packet belongs. In other words, before the filter spec can pass packets to the packet scheduler to obtain the QoS specified in the flowspec, it must first classify the packets based on their application level headers. Note that Version 1 of the RSVP specification does not specify filter specs for inspection of application layer fields due to simplicity reasons. Nevertheless, the concept of a filter spec inspecting fields at any layer is accepted in the specification.

Filter Spec Scenario 2

Consider the example of a multi point H.323 system, where there are two senders (EP 1 and EP 2) and three receivers (EP 3, EP 4, EP 5) as shown in Figure 17.13. Because each destination receives media from each sender, separate reservations can be made for media by each sender. The filter spec within each router can then classify the packets based on their source IP addresses. In addition, the packet schedulers in each router can then suitably treat the packet so it obtains the desired QoS.

Reservation Styles

RSVP lists three reservation styles:

- *Wildcard Filter (WF).* A reservation shared by all senders
- *Fixed Filter (FF).* Reservations apply only to a set of senders, and the specific reservation for each sender is also known.
- *Shared Explicit (SE).* Reservations apply to a set of senders who share the reservation

For the WF reservation style, no filter spec is required, but a filter spec is required for each identified sender in the FF or SE reservation styles.

RSVP does not permit different reservation styles to be used within the same RSVP session. Because RSVP does not permit different reservation styles

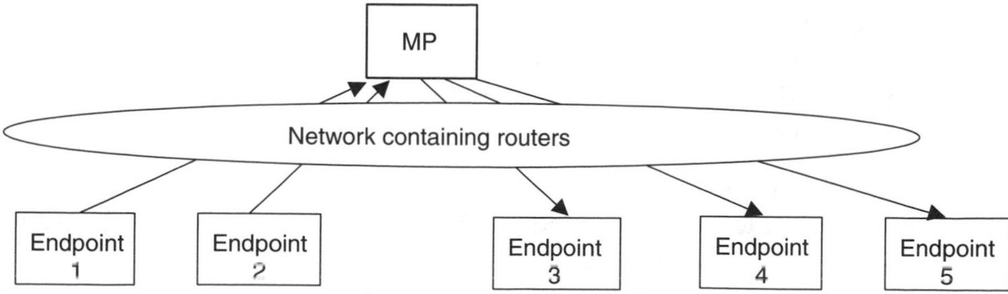

Figure 17.13 A Multi-Point Conferencing Scenario.

within the same session, H.323 had to specify a reservation style for use. H.323 mandated the use of the *Fixed Filter* (FF) reservation style. A WF or an SE reservation style is usually chosen for multicast applications where the number of senders transmitting media streams at any given time is fixed. For instance, in a multicast audio conference with multiple speakers, it is likely that only one participant is speaking at any given time. In Chapter 4, we discussed that H.323 specifies two types of multi-point conferences—centralized and distributed. Centralized multi-point conferences are point-to-multi-point in nature because the MCU acts as the source from the receiver's viewpoint. In this case, WF, FF and SE reservation styles are equivalent. In a distributed H.323 multi-point conference, it is usually difficult to restrict the number of participants that are transmitting media at any given time. Such a constraint rules out the applicability of WF and SE reservation styles. Hence, the FF reservation style is mandated by H.323.

H.323 and RSVP/Intserv

So far we discussed the operation of intserv and RSVP. We will now examine how RSVP and intserv can be invoked by an H.323 application. The various H.323 messages that are used for this purpose will be described.

Operational Overview

When an H.323 application wishes to use RSVP to reserve resources for a media stream which it wants to transmit, the H.323 application instance registers with RSVP and transmits the media stream's Tspec to RSVP. The H.323 application can optionally also supply RSVP with an Adspec initial value. This value contains information on the QoS capabilities and application. The application is then able to force the receiver to use a certain QoS service, say Guaranteed service, by including information in the Adspec that pertains only to this service. If H.323 does not provide RSVP with Adspec information, RSVP may then use its own default Adspec information. In this case, RSVP usually includes all the available QoS capabilities at the transmitting host. RSVP also includes the Tspec (after suitable formatting) and Adspec within the transmitted PATH message. Communication between H.323 and RSVP takes place across the RSVP *Application Programming Interface* (API) as shown in Figure 17.14.

As the PATH message traverses intermediate routers, the Adspec is extracted and passed to the traffic module. After suitable updating by the traffic module, the updated Adspec is inserted into the PATH message which is then transmitted to the next hop router. By inspecting various flags within the Adspec, the receiver can determine if network nodes exist in the data

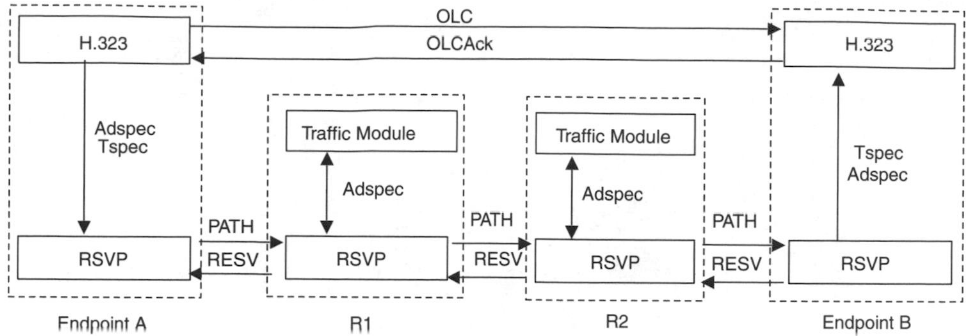

Figure 17.14 An interaction between the H.323 application and RSVP.

path that neither support RSVP/intserv or a particular intserv service (Guaranteed or Controlled-Load). When the PATH message arrives at the receiving endpoint, the RSVP of the receiving host passes the Tspec and Adspec to the H.323 application. The application then utilizes this information to determine various QoS-related parameters. For example, the values of Ctot and Dtot in Adspec can be used by the receiving H.323 endpoint to compute the end-to-end delay bound when a Controlled-Load service is used. Similarly, the MTU path in Adspec can be used to specify the maximum packet size in the RESV message. In addition, the receiver can also determine what QoS service type to use based on the flag information in the Adspec identifying end-to-end QoS capabilities. The receiving H.323 application then passes suitable parameters to RSVP that are used within the RESV message. These parameters include the type of service (Guaranteed service or Controlled-Load) and the flowspec (Tspec and optionally Rspec).

Use of H.245

In addition, Figure 17.14 also shows the OLC/OLCAck message sequence between the two H.323 endpoints. Only after this message sequence completion (i.e. after the logical channel opening) does the transmitting endpoint communicate with RSVP. This is because the destination port number for the media stream is only known by the transmitting endpoint after it receives the OLCAck. Without a destination port number, an RSVP PATH message cannot be transmitted.

As shown in Figure 17.15, the QoS parameters are carried by the OLC message. The traffic specification (r,b,p,M,m) along with an optional QoS mode is included specifically for RSVP/intserv. The QoS mode, which is a choice of the Guaranteed or Controlled-Load service, may be included if the transmitter wishes to choose the QoS service type used by the media stream.

```
OpenLogicalChannel     ::=     SEQUENCE
{
       ...
       forwardLogicalChannelParameters     SEQUENCE
       {
              ...
              multiplexParameters   CHOICE
              {
                     ...
                     h2250LogicalChannelParameters
                     H2250LogicalChannelParameters
                     ...
              }
              ...
       }
       ...
}

H2250LogicalChannelParameters ::=    SEQUENCE
{
       ...
       dynamicRTPPayloadType  INTEGER(96..127)       OPTIONAL,
       ...
       transportCapability    TransportCapability    OPTIONAL,
       ...
}

TransportCapability  ::= SEQUENCE
{
       ...
       qOSCapabilities        SEQUENCE SIZE (1..256) OF QOSCapability
       OPTIONAL,
       ...
}

QOSCapability  ::= SEQUENCE
{
       nonStandardData        NonStandardParameter   OPTIONAL,
       rsvpParameters         RSVPParameters         OPTIONAL,
       atmParameters          ATMParameters          OPTIONAL,
       ...
}

RSVPParameters ::= SEQUENCE
{
       qosMODE        QOSMode            OPTIONAL,
       tokenRate      INTEGER            OPTIONAL,
       bucketSize     INTEGER            OPTIONAL,
       peakRate       INTEGER            OPTIONAL,
       minPoliced     INTEGER            OPTIONAL,
       maxPktSize     INTEGER            OPTIONAL,
       ...
}

QOSMode::= CHOICE
{
       guaranteedQOS          BOOLEAN,
       controlledLoad         BOOLEAN,
       ...
}
```

Figure 17.15 Relevant H.245 fields for conveying desired QoS in OLC messages.

For instance, when the QoS mode is Controlled-Load service, it implies that the sender only supports (or wishes to use) Controlled-Load service and not Guaranteed service. In this case, when the sender subsequently sends Adspec information to its RSVP module, it includes only the Controlled-Load service fragment. In addition to other information, the receiver utilizes the traffic specification and optional QoS mode (included in the OLC message) to determine whether to accept (OLCAck) or reject (OLCRej) the OLC request. The inclusion of QoS parameters in the OLC message thus approximates (to a limited extent) the information included in the RSVP PATH message. Therefore, the Adspec within the PATH message is updated by each node along the path, yet the only conveyable information within an OLC message is the information available at the transmitting endpoint.

Another advantage of transmitting the QoS parameters in the OLC message is that it facilitates QoS setup simultaneously from both ends. This advantage is particularly useful when local networks containing the two endpoints use only RSVP/intserv, while the core network itself utilizes other QoS mechanisms (such as Differentiated Services).

H.323 with RSVP/Intserv over 802 LANs

Both RSVP signaling and intserv service specifications are independent of the underlying link layer technologies. An H.323 application wishing to use RSVP/intserv can do so without any explicit consideration or knowledge of the underlying link layer. Examples of link layers that can be used include 802.1 LANs, 802.3 LANs and ATM networks. In order to obtain QoS, the RSVP signaling and the intserv service specifications must be mapped onto specifications understood by the link layer. Figure 17.16 shows how mapping differs depending on the underlying link layer.

Consider an example where the link layer is an 802.1 LAN. When RSVP/intserv is used over a LAN, a map from RSVP/intserv reservations to the mechanisms understood by the LAN is needed. LANs may be shared (traditional Ethernet), switched (switched Ethernet) or have a priority associated with them (802.1p). The *Subnet Bandwidth Manager* (SBM) is a signaling protocol which enables the mapping of RSVP/intserv specifications onto 802.1 style LANs. Thus, it is easier to reserve resources for RSVP/intserv-enabled data flows during their traversal over an 802.1 style LAN.

Figure 17.17(a) shows a scenario where Endpoint A and Endpoint B are located on different 802.1 style LANs. Each LAN may have one or more SBMs, one which is a *Designated SBM* (DSBM). The DSBM may be physically located with another entity such as the endpoint or R. A typical operation

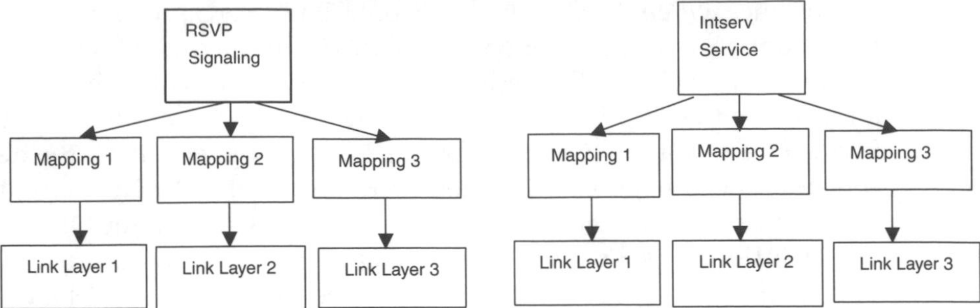

Figure 17.16 An example of the mapping of common (a) RSVP signaling and (b) intserv service specification to different specifications depending on the underlying link layer technology.

scenario for the topology in Figure 17.17(a) is illustrated in Figure 17.17(b). In this operation scenario, DSBM A and DSBM B are initialized with the fraction of bandwidth which can be utilized for streams with reservation. For instance, DSBM A may be initialized to use a maximum LAN bandwidth of 60 percent for streams with reservation, implying that at least 40 percent of the available bandwidth is for best-effort streams. Endpoint A and Endpoint B are initialized as DSBM clients. In other words, they are aware of the DSBM on their segment. The PATH message which Endpoint A would normally send to Endpoint B is sent to DSBM A instead. After creating a suitable state and appropriately modifying the PATH message, DSBM A then forwards the PATH message toward the destination Endpoint B. Router R1 receives the PATH message, creates suitable state and then forwards the modified PATH message to R2. Instead of forwarding the message to Endpoint B, R2 forwards it to DSBM B, which forwards it to Endpoint B. In other words, DSBM A and DSBM B are inserted into the signaling path. Because a RESV message retraces the route traversed by a PATH message, DSBM A and DSBM B can process the RESV message. In addition, based on the local link layer technology and the DSBM configuration, DSBM A and DSBM B can also determine how to handle the RESV message.

Diffserv-based QoS for H.323 Systems

Diffserv, rather than intserv, is the preferred mechanism to provide QoS in core IP networks. It is preferred because diffserv is known to scale better than intserv, and scalability is an important consideration in the network core where many flows are involved. At the network edges, it is likely that neither one nor both mechanisms (diffserv and RSVP/intserv) may exist. Although RSVP was originally envisioned to be used as the signaling protocol for intserv networks, RSVP can also be used to provision diffserv networks. In

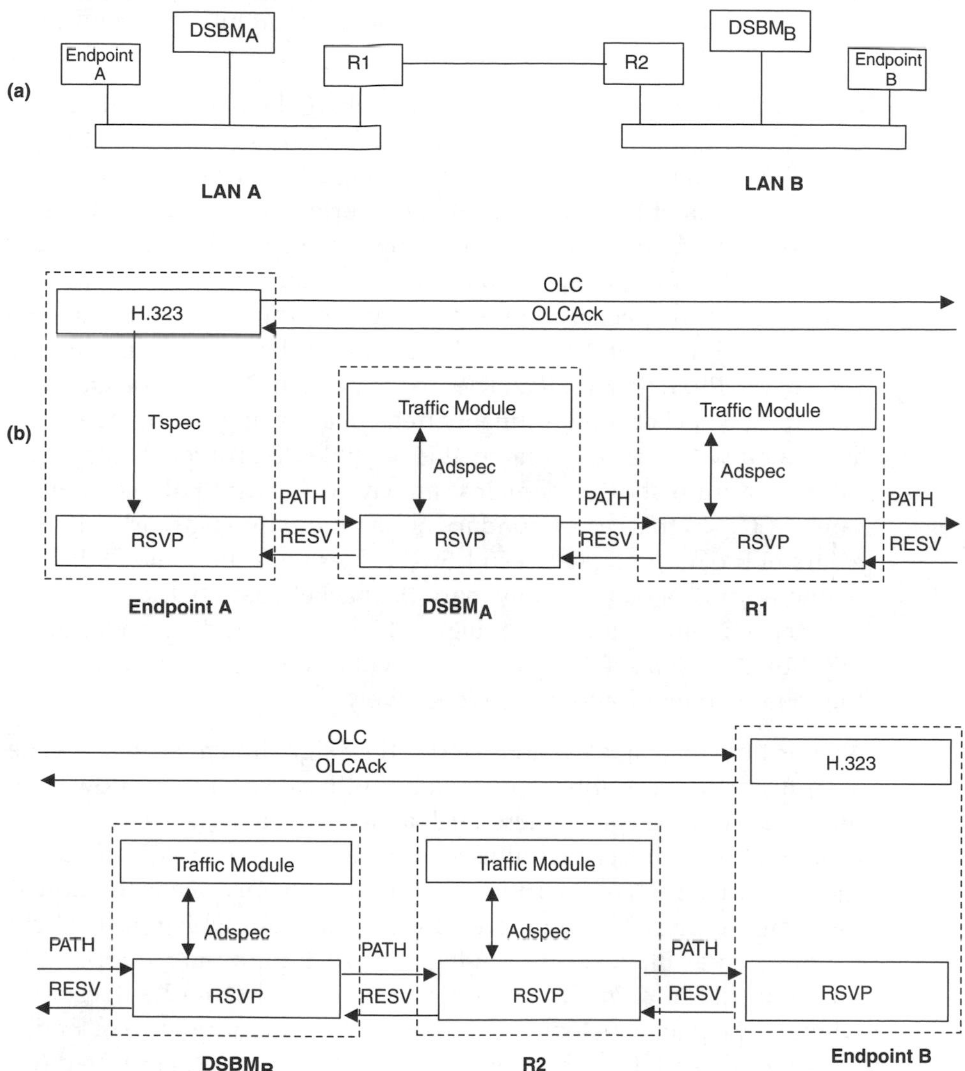

Figure 17.17 (a) LAN topology showing DSBM (b) message lows involving DSBM.

addition, RSVP may also be used to return diffserv information such as the *Differentiated Services CodePoint* (DSCP). In this section, we discuss an example where diffserv is used throughout the network.

The diffserv framework defines *a Differentiated Services CodePoint* (DSCP) and a *per-hop behavior* (PHB). The DSCP is a six-bit value which is carried within the IP header. A PHB is associated with each DSCP value, and it determines how the packet is treated at the router. A diffserv capable router examines the DSCP in the IP header of traversing packets and appropriately treats the packet according to how the PHB is associated with the DSCP. In order to obtain a certain forwarding behavior and consequently a certain QoS, packets are marked with the appropriate DSCP.

Look at the scenario in Figure 17. 6 and where the networks are diffserv capable. Consider a media stream flowing from Endpoint A to Endpoint B, and allow it to require a certain forwarding behavior at the routers. In order for the packets of this stream to obtain a certain forwarding behavior, they must be suitably marked. Such marking may occur either at the source (Endpoint A) or at the first-hop router (R1). Marking the packet sets the DSCP within the packet's IP header to the appropriate value. As the packet flows from Endpoint A to Endpoint B, each of the intermediate routers (R1, R3, R6, R8, R9, R10, R16, R17, R19) examines the DSCP associated with the packet. The packet is then suitably treated according to how the PHB is associated with the DSCP value. It is possible that routers belonging to different administrative domains can have different PHBs associated with the same DSCP. In this case, boundary nodes at the two network boundaries are aware of the mapping between DSCP values with the same PHB. These boundary nodes may suitably mark the packet again before the packet enters another domain. In the case of Figure 17. 6, the boundary nodes R3 and R10 may suitably re-mark the packet so it will receive the appropriate PHB from the routers in Net 2 and Net 4 respectively.

No per-flow state at each node or per-flow signaling at each hop is needed for diffserv, thereby enhancing scalability. Because a no per-flow state is maintained in the core routers, such a mechanism scales very well. In contrast, RSVP/intserv requires a per-flow state to be maintained in the core routers. Thus, each of the routers in Figure 17.6 only needs to know the PHB associated with DSCPs and is not concerned about which packet belongs to the flow. Thus, if packets belonging to flows Endpoint A Endpoint B and Endpoint C Endpoint D are identically marked, Router R9 does not care whether the packet belongs to flow Endpoint A Endpoint B or Endpoint C Endpoint D, and it treats them identically. When several hundred (or even thousand) flows pass through the same router, the fact that a router does not care about the particular flow and only cares about the DSCP value is important from a scaling perspective.

End-to-end QoS using diffserv is achieved for flows by the combination of *service level agreements* (SLA) and PHBs associated with DSCPs. For instance, in Figure 17.6 Net 2 may have an SLA with Net 1, Net 3 and Net 4. Such an SLA can facilitate suitable end-to-end QoS for each flow depicted in the figure.

The TOS byte in the IPv4 header and the Traffic Class byte in the IPv6 header are used to carry the DSCP. A suitable DSCP, which depends on the PHB attributed to the packet, is entered in the TOS byte PHBs can be standardized and their associated can be standardized as well. Four PHBs and their associated DSCPs have been standardized to date: the Default PHB, the Class Selector PHB, *Assured Forwarding* (AF) PHB and *Expedited Forwarding* (EF) PHB. It is likely that EF PHB will be widely used for real-time media streams.

Default PHB

The default PHB depicts the case where no guarantees whatsoever are given to the packet treatment at the network node. These packets are treated as "best-effort" traffic, as is the case in non-QoS enabled networks. The recommended codepoint for the default PHB is 0x00000000.

Class Selector PHB

The Class Selector PHB prioritizes the packet-forwarding treatment according to the class (and its associated priority) in which the packet belongs. Eight different codepoints—0x000000, 0x001000, 0x010000, 0x011000, 0x100000, 0x101000, 0x110000, 0x111000—are used to identify one of eight classes that are mapped to priority levels for packet-forwarding treatment.

Table 17.1 illustrates two different cases of mapping codepoints (or classes) to priorities. In the first case, each class is mapped to a different priority level—codepoint 0x111000 having the highest priority, and so on. In the second case, the eight classes are mapped to one of the three priorities. The priority of a packet with the codepoint 0x101000 is the same as the priority with the codepoint 0x011000. Each packet has a higher packet-forwarding priority when compared with packets with the codepoints 0x010000, 0x001000 or 0x000000.

As an example, an *IP telephony service provider* (ITSP) can offer its customers a choice of one of three plans—gold, silver or bronze. The ITSP then uses Class Selector PHB as shown in the second part of Table 17.1. Gold service customers have their media stream packets marked with a DSCP of 0x111000 or 0x110000; silver service customers have their media stream packets marked with a DSCP of 0x101000, 0x100000 or 0x011000; and bronze service customers have their media stream packets marked with a DSCP of 0x010000, 0x001000 or 0x000000. As the number of subscribers increases, the ITSP may decide at a later time to increase the number of service offerings to, for example, six—premium gold, gold, premium silver, silver, premium bronze, and bronze. In this case, the ITSP then can decide to use a Class Selector DSCP for priority mapping as shown in Table 17.2.

Assured Forwarding (AF) PHB

The *Assured Forwarding* (AF) PHB determines the packet forwarding assurance according to the AF class in which the packet belongs and the

Table 17.1 Example of Two Different Cases of Mapping Class Selector codepoints to Priorities

CODEPOINT	000000	001000	010000	011000	100000	101000	110000	111000
PRIORITY	7	6	5	4	3	2	1	0

CODEPOINT	000000	001000	010000	011000	100000	101000	110000	111000
PRIORITY	2	2	2	1	1	1	0	0

Table 17.2 Example of mapping of Class Selector DSCP to Five Priority Values

CODEPOINT	000000	001000	010000	011000	100000	101000	110000	111000
PRIORITY	5	5	4	4	3	2	1	0

resources (buffer and bandwidth) allocated to that AF class at the diffserv-compliant node. Four AF classes have been defined, and packets belonging to the same AF class and micro-flow may not be reordered within the network. Packets belonging to an AF class can be assigned one of three drop precedence values. During network congestion, a packet in an AF class with a higher drop precedence value will have a higher probability of being dropped when compared to a packet in the same AF class with a lower drop precedence value. The recommended codepoints for the AF PHB are indicated in Table 17.3. The AF codepoint representing Class *i* and Drop Precedence *j* is usually denoted by AF*ij*. Although four AF classes and three drop precedence values have been defined for general use, additional AF classes or drop precedence values can be defined by a domain administrator for local use (i.e., no standardization is needed for local use.)

As an example of the possible packet re-ordering using AF classes, consider Figure 17.12 where an H.323 Endpoint A opens two logical channels to Endpoint B in order to transmit two layers of a media stream. Each stream (or layer) is packetized into IP datagrams that traverse two diffserv compliant routers. Packets belonging to the base layer are transmitted with the AF11 PHB codepoint, while packets belonging to the enhancement layer are transmitted with the AF21 PHB codepoint. Let us examine which of the following statements are true:

a. *Packets belonging to the base layer can appear at Endpoint B in an order that is different from the order in which they were transmitted from Endpoint A.* This statement is false because packets belonging to the same AF class and the same micro-flow (a layer in our case) cannot be reordered.

b. *Packets belonging to the enhancement layer can appear at Endpoint B in an order that is different from the order in which they were transmitted from Endpoint A.* This statement is false for the same reason as the previous statement.

c. *A packet belonging to the enhancement layer can appear at Endpoint B ahead of a base layer packet, even when it was transmitted from Endpoint A at a later time.* This statement is true because packet re-ordering (whether they belong to the same micro-flow) assigned to different AF classes is possible.

d. *A packet belonging to the base layer can appear at Endpoint B ahead of an enhancement layer packet, even when it was transmitted from Endpoint A at a later time.* This statement is true for the same reason as the previous statement.

Packets belonging to one AF class are treated independently of other AF class packets. The average rate at which packets belonging to an AF class are forwarded should equal the bandwidth that is assigned to the AF class at the forwarding node.

Table 17.3 AF Classes

	CLASS 1	CLASS 2	CLASS 3	CLASS 4
Low Drop Precedence (1)	001010	010010	011010	100010
Medium Drop Precedence (2)	001100	010100	011100	100100
High Drop Precedence (3)	001110	010110	011110	100110

In order to illustrate how an AF PHB can handle VoIP traffic, consider an example where a service provider wishes to provide two kinds of treatment to the voice traffic on his network. The first is a low loss, low delay service while the second is a low delay service that does not give too much consideration to loss. We examine how the AF PHB may be used to create such a service. A low loss, low delay service is created using AF PHB by over-provisioning the network nodes for the AF*ij* class under consideration. To provide such a service, the arrival rate of the AF*ij* PHB BA at any network node should be less than the configured bandwidth at the network node for this traffic class. Suitable admission control and traffic conditioning at the diffserv domain along with over-provisioning the network nodes for the AF*ij* class ensures that this is the case. In the second case where loss is not considered serious, low delay is achieved using AF PHB which keeps the buffer size for the AF*ij* class small at each network node within the diffserv domain. The extent of packet loss is determined by the rate at which packet arrives at the network node and its configured bandwidth for the AF*ij* class.

Expedited Forwarding (EF) PHB

The *Expedited Forwarding* (EF) PHB guarantees that the EF BA arriving at the network node will be processed at a rate lying within a preconfigured range. Processing within this range is assured irrespective of the node load. The recommended codepoint for EF PHB is 0x101110. The EF PHB can construct a *Virtual Leased Line* (VLL) service type.

For example, an H.323 Endpoint A opens a logical channel for transmitting a variable bit rate video stream to Endpoint B. The video stream is packetized into IP datagrams which are transmitted with the EF PHB codepoint 0x101110. The rate of video transmission is shown in Figure 17. 5. Let us examine the following two different scenarios within this example.

a. *Video packets traverse one intermediate differentiated services-compliant router which is configured with a minimum rate of R/2 and a maximum rate of R for the behavior aggregate with an EF PHB codepoint.* Assuming that no other packets belonging to this behavior aggregate traverse the router, determine the time it takes for the video packets to reach Endpoint B when the router assigns only the minimum rate of R/2 throughout. Because the router assigns a rate of R/2 for EF PHB traffic and the only traffic with this codepoint which traverses this router is the video stream under consideration, a total traffic volume of (R/2)T + RT would take a time of 3T to transmit. Now determine the time it takes when the router assigns a rate of 0.75R until t=T, and beyond that a rate of R. In this case, the assigned rates of 0.75R and R at least equal the traffic rate, hence there is no traffic buildup at the router. Thus, all traffic belonging to the video stream will have traversed the router by 2T. Note that we have ignored transmission and propagation delays

b. *Video packets traverse an additional intermediate differentiated services-compliant router which is configured with rates similar to the first router.* Determine the time taken for the video packets to reach Endpoint B for each case in a., again ignoring the transmission and propagation delays. As seen in the previous scenario, the rate of the media stream out of the first router and into the second one is R/2. Because the second router is configured with a rate of R/2 for EF traffic, the total time taken for the last video packet to reach Endpoint B is identical to the previous scenario which is 3T. Therefore, this scenario is the same as the first and thus takes a time of 2T.

For another example, within a multi-point H.323 conference an Endpoint A opens a logical channel to a MP, which in turn opens a logical channel each to Endpoint B and Endpoint C for video transmission purposes. The video streams traverse one intermediate (differentiated services-compliant) router prior to its arrival at the endpoints as shown in Figure 17. 18(a). Each video stream is packetized into IP datagrams and is transmitted with the EF PHB codepoint 0x101110. The video transmission rate is indicated in Figure 17.18(b)—the dashed line denotes the rate of Endpoint B, and the thick line

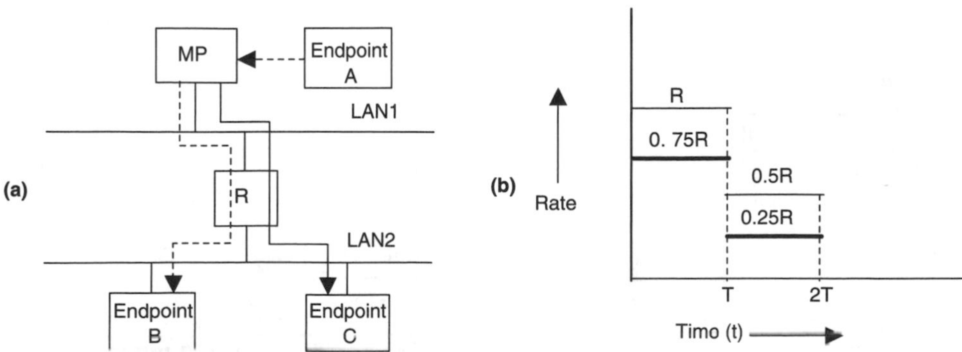

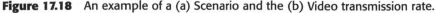

Figure 17.18 An example of a (a) Scenario and the (b) Video transmission rate.

denotes the rate of Endpoint C. (It is possible, for instance, that this is the case when Endpoint C is connected to LAN2 by a lower bandwidth (wireless) interface.) The router is configured with a constant rate of 1.5R for the behavior aggregate with the EF PHB codepoint, assuming that no other packets belonging to this behavior aggregate traverse the router other than those considered as belonging to the two video streams. We can now determine several performance metrics, as discussed in the following.

a. *Determine the time needed for the router to complete transmission of both video streams.* As far as the router is concerned, it does not distinguish between packets destined to Endpoint B and packets destined to Endpoint C, because they have the same DSCP. By t=T, the router completes transmission of 1.5RT of traffic, which results in a traffic buildup of 0.25RT. This 0.25RT of traffic and the newly arriving 0.75RT of traffic are transmitted by t=2T. Thus, all traffic transmission is complete by t=2T.
b. *Determine the maximum delay that a packet can experience within the router.* Because the traffic buildup in the buffer is at its maximum at t=T, traffic arriving at t=T faces the maximum delay. Due to the fact that this arriving traffic hits a buffer of 0.25RT, transmission of this traffic faces a delay of (0.25RT)/(1.5R) = 0.167T.

Diffserv is capable of providing two types of services—quantitative performance and relative performance. The former deals with providing numerical values or ranges for parameters such as delay, bandwidth, etc. In the latter case, while no numerical values or ranges are provided, performance is relatively the same as other classes.

Figure 17.19 illustrates the use of diffserv within H.323. The OLC/OLCAck sequence carries the traffic description. As we see in the policy discussion, this information can be used by the gatekeeper to return a DSCP back to Endpoint A. An Endpoint A then utilizes this DSCP to mark its packets which are flowing toward Endpoint B.

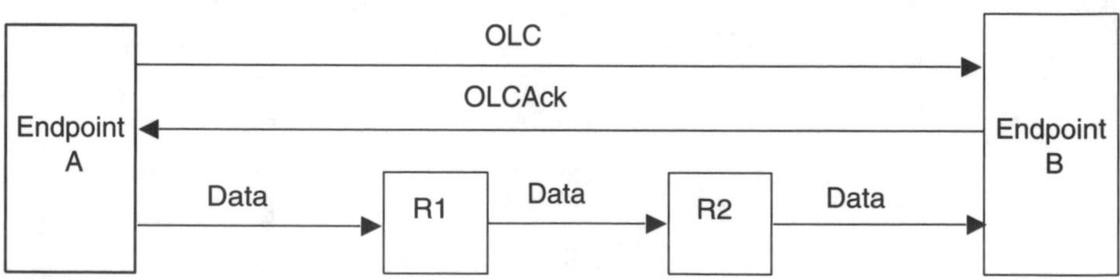

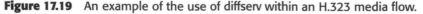

Figure 17.19 An example of the use of diffserv within an H.323 media flow.

Policy, Resource Management, and Multi-Domain Issues

In Section 17.3, we discussed the location where an endpoint and gatekeeper exchange QoS information prior to setting up a call. RAS messages are used for this purpose, which establish whether admission is granted for the call based on the total required bandwidth for the call as well as determines the QoS control entity (endpoint or gatekeeper). In Section 17.4, we discussed the use of RSVP/intserv to provide QoS for H.323 media streams, while in Section 17.5, we discussed the use of diffserv to provide QoS for those same streams. Although, the use of the OLC structure to convey an endpoint's desired QoS for a media stream to another endpoint was previously discussed in these sections, we did not discuss policy or multi-domain issues. We also did not take into consideration what the gatekeeper does upon receiving the OLC with the QoS parameters, or the case of the OLC traversing multiple gatekeepers that belonging to different administrative domains. In this section, we discuss some of these issues.

QoS Functional Entities and Reference Points

H.323 defines the following four QoS functional entities (as shown in Figure 17.20):

- *Endpoint QoS Entity (EPQoSE).* This functional entity resides within the endpoint and is responsible for QoS issues dealing with the endpoint. EPQoSE is responsible for issuing QoS requests on behalf of the endpoint, and for dealing with responses received to such requests.
- *QoS Manager (QoSM).* The QoSM is the functional entity which interacts with each of the other functional entities—EPQoSE, QoSPE, RM and another QoSM. The QoSM receives QoS requests from the EPQoSE, checks with the QoSPE whether such requests can be granted, suitably responds to the EPQoSE, and contacts an RM to reserve resources for the request.
- *QoS Policy Entity (QoSPE).* The QoSPE is responsible for determining if a certain QoS request from an endpoint can be authorized. Upon request from the QoSM, the QoSPE responds with authorization information.
- *Resource Manager (RM).* The RM is responsible for allocating/reserving transport resources within its administrative domain upon notification from the QoSM.

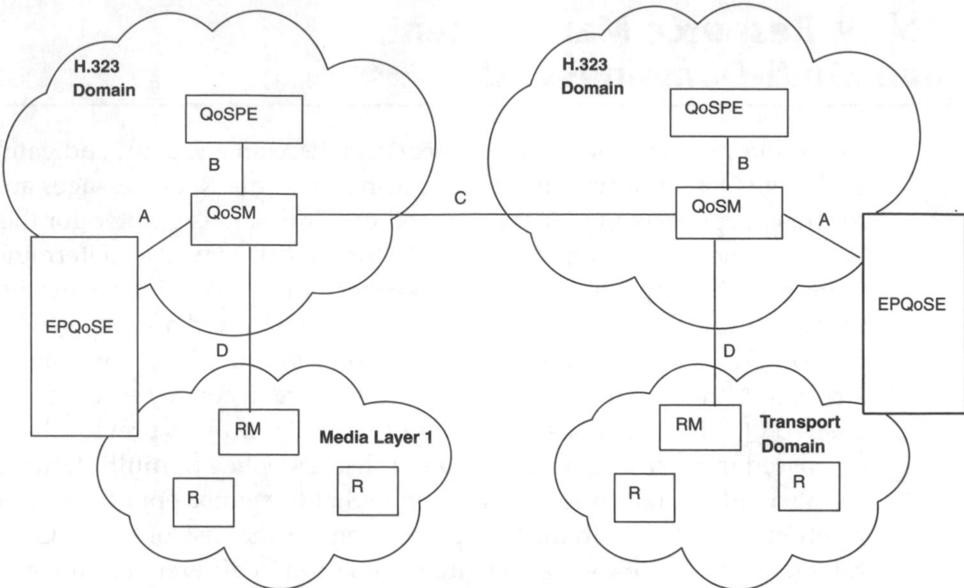

Figure 17.20 H.323 Functional Entities and Reference Points.

Although the physical location of these functional entities can vary, a typical implementation may have the EPQoSE located within the endpoint, the QoSM located within the gatekeeper, the QoSPE located within a policy server, and the RM located within a bandwidth broker.

Relevant reference points between these functional entities have also been defined as follows:

- Reference Point A exists between the EPQoSE and the QoSM.
- Reference Point B exists between pairs of QoSM.
- Reference Point C exists between QoSM and RM.
- Reference Point D exists between QoSM and QoSPE.

Role of Policy in H.323 QoS

Policy plays an important role within the QoS framework. It is responsible for determining whether an endpoint request for a certain QoS is authorized. For instance, a policy within an enterprise can exist that states engineers are entitled to bandwidths of 128 Kbps per call, while managers are entitled to bandwidths of 256 Kbps per call. When a H.323 endpoint representing an engineer user requests a bandwidth of 256 Kbps for a call, it is the policy server's responsibility to determine the allotted bandwidth according to the stipulated policy; the user making the call is not entitled to request the bandwidth. Policy decisions regarding QoS are made for both the cumulative bandwidth of the call prior to call setup as well as for individual media stream QoS after call setup.

The following three scenarios describe the role which policy plays in the QoS of H.323 systems.

Scenario 1

Endpoint A opens a logical channel to Endpoint B using OLC procedures after call setup as shown in Figure 17.21. Assume either the gatekeepers are absent at each end, or that while the gatekeepers are present a direct routed control channel is used at each end. Hence, the OLC/OLCAck exchange occurs directly between the two endpoints. Assume that the media stream from A to B traverses the two intermediate routers R1 and R2 and that the four entities (A, R1, R2, B) are RSVP capable.

Endpoint A needs a certain QoS for the media stream, which is indicated within the OLC message previously described in Section 17.3. Upon receiving the OLCAck message from Endpoint B, Endpoint A is aware of the RSVP capability of Endpoint B. Endpoint A then decides to use RSVP for resource reservation and it sends a PATH message addressed to Endpoint B.

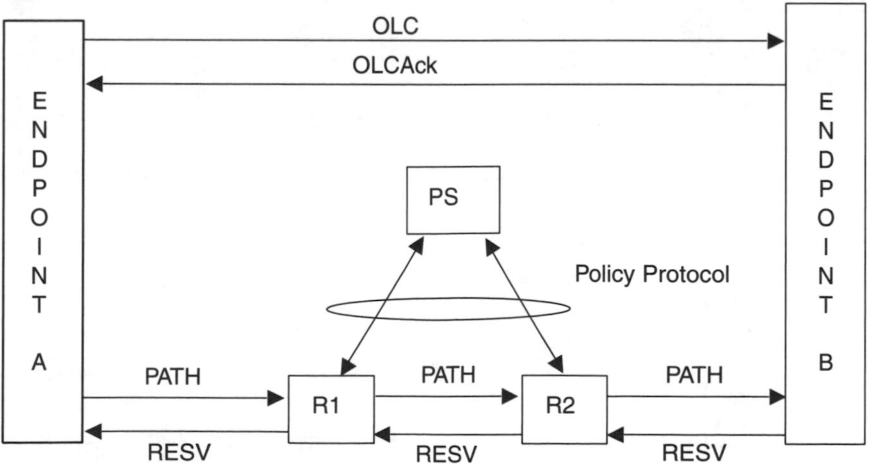

Figure 17.21 Scenario 1 of the policy illustration.

When Endpoint B sends a RESV message in the reverse direction, each of the intermediate routers (R1 and R2) query the policy server (PS) to determine whether resources can be reserved within the routers for this media stream. Admission, which is based on the PSs response, is then either granted or denied at R1 and R2. Thus, in this operational scenario the application (H.323 entities) is not directly concerned with policy issues, yet the network elements (R1 and R2) are policy clients.

Scenario 2

After setting up a call to Endpoint B, Endpoint A opens a logical channel as shown in Figure 17.22. Assume that the media stream from A to B traverses the two intermediate routers of R1 and R2 and that while R1, R2 and B each have RSVP signaling capability, A does not.

During the RAS registration phase, Gatekeeper A decides it is the QoS control entity for calls in which Endpoint A is involved in. Endpoint A needs a certain QoS for the media stream, which it indicates in the OLC message that is routed through Gatekeeper A. When Gatekeeper A receives the OLCAck from B (or B's gatekeeper), it initiates an admission control query to the PS. If admission is granted, the policy server provisions the first-hop router R1 with the necessary QoS resources for the media stream in addition to notifying the gatekeeper. R1 then issues a PATH message which reaches B, and then issues a RESV message back to R1. Upon receiving the RESV message from B, Router R2 queries the policy server for admission control.

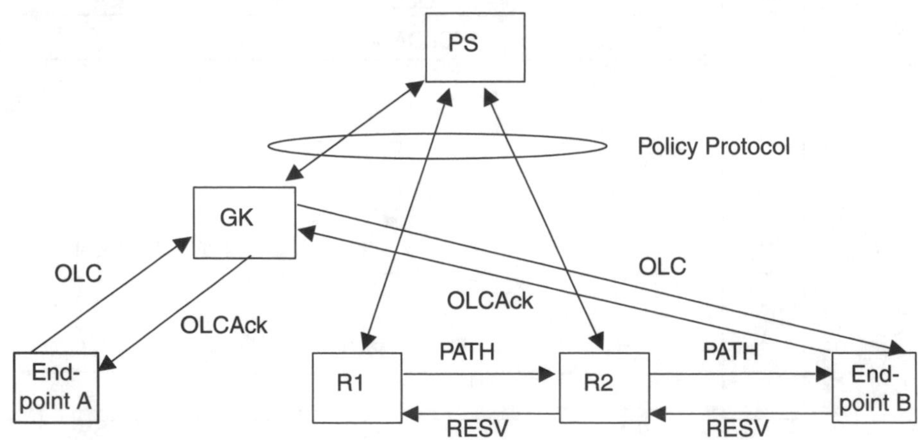

Figure 17.22 Scenario 2 of policy illustration.

Because the QoS control entity is gatekeeper A for calls involving Endpoint A, Endpoint A does not issue the PATH message even if it has RSVP capability in this scenario. A more likely usage of this particular scenario is the case where Endpoint A does not have RSVP signaling capability.

Scenario 3

Scenario 3, as shown in Figure 17.23, describes a case where the QoS control entity is the endpoint. As in the previous two scenarios, Endpoint A sets up a call to Endpoint B, and the media stream traverses routers R1 and R2. In addition, Endpoint A also has a policy client physically collocated and the four entities (A, R1, R2, B) are diffserv capable.

Because Endpoint A needs a certain QoS for the media stream, it queries the policy server with the desired QoS, after opening the logical channel (i.e., after receiving the OLCAck). The policy server then returns the DSCP that Endpoint A uses to mark its packets.

EP/GK Controlled QoS

In Section 17.3, we discussed how the QoS control entity is determined during registration/admission. The QoS control entity can be either the endpoint or the gatekeeper. We now provide some discussion on factors which could influence an endpoint to opt for controlling QoS. These factors depend on the capabilities of the endpoint—such as the presence of a policy client on the endpoint, RSVP capability, diffserv marking capability, etc.

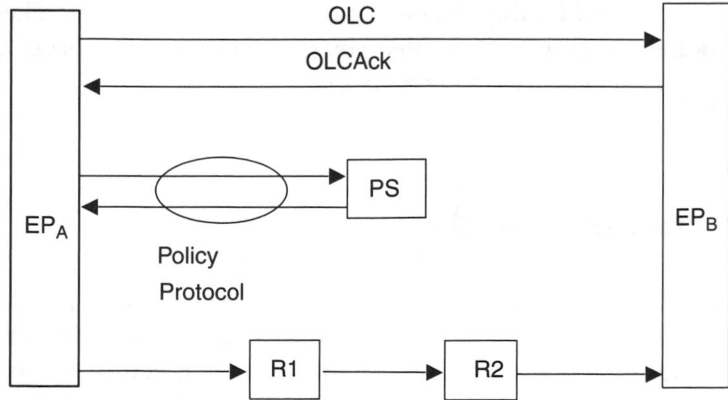

Figure 17.23 Scenario 3 of policy illustration.

Based on the combinations of these capabilities, several operational scenarios can be constructed and are classified into two kinds:

- The case where the endpoint handles QoS by itself (without assistance from the gatekeeper). Several scenarios can be envisaged here. The following two scenarios are some:
  - *Endpoint has a policy client and diffserv marking capability, but no RSVP capability.* In this case, the endpoint is able to query a suitable policy server which then returns the preferred DSCP profile(s) that the endpoint can use. The policy server also notifies the first-hop router of which traffic profile the endpoint can use; and it can also provision the network (usually, through a bandwidth broker) to handle the desired resources.
  - *The endpoint has RSVP capability but no policy client.* In this case, the transmitting endpoint sends an RSVP PATH message containing the desired intserv parameters toward the receiver after the OLC/OLCAck exchange. The first-hop router, upon receiving the PATH message and querying the policy server, then sets the ignore field in the PATH message and passes it on towards the receiver—only if the first hop router is an edge router bordering a diffserv network. In the RESV message, the first-hop router can include a DCLASS object. The sender may possibly be able to utilize the information in the DCLASS object, but it depends on whether the sender has marking capability.
- *The endpoint requires assistance from the gatekeeper to handle QoS.* This can occur when the endpoint only has diffserv marking capability. In such a case, the endpoint indicates the desired QoS for a particular media stream in the OLC (the H.323s current usage); the preferred DSCP profile(s) can be returned by the gatekeeper in the OLCAck. The gatekeeper then obtains such DSCP profile(s) by querying a policy server using the *Common Open Policy Server* (COPS) protocol.

Recommended Reading

Finally, there are some good textbooks circulating which deal with QoS techniques at the network level. Ferguson gives a good description of RSVP and the Integrated Service (intserv) architecture, while Kilkki describes the differentiated services (diffserv) architecture in great detail. Verma, on the other hand, describes the QoS building blocks quite well. In addition, you can also refer to several available RFCs for more information at http://www.ietf.org. RFCs 1633, 2205, 2210 and 2216 are good starting points to understand RSVP and the Integrated Services framework, while RFCs 2474, 2475, 2597 and 2598 describe the Differentiated Services framework. Other aspects such as the SBM and policy protocols such as COPS are also available from http://www.ietf.org.

Annex N of the ITU-T H.323 specification deals with QoS issues. The annex talks about the QoS functional entities and reference points, and also describes possible mapping between H.323 QoS classes to specific network QoS techniques such as diffserv, RSVP/intserv and MPLS. Appendix II of the H.323 standard also deals with H.323 QoS aspects such as RSVP and the use of H.245 for QoS. In addition, within the main H.323 standard you will find a discussion of the QoS control entity and bandwidth negotiation.

ETSI TIPHON has a QoS architecture which has been closely aligned with the H.323 Annex N document. TIPHON's QoS documents may be obtained from http://www.etsi.org/TIPHON.

References

Annex N H.323 Annex N, *End-to-End Quality of Service (QoS) Control and Signalling in H.323 Systems*. ITU-T Specification, November 2000.

Ferguson Ferguson, P. and Huston, G. *Quality of Service*. John Wiley & Sons, 1998.

Kilkki Kilkki, K., *Differentiated Services*. Macmillan Technical Publishing, 1999.

RFC 1633 Braden, R., Clark, D., and Shenker, S. *Integrated Services in the Internet Architecture: an Overview*. RFC 1633, ISI, MIT, and PARC, June 1994.

RFC 2205 Braden, R., et. al. *Resource Reservation Protocol (RSVP)—Version 1 Functional Specification*, RFC 2205, IETF, September 1997.

RFC 2210 Wroclawski, J. *Use of RSVP with IETF Integrated Services*, RFC 2210, IETF, September 1997.

RFC 2216 Shenker, S. and Wroclawski, J. *Network Element Service Specification Template*, RFC 2216, IETF, September 1997.

RFC 2474 Nichols, K., Blake, S., Baker, F., and Black, D. *Definition of the Differentiated Services Field (DS Field) in the Ipv4 and Ipv6 Headers*, RFC 2474, IETF, December 1998.

RFC 2475 Blake, S., Black, D., Carlson, M., Davies, E., Wang, Z., and Weiss, W. *An Architecture for Differentiated Services*, RFC 2475, IETF, December 1998.

RFC 2597 Heinanen, J., Baker, F., Weiss, W.,and Wroclawski J. *Assured Forwarding PHB*, RFC 2597, IETF, June 1999.

RFC 2598 Jacobson, V., Nichols, K., and Poduri, K. *An Expedited Forwarding PHB*, RFC 2598, IETF, June 1999.

TR 101 329-1 ETSI Technical Recommendation TR 101 329-1, *Telecommunications and Internet Protocol Harmonization over Networks (TIPHON); End-to-End Quality of Service in TIPHON Systems; Part 1: General Aspects of Quality of Service (QoS)*. ETSI, July 2000.

TS 101 329-2 ETSI Technical Specification TS 101 329-2, *Telecommunications and Internet Protocol Harmonization over Networks (TIPHON); End-to-End Quality of Service in TIPHON Systems; Part 2: Definition of Quality of Service (QoS) Classes*. ETSI, July 2000.

TS 101 329-3 ETSI Technical Specification TS 101 329-3, *Telecommunications and Internet Protocol Harmonization over Networks (TIPHON); End-to-End Quality of Service in TIPHON Systems; Part 3: Signalling and Control of End-to-End Quality of Service in TIPHON Systems.* ETSI, January 2001.

TS 101 329-5 ETSI Technical Specification TS 101 329-5, *Telecommunications and Internet Protocol Harmonization over Networks (TIPHON); End-to-End Quality of Service in TIPHON Systems; Part 5: Quality of Service (QoS) Measurement Methodologies*. ETSI, November 2000.

Verma, D. *Supporting Service Level Agreements on IP Networks*. Macmillan Technical Publishing, 1999.

Problems

1. Discuss the limitations of application level QoS techniques and then state the need for network level QoS techniques.
2. Under heavily loaded network conditions, the network using QoS enable routers can provide the promised good service quality to those applications which request it. Other applications which do not request QoS may end up receiving a worse service. Considering the system as a whole, determine the change in the average packet loss when the network provides QoS and does not. Assume that the packet arrival rate remains unchanged.
3. A traffic flow characterized by a token bucket of parameters (r,b,p,M,m) needs to satisfy the following conditions:

   Data Sent $\leq M + pt, \quad \forall t$

   Data Sent $\leq b + rt, \quad \forall t$

   Explain the reasoning behind these conditions.
4. A pair of communicating H.323 applications use Guaranteed service to bound the end-to-end delay experienced by an audio stream flowing between the two. The audio stream is characterized by a token bucket of

rate r and bucket depth b. State which of the following statements are true and why.

a. The sending H.323 application may be able to decrease the end-to-end delay bound by decreasing the token bucket depth b.

b. The sending H.323 application may be able to decrease the end-to-end delay bound by decreasing the token rate r.

c. The end-to-end delay bound may be decreased by decreasing the bandwidth R which is reserved for the audio stream.

d. The end-to-end delay bound may change if the route taken by the audio stream packets changes.

5. Prove the following: For a Guaranteed service class in the intserv architecture, the end-to-delay bound increases with an increase in maximum packet size M with all other parameters remaining unchanged.

6. A pair of communicating H.323 applications use Guaranteed service to bound the end-to-end delay experienced by two video streams flowing between the two. Each video stream is characterized by identical traffic flow parameters (r,b,p,M,m), the path they follow and the bandwidth R reserved for each stream is identical as well. Assuming that the flows conform to their traffic characterizations, state which of the following statements are true and why.

   a. The average end-to-end delay for the two streams is identical.

   b. The minimum end-to-end delay for the two streams is identical.

   c. The maximum end-to-end delay for the two streams is identical.

   d. The jitter experienced by the two streams is identical.

   e. The packet loss experienced by the two streams is identical.

7. Consider the scenario shown in Figure 17.13 which has been redrawn in Figure 17.24 to show the interfaces and intermediate routers. Figure 17.24 focuses on the MP which has two incoming interfaces (a and b) and two outgoing interfaces (c and d). Data from senders S1 and S2 arrive at interfaces a and b, respectively; data to receivers D1 and D2 exit out of interface c; and data to receiver D3 exit out of interface d. The router cloud can contain zero or more intermediate routers through which the data flows. Let the reservation requests received at interfaces c and d be as follows: D1 requests b11 for S1 and b12 for S2; D2 requests b21 for S1 and b22 for S2; D3 requests b31 for S1 and b32 for S3. Determine the reservations that the MP makes for each source at interfaces c and d in addition to the reservation requests that it sends upstream through interfaces a and b.

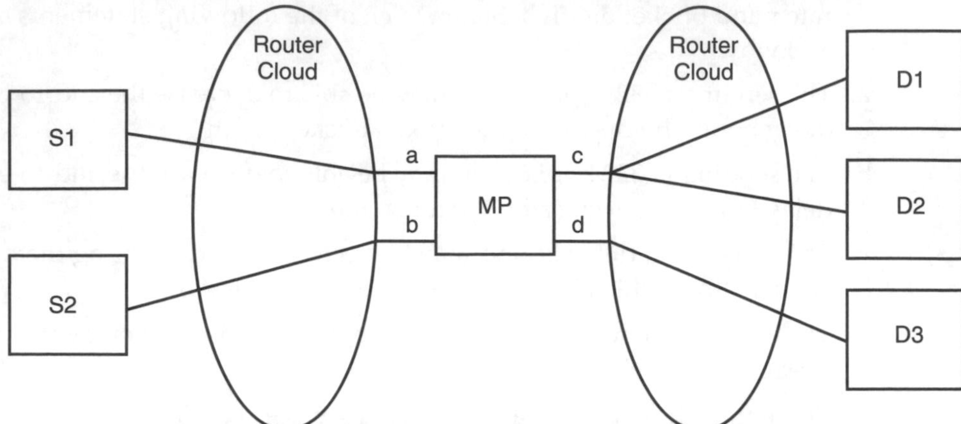

Figure 17.24 Figure 17.13 redrawn to show the interfaces at the MP and the router clouds.

8. Study the Multi-Protocol Label Switching (MPLS) technology by going to www.ietf.org. Discuss how it can be used to provide QoS for applications such as H.323.
9. Consider the topology of Figure 17.19 where a source (S) transmits media streams to a destination (D) via two intermediate routers (R1 and R2). In addition, also assume that the media streams are encrypted using IPSec ESP as described in RFC 2406. The use of IPSec ESP makes several fields including the source port number invisible to intermediate nodes such as R1 and R2. The filter specs in R1 and R2, in this case, cannot classify the packets based on source port information. Describe possible ways around this problem. Hint: See RFC 2207 for one possible solution.
10. While performing policy based admission control, the logic for the policy server is usually physically separate from the logic of the querier. Thus, it is necessary to define an open protocol such as COPS between the querier and the policy server. List the benefits in separating the logic for the policy server from the querier.

Glossary

Access-gateway A type of gateway that provides a User to Network interface (UNI), such as ISDN.

Activating call A signaling connection between an activating user and a served endpoint.

Activating endpoint The endpoint serving the activating user.

Active state The H.225.0 call state U10 'Active' (after CONNECT message).

Annex L endpoint An H.323 callable entity that can be controlled using the encapsulation method described in H.323 Annex L.

Application Protocol Data Unit (APDU) A sequence of data elements exchanged between peer application layer entities, such as ROS APDUs.

Back-haul The transport of signaling information from a media termination gateway, like an MG, to a signaling gateway, such as MGC. For example, a Layer 3 protocol such as Q.931 might be transported between MG and MGC so that the MGC terminates Layer 3, while the MG terminates Layers 1 and 2.

Busy, busy condition A busy condition exists when, in the absence of any supplementary services that might modify the behavior, a destination endpoint would respond to an incoming call by sending a Release Complete message containing a *ReleaseCompleteReason of inConf* or a Cause IE with cause value #17, "user busy." Note that an H.323 endpoint may be busy with one call or may be busy with more than one call depending on the implementation.

Call deflection The type of diversion invoked by the served user.

Call-independent signaling connection A signaling connection established between SS-Control entities located in different H.323 entities for the exchange of call-independent signaling information.

Call independent A property of information conveyed in a message that does not use the call reference of a call.

Call related A property of information conveyed in a message that uses the call reference of a call.

Call, Basic call A call in the sense of QSIG (see the ECMA-143 or corresponding ISO standard) and a (point-to-point) conference in the sense of H.323 (see ITU-T recommendation H.323). An H.323 call is that segment of a (point-to-point) conference that belongs to the H.323 domain. In a multi-point conference, the H.323 segment of each conference leg is a separate call.

Call A multimedia collaboration between two endpoints. *Refer to Recommendation H.323.*

Camp-on tone A special tone or announcement provided to the calling User A while the call is offered to the busy User B.

CheckRestriction call A signaling connection between a served endpoint and a diverted-to endpoint, for the purpose of checking call diversion restrictions.

Conference type connection A connection between the served user, User B, and User C, in which all users have user information connection with each other.

Conference A multimedia collaboration among three or more endpoints.

Consultation timer A timer governing the time in which the calling user is allowed to request the invocation of CO after being informed that a call has failed because of a busy signal at the destination. The duration of the timer is an implementation option.

Corporate telecommunication network (CN) Sets of equipment (Customer Premises Equipment and/or Customer Premises Networks) located at geographically dispersed locations and interconnected to provide telecommunication services to a defined group of users. A CN can be comprised of a PBX network, a private IP network (intranet), or a combination of the two.

Deactivating call The signaling connection between a deactivating user and the served endpoint.

Deactivating endpoint The endpoint serving the deactivating user.

Delayed invocation The invocation of CI (Call Intrusion) after the calling user has been informed that a call has failed because of a busy signal at the destination.

Destination entity In the context of a single one-way exchange of information between two SS-Control entities, the destination entity is the H.323 entity where the receiving SS-Control entity is located.

Diversion The redirection of a call, on request of a called (served) endpoint or user and prior to the receipt of an answer, to a number different from the number of the original endpoint/user.

Diverted-to endpoint The endpoint to which a call is diverted.

Diverted-to number The number to which a call is diverted.

Diverted-to subaddress The subaddress to which a call is diverted.

Diverting cause The parameter that contains the reason for the diversion, such as CFU, CFB, or CFNR.

Diverting number The number of the served endpoint/user.

Endpoint A The calling endpoint of a call that is subject to call diversion.

Endpoint B The served (diverting) endpoint of a call that is subject to call diversion—endpoint B1, endpoint B2, endpoint B3, etc.

Endpoint C The diverted-to endpoint with respect to the final stage of call diversion.

Endpoint; gatekeeper; gateway; terminal; user *See Recommendation H.323.*

Endpoint; terminal; user *See Recommendation H.323.*

Established call The active call that is selected for intruding.

Far-end call hold Same as remote-end call hold. An SS-HOLD scenario in which the served user asks the held endpoint to provide MOH to the held user.

Feature server A functional entity that uses the encapsulation method described in this annex to provide features to an Annex L endpoint. A feature server may reside anywhere on the network, may be collocated with a gatekeeper, or may reside on a gateway or other H.323 callable entity. A feature server may provide interworking between the stimulus protocol and H.450 services.

Feature A transaction that can affect the user interface and that may alter media streaming

Forced release The release of the established call on request from the served user.

Forwarded call The call leg from a rerouting entity toward the diverted-to user.

Forwarding call The call leg between a rerouting entity and a served endpoint/user.

Forwarding The type of diversion invoked automatically by the served endpoint in accordance with information previously registered in the served endpoint against the called number.

Free A property of a user, who can accept an attempt to present a call to that user (that is, allow the call to reach the alerting or answered state).

Gatekeeper (GK) A functional entity serving as a gateway and providing services such as authentication, authorization, alias resolution, and call routing.

Gateway A gateway as defined in H.323; present specifically for the purpose of interworking with a network using QSIG.

H.323 call, H.323 signaling This function in the decomposed gateway supports normal H.323 signaling, such as H.225.0, H.245, or H.450.x as described in H.323.

H.323 endpoint A terminal that is attached to a packet-based network, such as an IP Network, for example, and follows the H.323 recommendation as the attachment protocol. Examples are multimedia PC, LAN telephone, messaging server, and PSTN gateway that comply with the H.323 standard.

H.323 Entity *See* H.323 endpoint

H.450 Supplementary Service Control (SS-Control) entity An entity that exists within an H.323 entity and provides the procedures associated with the support of a particular supplementary service.

H.450.1 Supplementary Service APDU (H.450.1 APDU) A specific APDU defined by H.450.1 for the transport of supplementary service data elements

Held type of connection The breaking of the user information connection to and from user C during the intrusion state by means of isolating user C. As an example, user C may be held using the procedures of Recommendation H.450.4.

Held user The user who has been put on hold.

Holding user The user who has put a party on hold.

Immediate invocation The invocation of Call Intrusion as part of the initial call set up.

Interpretation APDU A specific APDU defined by H.450.1 that describes what a receiver of an H.450.1 APDU has to do if the receiver does not understand the contents of an APDU.

Interrogating call The signaling connection between an interrogating user and the served endpoint.

Interrogating endpoint The endpoint serving the interrogating user.

Intruding call A call in which the served user requests Call Intrusion.

Intrusion state The condition after communication is established between the served user and user B using Call Intrusion and prior to the termination of Call Intrusion.

Invocation A request by an SS-Control entity to perform an operation in a remote SS-Control entity.

IP network A public or private network offering connectionless packet-mode services based on the Internet Protocol (IP) as the network layer protocol.

Last diverting endpoint The served endpoint from the point of view of the diverted-to endpoint for a particular stage of call diversion. In the case of a call subject to a single stage of call diversion, Endpoint B is the last diverting endpoint from the point of view of Endpoint C. In the case of a call subject to multiple stages of call diversion, Endpoint B1 is the last diverting endpoint from the point-of-view of Endpoint B2; Endpoint B2 is the last diverting endpoint from the point of view of Endpoint B3, and so on. The served endpoint for the final stage of call diversion is the last diverting endpoint from the point-of-view of Endpoint C.

Media Gateway (MG) The media gateway converts media provided in one type of network to the format required in another type of network. For example, an MG could terminate bearer channels from a switched circuit network (for example, DSOs) and media streams from a packet network (for example, RTP streams in an IP network). This gateway may be able to process audio, video, and T.120 alone or in any combination and can do full-duplex media translations. The MG may also play audio/video messages and perform other IVR functions or may perform media conferencing.

Media Gateway Controller (MGC) Controls the parts of the call state that pertain to connection control for media channels in an MG.

Media on Hold (MOH) The media pattern that may be provided to the held user during hold condition. This pattern may include music, announcements, video, freeze (blank) frame, and other indications.

Message Waiting Indication An indication sent to the served user when messages are waiting for the served user.

Messaging server endpoint The endpoint that handles the H.323 signaling on behalf of the messaging server. For example, this may be the messaging server itself if it is directly attached to the H.323 network; it may be the originating user's endpoint; or it may be a gateway.

Messaging server The entity that requests activation or deactivation of the Message Waiting Indication. When a callback request is issued using the mechanism provided by MWI, the originating user acts as a messaging server.

mistyped A property of an APDU whose structure does not conform to the structure defined in the Recommendation or the structure defined for a particular supplementary service.

Multi-point Control Unit (MCU) A gateway that controls the setup and coordination of a multi-user conference, which typically includes processing of audio, video, and data.

Near-end call hold An SS-HOLD scenario in which MOH is provided from the holding endpoint to the held user.

Network access servers A gateway function in an MG that converts modem signals from an SCN network and provides data access to the Internet.

Network Facility Extension APDU A specific APDU defined by H.450.1, which describes the intended receiver of the H.450.1 APDUs sent in the message.

Object identifier *See Recommendation X.680.*

Offered call A call that is in a waiting condition as a result of an invocation of CO against a busy called user.

Original called endpoint The first served endpoint of a call, which is subject to multiple stages of call diversion, such as Endpoint B1.

Original called number In case of multiple call diversion, the number of Endpoint B1.

Originating call The call leg between the calling user and a rerouting entity.

Primary call A call between the transferring User A and the transferred User B.

Private Integrated Services Network (PBX Network) A private switched circuit network (SCN) that consists of ISDN PBXs.

Proxy An entity that acts on behalf of an endpoint for the CO procedures. A proxy in conjunction with SS-HOLD is an entity on the call signaling path that intercepts messages for the remote-end call hold in order to act on behalf of User B for SS-HOLD. The proxy entity may be collocated with the gatekeeper or may be located in a separate transit entity.

Receiving side Within the context of a single information exchange through a gateway, the side of the gateway on which the information arrives.

Remote Authentication Dial-In User (RADIUS) RADIUS is a client-server protocol that is used for Authentication, Authorization, and Accounting (AAA) services.

Rerouting entity The entity (that is, endpoint) that executes call diversion.

Residential gateway A gateway that interworks an analog line to the packet network.

Resource Reservation Protocol (RSVP) A signaling protocol that was originally designed to establish reservations for services based on the Intserv framework. It was developed as a general-purpose signaling protocol that may be easily extended for setting up reservations for services based on other frameworks as well.

ROS APDU An APDU defined by the Remote Operations Service (ROS).

Secondary call A call between the transferring User A and the transferred-to User C associated with the primary call (this association is an implementation matter within Endpoint A).

Sending side Within the context of a single information exchange through a gateway, the side of the gateway through which the information is transmitted.

Served (diverting) endpoints The endpoint that hosts the served user and where diversion is invoked. This endpoint may also be referred to as the diverting endpoint or the called endpoint. B1 is the first served endpoint; B2 is the second served endpoint; B3 is the third served endpoint, and so on.

Served user In Message Waiting, the user to whom the Message Waiting Indication is sent when initiated by the Message Center. In Call Intrusion, the user who requests Call Intrusion. For SS-CFU, SS-CFB, and SS-CFNR, the user for whom forwarding can be activated. For SS-CD, the user who can invoke deflection.

Service Level Agreement (SLA) The portion of the contract between an ITSP and a clearinghouse that deals with the set of services provided, the associated service quality, service monitoring procedures and recourse mechanism.

Side A single protocol stack (QSIG or H.323) within a gateway.

Silent monitoring type of connection A connection between the served user, User B, and User C, similar to a conference type of connection, but with the served user monitoring the established call with Users B and C not being informed.

Source entity In the context of a single one-way exchange of information between two SS-Control entities, the H.323 entity where the sending SS-Control entity is located.

Supplementary Service Control (SS-Control) entity An entity that exists within an H.323 entity and provides the procedures associated with the support of a particular supplementary service.

Transferred call A call between transferred User B and transferred-to User C which results from the successful completion of a call transfer.

Transferred endpoint; User B The remote endpoint/user of the call with user A, which is transferred by User A to User C.

Transferred-to endpoint; User C The endpoint/user to which User B, originally having called User A, is transferred.

Transferring endpoint; User A The user/endpoint transferring a call with Terminal B, to User C.

Trunking gateways A gateway between an SCN network and packet network that typically terminates a large number of digital circuits.

Trunk A communication channel between two switching systems, such as a DS0 on a T1 or E1 line.

Unrecognized A property of a message, information element, APDU, or operation value whose type identifier is not one supported by the destination entity.

User B (in Call Intrusion) The wanted user who is subject to the call intrusion.

User C (in Call Intrusion) The other user in the established call, also referred to as the unwanted user.

User An application that uses one or more of the services defined in this recommendation (activation, deactivation, interrogation, or invocation) via an application-programming interface.

Acronym List

A/D	Analog/Digital
AAA	Authentication, Authorization, and Accounting
ACF	Admission Confirm (see H.225.0)
ADPCM	Adaptive Differential Pulse-Code Modulation
Adspec	Advertisement Specification
AES	Advanced Encryption Standard
AF	Assured Forwarding
AMR	Adaptive Multi-Rate Codec
ANSI-41	American National Standards Institute Mobile Networks specifications—41
APDU	Application Protocol Data Unit
API	Application Programming Interface
ARJ	Admission Reject
ARQ	Admission Request (see H.225.0)
ASN.1	Abstract Syntax Notation No. 1
AuF	Authentication Function
B/s	Bytes per Second
BA	Behavior Aggregate
BCF	Bandwidth Confirm
BE	Border Element
BICC	Bearer-Independent Call Control

BN	Boundary Node
BRJ	Bandwidth Reject
BRQ	Bandwidth Request
BS	Base Station
Call	Multimedia collaboration between two endpoints
CBC	Cipher Block Chaining
CBQ	Class-Based Queuing
CCBS	Call Completion on Busy supplementary service
CCNR	Call Completion on No Reply supplementary service
CD	Call Deflection
CDA	Call Diversion Activating
CDD	Call Diversion Deactivating
CDF	Call Diversion diverted (Forwarded)-to
CDI	Call Diversion Interrogating
CDO	Call Diversion Originating
CDR	Call Detail Record
CDR	Call Diversion Rerouting
CDS	Call Diversion Served
CFB	Call Forwarding Busy
CFB	Cipher Feed Back
CFNR	Call Forwarding No Reply
CFU	Call Forwarding Unconditional
CI	Call Intrusion supplementary service
CI	Supplementary Service Call Intrusion
CICL	Call Intrusion Capability Level
CIF	Common Intermediate Format
CINT	Call Interception supplementary service
CIPL	Call Intrusion Protection Level
CNG	Comfort Noise Generator
CO	Call Offering supplementary service
Conference	Multimedia collaboration among three or more endpoints
COPS	Common Open Policy Server
CPL	Call Processing Language
CSRC	Contributing Source
CT	Call Transfer supplementary service
CTI	Computer-Telephony Integration
D/A	Digital/Analog
DCF	Disengage Confirm
DCT	Discrete Cosine Transform
DES	Digital Encryption Standard
DES	Data Encryption Standard
DFD	Displaced Frame Difference

DH	Diffie-Hellman
DIV	Diversion
DNDO	Do Not Disturb Override supplementary service
DNS	Domain Name Server
DRQ	Disengage Request
DS	Differentiated Services
DSA	Digital Signature Algorithm
DSBM	Designated SBM
DSCP	Differentiated Services Codepoint
DSS1	ISDN D-Channel signaling protocol for S/T-Reference point
DTMF	Dual-Tone Multi-Frequency
DV	Digital Video
EASE	Endpoint A Signaling Entity
EBSE	Endpoint B Signaling Entity
ECB	Electronic Code Book
ECDSA	Elliptic Curve Digital Signature Algorithm
ECSE	Endpoint C Signaling Entity
EF	Expedited Forwarding
EP	Endpoint
EPQoSE	Endpoint Quality of Service Entity
ESP	Encapsulating Security Payload
ETSI	European Telecommunication Standards Institute
FCS	Frame-Check Sequence
FEC	Forward Error Correction
FF	Fixed Filter
FIFO	First In, First Out
GCF	Gatekeeper Confirm
GK	Gatekeeper
GK/GKp/GKs	Gatekeeper/Gatekeeper on primary call/Gatekeeper on secondary call
GOB	Group of Blocks
GRJ	Gatekeeper Reject
GRQ	Gatekeeper Request
GSM	Global System for Mobile communication
GUID	Globally Unique Identification
GW	Gateway
HDSE (User)	Held Signaling Entity (User)
HGSE (User)	Holding Signaling Entity (User)
HLF	Home Location Function
HLR	Home Location Register
HMAC	Hashed Message Authentication Code
HOLD	Call Hold supplementary service

HTML	Hypertext Markup Language
HTTP	Hypertext Transfer Protocol
IACK	Information request Acknowledgement
IANA	Internet Assigned Numbers Authority
IE	Information Element
IETF	Internet Engineering Task Force
IKE	Internet Key Exchange
IMSI	International Mobile Subscriber Identity
IMTC	International Multimedia Teleconferencing Consortium
INAK	Information Request Negative Acknowledgement
IP	Internet Protocol
IPPM	IP Performance Metrics
IPSec	IP Security
IRR	Information Request Response
ISDN	Integrated Services Digital Network
ISO	International Organization for Standardization
ISP	Internet Service Provider
ITSP	IP Telephony Service Provider
ITU-T	International Telecommunication Union—Telecommunication
IV	Initialization Vector
IVR	Interactive Voice Response
IWF	Interworking Function
JPEG	Joint Photographic Experts Group
JTAPI	Java Telephony API
kb	kilobits
kB	kilobytes
kbps	kilobits per second
kBps	kilobytes per second
LAN	Local Area Network
LDAP	Lightweight Directory Access Protocol
MAC	Message Authentication Code
MB	Macroblock
MC	Multi-Point Controller
MCU	Multi-Point Control Unit
MD5	Message Digest 5
MF	Multi Field
MGC	Media Gateway Controller
MIME	Multipurpose Internet Mail Extensions
MIN	Mobile Identification Number
MIPS	Millions of Instructions per Second
MOH	Media on Hold
MOS	Mean Opinion Score

MP	Multi-Point Processor
MPEG	Motion Pictures Expert Group
MSC	Mobile Switching Center
MSI	Manufacturer-Specific Information
MTU	Maximum Transmission Unit
MWI	Message Waiting Indication
NAT	Network Address Translator
NFE	Network Facility Extension
NIST	National Institute of Standards and Technology
NTP	Network Time Protocol
NTSC	Networking and Telecommunication Standing Committee
OFB	Output Feedback
OID	Object Identifier
OLC	Open Logical Channel
OLCAck	OLC Acknowledgement
OLCRej	OLC Reject
OS	Operating System
PAL	Phase-Alternating Line
PBX	Private-Branch Exchange
PC	Personal Computer
PCM	Pulse-Code Modulation
PDA	Personal Digital Assistant
PDC	Personal Digital Cellular
PHB	Per-Hop Behavior
PISN	Private Integrated Services Network
PLMN	Public Land Mobile Network
POTS	Plain Old Telephone System
PPP	Point-to-Point Protocol
PSTN	Public Switched Telephone Network
PT	Payload Type
QCIF	Quarter CIF
QoS	Quality of Service
QoSM	QoS Manager
QoSPE	QoS Policy Entity
QSIG	ISDN D-Channel signaling protocol for PBX networking at Q-Reference point
R	Router
RA	Routing Area
RADIUS	Remote Authentication Dial-In User Service
RAM	Random Access Memory
RAS	Registration, Admission and Status
RC2	Rivest's Cipher 2

RCF	Registration Confirm
RIP	Request In Progress
RM	Resource Manager
RMS	Root Mean Square
ROM	Read Only Memory
ROS	Remote Operations Service
RRJ	Registration Reject
RRQ	Registration Request
RSA	Rivest, Shamir, Adleman
Rspec	Reservation Specification
RSVP	Resource Reservation Protocol
RTCP	Real-Time Control Protocol
RTP	Real-time Transport Protocol
RTT	Round-Trip Time
SBM	Subnet Bandwidth Manager
SCIF	Sub-CIF
SCN	Switched-Circuit Network
SDES	Source Description
SDL	Specification and Description Language
SDP	Session Description Protocol
SE	Shared Explicit
SET	Simple Endpoint Type
SGML	Standard Generalized Markup Language
SHA-1	Secure Hash Algorithm 1
SIM	Subscriber Identity Module
SLA	Service Level Agreement
SMS	Short Message Service
SN	Sequence Number
SNR	Signal to Noise Ratio
SS	Supplementary Service
SS-CT	Supplementary Service Call Transfer
SS-HOLD	Supplementary Service Hold
SSL	Secure Socket Layer
SSRC	Synchronization Source
TAPI	Microsoft Telephony API
TCP	Transmission Control Protocol
TIPHON	Telecommunication and IP Harmonization over Networks
TLS	Transport-Layer Security
TOS	Type of Service
TRDSE	Transferred Signaling Entity
TSP	Telephony Service Provider
Tspec	Traffic Specification

TTL	Time to Live
UCF	Unregistration Confirm
UDP	User Datagram Protocol
UIM	User Identity Module
ULP	Uneven Level Protection
URJ	Unregistration Reject
URL	Uniform Resource Locator
URQ	Unregistration Request
UTC	Coordinated Universal Time
VAD	Voice Activity Detector
VAS	Value-Added Service
VLF	Visitor Location Function
VLR	Visitor Location Register
VRC	Video Redundancy Coding
WAP	Wireless Application Protocol
WF	Wildcard Filter
WFQ	Weighted Fair Queuing
XML	Extensible Markup Language

Index

Symbols

802 LANs (RSVP/Intserv QoS), 555–556

A

AAA servers, 4
accounting, H.225.0 message flow, 129–130
acknowledgments, 358
ad hoc conferences, 146
  centralized, 179
  decentralized, 176, 178
  H.323, 153
Add command, 365, 368
address resolution
  authorization, 239–240
  call routing (inter-domain communication), 235–238
  H.225.0 message flow, 127
  servers, 4
address templates (call routing), 225, 228–234
addressing, private, 471
  network address translation, 471–473
  Realm Specific IP, 473, 475
Administrative Domain X, 7
  basic service, 7
  supplementary services, 8
Administrative Domain Y, 9
Administrative Domain Z, 9
administrative domains, communication between, 215, 217, 219–220
  address resolution tables, 235–238
  address templates for routing calls, 225, 228–234
  authorization, 239–240
  H.225.0 Annex G protocol, 220, 223–224
  resource usage reporting, 240–241
admission control (H.225.0 message flow), 125–127
adspec, *see* advertising specification
advertising specification, 549
AES (Advanced Encryption Standard), security algorithms, 456
AF, *see* Assured Forwarding PHB
alerting calls, 141
algorithms, security, 443–458
  AES (Advanced Encryption Standard), 456
  DES (Data Encryption Standard), 456
  DSA (Digital Signature Algorithm), 458
  hash, 457
  Message Digest 5, 457
  operation modes, 454
  RSA, 456, 458
  Secure Hash, 458
  signature, 457

alternating supplementary services, 284
Annex L encapsulation, 357
Annex L Endpoints, 355
anonymity, 432, 434
APDUs (Application Protocol Data Units), H.450.1, 263
application level gateways, 467–468
application level QoS, 503–520
  feedback mechanisms, 513–515
  source response to feedback, 515–519
Application Protocol Data Units, *see* APDUs
application scenarios (HTTP), 373–374
applications, call control, 247–248
  call management, 250
  first-party, 248
  third-party, 249–250
architecture, mobility, 487
  authenticating function, 491
  call signaling, 490
  GK discover and registration, 487, 489
  interworking function, 491
  location updates, 489–490
  types of, 483–485
associatedSessionID field, 88
Assured Forwarding PHB, 559, 562
audible tones, return of, 359
audio unit (stimulus terminals), 354
AuditCapabilities command, 368
AuditValue command, 368
authenticating function (mobility), 491
authentication
  H.225.0 message flow, 124
  H.323 security, 410–411
    digital signatures, 414
    message integrity, 415–416
    shared secret-based encryption, 411, 413
    shared secret-based hash, 413
authorization, 239–240
automatic recall, 314

B

baseline security profile, 436
basic service (Administrative Domain X), 7
Bearer Independent Call Control, *see* BICC
Behavior Aggregate classifiers, 533
BICC, 402
  interworking, 402
  ISUP trunking, 403
bit rates (voice coders), 22
bit-stream syntax (digital video), 33–34
book outline, 11–17
border element discovery (address resolution tables), 235
building blocks (network)
  QoS, 527
    packet classifiers, 533–534
    packet schedulers, 536–541
    queue, 536–541
    rate controllers, 534, 536
    Token Bucket, 527–533
busy condition (call completion services), 321–323

C

call bandwidth (QoS RAS operations), 544
Call Completion Services-H.450.9, 331–335
call control
  applications, 247–250
  centralized vs. distributed, 349–350
  embedding H.245
    Fast Connect, 111–114
    tunneling, 110–111
  protocols (H.245), 69–70
    H.323 usage scenarios, 99, 102–110
    messages, 71–99, 143
Call Deflection, 302, 307
  signaling protocol, 308
Call Detail Records (CDRs), 372
call diversion services, 301, 303–304, 307–309, 311, 314
  Call Deflection, 307
    signaling protocol, 308
  Call Forwarding, 307, 313–314
    gatekeeper, 309–310, 312
    signaling protocol, 308
  Call Forwarding on All Calls, 304–305
    signaling protocol, 306–307
  common characteristics, 302
  terminal out of service, 312–313
Call Forwarding, 313–314
  remote registration, 303
call forwarding notifications, 302
Call Forwarding on All Calls
  call diversion services, 304–305
  signaling protocol, 306–307
Call Forwarding on Busy, 301
Call Forwarding on No Answer, 302
Call Forwarding on No Reply, 307
  gatekeeper, 309–310, 312
  signaling protocol, 308

Call Forwarding
  Unconditional, 301
Call Hold supplementary
  services, 276–277, 314
  near-end, 277, 279
    gatekeepers, 281
  remote-end, 279, 281
    gatekeepers, 281–282
Call Intrusion-H.450.11, 341,
  343–344
Call management
  applications, 250
call models, 134
  gatekeeper-routed call
    signaling, 135,
    139–140
    alerting, 141
    connections, 141
    initiation, 135, 138–140
    termination, 142
Call Offering-H.450.10,
  336–340
Call Pickup, 361, 363
Call Reference (stimulus
  signaling), 356–357
call rerouting requests, 302
call scenarios, 9–10
call signaling
  embedding call control in
    Fast Connect, 111–114
    H.245 tunneling, 110–111
  H.225.0–Q.931 protocol,
    60–62, 64
    call alerting, 65
    call initiation, 64–65
    call proceeding, 65
    call termination, 66
    messages, 66–68
  mobility, 490
  protocol (conferencing
    additions), 170–171
call termination (H.225.0
  message flow), 131
Call Transfer supplementary
  services, 285–286
  gatekeepers, 288–290
  signaling protocol, 286
  unsuccessful transfers, 287
call waiting, 314, 379
  call waiting-H.450.6,
    323, 325
callIdentifier field, 68
Calls
  control applications,
    247–248
    call management, 250
    first-party, 248
    third-party, 249–250
  routing
    address resolution tables,
      235–238
    address templates, 225,
      228–234
    authorization, 239–240
  unsuccessful (call
    completion services),
    317–344
callSignalAddress field,
  122–123
CBQ, *see* Class-Based
  Queuing
CD, *see* Call Deflection
centralized ad hoc
  conferences, 179
centralized Call Control,
  349–350
CFB, *see* Call Forwarding on
  Busy
CFNA, *see* Call Forwarding
  on No Answer
CFU, *see* Call Forwarding
  Unconditional
circuit gateways, 466–467
Class Selector PHB, 559
Class-Based Queuing (QoS),
  539, 541
CloseLogicalChannel
  message, 93
CloseLogicalChannelAck
  message, 94
coders
  digital video
    H.261, 34
    H.263, 34
    H.263 version 2, 35–36
  voice, 20
    bit rates, 22
    complexity, 23
    delay, 23
    end-to-end delay, 24–25
    G.711, 21
    G.723.1, 21
    G.726, 21
    G.728, 22
    G.729, 22
    quality, 23
comfort noise format (RTP
  payload), 42
commands
  Add, 365, 368
  AuditCapabilities, 368
  AuditValue, 368
  Modify, 368
  Move, 365, 368
  Notify, 368
  ServiceChange, 368
  Subtract, 365, 368
communication, inter-
  domain, 215, 217,
  219–220
  address resolution tables,
    235–238
  address templates for
    routing calls, 225,
    228–234
  authorization, 239–240
  H.225.0 Annex G protocol,
    220, 223–224
  resource usage reporting,
    240–241
complexity (voice coder), 23
compression (RTP header),
  51–52
Conference Out of
  Consultation
  supplementary services,
  295–296
  signaling protocol, 297–298

conferences, 145, 181–182
 ad hoc, 146
  centralized, 179
  decentralized, 176, 178
  H.323, 153
 H.323 protocol, 154–155, 206, 210, 212
  call signaling additions, 170–171
  H.245 protocol additions, 155–162, 164–166
  RTP additions, 166–167, 169–170
 interactive-broadcast, 147
 MCU-based, 171–172, 174–175
 meet me, 146
 network configurations, 148, 150–151
  H.323, 151–152
 RTCP (RTP Control Protocol), 187, 189–190
  packets, 194–199, 201–209
  report interval rules, 193–194
  scalability, 209
  SSRC collision detection and resolution, 192
 scalability (voice and video), 180–181
 SDP (Session Description Protocol), 182, 184–187
connections (calls), 141
consultation (supplementary services), 283
consultation hold, 314
Consultation Transfer (QSIG), 390, 394
Consultation Transfer supplementary services, 290
 gatekeepers, 292–293, 295
 signaling protocol, 291
Context (H.248 connection model), 364
Controlled-Load service, 548–549
conversational text, 26
 end-to-end delay, 27
 T.140 as coder, 26–27
Corporate Network (CN), 387
CryptoHashdtoken, computing, 413
CryptoSignedToken, computing, 415
CryptoToken, 68
CryptowdEncr, computing, 413

D

Data Encryption Standard, *see* DES
deactivation procedures, 359
decentralized ad hoc conferences, 176, 178
default PHB, 559
delay (end-to-end)
 conversational text, 27
 RTP, 51–52
 voice coders, 23–25
delayed call forwarding, 308
DES (Data Encryption Standard), security algorithms, 456
descriptors, Terminations, 365–366
DestExtraCallInfo field, 67
DestinationAddress field, 67
Diffie-Hellman key generation, 408, 410
diffserv-based QoS, 556, 558
 Assured Forwarding PHB, 559, 562
 Class Selector PHB, 559
 default PHB, 559
 Expedited Forwarding PHB, 562, 564
digital signatures (user authentication), 414
digital video, 30, 32
 bit-stream syntax, 33–34
 coders
  H.261, 34
  H.263, 34
  H.263 version 2, 35–36
digitized voice, transmission of, 20
distributed Call Control, 349–350
distributed peer-to-peer signaling
 H.450 protocol, 256–257
domains
 Administrative Domain X, 7
  basic service, 7
  supplementary services, 8
 Administrative Domain Y, 9
 Administrative Domain Z, 9
 communication between, 215, 217, 219–220
  address resolution tables, 235–238
  address templates for routing calls, 225, 228–234
  authorization, 239–240
  H.225.0 Annex G protocol, 220, 223–224
  resource usage reporting, 240–241
drivers (QoS), 503–504, 506
DSA (Digital Signature Algorithm), 458
dynamicRTPPayloadType field, 88

E

EF, *see* Expedited Forwarding PHB
embedding
 call control in call signaling
  Fast Connect, 111–114
  H.245 tunneling, 110–111
 H.450 within H.323, 260

Encapsulating Security Payload (ESP), 534
encryption
  media-stream, 421, 425, 427, 429, 431–432
  shared secret-based (H.323 security), 411, 413
end-to-end delay
  RTP, 51–52
  text transmission, 27
  voice coders, 24–25
Endpoint QoS Entity, 565
Endpoint, *see* EP/GK controlled QoS
endpointAlias field, 122
endpointIdentifier field, 68, 123
entities (H.323), 3–4
EP/GK controlled QoS, 569–570
error conditions, responses during, 359
error correction, mobility (nonapplication layer), 499–500
ESP (Encapsulating Security Payload), IPSec, 445
exchanging security capabilities, 419
Expedited Forwarding PHB, 562, 564
Extension fields, 39

F

Fast Connect (H.245 protocol), 111–114
FastStart field, 68
Fax machines, 27
  G3 architecture, 27
    protocol, 28–29
  Internet transport, 54
feature activation requests, multiple, 359
feature identifier list, H.450.12, 268
feature indications, 358
  independent, 359
feature interworking, 360
feature key management (stimulus signaling), 349
feature keys
  handling, 358
  management
    extensions, 355
feature servers, 4, 351
features of service-independent transport, 373
FEC (Forward Error Correction) format, RTP payload, 49, 51
feedback mechanisms (application level QoS), 513, 515
feedback response (application level QoS), 515, 517, 519
FF, *see* Fixed Filter
FIFO queue, 536
filter specification, 549
  QoS, 550–551
firewalls
  application level gateways, 467–468
  circuit gateways, 466–467
  packet filters, 462
    stateful, 465
    static, 462, 464–465
  placement, 469–470
  traversing, 458–460
first-party call control applications, 248
Fixed Filter (reservation style), 551
flow specification, 549
FlowControlCommand message, 94
function keys (stimulus terminals), 354
functional entities (QoS), 565
functional units (stimulus signaling), 354
  audio, 354
  function keys, 354
  indicators, 354
  keypad, 354
  messages, 354–355
  soft keys, 354
  text displays, 354

G

G.711 voice coder, 21
G.723.1 format (RTP payload), 41
G.723.1 voice coder, 21
G.726 voice coder, 21
G.728 voice coder, 22
G.729 voice coder, 22
G3 facsimile architecture, 27
  Internet transport, 54
  protocol, 28–29
GatekeeperIdentifier field, 121–123
gatekeepers
  Call Forwarding on No Reply performed in, 309–310, 312
  call transfers, 288–290
  consultation transfers, 292–293, 295
  discovery, 120, 122, 487, 489
    endpointAlias, 122
    gatekeeperIdentifier field, 121–122
    rasAddress field, 121–122
  failure (H.225.0 message flow), 132–133
  layer architecture
    ISUP, 399
    QSIG, 38
  near-end hold services, 281
  remote-end hold services, 281–282
  signaling
    ISUP, 399
    QSIG, 389–390
gateways
  application level, 467–468

circuit, 466–467
residential, 402
trunking, 401
ISUP, 401
QSIG, 401
generic security protocols, 443–445, 447–451, 453
IKE (Internet Key Exchange), 453
IPSec, 444, 446–448
ESP (Encapsulating Security Payload), 445
IPSec AH, 444
ISAKMP (Internet Security Association and Key Management Protocol), 451
TLS (Transport Layer Security), 449, 451
goodbye packets (RTCP), 203
GRQs (Gatekeeper Request) messages, 120, 122
endpointAlias, 122
gatekeeperIdentifier field, 121–122
rasAddress field, 121–122
guaranteed service, 546, 548

H

H.225.0 Annex G protocol, messages, 220, 223–224
H.225.0 channels (security), 417, 419
H.225.0–Q.931 protocol, 60–62, 64
call alerting, 65
call initiation, 64–65
call proceeding, 65
call termination, 66
messages, 66–68
H.225.0–RAS protocol, 115–117
accounting, 129–130
address resolution, 127
admission control, 125–127
call termination, 131
gatekeeper failure, 132–133
lightweight registration, 132
load balancing, 132–133
message flows, 117, 120
authentication and message integrity, 124
gatekeeper discovery, 120–122
user registration, 122–123
QoS, 128–129
transport protocol (UDP), 133
user deregistration, 131
H.235.0 protocol, 7
control channel security, 419
H.240 stimulus signaling, 254
H.245 protocol, 69–70, 553, 555
conferencing additions, 155–162, 164–166
Fast Connect, 111–114
H.323 usage scenarios, 99–110
messages, 71–99, 143
CloseLogicalChannel, 93
CloseLogicalChannelAck, 94
FlowControlCommand, 94
MasterSlaveDetermination, 71–72
MiscellaneousCommand, 98–99
OpenLogicalChannel, 86, 88–89
OpenLogicalChannelAck, 91–92
TerminalCapabilitySet, 72–86
UserInputIndication, 95–97
securing, 417, 419
tunneling, 110–111
H.248 connection model
context, 364
stimulus signaling, 363
Terminations, 364
commands, 365–366
descriptors, 365–366
packages, 365
properties, 365–366
signals, 365
H.261 digital video coder, 34
H.263 digital video coder, 34
version 2, 35–36
H.263 format (RTP payload), 43–44
H.323
AAA servers, 4
ad hoc conferences, 153–155
call signaling additions, 170–171
H.245 protocol additions, 155–162, 164–166
RTP additions, 166–167, 169–170
address resolution servers, 4
border elements, 4
embedding H.450, 260
endpoints, 4
feature servers, 4
gatekeepers, 4
gateway, 3
GSM gateway, 3
interworking with QSIG, 387–398
interworking with ISUP, 398–403
MCUs (Multi-Point Control Units), 3
mobility architecture, 487–492
network configurations, 151–152
PBX gateway, 3
protocols, 5
H.225.0–Q.931., 5
H.225.0 Annex G., 6
H.225.0-RAS (Registration, Admission, and Status), 6
H.235.0, 7
H.245.0, 5
H.323 Annex K., 6

H.323 Annex L., 6
H.450.0, 6
RTCP (Real-Time Transport Control Protocol), 6
RTP (Real-Time Transport Protocol), 6
PSTN/fax gateway, 3
PSTN/H 324 gateway, 3
PSTN/voice gateway, 3
security, 405–406
H.225.0 and H.245 channels, 417, 419
key generation, 406–408, 410
message integrity, 415–416
user authentication, 410–411, 413–414
system model
Administrative Domain X, 7–8
Administrative Domain Y, 9
Administrative Domain Z, 9
terminal, 3
H.323 Annex L. protocol, 6
H.323 protocol
Fast Connect, 111–114
H.245 tunneling, 110–111
H.245 usage scenarios, 99–110
signaling architecture
H.450 distributed peer-to-peer approach, 256–257
stimulus signaling, 252–254
Web-based HTTP, 255
H.332, 210
H.450 protocol
distributed peer-to-peer signaling, 256–257
supplementary services, 258–259
embedding in H.323, 260
H.450.1, 261, 263, 265–266
H.450.12, 267–268
H.450.8, 269–271
recommendation status, 261
H.450.0 protocol, 6
H.450.1, 261
APDUs (Application Protocol Data Units), 263
reception rules, 266
sending rules, 265
transport connections, 263
valid messages, 265
H.450.12, 267–268
feature identifier list, 268
H.450.6–call waiting, 323, 325
H.450.7–Message Waiting Callback, 329, 331
H.450.7–message waiting indication, 326, 328
H.450.8, 269–271
H245 Address field, 68
hash, 457
shared secret-based (H.323 security), 413
headers, RTP, 39–40
compression, 51–52
HTTP (HyperText Transfer Protocol)
H.323 protocol, 255
service-independent transport, 371
application scenarios, 373–374
characteristics, 371–372
features, 373
protocol mechanisms, 375–382

I

identification services, 314
Internet Security Association and Key Management Protocol, *see* ISAKMP
IKE (Internet Key Exchange), 453
indicators, stimulus terminals, 354
information prompts, 358
Information Request Response (IRR) message, 376
initiation calls, 135, 138–140
integrated services
Controlled-Load, 548–549
Guaranteed, 546, 548
QoS, 545
integrity, 124
H.323 messages, 415–416
inter domain communication, 215, 217, 219–220
address resolution and authorization, 239–240
address resolution tables, 235–238
address templates for routing calls, 225, 228–234
protocols
H.225.0 Annex G, 220, 223–224
resource usage reporting, 240–241
inter-VLF mobility, 490
inter-zone mobility, 489
Interactive Voice Response units, 363
interactive-broadcast conferences, 147
International Standards Organization (ISO), 387
Internet Assigned Numbers Authority (IANA), 534
Internet Key Exchange, *see* IKE
Internet media
RTCP (Real-time Transport Control Protocol), 53
RTP, 36–37
end-to-end delay, 51–52
header, 39–40
payload, 41–47, 49, 51
synchronization of streams, 53
interworking
ISUP, 398–399
gateway signaling, 399

gateway-layer architecture, 399
principles of, 385–401
QSIG, 387–388
capabilities, 391
Consultation Transfer, 390, 394
gateway signaling, 389–390
gateway-layer architecture, 388
Single-Step Call Transfer, 396, 398
interworking function, 483
mobility, 491
intra-VLF mobility, 489
intra-zone mobility, 489
intrusion, 314
IP/UDP/RTP header compression
multi-frame packets, 519
overhead reduction technique, 519
IPSec protocol, 444, 446–448
ESP (Encapsulating Security Payload), 445
IPSec AH, 444
ISAKMP (Internet Security Association and Key Management Protocol), 451
ISUP interworking, 398–399
gateway signaling, 399
gateway-layer architecture, 399
ISUP trunking, 401–402
BICC, 403
ISUP/BICC interworking, 403
IWF, 491
functionality, 496
location and appearance, 495

K–L

Key generation (H.323 security), 406
Diffie-Hellman, 408, 410
from a password, 407–408
keypad stimulus, 348, 354
large scale conferences, 181–182
H.332 protocol, 206, 210, 212
RTCP (RTP Control Protocol), 187, 189–190
packets, 194–199, 201–209
report interval rules, 193–194
scalability, 209
SSRC collision detection and resolution, 192
SDP (Session Description Protocol), 182, 184–187
lightweight registration (H.225.0 message flow), 132
link and network layer handoff (mobility), 500
load balancing (H.225.0 message flow), 132–133
local keys, handling, 358
location updates (mobility), 489–490

M

MaintainConnection, 68
Marker field (RTP header), 40
MasterSlaveDetermination message, 71–72
Maximum Transmission Unit, *see* MTU
MCU-based conferences, 171–172, 174–175
MCUs (Multi-Point Control Units), 3
media
conversational text, 26
end-to-end delay, 27
T.140 as coder, 26–27
fax machines, 27
G3 architecture, 27
G3 fax protocol, 2,8–29
Internet transport, 54
Internet
RTCP (Real-time Transport Control Protocol), 53
RTP, 36–53
video, 30
digital, 30, 32–36
scalability, 180–181
voice, 19
coders, 20–23
digitized, transmission of, 20
end-to-end delay, 24–25
scalability, 180–181
Media Gateway Controllers, 352
media stream quality, 509, 511, 513
media stream encryption, 421–432
mediaControlChannel field, 88
mediaPacketization field, 88
meet me conferences, 146
Message Digest 5, 457
message waiting call back, 314
Message Waiting Callback-H.450.7, 329, 331
Message Waiting Indication (MWI), 499
message waiting indication-H.450.7, 326, 328
messages
H.225.0 Annex G protocol, 220, 223–224
H.225.0–RAS flow, 117, 120
accounting, 129–130
address resolution, 127
admission control, 125–127
authentication and integrity, 124
call termination, 131
gatekeeper discovery, 120–122

gatekeeper failure, 132–133
lightweight registration, 132
load balancing, 132–133
QoS, 128–129
transport protocol (UDP), 133
user deregistration, 131
user registration, 122–123
H.225.0–Q.931 protocol, 66 68
H.245 protocol, 71–99, 143
CloseLogicalChannel, 93
CloseLogicalChannelAck, 94
FlowControlCommand, 94
H.323 usage scenarios, 99–110
MasterSlaveDetermination, 71–72
MiscellaneousCommand, 98–99
OpenLogicalChannel, 86, 88–89
OpenLogicalChannelAck, 91–92
TerminalCapabilitySet, 72–86
UserInputIndication, 95–97
H.450.1, 265
reception rules, 266
sending rules, 265
integrity (H.323 security), 415–416
MGC, *see* Media Gateway Controllers
MiscellaneousCommand message, 98–99
mobility, 483–502
H.323 architecture, 487–492
authenticating function, 491
call signaling, 490
GK discovery and registration, 487, 489
interworking function, 491
location updates, 489–490
types of, 483–485
inter-VLF, 490
inter-zone, 489
intra-VLF, 489
intra-zone, 489
nonapplication layer issues, 499
error correction, 499–500
link and network layer handoff, 500
service, 484–486
terminal, 484–485
types, 483–484
user, 483–484
user, between PLMN and H.323, 492
subscriber identifiers, 492–493
user, with IWF, 493–499
models, call, 134
gatekeeper-routed call signaling, 135, 138–142
modes, security (receiver requests), 421
Modify command, 368
motivation (QoS), 503–527
Move command, 365
MP/Mixed packets (RTCP), 205–209
MTU (Maximum Transmission Unit), 37
multi-domain issues (QoS), 565
EP/GK controlled, 569–570
functional entities, 565
policy, 566, 568–569
multi-field classifiers, 533
multi-point conferences, 145, 181–182
ad hoc, 146
centralized, 179
decentralized, 176, 178
H.323, 153
H.323, 154–155
call signaling additions, 170–171
H.245 protocol additions, 155–166
RTP additions, 166–170
interactive-broadcast, 147
MCU-based, 171–175
meet me, 146
network configurations, 148, 150 –151
H.323, 151–152
RTCP (RTP Control Protocol), 189–190
H.332 protocol, 206, 210, 212
packets, 194–209
report interval rules, 193–194
scalability, 209
SSRC collision detection and resolution, 192
scalability (voice and video), 180–181
SDP (Session Description Protocol), 182–187
Multi-Point Control Units, *see* MCUs
multiple calls, handling, 321–323
MultipleCalls, 68

N

near-end hold services, 277, 279
gatekeepers, 281
network building blocks
QoS, 527
packet classifiers, 533–534
packet schedulers, 536, 539–541
queue management, 536, 539–541
rate controllers, 534, 536
Token Bucket, 527–533
network-provided QoS, 523–569

networks
conference configurations, 148, 150–151
H.323, 151–152
firewalls, placing, 469–470
nonapplication layer mobility, 499
error correction, 499–500
link and network layer handoff, 500
nonroutable alias address (resolution tables), 235
border element discovery, 235
population, 237–238
service relationship establishment, 236–237
Notify command, 368

O

OpenLogicalChannel (OLC) message, 86, 88–89, 529
OpenLogicalChannelAck message, 91–92
operation modes (security algorithms), 454
out-of-service terminals (call diversion), 312–313
overhead reduction techniques
IP/UDP/RTP header compression, 519
multi-frame packets, 519
QoS, 519

P

packages (Terminations), 365
packets
classifiers (QoS), 533–534
filters, 462
stateful, 465
static, 462–465
RTCP, 194–196
Goodbye, 203
MP/Mixer use, 205–209
Receiver Report, 199–203
Sender Report, 197
sending rules, 204–205
version, 198
Padding field (RTP header), 39
passwords (key generation), 407–408
Payload Type field, 518
payload Type field (RTP header), 40
payloads (RTP), 41
comfort noise format, 42
FEC (Forward Error Correction) format, 49, 51
G.723.1 format, 41
H.263 format, 43–44
redundancy format, 45–47
T.140 format, 42
PCM (Pulse Code Modulation), 20
Personal Computer Memory Card International Association (PCMCIA), 496
PLMN, mobility between H.323, 492
subscriber identifiers, 492–493
Point-to-point calls (call models), 134
gatekeeper-routed call signaling, 135, 138–142
protocols, 59–60
H.225.0–RAS, 115–117, 120–133
H.225.0–Q.931, 60–62, 64–68
H.245, 69–99, 102–114, 143
H.323, 110–114
policy, role of QoS, 566, 568–569
populating (address resolution tables), 237–238
PreGrantedARQ field, 123
private addressing, 471
network address translation, 471–473
Realm Specific IP, 473, 475
profiles, security, 436
baseline, 436
signature, 437–438
programming model (stimulus signaling), 351, 353
properties (Terminations), 365–366
protocol framework (stimulus signaling), 355
Call Reference, 356–357
examples, 360–361, 363
guidelines, 358, 360
protocol mechanisms (HTTP), 375
service control, 376–382
protocols, 5, 59–60
323 Annex K., 6
call signaling (conferencing additions), 170–171
G3 fax, 28–29
H.225.0 Annex G (messages), 220, 223–224
H.225.0–Q.931, 5
H.225.0–RAS, 115–117
message flows, 117, 120–133
transport protocol (UDP), 133
H.225.0 Annex G., 6
H.225.0-RAS (Registration, Admission, and Status), 6
H.225.0–Q.931, 60–62, 64
call alerting, 65
call initiation, 64–66
call proceeding, 65
messages, 66–68

H.235.0, 7
H.245, 69–70
  conferencing additions, 155–162, 164–166
  Fast Connect, 111–114
  H.323 usage scenarios, 99, 102–104, 106–108, 110
  messages, 71–99, 143
  tunneling, 110–111
H.245, 5
H.323
  Fast Connect, 111–114
  H.245 tunneling, 110–111
  H.450 distributed peer-to-peer approach, 256–257
  signaling architecture, 252–254
  Web-based HTTP, 255
H.323 Annex L., 6
H.332 (large-scale conferencing), 206, 210, 212
H.450.0, 6, 258–271
RTCP (RTP Control Protocol), 53, 187, 189–190
  packets, 194–199, 201–209
  report interval rules, 193–194
  scalability, 209
  SSRC collision detection and resolution, 192
RTP, 36–37
  conferencing additions, 166–170
  end-to-end delay, 51–52
  header, 39–40
  payload, 41–51
  synchronization of streams, 53
RTP (Real-Time Transport Protocol), 6
SDP (Session Description Protocol), 182–187
security
  generic, 443–453
  IKE (Internet Key Exchange), 453
  IPSec, 444, 446–448
  IPSec AH, 444
  IPSec ESP, 445
  ISAKMP (Internet Security Association and Key Management Protocol), 451
  TLS (Transport Layer Security), 449, 451
stimulus signaling, 363
  H.248 connection model, 363–364
proxies, 467–468
pull
  service delivery, 378
  service delivery by, 376
Pulse Code Modulation, *see* PCM
pure stimulus, 348
push
  service delivery, 378
  service delivery by, 376

Q

QoS (Quality of Service)
  application level, 513–520
    feedback mechanisms, 513, 515
    source response to feedback, 515–519
  diffserv-based, 556, 558
    Assured Forwarding PHB, 559, 562
    Class Selector PHB, 559
    default PHB, 559
    Expedited Forwarding PHB, 562, 564
  drivers, 503–504, 506
  H.225.0 message flow, 128–129
  motivation, 503–504, 506, 523, 525, 527
  multi-domain issues, 565
    EP/GK controlled, 569–570
    functional entities, 565
    policy, 566, 568–569
  network building blocks, 527
    packet classifiers, 533–534
    packet schedulers, 536, 539–541
    queue management, 536, 539–541
    rate controllers, 534, 536
    Token Bucket, 527, 529, 531, 533
  network-provided, 523–546, 550–569
  overhead reduction techniques, 519
    IP/UDP/RTP header compression, 519
    multi-frame packets, 519
  principles, 503–520
  RAS operations, 541
    call bandwidth, 544
    entity controlling, 541, 543–544
  resource management
    EP/GK controlled, 569–570
    functional entities, 565
    policy, 566, 568–569
  RSVP/Intserv based, 544, 549
    802 LANs, 555–556
    filter specification, 550–551
    H.245, 553, 555
    integrated services, 545–549
    invoking, 552
    operational overview, 549–553
    reservation styles, 551–552
QoS Manager, 565
QoS Policy Entity, 565

QoS, resource
management, 565
QSIG interworking, 387–388
capabilities, 391
Consultation Transfer,
390, 394
gateway signaling, 389–390
gateway-layer
architecture, 388
Single-Step Call Transfer,
396, 398
QSIG trunking, 401
quality (voice coder), 23
Quality of Service, *see* QoS
queue management (QoS),
536–541

R

RADIUS (Remote
Authentication Dial-In
User Service), 475–479
RAS channel (quality),
508–509
RAS operations
entity-controlling QoS,
541–544
QoS, 541
call bandwidth, 544
RasAddress field, 121–122
rate controllers (QoS),
534, 536
Real-Time Transport Control
Protocol, *see* RTCP
Real-Time Transport
Protocol, *see* RTP
Realm Specific IP, 473, 475
Receiver Report packets
(RTCP), 199, 201–203
receivers (security mode
requests), 421
receiving H.450.1 messages,
rules, 266
recommendations
(H.450), 261
redundancy format (RTP
payload), 45–47
redundancyEncoding
field, 88
redundancyEncodingMethod
field, 88
reference points (QoS), 565
registering users (H.225.0
message flow), 122–123
callSignalAddress field,
122–123
endpointIdentifier field, 123
gatekeeperIdentifier
field, 123
preGrantedARQ field, 123
terminalAlias field, 123
Registration, Admission and
Status protocol, *see*
H.225.0–RAS protocol
Remote Authentication Dial-
In User Service, *see*
RADIUS
remote registration (Call
Forwarding), 303
remote-end hold services,
279, 281
gatekeepers, 281–282
RemoteExtensionAddress
field, 67
report interval rules (RTCP),
193–194
reservation specification, 550
reservation styles (QoS),
551–552
residential gateways, 402
resource management
(QoS), 565
EP/GK controlled,
569–570
functional entities, 565
policy, 566, 568–569
Resource Manager, 565
resources, usage reporting
(inter-domain
communication),
240–241
responses (error
conditions), 359
routing calls
address resolution tables,
235–238
address templates, 225,
228–234
authorization, 239–240
RSA security algorithm,
456, 458
Rspec, *see* reservation
specification
RSVP/Intserv based QoS,
544, 549
802 LANs, 555–556
filter specification, 550–551
H.245, 553, 555
integrated services, 545
Controlled-Load, 548–549
Guaranteed, 546, 548
invoking, 552
operational overview,
549–550, 552–553
reservation styles, 551–552
RTCP (RTP Control
Protocol), 187, 189–190
packets, 194–196
Goodbye, 203
MP/Mixer use, 205–209
Receiver Report, 199,
201–203
Sender Report, 197
sending rules, 204–205
version, 198
report interval rules,
193–194
scalability, 209
SSRC collision detection
and resolution, 192
RTP (Real-Time Transport
Protocol), 6, 36–37
conferencing additions,
166–167, 169–170
end-to-end delay, 51–52
header, 39–40
compression, 51–52
payload, 41
comfort noise format, 42

FEC (Forward Error Correction) format, 49, 51
G.723.1 format, 41
H.263 format, 43–44
redundancy format, 45–47
T.140 format, 42
synchronization of streams, 53
RTP Control Protocol, *see* RTCP

S

scalability
RTCP, 209
voice and video, 180–181
schedulers (QoS), 536, 539–541
SDP (Session Description Protocol), 182, 184–187
Secure Hash security algorithm, 458
security
algorithms, 453–458
AES (Advanced Encryption Standard), 456
DES (Data Encryption Standard), 456
DSA (Digital Signature Algorithm), 458
hash, 457
Message Digest 5, 457
operation modes, 454
RSA, 456, 458
Secure Hash, 458
signature, 457
anonymity, 432, 434
encryption (media-stream), 421–432
exchanging capabilities, 419
firewalls
application level gateways, 467–468
circuit gateways, 466–467
packet filters, 462, 464–465
placement, 469–470
traversing, 458–460
H.225.0 and H.245 channels, 417, 419
H.235 control channel, 419
H.323, 405–406
key generation, 406–408, 410
message integrity, 415–416
user authentication, 410–411, 413–414
private addressing, 471
network address translation, 471–473
Realm Specific IP, 473, 475
profiles, 436
baseline, 436
signature, 437–438
protocols
generic, 443–445, 447–451, 453
IKE (Internet Key Exchange), 453
IPSec, 444, 446–448
IPSec AH, 444
IPSec ESP, 445
ISAKMP (Internet Security Association and Key Management Protocol), 451
TLS (Transport Layer Security), 449, 451
RADIUS (Remote Authentication Dial-In User Service), 475–479
receiver mode requests, 421
Sender Report packets (RTCP), 197
sending
H.450.1 messages (rules), 265
packets (RTCP), 204–205
Sequence Number field, 518
RTP header, 40
service control
call-related, 378, 380
non-call-related, 376, 381
service interactions, 381
service interactions, 381
Service Level Agreement, 504
service mobility, 484–486
Service relationships, establishing (address resolution tables), 236–237
service-independent transport (HTTP), 371
application scenarios, 373–374
characteristics, 371–372
features of, 373
protocol mechanisms, 375–382
stimulus signaling, 372
ServiceChange command, 368
Session Description Protocol, *see* SDP
sessionID field, 88
Shared Explicit (reservation style), 551
Short Message Service (SMS), 499
signaling architecture (H.323 protocol)
H.450 distributed peer-to-peer approach, 256–257
stimulus signaling, 252–254
embedding call control in
Fast Connect, 111–114
H.245 tunneling, 110–111
H.225.0–Q.931 protocol, 64
call alerting, 65
call initiation, 64–65
call proceeding, 65
call termination, 66
TTP, 255
signaling protocol
Call Deflection, 308
Call Forwarding on All Calls, 306–307
Call Forwarding on No Reply, 308

signals for Terminations, 365
signature security algorithm, 457
signature security profile, 437–438
Single-Step Call Transfer (QSIG), 396, 398
SLA, *see* Service Level Agreement
soft keys (stimulus terminals), 35
SourceAddress field, 66
SourceCallSignalAddress field, 67
SSRC collision detection (RTCP), 192
stateful packet filters, 465
static packet filters, 462, 464–465
static priority scheduler, 537
  QoS, 537
stimulus signaling, 252–256, 347–368, 372
  Call Control, 349–350
  Feature Server, 351
  functional units, 354
    audio, 354
    function keys, 354
    indicators, 354
    keypad, 354
    messages, 354–355
    soft keys, 354
    text displays, 354
  goals of, 350–351
  H.232 to H.450, 351
  H.323 protocol, 252–253
    H.240 stimulus, 254
  H.323 to H.248, 351
  H.323 to HTTP, 351
  programming model, 351, 353
  protocol, 363
    H.248 connection model, 363–364
  protocol framework, 355
    Call Reference, 356–357
    examples, 360–361, 363
    guidelines, 358, 360
  variants of, 348
    feature key management, 349
    keypad, 348
    Pure, 348
streams, synchronization of (RTP), 53
Subnet Bandwidth Manager, 555
subscriber identifiers, 492–493
Subtract command, 365, 368
supplementary services, 245–247
  Administrative Domain X, 8
  call completion, 317–319, 321
    busy (definition), 321–323
    Call Completion Services-H.450.9, 331–335
    Call Intrusion-H.450.11, 341, 343–344
    Call Offering-H.450.10, 336–340
    call waiting-H.450.6, 323, 325
    Message Waiting Callback-H.450.7, 329, 331
    message waiting indication-H.450.7, 326, 328
  call control applications, 247–248
    call management, 250
    first-party, 248
    third-party, 249–250
  H.323 signaling architecture
    H.450 distributed peer-to-peer approach, 256–257
    stimulus signaling, 252–254
    Web-based HTTP, 255
  H.450, 258–259
    embedding in H.323, 260
    H.450.1, 261, 263, 265–266
    H.450.12, 267–268
    H.450.8, 269–271
    recommendation status, 261
  three-party, 275
    Alternating, 284
    Call Hold, 276–282
    Call Transfer, 285–290
    Conference Out of Consultation, 295–298
    Consultation, 283
    Consultation Transfer, 290–293, 295
supplementary services interactions, 313–314
Switched-Circuit Network (SCN), 386
synchronization of streams (RTP), 53
system quality (factors affecting), 506, 508
  media stream, 509, 511, 513
  RAS channel, 508–509

T

T.140 format, 26–27
  RTP payload, 42
terminal mobility, 484–485
terminalAlias field, 123
TerminalCapabilitySet message, 72–86
Terminations
  calls, 142
  H.248 connection model, 364
    commands, 365–366
    descriptors, 365–366
    packages, 365
    properties, 365–366
    signals, 365
text displays (stimulus terminals), 354
Text, conversational, 26
  end-to-end delay, 27

T.140 as coder, 26–27
third-party call control applications, 249–250
three-party supplementary services, 275
Alternating, 284
Call Hold, 276–277
near-end, 277, 279, 281–282
remote-end, 279, 281
Call Transfer, 285–286
gatekeepers, 288–290
signaling protocol, 286
unsuccessful transfers, 287
Conference Out of Consultation, 295–296
signaling protocol, 297–298
Consultation, 283
Consultation Transfer, 290
gatekeepers, 292–293, 295
signaling protocol, 291
Timestamp field (RTP header), 40
TLS (Transport Layer Security) protocol, 449, 451
Token Bucket (traffic characterization with), 527, 529, 531, 533
traffic specification, 549
translation (network addresses), 471–473
transmission (digitized voice), 20
Transport connections (H.450.1), 263
Transport Layer Security, *see* TLS
TransportCapability field, 88
trunking gateways, 401
Tspec, *see* traffic specification
tunneling H.245 protocol, 110–111

U

uneven Level Protection (mobility), 500
uninterruptable power sources, 312
unsuccessful calls (call completion services), 317–319, 321
busy (definition), 321–323
Call Completion Services-H.450.9, 331–335
Call Intrusion-H.450.11, 341, 343–344
Call Offering-H.450.10, 336–340
call waiting-H.450.6, 323, 325
Message Waiting Callback-H.450.7, 329, 331
message waiting indication-H.450.7, 326, 328
UPS, *see* uninterruptable power sources
user mobility, 483–484
between PLMN and H.323, 492
subscriber identifiers, 492–493
IWF, 493, 496–497, 499
UserInputIndication message, 95–97
users
authentication (H.323 security), 410–411, 413–414
deregistration (H.225.0 message flow), 131
registering (H.225.0 message flow), 122–123
callSignalAddress field, 122–123
endpointIdentifier field, 123
gatekeeperIdentifier, 123
preGrantedARQ, 123
terminalAlias, 123

V

Value Added Services, 350
Version field (RTP header), 39
version packets (RTCP), 198
video, 30
digital, 30, 32
bit-stream syntax, 33–34
coders, 34–36
scalability, 180–181
voice scalability, 180–181
voice media, 19
coders, 20
bit rates, 22
complexity, 23
delay, 23
end-to-end delay, 24–25
G.711, 21
G.723.1, 21
G.726, 21
G.728, 22
G.729, 22
quality, 23
digitized, transmission of, 20

W

Weighted Fair Queuing (QoS), 538–539
Wildcard Filter
mobility, 493, 496–497, 499
reservation style, 551